The Self-Disclosure of God

SUNY Series in Islam
Seyyed Hossein Nasr, editor

PRINCIPLES OF IBN AL-ʿARABĪ'S COSMOLOGY

The Self-Disclosure of God

WILLIAM C. CHITTICK

State University of New York Press

Published by
State University of New York Press, Albany

Printed in the United States of America

For information, address State University of New York Press
State University Plaza, Albany, NY 12246

Production by Dana Foote
Marketing by Nancy Farrell

Library of Congress Cataloging-in-Publication Data

Chittick, William C.
The self-disclosure of God : principles of Ibn al-ʿArabī's cosmology / William C. Chittick.
p. cm. — (SUNY series in Islam)
Includes bibliographical references (p.) and index.
ISBN 0-7914-3403-6 (hardcover : alk. paper). — ISBN 0-7914-3404-4 (pbk. : alk. paper)
1. Ibn al-ʿArabī, 1165–1240. Futūḥāt al-Makkīyah. 2. God (Islam)—Early works to 1800. 3. Islamic cosmology—Early works to 1800. 4. Sufism—Early works to 1800. 5. Islam—Doctrines—Early works to 1800. I. Title. II. Series.
BP189.26.I2623C47 1998
297'.4—dc21 97-30521
CIP

CONTENTS

INTRODUCTION

This book continues the investigations I began in *The Sufi Path of Knowledge* (hereafter SPK). There I promised a volume on Ibn al-ʿArabī's "Cosmology," concerning which I had already prepared a good deal of material.[1] In 1993, I applied to the National Endowment for the Humanities for a fellowship to write a book on Ibn al-ʿArabī's cosmological teachings. I received the generous support of the Endowment during the academic year 1994–95, and for that I am extremely grateful. Without this support it is doubtful that this book could ever have been written. During that year I was able to put together a series of some twenty chapters dealing with the topic, ten of which are presented here. I hope to offer the remaining chapters as *The Breath of the All-Merciful: Ibn al-ʿArabī's Articulation of the Cosmos.*

In this introduction, after discussing what I have tried to do in the present volume, I reflect on the distinction between "cosmology" in a modern, scientific sense—the sense that informs contemporary culture—and in the sense in which the idea is understood by Ibn al-ʿArabī. Then I summarize the contents of SPK, the present book, and *The Breath of the All-Merciful.* Finally I turn to some of the problems that translators need to face when attempting to render the writings of Ibn al-ʿArabī into English.

The present book adds few basic terms and ideas to SPK. Practically every important term mentioned here was at least touched upon there. Many of the discussions will be familiar to readers of that book. Nevertheless, none of this book simply repeats what was said in the earlier volume, and, with few exceptions, all texts are translated into English for the first time.

One major difference between this volume and SPK is the manner in which I have attempted to contextualize the discussions. It is relatively easy to have Ibn al-ʿArabī say what one wants him to say. Critics and devotees have quoted him selectively for centuries, and modern scholarship has continued in the same path. Given that Ibn al-ʿArabī constantly shifts his perspective, it is a simple matter to choose words that pertain to one perspective, or some perspectives, and to claim that this is his view of things. Indeed it is, but he has many other views as well. If we make no attempt to take those views into account, we will misrepresent him.

It was my purpose in SPK to let Ibn al-ʿArabī speak for himself, and to this end I relied as much as possible on translating his words. In several essays over the years, some of which were published as *Imaginal Worlds,* I tried to speak for him, and in these my voice was no doubt louder than his. The best way to allow him to speak for himself would be, of course, simply to translate his works, but several major problems make this route difficult if not impossible to follow. Foremost among these is that the translator needs to understand what Ibn al-ʿArabī is saying, and this is not a qualification as common as one might expect.

Ibn al-ᶜArabī's writings are full of obscurities. Some of these go back to the richness of his teachings and the vast possibilities of the Arabic language, and others to the intense brilliance of the inspiration that seized the author in particular passages. In studying his works, the easiest way to deal with these obscurities is to ignore them and to focus on what is clear. In translating—as long as one is not attempting a complete translation—one can, as I did in SPK, simply drop such passages and all unwelcome digressions and replace them with an ellipsis.

Several of Ibn al-ᶜArabī's short works have been translated, but for a number of reasons few, if any, have been translated as well as one might have hoped. The major problem has not been knowledge of Arabic, but knowledge of Ibn al-ᶜArabī's teachings and perspectives. The context of his short works, after all, is not only the Islamic intellectual tradition of the thirteenth century—especially in its juridical, theological, philosophical, and Sufi modes—but also Ibn al-ᶜArabī's long works, in which he provides the background for what he says in his short works. Another problem with translating Ibn al-ᶜArabī is the profusion of technical terms and constant reference to Koran, Hadith, and other sources with which English readers are not normally conversant. James Morris has suggested eloquently in a number of articles some of the difficulties that these sorts of problems raise for readers and translators.[2]

Ibn al-ᶜArabī's major surviving work is *al-Futūḥāt al-makkiyya*, "The Meccan Openings." People sometimes ask me why I do not simply translate that, and my first answer is that I have only one lifetime to devote to it. The work is enormously long and, in places, extraordinarily difficult. When Ibn al-ᶜArabī's waxes poetical, as he often does, it is sometimes impossible (for this reader at least) to understand what he is getting at. The richness and profusion of the imagery, the constant allusions to diverse waystations of the spiritual journey, the strange symbolism mixed with classical literary tropes, make the task of deciphering the passages truly daunting. Even supposing the translator has understood what is being said, the problems of rendering the words into comprehensible English, without mountains of commentary, are, at this point, insurmountable.

My first major attempt to solve a few of the problems related to rendering Ibn al-ᶜArabī's ideas accurately into English is found in SPK. Most of that book is translation, but by selecting certain passages, I was able to define basic concepts in Ibn al-ᶜArabī's own words and then cite other passages to illustrate how he employs the concepts. However, most of those passages are short and incomplete. Ibn al-ᶜArabī does not develop his ideas gradually. Wherever one may enter into his writings, the ideas are already full blown. Only by quoting him out of context can one suggest that he is a systematic thinker, who develops his ideas in a way that would allow someone unfamiliar with them to be introduced to them step by step.

Many of the problems translators face can be examined closely in the volume *Les Illuminations de La Mecque/The Meccan Illuminations*, in which four of us translated passages from the *Futūḥāt* into English and French under the general editorship of Michel Chodkiewicz. Although we made some attempt to agree on how to render certain basic terms, for the most part we followed our own inclinations, both in translation and presentation. I, for example, tried to render whole chapters or sections, without interruption, whereas James Morris preferred to summarize some parts and translate others. Most of us made judicious use of ellipses—three small dots that in every case saved some sort of headache.

In this work I have attempted, as much as possible, to put discussions into the context not only of Ibn al-ᶜArabī's grand project, but also of the specific topic that he is presenting. In contrast to SPK, I have seriously tried to avoid quoting snippets of text and brief passages. Moreover, in contrast to that work, I have tried *not* to drop anything in the midst of a passage. This has made my task much more difficult, and it will not make things easier for the reader. Nevertheless, I think the struggle is worth the effort on both sides—if our goal is truly to understand what Ibn al-ᶜArabī is getting at.

In the attempt to avoid offering passages out of context, I have quoted many full chapters or full sections from chapters. These illustrate in some detail the manner in which Ibn al-ʿArabī employs terminology and ideas in concrete applications. Most of these passages digress from the announced topic in my own chapters, but this pertains to the nature of Ibn al-ʿArabī's writings. One cannot avoid it except by abstracting the ideas out of the context, a process that, as I argue shortly, seriously distorts his project.

Because of my attempt to preserve the exact content and even flavor of the original, I have not dropped the numerous lines of poetry that dot the text. Often, in struggling to understand these lines, I have regretted my decision to avoid the liberal use of ellipses. At least one of my friends, Professor Wolfhart Heinrichs, must have regretted my decision along with me, when I asked him to help me decipher a few of these lines. Nonetheless, the struggle has been valuable for me, and I hope readers will gain some appreciation of Ibn al-ʿArabī's poetical talents and goals through these passages. They may also be sure that Ibn al-ʿArabī himself considered the poetry, especially the lines that begin each chapter, an important part of the work. As he writes,

> Pay close regard to every versification at the beginning of each chapter of this book, for it contains the knowledges of the chapter in the measure that I desired to call attention to it there. You will find in the verses what is not found in the text of that chapter, and you will increase in knowledge of what the chapter contains through what I have mentioned in the verses. (IV 21.22)

At least one reviewer of SPK complained that he found "several passages [translated there] from the *Futūhāt* unduly long for the presentation of the point under consideration." Those who are looking for quick explanations of "the point under consideration" will find this book much more disappointing than SPK. Although I do indeed try to explain certain points, this has less to do with making the point than with explicating basic concepts so that the reader may see how these are employed by Ibn al-ʿArabī. My point is not to make the point, but to let Ibn al-ʿArabī say what he wants to say in the way he wants to say it.

Those who would prefer that I get to the point will have to be satisfied with other works or with the bare-bones outline of Ibn al-ʿArabī's cosmology later on in this introduction. Even then, it should be kept in mind that Ibn al-ʿArabī employed the bare bones to hold up the flesh and blood, and it is the flesh and blood that give life to his writings. The living body of his works is woven from the Koran, the Hadith, the Shariah, the Islamic intellectual tradition in general, and the Sufi tradition in particular. God's self-disclosure is found in the embodiment of Islamic experience much more clearly than in the dry bones that can be, if we are so minded, extracted from the body to be studied anatomically or, as one says nowadays, "architectonically."

One of the reasons for Ibn al-ʿArabī's extraordinary stress on the importance of imagination is his attempt to make people aware of the disservice to understanding done by rational extraction and abstraction. Not that he does not appreciate reason. On the contrary, he considers the rational faculty one of the two eyes with which the travelers to God see where they are going, and without both eyes they will never reach their goal. However, much of the Islamic intellectual tradition—like the Christian and post-Christian—has employed reason to separate the bones from the flesh. In effect, this destroys the living body.

Too often, in the case of studying Ibn al-ʿArabī, "getting to the point" is to kill. To get to the point is to bring about closure, but there is no closure, only *dis*closure. Ibn al-ʿArabī has no specific point to which he wants to get. He is simply flowing along with the infinitely diverse self-disclosures of God, and he is suggesting to us that we leave aside our artificialities and recognize that we are flowing along with him. There is no "point," because there is no end.

The attempt to make Ibn al-ʿArabī come to the point, typically so that we can place him into this category or that, too often manifests our own desire to bring his writings into line with own predispositions and prejudices. In the traditional Islamic context, he and other great figures were almost never studied with the aim of classifying them, of dominating over them through overarching claims to intellectual authority. On the contrary, they were approached with humility and the recognition that they have something real and profound to teach, something that the rest of us do not have.

Knowledge of the Cosmos

The word *cosmology* is used nowadays to cover a vast range of topics in fields ranging from scientific cosmology and astronomy, to philosophy, anthropology, and religious studies. Norriss S. Hetherington defines cosmology as "The science, theory, or study of the universe as an orderly system and of the laws that govern it." This provides a fair picture of what I set out to investigate in Ibn al-ᶜArabī's works. However, Hetherington's definition goes on to add, "in particular, a branch of astronomy that deals with the structure and evolution of the universe."[3] Ibn al-ᶜArabī's cosmology is definitely not a branch of astronomy, whether that term is understood in modern or Islamic terms, though his cosmology does touch on what might be called the "evolution" of the universe.

There are, of course, many deep differences between what modern cosmologists study and what Ibn al-ᶜArabī was studying. Probably the most profound and telling of these differences is the approach to the cosmologist. In modern cosmology, the cosmologist, in effect, pretends to be a disembodied spirit who stands outside the cosmos. The quest is to achieve "objectivity," but no attempt is ever made to grasp the nature of the inescapable subject who is needed in order for the object to be known. For Ibn al-ᶜArabī, all pretense to disembodied, "objective" knowledge must be thrown aside. Knowing the subject that knows is all important—true knowledge of the cosmos is inaccessible without true knowledge of the self.

It should be obvious to anyone that what we as subjects can know about the cosmos depends to a large degree on our starting point, and this goes back to who we are. Of course it is also true that the tools and methods that we employ in our investigations determine what we will discover, just as the mesh of the net determines—in Eddington's famous analogy—what kind of fish we will pull from the sea. Nonetheless, more than anything else, the investigator himself is the net.

Any understanding of the world begins somewhere, and the where of the beginning determines the where of the journey and the ultimate destination. There are wheres that cannot take the investigator to certain goals. As they used to say in Boston, "You can't get there from here." To understand what Ibn al-ᶜArabī is trying to do, we need to understand where he is located, where he is trying to go, and how it is that he can get there from here. Much of SPK and Addas's outstanding biography of Ibn al-ᶜArabī, *Quest for the Red Sulphur*, among other works, deal directly or indirectly with this issue. This book continues the discussion. Indeed, this issue—where do we in fact stand and where can we go from here?—will be seen to be, for Ibn al-ᶜArabī, the most important and basic of issues.

The idea that we possess "objective knowledge" is one of the most impenetrable of veils. Those who hold it typically take a dogmatic position that leads them to discount everyone else. If our own position is "objective," then that of the others is "subjective," and hence it can be dismissed from consideration. But obviously, a subject is making this claim, and typically a subject who has no idea of who or what he or she is. The novelist Walker Percy provides some of the most hilarious and profound insights into the contemporary ignorance of the subject in his *Lost in the Cosmos: The Last Self-Help Book*, and readers who would like to reflect on—and laugh about—who they are and the absurd pretensions of the specialists to know the answer are referred to that book. Percy provides a number of alternative titles, including these:

> How you can survive in the Cosmos about which you know more and more while knowing less and less about yourself, this despite 10,000 self-help books, 100,000 psychotherapists, and 100 million fundamentalist Christians

or

Why it is that of all the billions and billions of objects in the Cosmos—novas, quasars, pulsars, black holes—you are without doubt the strangest

or

Why it is possible to learn more in ten minutes about the Crab Nebula in Taurus, which is 6,000 light-years away, than you presently know about yourself, even though you've been stuck with yourself all your life

Ibn al-ᶜArabī deals with the puzzle of the human subject—Arabic *nafs*, "self" or "soul"—constantly, and many of his statements could be dropped into Percy's book, or others of the same sort, without anyone noticing. Thus he says of people in general that they are "seized by terror when they are alone with themselves" (II 541.20). He if anyone provides the strongest arguments for the absurdity of claiming to know "what's what" about self or anything else in more than a tentative manner. It is not accidental that he calls the highest form of knowledge accessible to human beings the "station of bewilderment."

In modern forms of cosmology, we are told, the theory stands or falls on empirical observation, though insight and imagination obviously play an important role in the theory's formulation. The subject who makes the observations and builds the theory is to be ignored to the extent possible. It is claimed that the findings, inasmuch as they are empirically verifiable, are empirically verifiable by everyone, and if taken seriously, this claim would reduce the findings to an absurdly low common denominator. In fact, of course, only people with years of the requisite training can verify the findings. One can perhaps be excused for comparing the requisite training to the rigorous ascetic practices imposed on initiates in esoteric orders throughout history.

Ibn al-ᶜArabī is fundamentally concerned with explicating the source of knowledge and clarifying that the preparedness of the investigator is everything. The "preparedness" of the subject depends on who we are and what we have become—in modern terms, on the combination of nature and nurture. No two people have identical preparednesses for understanding anything, least of all their own selves. Not understanding oneself, one does not know where one stands and one cannot grasp the global implications of what one knows. Knowledge rooted in ignorance of the subject should not be called "knowledge" in any real sense of the term, and certainly not wisdom. This is not to deny that this truncated knowledge can be an extremely powerful tool for manipulation, and herein lies its great attraction in modern times.

Behind Ibn al-ᶜArabī's discussion of epistemological issues lies a basic insight—that the human self is unbounded in its becoming. "The self is an ocean without shore. Gazing upon it has no end in this world and the next" (IV 68.9). However, the self tends to lose sight of its own unboundedness and ties itself down to specific configurations. The particularized limitations that the self adopts as its own determine where it stands and what it can know. It can escape from these limitations only by means of objective standards provided by the external provider of the limitations, not by the self itself. That external provider is called by many names. The name that is especially relevant in the present context is "Guide." This Guide is God—not God as such, who creates evil along with good, ignorance along with knowledge, error along with truth—but God inasmuch as He offers diverse paths to deliverance from the limitations that make the unbounded self perceive itself as finite and constricted. God offers these paths through certain human beings whom He chooses as His emissaries, and they are called "messengers" and "prophets."

In short, Ibn al-ᶜArabī's cosmology is a prophetic cosmology, and it is rooted primarily in the world view confirmed by the Koran and the Hadith. This is not to say that Ibn al-ᶜArabī simply repeats the traditional accounts, far from it. It is rather a question of priorities. How do we come to know what we know? Basically, from three sources: following the authority of knowledge transmitted from others (whoever these others may be—prophets, scientists, teachers, parents, journalists), rational investigation, and direct experience of what is real. Ibn al-ᶜArabī makes thorough use of all three routes, but he recognizes transmission as the most basic. Then come direct experience, then rational investigation.

Many modern scientists and certainly the popularizers of science would like us to think that science puts experience of what is real—an experience which they call "experimentation" and "empirical verification"—first, but, as soon as one asks what is meant by the word *real*, one understands that the scientific conception of reality is already determined by a theory, which, in most cases, has been received by transmission from some authority, whether that authority be the "Zeitgeist," society at large, or various teachers and books.

The route of direct experience of what is "real"—as that term has always been understood in Islamic civilization—is, in fact, the most difficult of all routes to follow, and it is blocked to all those sensibilities—especially modern scientific sensibilities—that are rooted in ignorance of the self. Here Ibn al-ʿArabī constantly quotes the prophetic dictum, "He who knows himself knows his Lord." A person's Lord is that configuration of reality that determines the person's situation. One will never know the configuration of reality that makes one what one is without knowing oneself.

Prophetic knowledge is a form of transmitted knowledge. Ibn al-ʿArabī accepts this knowledge without reservation. He recognizes that in principle it includes all the knowledge received from the 124,000 prophets from Adam down to Muhammad, but in practice he limits it to the Islamic forms of prophetic knowledge, that is, the Koran and the Hadith. Ibn al-ʿArabī also knows perfectly well that prophetic knowledge cannot be understood without a subject to know it, and what the subject comes to understand from the knowledge depends upon who the subject is and how he or she goes about trying to understand. In coming to an understanding of prophetic knowledge, the same three routes are available—following the authority of teachers and forebears, rational investigation, and direct experience. Obviously, these three routes are themselves intertwined. I will differentiate among them here by giving them a specifically Islamic context.

In Islamic history, diverse intellectual schools have attempted to achieve knowledge by stressing one or more of these three routes in different ways. Among the major intellectual perspectives, both jurisprudence and Kalām (dogmatic theology) stress the authority of transmission from the Prophet and the rational understanding of what has been transmitted. Philosophy stresses rational investigation, but not the authority of revelation. Theoretical Sufism places primary emphasis on the direct experience of God's reality or, to use the Arabic expression, *kashf*, the "unveiling" of the Real by removing the ignorance and obscurities that separate the true subject from the true object. Ibn al-ʿArabī calls those who achieve unveiling in its full and authentic form the "Folk of God" or the "Realizers."

What the Folk of God "realize" is the knowledge of God, self, and cosmos that has been revealed through the prophets. This knowledge is "empirical" or "experienced" in an ultimate sense, because its objects are the ultimate experience. The realization is all important. Without the realization, people are simply transmitters or arm-chair theorizers or dreamers. On this issue Ibn al-ʿArabī likes to quote the response of the famous Sufi Abū Yazīd to unsympathetic critics: "You take your knowledge dead from the dead, but we take our knowledge from the Living who does not die."

The prophetic knowledge that needs to be verified establishes the contours of what is knowable about God, the self, and the cosmos. Any cosmology, after all, selectively chooses, from the plethora of data, what is considered significant because of some theory. One of the primary factors tying together the modern scientific theories is quantification—what is quantifiable is significant, and what cannot be expressed mathematically is extraneous to true knowledge. Nevertheless, there are an indefinite number of standpoints from which we can decide what is significant among the infinite objects accessible to our experience, or what should be abstracted out and employed as the principles of order and arrangement. The diverse world views of peoples and tribes all over the globe and throughout history give witness to this fact.

The Koran and the Hadith define the boundaries of significance for Muslim cosmologists and determine what they will employ, qua Muslims, as a framework for classifying and arranging. These boundaries are broad and have yielded a diversity of cosmological perspectives. Ibn al-ᶜArabī speaks of many of these perspectives and integrates them into his own vision, a vision that can best be described as the "Vision of No Vision"—that is, the vision of no specific vision. In the same way, Ibn al-ᶜArabī calls the highest stage of human perfection, the standpoint that embraces all standpoints, the "Station of No Station."

Prophetic knowledge establishes a universe of discourse for a community. By the time of Ibn al-ᶜArabī, the Islamic community was spread over most of the civilized globe and shared a common conceptual universe. Part of the secret of Ibn al-ᶜArabī's success—the rapid spread of his writings and terminology, the tremendous respect and awe in which he was held by many, the fear and antagonism that his works inspired in others—lies in his plumbing the depths of the Koranic universe and his representation of that universe in a language that not only spoke to many of his contemporaries, but also has continued speaking to seekers of knowledge throughout the centuries.

There were many causes for the negative reactions that Ibn al-ᶜArabī stirred up. One was certainly his challenge to the received authority of the ulama. Not that he denied the authority of transmitted knowledge, but he was harshly critical of all claims to have codified and rationalized Islamic knowledge with finality, and it was upon such claims that religious authority was built. His was a profound attack on the solidifications and closures of the received wisdom, and naturally many defenders of the status quo responded with virulent attacks on Ibn al-ᶜArabī's own claims to authority.

There were many other reasons for the criticisms of Ibn al-ᶜArabī. Even some of the Sufi teachers prohibited their disciples from studying his works, because they knew of the twin dangers facing any student. The first danger is loss of center and stability. In any society, people maintain their stability and sanity through dwelling on the bedrock of certainty—various truths that appear to be self-evident in the context of the culture and the times. In traditional cultures like those that dominated over the Islamic world, the certainties are largely those of religion. Many of these gain their wide acceptance because they can be formulated simply and powerfully and are accessible to everyone. The formulations are typically presented along with clear definitions of the ultimate points of reference. God, for example, is understood as an objective reality, totally distinct from the subject. Believers do not like to be told that the God they worship is not in fact the ultimate reality that they suppose He is but rather the God of their belief, distinct from the Gods of other people's beliefs. Ibn al-ᶜArabī's works are replete with statements that seem designed to throw the naive and the dogmatically minded into a tizzy.

The second great danger facing students of Ibn al-ᶜArabī is the intoxication of discovery and the risk of losing touch with proper psychological and spiritual balance. Take, for example, the famous doctrine of *waḥdat al-wujūd,* "the Oneness of Being," which was ascribed to Ibn al-ᶜArabī within a hundred years of his death—though the expression is not his—and which soon took on a life of its own. One common way of interpreting it, a way that has endeared it to many people in the modern West, was as an elite knowledge that bestowed upon its possessors a superiority that differentiated them from the commoners. Hence, what was expected from the commoners—adherance to the revealed law and observance of moral codes—was not to be expected from the elite, since they stood beyond such petty concerns. This reading of *waḥdat al-wujūd,* along with the false ascription of the idea to Ibn al-ᶜArabī, was particularly prevalent in India and led to significant attacks on his teachings, such as those made by the Sufi shaykh Aḥmad Sirhindī.[4]

The primary importance of prophetic knowledge in Ibn al-ᶜArabī's viewpoint explains his constant citations from the Koran and the Hadith. These sources, after all, were among the most important, if not the most important, points of intellectual reference for him and his contemporaries—and they have remained such for a large body of the human race. Traditional Muslims see the universe differently from traditional Christians or Hindus or Apaches, and, with all the more reason, from those with a modern, scientific education. In the Islamic case, elements of the world view antedate Islam, but this does not make these "pre-Islamic" elements "un-Islamic." It needs to be remembered that the Koran repeatedly stresses that it came to "confirm" the prophetic knowledge that had gone before, and this could be interpreted, and was interpreted by those who felt the need, to mean most of the knowledge of the ancients, whether they were Arabs, Christians, Iranians, Babylonians, Egyptians, Hindus, or whatever. To this perspective alludes the famous saying attributed to the Prophet, "Seek knowledge even unto China."

Although profoundly rooted in transmission and tradition, Ibn al-ʿArabī's teachings exhibit a freshness and novelty that proved irresistible to a large body of Muslim intellectuals. Many others, who were not so intellectually oriented, sensed the sacred origin of his teachings and perceived him as one of the great saints or "friends of God." He himself was well aware of both the oldness and the newness of what he was doing, and this helps explain his claim to be the "Seal of the Saints," a claim that was taken seriously by many Muslims in later centuries.[5] This did not mean that he was claiming to be the last friend of God on earth, but rather the last plenary inheritor of Muhammad before the second coming of Jesus. After Ibn al-ʿArabī, people would continue to climb to God and become His friends, but they would not attain to the full inheritance of the Muhammadan reality, which embraces all the knowledge of all the prophets. Rather, under the aegis of Muhammad, they would inherit their knowledge, stations, and states from Jesus, Moses, Abraham, or any of the other 124,000 or so known and unknown prophets.

One traditional criticism of Ibn al-ʿArabī has to with his meddling in affairs that are not accessible to human knowledge. A good body of Islamic learning focuses on the present, the practical, the "profitable"—that is, profitable for establishing individual and social equilibrium vis-a-vis God, which leads to salvation after death.[6] This sort of knowledge is codified primarily in the Shariah, Islamic law, but most of Ibn al-ʿArabī's writings, even when he deals specifically with the Shariah, focus on God and the cosmos as a whole, along with the manner in which these are interrelated with the self. This sort of knowledge may not seem "profitable" to many people, and Ibn al-ʿArabī would agree that it has no real profit for affairs of the present world, but the present world is hardly his focus. He is looking at human beings in the overall context of reality, and that includes their posthumous becoming—a becoming whose significance can only be understood by knowing the self. It is here that the profitability of his writings becomes apparent. He explains this as follows:

> The need of the self for knowledge is greater than the constitution's need for the food that keeps it wholesome. Knowledge is of two sorts: The first knowledge is needed in the same way that food is needed. Hence it is necessary to exercise moderation, to limit oneself to the measure of need. This is the science of the Shariah's rulings. One should not consider these rulings except in the measure that one's need touches on them at the moment, for their ruling property pertains only to acts that occur in this world. So take from this knowledge only in the measure of your activity!
>
> The second knowledge, which has no limit at which one can come to a halt, is knowledge that pertains to God and the homesteads of the resurrection. Knowledge of the resurrection's homesteads will lead its knower to a preparedness for what is proper to each homestead. This is because on that day the Real Himself will make demands through the lifting of the veils; that is *the Day of Differentiation* [37:21]. It is necessary for all intelligent human beings to be *upon insight* [12:108] in their affairs and to be prepared to answer for themselves and others in the homesteads within which they know that answers will be demanded of them. (I 581.29)

Ibn al-ʿArabī's Basic Themes

In SPK, I dealt with six basic terminological and conceptual sets that are interwoven in most of Ibn al-ʿArabī's writings. These are the names of God, existence and nonexistence, *tanzīh* and *tashbīh*, modes of knowing, human perfection, and the *barzakh*. In what follows, I outline each of these sets to provide a basic orientation. I am not suggesting that this is an adequate outline, but it should refresh the memory of those familiar with his teachings and introduce his basic notions to those who have had little previous acquaintance with his works. Technical terms of special importance are printed in small capitals the first time they are explained. Detailed definitions and explanations can be found in SPK. In order not to clutter the discussion, I refrain from mentioning most of the original Arabic terms. They can be found quickly by reference to the Index of Terms in this book or in SPK.

Names of God

GOD is a name that has two basic meanings. In one sense it denotes the ESSENCE, which is the ultimate reality that is the fountainhead of all other realities. The Essence cannot be known in positive terms. Human knowledge of the Essence amounts to an acknowledgment that the Essence is there and a recognition that we cannot know it.

In a second sense, the name God designates what Ibn al-ʿArabī calls the LEVEL, that is, God's specific position in relation to any other realities that we might want to take into account. Hence the Level is the Essence inasmuch as we can situate it over and against worlds and creatures, or inasmuch as we can know its relations with the things that are found in the COSMOS, which can be defined as "everything other than God." God's Essence is identical with God's Level, but, God's Essence is known only to God, while His Level is the object of discussion whenever we envisage Him in relation to others, or in relation to Himself. As soon as we mention "God and the cosmos," we are talking about God inasmuch as He can be differentiated from the cosmos. We are situating Him at a specific level, a level in which He may in fact stand. We have not exhausted the reality of God, but have simply mentioned an outlook on that reality. We can go on mentioning outlooks and standpoints ad infinitum, but we will never move closer to the Essence, since the Infinite stands infinitely beyond the finite always and forever.

When we discuss the Level, we do so in terms of attributes and attributions. In Koranic language, these are known as DIVINE NAMES. They are the relations that can be envisaged between God and the cosmos. Ibn al-ʿArabī sometimes says that negative names—that is, the names that tell us what God is not—refer to the Essence, but when he wants to be more careful, he says that strictly speaking, the Essence cannot be discussed and cannot be referred to. The divine names refer to God's Level or position vis-a-vis the cosmos and everything within it, not to His Essence as such.

Ibn al-ʿArabī employs three basic terms more or less interchangeably to refer to the divine names—names, ATTRIBUTES, and RELATIONS (or RELATIONSHIPS). A grammatical distinction can be drawn among these terms because *name* refers technically to adjectives by which God can be addressed, such as Alive, Knowing, Powerful, Compassionate, and Forgiver. Both attributes and relations (or "attributions") refer to the abstract nouns that these names specify—life, knowledge, power, compassion, and forgiveness. Thus God has the name "Alive" and the attribute of life. Life is a "relation" or "attribution" in that it can be conceptually distinguished from the one who is Alive and then attributed to Him. More commonly, Ibn al-ʿArabī has in view the relations that most of the names establish between God and the cosmos. Thus God is "Knowing," which is to say that He knows the objects of His knowledge (whether these are Himself or the cosmos and its contents). Hence the relation of knowledge is established between Him and what He knows. He is Creator, so the attribute or relation of creativity is established between Him and His creation.

The divine names and attributes are demanded by the reality of God and the cosmos. In other words, as soon as we see that there is a God on one side and a cosmos on the other, we need the attributes to differentiate the two sides and to explain how they are related. The names are applicable to both sides. All names of God, with certain exceptions, like "God" itself, can properly be applied both to God and to created things. Clearly, however, the names do not mean exactly the same thing in the two cases.

The basic formula for differentiating the two senses of a single attribute that is applied both to God and something else is the first Shahadah, "There is no god but God." Thus, for example, we can apply the term REAL to both God and created things, but in the light of the Shahadah, we recognize that "There is none real but the Real." That which is truly real is God, while the creatures at best possess a borrowed reality. Hence, a creature is real from one point of view, but UNREAL from another point of view. The attribute of unreality pertains only to the creatures, not to God.

In one sense, the divine attributes are all anthropomorphic, which is to say that we conceive of them in terms of ourselves. They must be anthropomorphic, because we can only conceive of things in terms of ourselves. In a more profound sense, however, human attributes are theomorphic. God, after all, is the truly real, and human beings are real only inasmuch as they possess a reality given to them by God. Hence, whatever names can be attributed to both God and creation belong first to God and only by extension to creatures. The creatures were created in God's form, not vice versa. Nevertheless, Ibn al-ʿArabī repeatedly reminds us that "God" and all pertinent names and attributes rise up from knowledge of ourselves. Although we depend upon the Real for our reality, the designation of His names and attributes depends in an important sense upon our knowledge of ourselves and, following upon that knowledge, our knowledge of God. This knowledge of God is, of course, knowledge of God's Level in relation to us, not knowledge of His Essence.

Traditionally, God is said to have ninety-nine names. Ibn al-ʿArabī respects this tradition and considers calling God by any name by which He has not called Himself (in the Koran and the Hadith) a lack of COURTESY. Nonetheless, he recognizes that every relation established between God and the cosmos can be named, and naming it establishes a divine name. From this point of view, there are as many divine names as there are creatures, since each creature manifests a specific relation between God and the cosmos that is not repeated exactly in any other creature. On God's side, there is a single reality. On the side of creation, there is an infinity of realities demanding an infinity of names.

All the names are prefigured in God's own reality, in His Essence, which is inaccessible and unknowable to us in itself. Within God, the names have interrelations, and we can know something about these interrelations by knowing how the pertinent attributes interrelate on our own level. One of the most commonly discussed intradivine relations is referred to in the hadith, "God's mercy takes precedence over His wrath." Clearly, mercy and wrath are both relations between God and His creatures, but the precedence of one over the other says something about the divine Level, the reality called "God" that to some degree is accessible to our understanding.

Ibn al-ʿArabī sometimes talks about intradivine relations in terms of four fundamental attributes upon which the existence of the universe depends—life, knowledge, desire, and power. Within God, these attributes interrelate in a specific manner. God is Alive, and life is a necessary precondition for knowledge. Were God dead, He would know nothing. God is the Knowing, so He knows everything that can be known, including all creaturely possibilities. He is the Desiring, so He desires to create certain things, but He can only desire to create what He knows. Did He not know a thing, He could never desire to create it. He is the Powerful, so He exercises power by creating things, but He creates only what He desires to create, not what He does not desire to create.

This way of looking at divine attributes allows Ibn al-ʿArabī to rank them according to scope. Life is wider in scope than knowledge, knowledge wider than desire, and desire wider than power. In a similar way, forgiveness is wider in scope than vengeance. All divine attributes can be interrelated in analogous ways. **ORDER** (HIERARCHY in SPK) is intrinsic to the Real's attributes, and the Real creates the universe in keeping with His own attributes, which designate His own reality. It follows that order is intrinsic to the cosmos.

When Ibn al-ʿArabī studies the cosmos, he does not study it in and for itself. He looks at it inasmuch as it illustrates the order that is found in its Origin. The things and beings found in the cosmos are taken as outward expressions of the relations that exist within God and between God and the cosmos. The laws that govern the things and beings of the universe are the same laws that govern the relations among the divine names. To know the cosmos in its full significance, we need to seek out its ROOTS and SUPPORTS within God Himself, and these are the divine names, in a broad sense of the term. The things of the cosmos are the names' PROPERTIES or TRACES (EFFECTS in SPK). Just as the names can be ranked in degrees according to their scope, so also creatures can be ranked in degrees according to their capacity to manifest the properties of the Divine Level. RANKING IN DEGREES OF EXCELLENCE goes back to roots in God.

Existence and Nonexistence

To talk of God in terms of names is to employ the key terminology of the Koran and the Hadith, but Ibn al-ʿArabī also adopts terms that entered Islamic civilization from the Greek heritage and were refined and expanded upon by generations of philosophers and theologians. Probably the most important of these is *wujūd,* which is typically translated as "existence" or "being" but which literally means "finding." If, for English speakers, "existence" has no necessary connection with awareness, this is not the case for Ibn al-ʿArabī. To speak of *wujūd* is to speak of finding and what is found, and finding is meaningless without knowledge and consciousness.

Wujūd, then, is that which finds and is found. In the strictest sense of the term, it applies only to God as Essence, the Real Being, who alone is true and real in every sense of the term. The word is also applied to the cosmos as a whole, the whole domain of "existence"—as contrasted with God as "Being." It is in this sense of the term that the Shaykh says that something is "in *wujūd*" or "enters into *wujūd.*" Once something enters into *wujūd,* we can speak of its existence, its specific *wujūd* that is differentiated from all other *wujūds.*

When the term *wujūd* refers to God, it must be understood as the true and actual reality of God. In contrast, when it refers to other than God, the word is being used conventionally or metaphorically. Strictly speaking, only God has *wujūd* and the OTHERS do not exist, are not found, and do not find. God knows all things, is found in all things, finds Himself in all things, and lends finding to the things as is appropriate to their realities. In and of themselves, things have no claim to finding or being found in any respect, but as God's creatures, they are given *wujūd.*

NONEXISTENCE is an inherent and essential characteristic of all things other than God. Things in themselves have no claim to any sort of existence. It is true that God knows the things as concomitants of His knowledge of Himself, but this does not give them existence apart from God's own *wujūd,* nor does it give them the finding of their own being found. In a similar way, our knowledge does not give self-existence to what we know. The objects of our knowledge, inasmuch as they are simply our own concepts, are found by us, not by themselves. If we subsequently give external existence to what we know, that is another discussion.

In themselves, THE OBJECTS OF GOD'S KNOWLEDGE are nonexistent. Ibn al-ʿArabī refers to them by several expressions, such as ENTITIES and THINGS. God knows what He knows as corollaries of *wujūd,* which is His own self-finding. *Wujūd*'s finding of itself is an inherent attribute of *wujūd,* so God is the Knower always and forever. It follows that the things are always and forever the objects of God's knowledge, because they have no *wujūd* apart from His *wujūd,* and His *wujūd* is eternal and unchanging. Moreover, the things never leave God's knowledge. What comes to exist in the cosmos is not the things in themselves, for nothing is found other than *wujūd.* The things are analogous to the fixed stars (*thawābit*), which leave their traces on earth without ever moving from their places in heaven. Hence the entities dwell in FIXITY (IMMUTABILITY in SPK) and are often called the FIXED ENTITIES (IMMUTABLE ENTITIES in SPK).

Things have two situations. Their own essential situation—the situation that belongs to them by their own essences—is to be nonexistent objects of God's knowledge. This is their THINGNESS OF FIXITY, the fact that they are forever fixed as things in God's awareness of Himself. God may, on the basis of His life, knowledge, desire, and power, give existence to things, and then, as Ibn al-ʿArabī often puts it, "They enter into *wujūd*." They come to exist through a *wujūd* that has been given to them by God. This is their THINGNESS OF *WUJŪD*, the fact that created things are found in an external world known as the "cosmos." Within the cosmos, they continue to be found by God, but now they are also found by themselves and others.

Ibn al-ʿArabī distinguishes between the two basic modes of *wujūd*—God's real *wujūd* and the entities' borrowed *wujūd*—in many ways. For example, he often follows the standard Avicennan distinction among three different ways of describing things in relation to *wujūd*—the NECESSARY, the POSSIBLE, and the IMPOSSIBLE. The "impossible" is that which can have no *wujūd*; it is not found, because it cannot exist. The "necessary" is *wujūd* in itself, which cannot not be found, because it is found through its own essential reality, and REALITIES do not change—otherwise they would not be realities. If the finders do not know what they are finding, this does not detract from *wujūd*'s necessity. Thus "the Necessary *Wujūd*" is a philosophical name of God.

Modalities of *wujūd* that are neither impossible nor necessary are "possible." These modalities include the *wujūd* of everything other than God, everything that is found apart from God in any mode of finding. These are the POSSIBLE THINGS, a term that is equivalent to "things" and "entities." They are "possible" because logically they stand equidistant between *wujūd* and nonexistence. If we look at them in terms of themselves, without regard to their existence or nonexistence in the cosmos, we have no way of judging whether or not God will give them existence. When God does give existence to a possible thing, this is known as PREPONDERATION—giving weight to the side of existence over the side of nonexistence. God is then the **PREPONDERATOR**, since a thing's coming into existence depends upon His knowledge, desire, and power.

A possible thing may or may not exist. If the thing does not exist, it may be called a "fixed entity" or an "object of knowledge," and everything other than God is always and forever a fixed entity. If it does exist, it is also called, in respect of its *wujūd*, an EXISTENT ENTITY or simply an EXISTENT THING. When Ibn al-ʿArabī is discussing "entities" or "things" without qualification, it may not be clear whether or not they exist. In many cases the question is irrelevant, because the attributes and properties of the entities remain the same whether or not they are found in the cosmos.

The distinction between the thing itself and the existence of the thing is well known to the Muslim philosophers (and, of course, to Western philosophers). The terms typically employed to make the distinction are QUIDDITY—a thing's "whatness" or "what-is-it-ness"—and *wujūd*. Here two different questions are posed: To grasp a thing's quiddity, we ask, "What is it?" Having understood what it is, we ask, "Is it?" In English, some ambiguity arises because the word *is* has two different senses in the two questions. In the first case it is a copula, and in the second it refers to a thing's existence. In Arabic, there is no ambiguity, because there is no copula. Literally, one says, "What it?" and "Whether it?" To the first question, one answers with a definition—one mentions the thing's whatness. To the second question, one answers yes or no, thus affirming or denying its *wujūd*.

The true whatness of a thing is the thing as it is known by God, that is, its fixed entity. If the thing exists, then we can talk about it as an existent entity. The term *reality* is used in the same sense as whatness. When Ibn al-ʿArabī refers to "the realities," he typically has in mind the fixed entities, the things as they are known by God. He also calls the realities in this sense the "divine roots" and "divine supports." Sometimes, however, he uses *reality* to refer to the existent entities, to the things as they are actually found in *wujūd*, in whatever modality they are found (e.g., external *wujūd*, mental *wujūd*, verbal *wujūd*, written *wujūd*). In short, "entity" and "reality" are often employed as synonyms—either may refer to an object of God's knowledge, a thing in the world, or both at once. Either may also be employed to refer to God, though Ibn al-ʿArabī is much more likely to use entity in this sense—especially in the expression THE ONE ENTITY.

Ibn al-ʿArabī calls the cosmos "ENGENDERED EXISTENCE" (*kawn*), a term that the philosophers employed to translate "generation" in the Greek expression that gives us "generation and corruption." From the same root we have terms like ENGENDERED THING, a synonym of existent entity or existent reality. In employing these terms, Ibn al-ʿArabī always has in mind the etymological connection with the word "Be" (*kun*), which is God's command to a thing when He desires to bring it into existence, that is, when He wants to "engender" it. This word *Be* is God's ENGENDERING COMMAND, which is differentiated from His PRESCRIPTIVE COMMAND. Through the engendering command, God gives existence to the things. Through the prescriptive command, He addresses human beings through MESSENGERS and PROPHETS, thereby establishing SHARIAHS, that is, systems of revealed LAW and modes of right conduct.

Tanzīh *and* Tashbīh

From one point of view, *wujūd* belongs strictly to God, and everything other than God is nonexistent. No comparisons can be drawn between what is and what is not. There is simply no common measure. This is the standpoint of *tanzīh* or declaring INCOMPARABILITY, and it was central to Islamic theological thinking from early times.

From a second point of view, *wujūd* appears wherever anything finds or is found, and there is nothing but finding and being found. We experience only *wujūd*, because experience is finding, and there is nothing there to experience or to be experienced save what is found. Our experience of the *wujūd* of our own entities is sufficiently real for us to function in the situations in which we find ourselves. Hence there is some common measure between us—who are busy finding ourselves and others—and God, who alone finds in a true sense. This is the perspective of *tashbīh* or declaring SIMILARITY, and, in Ibn al-ʿArabī's view of things, it is every bit as important as the perspective of incomparability, even if, in early Islamic theology, the term was most often employed to designate what was considered a heretical position.

When we look at the divine names, we see that they can be understood either in terms of incomparability or in terms of similarity, or in both ways at once. But to understand a name in both senses, we need to go forward one sense at a time. Because of the necessity of recognizing the overwhelming reality of the Real and observing courtesy toward the Creator, we begin with the perspective of *tanzīh*. From this point of view, the qualities designated by the divine names belong strictly to God, and human beings have no share in them. This perspective stresses the nonexistence of creatures and the *wujūd* of the Real. In the context of Islamic praxis, the response to God's reality and human unreality is known as SERVANTHOOD, or observing the requirements of the revealed Law, the Shariah.

From a second point of view, the divine names exhibit their properties and traces in creation. As the Prophet said, "God created Adam in His form," and as Ibn al-ʿArabī insists, this holds both for the great Adam, who is the cosmos in its entirety, and for the small Adam, who is the human being. The properties and traces of the divine attributes are indefinitely dispersed in the MACROCOSM, which is the cosmos as a whole. They are also concentrated into a single, relatively undifferentiated unity in the MICROCOSM, which is the human being. Inasmuch as human beings are full and integral embodiments of the DIVINE FORM in which they were created, they are worthy to be called VICEGERENTS of God. Those who have achieved this station are the PROPHETS and the great saints or FRIENDS of God.

In one respect, *tanzīh* denotes the utter lack of commonality between *wujūd* and nonexistence, or the fact that the Essence is inaccessible to the creatures. In another respect, *tanzīh* refers to a set of divine attributes that stress the difference between God and creation, while *tashbīh* designates another set that suggests a certain similarity. When human beings establish the proper relation with God in terms of these two categories, they are God's full servants and worthy vicegerents. These two groups of names are often called the names of "beauty and majesty," or "gentleness and subjugation," or "mercy and wrath." Sometimes Ibn al-ʿArabī refers to them as the TWO HANDS with which God created Adam.

Included among the divine names of *tanzīh* are names such as Majestic, Subjugating, Wrathful, Exalted, Independent, Holy, Glorified, King, and Great. In respect of these names, creatures are insignificant and, in effect, nonexistent. But God is also Beautiful, Gentle, Merciful, Compassionate, Near, Loving, Forgiving, and Kind. In respect of these names, God turns His face toward the creatures to ensure their happiness. His concern for human beings leads Him to create them in His own form and make them His vicegerents in the earth. And His concern outweighs everything else, for "His mercy takes precedence over His wrath," so *tashbīh*—God's presence in the cosmos—overrules the effects of *tanzīh*, His absence from it.

Looking more closely at the implications of the divine names, Ibn al-ʿArabī brings out the inherent worth of the cosmos. God is the NONMANIFEST and the MANIFEST. In respect of the first name, He is the incomparable Essence, but in respect of the second name, He displays Himself to the universe through the traces and properties of His names. The universe is nothing other than His display, His SELF-DISCLOSURE or His LOCUS OF MANIFESTATION. Hence in the last analysis, the cosmos is God as Manifest, while everything other than the cosmos is God as Nonmanifest.

Ibn al-ʿArabī makes the same points in terms of the terminology of *wujūd*. *Wujūd* is nonmanifest because it is "no thing" as opposed to each and every thing, and hence *wujūd* is not differentiated and distinct from any thing. It is UNBOUNDED (NONDELIMITED in SPK), while every created thing is BOUND (DELIMITED in SPK) and constrained by the specific characteristics that make it this and not that. However, since *wujūd* is unbounded in an absolute sense, it is not bound by unboundedness. Hence it binds itself in accordance with every possible mode of binding. The diverse modes in which *wujūd* binds itself are the existent things that fill the cosmos.

Modes of Knowing

As already noted, Ibn al-ʿArabī sees three basic routes to gain knowledge—acceptance of reports, rational investigation, and unveiling. REPORTS are everything transmitted to us from others. In evaluating the reliability of reports, we need to look at the source and the chain of transmission. Reports stemming from God by reliable chains are of course the most authoritative, and these include the scriptures, the Koran in particular. Other important sources include the prophets, whose words may be assimilated to those of God, and the friends of God. There are various SCALES by which reports and their transmitters can be weighed.

The second route of acquiring knowledge is REASON or the rational faculty. It is a means of understanding whose proper function is to accept reports and legal RULINGS from God and to keep the human being focused on the right path by restraining CAPRICE, which is the servant's self-will. In addition, reason has the innate tendency to separate and distinguish, and hence to see what God is not. Its guiding light steers it toward *tanzīh*, and, if left to itself, it will never accept that God can be similar to anything, so it rejects *tashbīh*.

UNVEILING, the third route, is knowledge that God gives directly to the servants when He lifts the veils separating Himself from them and "opens the door" to perception of invisible realities. There are several types of unveiling, and Ibn al-ʿArabī sometimes distinguishes among them, employing terms such as TASTING, WITNESSING, OPENING, and INSIGHT. Generally speaking, unveiling is associated with IMAGINATION, because it typically occurs through the imaginalization of various invisible entities or realities. In other words, things that are normally inaccessible to sense perception or to reason are given form by God and then perceived within imagination by those to whom the door to unseen things has been opened. Unveiling is an everyday occurrence for prophets. For the friends of God, it is an INHERITANCE from the prophets. The FOLK OF UNVEILING are the highest ranking friends of God.

One of Ibn al-ʿArabī's constant themes is the affinity between routes to knowledge and the understanding of God that rises up from following a specific route. In knowing anything at all, human PREPAREDNESS or RECEPTIVITY is of the utmost importance. Generally speaking, those with rational proclivities will understand God as distant and incomparable, and this explains the preoccupations of Kalām specialists, philosophers, mathematicians, and natural scientists. Those who are given unveiling will find God present and similar. They will see the cosmos and everything within it as God's self-disclosure. This helps explain the Sufi stress upon living in the presence of God.

Perfect knowledge of God demands seeing with TWO EYES. The highest of God's friends, whom Ibn al-ʿArabī calls by such terms as the GNOSTICS, the **FOLK OF GOD** (the **FOLK OF ALLAH** in SPK), and the **REALIZERS**, are those who recognize God in His self-disclosures and at the same time acknowledge His utter incomparability with everything found in the self and the cosmos. They have achieved knowledge of the HEART, whose beating signifies its constant FLUCTUATION between understanding God as different, far, and incomparable and seeing Him as same, near, and similar.

The Realizers reach their knowledge by FOLLOWING AUTHORITY. No knowledge is accessible without an initial acceptance of the authority of reports. If reason attains knowledge, it does so on the basis of accepting the reports transmitted to it by the senses and REFLECTION. Since all knowledge goes back to authority, Ibn al-ʿArabī maintains that the only rational route is to follow the authority of God, and we can only do this by accepting the reports brought by the prophets.

Human Perfection

Ibn al-ʿArabī's teachings come together on the issue of human PERFECTION, which is none other than for HUMAN BEINGS to be fully human. Humans are different from other creatures because they are forms of the whole, while other creatures are parts. "God created Adam in His form," and He likewise created the cosmos in His form. Both the cosmos and the human being are integral forms of God. But the cosmos displays the divine names and attributes in indefinite dispersion in all worlds and all space and time, so each individual thing in the cosmos can only be an infinitesimal part of the whole. In contrast, human beings are called upon to display the entirety of the divine form. The degree to which they achieve this goal establishes their worth as God's servants and vicegerents and determines their situation in this world and the next. It brings about the distinction between those who reach FELICITY, which is the Koranic term for the bliss of the people of paradise, and those who suffer WRETCHEDNESS, the attribute of those who go to hell.

Human beings are defined by the form of God. God is the Level that is named by all the divine names. Hence every attribute of God is found in the INNATE DISPOSITION (*fiṭra*) of the human being. The path to perfection involves bringing these attributes out from hiddenness to manifestation. Because of *tanzīh*, it is utterly impossible for people to understand their own innate disposition, made in the form of God, without God's help. This help comes as prophetic guidance. The only way to reach perfection is to follow the authority of the prophets. People go astray by following the authority of their own caprice or their own powers of reflection and rational thought.

People need to observe the revealed Law, the Shariah, in order to bring their activity and knowledge into conformity with God's scales of measurement. Even the Folk of God are not striving to know God as such, but rather to achieve felicity—their own everlasting happiness. In terms of the divine roots and supports of the universe, the quest to act correctly with the right intention brings about the actualization of NOBLE CHARACTER TRAITS, and these traits are nothing but the traces and properties of the divine names in the human being, who is the divine form. Hence Ibn al-ʿArabī often refers to the path to perfection as that of ASSUMING THE CHARACTER TRAITS OF GOD.

On the concrete, human level, the Shariah in its broadest sense provides the scale with which the appropriate and proper assumption of God's traits can be measured. The basic principle here is the notion of *ḥaqq,* which is a noun and an adjective that means truth and true, reality and real, propriety and proper, rightness and right. As a divine name, *al-ḥaqq* means the Real, the Truth, the Right, and it is typically juxtaposed with *khalq,* creation. But everything has a *ḥaqq* pertaining to it, which is to say that everything has a proper situation, a correct mode of being, an appropriate manner of displaying the Real to us. The sense of appropriateness and rightness in *ḥaqq* is very strong, and the words "real" or "truth" simply do not express it in English.

To say that everything has a *ḥaqq* is to say that everything has a right and appropriate mode of being and that, in addition, it is our duty before God, the Real, to recognize it and to act accordingly. The divine *Ḥaqq* makes demand upon us through the appropriate manifestations of itself, which are the *ḥaqq*s in creation. *Wujūd* is not simply "existence," that which is, it is also that which makes moral and ethical demands on us through its very nature. It is *ḥaqq,* which is to say that it is right, true, and appropriate, and it alone is real. Its realness makes it cognitively indefensible to busy oneself with the unreal, and its rightness and appropriateness make it morally absurd to take anything else into consideration in human activity. All the manifestations of *wujūd,* all the self-disclosures of the Real, address us personally, and we will be held responsible for recognizing the *ḥaqq* in each thing and acting accordingly, simply because the Real alone provides the standards for judging right and appropriate activity. Each thing has a right upon us, and hence each is our "responsibility" (another word that can translate *ḥaqq*). Given that all things manifest the *Ḥaqq,* each possesses a *ḥaqq,* and we will be held responsible for all the *ḥaqq*s that pertain specifically to us. Hence we need a scale by which we can recognize the *ḥaqq*s of things and from which we can learn the appropriate and proper manner for dealing with them.

The Prophet said, "Your self has a *ḥaqq* upon you, your Lord has a *ḥaqq* upon you, and your spouse has a *ḥaqq* upon you, so give to each that has a *ḥaqq* its *ḥaqq.*" In other words, "Give to each thing that has a rightful due"—and everything has something that is rightfully due to it—"its rightful due." This giving things their *ḥaqq*s is for Ibn al-ʿArabī the very definition of the human task in the cosmos. The word *taḥqīq,* which I have been translating here as "realization" ("verification" in SPK) means as well "giving things their rightful due" or "recognizing the *ḥaqq* of each thing and acting in an appropriate manner." The fifth form of the same root, *taḥaqquq,* which can also be translated as "realization," though it has a less transitive sense than *taḥqīq,* means finding the *ḥaqq* of each thing in oneself and living fully in accordance with that *ḥaqq.* If Ibn al-ʿArabī takes realization as the highest stage of human perfection, it is because the Realizers are those who live up to the Real, the Right, the True, the Proper, the *Ḥaqq.* They do so not only in their minds and their understandings, but also in every act that they perform and every word that they speak. Their activity wells up from their character traits, and their character traits are nothing save the human *ḥaqq* of the divine names, names that display their traces in human beings because people were created in the form of God, the *Ḥaqq.* The Realizers are those who recognize that each divine name names only *al-Ḥaqq,* the Real. They recognize that the named object, the *ḥaqq,* is present not only in the Divine Essence, but also in the divine self-disclosure, which is the cosmos and the self. They recognize that each name has a specific *ḥaqq* in each of its loci of manifestation, which is to say that each appears properly and appropriately in the created things and each makes demands upon them. When Ibn al-ʿArabī cites the Koranic verse, *He has given each thing its creation* (20:50), he typically means that the Real has given each created thing an appropriate measure, a rightful due, a glimmer of *wujūd*, a theophany of the divine names, a *ḥaqq*. In this respect the *khalq* or "creation" of each thing is identical with its *ḥaqq*, because the *Ḥaqq* has given the thing its *khalq*, so this creation makes demands on us. We must recognize the *ḥaqq* of each thing and act accordingly. Because human beings alone were made in the integral form of God, they alone are able to recognize and realize the *Ḥaqq* Itself and the *ḥaqq* of everything in *wujūd*, which is the whole cosmos.

In Itself, the *Ḥaqq*—which is the Real *wujūd*—has no form, or rather, through its infinity and unboundedness, *wujūd* assumes every binding and every form without becoming bound and constricted. Human beings were created in the form of God, which is to say that they were created in the form of the sum total of the divine names, or according to every aspect and every face of the *Ḥaqq*, such that each human being is the form of the Real *Wujūd*. By the same token, because *wujūd* is infinite and unconstricted, the perfect human form is the form of no form. To be a mortal human being is to be delimited and bound by specific attributes and qualities, but to be perfectly human is to be freed from all limitations and constrictions by virtue of having returned to the innate human disposition, which is *wujūd* itself. Hence the highest of the PERFECT HUMAN BEINGS are those who attain to the STATION OF NO STATION. Their *ḥaqq* is not to be bound and knotted by any specific *ḥaqq*, but to give each possessor of a *ḥaqq*—each thing in *wujūd*, each self-disclosure of the *Ḥaqq*—what properly belongs to it. They are the MUHAMMADAN friends of God. Like Muhammad, they manifest every divine and human perfection, and like God Himself, they are named by all names and display the appropriate activity in every situation, giving each possessor of a *ḥaqq* its *ḥaqq*.

The supreme importance that Ibn al-ʿArabī gives to the notion of *ḥaqq* helps explain why the most commonly quoted Koranic verse in his writings is 33:4, which is usually translated as *And God speaks the truth, and He guides on the path.* The Shaykh concludes most chapters, most sections of chapters, and most semi-independent discussions within chapters with this verse. At first sight, and given this translation, the implication of quoting this verse seems to be that he has just spoken on God's behalf and provided the truth of the matter, so his readers should accept it from him. However, I would rather translate the verse as *And God speaks the* ***ḥaqq****, and He guides on the path.* In other words, God's Koranic exposition gives the situation its rightful due. His revealed speech expresses how the face of the Real is found in all things, and it delineates the intellectual, spiritual, and moral duties of God's servants in the cosmos. Only by realizing these words can His servants hope to live up to their servanthood and vicegerency, and this means not only recognizing the truth of the words, but also putting them into practice on every level. Thus Ibn al-ʿArabī's constant repetition of this verse serves as a reminder to the reader that the purpose of human life is defined by the *Ḥaqq*, who is God; it is He alone who speaks the *ḥaqq*, which is not the "truth" in a cognitive, logical, or epistemic sense, but rather the existential truth that is exactly appropriate to the actual situation of human beings in respect of their purpose in the cosmos. It is the truth as God alone can express it, because only the *Ḥaqq* comprehends each and every individual *ḥaqq*—the rightful due of everything in the universe.

The Barzakh

Those who achieve and realize the highest station of human perfection play two basic roles in the cosmos. First, as prophets and friends of God, their function is to guide others to human perfection. Second, as full realizations of *wujūd*'s form, they play an ontological role. Only through human perfection does *wujūd* reach the fullness of its outward manifestation. If *wujūd* is to display its own attributes, appropriate receptacles must be found. Many of these attributes can only be actualized externally through their embodiment in human beings. The divine attributes have no meaning if they remain abstractions. They can become fully manifest only through the context of human existence.

This is especially obvious with attributes such as mercy, compassion, wisdom, and love.

By manifesting the divine attributes fully, perfect human beings make possible the unfolding of the full range of *wujūd*'s possibilities. This gives them a function that far transcends social and human relations. In fact, this world depends upon them for its existence. It was brought into existence in the first place only to actualize all the possibilities of manifestation that perfect human beings embody.

In their cosmic function, perfect human beings bring together God and creation. As fully actualized divine forms, they are the self-disclosures of the ALL-COMPREHENSIVE NAME, which is God (i.e., Allah), within the universe. In themselves, they stand fully with God and fully with the cosmos. They are both eternal and temporal, nonmanifest and manifest, divine and human, infinite and finite.

If we turn away from the individual instances of human perfection and look at their nonmanifest realities, we find a single archetype, which is God Himself inasmuch as He has turned His face toward creating human beings in His own form. This self-binding with the aim of bringing perfect human beings into existence is called the MUHAMMADAN REALITY or the REALITY OF REALITIES. This Reality is the single, nonmanifest whole which, through differentiated manifestation, becomes the entire cosmos. But this single whole also has many relatively undifferentiated loci of manifestation, and these are the perfect human beings. Each perfect human being is one with God and with the Reality of Realities. At the same time, each is unique in his or her historical actuality. Each is like a divine name in signifying nothing but the One Entity. At the same time, every divine name has specific referents in the cosmos, given that knowledge and power, for example, do not become manifest in exactly the same configurations.

Viewed as a cosmic principle that undergirds all of manifest existence, the Reality of Realities is called the BREATH OF THE ALL-MERCIFUL. As God speaks, saying "Be!" to each thing that He desires to engender, His one word becomes articulated as the existent things within His breath. His breath is His mercy, which, in Koranic terms, *embraces everything* (7:156). Each word is nothing but a possible thing given existence within the breath of God. Each is inseparable from the Breath and the specific articulation or binding that gives it form, yet each is uniquely itself. In respect of *tanzīh*, God is situated infinitely beyond the words that He speaks, but in respect of *tashbīh*, each word is nothing but God's self-expression or self-disclosure. Each is identical with God and different from God at one and the same time. Each is HE/NOT HE.

If each thing is He/not He at any moment of its existence, it shares in the divine uniqueness inasmuch as it is He. At each moment, the He is affirmed, only to be negated by the specific, nonexistent reality of the thing as not He. This incessant affirmation and negation becomes manifest to those with eyes to see as the NEW CREATION, the fact that the *wujūd* of the things is constantly renewed moment by moment. Each of these moments is a unique moment, because God is unique in His HE-NESS or Essence, so each successive moment is new not only in the sense that existence is newly given, but also in the sense that the actual existing entity is different in each instant, though its nonexistent entity remains the same. Hence the cosmos is in constant turmoil, fluctuation, and TRANSMUTATION.

The ontological ambiguity of all things, standing as they do in a *barzakh* or isthmus between *wujūd* and nonexistence and between this moment and the next, brings us back to imagination, one of whose outstanding characteristics is constant fluctuation and change. As a faculty of the soul, imagination is able to perceive the self-disclosures of God, recognizing the presence of God in each thing. Imagination, in other words, can perceive the words of the All-Merciful as God's self-articulation. It sees the things as He even as reason recognizes that they are not He.

As a cosmic reality, imagination is the characteristic both of each word articulated within the All-Merciful Breath and of the Breath itself, which is the SUPREME or Highest BARZAKH. All things are imagination, which is to say that everything is what it appears to be by disclosing something else. Like mirror images, all things are both distinct entities and reflections of things greater and lesser than themselves. They are at once fixed entities in God's knowledge and existent entities in manifest *wujūd,* both immutable and everchanging.

The Reality of Realities, or the Highest Barzakh, exists as the object of God's knowledge but, like any other reality, its *wujūd* is nothing but the *wujūd* of God. It is not identical with God, nor is it different from Him. Likewise, it is not identical with the total cosmos, nor is it different from the total cosmos. The cosmos makes manifest in differentiated detail all the realities that the Reality of Realities embraces, but its most perfect loci of manifestation are the perfect human beings and, most specifically, the prophet Muhammad. Hence the Reality of Realities, also called "the Breath of the All-Merciful," is identical with the Muhammadan Reality. Those who come to know it as their own reality are the Muhammadan friends of God. Standing in the Station of No Station, they actualize to the fullest possible extent the reality of He/not He.

The Principles of Ibn al-ʿArabī's Cosmology

The present book deals with what I have called the "principles" of Ibn al-ʿArabī's cosmology. In contrast, the volume now in preparation, *The Breath of the All-Merciful,* deals with the details of the cosmic degrees as they become articulated within the divine speech. It needs to be kept in mind, however, that both principles and articulations are, in themselves, the bare bones of rational structure. As already noted, these bones play an essential role, but we do violence to them when we remove them from their body, which is Ibn al-ʿArabī's text. In this text, his interest lies in illustrating how the bare bones become clothed in the flesh of experience, on whatever level and in whatever locus this "experience" may occur. One of God's Koranic names, it should be remarked, is *al-khabīr,* and the best way to translate this term, as Ibn al-ʿArabī understands it, is "the Experienced," in the double sense that this word has in English. God is the Experienced because He knows things through their actual manifest reality, and hence He experiences them as they are. And God is also experienced by us, because we become aware of *wujūd* through our presence within the All-Merciful Breath.

Ibn al-ʿArabī's discussions of cosmic structure are designed to help his readers become aware of how they actually experience the cosmos and how it may be experienced. In a profound sense, his cosmology is nothing but "empirical," because he has come to know what he knows through his own experience, and he is asking us to know it in terms of our experience.

In the present volume, I deal with three broad and interrelated themes, themes that are standard throughout much of the Islamic intellectual tradition—God, the world, and the human being; or metacosm, macrocosm, and microcosm. The skeleton can be described as follows, but what is of primary significance is not the skeleton, but the manner in which Ibn al-ʿArabī enfleshes it with clarifications of the nature of the human reality based on the Koran and the Hadith.

Part 1, "God and the Cosmos," deals with the basic concepts that aid in understanding God in terms of the cosmos, and vice versa. Many of these concepts and related themes were dealt with more briefly in SPK. In fact, the first two chapters of the present book all deal with concepts that will be familiar from that book, though, as mentioned, the passages cited here are, on the whole, much longer.

Chapters three and four, dealing with the face and the veil, present two fundamental themes of Ibn al-ʿArabī's writings that were only touched upon in SPK. The cosmos and the self, in brief, are the face of the Real, disclosing as they do His names and attributes, but they are also His veil, because they prevent us from seeing Him as He is.

Part 2, "The Order of the Worlds," investigates the divine Level inasmuch as it provides the principles for the orderly structure of the universe. Divine names such as Manifest and Nonmanifest leave their traces in the universe through two basic orders of existence—what we see and what we do not see, or the "unseen" and the "visible," terms that I translate here as the "absent" and the "witnessed." Dwelling in the absent domain are creatures such as angels and spirits, and dwelling in the witnessed domain are inanimate objects, plants, and animals—inasmuch as they are simply bodies. But all have invisible, absent dimensions to their realities, so all are absent as well as witnessed.

The worlds, Ibn al-ʿArabī tells us, are no more than two—the absent and the witnessed. But often he changes his standpoint and speaks of three worlds, because any two things are separated by a *barzakh* that is neither the one nor the other. Cosmically, the *barzakh* that separates the absent world from the witnessed world is called "the world of imagination."

Part 3, "The Structure of the Microcosm," investigates the nature of the human being considered as an image of the whole cosmos. Here I look at basic concepts such as spirit and body, the rational soul (a term that I translate more literally from the Arabic as "the rationally speaking soul"), the soul's faculties, the natural constitution, appetite, and the soul's everlastingness.

The Breath of the All-Merciful

In organizing *The Self-Disclosure of God,* I have been concerned from the outset to provide the broad picture to which the details can be related. The cosmos makes sense only in the context of *wujūd,* which is the Real. Our situation in the cosmos makes sense only in the context of orderly arrangements established by degrees of light and darkness, disclosure and curtaining, *tashbīh* and *tanzīh,* He and not He. Cosmic order makes sense only in the context of an overarching reality that is itself orderly and that establishes order, a reality that is *wujūd,* whose diverse modalities of order can be grasped by meditating on the divine names. Human order makes sense only in terms of cosmic order, which provides the context for differentiating among things on the basis of polar opposites such as absent and witnessed, light and darkness, subtle and dense, spirit and body, day and night. Our internal order parallels cosmic order, and both these orders disclose the Divine Level.

The forthcoming volume, *The Breath of the All-Merciful,* focuses on Ibn al-ʿArabī's detailed analysis of the structure of the cosmos in terms of the letters of the Arabic alphabet, letters that have their analogues in twenty-eight degrees of cosmic manifestation. A thorough understanding of this scheme presupposes a good knowledge of all the themes discussed in the present volume.

Ibn al-ʿArabī's twenty-eight letter scheme of cosmic degrees is discussed in Chapter 198 of the *Futūḥāt,* one of the longest chapters of the book. This scheme has been represented diagramatically by Titus Burckhardt in his short study, *Mystical Astrology According to Ibn ʿArabī.* The diagram, however, is not found in the *Futūḥāt* (in contrast to several other diagrams), and, as Burckhardt was well aware, it provides only the barest outline. And once again, Ibn al-ʿArabī's real contribution lies not in the scheme itself, but in his detailed analysis of the cosmos and the human reality with this scheme as the backdrop. The net result is to give the reader both a broad view of cosmic and divine interrelationships and a concrete picture of how these are explicated in the three books of God—the cosmos, the self, and the Koran, the last being the key that opens the door to the first two.

The Breath of the All-Merciful is not simply a study or translation of Chapter 198, because Ibn al-ʿArabī provides much of the explication of the scheme elsewhere in the *Futūḥāt,* and a good deal of this specific chapter is taken up by digressions which, however fascinating, would take us too far afield from the goal announced in the book's title.

Given that *The Breath of the All-Merciful* is far from complete and will not necessarily see the light of day, I summarize here the articulation of the cosmos as detailed there. This will be useful because most of the terminology is discussed or at least touched upon in the present volume, so an idea of how these realities are situated schematically in relation to degrees of manifestation found in the Breath of the All-Merciful may help provide a broad picture of what Ibn al-ʿArabī is saying.

Ibn al-ʿArabī arranges the twenty-eight letters according to their traditionally assigned places of articulation, beginning with the letter that is pronounced most deeply in the throat.[7] In other words, the arrangement represents the order in which the All-Merciful articulates the levels of the cosmos, beginning with the most internal of the letters. The deepest and most hidden letter is *hamza*, which corresponds to the First Intellect, the first thing created by God. Each succeeding degree apparently represents a logical rather than ontological progression in the direction of manifestation. I say "logical" because Ibn al-ʿArabī does not refer to all of these degrees as actually existing entities. Some are conceptual tools and have no external existence save in the traces that they leave in the cosmos or in our minds.

The arrangement of the universe in terms of twenty-eight letters is one of four basic ways in which Ibn al-ʿArabī orders the cosmic degrees, the other three being temporal (prior and posterior), spatial (higher and lower), and qualitative (more excellent and less excellent). He mentions in several contexts that he has realized the external existence of many of these cosmic degrees during his ascents (*miʿrāj*) to God in Muhammad's footsteps. In what follows, I list the twenty-eight letters of the alphabet, along with the corresponding cosmic degree and the relevant divine name. I add brief explanations when these will be helpful in the context of the present book. I have divided the twenty-eight levels into seven basic categories, though Ibn al-ʿArabī does not make this completely explicit. The original Arabic terms can be found by referring to the index of this book.

A. The Intellective World

1. *Hamza*, the First Intellect (also called the Highest Pen), the Innovator. The First Intellect was created directly by God, without any intermediaries. Hence it is the only created thing that is "innovated" (*mubdaʿ*) in the strict sense of the term, since everything else is created through one or more intermediaries.

2. *Hāʾ*, the Universal Soul (the Preserved Tablet), the Upraiser. The name Upraiser lifts up something that is already there, and hence it is associated with those human individuals who are "raised up" to be prophets and with all human beings at the resurrection, which is called the "Uprising." In this case, the Universal Soul is the first existent thing to be raised up from another existent thing, that is, the First Intellect. On the intellective or spiritual level, Intellect and Soul, or Pen and Tablet, are the prototypes of all cosmic activity and receptivity, all masculinity and femininity. The Soul reflects this cosmic polarity internally in its two basic faculties—knowledge, whereby it receives from the Intellect, and practice, whereby it displays its own traces in everything below itself.

3. *ʿAyn*, nature, the Nonmanifest. Nature represents the Nonmanifest within the cosmos because it remains forever hidden, despite its manifestation through the four primary cosmic qualities or tendencies, which are called the "four natures"—heat, cold, dryness, and wetness. The four natures, two of which are active (heat and cold) and two receptive, double the Soul's faculties. Nature is the Mother who exercises her ruling property over everything in the cosmos except her own parents—the Intellect and the Soul.

4. *Ḥāʾ*, the Dust Substance, the Last. Known in philosophical terms as "Prime Matter" and "First Hyle," the Dust Substance, like nature, remains unknown except through its traces. It fills the Void and is the underlying matter of everything in the universe, except the Intellect and the Soul. Its connection with the name Last has to do with the fact that the Last is the principle of the "next world," which, more properly, should be translated as the "last world." All things arise from the First and return to the Last. In the same way, all things arise from the Dust Substance and return to it moment by moment, only to be reborn through the new creation. Whatever a thing may be, at every instant it undergoes dissolution and goes back to the Dust, only to be given existence by God in the next instant.

B. Body, Shape, Throne, and Footstool

Ibn al-ʿArabī does not specify the "location" of the next four levels, but they clearly stand between spirits and bodies. Hence, to the extent that they can be considered as externally existing realities, they belong to the higher realms of the world of imagination.

5. *Ghayn,* the All Body, the Manifest. The All Body is the single corporeal substance from which every corporeal and imaginal body in the universe is shaped and formed. It can be pictured as a sphere that fills the Void, which itself is an "imagined extension"—the empty space that has never existed but that we imagine to have been filled by the universe. Imaginal bodies have sensory characteristics similar to those of corporeal bodies but without the "density," so they also are shaped from the All Body. The connection with the name Manifest is plain—that which is manifest to us is precisely corporeality, which is defined as that which is perceived through the sensory faculties (keeping in mind that these faculties do not depend on the external sense organs, as, for example, when we "see" during a dream).

6. *Khāʾ,* shape, the Wise. Shape is the next logical step in manifestation after the amorphous, uniform corporeality that is the All Body. Through shape, the bodily things of the universe become distinct from each other. The name Wise rules over every sort of order and has to do with putting each thing in its proper place. In this case, it determines the appropriate shape for every bodily thing.

7. *Qāf,* the Throne, the All-Encompassing. This is the Throne mentioned in the Koran upon which *the All-Merciful sat* (20:5). It is the first bodily thing that assumes a specific shape. It encompasses the entire manifest universe—which, once again, includes the world of imagination.

8. *Kāf,* the Footstool, the Grateful. This is the first imaginal thing within the embrace of the Throne. It is the locus where God lets down His "two feet," which are the foot of mercy and the foot of mercy mixed with wrath. Above the Footstool is found only mercy, but the Footstool *embraces the heavens and the earth* (2:255), which include manifestations of both mercy and wrath. Ibn al-ʿArabī provides no explicit explanation for the connection with the name Grateful, but it has to do with the division of the phenomena of the cosmos into two sorts as signified by the two feet. In other words, the manifestation of the cosmos demands both good and evil, both happiness and suffering. Moreover, at the two feet, the prescriptive command becomes differentiated into commands and prohibitions, thus providing the cosmic origin of shariahs. True gratitude becomes possible only after this division, because true gratitude demands recognizing and accepting God's mercy and guidance and thanking Him in every state, whether we consider the state beneficial or harmful. Human gratitude, in turn, is nothing but the cosmic reverberation of the divine gratitude mentioned, for example, in the verse, *Whoso volunteers good—God is Grateful, Knowing* (2:158).

C. The Celestial Spheres

Ibn al-ʿArabī enumerates the celestial spheres in a variety of ways. Most often he considers them as nine, that is, the starless sphere, the sphere of the fixed stars, and the spheres marked by the orbits of the seven visible planets—Saturn, Jupiter, Mars, the sun, Venus, mercury, and the moon. Sometimes he includes within them the four "globes" of the elements as well as the Throne and the Footstool. Then we have fifteen spheres, seven on either side of the celestial axis or "pole," which is the sun.

9. *Jīm,* the black satin sphere, the Independent. This is the starless sphere, which manifests the divine independence because it is free of the specification of stars or planets that designate the lower spheres, even though it can be divided (on the basis of what is below itself) into twelve sectors, known as the "towers," that is, the constellations of the zodiac. Paradise is located between this sphere and the next lower sphere.

10. *Shīn,* the sphere of the fixed stars, the Determiner. Within this sphere appear the moon's twenty-eight mansions or "waystations," each of which corresponds to one of the letters of the Breath. The interactions between the properties of the twelve constel-

lations and the twenty-eight waystations establish a disequilibrium (since the relation is not that of whole numbers), and this drives the constant movement and change in the lower realms.[8] The Koran explicitly ascribes the moon's waystations to God's determination (36:39).

11. *Yā*, the first heaven, the Lord. This heaven is associated with Saturn, Saturday, and Abraham.

12. *Ḍād*, the second heaven, the Knowing. Jupiter, Thursday, Moses.

13. *Lām*, the third heaven, the Subjugating. Mars, Tuesday, Aaron.

14. *Nūn*, the fourth heaven, Light. The sun, Sunday, Idris (Enoch).

15. *Rā'*, the fifth heaven, the Form-giver. Venus, Friday, Joseph.

16. *Ṭā'*, the sixth heaven, the Enumerator. Mercury, Wednesday, Jesus.

17. *Dāl*, the closest heaven, the Clarifier. The moon, Monday, Adam.

D. The Elemental Globes

The four elements, also called the "pillars," are depicted as four concentric globes within the sphere of the moon. Their arrangement has to do with the descent from subtlety to density and light to darkness.

18. *Tā'*, fire, the Gripper.

19. *Zā'*, air, the Alive.

20. *Sīn*, water, the Life-giver.

21. *Ṣād*, earth, the Death-giver.

E. The Progeny

These are the three kingdoms, the born things or "progeny"—a term I translated in SPK as "productions." They are the children of the "high fathers," who are the celestial spheres, and the "low mothers," who are the elements. The minerals are the first things to appear pertaining strictly to the corporeal world, not the imaginal world. The four elements themselves are "simple," which is to say that they are not compounded of anything, and noncompound things can have no purely corporeal manifestation. In contrast, the progeny are compounded of the four elements, and at each level the complexity of the compoundedness increases. The degree of compoundedness then determines the thing's preparedness for the "spirit" that is blown into it.

22. *Ẓā'*, minerals, the Exalted.

23. *Thā'*, plants, the All-Provider.

24. *Dhāl*, animals, the Abaser.

F. The Spirituals

These are the angels and the jinn, who are differentiated from each other by the fact that the bodies of angels are created from light and those of jinn from fire. This does not seem to be elemental fire, however, since the jinn are not classified as progeny. Angels and jinn are closest in configuration to human beings in that both are conscious subjects and hence, in principle, susceptible to forgetfulness and addressed by the prescriptive command. In practice, however, angels are too luminous and clear-seeing to disobey God, in contrast to the jinn, the first of whom was Iblis or Satan.

Apparently angels and jinn are articulated after the progeny for the same reason that God first molded the clay of Adam, then blew into him of His own spirit. The receptacle must be present before the divine spirit—the spirit of spirits—can be delimited and bound to accord with the specific receptacle. The angels, who are sometimes discussed as synonymous with "spirits" per se, are articulated before the jinn, who are a denser delimitation of spiritual reality in accordance with the characteristics of fire.

25. *Fā'*, the angels, the Strong.

26. *Bā'*, the Jinn, the Subtle.

G. Human Beings

Human beings can also be classified as "spirituals," since they are often distinguished from angels and jinn simply by the fact that their bodies were shaped from clay rather than from light or fire.

27. *Mīm*, human beings, the All-Comprehensive. The All-Comprehensive is both a divine name and the specific attribute of

the name God, which is called the "all-comprehensive name." Although Ibn al-ᶜArabī places "All-Comprehensive" in the title of this section, he also says, in explaining this title, "The name the All-Comprehensive is God" (II 468.8), and God is the name in the form of which human beings were created. Human beings are situated at the end of the created hierarchy because they are microcosms, containing in themselves the whole of the cosmos. Their "containment" of the macrocosm can be understood in a number of ways. In the present context, it can mean that all of the twenty-six preceding levels are necessary preconditions for human existence, and each level leaves its trace within the human configuration. It can also mean that all the divine names are brought together so as to configure the human being as the locus of disclosure for the name God, because the meaning of this name embraces the meanings of all the divine names. Just as God is the all-comprehensive name, so also the human being—or, more specifically, the perfect human being—is the "all-comprehensive engendered thing."

28. *Wāw*; the levels, the stations, and the waystations; the Uplifter of degrees. This final level refers to the differentiation of human beings into an indefinite number of types and individuals, each of which is ranked in degrees of excellence in relation to other human beings. Moreover, just as the macrocosm has many degrees in its unfolding, so also does every microcosm. Each moment of individual human existence is a waystation on the path of returning to God, so everyone stands in one of the stations of the journey. All the Shaykh's writings can be said to be focused on this last letter of the alphabet—the understanding of which demands an understanding of all the previous letters. His concern is precisely to designate the degrees of human possibility and to describe the stations and waystations of the human ascent to God. Hence he discusses nothing without taking it back to its relevance to the human self. Knowing the cosmos, we come to know the microcosm, and knowing our own microcosm, we come to know the infinite Being of the Real.

Cosmic Language

The importance that Ibn al-ᶜArabī gives to language can hardly be overestimated. Michel Chodkiewicz has done a great service to students of Ibn al-ᶜArabī by bringing out various aspects of this importance in his *An Ocean without Shore: Ibn ᶜArabī, the Book, and the Law*. Michael Sells has provided astute observations on the rhetorical goals of some of this language in two chapters of *Mystical Languages of Unsaying*. I present here a few of my own reflections on the problems that Ibn al-ᶜArabī's attention to language raises for those who would like to render his concepts into English.

The fundamental determinant of Ibn al-ᶜArabī's deeply Islamic perspective on language is of course the Book itself, that is, the Koran, which molds his psyche in a way that is simply unimaginable to contemporary observers, even those theorists who claim that language determines all of reality. Perhaps the problem for the modern theorists is that they have little idea of what "all of reality" might entail, or, if they do have an idea, they are extreme reductionists. From Ibn al-ᶜArabī's point of view, they are correct in situating all of reality in language, but they are mistaken in finding language's origin in the human self or in anything other than God. The self is nothing but a word articulated by the Essence, and the Essence remains always and forever beyond any articulation. So also, every language, whether meta-, cosmic, human, or infrahuman, is an articulation of Unarticulated *Wujūd*.

As for Ibn al-ᶜArabī, he does have a clear idea of what "all of reality" entails, and he can hardly be called a reductionist. His idea has resonated so profoundly with Muslims over the centuries that many of the most intelligent and reflective of them have called him al-Shaykh al-Akbar, "the Greatest Master." I will attempt to explain in abstract, conceptual terms, why language is so basic for him and for Muslims in general, and then suggest some of the difficulties faced by Ibn al-ᶜArabī's translators.

On the formal level, language is first an articulation of the breath. The breath (*nafas*) is the life force, and, in the human case, the life force is the self (*nafs*). Language articulates the contents of the self in a *barzakh*, an isthmus—i.e., the breath—that is neither immaterial like the self, nor material like the external world. We know the *barzakh* is there because we experience its articulation, not least through enunciating and hearing spoken words. Language is intelligible, because the self is intelligent, and it is sensory, because it is perceived by sensation. Hence it is a world of imagination, a *barzakh* between awareness and embodiment, meaning and form, reason and sensation, self and other. It is an image of the self and of the world outside the self. It is neither here nor there, neither this nor that. It clarifies and obscures, reveals and veils.

God created Adam in His own form. God is *wujūd*, that which cannot not be, and this *wujūd* is alive, knowing, desiring, powerful, and speaking. When this *wujūd* discloses itself—and it does nothing but disclose, because it is nothing if not found—it appears in an infinite array of configurations. Of these configurations, that which, in our experience, is most complete, perfect, and all-comprehensive is called "Adam," that is, "human being."

Wujūd is unbounded, which is to say that, in itself, it is not determined and defined by any articulation. Such is the Essence. But when *wujūd* discloses itself, it does so in conformity with the divine Level, of which human beings are the form. This divine self-articulation can be understood in many ways, but one of the most straightforward ways of understanding it is to think in terms of the creative power possessed by the divine form, which is the human being. This creativity appears first and foremost in speech, which is intelligence articulated and formalized within the imaginal world of the breath.

The human breath is the form (*ṣūra*) of a meaning (*maʿnā*) that is called, on the divine side, "the Breath of the All-Merciful." This divine Breath is attributed specifically to the name All-Merciful, because God is All-Merciful inasmuch as He displays His bounties and His *wujūd* within everything in the realm of possibility, which is precisely the cosmos, "everything other than God."

God reveals Himself in two basic letter configurations, the "letters" being the fundamental articulations of *wujūd* on the basis of which a cosmos—after the unknowable "chaos" of *wujūd* in itself—can be arranged and ordered. These two basic configurations are the macrocosm and the microcosm, the first of which is indefinitely deployed and differentiated, and the second of which is focused and relatively undifferentiated. When the microcosm finds itself, it finds itself as a whole, differentiated from the indefinite multiplicity and dispersion that is the macrocosm. Precisely this wholeness and all-comprehensiveness, the fact that it brings together all the divine attributes, gives the microcosm an awareness of self as differentiated from other selves and from the macrocosm. Just as God is aware of Himself, so also the microcosm, His form, is aware of itself, and this self-awareness is the root of the veiling and obscuration that prevent the self from seeing itself for what it is, just as it is the root of every self-knowledge.

The self, then, is a unique articulation of the divine Breath, an articulation that is aware of itself and the cosmos. Left to itself, this undifferentiated self-awareness in this indefinitely differentiated cosmos would find no dependable standards by which to differentiate its own divine form from that of the cosmos. However, this self has never been left to itself, at least not in the Islamic view of things. The myths of "the day of Alast" and of God's choosing Adam as a prophet make this abundantly clear. From the moment in which the self was differentiated within *wujūd*'s unboundedness, it was informed of who it is and why it is here. The problem arises because of Adam's "forgetfulness" and "heedlessness," attributes that are found in all his descendants.

Thus the divine Breath is articulated in two basic modes, which are the macrocosm and the microcosm, and there is also the reality of forgetfulness, which makes possible the realization of many modes of perfection not available to those who never forget. Beings who always remember cannot leave the Center, and hence they are fixed in the intense luminosity of the divine light. Those who do forget can fall far from the Center.

Once fallen, they establish a distant circumference with indefinite possible directions of movement that can be summarized as three basic paths—toward the Center, away from it, and wavering in between (three routes that the Koran mentions in the Fātiḥa).

The cosmos is a vast configuration of words telling a coherent story (for those who understand), and hence it is a book. So also the human being is a book, but human beings, by and large, have forgotten the story line (nowadays, many of them exult in their forgetfulness and tell us that all stories are arbitrary anyway, so take your pick). Given the fact of human forgetfulness, the All-Merciful articulates a third book through precisely the same creative process that brought the first two books into being. This book is the Book of Revelation, the Reminder or the Remembrance, given to Adam and to all the subsequent prophets and appearing in its most complete and comprehensive articulation in the Koran.

The Reminder is anything but a human invention. It is no more a human invention than are the cosmos and the self. Naturally, however, the recited and written Book appears in a form that corresponds with the macrocosmic and microcosmic books, which is to say that it appears in a linguistic form and a cultural language appropriate to the recipients. In support of this idea, Ibn al-ʿArabī often cites the Koranic verse, *We sent no messenger save with the tongue of his people* (14:4).

The human ability to articulate awareness within the imaginal forms of language, whether within the *barzakh* that is the breath, or the *barzakh* that is the self, appears coextensively with the human being. It is an essential attribute of human nature because God created Adam in His own form, and God speaks, which is to say that He articulates His awareness of self and others in the *barzakh*s that are the cosmos and the human being. Human language is no more a human concoction than is breathing. This is not to suggest that humans have no role to play in the differentiation of language and vocabulary, but it is to say that language is utterly central to reality in whatever form it takes, and most obviously so in human reality.

Ibn al-ʿArabī lived in the intimate awareness of the ongoing articulation of words within the divine Breath. When he refers to the Folk of God as the "Men of the Breaths" he is alluding precisely to this experience of the cosmos as speech. He was tremendously aware that everything is God's speech and that the most basic way we, as divine forms, have of communicating with reality is through speech. The most direct of all linguistic communications of the true nature of things is God's own communication through the prophets. Hence it is incumbent upon human beings to understand what the prophets are saying. Only then will it be possible to understand the cosmos and the self and to become truly realized and fully functional human beings.

What then is Ibn al-ʿArabī trying to communicate? In one word—the speech of God as articulated in the Koran. This means that the Koran, as Chodkiewicz has amply illustrated, is his constant point of reference. Over and over again, his basic intention is to bring out the meaning inherent in this divine speech, whose articulation is aimed specifically at establishing human awareness of self, cosmos, and God. Hence Ibn al-ʿArabī is constantly meditating on Koranic words and verses, as well as on the sayings of the most aware of all the Koran's readers, the Prophet Muhammad, whose "character was the Koran," as his wife ʿĀʾisha put it.

Ibn al-ʿArabī's writings are addressed primarily to his contemporaries, though he certainly had a sense of the historical role that he would play. The fact that he called himself "the Seal of the Muhammadan Friends" is an explicit expression of this historical awareness. He did not, of course, address his writings to all his contemporaries, only those who had the preparedness to understand, and they would have needed to be thoroughly trained in the Islamic sciences—no one else could read his books. Always he is trying to awaken his readers to the deep mysteries of the Koranic text, the fact that the words and verses open up to the Infinite, because they are the divine Speech, and, as he likes to say, God's Speech is His knowledge, and God's knowledge is His Essence.

Modern commentators have often remarked upon Ibn al-ʿArabī's surprising if not shocking interpretations of Koranic verses—a quality that is found especially in his often studied *Fuṣūṣ al-ḥikam*, but rarely in the *Futūḥāt*. These interpretations are not as scandalous as they might seem, however, as soon as we acknowledge that it is surely not God's intention in the Koran to confirm us in our "common sense," which is largely coextensive with the forgetfulness and heedlessness that define the human predicament. Not that Ibn al-ʿArabī wants to deny the apparent meaning of the text—he never does that. He simply maintains that God, unlike other authors, knows every plausible interpretation of His speech, and, moreover, He intends every plausible interpretation. Ibn al-ʿArabī defines this "plausibility" in terms of what is allowable in the Arabic language according to the rules of grammar and the limits of the meanings carried by the words. He does not mean "common sense," and hence his interpretations, when they fly in the face of common sense and the apparent meaning, can cause scandal to some. Nevertheless, a close reading of these passages shows that he stands within the boundaries of his definition of plausibility. And certainly, when he does provide surprising interpretations, the reader is forced to rethink his or her idea of the limits of the meaning of God's Speech. In any case, shock is a time-honored treatment for the spiritually ill in many traditions.

Ibn al-ʿArabī wrote because he was compelled to write—a point he makes repeatedly. The divine unveiling pushed him to the point of exploding, and he could only relieve the pressure by putting down what he saw on paper. At the same time, he—or He who exerted the pressure—had several obvious intentions in the writing, as already suggested. One of these is to critique the overrationalization of the intellectual traditions of the time, Kalām and philosophy in particular. But more than a critique of specific schools of thought, Ibn al-ʿArabī's writings are a critique of a one-eyed approach to interpretation. Reason is only one of the eyes through which we see our way to God. Imagination is the other, and certainly most schools of the Islamic intellectual tradition had pushed imagination off to the side. It was, of course, central to Sufism, but many forms of Sufism denigrated reason to an extent that Ibn al-ʿArabī could not accept. Such Sufis were also one-eyed, but they saw with the other eye. Ibn al-ʿArabī's project then, involved keeping both eyes open and explaining to his readers how they could do the same.

The Translator's Dilemmas

Once one understands Ibn al-ʿArabī's rhetorical purposes, one runs into an obstacle that stands before all translators of Islamic religious texts. Few people have paid much attention to this obstacle, but as soon as one becomes aware of it, it is obvious that it has played a major role in distorting not only translations of Ibn al-ʿArabī's writings, but also translations of other works, not least the Koran. This obstacle is the prevalence of abstraction in the English language and in our concepts of what amounts to elegant prose, and the fact that abstraction pushes the understanding in the direction of *tanzīh*.

Part of the problem in English is the diverse sources of the language and the fact that the learned language, extracted largely from Latin and Greek, employs words that are now understood as abstractions, even if the original terms were concrete. In contrast, the Arabic of the Koran, which Ibn al-ʿArabī is constantly uncovering, always has a concrete side to it, and this is true of Arabic in general, with the multifacetedness of its root system. An old joke among Orientalists tells us that every Arabic word has four meanings: It means what it means, then it means the opposite of what it means, then it has something to do with sex, and finally it designates something to do with a camel. Part of the truth of the witticism is the way it indicates how Arabic is grounded in everyday human experience. The rational mind tends to push the meaning of a word away from experience to "what it means," but the imaginal mind finds the self-disclosure of the Real in the sex and the camel. The concreteness of sex or the camel is always there, waiting to be brought to light for those who have drifted off into abstraction, and it is in the world's concrete realities that God is found, not its abstractions.

In Ibn al-ʿArabī's way of looking at things, reason can do nothing but abstract. It is precisely the mode of understanding that sees things in terms of abstraction. In other words, reason pulls things out of their discrete embodiments in the flow of *wujūd* and attempts to delineate their "essences." In the case of God, reason looks upon God as abstracted and pulled out of the world. The more that rational thinkers reflect upon God, the further away they push Him. This is Ibn al-ʿArabī's greatest objection to Kalām and philosophy. Both are so thoroughly grounded in the rational faculty that they cannot conceive of God's presence, except in abstract terms—and this immediately pushes Him far away again. Both Kalām and philosophy, in other words, are firmly rooted in *tanzīh*, the assertion that God is incomparable with all created reality.

This characteristic of rational thought explains one of the deepest reasons for the fact that "You can't get there from here." Scientific rationality will never find God, because it is inherently and essentially predisposed to remove Him from the scene. This predisposition is, if you will, the God-given characteristic of reason, and no rational thought, qua rational thought, can do away with it, any more than it can do away with itself. It is also true that mathematical and logical symbols are the ultimate abstractions. Few things are further from the universe as we experience it.

In contrast to reason, imagination embodies. It cannot conceive of God or anything else save in concrete terms. Imagination alone finds God really present. In other words, imagination is inherently and essentially rooted in *tashbīh*, the assertion of God's similarity.

As an example of the difference between rational and imaginal perception we can look at what is commonly called in English a "symbol." There are a number of words in Ibn al-ʿArabī's vocabulary that might be taken as equivalents for this term, such as *form, image,* and *locus of manifestation*. In any case, if a word is taken as a "symbol" for something else, rational analysis will attempt to tell us exactly how it is that *x* can be considered a symbol for *y*. The more effort we spend in analysis, the more the relation may seem far-fetched. At best we come to understand a certain logic.

In Ibn al-ʿArabī's view, by its own essence reason distinguishes between symbol and symbolized, Creator and creature, meaning and form, spirit and body, the Manifest and the locus of manifestation, the object and the image. In contrast, imagination perceives that the symbol is identical with what it symbolizes, creation is the same as the Creator, the form is none other than the meaning, the body is the spirit, the locus of manifestation is nothing but God as Manifest, and the image is the object. This perception of sameness is unmediated by any rational process—it is a tasting, an unveiling, a witnessing, an insight (to use some of Ibn al-ʿArabī's terms). It is best exemplified in human experience precisely by concrete experience—tasting food, being carried away by music, falling in love. Theologically, imagination perceives, through a direct vision, that the symbol is identical with what is symbolized; it achieves an incontrovertible understanding that the creature is God. But, at the same time, to see in this manner is to see with one eye. Unless this vision is balanced by the other eye—the rational perception of difference and otherness—it is blatantly erroneous and can lead to the worst sorts of confusion, ignorance, dispersion, and delusion.

Ibn al-ʿArabī's universe is governed by rational laws, no doubt, and he may even express some of these laws in simple mathematical terms (his favorite formula being 1x1=1). But by and large, these laws are embodied in the imagery of divine revelation, human speech, and everyday experience. However, even though the language is that of the Islamic universe, this does not mean that anyone familiar with that language will necessarily understand the words. We are dealing, after all, with the ultimate mysteries, and Ibn al-ʿArabī knows as well as anyone how difficult it is for people to grasp these mysteries, even if, as he claims, they were laid bare in his own case.

The mysteries of the universe do not lie primarily in the universal laws and principles, even though these are mysterious enough. What is most mysterious and miraculous about the universe is its concrete particularity, its every object and inhabitant, each of which is uniquely and ultimately unfathomable. The more we derive our abstract principles and lift them beyond everyday minuteness, the more we depart from the universe as it actually is. God is disclosed in the details, in the molecules and atoms, just as He appears in the grand, overarching syntheses and unities. Yes, reality is found in the grand abstractions achieved by reason, but it is also found in the concrete things that we experience, and these have an even greater claim to be called the reality of the Real.

The contrast between imaginal and rational perception is one of the major themes of both SPK and *Imaginal Worlds,* so I will not belabor it here. What I want to point out is the practical problem that this contrast raises for the translator: In choosing English equivalents, how do we balance abstraction and concrete, imagistic embodiment? This is an especially critical issue in Koranic terminology, which provides the backbone of Ibn al-ʿArabī's conceptual universe. One of his primary criticisms of the rational thinkers is precisely that they insist upon interpreting the Koran in abstract terms. In effect, they read every symbol and every concrete image found in the Koran in ways that harmonize with their understanding of *tanzīh,* God's incomparability and transcendence. They refuse to see that these same words have a different message if read in terms of *tashbīh,* as images and symbols that are meant not only to express but actually to embody God's similarity and immanence.

Excessive abstraction is especially a problem in translations of the Koran. This is a topic that would reward a researcher—to investigate how preconceptions of the importance of rational abstraction have affected translations of the Koran into English. In brief—and this is a vast topic—Muslim apologists, beginning especially in India in the past century, have been overawed by modern science and rationality and have considered it their duty to put these sorts of knowledge to use for social engineering. At the same time, they have correctly perceived that there is a current of Islamic intellectuality that is, in certain ways, congruent with scientific thinking. That current is the path of *tanzīh,* the rational abstracting of God from the universe, leaving it open for human manipulation without concern for God's presence save in a relatively distant, legal sense. Most of the translations of the Koran made by Muslims have been done by apologists of this rationalizing bent—and this includes the converts among them, such as Muhammad Marmaduke Pickthall and Muhammad Asad. Many contemporary Muslim intellectuals, educated, as they usually are, as doctors and engineers, find these abstracting translations quite congenial, since they confirm the rightness of the abstract rationality of their own professional choices.

Understanding the Koran exclusively in rational terms is precisely the type of distortion that Ibn al-ʿArabī is most concerned to criticize—and this is another reason that certain of the traditional ulama and many of the moderns have considered him a heretic. Interestingly, it is a translation of the Koran like that of the great Orientalist A. J. Arberry—which preserves to a large degree the concreteness and ambiguity of the original text—that is closest not only to the Arabic original, but also to the appropriate English idiom. Throughout this book (and in my other books) I have taken Arberry as my guide in translating the Koran, though it has often been necessary to modify his translation to maintain consistency in rendering technical terms.

In writing the present book, I have been more aware of the tension between abstraction and imagery, *tanzīh* and *tashbīh,* as a translator's problem than I was in writing SPK. Careful readers of both books will notice that I have changed the English equivalent for Arabic terms in a significant number of instances, even though I have tried to maintain consistency with that book (major changes in terminology are noted in Appendix II). Usually, I have made the changes in the attempt to bring the English closer to the concrete imagery of the original Arabic, or to indicate the etymological connections that play an important role in Ibn al-ʿArabī's thinking.

For example, in SPK, I translated the term *athar* as "effect." The English word is relatively abstract and suggests that it is contrasted with the Arabic word for "cause," which it is not. Here I render the term as "trace." In SPK I translated *tawajjuh* as "to turn the attentiveness" or simply "attentiveness." The term *attentive* is already abstract, and the suffix *ness* makes it doubly so. In this book I have rendered *tawajjuh* in its literal sense as "to turn the face" or "face-turning." It may seem strange to hear that God turns desire's face toward something, but not after one has thought about the implications of God's Koranic ascription of the term *face* (*wajh*) to Himself—which is the topic of Chapter 3. Another example is *ʿayn thābita*, which I translated in SPK as "immutable entity," but which I translate here as "fixed entity." "Immutable" is an abstract term, negative in form, that means "unchanging," and it does not have a significant range of meanings. In contrast, "fixed" is relatively concrete and covers a rather wide range of meanings, such as securely placed, stationary, settled, definite, unswerving, immobile. Among the English equivalents that Lane provides for *thābit* in his *Arabic-English Lexicon* are permanent, constant, firm, steady, stable, fixed, settled, and established (not "immutable"). Ibn al-ʿArabī uses the term *thābit* in a wide variety of contexts, most of which can be subsumed under English "fixed." But the term *immutable* is only appropriate in the case of the entities in God's knowledge, and even here, one can argue that Ibn al-ʿArabī's motivations for employing the term *thābit* include the wish to preserve the analogy between the fixed entities and the fixed stars—an analogy (*tashbīh*) that is lost when we translate the term as "immutable." As for "entity," I have kept that because, as explained in SPK, it is much more accurate than "archetype," and "thing" is needed for *shayʾ*. (Several authors have translated the term *ʿayn* in this context as "essence," but this is misleading.)[9]

As is well known, most translation falls between two poles, though a translator may aim for one or the other. One pole is to provide exact, literal equivalents of the translated terms and expressions. The other is to render the ideas in an appropriate corresponding idiom, without being too concerned whether or not the rendering has its literal equivalent in the original. Either approach is fraught with difficulties, and Ibn al-ʿArabī's writings pose special problems. There are no exact equivalents in English for many of his terms, and there are certainly, in many, many cases, no equivalent idiomatic expressions. You cannot get there from here.

From early on in my career as a translator of the works of Ibn al-ʿArabī and his school, I have preferred the first pole over the second. A major reason for this is the technical nature of the discussion—in contrast, for example, to most poetry. Authors such as Ibn al-ʿArabī were extremely careful in choosing the words they used. They kept in mind the Koran, the Hadith, and the intellectual tradition in general, and when they used one term rather than another, they usually did so with a purpose. We may not know exactly why they chose the terms they did, and this is especially true when we are not completely familiar with the topic under discussion. But, to be fair to the original, some attempt should be made to maintain the distinctions and nuances.

The problem is, of course, that few English terms have anything like the exact technical significance of the Arabic. In order to deal with this problem, I have long been attempting to establish an idiom in English that is adequate for the meanings that Ibn al-ʿArabī loads onto the words. It has been a constant learning process, and, given the opportunity, I would revise my earliest translations thoroughly. With SPK, I tried to provide adequate English equivalents for technical terms by paying close attention to the etymological and technical senses of the Arabic words, by explaining these senses in English as well as I could, and by choosing English terms to represent the Arabic term. As often as not, the English term in its normal English senses is not adequate to the Arabic. However, once the English word has been defined in terms of the Arabic, and once the English term has been used consistently in this sense in many examples, the English word should begin to acquire the sense of the Arabic expression. In order for this technique to be effective, however, consistency needs to be maintained.

One of my own primary standards for judging whether a translation is accurate or not is whether the reader is able to reconstruct, on the basis of the translation, the important technical terms in the original. The translator's success here depends on consistency and economy of words. In too many cases, translators do not keep track of how they have translated words in other parts of the text, thus making consistency impossible, and they tend to turn a single word into a phrase or a sentence in the attempt to bring out the nuances of the original. Unfortunately, the original term may have a slightly different nuance each time it is employed, so the translator is forced to flow with the text—if the translator catches the change. Moreover, translators themselves undergo constant change, so what they render one day as *x*, two weeks later they will feel like rendering as *y*. The net result is that the English is totally arbitrary, depending upon the translator's whims.

In addition, this sort of paraphrasing is too often used to justify ignorance of the exact technical sense of the passage. Translators of Ibn al-ʿArabī—and of others as well—should admit up front that they are not always sure of what he is trying to say, even in the literal sense of the words. In such situations, one is tempted to paraphrase so that the sentence makes good sense in English, but the result is likely to be misleading or totally erroneous.

Translators who paraphrase use a variety of techniques to improve the flow of the text and make it readable and comprehensible in English. But this is something like smoothing out a carefully written treatise on physics by getting rid of what appears to an amateur as "jargon." The result would be incomprehensible to the specialists in the field and worthless as a scientific statement. Perhaps the analogy is extreme, but there is a good deal of truth to it, and it does suggest the importance of exactness and consistency.

Another common technique, especially among translators of or commentators on Sufi texts, is to throw in modifiers to suggest that the Arabic term is elevated above its normal English equivalent. Translations and studies can be sprinkled with terms such as *spiritual, mystical,* or *symbolic* that are not found in the original. This is especially unfortunate with a word like *spiritual,* which has an extremely important technical significance and is never employed lightly in the original texts. Once such terms are used as salt and pepper, they lose their ability to convey any meaning at all.

Most of the passages translated in SPK and this book follow the original Arabic practically word for word. One negative result of this is the inevitable awkwardisms. Moreover, it may seem that simpler or more direct words and expressions could have been used to make the same point. However, my goal is always to make it possible for readers to see how the original language is used in a wide variety of contexts. When key terminology is translated primarily with a view toward English style, the possibility of tracking the use of important terms in various contexts is lost. Readers may often find certain translations of Ibn al-ʿArabī's short works easy to follow, but the translators of these works have, as a rule, given no thought to the broad context of the original terminology, so the translation can hardly be related to other translations, except in very general terms.

There remains the problem of abstraction as opposed to concrete imagery. It is probably fair to say that all those who have translated Ibn al-ʿArabī's prose works into English, myself included, have, by and large, tended toward expressing his ideas through abstract terms. He was, after all, enormously learned and totally immersed in the intellectual language of the Islamic tradition. It is only natural that people represent his ideas in English in the learned language of rational discourse, which is largely abstract. This is frequently justified, but not always, and certainly not nearly as often as it is done. I will not here attempt to go into any more details. A look at the foundational studies of Ibn al-ʿArabī's conceptual universe, such as those of Corbin and Izutsu, or at the translations of the *Fuṣūṣ,* such as the partial version by Burckhardt or the full version by Austin, should be enough to confirm the point. My attempts to deal with over-abstraction help explain many of the features of the translated texts in this book.

A Note on Format

I have made a number of minor changes from SPK in the way in which the translated texts are presented, all with the aim of removing as much clutter as possible. For the most part I have not cited Arabic words within the translations, and, in my own commentary, I limit these citations to the most important terms being discussed. The original Arabic for all important terms can be found by referring to the index.

I have cited Koranic passages in italics without quotation marks. This removes the excessive number of quotation marks, makes it easier to differentiate between the Koran and Ibn al-ʿArabī's text, and provides a fairer representation of the impression made by the Koranic verses on the Arabic reader of Ibn al-ʿArabī's writings. Although citations from the Koran are not marked in any way in the original text, save often with introductory words such as "He—high indeed is He!—said," the Koran has its own inimitable style, and any traditional reader of Ibn al-ʿArabī would practically know the Koran by heart, so it positively stands out in the middle of the discussion. Italics render this effect in English.

I have tried to limit the number of notes by referring to Koranic passages and hadiths only where absolutely necessary to clarify allusions. In many cases, I leave it up to the reader to track down the reference with the help of the indexes. I also use notes in order to indicate important parallel or clarifying discussions in SPK and other works. Sometimes, I use them to provide parallel passages drawn from other chapters of the *Futūḥāt*. Instead of providing sources for hadiths in the notes, I have cited sources in the Index of Hadiths and Sayings.

Quotations are from *al-Futūḥāt al-makkiyya*, except where otherwise noted. When I refer simply to a chapter, it belongs to the *Futūḥāt*.

Finally, I would like to express my gratitude, once again, to the National Endowment for the Humanities, for making possible the research that has led to this book. In addition, I am also grateful to the members of the Department of Near Eastern Languages and Civilizations at Harvard University—especially William Graham, Wolfhart Heinrichs, and Roy Mottahedeh—who invited me to teach two courses during the time I was busy with the final editing of the manuscript. Especially fruitful for me was my interaction with the students who enrolled in my seminar on Ibn al-ʿArabī—Whitney Bodman, Syed Akbar Hyder, Angela Jaffray-Shehrzad, Wayne Lee Jones, Tahira Qutbuddin, and Shafique Virani. Their meticulous attention to detail while we read together the text and translation of a few passages from the *Futūḥāt* saved me a number of embarrassing errors and convinced me to give the translations one final review. I am also grateful to Lawrence Sullivan, director of the Center for the Study of World Religions at Harvard, who provided me with a fellowship to stay at the Center during the same period.

I

God and the Cosmos

1. Wujūd *and the Entities*

The Arabic word for cosmos, *ʿālam*, derives from the same root as *ʿalāma* (mark), *ʿalam* (signpost), and *ʿilm* (knowledge). The derivation suggests that the cosmos is both a source of knowledge and a mark or a signpost pointing to something other than itself.

> We mention the "cosmos" with this word to give knowledge that by it we mean He has made it a "mark." (II 473.33)[1]

The Koran refers to all things as "signs" (*āyāt*) of God, which is to say that Koranically, the meaning of things is determined by the mode in which they signify God, the Real. Hence the term *cosmology* might be defined as knowledge of the marks and signs and the understanding of what they signify. Ibn al-ʿArabī's cosmology is then a science of signs, an account and a narration of the significance of marks.

In the most general sense, the word *ʿālam* means "world." It can refer to the whole universe, in which case I translate it as "cosmos," or to any coherent whole within the universe, in which case I render it as "world." In the first sense of the term, Ibn al-ʿArabī commonly defines *ʿālam* as "everything other than God" (*mā siwā Allāh*) or "everything other than the Real" (*mā siwā al-ḥaqq*). Thus the cosmos is "everything other than God, whether high or low, spirit or body, meaning or sensory thing, manifest or nonmanifest" (III 197.31). Within the cosmos, there are many worlds, but before looking at the worlds and entities within the cosmos and the internal structures that shape the cosmos, we can usefully look at how Ibn al-ʿArabī situates the cosmos in relation to God.

The most important synonym for "cosmos" is probably *creation* (*khalq*). Like its English equivalent, the Arabic term has two basic senses. It can refer to the act of creating, or to the result of the creative act. In the second sense, the word may be employed as a synonym for cosmos. It is everything other than God, or everything created by the Creator. The term is often juxtaposed with *al-ḥaqq*, "the Real." Sometimes the word is used with a plural verb, and in such contexts I translate it as "creatures." Then it is equivalent to *makhlūqāt*, "the created things."

Signs, Marks, and Proofs

More commonly than either *sign* or *mark*, Ibn al-ʿArabī employs the term *dalīl* to refer to the fact that the cosmos points to God. The term means guide, directive, pointer, indication, signifier, evidence, proof, denotation. Although found only once in the Koran, it becomes an important term in the Islamic sciences, where it is used to refer to the proofs and demonstrations that scholars marshal to argue their cases. I translate the term sometimes as "signifier" and sometimes as "proof." In the first and more general sense, the term means practically the same as "sign," but in the context of the rational sciences, it usually takes on the technical sense of a formal proof. In Ibn al-ʿArabī's view, these rational arguments and formal proofs are inferior to unveiling and tasting as sources of knowledge. In one passage, he contrasts the terms *sign* and *proof*, identifying the former with the direct cognition achieved by the folk of unveiling and the latter with the indirect understanding acquired by the rational thinkers. Here he has in view specifically the philosophers, who are commonly called the "sages" (*ḥukamāʾ*), while philosophy (*falsafa*) is also called "wisdom" (*ḥikma*).

> One of the knowledges comprised by this waystation is the difference between the *proof* and the *sign*. The companion of the sign is more worthy of having "wisdom" ascribed to him and of being called a "sage" than the companion of the proof, for the sign accepts no obfuscation, and it belongs only to the folk of unveiling and finding, but the proof is not like that. (III 240.31)

The superiority of signs over proofs is connected with the superiority of faith over rational understanding. Faith perceives with an interior light that accepts no darkening, while reason perceives with proofs that are not immune from counterproofs and obfuscations (*shubha*).[2]

> Part of the reality of the [revealed] report is the possibility of the property of the two attributes, truthfulness and falsehood—in respect of its being a report, not in respect of considering who gave the report. Hence we distinguish between those who maintain the truthfulness of the report-giver on the basis of proofs and those who maintain it through faith. After all, faith is a luminous unveiling that does not accept obfuscations, but the companion of the proof is not able to preserve himself from misgivings that detract from his proof, and these send him back to his rational consideration.
>
> This is why we consider the companion of the proof devoid of faith. After all, faith does not accept disappearance, for it is a watchful, divine light that *stands over every soul for what it earns* [13:33]. It is not a solar or stellar light that rises and sets and is then followed by the darknesses of doubt or something else.
>
> Those who know what we have just said know the level of knowledge in respect of faith and the level of knowledge that is gained from proofs. After all, the root, who is the Real, does not know things through proofs. He knows them only through Himself.
>
> The perfect human being is created in His form. His knowledge of God is a faith through light and unveiling, so he describes God with attributes that are not accepted by proofs. People who have faith in Him in respect of their proofs interpret these descriptions, so their faith is diminished to the degree that their proofs negate them from Him. (III 218.23)

Everything qualifies as a sign of God. As the Shaykh remarks, "Everything in engendered existence is a sign of Him" (IV 411.20). "All possible things are signs" (III 492.11). Those who grasp the significance of the signs "see that everything other than God is a locus for the flow of the Real's instructions to them" (III 372.34).

> The fluctuations of the states in the cosmos are all signs. People undergo these fluctuations while remaining unaware. (III 344.33)

> The "signs" are the signifiers that He is the Real who is manifest within the loci of manifestation that are the entities of the cosmos. (II 151.3)

The signs point to God, and each carries a message given to it by God. Each is a "messenger" (*rasūl*), even if this term refers technically to a specific type of prophet, as in "Muhammad is the messenger of God."

> In this waystation is found the knowledge of the messages scattered throughout the cosmos. Nothing walks in the cosmos without walking as a messenger with a message. This is an eminent knowledge. Even worms in their movements are rushing with a message to those who understand it. (III 210.2)

The cosmos is the sum total of the words of God articulated within the Breath of the All-Merciful. Hence each thing in the cosmos is not only a sign, a proof, and a messenger, but also a letter or a word spoken by God, and its ultimate meaning is God Himself in respect of His names and attributes.

> All the cosmos is a word that has come with a meaning, and its meaning is God, so that He may make His properties manifest within it, since He is not a locus in Himself for the manifestation of His properties. Hence, the meaning always remains intertied with the word, and God remains always with the cosmos. He says, *And He is with you wherever you are* [57:4]. (III 148.10)

The Koran employs the word *sign* to refer not only to the phenomena of the cosmos but also to its own verses. Just as the Koran is God's book displaying His signs or verses, so also the cosmos is His book, and the special knowledge given to the folk of unveiling has to do with their God-given ability to read this book. Their "wisdom" does not come from rational demonstration, but divine inspiration.

> The sage is he who does what is proper for what is proper as is proper. Even if we [sages] are ignorant of the form of what is proper in something, God puts it in the correct order at our hand. Thus we leave it and we do not enter into it with our own opinion, or with our rational faculties. God dictates to the hearts through inspiration everything that the cosmos inscribes in *wujūd*, for the cosmos is a divine *book inscribed* [52:2]. (II 163.26)

In discussing the Breath of the All-Merciful, Ibn al-ᶜArabī treats both speaking and writing as analogues of God's creativity. In the same way, the marriage act (*nikāḥ*), which produces children in our world, derives from a divine archetype that appears as what he calls "the marriage act that pervades every atom."[3] It should not be surprising, then, that sexual union is also an act of "writing" (*kitāba*) or a "book" (*kitāb*). The Shaykh employs this terminology in Chapter 559, the penultimate chapter of the *Futūḥāt*, and the fourth longest. He calls it, "On the true knowledge of the mysteries and the realities from diverse waystations." He writes, "In this chapter I have included everything that must be called to the reader's attention in all the chapters of the book, arranged from the first chapter to the last" (IV 327.4). Unfortunately, except for the first few chapters, the correspondence between the sections of this chapter and the 558 chapters that precede it are not always clear, and, although the text provides numbers up to 475, most of these do not coincide with the actual chapter numbers in the printed text. In any case, these sections are richly allusive, and many of them are written in rhymed prose. Some are clear, some unfathomable. A large number begin, or mention in several places, the words, "He says," presumably referring to Ibn al-ᶜArabī's own words in the relevant chapter (though these are certainly not direct quotations). When I quote one of the sections of Chapter 559, I title it "A Mystery." In the following, Ibn al-ᶜArabī alludes to the hadith of the Hidden Treasure, according to which God created the universe out of love for it.

A Mystery

Some inheritors of the
Folk of the Book taste the
lovers' chastisement.

The chastisement becomes sweet
through the lovers' vision,
for their eyes witness
my place of return.
Chastisement is nothing but separation
from my lovers,
joy the seeing
of friends.

> He says: Among the inheritors of the Book is he who wrongs his own self through that in which he makes it struggle. Hence he wrongs his own self because of the *ḥaqq* that it has that belongs to himself. At that moment he is the companion of chastisement and pain, but he does not desire to repel it from himself, because he finds it sweet, and next to what he seeks, it is easy to endure, for he is seeking his own felicity.
>
> The "Book" is the joining of meanings to meanings, but meanings do not accept joining to other meanings until they are deposited within letters and words. When they are enclosed in words and letters, some of them accept joining to others. Then the meanings join together by virtue of following the joining of the letters. This joining of letters is called "writing."

Were it not for the joining of the spouses, there would be no marriage act. The marriage act is a writing.

The cosmos, all of it, is *a book inscribed* [52:2], since it is an orderly arrangement, parts of which have been joined to other parts. Instant by instant in every state it gives birth. There is nothing but the appearance of entities perpetually.

No existence-giver ever gives existence to anything until it loves giving it existence. Hence everything in *wujūd* is a beloved, so there are nothing but loved ones. (IV 424.21)

Selves and Horizons

The signs and verses are found both in the outside world and within ourselves. The Koran says, *We shall show them Our signs upon the horizons and in themselves, until it is clear to them that it/He is the Real* (41:53). *Horizons* refers to the world that we see outside us, while *themselves* refers to the world of inner experience. The antecedent of the pronoun *hu*, translated as "it/He," is ambiguous. It may refer to an implied "everything," or it may refer to God. Ibn al-ᶜArabī's seems to understand it either way, depending on the context in which he cites it, but it is not always clear that he has one meaning rather than the other in mind.

In the Shaykh's view, the basic sense of this verse is, "Your signifier of the Real is yourself and the cosmos" (IV 307.1). Self and cosmos are the two realities within which the Real's self-disclosure may be witnessed. Some Islamic texts mention *horizons* and *selves* as Koranic expressions that are equivalent to "macrocosm" and "microcosm," philosophical terms that go back to Greek sources. Study of cosmology entails the attempt to understand the significance of both the horizons and the selves, both the great world and the small world.

The Lawgiver turned you over to knowledge of yourself in knowledge of God through His words, *We shall show them Our signs*, which are the signifiers, *upon the horizons and in themselves*. Hence He did not leave aside anything of the cosmos, for everything of the cosmos that is outside of you is identical with the *horizons*, which are the regions around you. *Until it is clear to them that it is the Real*, nothing else, because there is nothing else. (III 275.32)

Ordinary people differ from the friends of God in that they miss the significance of the signs, not only in the great world, but also in the small world. Not that God's friends simply choose to recognize the signs for what they are. In the last analysis, God inspires them with knowledge of this significance.

[The friend of God] exceeds those who are veiled only because of what God inspires into his secret heart. This may be a consideration of his rational faculty or his reflection, or it may be a readiness, through the polishing of the mirror of his heart, for the signs to be unveiled through unveiling, witnessing, tasting, and finding. (III 344.34)

From one point of view, God's signs can be divided into two basic sorts—those that appear constantly such that we do not notice them, and those that impinge upon our awareness because they break with our concept of normalcy. Ibn al-ᶜArabī sometimes calls these two sorts "habitual" (*muᶜtād*) and "non-habitual" signs. People see the first sort all the time, but only the friends of God notice them. The second sort catch everyone's attention. They include certain natural events and what are commonly called "miracles" or, in Arabic, "the breaking of habit" (*kharq al-ᶜāda*), a term that means, in a more general sense, an extra-ordinary event. The expression *Folk of God*, which the Shaykh employs to refer to the highest of God's friends, derives from the hadith, "God has folk among the people—the Folk of the Koran, who are the Folk of God and His elect."

God has placed His signs in the cosmos as the habitual and the non-habitual. No one takes the habitual into account save only the folk of understanding from God. Others have no knowledge of God's desire through them.

God has filled the Koran with [mention of] the habitual signs, such as the alternation of day and night, the descent of the rains, the bringing forth of vegetation, the running of ships in the sea, the diversity of tongues and colors, sleep during the night, and the daytime for seeking after God's bounty. So also is everything He has mentioned in the Koran as signs *for a people who have intelligence* [13:4], *who hear* [10:67], *who understand* [6:98], *who have faith* [6:99], *who know* [6:97], *who have certainty* [2:118], and *who reflect* [13:3]. Despite all this, no one gives it any notice save the Folk of God, who are the Folk of the Koran, God's elect.

The non-habitual signs—that is, those that break habits—are those that display traces within the souls of the common people, such as earthquakes and tremblers, eclipses, the rational speech of animals, walking on water, passing through the sky, announcing events in the future that happen exactly as announced, reading thoughts,[4] eating from engendered existence,[5] and the satiation of many people with a small amount of food. Such things are taken into account only by the common people.

When miraculous breaking of habits occurs not on the basis of uprightness, or if it does not alert people and incite them to return to God such that they return and exert themselves in returning, then it is a deception and a *leading on step by step from whence they know not* [7:182]. This is the *sure guile* [7:183]—God's gifts, despite [the servant's] acts of opposition.[6] (II 372.10)

The Folk of God, also known as the "gnostics," recognize the things of the universe as signs and grasp the messages that the signs convey. It is they, for example, who understand the meaning of God's two names, All-Encompassing (*muḥīṭ*) and Aeon (*dahr*). They have actualized the station referred to in the *ḥadīth qudsī*: "Neither My heaven nor My earth embraces Me, but the heart of My servant with faith does embrace Me."

God has unveiled the covering of ignorance from the eyes of their insights and has made them witness the signs of *themselves* and the signs of *the horizons*. Hence it has become *clear to them that it is the Real* [41:53], nothing else. So they have faith in Him, or rather, they know Him through every face and in every form, and they know that *He encompasses everything* [41:54]. The gnostics see nothing unless in Him, since He is the container that encompasses everything. And how should He not be? He has alerted us to this with His name Aeon, within which enters everything other than God, so he who sees something sees it only in Him. That is why Abū Bakr said, "I see nothing without seeing God before it," for he did not see it until it had entered into Him. Necessarily, his eye saw the Real before the thing, for he saw the thing proceed from Him. So the Real is the house of all existent things, because He is *wujūd*. And the heart of the servant is the house of the Real, because it embraces Him—that is, the heart of the one who has faith, none other. (IV 7.30)

The Prophet confirmed the importance of seeing the signs of the self in his famous saying, "He who knows [*ʿarafa*] himself knows his Lord." Hence one definition of *maʿrifa* (knowledge or gnosis) is true knowledge of God through knowing oneself. One seeks to know the signs with the aim of knowing God. Knowing the signs of the self, one comes to know one's Lord. The self is one's basic *dalīl*, one's proof or signifier of God. "What I signify is the *wujūd* of the Real that supports me" (IV 31.23).

In some passages, the Shaykh tells us that this knowledge of self is achieved by the rational faculty (*ʿaql*) through its power of remembrance (*dhikr*), which, in the philosophical sciences, is called the "remembering faculty" (*al-quwwat al-dhākira*), i.e., memory. In his view, when the Koran addresses the "possessors of minds"—literally, "the possessors of the kernels" (*ulu'l-albāb*)—it means those with discerning rational faculties.

In this waystation is found the knowledge of the rational proofs and demonstrations that judge their Existence-Giver as is worthy of Him and [the knowledge of] His acknowledgment of their truthfulness in what they judge. After all, God set up some signs only for the Possessors of the Kernels, who are those who understand the meanings of the signs through the rational faculty that God has mounted within them.

Moreover, God made reason itself a sign of reason, and He bestowed upon it the remembering and reminding faculty that reminds it of the Real who discloses Himself to it so that it knows Him through witnessing and vision. Then He lets down the veils of nature upon it, and then He calls it to His knowledge through the signifiers and the signs. He reminds it that its own self is the first signifier of Him, so it should consider it. (III 291.2)

Although the Koranic verse on knowledge of the self and the horizons seems to place these two knowledges on the same level, Ibn al-ʿArabī sees knowledge of the cosmos as secondary to knowledge of the self, because everything in the cosmos is already found in the self, which was created in God's form. "There is nothing outside of you, so do not hope to know yourself through other than yourself, for there is no such thing. You are the signifier of you and of Him, but there is nothing that signifies you" (III 319.23). One might object that the macrocosm signifies the microcosm, but the macrocosm is unknowable in its totality, because of its indefinite dispersion in time and space. In one passage, the Shaykh suggests how one can read the verse on horizons and selves to support the primacy of the self. In the process, he tells us that through knowing self, one comes to know God in two basic ways, which correspond to *tanzīh* or declaring His incomparability and *tashbīh* or asserting His similarity, or to the actualization of both vicegerency and servanthood. We know ourselves as similar to God because we are created in His form to be His vicegerents, and we know ourselves as utterly incomparable with Him and insignificant before Him because He is the source of all that we are, so we can only submit to Him.

Toward the end of the passage, the Shaykh al-Akbar alludes to a hadith that he quotes more commonly than any other. This is the well-known *ḥadīth qudsī* that mentions obligatory and supererogatory works. In particular he constantly comes back to the words of God in the hadith, "When I love him [i.e., My servant], I am his hearing through which he hears, his eyesight through which he sees, his hand through which he holds, and his foot through which he walks." Here we have the mystery of God's nearness to the servant expressed in a language that provides the Shaykh endless opportunities to meditate upon the divine/human relationship. One meaning that he frequently attributes to the hadith is that "None knows God but God." The servant, qua servant, can never know God, because he is existentially locked into *tanzīh*. But inasmuch as God becomes the eyesight through which he sees, he is God's representative and vicegerent, and because of the *tashbīh* involved he can see God. Or rather, none sees God but God—only the divine in the human sees and recognizes the signs for what they are. Throughout such meditations, there is a constant tension and dialogue between affirmation and negation, nearness and distance, the He and the not He.

> The Messenger of God said that there is no path to knowledge of God but knowledge of self, for he said, "He who knows himself knows his Lord." He also said, "He who knows himself best knows his Lord best." Hence he made you a signifier. That is, he made your knowledge of yourself signify your knowledge of Him. This is either by way of the fact that He described you with the same essence and attributes with which He described Himself and He made you His vicegerent and deputy in His earth; or it is that you have poverty and need for Him in your existence; or it is the two affairs together, and inescapably so.
>
> We also see that, concerning the knowledge of God that is called *maʿrifa*, God says, *We shall show them Our signs upon the horizons and in themselves until it is clear to them that He is the Real.* Hence the Real turned us over to the *horizons*, which is everything outside of us, and to *ourselves*, which is everything that we are upon and in. When we come to understand these two affairs together, we come to know Him and it becomes clear to us *that He is the Real.* Hence the signifying of God is more complete.
>
> This is because, when we consider ourselves to begin with, we do not know whether consideration of the cosmos outside ourselves—indicated by His words, *in the horizons*—gives us a knowledge of God that is not given by ourselves or by everything in ourselves. If it did give us such a knowledge, then, when we considered ourselves, we would gain the knowledge of God that is gained by those who consider the horizons. As for the Lawgiver, he knew that the self brings together all the realities of the cosmos. Hence he focused you upon yourself because of his eager desire—since, as God said concerning him, *He is eagerly desirous for you* [9:128]. He wanted you to approach the signifier so that you would win knowledge of God quickly, and through it reach felicity.
>
> As for the Real, He mentioned the *horizons* to warn you of what we mentioned—lest you imagine that something remains in the horizons

giving a knowledge of God that is not given by your self. Hence He turned you over to the horizons. Then, when you recognize from them the very signifier of God that they provide, you will consider yourself, and you will find that the knowledge of God that is yielded by your consideration of the horizons is exactly the same as that yielded by your consideration of yourself. Then no obfuscation will remain to cause misgivings in you, because there will be nothing but God, you, and what is outside you, that is, the cosmos.

Then He taught you how to consider the cosmos. He said, *Do you not see how your Lord draws out the shadow?* [25:45]. *What, do they not consider how the clouds were created,*[7] and so on [88:17 ff.]. *Have they not considered the sovereignty of the heavens and the earth?* [7:185]. Such is every verse in which He urges you to consider the signs. In the same way He says, *Surely in that are signs for a people who have intelligence* [13:4], *who reflect* [13:3], *who hear* [10:67], and *who understand* [6:98], and *for the knowers* [30:22], *for the faithful* [15:77], *for the possessors of understanding* [20:128], and *for the possessors of the kernels* [3:190]. He knew that He created the creatures in stages, so He enumerated the paths that lead to knowledge of Him, since no stage oversteps its waystation, because of what God has mounted within it.

The Messenger turned you over to yourself alone because he knew that the Real would be your faculties and that you would know Him through Him, not through other than He. For He is the Exalted, and the "Exalted" is the forbidden through its unreachability. When someone attains someone else, the latter is not forbidden in its unreachability, so he is not exalted. That is why the Real is your faculties. When you know Him and you attain to Him, none will have known and attained to Him save He. Hence the attribute of exaltation never leaves Him. Such is the situation, for the door to knowledge of Him is shut, unless it comes from Him, and inescapably so. (II 298.29)

Even though knowledge of self is the primary goal, the Koran's mention of *horizons* before *selves* is not without wisdom, given the danger of self-absorption. Without the support of the external world, the seeker may be led to focus only on himself and ignore all input from the outside. Clearly, in any balanced psyche, both inside and outside have significant roles to play. The Shaykh refers to the importance of the horizons in his chapter on *khalwa*, the Sufi practice of "seclusion" or spiritual retreat.

God says, *We shall show them Our signs upon the horizons and in themselves* so that they will know that the human being is a microcosm of the cosmos containing the signs that are within the cosmos. The first thing that is unveiled to the companion of the seclusion is the signs of the cosmos, before the signs of his own self, for the cosmos is before him, as God has said: *We shall show them Our signs upon the horizons.* Then, after this, He will show him the signs that he saw in the cosmos within himself. If he were to see them first in himself, then in the cosmos, perhaps he would imagine that his self is seen in the cosmos. So God removed this confusion for him by giving priority to the vision of the signs in the cosmos, just as has occurred in *wujūd*. After all, the cosmos is prior to the human being. How should it not be prior to him? It is his father. Thus the vision of those signs that are in the horizons and in himself clarify for him that *He is the Real,* nothing else. (II 150.33)

Just as each thing in the cosmos is a sign, signifier, and proof of God, so also it names Him. Ibn al-ᶜArabī explains this by commenting on the first Shahadah, "(There is) no god but God," which is divided into two basic parts—the negation ("no god") and the affirmation ("but God"). The negation is directed toward any attributes of divinity, any claim to be a god, by anything in the cosmos. And since everything in the cosmos is a sign of God, displaying something of the divine attributes, the negation is directed toward all things. The "He-ness" of God is the Essence, or that which is signified by the pronoun *He* in such Koranic verses as, *He is the First and the Last* (57:3).

The negation is turned toward the indefinite noun, which is *god,* while the affirmation is turned toward the definite noun, which is *God.* The negation is turned toward the indefinite—that is, *god*—only because all things are included within it. There is nothing that does not have a share of divinity to which it lays claim. This is why the negation is turned toward it, since the "god" is he whose shares do not become designated, because all shares belong to him. When people recognize that the god possesses all shares, they recognize that he is called by the name *God*.

Everything has a share and each share is one of the names of what is called "God," so all are His names. Every name signifies His He-ness, or rather, is identical with His He-ness. This is why He says, *Call upon God, or call upon the All-Merciful; whichever you call upon, to "Him" belong the most beautiful names* [17:110]. This is the property of every name you call upon—*to Him belong the most beautiful names.* So to Him belong all the names of the cosmos, and the whole cosmos has the most beautiful level. (IV 89.16)

The fact that the whole cosmos signifies and names God explains its beauty and goodness. The cosmos has an innate eminence (*sharaf*), so it must never be condemned. The only thing that can be condemned is ignorance of the true nature of things. The Koran says that, on seeing God's "waymarks" (*shaʿāʾir*), those who possess "godwariness" (*taqwā*)—an attribute that it constantly praises—should "magnify" (*taʿẓīm*) these waymarks, which is to say, in Ibn al-ʿArabī's reading, that they should acknowledge the majesty and greatness of everything that signifies God, not because of its own worth, but because of what it signifies.

Know—God confirm us and you with the spirit of holiness—that contempt for anything of the cosmos does not proceed from any godwary person who is wary of God. What then if someone knows God, whether through the knowledge of proofs or the knowledge of tastings?

After all, there is no entity in the cosmos that is not among God's waymarks inasmuch as the Real has put it there to signify Him. God has described those who magnify His waymarks with His words, *Whoever magnifies God's waymarks, that is of the godwariness of the hearts* [22:32]. In other words, either the magnificence of the waymarks is of the godwariness of the hearts, or the waymarks themselves are of the godwariness of the hearts.

God has delineated limits for all His waymarks in the abode of religious prescription. These limits pertain to those for whom prescription is made, in all their manifest and nonmanifest movements, and include everything in which they act freely, on both the spiritual and sensory levels, through the ruling [the prescribed limit]. God made these His "inviolable things" for those for whom prescription is made, for He says, *Whoever magnifies the inviolable things of God [that is a good for him with his Lord]* [22:30]. Their magnifying them is to keep them inviolable, just as God has determined them as such in the ruling, for there are affairs that remove them from being inviolable. For example, we will be in the last abode in the Garden without any forbidding, as indicated by His words, *We dwell in the Garden wherever we will* [39:74]; *Therein you shall have everything for which your souls have appetite* [41:31]. So also are His words, *Today the companions of the Garden are in an occupation rejoicing* [36:55], while interdiction has been lifted.

It may happen that within the abode of religious prescription the servant is made to stand in this homestead, so he desires to act freely in it, just as its reality demands—but in its own homestead. Then the servant overthrows the inviolable things of God in this, so he gives them no notice and does not find that he should magnify them. Hence he loses their good—if he does not magnify them—with his Lord. Thus God says, *Whoever magnifies the inviolable things of God, that is a good for him with his Lord* [22:30].

God says this without making any threats only because the companions of states, when they are overcome by their states, are like madmen. As a result they are no longer answerable to the Shariah. Thereby much good with God escapes them. That is why none of the great ones ever seek states. They seek only stations.[8]

We are in the abode of prescription. When something of prescription escapes us in this abode, its good escapes us in the last abode. Then we will know for certain that we are not among the folk of solicitude with God—through the escape of that good.

Such is the situation if we have not exerted ourselves to gain the state that makes the good escape from us. What then will be our situation if we become qualified by the property that makes the good escape from us because we have exercised rational consideration in the roots of affairs after having come to know a few of their realities, and in these few themselves lies what makes the good escape from us? I have seen many of the considerative thinkers in such a situation without any state given by tasting—God give us refuge from that in tasting and consideration!

Since a signifier gains its eminence from what it signifies and since the cosmos signifies the *wujūd* of God, all of the cosmos is eminent. Nothing in it is worthy of contempt or disdain. This is if we take it in respect of reflective consideration. In the Koran, this is indicated by His words, *What, do they not consider [. . .] how heaven was lifted up, and how the mountains were hoisted?* [88:19], and by all the verses of consideration that are found in the Koran. So also are His words, *Have they not considered the sovereignty of the heavens and the earth?* [7:185]; His words, *Surely in the creation of the heavens and the earth and the alternation of night and day* and so on [2:164]; His words, *Do you not see how your Lord draws out the shadow?* [25:45]; His words, *Do you not see how to God prostrate themselves all who are in the heavens and all who are in the earth,* and so on [22:18]; and His words, *We shall show them Our signs upon the horizons and in themselves, until it is clear to them that He is the Real* [41:53], and other verses of the same sort.

As for the folk of unveiling and finding, in their view every part of the cosmos, or rather, everything in the cosmos, was brought into existence by God. Inescapably it is supported in its *wujūd* by a divine reality. Those who have contempt or disdain for it have had contempt and disdain for its Creator, who has made it manifest. Everything in *wujūd* is a wisdom that God has brought into existence, for it is the artisanry of one who is Wise. So nothing becomes manifest save [wisdom, which is] "what is proper for what is proper as is proper." Those who are blind to the wisdom of things will be ignorant of the things; and those who are ignorant that the affair is a wisdom are ignorant of the Wise who has put it there. There is nothing uglier than ignorance.[9] (III 527.17)

Although the cosmos signifies and proves God, this means that it signifies His "Level" (*martaba*), not His Essence. In other words, it gives us knowledge of God's names and attributes, but God in Himself remains forever unknown. In respect of the Essence, or the very Selfhood of God, the cosmos signifies only that there is such a reality. When Ibn al-ʿArabī says that the cosmos signifies God in respect of the fact that "God" is the all-comprehensive name, the name that brings together all opposites, he clearly means that the cosmos signifies God in respect of His many names. Nothing can signify God as He is in Himself, because only God Himself can signify His own Self.

In one of the many passages where Ibn al-ʿArabī explains that the cosmos cannot act as a signifier for God's Essence, he does so while explaining "intimacy" (*uns*) with God, an attribute that is much desired by those who are seeking to reach Him. Although intimacy can be achieved, it cannot be achieved with God, because, properly speaking, God is the Essence, and the Essence is, in the Koranic expression, *Independent of the worlds* (3:97). Hence the "intimacy" that can be experienced is with God's self-disclosure, which is to say that it is experienced on the basis of the relations that exist between God and the cosmos, relations that are denoted by His names.

The Koran calls God *Independent of the worlds.* We make Him independent of signification. It is as if He is saying, "I did not bring the cosmos into existence to signify Me, nor did I make it manifest as a mark of My *wujūd.* I made it manifest only so that the properties of the realities of My names would become manifest. I have no mark of Me apart from Me. When I disclose Myself, I am known through the self-disclosure itself. The cosmos is a mark of the realities of the names, not of Me. It is also a mark that I am its support, nothing else."

Hence the whole cosmos possesses an intimacy with God. However, parts of it are not aware that the intimacy they have is with God.

Each part of the cosmos will inescapably find an intimacy with something, whether constantly, or by way of transferal to an intimacy that it finds with something else. However, nothing other than God among the engendered things has any properties. Hence, a thing's intimacy can only be with God, even if it does not know this. When the servant sees his intimacy with something, that thing is one of the forms of His self-disclosure. The servant may recognize this, or he may deny it. So the servant feels repelled by the same thing with which he is intimate, but he is not aware, because of the diversity of the forms. Hence, no one lacks intimacy with God, and no one is terrified of any but God. Intimacy is an expansiveness, while terror is a contraction.

The intimacy of the knowers of God is their intimacy with themselves, not with God, for they have come to know that they see nothing of God but the form of what they are and that they have no intimacy with anything but what they see. Those who are not gnostics see intimacy only with the other, so they are seized by

> terror when they are alone with themselves. (II 541.11)

In short, everything in the cosmos names, denotes, signifies, and proves God. In this perspective, in which *tashbīh* is stressed, everything is good and praiseworthy, because everything manifests the Real. There is nothing but the self-disclosure of God, who is *wujūd*. Wherever we look, whether on the horizons or in ourselves, we find existent things, which, in respect of their existence, are nothing but the shining light of *wujūd*. Only darkness can be blamed, but darkness cannot be found. It follows that every act performed by every creature is also a sign and mark of God, an affirmation of *wujūd*, which is Sheer Good. Unmixed evil cannot exist.

> Know that there is no deed that is not an affair of *wujūd*, and there is no affair of *wujūd* that does not signify the *wujūd* of God and His *tawḥīd*, whether the affair is blameworthy according to common consent and the Shariah, or praiseworthy according to common consent and the Shariah. If it is a signification, then it is a light, and light is praiseworthy by its essence. Hence nothing can be blamed in an absolute sense. (II 203.17)

Wujūd

To say that the cosmos is "everything other than God" is to say that it is everything other than *wujūd*. Strictly speaking, *wujūd* belongs only to God, because *wujūd* is God. "The Real is identical with *wujūd*" (I 328.25). "In actual fact, *wujūd* is identical with the Real, not other than He" (III 566.30).

Although "*Wujūd* is not identical with the existent thing except in the case of the Real" (II 588.2), anything in the cosmos can be called a *mawjūd*, an existent thing, because it is found. Hence, every existent thing manifests *wujūd*, and Ibn al-ʿArabī often employs the term *wujūd* to mean "all existent things" (III 384.10), everything that exists in any mode whatsoever. Nevertheless, when *wujūd* is ascribed to the cosmos, it needs to be remembered that, "As for the Real in respect of Himself, He is not qualified by anything by which the *wujūd* of the cosmos is qualified" (III 537.21), because the things that fill the cosmos are inherently nonexistent, which is to say that they do not exist on their own. The *wujūd* they possess has been loaned to them by God. Inasmuch as the cosmos is found, it is *wujūd*, but inasmuch as it is considered in and of itself, it is nonexistence. "The nonexistent thing becomes manifest in the form of the existent thing, but it is distinct in *wujūd* from true *wujūd*" (III 307.29).

If, in a certain respect, everything that exists in any mode whatsoever can be said to possess *wujūd*, this means that whatever can be known, whether or not it is found in itself, has some mode of existence.

> There is no object of knowledge that is not qualified by *wujūd* in some respect. The occasion of this is the strength of *wujūd*, which is the root of roots, that is, God, because through it all the levels become manifest and all the realities become entified. (II 309.33)

Although it is proper to speak about the *wujūd* of the things in a certain sense, in the last analysis, all *wujūd* is the Real, because *wujūd* is a single reality. Hence, "There is nothing in *wujūd* but God" (I 272.15, II 148.17, 470.16, III 80:14)—a formula that was used by al-Ghazālī and has been traced back to Maʿrūf al-Karkhī in the second/eighth century.[10] Nonetheless, "It should not be said, 'There is nothing in *wujūd* but God,' because the possible things and the creatures are manifest" (III 299.28). From the first standpoint, God alone is real; from the second, the cosmos and everything within it are infused with His reality, because He has given them existence and attributes. Hence they are His self-disclosure.

The fact that God is *wujūd* explains the deepest meaning of the Koranic divine name *al-muḥīṭ*, the All-Encompassing. "Since the Real is identical with *wujūd*, He has the attribute of encompassing the cosmos" (IV 193.16). Everything in the cosmos is embedded in *wujūd* and embraced by *wujūd*.

> Hence—if you have understood—nothing is understood by imagination, reason, or sensation save the Real *Wujūd* that supports us in our *wujūd*. (III 547.5)

In his chapter on "separation" (*farq*), the Shaykh sets out to explain several definitions of separation provided by classical Sufis. According to one of them, "Separation is the affirmation of creation," because, by affirming the reality of creation, we separate it from the Real. In a similar way, "bringing together" (*jamᶜ*), the correlative of separation, is "affirmation of creation as abiding through the Real" (II 516.17). But, according to the Shaykh, affirmation of creation does not mean the affirmation of its *wujūd*, since *wujūd* belongs only to the Real. Hence, to affirm creation is to affirm the fixed entities, which are inherently nonexistent.

> He says "affirmation of creation," not "affirmation of the *wujūd* of creation," because creation's *wujūd* is identical with the Real's *wujūd*. In respect of its own entity, creation is fixed, and its fixity belongs to itself from eternity without beginning. The fact that it is qualified by *wujūd* is a newly arrived affair that overtakes it, and we have already let you know what this means. Hence, his words, "the affirmation of creation," mean that in eternity without beginning separation occurred between God and creation. Hence the Real is not identical with the fixed entities, in contrast to the state when they become qualified by *wujūd*, for He is identical with that which is described by *wujūd*, not with the entities. (II 519.5)

People commonly ask when the universe began. If we consider the cosmos in relation to Real *Wujūd*, the question is meaningless, because the question "when" only makes sense in the context of the cosmos itself, given that time (*zamān*) is created along with place (*makān*).

> The cosmos is existent through God, neither through itself nor by itself. In its very essence it is bound in *wujūd* through the *wujūd* of the Real. Hence, the *wujūd* of the cosmos can never be correct save through the *wujūd* of the Real.
>
> Since time is negated from the *wujūd* of the Real and from the *wujūd* of the origination of the cosmos, the cosmos did not come into *wujūd* within time. Hence we do not say, in respect of the actual situation, that God existed "before" the cosmos. For it is affirmed that "before" is one of the modalities of time, and there is no time. Nor do we say that the cosmos came to exist "after" the *wujūd* of the Real, since there is no afterness; nor [do we say] "with" the *wujūd* of the Real, for the Real is He who brought the cosmos into existence and He who is its agent and deviser when it is not a thing. Rather, as we said, the Real is existent through His own Essence, and the cosmos is existent through Him.
>
> A possessor of fantasy may ask, "When did the *wujūd* of the cosmos derive from the *wujūd* of the Real?" We would reply: "When" is a question pertaining to time, and time belongs to the world of relations, which is created by God. After all, the world of relations possesses the creation of "determination," not that of "existence-giving."[11] Hence this question is absurd. So consider how you question! Let not these grammatical particles veil you from realizing these meanings and gaining them in yourself!
>
> Nothing remains but a sheer, pure *wujūd* not following upon a nonexistence, and this is the *wujūd* of the Real; and a *wujūd* following upon the nonexistence of the entity of the existent thing, and this is the *wujūd* of the cosmos. There is no in-betweenness [*bayniyya*] between the two *wujūd*s, nor is there any extension, save in the fantasy of supposition, which knowledge shows to be impossible. There is an unbounded *wujūd* and a bound *wujūd*, a *wujūd* that acts and a *wujūd* that is acted upon. Such is given by the realities, and so it is. (I 90.13)

The exact manner in which *wujūd* is identical with the cosmos is not at all clear to the rational mind, and Ibn al-ᶜArabī does not claim to explain it in any exhaustive fashion, though he frequently provides suggestive analogies. In any case, real knowledge of *wujūd*'s omnipresence comes by way of unveiling, not reason. Reason's powers—consideration and reflection—force rational thinkers to declare God incomparable with all things. As long as they employ reason to the exclusion of unveiling, they are locked into *tanzīh*. Only God's friends see God in His self-disclosure, recognizing *tashbīh*. Even so, not everyone worthy of being called a friend of God necessarily sees or understands His self-disclosure. In one passage, the Shaykh points out that the full vision of *wujūd*'s omnipresence is achieved only by a small elite among God's friends—those whom he calls here the "chosen" (*muṣṭafā*). These are the friends whom God protects from acquiring rational knowledge concerning Him before He lifts them up to Himself. Ibn al-ʿArabī certainly has his own experience in mind, given that he received his grand opening long before he had studied any of the sciences. In employing the word "knotting" (*ʿaqd*), he has in view the etymological sense of the words *ʿaqīda* and *iʿtiqād*, the standard terms for "creed" and "belief."[12]

Know that, before his prophecy, no prophet ever knew God through rational consideration, and it is not proper for any prophet to do so. In the same way, the chosen friend of God has no prior knowledge of God through rational consideration. Any friend of God who has prior knowledge of God in respect of reflective consideration is not "chosen," even though he is a friend of God, nor is he one of those to whom God has given the inheritance of the Divine Book.

This is occasioned by the fact that rational consideration binds the friend's view of God by some affair that distinguishes God from other affairs. He is not able to attribute the all-inclusiveness of *wujūd* to God. Hence he has nothing but naked *tanzīh*. Then, when he has tied his knot upon Him, he rejects anything that comes from his Lord that diverges from his knotting, for it detracts from the proofs with which he supports what has come to him from his Lord.

When God shows solicitude to someone, He preserves him, before He chooses him, from the sciences of consideration and He *employs* him *for* Him*self* [20:41]. He comes between him and the search for considerative sciences and provides him with faith in God and in that which has come from God on the tongue of God's Messenger. This is the situation of this community, whose messenger's call is general.

In the former prophecy, when a person lived in a gap between prophets, God would provide for him and make him love occupying himself with seeking provision or the practical arts, or occupying himself with the preparatory sciences, such as arithmetic, geometry, astronomy, medicine, and anything of the same sort that does not attach itself to the God. If the person was chosen and in God's knowledge he was to be a prophet in the time of prophecy, then revelation would come to him while his heart was pure of being bound by a God restricted within the compass of his rational faculty. If he was not a prophet, but a messenger had come to a community to which he belonged, he would accept what his prophet brought him because of the unobstructedness of his locus.[13] Then he would practice in accordance with his faith and would have godwariness toward his Lord, and at that God would provide him with a discrimination in his heart possessed by no one else.[14] In this manner God has caused His habit to occur in His creation.

Even if the companion of rational consideration reaches felicity, he will never achieve the level of the one who is unobstructed, who has no knowledge of God except in respect of his faith and his godwariness. Such a person is an heir to the prophets in this attribute, so he is with them and stands in this degree of theirs. So know this, and say, *My Lord, increase me in knowledge!* [20:114]. (III 402.13)[15]

Although the chosen are able to see that *wujūd* is all-comprehensive and all-inclusive, neither they nor anyone else can discern the exact manner in which *wujūd* becomes manifest through the *mawjūdāt*, the existent things. *Wujūd* in itself, after all, is God's own Self—His Essence—and His Essence is unknowable. *Wujūd* as *wujūd* is no less unknowable when present in an existent thing that we know, because we know only the entity or reality of the thing, not the *wujūd* through which the thing is present to us. This should help us understand why the Shaykh maintains that the Folk of God do not seek God.

A Mystery

The long interval impedes.

When the Men who have no impediment
reach the long interval,
you will see among their warriors
a servant whose state brings
the pain of distance,
thus cutting him off from them.

He says: Since God created *human beings hasty* [17:11] and He created in them seeking, but they do not gain the object of their search in the first step, the interval draws out for them because of their hastiness. They halt because of the length of the interval, and they are held back from gaining benefit.

After all, God is not reached through seeking. Hence the gnostic seeks his own felicity, not God. One does not aspire for what one already has. God is greater than that He should be sought through the distance of steps, the hardship of deeds, and reflective thoughts. Just as He does not become spatially confined, so also He does not become distinct. He is known to us in the sense that in each thing He is identical with each thing but unknown in the distinction, because of the diversity of the forms that we witness.

As soon as you say concerning a form, "He is this," another form with which He is identical will veil you from that form. Concerning it you will also say, "He is this," and His He-ness will absent itself from you through the form that goes. Then you will not know what you depend upon, exactly like the person who is bewildered by reflective consideration and does not know what he believes. As often as a proof shines forth to him, an obfuscation also shines forth.

No proof of Him can ever be safe from obfuscation, because He is the Greatest Proof, and we are His obfuscation. (IV 442.31)

Given that people cannot understand *wujūd*, whether in itself or in its relations with the cosmos, those who study the actual situation of things are sure to end up in bewilderment, a situation which, for Ibn al-ᶜArabī, can be one of the highest stations of knowledge, provided it is the right sort of bewilderment. In discussing the meaning of God's "independence" (*ghinā*) from the worlds, he suggests the various positions that people will take concerning *wujūd* and the entities.

The cosmos never ceases being preserved by God, so He never ceases being its preserver. Were the preservation cut off, the cosmos would disappear. After all, God is Independent of the cosmos only because He becomes manifest through Himself to the cosmos. So He is independent of being known through the cosmos, because He cannot be signified by the other. On the contrary, He signifies Himself through His manifestation to His creatures.

Among the creatures are those who know Him and distinguish Him from His creation.

Among them are those who make Him identical with His creation.

Among them are those who become bewildered in Him. They do not know if He is identical with His creation or distinct from it.

Among them are those who know that He is distinct from His creation and that the creation is distinct from Him, but they do not know through what creation is distinct from the Real or the Real from creation. This is why Abū Yazīd became bewildered, for he knew that there was some sort of distinction, but he did not know what it was until the Real said to him, "The distinction lies in abasement and poverty." Then he became still. God did not speak to him of the other half of the distinction, and that is the divine independence from the cosmos. (III 405.8)

The exact mode of a thing's becoming manifest is unknowable, because knowing it would demand knowing *wujūd* in itself. What Ibn al-ᶜArabī does try to explain repeatedly is that it is easy to see from the signs and marks that everything is the self-disclosure of *wujūd*. One of his favorite analogies for this self-disclosure is the mirror, or, more specifically, what we would recognize as funhouse mirrors.

There is nothing in *wujūd* but God. In the same way, if you were to say, "There is nothing in the mirror except the one who is disclosing himself to it," you would be speaking the truth. Nevertheless, you know that there is nothing at all "in the mirror," nor is there anything of the mirror in the viewer. But within the very form of the mirror, the display of variations and traces is perceived. At the same time, the viewer is as he was, and he displays no traces. So glory be to Him who strikes likenesses and makes the entities appear so as to signify that nothing is similar to Him, and that He is similar to nothing!

There is nothing in *wujūd* but He, and *wujūd* is acquired only from Him. No entity of any existent thing becomes manifest except through His self-disclosure. So the mirror is the Presence of Possibility, the Real is the one who looks within it, and the form is you in keeping with the mode of your possibility. You may be an angel, a celestial sphere, a human being, a horse. Like the form in a mirror, you follow the guise of the mirror's own essence in terms of height, breadth, circularity, and diverse shapes, even though it is a mirror in every case.

In the same way, the possible things are like shapes in possibility. The divine self-disclosure imparts *wujūd* to the possible things. The mirror imparts shapes to them. Then angel, substance, body, and accident become manifest, but possibility remains itself. It does not leave its own reality. (III 80.14)

From Chapter 73: The One Hundred and Third Question

Ibn al-ʿArabī connects God's unknowability specifically to the issue of *wujūd* while commenting on a *ḥadīth qudsī*: "Exaltation is My loincloth and magnificence My mantle. When someone contends with Me in either of them, I shatter him." The passage pertains to his answers to a series of 157 questions that had been posed three hundred years earlier by al-Ḥakīm al-Tirmidhī, who maintained that only the Seal of God's Friends would be able to answer them.[16] The Shaykh provided answers in a treatise that he later incorporated into the *Futūḥāt*.

Question: What are His words, "Exaltation is My loincloth"?

Answer: The Real blessed His servants when He called them to know Him by descending to strike likenesses for them so that they may gain knowledge from Him in the measure that He desires. Such, for example, is His words, *The likeness of His light is as a niche, within which is a lamp* [24:35]. This is because of His words, *God is the light of the heavens and the earth* [24:35], whereby He made Himself light, for it is the predicate of the subject, that is, its attribute. His He-ness is light in respect of the fact that He is God, the Light. But what does the light of the lamp have to do with His words, *God is the light*?

Similar to this is the report that when God speaks through revelation it is "like a chain across pebbles." What does the speech of the Real have to do with striking a chain across pebbles?

Such also are His words, "Exaltation is My loincloth." For the sake of His servants, He put Himself in the waystation of someone who receives qualification by a loincloth. What He desires them to know about Him in the like of this corresponds to a loincloth and what it curtains.

Know that a loincloth is worn for the sake of three affairs—first, for adornment; second, for protection; and third, for curtaining. Of these three, what is meant in this report is specifically protection. This is shown by the word *exaltation*. Here exaltation demands the impossibility of reaching Him, because the loincloth protects the site of embarrassment from being seen by the eyes.

Exaltation is forbidden through its unreachability, so in reality it cannot become the quality of any created or innovated thing, because abasement is the constant companion of created and innovated things, and abasement contradicts exaltation. Hence, when the Real put on the loincloth of exaltation, rational faculties were prevented from perceiving the entities' reception of existence-giving, by which they became qualified and through which they became distinct to themselves. Hence nothing apart from God knows the form of His giving existence or its reception, nor how the thing comes to be a locus of manifestation for the Real, nor how it is described by *wujūd*—for now it is said concerning it, "existent thing," but it used to be said, "nonexistent thing."

Hence the Real said, "Exaltation is My loincloth," that is, it is a veil over what souls can properly expect to gain.

That is why He says, "When someone contends with Me in either of them, I shatter him." He reports that He is contended with in attributes of this sort that are appropriate only for Him—like exaltation, magnificence, and greatness. So exaltation is the subjugating force that you find preventing perception of the mystery through which the cosmos becomes manifest. (II 102.33)

Causality

Ibn al-ʿArabī describes the cosmos as God's sign, signifier, mark, waymark, and image. In all these cases, the relationship is one of *tashbīh*, in the sense that the cosmos is understood to be a reflection or shadow of the Real in a manner that cannot fully be grasped by the rational mind. These terms are all Koranic, and they are rooted in the concreteness of the Arabic language and actual human experience of the world. Of course many rational explanations for the relation between God and the cosmos were offered by the philosophers and theologians, but the Shaykh tends to look upon these with a critical eye, especially if the terminology is not drawn from the Koran or the Hadith. Thus, for example, the Muslim philosophers often called God the "cause" (*ʿilla*) of the universe and the universe God's "effect" (*maʿlūl*). So important is this doctrine for their position—in Ibn al-ʿArabī's view at least—that he sometimes refers to them as "the Companions of the Causes" (IV 307.18) or "the Affirmers of the Causes" (III 212.35).[17] But he considers application of the term *cause* to God as misguided and mistaken, because cause and effect are inextricably correlative. There can be no cause without an effect. It follows that by calling God a "cause" the philosophers are maintaining that God demands the existence of the cosmos, but this contradicts the independence of the Essence. Hence cause and effect play roles within the cosmos, but not in the relation between God and the cosmos.

> The Real is existent through His own Essence for His own Essence, unbounded in *wujūd*, not bound by other than Himself. He is not caused by anything, nor is He the cause of anything. On the contrary, He is the Creator of the effects and the causes, the King, the All-Holy who always was. (I 90.12)

> We do not make Him a cause of anything, because the cause seeks its effect, just as the effect seeks its cause, but the Independent is not qualified by seeking. Hence it is not correct for Him to be a cause. (II 57.26)

> The Author is He who is not the cause of anything. Hence the words of those who say, "O Cause of causes," is absurd. After all, the cause is equal to its effect in *wujūd*, but the situation is not like that. (*ʿAbādila* 163)

> It is not appropriate that the Real's acts be assigned causes, for there is no cause that makes necessary the engendering of a thing save the very *wujūd* of the Essence and the fact that the entity of the possible thing is a receptacle for the manifestation of *wujūd*. (II 64.8)

> The cosmos is identical with the cause and the effect. I do not say that the Real is its cause, as is said by some of the considerative thinkers, for that is the utmost ignorance of the affair. Whoever says so does not know *wujūd*, nor who it is that is the Existent. You, O so-and-so, are the effect of your cause, and God is your Creator! So understand! (IV 54.8)

Ibn al-ʿArabī makes use of the idea that cause and effect demand each other in *wujūd* while explaining why he rejects the opinion that in order to know oneself, one must first know God.

> Some of the reflective thinkers have held that knowledge of God is the root in knowledge of the self, but this can never be correct for the creature's knowledge of God. This is so only in the Real's knowledge, and here it is a priority and a root in level, not in *wujūd*, because in *wujūd*, His knowledge of Himself is identical with His knowledge of the cosmos. Although knowledge is a root in level, it is not so in *wujūd*.
>
> You say a similar thing in the rational consideration of a cause and an effect, even though they are coextensive in *wujūd* and cannot be otherwise. It is known that the level of the cause is prior to the level of its effect in rational conception, but not in existence.
>
> The same is the case with two correlatives inasmuch as they are two correlatives, and this is even more complete in what we mean. For each of the two correlatives is a cause and an effect of that through which the correlation abides. Thus each is a cause of that of which it is the effect, and an effect of that of which it is the cause. Thus, as a cause, "sonship" makes necessary that "fatherhood" be its effect, and fatherhood as a cause makes necessary that sonship be its effect. But in respect of their entities, there is no cause and no effect. (III 121.28)

A well-known philosophical maxim, apparently used first by Avicenna, maintains that "Nothing proceeds from the One but one."[18] Ibn al-ʿArabī frequently cites or refers to this maxim, most often rejecting it. In the present context he understands it to mean that God is the cause of a single effect, which "proceeds" (*ṣudūr*) from Him, and that this Proceeder (*ṣādir*) is then the cause of the cosmos. When the issue is posed in these terms, it may appear that this Proceeder is identical with Ibn al-ʿArabī's Breath of the All-Merciful. He addresses this issue, though somewhat obliquely, in Chapter 368, "On the true knowledge of the waystation of the Acts, like *[God's command] came* [16:1] and 'did not come,' and the Presence of the Command alone." Here he takes up the technical term *al-ḥaqq al-makhlūq bihi*, "The Real Through Which Creation Occurs," which elsewhere he treats as a synonym for the Breath of the All-Merciful. The term is derived from a number of Koranic verses, and the Shaykh acknowledges that he has taken it from Ibn Barrajān of Seville.[19] In this particular chapter, he says that some of the Folk of God have been mistaken in understanding this term, for, "Having heard God words, *He created the heavens and the earth through the Real* [16:3] and other similar verses in the Koran, they made the Real Through Which Creation Occurs an existent entity" (III 354.28). Having done so, they were guilty of *shirk*, because there cannot be two *wujūd*s. Their mistake lay in reading the pronoun *bi* ("through"), which they took to mean that God needed this second Real to create the universe. What they failed to understand was that *bi* here means *li*, "for the sake of." In other words, the term means the Real For the Sake of Which Creation Occurs. This Real is the truth, the right, and the proper, or God's wisdom in creation. This is why, he says, the same verse continues by negating that there should be another existent thing—an associate of the Real—for it says, *High indeed is He above what they associate!* Having explained this and a number of other relevant points, Ibn al-ʿArabī summarizes his objections, which come down to the issue of causality.

> They have stipulated the Real Through Which Creation Occurs in two meanings.
>
> Some of them make this Real Through Which Creation Occurs identical with the cause of creation. But the Real's creation cannot be assigned a cause; this is what is correct in itself, so much so that in Him nothing can be rationally conceived of that would require the causation of this creation of His that becomes manifest. On the contrary, His creation of the creatures is a gratuitous favor toward the creatures and a beginning of bounty, and He *is independent of the worlds* [3:97].
>
> Others make this Real Through Which Creation Occurs an existent entity through which God created what is apart from Him. These are those who say that "Nothing proceeds from the One save one" and that the procession of this one is the procession of an effect from a cause, a cause that demands that procession. As for this—in it is what is in it [i.e., error].
>
> As for me, I say,
>
> *When God's command comes* [40:78], the Commander is the command,
> and this is the *tawḥīd* of Him who possesses the command.
> So associate not, for association is a proven wrongdoing,
> a wrongdoing that all have condemned. (III 355.30)

Ibn al-ʿArabī devotes several passages in the penultimate chapter of the *Futūḥāt* to the issue of causality. In three of the following four mysteries, he rejects the ascription of the term *cause* to God. But in the last, he accepts it and says that the really important point is not whether or not one uses it, but whether or not one preserves courtesy (*adab*) toward God. No doubt this means that one should be careful to observe the limits of God's revealed language, and one should not interpret (*taʾwīl*) God's speech in ways that go against the words. If God speaks of creation, we should speak of creation, at least in the context of the Koranic text. As long as we do not fall into association or some other error, it is all right to speak of God as "the Cause" in appropriate contexts. The term *ʿilla* in Arabic means not only "cause," but also "infirmity," just as *maʿlūl* means not only "caused thing" or "effect" but also "infirm." Thus he writes, "The root of the cosmos is infirm, so illness clings to it forever. There is no remedy that could rid it of its infirmity" (*ʿAbādila* 67). In the second and third passages below, the Shaykh has a view toward both meanings of the terms. In the third and fourth passages he refers to the fact that the term *condition* (*sharṭ*) has been preferred by some of the Realizers to avoid the problems connected with the term *cause*.

Thus God is considered as a necessary condition for the existence of the cosmos, but not as its cause.

A MYSTERY
The secret of eternity without beginning is in the causes.

Were He a cause, the effect would be coextensive with Him in *wujūd*, but it is posterior to Him, for the names Prior and Posterior are affirmed.

Were He to demand the *wujūd* of the cosmos because of His Essence, none of its newly arrived things would be posterior to Him.

Were it correct that nothing proceeds from Him save one, the relations and the witnesses would be nullified. Those who assign relations to the Proceeder, despite its unity, have affirmed relations and properties. The Proceeder is a known existent, but the relations are a nonexistent affair, and nonexistence does not abide through *wujūd*, for the demonstrations nullify this. But limits and manyness are intelligible, and there is no cause that is not an effect. (IV 336.4)

A MYSTERY
He who witnesses finds.

No one gains *wujūd*
save him who renounces the existent thing.
He who sees that engendered existence has an independent entity
is the companion of a cause, not the companion of a tenet.
No one professes causes
save him who says that the cosmos has no beginning.
But how should the cosmos have eternity?
It has no entrance into the self-necessity of *wujūd*.
It has only a secondary level,
which is the subsistent, the annihilated.
Were eternity affirmed for the cosmos,
nonexistence would be impossible for it,
but nonexistence is possible, or rather, it actually happens
for all the cosmos.
However, most of the servants
are uncertain of a new creation [50:15].
No one recognizes the renewal of the entities
save the Folk of Ḥusbān.
Al-Ashʿarī affirmed it in the accidents
but the philosophers imagine that he was the companion of a disease,
so they considered him ignorant of the black of the African and the yellow of gold
and thought that his position had led him astray.[20] (IV 378.33)

A MYSTERY
Those who profess the cause do not belong to the community.

For the Folk of the Community,
it is not correct for the Real to be our cause,
since He was when I was not,
so why do you trouble yourself?
No cause is separate from its effect
just as no signifier is separate from the signified.
Were this to become separate from that, it would not be a signifier,
nor would the other be a causer.
Healing is one of the properties of causes ["infirmities"]
in eternity without beginning.
No one professes the cause
except those ignorant of what proofs bestow.
The firm and fastened affair
lies in the knowledge of the condition and the conditioned.
Upon this depend the Folk of Realization
in this path.
Professing the cause is an effect ["an infirmity"]
according to the plainest proof.
The properties of the Real in His servants are not given causes,
but He is the intended through aspirations and hopes.
Were it correct for someone to hope for something other than He
it would not be affirmed that He is the God,
but it has been affirmed that He is the God,
so none hopes for any but He.
In the same way, He—exalted and majestic is He—
has troubled His servants as He has troubled them,
for He desires the deferred, last world,
but we desire the hurried, close world.
(IV 373.19)

A MYSTERY
Affirming the cause is a tenet.

He says: Although the cause requires the effect by its essence, it has priority in level. Although the effect is coextensive with the cause in *wujūd*, it is not coextensive with it in essential self-necessity. Once you have understood this, have no concern, save as courtesy restrains you.

He says: Those who fled to professing conditions fled only in fear of the coextensiveness of *wujūd*. They did not know that the existent thing has the property of *wujūd*, whether it is posterior or prior, in contrast to self-necessity, for that belongs to Him, but it does not belong to you. So "God was" in that, "but nothing was with Him" in that, and nothing will be, in contrast to *wujūd*.

If you were to say, "God was, and nothing was with Him," you would not say, "and He is now, and there is nothing," because of the *wujūd* of the things. But concerning essential necessity, you will say in every state, "God was and nothing was with Him, and He is now, and there is nothing."

Now that you know the separating factor, say "condition" or "cause," unless you are restrained by the Shariah. (IV 413.28)

God's Knowledge

Although God is not the cause of the cosmos, He is its necessary condition. Without Him, there is no cosmos. Not only does the *wujūd* of the cosmos derive from God, but also the specific attributes, characteristics, and limitations of the cosmos. Before they come to exist in the universe, all the entities are present to the Real *Wujūd*. This presence to God is known as His "knowledge."

Wujūd, as the source of every reality, is the source of every conceivable attribute that denotes the presence of one thing to the awareness of another thing—such as knowledge, consciousness, witnessing, perception, wisdom, hearing, sight, and so on. As for knowledge, the Koran tells us repeatedly that God is *Knower of all things*. In contrast, the things *encompass nothing of His knowledge save such as He wills* (2:255). One of the implications of this is that God's knowledge alone is perfect and complete. Only God knows any given thing as it truly is. "No one knows a thing in every respect except God, who *encompasses everything in knowledge* [65:12], whether the thing be fixed or existent, finite or infinite" (III 382.21). This leads to Ibn al-ʿArabī's radical agnosticism concerning the realities of the cosmic things. He expresses it succinctly in a line of poetry:

I have not perceived the reality of anything—
How can I perceive something in which
You are? (*Dīwān* 96)

God's omniscience means that *wujūd* finds all things as potentialities within itself and as actualities within their own specific modes of *wujūd*. The term *wujūd* denotes not only the fact that God is found, but also the fact that He finds all things. Through self-finding, the Real perceives within Himself the presence of every possible modality of reality. These modalities, once they become manifest to human beings, are called by such terms as things, entities, realities, possible things, existent things, properties, traces, and occasions.

On the basis of what He knows, the Real gives existence to the things in the manner that He knows them, and they come into *wujūd* manifesting His properties. He creates the cosmos, like Adam, in His own form.

In Himself, God's knowledge of the cosmos brings together His knowledge of Himself, so the cosmos emerges in His form. This is why we say that the Real is identical with *wujūd*. (IV 306.22)

The cosmos is a mark of God's knowing His own Essence. In knowing Himself, God knows all the marks of *wujūd*, all its possible permutations and manifestations. In expressing His knowledge through His creative word *Be!*, He articulates the things within *wujūd*, which, as the substrate of all existential words, is known as the "Breath of the All-Merciful."

Knowledge—every knowledge—is gained through a signifying, because *ʿilm* [knowledge] is derived from *ʿalāma* [mark]. That is why knowledge of the things is attributed to God, for He knows Himself, and thereby He knows the cosmos. Hence He is a signifier and a mark of the cosmos.

In a similar way, the cosmos is a mark of Him in our knowledge of Him. This is indicated by the Prophet's words, "He who knows himself knows his Lord." Hence He made you your signifier of Him, and you come to know Him. Likewise, His Essence is His signifier of you, so He knew you and then brought you into existence. (II 479.3)

Given that God knows all things in Himself and that the cosmos is the exteriorization of this knowledge, and given that God's knowledge is the root of all knowledge, no knowledge of God is conceivable without the cosmos.

Do you not see that the *wujūd* of the servant—by which I mean the cosmos—becomes manifest only through the *wujūd* of the Real and His existence-giving? For the ruling property belongs to Him.

Then He who was prior became posterior, and he who was posterior became prior, for no entity becomes manifest for knowledge of God until knowledge of the cosmos makes it manifest. (IV 43.34)

God is present with the things both in the state of their nonexistence, when they are known to Him but not manifest in the cosmos, and in the state of their *wujūd*. God is always present with the cosmos, but the cosmos is not present with Him so long as it does not witness Him.

A Mystery

He who is certain of emergence will never seek ascent.

He says: Since you have no escape from returning to Him, you should know that you are at Him from the first step, which is the first breath. So do not weary yourself by seeking ascent to Him, for that is nothing but your emerging from your desire such that you do not witness it. For *He is with you wherever you are* [57:4], so your eyes will fall on none but Him. However, it remains for you to recognize Him. Were you to distinguish and recognize Him, you would not seek to ascend to Him, for you have not lost Him.

When you see those who are seeking Him, you will see that they are seeking their felicity in their path. Their felicity is the repulsion of pains from them, nothing else, wherever they may be.

The one who is completely ignorant is he who seeks what is already there, so no one is more ignorant than he who seeks God. If you have faith in His words, *He is with you wherever you are,* and His words, *Wherever you turn, there is the face of God* [2:115], you will recognize that no one seeks God. People seek only their felicity so that they will be safe from what they detest. (IV 424.15)

The fact that God is with all things helps explain why He brings them from nonexistence in knowledge to existence in the cosmos. Sufis typically understand love as God's motive for creating the cosmos. Like others, Ibn al-ᶜArabī often refers to the famous *ḥadīth qudsī* that speaks of God as a Hidden Treasure. The version he usually cites reads, "I was a Treasure but was not known, so I *loved* to be known; I created the creatures and made Myself known to them, so they came to know Me." But the Shaykh often reminds us that the object of love remains nonexistent, whether the love be human or divine.[21] Of course, objections quickly arise when it is said that the object of love does not exist.

You may object and say: We loved sitting with a person, or kissing, or embracing, or intimacy, or conversation. Then we saw that it was achieved, but love did not disappear, even though there was embracing and mutual arrival. Hence, the object of love does not have to be nonexistent.

We would reply: You are mistaken. When you embrace the person, and when the object of your love had been embracing, or sitting together, or intimacy, you have not achieved the object of your love through this situation. For the object is now the continuance and permanence of what you have achieved. This continuance is nonexistent. It has not entered into *wujūd,* and its period has no end. Hence, in the state of arrival, love attaches itself only to a nonexistent thing, and that is its permanence.

How beautifully the Koran has expressed this with His words, *He will love them and they will love Him* [5:54]. For it employs pronouns of absence [i.e., third person] and future tense verbs. Hence it ascribes love's connection only to that which is absent and nonexistent. And every absent thing is a nonexistent thing in a relative sense. (II 327.8)

In the Shaykh's view, when God loves creation, He loves nonexistent things. This love then brings them into *wujūd* in the mode of their temporal unfolding.

God's love for His servants is not qualified by origin or end, for it does not accept qualities that are newly arrived or accidental. His love for His servants is identical with the origination of their engendered existence, whether they be prior or posterior, ad infinitum. Hence the relation of God's love to them is the same as the fact that He is *with* them *wherever* they *are* [57:4], whether in the state of their nonexistence or the state of their *wujūd*. Just as He is with them in the state of their *wujūd*, so also He is with them in the state of their nonexistence, for they are the objects of His knowledge. He witnesses them and loves them never-endingly. No property comes to Him newly that He did not already possess. On the contrary, He has always loved His creatures, just as He has always known them.

His words, "So I loved to be known," instruct us concerning the affair as it is in itself—[when these words are understood] as is proper to His majesty. He can only be conceived of as Agent and Creator.

Every entity was nonexistent in itself and known to Him, and He loved to bring it into existence. Then He made *wujūd* arrive for it newly, or rather, He made *wujūd* arrive in it newly, or rather, He draped it in the robe of *wujūd*. So an entity came to be, then another, then another, continually and successively, from the first existent thing supported by the Firstness of the Real. And there is no last existent thing, but rather, a continuing *wujūd* in individuals, for the "last" is in genera and species. Individuals among created things are not finite in the last world except in certain specific kinds.

Although this world is finite, the engendered things are new, without any end to their engendering, because the possible things have no end. Their endlessness is perpetual, just as beginninglessness in the case of the Real is fixed and necessary. His *wujūd* has no first point, so His love for His servants has no first point. (II 329.5)

Chapter 475: God's Waymarks

It was noted in a previous section that Ibn al-ʿArabī understands "waymarks" in the Koranic passage *Whoever magnifies God's waymarks* (22:32) as a reference to the signs on the horizons. Naturally, they also refer to the signs in the selves. These microcosmic signs tell us that we ourselves signify God's knowledge. The Shaykh explains this in the course of Chapter 475, which he calls, "On the true knowledge of the state of the Pole whose waystation is, *Whoever magnifies God's waymarks*." This is one of the ninety-three chapters in Part Six that he dedicates to explaining how various Koranic verses have their highest human manifestations in the Muhammadan Poles, friends of God who inherit certain sciences and states from Muhammad that were not possessed by any previous prophets. Each of these Poles has a word or a formula, typically a Koranic verse, that provides him with a constant invocation (*hijjīr*) and determines his degree in knowledge and witnessing.

God's waymarks are signposts for us,
set up that we may know
the difference between
the Real and the creation.
They are the limits
whose partitions abide
as a protection for him
who upholds difference.
When someone magnifies them,
they protect him—
he is the one who is wary
of the things through the Real.
On the Day of the Droves,
God will give him a station
apart from the creatures
called the *Seat of Truthfulness* [54:55].
He comes to possess it through
what he won in the race
during all that happened
in the racetrack of precedence.[22]
He annihilates and makes subsistent
him who calls upon Him,
while He is qualified by His names
Annihilator and Subsistence-giver.

God says concerning the magnification of the waymarks, or rather, concerning the waymarks themselves, that they are *of the godwariness of the hearts.* [He continues:] *For you are benefits therein,* that is, in the waymarks, *to a named term; thereafter their lawful place* [of sacrifice] *is at the Ancient House* [22:33], which, for the Folk of Allusions, is the house of faith, which is none other than the heart of the person of faith that embraces the magnificence and majesty of God.

God's waymarks are His signposts, and His signposts are the signifiers of Him that allow someone to arrive at Him. How strange! How can someone arrive at Him when he is with Him? Thus Abū Yazīd, having heard a reciter recite, *On the day when We shall muster the godwary to the All-Merciful in droves* [19:85], cried out and wept until blood flowed from his eyes and struck the pulpit. He said, "How can he who is sitting with Him be mustered?"

Thus God spoke the truth concerning perfection, because the "godwary" is not wary of the All-Merciful. And Abū Yazīd spoke the truth, for, in that state, his object of witnessing was nothing but the All-Merciful, and the friend of God does not transgress his tasting or speak of other than his state. Everything he hears arrives at the state that has overcome him. At that moment, Abū Yazīd's state was that through which he spoke, for a man is concealed beneath his tongue, since the tongue is the spokesman for the states of the speaker.

Then you should know concerning *the sacrificial camels*—that God *has made them among* His *waymarks* [22:36]. Hence they are "marked"[23] so that it may be known that they are among God's waymarks. That which is given to God cannot be taken back. Do you not see that, should the camel die before it reaches the House, its owner butchers it and separates it from the people, and he does not eat anything of it? This is part of God's gratuitous favor, for He has made you a likeness, distinguished you from Him, appointed for you a kingdom, and sought from you that you lend it to Him. But at root, the blessing is His blessing.

All this is among the waymarks of God, for each of these waymarks is a signifier of God in respect of a specific affair that God desires and that He has clarified for the folk of understanding among His servants. They are ranked in degrees in this to the measure of their understanding.

When you see something concerning which it is said that it is among the waymarks of God, but you are ignorant of its form among the waymarks and you do not know what it signifies, you should know that the Real has not addressed you through this waymark and has not established it for you. Rather, He has established it for those who understand it from Him. But you also have a waymark other than that, which is everything you know that signifies Him for you. Thus Abu'l-ʿAtāhiyya has said,

In each thing is a sign
  signifying that He is one.

So, stop at this sign and say, *My Lord, increase me in knowledge!* [20:114]. Then He will strengthen your understanding in that which He sends down and *He will teach you what you did not know* [4:113].

When the Real gives you the ability from yourself, you will know that you are one of the strongest and clearest of waymarks of Him. This is why the Shariah has come with the saying, "He who knows himself knows his Lord." When you reach what the waymarks of yourself allow you to reach and when you witness what they mark, then you will see Him in your own form. Thereby you will know that you are the root in His knowledge of you and that He discloses Himself to you only in the form of His knowledge of you. He does not know you except through you. Through your own essence you give Him knowledge of you. Hence for Him you are a waymark of you, so if you see Him in other than your own form, you will not have seen Him in respect of the fact that for Him, you are a waymark.

[On the day of resurrection] do not deny Him when you see what you do not recognize and when others deny Him. In that Presence, there is no locus of disclosure for any but God. When this occurs, bring your gaze back from Him to yourself. You will see yourself in the form in which you saw Him. You will not have become colored by that form from Him, for it also is your form in your fixity. It is what arrived at the entrance into it and your manifestation through it. For the forms undergo constant fluctuation over you ad infinitum, and you fluctuate in forms and become manifest through them ad infinitum, but this occurs in state after state, through unending transferal. God knows you in these forms in their infinity, and He discloses Himself to you in a form before the arrival of the moment of your becoming manifest within it, for you are bound, but He is not bound. Or rather, His unboundedness has bound Him.

God does this with His servants only so as to become manifest to them in the state of denial.

Hence they deny Him, except the gnostics of this station, for they do not deny Him in whatever form He becomes manifest, since they have preserved the root, which is that He discloses Himself to the created thing only in the form of the created thing.

When [He discloses Himself] in the form that the thing has in the [present] state, it recognizes Him, but if it is in the form that it will have after that, it denies Him, until it sees that it has entered into that form. Then it recognizes Him. God knows the created thing and He knows that to which it goes back. But the created thing knows nothing of its own states save what it has at the moment. This is why it says, *My Lord, increase me in knowledge!* [20:114].

Some of the servants know this. When one of them sees the Real in a form that he does not recognize, he knows, by virtue of the homestead and his own receptivity, that the Real has disclosed Himself to him in a form that belongs only to him but whose moment has not yet arrived. Hence he knows the form before he enters into it. This is part of the "increase" in knowledge that God gives. So he thanks God, whom he has recognized in the homestead of denial. This is why God magnifies this bounty, for He says, *He will teach you what you did not know, and God's bounty to you is ever magnificent* [4:113]. Thus in this homestead the Real is one of the waymarks of yourself. You know yourself through Him, just as you know Him through yourself. So think about this!

We have come together in the waymarks,
 we have kept apart in the secret hearts.
From Him we have self-disclosure,
 from us He has the deepest selves.
For the like of this a servant
 should be enraptured in Him and hurry.
When you come to know it,
 you will not be proceeding from Him,
For He proceeds from you,
 like the pages of a notebook,
Some curtaining others,
 through the first parts and the last.
Let him who makes haste make haste,
 and let him who wants to boast boast!

God did not magnify His waymarks for nothing. After all, He magnifies only that which accepts such magnifying. As for the magnificent, it is not magnified, for the Existent does not come into existence. God is Magnificent, and all the cosmos, because of its possibility, is lowly, except that it is receptive to magnifying. It has no path in magnifying save to be one of God's waymarks of Him. Given that, in actual fact, it is His waymark, we recognize the Real through it. Thus we come to see the rightness of the words, "We sought the signifier of Him in us and in Him when He became manifest to us in the denial."

From Him to me there is a signifier of me
 and from me to Him a signifier of Him.
We are with Him, as He has said,
 through His acts, then we are with Him.
His acts are the same as our entities,
 so my origin is from Him and my return to Him.

Were this not the affair, your taking Him as a trustee would not be true.[24] But the possessions are His possessions, so the possessions are your possessions. The allusion is that the form is your form.

Hence the words *Thou shalt not see Me* tell the truth, when Moses said to Him, *O my Lord, show me, that I may look upon Thee!* [7:143]. He said, *Thou shalt not see Me,* and the words *shalt not* negate future acts. The allusion [through the use of the future tense] is that anyone ignorant of You in the [present] state will be ignorant of You at the final issue. After all, when You become manifest to him at the final issue, You will not become manifest to him in the form of the state in which he had been ignorant of You when he sought vision of You. Rather, You will become manifest to him in the form of the state of that final issue. Hence, he will never cease denying what he sees until he recognizes the homestead and its property. Then he will know what he sees and what is the property ruling over him.

God remains forever manifest to the Possessor of Two Eyes and Eyes. As for the possessor of one eye, he is a one-eyed Dajjāl and will remain forever fettered by the noose of binding. But God may open a person's two eyes, [and it is these] with which He has favored him in His words, *Have We not appointed for him two eyes?* [90:8], i.e., with which to witness Me in the two states—the present state and the future state. As for him who does not see Me in the [present] state while he is gazing upon Me, he is even more unlikely to see Me in the state of the final issue. He will see Me, but he will not recognize that I am the object of his search. The occasion of this is that he seeks Me through the mark.[25] Is this anything other than ignorance of Me?

Is there any other than I,
is there any that is not I?
Oh the insights' loss
through the eyesights!
Beware of reflective thoughts
if you are a seeker,
for the locus of trial
is the secret hearts!

*And God speaks the **haqq**, and He guides on the path* [33:4]. (IV 109.11)

Chapter 411: The Precedent Book

"The whole cosmos is *a book inscribed on a parchment unrolled* [52:2–3], and it is *wujūd*" (III 455.21). The words that God writes on this parchment are present in their Author's knowledge before He writes them. Unlike human authors, God never revises His manuscript. He writes out the book as He has known it for all eternity. Any word in the book—any entity or creature—is found in the text in its proper place. The book, like every entity, is immutably fixed in God's knowledge. "The cosmos becomes manifest only in accordance with its actual situation in the divine knowledge, and nothing in knowledge changes" (III 365.15). In the Shaykh's view, God's fixed knowledge is alluded to in the verse, *Had it not been for a Book from God that had preceded, there would have afflicted you, for what you took, a great chastisement* (8:68). The "precedent Book" is God's foreknowledge of what enters *wujūd* to become the *book inscribed on a parchment unrolled.* The Shaykh explains this in Chapter 411, which he calls, "On the true knowledge of the mutual waystation of 'The Book will take precedence over him, so he will enter the Fire.' This is from the Presence of, 'He almost did not enter the Fire, so fear the Book, but do not fear Me, for I and you are equal in the like of this.'" A "mutual waystation" is a visionary encounter in which God descends toward the servant and the servant ascends toward God. They meet in the middle, and God speaks to the servant, typically—if Ibn al-ʿArabī's chapter headings are to be taken at face value—in aphoristic and enigmatic fashion. Ibn al-ʿArabī devotes Part Five of the *Futūḥāt*—seventy-eight chapters—to these mutual waystations.[26]

God says, *The word is not changed with Me, and I do not wrong My servants* [50:29], because the Book exercises its ruling property over and against everyone—*he against whom the word of chastisement is realized* [39:19]. So how difficult is the affair for the intelligent, the experienced!

Fear of the Book is the worst of my sins,
for the Book rules over *wujūd* and us.
We have read this explicitly in the Koran
and saw it there as a truth of certainty.
God is not feared save for events
that arrive newly from Him and are visited
upon the worlds.

The Messenger of God said in a sound hadith, "A man will do the deeds of the folk of the Garden in what appears to the people until nothing remains between him and the Garden save a span, but then the Book will take precedence over him and he will do the deeds of the folk of the Fire, so he will enter the Fire." Then he said a similar thing about the folk of the Garden. Then he said, "Deeds are judged only by the conclusions," and these follow the ruling property of the precedents.

God decrees no decree save in accordance with the precedent decree of the Book, for His knowledge in the things is identical with His word in giving engendered existence. *The word is not changed with Me* [50:29], so no creator and no created thing has any ruling property except through what had been given precedence in the Divine Book. This is why He continues by saying, *and I do not wrong My servants* [50:29]. In other words, "In them We bring to pass only what precedes in knowledge, and I judge them only through what precedes." This is the "halting place of equality," in which the servant is made to halt.[27]

Since the Real's knowledge
rules the Real,
what could be more worthy
to rule creation?
If this is the case,
no one has any choice.
All submit
to the Precedent Book.

There is nothing to fear
save the Book,
for its suras and verses concerning us
have gone before.
Had He choice, we would be safe,
for He is the Clement,
the Compassionate toward the servants,
the Most Merciful.
And in the Good News,
He has reported about His mercy,
which has generous
precedence over
the wrath that is made to appear
by His servants' acts.
It will vanish—praise to God—
from Him and from them.
"My book is nothing but My Essence—
so understand!"
What He has shown me in likenesses,
divulge and keep secret!

Nay, man is an insight against himself [75:14]. So, dear friend, consider what is woven into your breast.[28] Do not consider the accidental qualities, for you accord with what is woven. If faith is woven, you are one of the faithful, and if what is woven is turning away from what faith requires and toward what is not demanded by the outward sense of the ruling, then you accord with that, and through that you will reach your conclusion.

Do not consider what appears to the people from you. Depend only upon what is woven into your own breast, for nothing is woven into your breast save your conclusion that has been given precedence in the Book. However, people are heedless of that to which I have called their attention.

None repels His command, *None holds back His ruling* [13:41]. That which is woven into your breast is identical with the self-disclosure of the command pertaining to you and your portion of the Real *Wujūd.*

One of them said concerning abstinence, "I have seen nothing easier for me than abstinence. Whenever something disquiets me, I leave it aside."[29] This is confirmed by the words of the Prophet, "Leave what disquiets you for that which does not disquiet you." He also said, "Seek a pronouncement from your heart [. . .], even if the pronouncers make pronouncements for you."

Know that God writes only what He knows, and He knows only the forms of the objects of knowledge that He witnesses as they are in themselves—that which changes and that which does not change. He witnesses all of them in the state of their nonexistence according to the variations of their changes ad infinitum. He brings them into existence only as they are in themselves. From here you will know God's knowledge of the things—whether they are nonexistent or existent, whether necessary, possible, or impossible.

Thus, as we have stipulated, there is no Book that "precedes" other than that "the Book" is ascribed to that through which the thing becomes manifest in *wujūd* just as the Real has witnessed it in the state of its nonexistence. This, in reality, is the precedence of the Book. The Book precedes the *wujūd* of the thing.

The tasting of this is known by him who knows engendered events before they are engendered. They are witnessed by him in the state of their nonexistence when they have no *wujūd.* He who has this knows the meaning of the precedence of the Book, so he does not fear the Book's preceding him. He fears only himself, for the Book and knowledge have precedence over him in keeping only with his form in which he becomes manifest in his *wujūd.* So blame yourself![30] Do not protest against the Book!

From here—if you understand—the Real has described Himself as having *the conclusive argument* [6:149] if anyone should contend with Him. After all, it is impossible for knowledge to be connected to anything other than the situation of the object of knowledge in itself. If anyone brings an argument against God—saying, "You had precedent knowledge that I would be such and such, so do not take me to task"—the Real will say to him, "Did I not know you as you are? If you were otherwise, I would have known you as you were." This is why He says *[And We shall assuredly try you] until We know [those of you who struggle and are steadfast]* [47:31].

So turn back to yourself and be fair in your speech!

When the servant turns back to himself and considers the affair as we have mentioned, he will know that he has been defeated by the argument, and that the argument belongs to God against him. Have you not heard Him saying, *God wronged them not* [16:33]? *We wronged them not* [16:118, 43:76]. He also says, *But they wronged themselves* [16:33, 16:118], just as He says, *But they were the wrongdoers* [43:76], that is, against themselves, for they did not become manifest to Us until We knew them. They were nonexistent things save only through the states through which they became manifest in *wujūd.* Knowledge follows the object of knowledge; the object of knowledge does not follow knowledge. So understand this!

> This is a delicate and magnificent issue. I do not know that anyone has called attention to it, though it may be that someone has, and it has not reached us. No one, if he realizes it, can deny it.
>
> So distinguish, my brother, between a thing when it is existent, such that knowledge takes priority over its *wujūd*, and the thing when it has these forms in the state of its beginningless nonexistence, so that it is coextensive with God's knowledge of it and it takes priority over the knowledge through the level, because through its very essence it bestows knowledge of itself upon Him.
>
> Know what we have mentioned! It will benefit you and strengthen you in assenting to and trusting in the decree and the measuring out that is decreed by your state. Were there nothing in this book save this issue, it would be sufficient for every companion of proper consideration and healthy intelligence. *And God speaks the ḥaqq, and He guides on the path* [33:4]. (IV 15.19)

God's Form

A famous hadith tells us, "God created Adam in His form [*ṣūra*]." The word *form* itself occurs three times in the Koran, once in the singular and twice in the plural: *[God] created you, then proportioned you, then balanced you; in whatever form He willed He mounted you* (82:7–8). *He formed you, and He made your forms beautiful* (40:64, 64:3). God is the subject of the verb *to form* (*taṣwīr*) four times, and He is also called the "Former," i.e., "Form-Giver" (*muṣawwir*), once (59:24). As a technical term in Islamic philosophy, *form* was used in an Aristotelian sense as the correlative of matter, and hence it was taken as a synonym of words like *reality* and *quiddity*. In Sufism, form was typically paired with "meaning" (*maᶜnā*), and meaning was taken as a synonym of reality and quiddity. Then the form would be the outward, witnessed aspect of a thing and the meaning its inward, absent dimension. Ibn al-ᶜArabī often uses the term *form* in this sense, though he rarely juxtaposes it with meaning. Sometimes he pairs it with the term *entity*, that is, the fixed entity, which is the form's reality with God. Thus he writes, "Manifestation belongs to the forms, not to the entity. The entity is forever absent, the forms are forever witnessed" (III 161.34).

In general, Ibn al-ᶜArabī employs the term *form* to refer to anything that becomes manifest, anything or any quality or attribute that can be distinguished or differentiated, "whether the form pertains to the genus, the species, or the individual" (II 652.27). Every "thing" that we perceive in any mode whatsoever is a form inasmuch as we perceive it. Even the fixed entities themselves, though they may be juxtaposed with the term *form*, may be called forms, because they can be differentiated from a reality that they make manifest, i.e., the Essence of God.

The cosmos is a vast collection of forms that make the fixed entities manifest. "As we have often said, the forms that are called the 'cosmos' are the properties of the entities of the possible things in the *wujūd* of the Real" (IV 141.21). The forms display the entities, and the entities display the properties of the Real. Hence, everything in the cosmos can be looked upon as a form of the Real.

> Whatever the situation of anything in the cosmos, it is the form of the Real because of what He has given to it, for it is not correct for anything in the cosmos to have a *wujūd* that is not the form of the Real. (III 409.31)

> He is *wujūd* and everything
> in engendered existence is His form,
> for there is no existent thing
> but the All-Merciful. (III 245.23)

> Engendered existence became manifest in the form of *Be! Be* is His command, His command His speech, His speech His knowledge, and His knowledge His Essence. Hence the cosmos became manifest in His form. (II 403.11)

Each individual thing in the cosmos is a form of God in respect of *wujūd*, but strictly speaking, only human beings—and perfect human beings at that—manifest the form of God in its full splendor. It is from this point of view that Ibn al-ᶜArabī writes, "Not every part of the cosmos is in the form of the Real" (IV 8.1). Beside the human being, only the cosmos as a whole, viewed as a single form, is in the form of "God," the all-comprehensive name that embraces the meanings of all the divine names. "Nothing in the cosmos is without a share of the divine form, but the cosmos as a whole is in the divine form" (IV 231.5). Thus, for Ibn al-ʿArabī, "God created Adam in His form" means "Every attribute accepted by the Divine Presence is accepted both by the small human being and by the great human being" (II 139.30), that is, both by the microcosm and by the macrocosm.

I saw in [this waystation] the knowledge of mutual interpenetration and the vicious circle. In His acts the Real can only be in the form of creation, and in its acts creation can only be in the form of the Real. Hence we have a vicious circle, but this does not give rise to the impossibility of occurrence. On the contrary, this is what occurs in the actual situation. (III 352.11)

Know that the divine beauty through which God is named "Beautiful" and by which He described Himself in His messenger's words, "He loves beauty," is in all things. There is nothing but beauty, for God created the cosmos only in His form, and He is beautiful. Hence all the cosmos is beautiful. (II 542.19)

Know that God created the cosmos in the furthest limit of good making and sound arrangement. Thus Imam Abū Ḥāmid Ghazālī said that nothing remains in possibility more wondrous than this cosmos.[31] For the Prophet reported that God created Adam in His form, and the human being has brought together the whole cosmos. God's knowledge of the cosmos is none other than His knowledge of Himself, since there is nothing in *wujūd* but He. Inescapably the cosmos is in His form. When God made the cosmos manifest in its entity, it was His locus of disclosure, so He saw nothing within it but His own beauty, and He loved the beauty. Thus the cosmos is God's beauty. So He is the beautiful, the lover of beauty. Anyone who loves the cosmos in this regard has loved it with God's love and has loved nothing but God's beauty, for the beauty of the artisanry is not ascribed to itself; it is ascribed only to the artisan. Hence the beauty of the cosmos is God's beauty. (II 345.21)

A sound report has come in the *Ṣaḥīḥ* of Muslim from God's Messenger that he said, "God is beautiful and He loves beauty." He is the artisan of the cosmos and He gave it existence in His form. So the whole cosmos is in the furthest limit of beauty, and there is nothing of ugliness within it. On the contrary, God brought together for it all comeliness and beauty, so there is nothing in possibility more beautiful, more wondrous, and more comely than the cosmos. If He were to bring into existence what He brings into existence ad infinitum, it would be like what He has brought into existence, because the divine comeliness and beauty has possessed it and become manifest through it. After all, as He says, *He gave each thing its creation* [20:50], so that is its beauty. Were it to lack anything, it would descend from the degree of the perfection of its creation and be ugly. *Then He guided* [20:50], that is, He clarified this for us through His words, *He gave each thing its creation.* (III 449.7)

Since God created the cosmos in His own form, all God's names come to be applied to it, or rather, to the various entities that become manifest within it. For the Shaykh, God is the source of every attribute in *wujūd,* even if the theologians and philosophers insist on declaring Him incomparable with many of these attributes. "None knows God but God," after all, so no one truly knows what attributes belong to God but God Himself. If He declares in His revelation that He laughs or thirsts, then these are His attributes, even if rational minds would like to protect His holiness from such mundane affairs.

God has described Himself with attributes that the considerative thinkers consider to be true for creation but metaphorical for God. These range from hunger, thirst, illness, wrath, good-pleasure, anger, wonder, joy, and receiving joyfully to foot, hand, eye, arm, and so on. Reports about these have come from God on the tongues of the messengers and in the speech attributed to God that is called scripture, Koran, Furqān, Torah, Gospel, and Psalms.[32]

For the Realizers, the situation is that all these are attributes of the Real, not attributes of creation. Creation has become qualified by them through jostling the Real. In the same way, the cosmos has become qualified by all the most beautiful divine names, and the considerative thinkers have reached consensus on these. All are His names without specification.

This is the position of the Realizers, for it is truthful. That is why we maintain conditionality [in knowledge of the names]: We describe Him only as He has described Himself, and we name Him only as He has named Himself. We do not devise any names for Him, bring forth any properties for Him, or make Him stand in any attributes. For we have already told you that He is not like us, nor are we like Him. So *nothing* of us *is as His likeness* [42:11], and nothing of Him is as our likeness. He belongs to Himself through Himself, and we belong to us through Him, for in our *wujūd* we are not independent as He is independent.

However, He created the cosmos in His form, so it accepts to be named by His names. What is ascribed to the Real—in respect of what the Real has ascribed to Himself—is ascribed to the cosmos. Thus we know that He is the root in His names, not we. He has not taken anything that belongs to us, nor are we worthy of anything. On the contrary, all of it belongs to Him.

Among the things that God has created is imagination. He became manifest to us within it through these names and attributes. Hence we differentiated, divided, lifted up, and put down. Imagination left nothing of the attributes of the cosmos with us by which we did not describe our Creator. Then unveiling occurred for us, and behold, all were His attributes, not our attributes.

In reality, the attributes of the cosmos are the He-ness of the Real. The diversity in the divine self-disclosures belongs to the realities of the possible things in the Entity of the Real, for He is identical with the form that we perceive. After all, we do not doubt in what we see that we have seen the Real, through the mark that is between us and Him,[33] when He—in respect of His He-ness—is our eyesight and our hearing. So we see Him only through Him, not through our own eyesight. We hear His speech only through Him, not through our own hearing.

There is no escape from an entity named "the cosmos," and there is no escape from an entity named "the Real." *Nothing* of the one *is as the likeness* of anything of the other. (III 538.9)

The Nonexistent Entities

Wujūd's opposite is *ʿadam*, nonexistence. Nonexistence is an inherent, essential property of the cosmos and all things, given that everything other than God is other than *wujūd*. However, in creating the cosmos and the entities, God "gives them existence" (*ījād*), which is to say that they "acquire" (*istifāda*) or "receive" (*qabūl*) *wujūd* from Him. The question then arises as to the exact relation between the *wujūd* of the Real and that of the existent things. What sort of *wujūd* does the cosmos acquire from God? How exactly is the cosmos related to Real *Wujūd*? Ibn al-ʿArabī offers a variety of answers, all the while maintaining that the ultimate mystery of *wujūd*'s presence in the things is unknowable. However, he does insist that the things never become qualified (*ittiṣāf*) by *wujūd* in the same mode that the Real is qualified by *wujūd*. The Real, after all, is identical with *wujūd*, whereas the things merely become draped (*iktisāʾ*) in *wujūd*. God is the Manifest, but they are simply the loci in which He becomes manifest. They remain totally different from God in that He is *wujūd*, while their *wujūd* is He. Inasmuch as they are nonexistent, they are distinct from Him, but inasmuch as they exist, they are identical with Him. The cosmos is, in Ibn al-ʿArabī's most succinct expression, "He/not He," both the same as *wujūd* and other than *wujūd* at one and the same time.

As the counterpart of His *wujūd* are fixed entities that have no *wujūd* except by way of acquisition from the *wujūd* of the Real. Hence they are His loci of manifestation in this qualification by *wujūd*. They are entities by their own essences, not by a necessitating factor or a cause. In the same way *wujūd* belongs to the Real by His Essence, not by a cause. Just as independence belongs to God absolutely, so also poverty toward Him who is Independent—who is necessarily Independent through His Essence by His Essence—belongs to these entities absolutely. (II 57.15)

He who has not been given an overview of the form of the affair as it is in itself imagines from God's words, "I have divided the *ṣalāt* into two halves between Me and My servant," that perhaps his own entity, fixed in nonexistence, gains *wujūd*. For he has seen that his entity has properties in the *wujūd* of the Real such that the name of his entity is ascribed to that *wujūd*. He does not know that *wujūd* is the Real's *wujūd*, and that the property is the pos-

> sible thing's property, though the possible thing remains fixed in its nonexistence. (III 566.26)

> Although the possible thing exists, it has the property of the nonexistent thing. "The truest verse spoken by the Arabs is the words of Labīd, 'Is not everything other than God unreal?'," and the unreal is nonexistence. (I 716.16)

The entities are essentially nonexistent, which is to say that in their very essences they are other than *wujūd*. Since, as the Arabic proverb has it, "Things become distinct through their opposites," to understand *wujūd* we need to understand nonexistence. One place to begin is to keep in mind that nonexistence can be divided into two basic kinds—bound or relative (*muqayyad*) and unbounded or absolute (*muṭlaq*). Absolute nonexistence has no mode of existence whatsoever. Relative nonexistence is the situation of the possible things, which are nonexistent relative to Real *Wujūd*, but existent relative to absolute nonexistence. In other words, all entities are nonexistent in themselves, but existent through the Real.

From a certain point of view, the possible things have two modes of relative nonexistence, which is to say that they have two modes of relative existence. In the first mode, they are nonexistent in the cosmos but existent as objects of God's knowledge. They are concomitants of God's knowledge of Himself, while having no separate existence of their own. In this situation, they are known by God alone. In the second mode, they exist both as objects of knowledge and as entities in the cosmos. God knows them, and they also know each other by finding and being found. However, Ibn al-ʿArabī looks on this existence in the cosmos as metaphorical (*majāzī*), not true (*ḥaqīqī*). He is willing to employ terminology that affirms the *wujūd* of the cosmic things, but he does this more as convention or an acknowledgment of common usage than as a precise statement of the situation. In fact, *wujūd* is the Real, and any mode of *wujūd* can be nothing but the Real. Hence, everything that is not the Real is nonexistent.

Although the things have no *wujūd* of their own, they exist as fixed entities known by God. Hence, when God gives them existence, He brings them from *wujūd* in His knowledge to *wujūd* in the cosmos. He creates things from "nothingness" only in the sense that they are not found in the cosmos before He puts them there. But even when they come to be found, they remain a nothingness in themselves, because their *wujūd* is not their own. In the following the "Cloud" is the Breath of the All-Merciful, or the manifestation of the Breath.

> The forms of the genera of the cosmos never cease becoming manifest within the Cloud, one thing after another and stage after stage, until the cosmos becomes perfect in respect of its genera. When it is perfect, the individuals of these genera remain. They come into being perpetually through an engendering that is a transmutation from a *wujūd* to a *wujūd*, not from a nonexistence to a *wujūd*. Thus He *created* Adam *from dust* [3:59], He created the children of Adam *from a sperm-drop* [16:14]—which is the *vile water* [32:8]. *Then* He *created of the sperm-drop a clot* [23:14]. This is why we say concerning the individuals that they are created from a *wujūd*, not from a nonexistence. For the root—that is, the Cloud—comes to be as such. It is from the Breath, which is a *wujūd*; in other words, it is the same as the Real Through Which Creation Occurs. The genera of the cosmos are created from the Cloud, and the individuals of the cosmos are also created from the Cloud and from the species of its genera.
>
> Nothing was created from a nonexistence whose *wujūd* is impossible. On the contrary, things became manifest in fixed entities. This is our words at the beginning of this book, "Praise belongs to God, who brought the things into existence from a nonexistence and from its nonexistence."[34] "From a nonexistence," in respect of the fact that they had no manifest entity, "and from its nonexistence," since the nonexistence of a nonexistence is a *wujūd*. In other words, although the things had no entity, in reality the entity became manifest from a *wujūd*, so the entity made the first nonexistence—which it affirmed in one relation—nonexistent. Hence, in respect of the first relation, the thing is fixed, and in respect of the other relation, it is negated. Once you have realized this, then, if you wish, say "from a nonexistence," and if you wish, say "from a *wujūd*"—after your knowledge of the actual situation. (II 310.28)

All existent things stand between absolute nonexistence and *wujūd*. They are neither the one nor the other. One of the many signs of their intermediate status is the renewal of their creation at each instant. Since God loves only nonexistent things, He does not love existent things, and hence nothing supports their *wujūd*. However, the next moment of the thing is not yet existent, so God turns His love toward that, thus bringing it into existence. Hence He brings the nonexistent things into existence moment by moment, but the specific entity present at one moment does not subsist, because God's love no longer supports it. It is followed in the next moment by its similar, and so it continues, ad infinitum.

In their new creation, the things are not exactly what they were in the previous creation because "Self-Disclosure never repeats itself." *Wujūd*'s infinity demands that it never display itself in an identical manner in two successive moments or in two different things. As a result, all creatures dwell in constant change and "fluctuation" (*taqallub*). For human beings, the perception of constant change is located in the heart (*qalb*). The very word *qalb* indicates this, for it comes from the same root as *taqallub* and can mean the same thing. The Shaykh makes some of these points while discussing eminence (*sharaf*) and "magnifying things" (*ta^cẓīm*), the latter of which is to acknowledge the greatness and magnificence of things because of their situation in relation to *wujūd*.

> All things have a relation with eminence and magnification, as does nonexistence. The eminence of absolute nonexistence is that it signifies absolute *wujūd*, so it is magnified in respect of this signifying. This is a point people often make, and someone has versified it:
>
> Through their opposites
> things become distinct.
>
> Thus nonexistence makes *wujūd* distinct, and *wujūd* makes nonexistence distinct.
>
> As for relative nonexistence, it has an attribute that allows it to receive *wujūd*, and *wujūd* is eminent in itself. Hence *wujūd* is one of the descriptions of the Real. So relative nonexistence is more eminent than absolute nonexistence inasmuch as it receives *wujūd*. Hence it signifies the Real in two ways—a signifying in the state of its nonexistence and a signifying in the state of its *wujūd*.
>
> Absolute nonexistence is more eminent than relative nonexistence in a certain respect, and that is that, in its magnification of God and in the strength of its signifying Him, it does not receive *wujūd*. It remains in its root and entity, out of jealousy[35] lest it be the associate of the Divine Side in the attribute of *wujūd* and lest the names that are ascribed to God be ascribed to it.
>
> Since this is the actual situation, the Real made glorification of Him a shariah for the existent things. Glorification is to assert God's incomparability [*tanzīh*]. It is for Him to be described such that the attributes of newly arrived things have no connection with Him. *Tanzīh* is a description by nonexistence. Hence He made absolute nonexistence eminent by describing Himself by it, for He says, *Glory be to thy Lord, the Lord of exaltation, above what they describe* [37:180]. Thereby He gives eminence to nonexistence because of this realized intention on its part to magnify God. After all, absolute nonexistence is better at making known what is worthy of God than the relatively nonexistent, because it has the attribute of eternity without beginning in its nonexistence, just as the Real has the attribute of eternity without beginning in His *wujūd*. This is the description of the Real by the negation of firstness, which is the description of nonexistence by the fact that *wujūd* is negated from it through its own essence. Hence nothing other than God makes God known with greater knowledge than does absolute nonexistence.
>
> Given that nonexistence has such eminence, and given that making claims and associating things [with God] belong to the existent things, God says to us, *I created you aforetime, when you were not a thing* [19:9], that is, you were not an existent thing. He says: So be with Me in the state of your *wujūd* by not protesting to the ruling and by consenting to the flow of what is measured out, just as you were in the state of your nonexistence. He made human eminence to be the return within their *wujūd* to the state of their nonexistence. Were it not for the eminence of nonexistence that we have mentioned, the Real would not have admonished the existent, created thing to return to that state—in property, not in entity. No one has the ability to achieve this sort of return to nonexistence in property, while he is in entified *wujūd*, save him who knows from whence he has come,

what is desired from him, and why he was created.

Enough has become clear to you concerning the eminence of absolute nonexistence. This is an issue of which people are heedless. They do not understand it from God when He mentions it to them.

Once it becomes clear that eminence belongs to the existent and nonexistent things in respect of their signifying, it becomes necessary to magnify them, for God said, *Whoever magnifies God's waymarks, that is of the godwariness of the hearts* [22:32]. "Waymarks" are signposts, so they are signifiers.

He who magnifies the waymarks has shown godwariness in all his fluctuations. For "heart" derives from "fluctuation." God did not say, "That is of the godwariness of the souls" or "the godwariness of the spirits." On the contrary, He said, *the godwariness of the hearts,* because the human being undergoes fluctuations in his states breath by breath. This is the bringing of nonexistent things into existence breath by breath. When someone is wary of God in each fluctuation that he undergoes, this is the furthest limit of what God seeks from the human being. None reach it but the strong, the perfect among the creatures, for "awareness" [*shuʿūr*] of this fluctuation is exalted. That is why He said *God's "waymarks"* [*shaʿāʾir*]. In other words, they give "awareness" of what they signify, but they are waymarks only in the case of those who are aware of them. As for those who are not aware of the waymarks—that is, most creatures—they do not magnify them.

Since those who magnify the waymarks are those who betake themselves to God in everything they face and in all their activities, God mentioned the waymarks only in the context of the hajj, which means [literally] "repeatedly betaking oneself." (II 672.13)

In discussing the things of the cosmos, Ibn al-ʿArabī often refers to God's speech to them when they were nonexistent. In particular, he likes to quote the verse, *Our only word to a thing, when We desire it, is to say to it "Be!," so it comes to be* (16:40). Another Koranic verse that speaks of "things" is 17:44: *There is no thing that does not glorify Him in praise.* In explaining some of the implications of the latter verse, Ibn al-ʿArabī assures us that things are always just things. In other words, the entities are always simply entities, whether we speak of them as nonexistent in fixity or existent in the cosmos. However, there is a certain difference between the states of the entities in the two situations.

God says, *There is no thing that does not glorify Him in praise.* He brought the indefinite form of the word, so He did not specify the fixed thing apart from the existent thing. This is because the things receive the thingness of *wujūd* according to the state they have in their thingness of fixity.

God has given us knowledge that He addressed them in the state of their nonexistence and that they obeyed His command when they were addressed. Hence they hastened to obey what He commanded them. Had they not been described in the state of their nonexistence by the descriptions that they possess in the state of their *wujūd*, the Real would not have described them as He described them. But He is the truthful Report-Giver concerning the realities of the things as they are in themselves. So the entities of the existent things become manifest only in the state that they had in the state of nonexistence. They acquire nothing but *wujūd* in respect to their entities and in respect to that through which they subsist.

Everything that belongs to the entities and abides through them is essential to them, even if their accidental qualities should change through likenesses and opposites. However, their property in the state of their nonexistence is not the same as their property in the state of their *wujūd* in respect to a certain affair. This is because their property in the state of their nonexistence is essential to them, so the Real has no property within them. If He did, nonexistence would not be one of their essential attributes.

In the state of their nonexistence, the possible things remain forever gazing upon God through their own states. No state changes for them that they might become qualified by *wujūd*. Then states would alter for them, because of the nonexistence that would rush to that through which the entity subsists. But this is not so in the state of nonexistence, because nothing alters for them in the state of nonexistence. On the contrary, their situation in themselves is fixed, since, were the situation to depart from them, they would only depart into *wujūd*. But no entity departs into *wujūd*, except when the entity through which this specific possible thing abides becomes qualified by *wujūd*.

The actual situation dwells between *wujūd* and nonexistence within entities that are fixed in specific states. When you realize what I have made apparent to you, you will come to know creation and the Creator, the property that is appropriate for the creation, and that by which the Creator should appropriately be described. For *Nothing is as His likeness* [42:11] and *Each day He is upon some task* [55:29], so He is not similar to any fixed thing nor any existent thing. (III 263.21)

From Chapter 463: The Third Pole

Ibn al-ʿArabī calls this chapter "On the true knowledge of the twelve poles around whom revolve the world of their time." It is the second chapter of Part Six, which deals with the Muhammadan Poles. In most of the remaining chapters of this Part, each Pole is assigned a Koranic verse, but in this chapter, the Shaykh explains that each of the twelve poles is "upon the heart of" (*ʿalā qalb*) or "upon the footsteps of" (*ʿalā qadam*) one of the prophets, which is to say that each is the inheritor of the knowledges, stations, and states of a specific prophet. The Poles are the analogues in the absent domain of the twelve constellations that rule over the witnessed domain, and each of them corresponds to a surah of the Koran. In order, the twelve Poles (along with their surahs) are Noah (Yāsīn: 36) , Abraham (al-Ikhlāṣ: 112), Moses (al-Naṣr: 110), Jesus (al-Kāfirūn: 109), David (al-Zilzāl: 99), Solomon (al-Wāqiʿa: 56), Job (al-Baqara: 2), Elias (Āl ʿImrān: 3), Lot (al-Kahf: 18), Hūd (al-Anʿām: 6), Ṣāliḥ (Ṭāhā: 20), and Shuʿayb (al-Mulk: 67).

In discussing the knowledge that is bestowed upon the Third Pole, the Shaykh provides some rather exotic details of the situation of the nonexistent entities and the way in which they are enticed into existence. Many of the entities, if given the choice, would rather not enter into *wujūd* because of the suffering they must undergo when they do so. In explaining these details, the Shaykh brings out a fundamental difference between the state of the things in *wujūd* and their state in fixity. Although the things in *wujūd* are identical with the things in fixity, they find themselves and others when they enter into *wujūd*. The "others" are not only entities like themselves, but also entities that stand or abide (*qāʾim*) through them. Thus, for example, if a human being is an entity, various accidents and attributes that come over the human being are also entities, but these entities abide through the human being. Ibn al-ʿArabī uses the example of the specific states that people experience as pleasure or pain.

The Third Pole is upon the footsteps of Moses. His surah is, *When comes the help of God, and opening* [110]. His waystations accord with the number of this surah's verses; to this surah belongs one-quarter of the Koran.[36]

This Pole was among the [four] Pegs,[37] then was transferred to Polehood, just as the second Pole was among the Imams, then was transferred to Polehood. This Pole is the companion of effort and endurance. He never ceases being occupied with the creatures at God. In the Waystation of the Call, God bestowed upon him twelve thousand knowledges by way of tasting in one night. The Waystation of the Call is among the greatest of waystations. We have designated it in the "Waystation of Waystations" in this book, and we also have a separate fascicle that deals with it, that is, "On the Grades of the Waystations and Their Number."[38]

One of the knowledges of this Pole is the knowledge of poverty toward God through God. This is an eminent knowledge, and when I tasted it I did not witness anyone else who was tasting it. Its meaning and mystery are that God lets the Pole see that the need of the divine names to leave traces among the entities of the possible things is greater than the possible things' need for the manifestation of traces within themselves.

This is because, through the manifestation of their traces, the names have authority and exaltation. But the possible things may gain a trace through which they will suffer harm, or one through which they will benefit. So they are in danger, and their remaining in the state of nonexistence would be more loved by them, were they given the choice. For in the fixed witnessing of their states they take pleasure through a fixed pleasure while each of the states is far removed from every other state. No one entity brings the states together in the state of fixity. But, within the thingness of *wujūd*, the states become manifest in one entity. For example, at one moment Zayd is healthy and at another moment he himself is infirm in the same entity. Someone who is relieved at one moment is afflicted in his entity at another moment.

In fixity, the situation is not like this. In fixity, pain is not in the entity of the one who suffers pain. Rather, it is only in its own entity. So pain takes pleasure through its fixity, just as it takes pleasure through its *wujūd* in the one who suffers pain, but the locus suffers pain through it. The occasion of this is the fact that fixity is noncompound and solitary, so nothing abides through other things, but in *wujūd,* there is nothing but mountedness,[39] so there is a carrier and a carried. In *wujūd,* the situation of the carried is always like its situation in fixity—it dwells in perpetual bliss. But the carrier is not like this because, if the carried necessitates pleasure, the carrier takes pleasure, but if it necessitates pain, the carrier suffers pain.

This was not the carrier's situation in the state of fixity. On the contrary, in its fixity, the carrying entity became manifest in what it has in its *wujūd* ad infinitum. Every state that it would come to possess was off to the side, gazing upon it, but not carried by it. Thus the entity took pleasure in its own essence, and the state took pleasure in its own essence. These states do not undergo change in their tasting through *wujūd,* but the state of the carrier does change through *wujūd.*

This is an exalted knowledge. The entities know this in their fixity only through the gazing of the state upon them. However, they do not know that when they carry the state, they will suffer pain through it, because they dwell in a Presence where they do not know the flavor of pains. Or rather, they take the state as a companion. If the entity were to know that it will suffer pain when it becomes qualified by that state, it would suffer pain in the state of its fixity through the state's gazing upon it, because it would know that it will become clothed in it and carry it in the state of its *wujūd.* Thus its familiarity with the state in fixity is a joy for it.

This variety of knowledge is one of the greatest mysteries of God's knowledge concerning the things. I witnessed it through a divine tasting, for there are servants of God whom God gives to see, through unveiling, the fixed entities. Then they see them in the form of the adjacency that we have mentioned. But rational consideration does not see that the entities have either state or locus.

No, every essence is solitary
  without contamination or unification,
no indwelling, no transferal,
  no coinciding, no obstinacy.

Once you have understood the difference between *wujūd* and fixity and you know what properties are possessed by the entities in *wujūd* and fixity, then you will know that some of the entities do not desire the manifestation of traces in themselves through the state. The tasting they have in that is through the state. Were they to taste pain in the state of fixity, they would scream, for their situation in the state of *wujūd* may or may not carry patience when it carries pain. But we suppose that in the state of their fixity they are carriers that lack patience. Thus, through the tongue of their state, they do not have the poverty toward seeking *wujūd* [that the names have], even if they do seek it through the fixed word from God. Hence, when they come to exist, they will say—as has been transmitted from one of them—"Would that I had not been created, would that ʿUmar's mother had never given birth to him, would that she had been barren," and the like of this.

So the entities have less poverty than the divine names, while the names have a more intense poverty, because of the bliss they have through that. This is especially true because of the essential delight in perfection that the names witness from the Real in respect of their companionship with the possible things in their fixity through His Essence. But He is incomparable with their trace and with receiving traces because of them. Hence, in respect of His Essence, His perfection allows no reception of traces in the state of the entities' fixity and the state of their *wujūd,* because in Himself He does not increase in the knowledge of what they are, for they have given Him knowledge of their situation from eternity without beginning, and in that form they come to exist.

That which, in fixity, is an adjacency is, in *wujūd,* an indwelling. In fixity, the states are off to the side of the entities, and in *wujūd* they dwell within them.

This then is one of those twelve thousand knowledges. So know this! (IV 81.2)

Chapter 493: New Arrival

In attempting to provide intimations of how the entities are related to *wujūd,* Ibn al-ʿArabī frequently resorts to analogies. In Chapter 493, he compares the relation between *wujūd* and the entities to that between water and ice. He calls it "On the true knowledge of the state of the Pole whose waystation is *Say: Everything is from God. What is it with these people that they scarcely understand any speaking?* [4:78]." The word that Koran translators render here as "from" is in fact two words, *min ʿind,* and the expression can be translated more literally as "from at." The word *ʿind* or "at," as Lane points out in his *Lexicon,* "is primarily used in relation to that which is present with a person or thing." In this chapter, the Shaykh sets out to explain the meaning of "at-ness" (*ʿindiyya*), the state of being present with God. The term can be contrasted with "withness" (*maʿiyya*), which the Shaykh often discusses. At-ness is the situation of things present with God before they enter into existence, whereas withness is God's presence with all things once they enter into existence.

Ibn al-ʿArabī begins the chapter by addressing an issue closely related to at-ness, that is, *ḥudūth,* which basically means to occur, to happen. Before something occurs, it is "at" God. *Ḥudūth,* however, is a technical theological term that I translate as "new arrival" ("temporal origination" in SPK). It is for a thing to happen, and when something happens, it happens for the first time, that is, newly. *Ḥudūth* is contrasted with *qidam,* "eternity," which is to have no beginning or to be outside of time. However, in a nontechnical sense, the term *qidam* means oldness or ancientness. It is written the same as *qadam,* "foot," and the basic verbal sense of the root of the two words is to step, to go forward, to have gone before (and hence to be ancient). From the same root we have a term that the Shaykh often discusses, *taqaddum,* "priority," which is contrasted with *taʾakhkhur,* "posteriority."

In Islamic theology, the Koran is *qadīm,* "eternal." Nevertheless, in two instances the book speaks of its verses as *muḥdath,* "newly arrived," a word Koran translators render by such terms as "fresh" (Arberry, Pickthall), "new" (Muhammad Ali, Pickthall), "recent" (Palmer), and "of late" (Palmer). The standard theological formula that solves the contradiction between eternity and new arrival holds that the Book has no beginning with God, but it is newly arrived with the creatures. For Ibn al-ʿArabī, this formula expresses the situation of all things, which are fixed and eternal entities with God, yet newly arrived as existent entities in their temporal situation. The Koran is not alone in being the speech of God—both macrocosm and microcosm are divine books.

In the title of the chapter and in the rather enigmatic opening lines of poetry, Ibn al-ʿArabī mentions *ḥadīth,* another word from the same root as *ḥudūth.* The basic meaning of the term is new or newly said (as in "news"). The term is, of course, employed to refer to the sayings of Muhammad, but the Shaykh typically uses it as a virtual synonym for *kalām,* "speech," so I translate it in this sense as "speaking." In the second line of the poetry, he uses the term in this meaning in alluding to the Koranic verse cited in the title of the chapter—*What is it with these people that they scarcely understand any speaking?* In the last line, he uses the same word to mean "new."

Everything in engendered existence
comes from its Creator,
so there is no new arrival
in the engendered world.
Do you not see that He has negated
knowledge of Him
when "speaking" is not understood
among the engendered things?
They do not find it
newly arrived—
this is why traveling in that
is hurried.
No one's knowledge of Him
is negated
save an ignorant imbecile
or an unwholesome wretch.
All that is known of Him
is the fact
that He is one in entity,
though idle talk goes on.
God ennobled
a messenger through
spreading among us
the "new" Remembrance.

God says, *No remembrance comes to them from the All-Merciful newly arrived but they turn away from it* [26:5]. He says, *No remembrance comes to them from their Lord newly arrived, but they listen to it yet playing, their hearts diverted* [21:2]. Thus the remembrance came from "the Lord" and "the All-Merciful," and He reports that they listened and gave ear to the remembrance of the Lord in the state of diversion. He mentioned their turning away from the All-Merciful's remembrance, despite their knowledge that it is the Koran. It is God's speech, and speech is His attribute, so it possesses eternity, even if the coming arrives newly.

Know that the "new" [*ḥadīth*] may be new in actual fact, or it may be new in relation to its *wujūd* at you in the state, though it is more ancient in itself than this new arrival. This is when you mean by "ancientness" [*qidam*] the negation of firstness. This is nothing but God's speech, and it is nothing but exactly what receives the forms of self-disclosure.

When you mean by "ancientness" other than the negation of firstness, the thing may be newly arrived in itself before its new arrival at you, or it may be newly arrived through its new arrival at you, which is to say that this is the time of its new arrival. This is the accidents in the state that abide through you or through him who addresses you or sits with you.

As for the at-ness of God—here I mean everything that is "at God"—it is of two sorts. The first sort is everything that is understood as superadded to His He-ness, even if we do not say concerning it that it is other than He or the same as He. Such, for example, are the attributes that are attributed to Him—"They are neither He nor other than He." [The second sort of] what is at Him is what He makes arrive newly in us and for us. This is like His words, *There is no thing whose storehouses are not at Us [and We send it not down but in a known measure]* [15:21].

As for what is at us, it is of two sorts: In one sort, its form is newly arrived, but not its substance. Take rain, for example. We know what it is in respect of its substance and what it is in respect of its form. The whole cosmos is either of this sort or of the other sort, in which the substance itself is newly arrived. This is nothing but the substance of the form, or the *wujūd* of the substance of that entity through which the form abides. For the entity of the form's substance, through which the form abides, has no *wujūd* save at the abiding of the form through it. Before that, the substance is intelligible, not existent in entity. So *wujūd* arrives newly for the site of the form, or for the locus of the form—which is its matter—through the new arrival of the form in a certain state, but not in every state. Then the locus leaves *wujūd* through the nonexistence of the form, so long as there is not another form through which it abides.

Each is "at God," for God is identical with the thingness of each. No intelligible thing or existent thing arrives newly at Him. On the contrary, He witnesses the entities of all things between fixity and *wujūd*. So fixity is His storehouses, and *wujūd* is everything that arrives newly at us from the storehouses.

The form of water is intelligible in ice, but the name "ice" is ascribed to it. The water is potential in the ice, for when something happens to the ice that melts it, it becomes water. Thereby the form of the water becomes manifest and arrives newly in it and from it, and the name *ice* disappears from it, along with the form, definition, and reality of ice.

In our view, before the ice melted, it was one of the storehouses of rain. Then it became manifest that the ice is identical with what was stored away. Hence it was a storehouse through one form and something stored away through another form. Such also is the property of everything that undergoes transmutation. It is identical both with what undergoes transmutation and with what it is transmuted into.

We have brought this realized analogy because of the forms of self-disclosure that we examine in the Real *Wujūd*. We want to connect to it the forms of the whole cosmos in the *wujūd* of the Real. We ascribe the term *creation* to the cosmos just as we ascribe the term *water* to the water that has melted from the ice. And this is a true ascription, since the water is none other than what has melted and what was called "ice."

Hence the cosmos is the Real in one respect and creation in another respect.

This and its like in the divine science are the result of this formula of remembrance. From here you will know all newly arrived things—what they are, when the name *new arrival* is ascribed to them, and when they accept the name *eternity*. This is a precious knowledge that God specifies for those of His servants whom He wills, and it is the clear bounty. *And God speaks the* ***ḥaqq****, and He guides on the path* [33:4]. (IV 129.17)

From Chapter 369: The Storehouse of Lights

This chapter, "On the true knowledge of the waystation of the keys to the Storehouses of

Munificence," has twenty-three subchapters in which Ibn al-ᶜArabī describes various aspects of God's generous giving. In the fifteenth subchapter, he looks at bodily things as the storehouses of lights. *Wujūd*, after all, is light, while nonexistence is the absence of light, and absolute nonexistence is sheer and utter darkness. The cosmos is light in one respect and darkness in another respect. Inasmuch as it manifests the Real, it is light, but inasmuch as it hides the Real, it is darkness. God's "withness" (*maᶜiyya*), the fact that He is with all things, is confirmed by the presence of *wujūd*'s light in all that exists.

The natural bodies are storehouses of the lights through which their engendered existence is brightened, even if they become manifest to our eyes as dark. In the same way, milk comes forth from *between filth and blood, pure milk, sweet to the drinkers* [16:66], a milk that has been stored away for them by the udders of their cattle and their camels. So also, *There comes forth from the bellies* of the bees *a drink of diverse hues, within which is a healing for the people* [16:69].

God also says, *God is the light of the heavens and the earth* [24:35]. Were it not for light, no entity would become manifest for the possible things. The Messenger of God said in his supplication, "O God, place in my hearing a light, in my eyesight a light, in my hair a light" to the point where he said, "and make me into a light," and so he was. He sought only the witnessing of that, so that it would become manifest to the eyesights. For suprasensory light is hidden, and *The eyesights perceive it not* [6:103]. The Messenger of God desired to perceive through sensation what he perceived through faith and reason. This does not become manifest except to the lords of struggle.

Fire is concealed in stones—
it flames up only when kindled by steel.

We know that fire is there, but we do not see any warmth in the stone or burning in the [tinder, whether it is made of] *markh* or *ᶜafār*.[40] So also is the situation of all existent things for those who consider and look carefully, or who witness and then take heed. For the Real is concealed within creation in respect of His being a light. When you strike the flint of creation with reflective thought, the light of the Real becomes manifest. "He who knows himself knows his Lord." When someone knows the striking and distinguishes the flint, the fire is at him, *so he is upon a light from his Lord* [39:22].

Whenever God wills, He makes the fire manifest, for He is the Manifest. And whenever He wills, He hides it, for He is the Nonmanifest. When He is nonmanifest, *Nothing is as His likeness*, and when He is manifest, *He is the Hearing, the Seeing* [42:11]. The "striker" is what brings light from Him, for the Real is *with* us *wherever* we *are* [57:4], whether in nonexistence or *wujūd*. Through His withness we become manifest. So we are possessors of light, but we have no awareness.

To God belongs our engendered existence
that is God's own,
and to the engendered existence belongs
His Essence's light that belongs to it.
We are many, and the Guardian is one—
He is one in His names and His attributes.

I say that "We are many and He is one" only because the flints are many, but the fire of each is one in entity. It makes no difference whether it is wood or stone. That is why the doctrines concerning God are diverse, but what is sought is one. Everything that becomes manifest to every seeker is nothing but God, not other than He, for everything originates from Him and returns to Him.

He who seeks fire from the flint is called a "striker" only because seeking the Real from creation so as to know His Essence is to "strike out" against sound knowledge of His Essence, for nothing can be known of the Real but the Level, which is simply the fact that He is one God.

If someone covets knowledge of His Essence, this is "witnessing." But witnessing occurs only through His self-disclosure, and that takes place only by "striking out" against Him, since you will see Him only as bound—your rational faculty binds Him through its consideration. He discloses Himself to you in the form of your binding. This is a striking out against what He is in actual fact.

If you did not possess in yourself the rational light, you would not know Him, and if you did not possess the visual light, you would not witness Him. So you witness Him only through light, and there is no light but He. You witness Him and you know Him only through Him, for He is the *light of the heavens* in respect of rational faculties and *of the earth* in respect of the eyesights. God placed the attribute of His light only in the light that is the *lamp* [24:35], and that is an earthly light, not heavenly. For He declared His light similar to the lamp. Our vision of Him is like our vision of the sun and the moon. In other words, although He is like the lamp, He is higher in vision and perception than vision of the lamp. Thus through Himself He is earthly, because, if He had not descended to us, we would not have known Him. But through vision He is heavenly. So consider how the Lawgiver has ascribed properties to God! What does He have to do with rational consideration?

This is why God says, *Eyesights perceive Him not,* because He is light, and light can only be perceived through light, so He is perceived only through Him. *But He perceives the eyesights,* because He is light; *and He is the Subtle,* because He is subtle and hidden in His very manifestation, so He is not known and not witnessed as He knows and witnesses Himself; *the Experienced* [6:103] through a knowledge of tasting. He did not say, "Lights perceive Him not."

If not for light,
  no eye would witness Him;
    if not for reason,
      no engendered thing would know Him.

Through the engendered and divine lights, the existent things become manifest, though they remain forever manifest to Him in the state of their nonexistence, just as they are manifest to us in the state of their *wujūd*. So we perceive them rationally in the state of their nonexistence, and we perceive them in entity in the state of their *wujūd*. But the Real perceives them in entity in both states.

If the possible thing had no light of its own in the state of its nonexistence, it would not receive *wujūd* and it would not become distinct from the impossible. So the Real witnesses it through the light of its possibility, but creation witnesses it through the light of its *wujūd*. Between the Real and creation stands what is between the two witnessings. The Real is a light within a light, but creation is a light within a darkness in the state of its nonexistence. As for the state of its *wujūd*, it is *a light upon a light* [24:35], because it is identical with the signifier of its Lord.

This section cannot carry more than this, for within it is a hidden deception, because the Real has no likeness, though He cannot be witnessed or known save through striking a likeness. This is why He made for us the *likeness of His light* in the heavens and the earth *as a niche, within which is a lamp—the lamp in a glass, the glass as it were a glittering star—kindled from a blessed tree, an olive that is neither of the east nor of the west, whose oil well-nigh would shine, even if no fire touched it.* Then He says, *A light upon a light, God guides to His light,* i.e., to one of these two lights, *whom He will,* and then he comes to know that which is declared similar and that to which it is declared similar. *And God strikes likenesses* [24:35].

He made the striking of likenesses for conveying knowledge. In the striking of likenesses, the impossible thing that cannot occur is permissible. Just as that whose *wujūd* is impossible does not become a *wujūd* through supposition, so also creation does not come to be Real through the striking of likenesses. It may happen that what is existent through supposition cannot be existent through entity. If what is declared similar itself strikes the likeness, it is a striking of likeness only in one respect, so it is not correct here for that to which similarity is declared and with which the likeness is struck to be existent, except through supposition.

Thus we come to know through the striking of this likeness that in the furthest limit of distance from Him we also dwell in the furthest limit of nearness. That is why we receive the striking of the likeness, so we bring together distance and nearness, and He is named for us "the Near" and "the Distant." Just as *Nothing is as His likeness* [42:11], so He is *nearer than the jugular vein* [50:16], *and He is the Hearing, the Seeing* [42:11]. Thus He is the Near through the likeness and the Distant through the form, since supposing the thing is not like the thing or identical with it. (III 391.35)

The Shaykh now turns to another issue that he finds relevant to the lights found in corporeal bodies, and that is a certain part of the hajj, where the pilgrims move from Mt. Arafat to Jam^{c} (also called Muzdalifa), which is the plain between Arafat and Minā, and from Jam^{c} to Minā. As Ibn al-ʿArabī explains in his chapter on the hajj, the "day of ʿArafa" is the only day of the year whose nighttime is considered to follow its daytime. In all the other days, the night before the day belongs to the day. For the Shaykh, this has to do with the *ma^{c}rifa* or "knowledge" that is signified by the very word *ʿArafa*. He seems to be taking the hajj as an explicit means for actualizing the knowledge both of *tanzīh* and *tashbīh,* both God's distance and nearness, both the differentiation achieved by reason and the bewilderment attained by unveiling, when the absent is seen to be present and the present absent.

In this section is the pilgrim's *pressing on from Arafat* [2:198] to Jamᶜ and from Jamᶜ to Minā, for the pressing on of Arafat is by night and the pressing on of Jamᶜ is by daytime for the fasting person, or, if you like, say "by the daytime" without the attribution.

The hajj brings all this together. It accepts the differentiation of the temporal day, which is the night and the daytime. In the same way, something within it confuses rational faculties, preventing their light from penetrating to the vision of the sought object. This is a subtle veil because of the nearness to the object. After all, yearning distresses most when the lover sees his beloved's abode. The poet says,

Yearning distresses most on the day
when you approach the abode.

One of the most marvelous of affairs is that the human being curtains the Real, so He is not witnessed, but through the human being He becomes manifest that He might be known. Hence the human being brings together the veil and manifestation. He is the manifester/the curtainer, the sharp/the blunt sword. The Real witnesses that from him, because He created him so, and the human being witnesses that from himself, for he is not absent from himself. He desires to reach what he already knows he will not reach. He is like the Real in His command when He commands someone to do something that He desires not to occur from him, so He is desiring/not desiring.[41]

Were it not for the fact that the Real is the shell of our entities, we would not be the shell of the entity of knowledge of Him. Pearls are engendered within shells, and we are engendered only in *wujūd,* and *wujūd* is nothing but He. However, He curtains us in order to preserve us, then He makes us manifest. Then He makes Himself known to us through us, and He turns us over to us for knowledge of Him. When we come to know us, we curtain our knowledge of Him. Hence the affair never emerges from the shell that curtains pearls, except from time to time.

That is the metal, and we are the rust—
we have nothing of engendered existence save a call.
Whomever He calls will come to be like Him,
but this coming to be does not begin from him.
For he arrives newly from His word,
and His word *Be* is not aimless.
We come to be from Him, and through Him has appeared
what has already appeared in His Entity.
He is the dew at night, as am I,
just as I am His dew by day.
If you wish, reverse what I said,
for He is the night, and we are the dew.

And God speaks the **ḥaqq**, *and He guides on the path* [33:4]. (III 393.5)

The Entities and the Names

Ibn al-ᶜArabī often describes the relation between *wujūd* and the nonexistent things in terms of the divine names. The names denote *wujūd*'s perfections, such as life, knowledge, desire, and power. The traces of these perfections are observable in the cosmos. But the names themselves have no independent existence, since they are simply words that designate relations. And the relations themselves, as Ibn al-ᶜArabī often reminds us, are not entities. So the names are words that signify the manner one thing is connected with another thing. The "things" between which connection is established may be said to have *wujūd,* but the actual connections do not. Nevertheless, the traces and properties of the relations are observed everywhere. Hence a nonexistence—the relation—leaves its traces in *wujūd.*

The cosmos is restricted to entities and relations. The entities pertain to *wujūd,* while the relations are intelligible and pertain to nonexistence. This is everything other than God. (III 66.2)

The forms are diverse because of the diversity of the relations, or the relations are diverse because of the diversity of the forms. Were it not for the relations, the forms would not arrive newly, and were it not for the forms, the diversity of the relations would not be known. (IV 130.32)

Relations arise as soon as we conceptualize the entities that can be said to have *wujūd* or to be in *wujūd*. Ibn al-ᶜArabī suggests something of how this occurs in the following:

When God ascribed greatness to Himself, He made its locus only the heavens and the earth, for He said, *To Him belongs the greatness in the heavens and the earth* [45:37]—He did not say, "in Himself." Hence the locus is described by the greatness that belongs to God.

When the cosmos considers itself as small or sees its Existence-Giver as incomparable with what is worthy of itself, it names its Lord "Great" and "Possessor of Greatness" because for it the display of traces and the subjugating force that He possesses within it are great. If the cosmos did not receive God's traces, it would not know that it is small or that its Lord is great.

In the same way, when the cosmos sees that need and poverty toward others abide in itself, then it needs to believe and to know that the one by whom it is supported in its poverty possesses independence. Hence, He is the Independent in the self of His servant. But in regard to His Essence, He is naked of gazing upon the cosmos and not qualified by independence, because there is no one to be independent *from*.

So also, when the cosmos gazes upon its own abasement, it knows that it is not abased in itself, but rather it is abased under the other's authority over it. Hence it calls Him "exalted," since the Real is exalted in the self of this servant because of his own abasement.

Thus the servant is the locus of the greatness, independence, magnificence, and exaltation that belong to God. The servant describes his Lord by that which abides through himself. Hence the meaning necessitates its property in other than the one through whom it abides. (III 537.22)

The names arise from the traces that are perceived in the things, so they arise from the things. But the things arise from *wujūd*, so the traces in fact belong to God.

None leaves traces except God, so here we have a creation that has become manifest in the form of the Real. Thus the locus of receiving activity is acted upon because of the form of the Real, not because of creation. In the activity, creation has become clothed in the Real in giving existence, and the Real has become clothed by creation in the form from which the trace becomes manifest in the witnessed domain—just as, rationally, it becomes manifest from the Real. *They are a clothing for you, and you are a clothing for them* [2:187]. The word *they* is an allusion to the divine names, even if, according to exegesis, it refers to wives.[42]

If you say, "This is the Real,"
you have made manifest something absent,
and if you say, "This is creation,"
you have hidden Him within it.
If not for the *wujūd* of the Real
no engendered thing would have appeared,
and if not for the *wujūd* of creation,
you would not have hidden Him. (IV 226.31)

In a context framed by the rational language of the Kalām authorities, Ibn al-ᶜArabī explains how divine attributes are employed to specify the relations between God and the possible things.

The poverty of the possible thing toward the Necessary through the Essence and the essential independence of the Necessary, apart from the possible, is called "a God."

The Essence's connection to Itself and to the realities of every realized thing, whether it be a *wujūd* or a nonexistence, is called "knowledge."

Its connection to the possible things in respect of their actual situation is called "choice."

Its connection to the possible thing in respect of knowledge's priority over the engendered existence of the possible thing is called "will."

Its connection to specifying exactly one of the possible thing's two permissibles is called "desire."

Its connection to giving existence to the possible thing is called "power." . . .

In all this the Entity is one. The connections are plural because of the realities to which they are connected, and the names are plural because of the objects they name. (I 44.21)

Chapter 406: Nothing Has Become Manifest

God's most beautiful names designate the basic relations that are established between *wujūd* and the nonexistent entities. Ibn al-ʿArabī discusses some of these names as nonexistent relations in Chapter 406, "On the true knowledge of the mutual waystation of 'Nothing has become manifest from Me to anything, and it is not proper for anything to become manifest.'" He begins by paraphrasing God's words to him in the waystation:

> Were We to become manifest to the thing
> it would be other than We,
> but there is no "other than We,"
> so where is manifestation?
> You are identical with *wujūd*,
> there is no "other,"
> and that is why I
> am the Jealous God.
> Say not, My servants,
> "Surely you, surely I,"
> for I subsist,
> but you are annihilated and disappear.
> At every moment
> you are a new creation—
> that is why to you belong
> annihilation and upstirring.

The Real says, "There is no thing to which I manifest Myself, because I am identical with each thing. Hence I become manifest only to the one who does not have the thingness of *wujūd*, so no one sees Me save the possible things in the thingness of their fixity. Hence I do not become manifest to them, because they remain nonexistent, and I am forever existent. So My *wujūd* is identical with My manifestation, and it is not appropriate for the affair to be other than this.

"The properties of what becomes manifest belong to My names. But in actual fact they belong to the entities of the possible things, while *wujūd* is identical with Me, none other than I.

"The possible properties differentiate the forms in the One Entity. In a similar way, the considerative thinkers speak of the differentiation of the species within the genus, and the differentiation of the individuals within the species. So also is the differentiation of the possible forms within the Entity.

"You see the names by which I am named—I mean the most beautiful names. The trace is assigned to the names, but in reality, the trace belongs only to the entities of the possible things. That is why it is ascribed to the forms of the names of the possible things."

Among the names of the possible things are the names of God. They have two relations—a relation to God, and a relation to the forms of the possible things. The Real is not manifest to the entities of the possible things' forms in respect of the fact that they are their forms, but rather in respect of the fact that they become manifest in the entity of the Real *Wujūd*. When something is in something else through this sort of nearness, it cannot see it, so the one cannot become manifest to the other. We see the same sort of thing with air. What prevents us from seeing it is only excessive nearness. It is impossible for us to see it, and it is impossible for it to become manifest habitually. If it were to become distant from us, we would see it.

It is impossible for the forms to be distant from the Entity within which they exist, for, were they to be separate from it, they would cease to exist, as is in fact the actual situation, for the forms in this Entity cease to exist, but they are *uncertain of a new creation* [50:15].

The possible things, in respect of having the divine names, constantly bestow these forms that are manifest to each other in the entity of *wujūd*. Hence these possible entities make no form manifest except through the divine names, such as Speaker, Powerful, Creator, Provider, Life-Giver, Death-Giver, Exalter, and Abaser.

As for independence and exaltation, these belong to the Essence, and He is the Independent, the Exalted. Independence belongs to the Essence because the Essence gives these forms but does not receive gifts, because of what is given by the reality of Its Essence. As for Its exaltation, that is because these forms do not give It, nor do they display within It any trace of the knowledge of what they have acquired in their state of having *wujūd* one from another. After all, it is the entities that bestow upon the forms the knowledges that they acquire through the divine names. This is the meaning of God's words, *until We know* [47:31], while He is the Knower, without doubt. So the Real is a Knower, and the entities are knowers and acquirers. "Knowledge" is nothing but the very forms and their acquisition from the divine names, which were given knowledge by the entities of the possible things.

From here you will know the property of manyness and oneness; the displayer of the trace, the recipient of the trace, and the trace; the relation of the cosmos to God; the relation of the manifest forms undergoing variation; what becomes manifest and who becomes manifest; what remains nonmanifest and who remains nonmanifest; the reality of *the First and the Last and the Manifest and the Nonmanifest* [57:3], and the fact that these are descriptions of Him who possesses the most beautiful names. So realize what we have mentioned in this chapter, for it is beneficial in the extreme. It comprises a magnificent affair whose measure none measures but God.

He who knows this chapter will know himself: Is he the form? Is he identical with the Bestower of the form? Or is he identical with the possible, fixed entity that possesses nonexistence from its own essence? Necessarily, "He who knows himself knows his Lord," for none knows the Real but the Real.

There is no priority and no posteriority, because the possible thing, in the state of its nonexistence, is not posterior to the beginninglessness that is ascribed to the *wujūd* of the Real. Just as beginninglessness is necessary for the *wujūd* of the Real, so it is necessary for the nonexistence and fixity of the possible thing and its being entified at the Real. Were the possible thing not entified at the Real and not distinct from other possible things, He would not have singled it out for the address in the word *Be*.

He who knows this chapter will know who says *Be*, him to whom *Be* is said, who comes to be from the word *Be*, and who receives the property of the *B* and the *E*. *And God speaks the* ***ḥaqq***, *and He guides on the path* [33:4]. (IV 8.29)

Chapter 451: The Stairs

The full title of this chapter is "On the true knowledge of the mutual waystation of 'Within the articulations is the true knowledge of the stairs.'" The term *maʿārij* or "stairs" is the plural of *miʿraj*, which designates any means of ascent. The Koran employs the term twice, once in reference to houses (43:33), and once as an attribute of God, whom it calls *Possessor of the Stairs* (70:3). Commentators have taken the latter as a reference to the means of descent and ascent whereby the angels come down from God and return to Him. In this mutual waystation, God tells Ibn al-ʿArabī that the "Stairs" are the "points of articulation" (*makhārij*), that is, the places in the throat, mouth, and lips where the letters of the alphabet become articulated during speaking. Thus the breath descends on these stairs in becoming articulated as words. In God's case, the twenty-eight levels of the cosmos are the stairs upon which the Breath of the All-Merciful descends in order to create the universe. In the chapter, Ibn al-ʿArabī develops the analogy of the Breath to explain how certain cosmic words ascend back to God. Since they are words, they are coined or established (*waḍʿ*) by the founder of the language, who is God. Hence the words are perfect expressions of their meanings, and the meanings are the entities known in God's beginningless knowledge. These cosmic words are determined by fixed entities, or fixed words articulated within God's knowledge, so they are referred to in the verse, *The word is not changed with Me* (50:29). The discussion eventually leads to the mysteries of the intertwining of the Real and creation through the descent of God to us and our ascent to Him.

Were it not for the *wujūd* of engendered
existence in the stairs,
no letter's entity would come forth in the
points of articulation.
He made it emerge striking a likeness
for him who climbs the levels of the stairs.
The breath that goes forward in its path
clarifies the waystations of the roads.

God says, *The angels and the Spirit ascend to Him* [70:4]. He says, *To Him climb up the pleasant words* [35:10]. He says, *Uplifter of degrees, Possessor of the Throne* [40:15].

You should know that the possible things are the *words of God* that do *not run out* [31:27], and through them becomes manifest their authority that is not taken away. They are compound things, because they have come for bestowing benefits. They have proceeded from a composition that is expressed in the Arabic language with the word *Be*. Nothing is engendered from this word save that which is compounded of spirit and form. Then some of the forms become conjoined with others because of the correspondences among them.

Meanings arrive newly within us because of the new arrival of the established combination of the words. But this establishment does not occur for them in specific forms save through their own essences, not by the property of coincidence, nor the property of choice. For they, through their own entities, bestow the knowledge that does not undergo transmutation, *the word* that *is not changed* [50:29], and the will that is effectuated. Hence, in the witnessed domain, they accord with what they are in the absent domain, and in the absent domain, they take the form of everything that fluctuates in the manifest domain, a fluctuation which, in the absent, is infinite. In the manifest, it appears instant by instant, because the infinite cannot enter into *wujūd,* for the infinite does not come to an end, so it does not halt at a limit.

The matter within which the words of God—which are the cosmos—become manifest is the Breath of the All-Merciful. This is why they are called "words," and it is said concerning Jesus that he is *the word* of God [4:171].[43]

You should also know that when God makes manifest those of His words that He makes manifest, He determines for them the levels that He determines. Among them are the luminous, the fiery, and the earthy spirits. These have diverse levels, but He has made all of them halt with themselves and given them to witness themselves, and He has veiled Himself from them within them. Then He has sought from them that they seek Him. He has set up for them stairs upon which they ascend when they seek Him.

Through these stairs He enters for them into the ruling property of limit. He assigns to them *hearts through which they use intelligence* [22:46] and, to some of them, reflective thought through which they reflect. He assigns among their stairs the negation of likeness from Him in every respect, and then He makes Himself similar for them through them, so He affirms exactly what He negates. Then He sets up for them proofs of the truthfulness of His report when He gives them reports. Thus their understandings are ranked in excellence because of the ranking in excellence of their realities in their configurations. Each group who travel in Him on paths never emerge from what they are in those paths. At the end of their seeking they find nothing but themselves.

Among them are those who say that they are He.

Among them are those who speak of incapacity in this. They say, "What is sought from us is only that we come to know that He is not known." This is the meaning of "incapacity."

Among them are those who say that He is known in one respect but incapable of being known in another respect.

Among them are those who say that every group is correct in what they maintain, and that it is the *ḥaqq,* whether they reach felicity or wretchedness. After all, felicity and wretchedness are among the relations that are ascribed to creation. In the same way, we know that *ḥaqq* and truthfulness are two praiseworthy relations, yet they have homesteads in which they are blamed by both the Shariah and reason. So there is nothing that belongs to itself, and there is nothing that does not belong to itself.

In short, every creature is tied to God as the possible is tied to the Necessary, whether the creature is nonexistent or existent, felicitous or wretched. The Real also, in respect of His names, is tied to creation, for the divine names seek the cosmos with an essential seeking. Hence there is no departure in *wujūd* from binding on both sides. Just as "We are through Him and for Him," so also He is through us and for us. Otherwise, He would not be a Lord or a Creator for us, but He is our Lord and our Creator.

He is "through us" because He is "through Him," and He is "for us" because He is "for Him." However, He gives us assistance in *wujūd,* and we give Him assistance in knowledge. So His prescribing [the Shariah] for us is a prescription for Him, because through us He prescribes for Himself prescription for us.[44] So nothing prescribes for us save us, but through Him, not through us. Thus the levels have interpenetrated.

He is the Uplifter of Degrees along with essential descent, while creation is in descent along with essential ascent and rising. No existent thing departs from leaving traces in both *wujūd* and nonexistence. But in reality, nothing displays any traces except relations, and they are affairs of nonexistence that carry whiffs of *wujūd.* Hence nonexistence leaves no trace except inasmuch as the whiffs of *wujūd* are smelt from it, and *wujūd* leaves no trace except through a relation of nonexistence.

Given that the two contradictories—*wujūd* and nonexistence—are intertied, the intertying between two existent things is even nearer. So there is nothing but intertying and intertwining, as He has alerted us: *The leg is intertwined with the leg* [75:29]. In other words: Our affair is intertwined and knotted with His affair, so we will never be untied from His knot.

He completed [this passage]—and He is the truthful in His words—by saying: *Unto thy Lord,* thereby affirming the *wujūd* of His level through you, *on that day is the driving* [75:30], that is, *on the day when the leg is unveiled* [68:42]. [The driving] is the return of everyone to Him, those who are felicitous and those are wretched, those who are troubled and those who are at ease.

The Prophet said concerning al-Dajjāl, "His Garden is a Fire, and his Fire is a Garden," so he affirmed the two affairs and did not eliminate them. The Garden is a fixed Garden, and the Fire is a fixed Fire, and the forms manifest to the view of the eye may correspond exactly with the actual situation in itself, or they may not correspond. In either case, these two affairs are inescapable, whether they be imagination or other than imagination.

When the two affairs are intertied in the manner that we said, there is no escape from something that brings the two together, and this is the tie. It is nothing but what is required by the essence of each. There is no need for an additional affair of *wujūd*. Thus they are intertied through themselves, since there is nothing but creation and Real.

The tie must be one of them, or both of them. It is impossible for one of them to possess this property alone, without the other, since both of them must have it, because of the acceptance of this intertying. Through the two it becomes manifest, not through one of the two.

Despite this intertying, the two are not likenesses. On the contrary, neither of them is like the other. So they must be distinguished through something else, a something else that is not in one of them, but through which both are alluded to.

Thus, poverty necessitates inclination and acceptance of movement, but that is not the property of independence in the Independent. Thus we know that between a magnet and iron there is a correspondence and an intertying, from which there is no escape, like the intertying between creation and the Creator. However, when we grasp the magnet, it attracts the iron toward it, so we come to know that there is an attraction in the magnet and a reception in the iron. That is why the iron is acted upon by the movement toward it. But when we grasp the iron, it does not attract the magnet toward it. So the two, though they are intertied, are different and distinct. So the *people,* or rather, the cosmos, are *the poor toward God* [35:15], and *God is independent of the worlds* [3:97].

Such is the form of *wujūd*
so pay no regard to anything else.
Through it is our duality
and He is the One, the God.

And God speaks the ***ḥaqq****, and He guides on the path* [33:4]. (IV 65.21)

Thingness of Fixity

The entities may be known only by God, or they may be found in the cosmos and thereby known by others as well. Thus we can speak of things in two different states or situations—fixity and *wujūd*. In either case they are called "things," and the fact that they are things is called their "thingness."

The word *thing* is the "most indefinite of the indefinites" (*ankar al-nakirāt* [III 289.12]), which is to say that it applies to everything. There is nothing that cannot be called a thing. When the word is employed to refer to a specific thing, it indicates that the object of discussion has a reality that distinguishes it from other things. Hence the word points to unity (*aḥadiyya*).

> God created no thing except in the station of its unity through which it is distinguished from other things. Through the duality that is found in each thing, things share with each other. But through the unity of each thing, each becomes distinct from the thingness of other things. What is taken into account in each thing is only that through which it becomes distinct. Then it is named a "thing." If the duality were meant, then it would not be a "thing," but rather, "two things." God says, *Our only word to a thing* [16:40]. He did not say, "two things." (IV 232.32)

Since the word *thing* can be applied to anything at all, it can also be used in reference to God. However, Ibn al-ʿArabī rarely calls God a thing, because that would be discourteous, given that God has not called Himself a thing. Thus, in a passage in which he is discussing which divine name applies to God before any other, He suggests that it is "One" (*al-wāḥid*), though "thing"—were it a divine name—would do as well, because it also denotes a single, indefinite reality that accepts no multiplicity in respect of its specificity.

> It is not correct for "God" to be the first of His names. That leaves only "One" in the respect that nothing is understood from it except

the Entity without composition. If God had named Himself "Thing," we would call Him "Thing," and it would be the first of His names. However, "O Thing!" has not come down to us among the divine names. But there is no difference between what is signified by "one" and what is signified by "thing." (II 57.11)

When the word *thing* is employed, this affirms that something has a mode of *wujūd*, whether in fixity or in the cosmos. Everything known or conceived of by a human being, after all, is already known by God. If human beings can conceive of "impossible things," God has a much greater ability to do so, given that God created people and their conceptual powers. Hence, to speak of "nothings" is to affirm the thingness of fixity. And since fixity is a mode of *wujūd* in God's knowledge, there is no absolute nonexistence, only relative nonexistence.

A MYSTERY
Nonexistence is not there, so understand!

He says: There is nothing but God and the possible things. God is existent, and the possible things are fixed. So there is no nonexistence.

He says: Were the entities not witnessed by the Real, the *wujūd* of what comes into existence from them would not be preferred over its nonexistence and the *wujūd* of something else. He witnesses only what there is.

He says: Nothing enters more into the property of negation than the impossible thing. Nevertheless, there is a Presence that stipulates it, gives it form, and shapes it. Nothing accepts form-giving and shaping save what is there. So the impossible is there.

He says: Absolute nonexistence is that within which no form is intelligible, and it is not there. There are only three—the necessary, the impossible, and the possible, or necessity, impossibility, and possibility. All this is intelligible, and everything intelligible is bound. Every bound thing is distinct, and every distinct thing is separate from that from which it is distinct. Hence there is no nonexistent thing that does not become distinct, so there is no nonexistence.

He says: For the Kalām authorities, the "states" are neither existent nor nonexistent. It is known that there is only a locus and a state. For example, there is nothing but color and what accepts color, so what is the colored thing? There is nothing but life and what accepts life, so what is the living thing? There is nothing but movement and what accepts movement, so what is the moving thing? (IV 410.30)

The Koran employs the word *thing* in 280 verses, but it is not always clear if it is discussing existent things or nonexistent things. In any case, the use of the word has important theological implications. Take, for example, the Gospel notion that "With God all things are possible" (Mt. 19.26). This is perfectly acceptable to Ibn al-ʿArabī, but he would insist that we pay close attention here to what is meant by the word *thing*. Koranic equivalents to this statement are found in the thirty-five verses that assert that God is *powerful over each thing*. Notice that the divine attribute of power applies specifically to the "thing," not to the nothing (*lā shayʾ*). "With God all *things* are possible," but all nothings are impossible, because nonexistence is not there—whether in fixity or in *wujūd*.

God is powerful over each thing [2:20], not over what is not a thing, for a nothing does not accept thingness. If it did accept thingness, its reality would not be a nothing. But no object of knowledge departs from its reality, so the ruling property of a nothing is to be a nothing forever. As for that which is a thing, its ruling property is to be a thing forever. (II 171.15)

The things are the objects of God's knowledge. The imaginal language of the Koran puts them in a specific "place," which is God's "storehouses." *There is no thing whose storehouses are not at Us* (15:21). In the Shaykh's understanding, the things "at" God are the fixed entities, and they always remain at Him. When they enter into *wujūd*, they are still at Him, but they are also found at us. They never leave their at-ness with God, even in the transition stage from fixity to *wujūd*.

The entities of the cosmos are preserved in His storehouses at Him. His storehouses are His knowledge, and we are His stores. Hence it is we who have affirmed for Him the property of

> storing up, because He knows us only from us.
>
> He is a middle path between the thingness of our fixity and the thingness of our *wujūd*. When He desires to transfer us to the thingness of our *wujūd*, He commands this and we acquire *wujūd* from Him. Then we become manifest in His form in the thingness of our *wujūd*. His form is what we have in the thingness of our fixity, for His knowledge is identical with His Essence. It is called "knowledge" only because of its connection to the object of knowledge, and the connection is "love."
>
> If nonexistence were the middle between the thingness of fixity and the thingness of *wujūd*, then, when He desired to bring us into existence, He would make us pass by nonexistence. We would acquire from it the negation of the thingness of fixity. Then we would not exist either in fixity or in *wujūd*. Thus our only path goes by the *wujūd* of the Real so as to acquire *wujūd* from Him. (IV 108.9)

Whether we dwell in the thingness of fixity or the thingness of *wujūd*, we are "at" the *wujūd* of the Real. However, in the first situation, we are not aware of ourselves, because our knowledge in the domain of fixity does not allow for knowledge of any self other than God. Once God gives us the thingness of *wujūd*, then we perceive ourselves and others. In this situation, we know and perceive only the Real *Wujūd*, but we do not and cannot know It in Itself, since none knows the Essence but God. Therefore we know *wujūd*'s self-disclosures. In other words, we know the *wujūd* of the Real inasmuch as it is colored and given properties by the entities, which are ourselves and our situations. At every stage of our thingness of *wujūd*, we see nothing but the Real's self-disclosures, and our knowledge is always conditioned by the world or domain in which we dwell or which we perceive—what Ibn al-ʿArabī often calls the "homestead" (*mawṭin*). Thus the homestead of this world is different from the homestead of the last world, and the homestead of reason is different from the homestead of imagination. In each case, our perception of *wujūd* is conditioned by our situation, or our position vis-a-vis the other self-manifestations of *wujūd*.

Ibn al-ʿArabī continues the above passage by insisting on the importance of the specific relation that is established between the thingness of fixity and the thingness of *wujūd*. He calls it here a *tartīb*, an "order"—or the relating of some "levels" (*rutba, martaba*) to other levels. The different situations of a single entity in fixity and *wujūd* alert us to the fact that the homestead plays an important determining role. Moreover, once things enter into *wujūd*, they do not remain permanently at themselves, because their situation is constantly changing as they move from homestead to homestead. What they have at one time they lose at another time. Thus the Koran says, *What is at you runs out, but what is at God subsists* (16:96).

> Understand the order here, for it is useful and beneficial! It will give you knowledge of the property of the homesteads and the fact that they exercise ruling properties through themselves over everyone who becomes manifest within them. He who passes over a homestead becomes colored by it. The lucid proof of this is the vision of God that you have in a dream, which is the homestead of imagination. You will never see the Real in a dream except in a corporeous form, whatever the form may be. This is the property of the homestead. It has exercised its property over you such that you see the Real only in that way. So also, when you enter the homestead of rational consideration and leave the storehouse and homestead of imagination, you will perceive the Real only as incomparable with the form in which you perceived Him in the homestead of imagination.
>
> Since the ruling property belongs to the homestead, you will know when you see the Real what you are seeing, and you will affirm that this—I mean the property—belongs to the homestead, so the Real will remain unknown to you forever. You will gain no knowledge of Him in yourself save through the *tawḥīd* of the Level that belongs to Him. As for knowing His Essence, that is impossible, for you will never cease being in a homestead. It will exercise its ruling property over you such that you will see the Real only in keeping with it, for you will be separate from the knowledge of Him that He gives to you in another homestead. Hence in every homestead you judge that the Real has properties that are not identical with those that you judged He had in the previous homestead. Then you will know that

you do not know Him in the respect that He knows Himself.

This is the furthest limit in our knowledge of Him. So, *What is at* us from Him in a homestead *runs out* in another homestead. *What is at* us *runs out, but what is at God subsists,* that is, His knowledge of Himself. It does not change and alter, and He does not undergo variation for Himself in Himself through the variation of the homesteads, for the variation of the homesteads pertains to their own essences. If they did not vary, they would be a single homestead. In the same way, if the meanings of the names were not diverse, they would be one name, just as they are one in respect of what they name, as, for example, in His words, *Call upon God, or call upon the All-Merciful.* This is in respect of what they name, for He continues by saying, *whichever you call upon, to Him belong the most beautiful names* [17:110]. He declares one because He means what is named by them, so He did not take into account the diversity of the realities signified by the words of the most beautiful names. (IV 108.14)

2. *Perpetual Self-Disclosure*

To speak of the cosmos is to speak of something that is found, of an entity and its relation with *wujūd.* Having looked at a few of the issues involved in thinking about *wujūd* and entities, we can investigate relations in a bit more detail. Ibn al-ᶜArabī deals with these in terms of the divine names and their concomitants. More generally, he discusses the attributes of *wujūd.* These become manifest in the cosmos, and their divine roots are given linguistic expression by the Koran and the Hadith. In the present chapter, we look at some of the Shaykh's most often discussed themes in describing the relation between God and the cosmos.

Creation

All Muslims agree that God created the cosmos and everything within it. The Koran employs the word *creation* as verb or noun in well over two hundred verses, and in several verses it refers to God as "Creator." But it is important to remember that the Arabic word *khalq* has two basic meanings. First it means to determine (*taqdīr*), that is, to give "measure" (*qadar*) to something or to take something's measure. Second, in the more commonly understood sense, it means to give existence to something (*ījād*). "'Creator' has two meanings—the one who determines, and the one who gives existence. He who has 'created' has either determined or given existence" (II 430.9).

Commentators see the first meaning of the term in these Koranic words of Jesus: *I will* ***create*** *for you from clay as the guise of a bird, then I will blow into it, and it will be a bird, by the leave of God* (3:49). Clearly, this means that Jesus will give measure and shape to a pre-existent piece of clay, not that he will bring it into existence. Thus Ibn al-ᶜArabī tells us that when the Koran calls God "the most beautiful of creators," it is comparing Him with others and attributing creation also to them, and this can only be the creation of determination. In contrast, when it affirms that God alone creates, it means that He alone gives *wujūd* to things.

> God says, *[Blessed is God,] the most beautiful of creators* [23:14], and He says, *Is He who creates like him who does not create?* [16:17]. Creation by people is determining. The other creation is existence-giving. (*Naqsh* 11)

Although Ibn al-ᶜArabī usually says that creation in the sense of giving existence is exclusively a divine attribute, while the creation of determination is a shared attribute, he also speaks of human participation in the divine existence-giving. Thus, according to a hadith, people in paradise will be given the power to say to things *Be!*, and those things will come to be.[1] This helps explain the sense of the Koranic verses that tell us that the blessed will have everything they desire, every object for which they have appetite (*shahwa*).

This power of engendering (*takwīn*), or saying *Be* to a thing so that it comes to be, is possessed by some of the friends of God already in this world. Through their Aspiration (*himma*), they bring into existence whatever they desire. In one passage, the Shaykh acknowledges that every attribute of *wujūd* can become manifest within the servant. In such a situation, the only difference between the Lord and the servant is that the first is *wujūd* as such, while the second is nonexistence. In other words, the first is Necessary and the second possible, or, in Koranic language, the first is the Wealthy or the Independent (*ghanī*) and the second the needy or the poor (*faqīr*).

> There is nothing but a servant and a Lord. The servant is not distinguished from the Lord save through poverty. When God takes away his poverty, He drapes him in the robe of the lordly attribute. Then He gives to him to say to a thing, when he desires it, *"Be!," so it comes to be* [16:40].
>
> This is the mystery of the *wujūd* of wealth in poverty, and not everyone is aware of it. After all, he does not say to a thing, *"Be!," so it comes to be,* until he has appetite for it. That is why God says, *Therein you shall have everything for which your souls have appetite* [41:31]. Someone seeks to have what he does not have only out of poverty for what he seeks, for his appetite makes him poor toward it and incites him to seek it. The object of appetite does not seek him, but he has the lordly attribute that necessitates for him the strength to bring this sought object of appetite into existence in its entity. So he says *Be!* to it out of poverty toward a divine attribute, and this is the sought object itself. Then from it he partakes of that for the sake of which he sought its *wujūd*.
>
> Such is not the affair in the case of the Real, because God does not seek to engender the existent things out of His poverty toward them. Rather, in the state of their nonexistence in the possible domain, the things seek their own *wujūd*. They are poor in essence toward God, who is their Existence-Giver. They know no one else. Hence they seek, through their own essential poverty, their *wujūd* from God. The Real accepts their request, and He brings them into existence for themselves and for the sake of their request, not out of any need for them that abides in Him, for they are witnessed by Him in the state of both their nonexistence and their *wujūd*. But the servant is not like this, for he lacks any sensation of the things in the state of their nonexistence, even if he does not lack them in knowledge—since, if he had no knowledge of them, he would not designate one thing apart from another thing to bring it into existence.
>
> However, the servant is compounded of two essences—a meaning and a sensory domain—and this is his perfection. As long as the known thing does not come into existence in the sensory domain, his perception of that thing is not perfected through the perfection of his essence. But when he perceives it after its *wujūd*—and he had already been perceiving it in knowledge—then his perception of the thing is perfected in his essence. His compoundedness is the occasion of his poverty toward that whose *wujūd* he desires, and his possibility is the occasion of his poverty toward its Preponderator.
>
> As for the Real, He is not compounded. On the contrary, He is one. His perception of the things, in accordance with what the things are in their realities in the state of both their nonexistence and their *wujūd*, is one perception. Hence there is no poverty in His giving existence to the things, in contrast to what there is in this servant upon whom the attribute of the Real has been conferred.
>
> This problem is such that, were your entity to disappear as a recompense for grasping it, this would be little for its sake, for it is a place where feet slip. Many of the folk of our path have slipped here and thereby joined up with those whom God has blamed in His Book for their words, *Surely God is poor* [3:181]. This is the occasion of that.
>
> Thus the possible thing and newly arrived knowledge come into existence only for the sake of the perfection of the level of *wujūd* and the perfection of the level of knowledge, not the perfection of God. On the contrary, He is the Perfect in Himself, whether or not the cosmos comes to exist and whether or not He is known through newly arrived knowledge. In the same way, in reality, He is not known, and no possible thing knows anything of Him save itself. (I 733.35)

From Chapter 73: The Thirtieth Question

In a number of contexts, the distinction between the two meanings of the word *creation* helps Ibn al-ʿArabī bring out nuances in the sense of Koranic verses and hadiths. For example, it provides him with a way to differentiate between the two basic states of the entities, which are "created" things. Thus the nonexistent, fixed entities are created in the sense of having been determined and measured by God, but the existent entities are created in both senses of the term, since they have also been given existence. The Shaykh makes use of this distinction in one of his answers to al-Ḥakīm al-Tirmidhī, who asks the meaning of the hadith, "God created the creation (or "the creatures") in darkness." In the first paragraph, the Shaykh reminds us that *wujūd* means not only "existence," but also "finding," because he treats it as a synonym for the term *perception* (*idrāk*).

The thirtieth question: "God created the creation in darkness."

The answer: This is like God's words, *God brought you forth from your mothers' bellies, not knowing anything, and He appointed for you hearing, eyesight, and hearts* [16:78]. These are all lights within you through which you perceive things. Hence you perceive only through what He has appointed within you, and He has appointed nothing within you but yourself. So, of what you are, to Him belongs the *wujūd*, and of that *wujūd*, you are the one who perceives through it, the nonexistent/the existent, that which is qualified neither by nonexistence nor by *wujūd*, but He is the perception of the hearts, as mentioned.

The possible things, in all their infinity, dwell in a darkness deriving from their essences and entities. They know nothing as long as they are not loci of manifestation for His *wujūd*. *Wujūd* is what the possible things acquire from Him, and this is indicated by His words, *upon a light from his Lord* [39:22].

Hence, in this hadith, "creation" means "determination." God says, *He created each thing, so He determined it with a determination* [25:2]. Thus He determined them, but they were not a locus of manifestation. Rather, they were receptacles for His determining. So the first divine trace in the creatures is determination before their *wujūd* and their taking on the qualities of being loci of manifestation for the Real.

In the case of the creatures, the divine determining is like the architect who makes present everything he has devised in his mind concerning what he wants to bring into appearance. Hence, the first trace in that form is what the architect has conceptualized without any model.

The verse of this station is His words, *He governs the affair, He differentiates the signs; perhaps you will have certainty concerning the encounter with your Lord* [13:2]. In other words, your transferal from the *wujūd* of this world to the *wujūd* of the last world will be nearer to knowledge if you have certainty concerning your transferal from the state of nonexistence to the state of *wujūd*. For you are in darkness in you, but you are in *wujūd* in Him. However, you have transferals in His *wujūd*, but your darkness remains your constant companion and never parts from you. *And a sign for them is the night; We pull out from it the daytime, and behold, they are dark* [36:37]. He did not say, "We place them in darkness." Rather, the disappearance of the entity of light—which is *wujūd*—is the very fact that you are dark. In other words, your entities remain without any light, that is, without any *wujūd*.

Were darkness not a relation of nonexistence—the fact that your entified essences are nonexistent—darkness would be part of creation. Then darkness would demand that it be in darkness, and what is said about this darkness would be like what is said about the first darkness, and there would be an infinite regression. After all, in his words, "God created the creation in darkness," the Prophet may mean by *creation* the created things. If darkness were an affair of *wujūd*, it would be a created thing, so it also would be in darkness.

If, however, *creation* here is a gerund, then it is as if he is saying, "God determined the determination in darkness;" in other words, not in existent things, that is, the entities. Consider God's words, *He creates you in your mothers' bellies, creation after creation, in three darknesses* [39:6].

Then in the *wujūd* of the last world, when God desires to change the earth [*into other than the earth* (14:48)], the creatures will be "in the darkness" before the Bridge. Thus darkness accompanies them between every two stations. When God desires to bring them into existence in another world, He configures them in another configuration that was not in their entities, and they come to know through the states that change for them that they are under the ruling property of one who is All-Subjugating. Thus in the state of their *wujūd* they are like their state in nonexistence.

This is why the Real admonished our rational faculties with His words, *Will not the human being remember that We created him before, when he was not a thing?* [19:67]. In other words, We determined him in the state of his thingness, toward which was turned the face of God's command to [enter into] another thingness, in accordance with His words, *Our only word to a thing, when We desire it,* that is, in the state of its nonexistence, *is to say to it "Be!"* [16:40]. *Be* is a word that demands *wujūd,* that is, engendering. Thus God named the thing a "thing" in the state in which it did not have the thingness that is negated from it with His words, *when you were not a thing* [19:9].

Inescapably the gnostic comes to understand which thingness is fixed for him in the state of his nonexistence—in His words, *Our only word to a thing*—and which thingness is negated from him in the state of his nonexistence—in His words, *when you were not a thing.* Thus the "darkness" within which "God created the creatures" is the negation of this thingness from them, and negation is a sheer nonexistence, without any *wujūd.*

The commentators have mentioned the meaning of His words, *in three darknesses* [39:6]. But our intention here is only [to explain] what has been mentioned by him who asked the question [al-Tirmidhī]. As for this verse, its affair is known by the knowers of God concerning a specific creation, that is, creation in the womb, nothing else. (II 61.33)

From Chapter 558: The Presence of the Creation and the Command

In his chapter on the divine names, Ibn al-ʿArabī ascribes creation in the sense of existence-giving specifically to the name Author (*bāriʾ*), and he attributes the creation of determination to the name Creator itself. While discussing the latter name, he clarifies the connection between *taqdīr* (determination) and *qadar* (measuring out), the Koranic doctrine that everything in creation is measured out by God. The term *qadar* is typically translated as "predestination," and this may be appropriate in discussions of the theological debates where it played a major role, but the Shaykh is careful to keep the Koranic meaning in view.

Toward the Creator of the spirits
I aimed my Aspiration
that I might enjoy Him
while the witnesses are present.
O you who see me aiming and assuming
the traits [of the divine names],
verily I am with Him
a shadow and a light:
If this not be
my speech,
yet I am His servant,
well experienced of the worlds.
Though these not be my words,
yet I speak them as deputy,
or I, by the Lord of the Dancers,
would be a concealer.[2]
If they be my words,
wujūd is realized,
and I am a knower of the doctrine,
a seer.

The companion of this Presence is called "Servant of the Creator."

"Creation" is of two sorts. [The first is] the creation of determination, which is prior to the divine command. God has made it prior, and the command posterior, for He says, *Verily, His are the creation and the command* [7:54]. The second creation means "existence-giving." It is that which is coextensive with the divine command, even if the divine command is prior to it in level.

The divine command of engendering is between two creations, the creation of determination and the creation of existence-giving. That to which the command is connected is the creation of existence-giving. Its Presence will be discussed in [this chapter under] "The Presence of the Author."

The creation of determination is connected to the designation of the moment in which the entity of the possible thing becomes manifest. Hence the command [that gives it existence] depends upon this determination. A hadith has come saying, "Everything accords with the decree and the measuring out, even incapacity and cleverness." The "moment" is an affair of nonexistence, because it is a relation, and relations have no entities in *wujūd.*

The possible entities in the state of nonexistence have a temporal order just as has occurred and will occur in *wujūd*. Each entity receives changes of states, qualities, accidents, and the like, for it becomes clothed in the affair that is off to its side and toward which it changes. The entity that receives this diversity in fixity has a plurality of entities. Each affair toward which it changes has an entity in fixity. Hence the entity becomes distinct in its states and plural in accordance with the plurality of its states, whether its affair is finite or infinite.

In this manner the knowledge of the Author is connected to the entity from eternity without beginning. Hence He brings it into existence only in the form of what He knows within the entity's fixity in its state of nonexistence—state after state, and state within state—in states that are not contrary. After all, the entity's relation to one of the contrary states is other than its relation with the state that is contrary to it, so an entity must be affirmed for it in every state. Since the states are not contrary, it has one entity in diverse states, and so it comes to exist.

The divine command is coextensive in *wujūd* with the creation of existence-giving, so the word *Be* is identical with the reception of engendering by the engendered thing. God's word *so* in *[He says to it "Be!,"] so it comes to be* [16:40], is the answer to His command *Be!* This is the *so* of outcome. This answer and outcome pertain only to the level. Thus it is imagined that the Real does not say *Be!* to a thing until He desires it. You see that the *wujūd* of certain existent things is posterior to that of others, that each existent thing must have been desired for *wujūd*, and that none comes to be save through the divine word as a command. Hence the human being, or the possessor of the faculty of imagination, imagines that there are many commands and that everything that is engendered has a divine command that God utters only when He desires the engendering of that thing. Through this very imagination the command has priority over the giving of existence, that is, the *wujūd*. For the divine address on the tongue of the Messenger requires this. Hence it must be conceived of, even if rational proofs do not conceive of it and do not accept it. Nevertheless, imagination makes it present and conceives of it, just as it conceives of the impossible and imagines it as a form in *wujūd*. Although it can never occur in sensory *wujūd*, it occurs in imagination. In the same way, it is differentiated within the fixity of the possible domain.

After all, for the faculty of imagination, nothing whatsoever is impossible, and it knows no such thing. It has absolute free activity in the Necessary *Wujūd* and the impossible thing. In imagination, all this is receptive in essence toward the possibility of assuming form. And this faculty, though it has this ruling property in Him who created it, is itself created. This property is an essential description of this faculty itself; the faculty has no *wujūd* in entity within those in whom it has been created unless they possess this property, for this property is identical with the faculty itself.

None possesses this faculty save the human configuration. Through it the human being recognizes the order of the fixed entities in the state of their nonexistence just as if they were existent, and so they are, for they have an imaginalized *wujūd* within imagination. Because of this imaginal *wujūd*, the Real says to the thing, "Be in entified *wujūd*!" The one who hears this divine command comes to be as an entified *wujūd* that is perceived by sensation. In other words, sensation becomes connected to it in sensory *wujūd*, just as imagination becomes connected to it in imaginal *wujūd*.

Here minds are bewildered. Is the thing qualified by the *wujūd* that is perceived by these perceptions the fixed entity, which is transferred from the state of nonexistence to the state of *wujūd*? Or, has the entity's property become connected to manifestation through the entity of the Real *Wujūd*—just as the form of something seen in a mirror becomes connected—while it remains fixed as it was in the state of its nonexistence, still described by this attribute? Then some of the possible entities would perceive others in the entity of the mirror of the Real's *wujūd*, while the entities, fixed in the order that they have with us in perception, would remain as they were in nonexistence. Or, is it the Real of *Wujūd* that is manifest in these entities, while they are loci of manifestation for it? Then some of them would perceive others when the Real becomes manifest within them. It would be said, "The entities have acquired *wujūd*," but this is only the Real's manifestation. This is nearer to the actual situation in one respect, while the other is nearer in another respect, and that is that the Real is the locus for the manifestation of the properties of the possible things. However, in both judgments, the things are nonexistent in entity and fixed in the Presence of fixity.

The unveiler unveils both these respects, and this is the perfect unveiling. Some of them unveil only one of the two respects, whichever it may be. The companion of each unveiling speaks in keeping with what he unveils.

The property of unveiling pertains only to the folk of this path. As for others, they are of two sorts. One group says, "The possible thing has no entity in the state of nonexistence. It has an entity only when the Real brings it into existence." These are the Ash'arites and those who accept their position. Another group says, "They have entities of fixity, and it is these that come into existence after they were not. As for that whose *wujūd* is not possible, such as the impossible thing, it has no fixed entity." These are the Mu'tazilites.

The Realizers among the Folk of God affirm fixed entities through the fixity of the things. These entities also have fixed properties through which each of them becomes manifest in *wujūd* to the extent that we said, that is, such that it is a locus of manifestation, or such that it has a property in the entity of the Real *Wujūd*.

This is what is given by the Presence of the creation and the command. *Verily, His are the creation and the command* [7:54], just as *To God belongs the command before and after* [30:4]. *And God speaks the* ***ḥaqq****, and He guides on the path* [33:4]. (IV 210.13)

Self-Disclosure

Ibn al-ʿArabī's frequent use of the word *creation* puts him in the mainstream of Islamic thought. What differentiates him from earlier figures is the manner in which he elucidates the meaning of the term. Thus, for example, he maintains that to say that God "creates" the universe—that is, gives existence to it—is to say that God discloses Himself in the forms that are called "creatures." The term *self-disclosure* (*tajallī*)—often translated as "theophany"—plays such a central role in Ibn al-ʿArabī's teachings that, before he was known as the great spokesman for *waḥdat al-wujūd*, he had been called one of the Companions of Self-Disclosure (*aṣḥāb al-tajallī*).[3] He employs the term to mean that God shows Himself to the universe inasmuch as *wujūd* is present in all things, or inasmuch as His names and attributes display traces (*āthār*) and properties (*aḥkām*) in the cosmos; the configurations and forms left by these traces and properties are then known as "the creatures." It follows that everything in the universe, everything other than God, is God's self-disclosure, because everything displays *wujūd*, and, by having specific characteristics, it displays the traces of God's names. In using the word *tajallī*, sometimes the Shaykh stresses the side of manifest reality, thereby emphasizing that everything is as it is because God has disclosed Himself in that form. At other times he employs the term *self-disclosure* as a synonym for unveiling, thereby stressing the awareness or "witnessing" (*shuhūd*) that is the human perception of God's self-display.

The Koran employs the term *tajallī* in two verses. The first is discussed frequently by Sufis in general and the Shaykh in particular, because it occurs in one of the few Koranic references to the vision (*ruʾya*) of God in this world. According to the Kalām authorities, this verse proves that God cannot be seen in this world, but the Sufis have always found a more ambiguous text.

> *And when Moses came to Our appointed time and his Lord spoke to him, he said, "O my Lord, show me, that I may look upon Thee!" Said He, "Thou shalt not see Me; but behold the mountain—if it stays fast in its place, then thou shalt see Me." And when his Lord* ***disclosed Himself*** *to the mountain, He made it crumble to dust, and Moses fell down thunderstruck.* (7:143)

Although everything in the cosmos is God's self-disclosure, only the Folk of God perceive God in the things. Others either deny that the cosmos discloses God or, if they know this theoretically, are unable to distinguish in practice the exact mode in which God discloses Himself. In other words, self-disclosure is the name of the "situation as it is in itself" (*al-amr ʿalā mā huwa ʿalayhi fī nafsihi*), the actual situation of the creatures in *wujūd*. But the perception of self-disclosure is the unveiling given to the Folk of God. Those travelers on the path who have not yet achieved a firm footing cannot bear God's self-disclosure, so they fall down thunderstruck when they glimpse it. Not that the Folk of God are greater than Moses—far from it. Ibn al-ʿArabī is careful to point out that the highest stages of the friends of God are simply the beginning stages of the prophets, and Moses, like other prophets, stands beyond the friends. When Moses was thunderstruck, this pertained to certain specific prophetic capacities that lie beyond what the Folk of God can achieve.

> Someone may say: Moses is more worthy of this attribute [i.e., witnessing God] than the friends of God, and he asked for vision.
>
> We would reply: It has been affirmed for you—if you have faith and even if you are not one of the folk of unveiling—that the Prophet reported that God discloses Himself in a form and transmutes Himself into another form and that He is recognized and denied. If you have faith, you do not doubt this, nor do you doubt that he has explained that self-disclosure in forms accords with the measure of the locus of self-disclosure.[4] Since you know this, you know that Moses may have seen the Real as He discloses Himself to the friends of God, for Moses knew that He discloses Himself to the friends in diverse forms, because he was a friend of God. He could have known this and its like, for it is not hidden.
>
> Moses asked for self-disclosure only in the form perceived solely by the prophets. Among the prophets are those whom God has specified for a station that no other prophet reached, such as God's speech to Moses through lifting the intermediaries.[5] So Moses sought from his Lord to see Him in the form that is sought by his station. As for the vision of Him in the form that the friends see, that was his experience and his wont.
>
> The only thing that makes you say something like this by way of protest is that you are not a gnostic friend of God. If you were one of the gnostics, you would witness it, and the knowledge through which we separate ourselves [from you] in the answer to your question would not be absent from you. (III 541.12)

Self-Disclosure along with the term *curtaining* (*satr*) forms one of several pairs of terms that Ibn al-ʿArabī employs to refer to the basic polarity that establishes the cosmos. *Wujūd* as *wujūd* is unknowable, which is to say that the Essence of the Real remains forever curtained. This perspective correlates with *tanzīh*, the assertion of God's incomparability. However, God shows Himself through His creative activity, so creation is *wujūd*'s self-disclosure. *Wujūd* can be known inasmuch as it is bound and constrained by the entities. From this point of view, we are justified in saying that God is, in a certain sense, similar to the things (*tashbīh*). These two viewpoints, then—*tanzīh* and *tashbīh*—are the "two eyes" by means of which the Folk of God look upon all things. They are the perspectives of reason, which declares God absent from things, and imagination, which sees Him present.

When God discloses Himself to the cosmos or to specific creatures within the cosmos, He does so in terms of His names. Thus the properties that appear within the created things—such as life, knowledge, compassion, and wrath—can be traced back to the divine attributes. All God's names can disclose themselves, save *al-aḥad* and God itself. The first, like the divine name *al-wāḥid*, means One, but *al-aḥad* designates the One inasmuch as He is uniquely, exclusively, and incomparably One. It is as close as we can get to a name that denotes the Essence Itself. And the name God, as Ibn al-ʿArabī understands it in this context, designates the divine Essence inasmuch as It comprehends all attributes in an exclusive manner.

> God does not disclose Himself in the name One, and there cannot be self-disclosure within it, nor in the name God. But self-disclosure does occur in the other names that are known to us. (III 180.23)

Ibn al-ʿArabī finds allusions to the fact that God never discloses Himself as such in the Koran's use of the word *ilāh* or "god." In the following discussion, he alludes to his controversial teaching that Pharaoh, the chief villain of the Koran, had a genuine knowledge of God that allowed him to reject some of the teachings of Moses.

> Under this heading come the words of the Samaritan concerning the Calf, *This is your god, and the god of Moses* [20:88]. He did not say, "This is God, to whom Moses has been calling you." So also are the words of Pharaoh, *So that perhaps [. . .] I may look upon the god of Moses* [40:37]. He did not say, "upon God, to whom Moses has been calling." Pharaoh also said, *I do not know that you have any god but me* [28:38].

How beautiful is this investigation for you to understand that Pharaoh had a knowledge of God! However, chieftainship and love for it had overcome him in his affairs in this world. After all, Pharaoh said, *I do not know that you have*; he did not say, "I do not know that the cosmos has," since he knew that his people believed that he was a god for them. Hence, he reported the actual situation and he was truthful in his reporting, for he knew that they did not know that they had any god other than Pharaoh.

Given that in the actual situation, there are degrees related to God through lifting up, for He is *the Uplifter of degrees* [40:15], the forms of self-disclosure become many in diversity. This is what the Samaritan spoke of when he said, *And the god of Moses* [20:88]. For the divine self-disclosure belongs only to the God [*al-ilāh*] and the Lord. It never belongs to God, for God is the Independent. *Say: He is God, One, God, the Everlasting Refuge. He gives not birth, nor was He born, nor is His equal any one* [112]. "He never discloses Himself twice to a single individual in one form, nor to two individuals in one form."

That is why the Samaritan said, *And the god of Moses*, for His self-disclosure to the prophets is diverse in forms but unitary in the property that He is the God in whatever form He discloses Himself. Do you not see that at the resurrection, when He discloses Himself, He will be denied and known through the diversity of the forms?

You may say: It may be that when He is denied, He returns to the form so that He may be recognized. We would reply: If you only knew the meaning of His words, "Is there between you and Him a mark?" The mark is their proof. When they see it upon Him, they know that He is their Lord. The mark is called a "form" because the name *form* is applied to every known thing. Thus they recognize Him through the mark. It is not that He repeats the form for them; on the contrary, that form itself is the mark.

The degrees of the Real have no end, because the self-disclosure occurs within them and it has no end, for the subsistence of the cosmos has no end. Hence, the degrees have no end on the two sides—I mean eternity without beginning and eternity without end, which become manifest through the [present] state, which is the cosmos. Were the cosmos to disappear, eternity without beginning would not be distinct from eternity without end, just as the actual situation is in itself. For there is no origin for the Real, and the negation of origin from Him is one of His degrees through which He is lifted up from interrelation with the cosmos. The degrees of the cosmos, which are identical with His degrees, are infinite in their eternity without end, even if the descent of the cosmos into a degree is one of them. This degree is an origin for the cosmos. It is not that the degrees have an origin. Rather, the manifestation of the cosmos within them has an origin. (III 178.15)

Self-Disclosure is always confined and constricted by the form or the meaning in which it occurs. In other words, only *wujūd* itself is unbounded, and anything other than sheer *wujūd* is forever bound. Any form that appears in the cosmos designates a limited property that belongs to *wujūd*'s self-disclosure.

The property that rules over God always accords with the form within which He discloses Himself. Whenever an attribute occurs for a receptive form, the Real is described by that attribute, and He describes Himself by it. This happens for the common people when someone dreams about the Real in a form, whatever the form may be. The dreamer applies to Him whatever attributes that are necessitated by the form within which he sees Him. No one denies this in the case of dreams. But some of the Men of God see this form in the state of wakefulness—though within the Presence within which the dreamer sees it, no other. This is a level within which come together the prophets and the friends of God. (IV 200.23)

"The Presence within which the dreamer sees" God's self-disclosure is the Presence of Imagination. Thus Ibn al-ʿArabī is referring here to the fact that only the faculty of imagination perceives God in His self-disclosure. In contrast, reason declares Him incomparable with all forms and all self-disclosures. However, the imagination that truly perceives the Real is not just any imagination. The seeker needs the imaginal vision that Ibn al-ʿArabī most typically refers to as "unveiling." This sort of unveiling belongs strictly to the gnostics, the Folk of God. They alone recognize God's self-disclosures in the cosmos because they alone have had the eye of their insight opened by God. This vision can never be achieved by the rational faculty, no matter how refined it may be.

Some maintain that the "vision of the Real" is only an increased lucidity in considerative knowledge of God, nothing else. This is the doctrine of him who has no knowledge of God by way of unveiling and self-disclosure—unless he has said this because he is present with someone for whom it is not proper to hear this sort of thing. (III 395.17)

The Folk of God who sit with God report about His self-disclosures. But this God that they witness is the God that appears specifically to them, which is to say that they see God in keeping with their own preparedness and understanding. God in Himself remains forever beyond the knowledge of all creatures.

He is too high to be limited
by reflection and reports,
too majestic for the property
of insight and eyesight.
We have nothing of Him
save what He wishes
in every state
in the signifiers and the expressions.
Know that I have realized
none but Him
and I know none
but mortal man.
This is why the All-Merciful forbade
considering His Essence
in His revelation on the tongue
of the Messenger.
He said not to pursue
what you cannot know—
those who consider [the Essence]
are in danger,
For He *is not born* in knowledge
and *gives not birth* [112:3]
in *wujūd*. So realize who prohibits
and who commands!

It does not lie in the possible domain for God to create in what He creates a faculty in an existent thing through which the thing would encompass God in knowledge—in respect of this faculty abiding within it. The inmost center of His majesty is not perceived by any rational faculty, nor is the inmost center of His Essence perceived by eyesight when He discloses Himself, wherever He should disclose Himself to His servants. He is the Self-Discloser whose Self is not perceived by the perception that perceives Him, whether in knowledge or vision. So it is not proper for human beings to pursue knowledge of what they know they cannot reach. Abū Bakr said, "The incapacity to attain perception is itself perception." When someone is perceived only through incapacity, how can this perceiver be described as having perceived?

Whenever there is marriage
and coupling in a thing,
that is the goal
of the people of arguments.
When He produces me as offspring,
I produce Him,
so you see us in marriage
and reproduction.
Our states that come
to be manifest
stand between lucidity
and indistinction.
As "We are through Him,"[6]
He is through us—
constriction is the same
as release. (III 371.13)

Like everyone else, the Folk of God see God through the limits (*ḥadd*) that He assumes through disclosing Himself. But they know exactly what they are seeing, and they know that no limit is God. In the midst of perceiving *tashbīh* through imagination, they acknowledge *tanzīh* through reason.

Someone who curtains the Real,
not divulging Him,
is the individual
who has shown unbelief.
God is not hidden
from those who look upon Him
with the eye of reason
or eyesight.
Blessed is God
who becomes manifest without cease
in every form
that appears,
for He configures them
constantly
in everything that becomes manifest
or is manifest!

Know—God confirm you—that worshiping God in the absent domain is identical with worshiping Him in the witnessed domain, since neither human beings nor any other worshipers can worship their object of worship except as witnessed, whether through reason or through eyesight or insight. Through insight the worshiper witnesses Him, so he worships Him. Otherwise, it is not correct for him to worship. Hence he worships only something witnessed, not something absent. If God gives His servants knowledge of His self-disclosure in the forms of eyesight so that they distinguish Him, then they also worship Him while witnessing Him through eyesight. This takes place only after they have seen Him with the eye of their insight. Whoever brings together insight and eyesight has perfected his worship in the manifest and nonmanifest domains.

Those who say that the Real indwells [*ḥulūl*] in forms are ignorant of both affairs. The truth is that the Real is identical with the forms, for no container encloses Him and no form is absent from Him. His "absence" is nothing but ignorance of Him by those who are ignorant. The ignorant see Him, but they do not know that He is the object they seek. Hence the Messenger of God said to such people, "Worship God as if you see Him." He commanded them to consider Him present, for they know that no one is considered present who cannot be present. The servants' considering their Lord present in worship is identical with the presence of the object of worship with them.

If the servants do not know Him save within limit and measure, they limit and measure Him. If they know Him as incomparable with that, they do not limit or measure Him, even though they consider Him present as if they see Him. The gnostics who know Him do not limit Him and do not measure Him, because they see Him as all forms. Whenever they limit Him through a form, another form protests, so the limit falls apart for them. The gnostics cannot restrict the affair, for they do not encompass all engendered and non-engendered forms. Hence they do not encompass Him in knowledge, as He says, *And they encompass Him not in knowledge* [20:110], even though He described Himself as *nearer* to human beings *than* their *jugular vein* [50:16]. So the Real is nearer to them than their own self, for He employed the comparative form, because there is something near.

The nearest of things is the nearness of the manifest to the nonmanifest. So there is nothing nearer to the manifest than the nonmanifest, save the manifest itself, and there is nothing nearer to the nonmanifest than the manifest, save the nonmanifest itself. But He is *nearer to him than the jugular vein*, so He is identical with him who is described as having a jugular vein. Thus we come to know that He is identical with every form, but we do not encompass the forms in *wujūd*. So we *encompass Him not in knowledge*.

You may say: You are one of the forms.

I would reply: That is exactly what I say. However, although the forms are identical with the sought object, they are the properties of the possible things in the entity of the sought object, so I do not care whether ignorance, knowledge, or any other description is ascribed to them, for I know how I should ascribe, depict, and describe, for *To God belongs the command before and after* [30:4]. (III 375.29)

It should not be imagined that Ibn al-ʿArabī, when he speaks of the gnostics or the Folk of God, means those commonly referred to as "Sufis." On the contrary, he has in view a tiny minority—those who have attained to the station of realization, or the Station of No Station. Such people were extremely rare in Ibn al-ʿArabī's own day, much less in later times. He alludes to this point after having explained that God has two relations with *wujūd*. In respect of the first relation, God is *wujūd* in itself, and it is impossible for there to be self-disclosure. This is the respect in which God is God as such, the exclusively One. In respect of the second relation, God discloses Himself within formal *wujūd*, that is, the *wujūd* that assumes the forms of the cosmos, or the Breath of the All-Merciful.[7] Having explained this, the Shaykh offers a sort of apology even for speaking about the second relation. After all, from the point of view of Kalām, it appears scandalous, and even many Sufis have not understood it.

So, my friend, consider this homestead, for it is a homestead that is extremely hidden. If not for the tongue of the Shariah that has pointed toward it and called attention to it, I would not have expounded it eloquently to the folk of our path. For many of the folk of the Path of God, even if they witness the Real's self-disclosure, have no knowledge of that, nor of what they see, nor of the form of the actual situation.

He who knows what we have stipulated concerning the clarification of the Shariah's intention will know how the cosmos proceeds [from God], what it is, what of the cosmos subsists in entity, and what of it is annihilated. He will also know what it is that the Real inherits from the cosmos, for He says, *Surely We shall in-*

herit the earth and all who are upon it, and unto Us they shall be returned [19:40]. In reality, He inherits nothing but the *wujūd* within which He discloses Himself to those of His creatures that become manifest and from which the forms and accidents of the possible things are dismissed. For there is no inheritor as long as those from whom inheritance is taken have *wujūd* and subsistence. Inheritance takes place only after their transferal from this homestead and their nonexistence within it, and that is their becoming qualified by nonexistence. But this belongs only to the forms and the accidents. So He is the Inheritor perpetually, the dismissing occurs perpetually, the reception is made present perpetually, and the [divine] marriage act [at the root of engendering] is imperative perpetually. This is the meaning of the "perpetuity" ascribed to the Real. (III 516.18)

God in Himself is unknowable, although He can be known when He discloses Himself. However, the self-disclosure partakes of the divine unknowability in that it is never the same, because it is never repeated. Anything one knows has already entered one's experience and awareness, but God's self-disclosure can never be known beforehand because, whenever it arrives, it is new. One of the implications of this is that no one perceives self-disclosure for what it is save as a gratuitous favor (*imtinān*). No one can achieve it through striving (*sa ᶜāya*) to achieve it, because one already knows what one is striving to achieve.

When something is achieved through striving, there is nothing of gratuitous favor in it. Seeking is a striving, while vision is a gratuitous favor, so it cannot be sought. When something of vision occurs as the result of seeking, in reality this vision has not been gained through the seeking. After all, when people seek to see the object of vision, they seek to see Him only as He is to Himself. But He discloses Himself to them only in the form of their knowledge of Him because, were this not the case, they would deny Him.

So He discloses Himself to them only in something other than what they have sought. The vision is a beneficence, for exactly what was sought has not come to them. They imagine that it is exactly what they had sought, but it is not. When they take pleasure in what they see and they imagine that it is the object of their seeking, then, after that, He discloses Himself to them without any seeking. This self-disclosure is also a divine gratuitous favor. Through it He gives them a knowledge of Him that was not present with them and that had not occurred to their mind.

Once you have understood what I have said, you will know that the vision of God does not take place through seeking and is not reached through recompense, in contrast to the blessings in the Gardens. This is a question to which, so far as I know, none of God's creatures has called attention, only God. The Men of God know it, but they have not called attention to it, because they imagine that this question is near to grasp and easy for the taking, or that it cannot possibly occur—there must be one of these two judgments. For God has not treated the creatures equally in knowledge of Him, so God's servants must be ranked in degrees of excellence in that.

The Mu'tazilites refuse to accept vision, the Ash'arites permit it rationally and affirm it according to the Shariah as required by their consideration, the philosophers negate it rationally, since they have no entrance into the Shariah and faith, and the Folk of God affirm it through unveiling and tasting.

Whatever there may be before unveiling, unveiling rejects it because of what it gives. It does not allow them to remain as they were, unless they are among those who uphold what the folk of unveiling bring. In that case, the state will not change for them, save in the measure of the difference between knowledge and the vision of knowledge's object. (III 464.27)

Unending Renewal

To see God in His self-disclosure is to see a perpetual and never-repeated display of novel forms. Ibn al-ᶜArabī explains the implications of the constant renewal of creation in many different connections, citing as one of his primary proof texts the verse, *No indeed, but they are uncertain of a new creation* (50:15). Although the immediate context of this verse makes it apply to the resurrection, the Shaykh reads it as an allusion to the constant and never-ending bestowal of *wujūd* upon the possible things in this world. He refers to the fact that most people would not understand the verse in this way while discussing the manner in which God's mercy bestows a special pleasure on the sinners.

A Mystery
That Within Which There is No Illness, that is, the Healthy Mind

The pleasure of the moment
belongs to him who plucks
the fruit of nearness
when he sins.
When someone asked how,
I said to him,
"Were the world to know
what I mean,
"They would be enraptured
by ecstasy in Him, so what of me?
That is why I have curtained it
on my part."

The poet says, "Sweeter than security for the frightened and timorous!" When the Arriver that gives security arrives at a frightened person, he has greater pleasure than those who are constantly secure. This is because security is renewed for him after fear. It comes in contrast to the frightening affair whose occurrence he had been expecting and anticipating. Hence he finds a pleasure that could not be more pleasurable.

Were God to open the eye of a person's insight and were he to see the renewal of his configuration at every breath along with the permissibility of nonrenewal and of joining with nonexistence, then he would be in perpetual pleasure. However, not everyone is given this level. On the contrary, as God says, the human being is *uncertain of a new creation,* though here the common people understand the configuration of the last world.

The sinner is he who anticipates punishment. If he is a person of faith, he anticipates either punishment from God for his sin, or pardon and forgiveness. When forgiveness comes to him, he finds with it a joy whose measure cannot be measured save by him who tastes it. (IV 439.10)

It was obvious to Muslim thinkers, as it had been obvious to the Greeks and others, that the cosmos undergoes generation (*kawn*) and corruption (*fasād*). Everything within it comes into existence and eventually disappears. The Ash'arite theologians in particular insisted that accidents (as opposed to substances) were constantly being recreated and renewed. Ibn al-ʿArabī's theoretical contribution was simply to insist that this generation and corruption occurs at every instant in everything other than God and to find support for this observation in the basic texts of the tradition. The Shaykh's perception of perpetual renewal is inextricably tied to his fundamental insight about the cosmos, that is, its ambiguous ontological situation, the fact that it can neither be totally affirmed nor totally denied, that it is neither *wujūd* nor other than *wujūd*—He/not He. On the temporal plane, this fact becomes manifest as the incessant affirmation of *wujūd* followed by its immediate negation.

God says, *There is nothing that does not glorify Him in praise* [17:44], so there is no form in the cosmos—and there is nothing in the cosmos but forms—that does not glorify its Creator with a specific praise that He inspires within it. And there is no form in the cosmos that undergoes corruption without its very corruption being the manifestation of another form within those substances themselves, glorifying God, so that none of engendered existence may be empty of the glorification of its Creator. The entities of the parts of the form glorify Him as is worthy of the form.

The forms in the cosmos are all relations and states that are neither existent nor nonexistent. Although they are witnessed in one respect, they are not witnessed in another respect. The time of the annihilation of the forms is identical with the time of the *wujūd* of the forms. In other words, the corruption of the forms is identical with other forms—it is not that after the corruption, the other forms arrive newly. (II 682.20)

The Shaykh finds one of the most explicit scriptural references to God as the root of all creaturely activity in the *ḥadīth qudsī* in which God says that He is the hearing and the eyesight of the one whom He loves. In one passage, he brings up this hadith while discussing the issue of human will (*mashīʾa*) and choice (*ikhtiyār*). Muslim theologians and philosophers often discussed the tangled issues that arise as soon as we try to analyze the exact source of human movement and activity. The Ash'arites and Mu'tazilites are typically represented as taking two opposing positions on the issue, the former asserting predestination and the latter choice.[8] On the issue of movement (*ḥaraka*), various explanations were offered by theologians to explain the two sorts that people commonly experience—free or chosen (*ikhtiyārī*) and compulsory (*majbūr*) or constrained (*iḍṭirārī*). The Shaykh's discussion begins in a theological mode by offering various rational explanations for what we experience. Then he turns to unveiling and describes the constant change of all things perceived by the Folk of God.

There remains the issue of who brings about the movement. Is it the moving thing, or something else?

Some people say that what brings about the movement is the movement. It abides through the body and makes it necessary for it to undergo movement and transferal. But they disagree concerning the movement that makes it necessary for the body to undergo movement. Is the servant's will connected to it, so that it is called "chosen," that is, a movement of choice? Or is the mover's will not connected to it, so that it is called "constrained," like the movement of someone with a tremor? All of this is when it has been affirmed that there is a movement, as some suppose.

They do not disagree that these engendered qualities are accidents, whether they are relations or meanings abiding within the loci that are described by them. After all, we do not doubt that a state which the body did not have has occurred to it as an accident. It is impossible that any of these accidents be essential to it. Rather, what is essential to it is its reception of accidents.

They disagree as to who brings the movement and stillness into existence—if it is affirmed that the thing is an existent entity. Is it God, or other than God? Some say that, some say this, and it is the same whether or not it is someone with a tremor.

Some say that the engendered qualities have no *wujūd* but are only relations, so by whom are these qualities supported?

We say, concerning the relation of choice, that God created for the servant a will through which he wills as a property of this relation. This newly arrived will derives from God's will. God says, *You will not will unless God wills* [76:30]. Thereby He affirms will for Him and for us, and He makes our will dependent upon His will. This is movement by choice. As for compulsory movement, in our view the actual situation is one. The first occasion is the will of the Real, and the second occasion is the will that comes to exist from the will of the Real.

However, there is a subtlety here that is given by unveiling. God alludes to it from behind the veil of engendered existence with His words, *You will not will unless God wills*. In unveiling, God is the Willer. If the servant finds the desire for something in himself, the Real is identical with his desire, nothing else. In the same way, it has been affirmed that when God loves the servant, He is his hearing, his eyesight, his hand, and all his faculties, so the property of the will that the servant finds in himself is nothing other than the Real. When God wills, what He wills comes to be, for He is identical with the will of every willer.

In a similar way, those who affirm movement say that Zayd moved, or that he moved his hand. But when you realize their view in keeping with their position, you will find that what moves Zayd's hand is the movement that arises through his hand. Even if you do not see that movement, you perceive its trace. Nevertheless, you say that Zayd moved his hand. In the same way, you say that Zayd moved his hand, but the mover is only God.

Know also that there is no stillness whatsoever in the cosmos. It fluctuates endlessly and perpetually from state to state, in this world and the last world, outwardly and inwardly. However, there is a hidden movement and a witnessed movement. The states come and go for the entities that receive them, and the movements bestow diverse traces in the cosmos. If not for these states, periods would never come to an end, numbers would have no ruling property, things would not run *to a named term* [31:29], and there would be no transferal from abode to abode.

The root of the *wujūd* of these states is the divine descriptions, such as the Real's descent to the closest heaven every night, His sitting upon a newly arrived Throne, and His coming to be in a Cloud when there was no Throne. It is this that necessitates that the Real be the hearing and eyesight of the servant and identical with his will, so that through Him he hears, sees, moves, and wills.

So glory be to Him who is hidden in His manifestation and manifest in His hiddenness and who described Himself by saying that He is the *Everlasting Refuge* [112:2]! There is no god but He. *He forms* us *in the wombs as He* wills [3:6], *He makes the night and day fluctuate* [24:44], *He is with* us *wherever* we *are* [57:4], and He is nearer to us than we are.

We declare His multiplicity [*takthīr*] through us and we declare His unity [*tawḥīd*] through Him. Then He sought from us that we declare His unity through "There is no god but God," so we declared His unity through His command and we declared His multiplicity through us.

The Real does not show you His wisdom
every moment,
even if none of His moments
is empty of wisdom.
Consider a joy in the heart,
arising from grief,
coming from the heavens,
the tablets, the Pen,
Brought by the spirit messengers
descending
on our secret hearts
from the Presence of the Words.
The object of every hidden knowledge
is exalted
beyond rational faculties
that enjoy not Eternity's favor.
So I stand in love and honor
for their station,
I walk striving at the head,
not in the footsteps. (III 303.19)

In the context of the new creation, Ibn al-ʿArabī often refers to the cosmos as "imagination," because it is a never-ending fluctuation of forms, each of which provides a new image of *wujūd*. Like dream images, which appear to us in what he calls "contiguous imagination," cosmic imagination refuses to stay fixed. As manifest in the Breath of the All-Merciful, the cosmos is "the dream of the Real" (II 380.17) or "Unbounded Imagination" (*al-khayāl al-muṭlaq*).[9] It undergoes constant "transmutation" (*istiḥāla*), which means to change from one state (*ḥāl*) to another.

Were it not for the faculty of imagination, none of what we have made manifest to you would have become manifest. For imagination is the most all-embracing of engendered things and the most perfect of existent things, and it accepts spiritual forms. It is for things to assume shape in the diverse forms of engendered transmutation.

Some transmutation is speedy, like the transmutation of spirits into corporeous forms and of meanings into the corporeous forms that become manifest in the engendered existence of the Cloud.[10] Other transmutations are slow, like the transmutation of water into air, air into fire, the sperm-drop into a human being, and the elements into a plant or an animal. Although all this is transmutation, it does not have the speed of the transmutation of forms within the human imaginal faculty, which is "contiguous imagination," nor that of the transmutation of the forms of spirits within the forms of bodies into corporeous bodies, such as the angels within the form of mortal man. For the speed here is greater and, in the same way, its disappearance is quicker, than the transmutation of bodies after death into that into which they become transmuted.

Once you have understood this root, you will know that the Real is He who speaks, brings into movement, stills, gives existence, and takes away. Thus you will know that all forms, through that which is attributed to them as belonging to them, are raised-up imagination, and that the reality of *wujūd* belongs to Him—high exalted is He!

Do you not see the one who sets up "the image on the screen"?[11] He sets it up only so that the viewer will realize the knowledge of *wujūd*'s actual situation. The viewer sees numerous forms whose movements, activities, and properties belong to one entity that has none of this. What brings these things into existence, making them move and stand still between us and Him, is the screen that is set up. It is the separating limit between us and Him, through which the distinction occurs. Concerning Him it is said, "a god," and concerning us, "servants" and "a cosmos"—whichever word you like. (II 311.2)

The ever-renewed states that become manifest in the cosmos fill the "Void" (*al-khalaʾ*), which Ibn al-ʿArabī defines as "an imagined extension that is not within a body" (II 310.25, 433.27), or "an imagined roundness that is not within a body" (III 119.31), or "an extension without edges that is not within a body, but within which corporealization is imagined" (I 291.7). He seems to be saying that in order for us to conceive of bodily things, we have to imagine an empty space that they occupy. But of course, if there were no bodily dimensions whatsoever—if there were an absolute nothingness—we would not find the empty space. An absolute nothingness cannot exist for us to find. Hence the Void remains a useful supposition, whereby we can talk about the place of the cosmos in general terms, but it has no existence except in imagination.

The Void is contrasted with the "plenum" (*mala*ʾ) that fills it. Often the Shaykh speaks of the higher and lower plenums, or the two plenums, meaning the angelic or spiritual beings and the corporeal things, that is, the two basic kinds of existent things that occupy the cosmos. At least once he mentions the "middle plenum" (IV 198.14), meaning the spirits that dwell in the seven heavens, which pertain to the imaginal world.

> Perpetual existence-giving belongs to God, and perpetual reception of activity belongs to the possible things, which are the cosmos. So engendering never ceases perpetually, and the entities become manifest perpetually. The Void never ceases to extend ad infinitum, because the entities of the possible things come into existence ad infinitum. Through their entities they inhabit nothing but the Void.
>
> When I said earlier that the cosmos inhabits nothing save the Void, I meant that it is impossible for it to occupy a plenum, for the plenum is the inhabitant. Hence it does not inhabit a plenum, and there is nothing but plenum or void.
>
> The cosmos undergoes renewal endlessly, so the last world has no end. If not for us, no one would say "this world" and "last world." Rather, it would only be said that the possible things have come into existence and will come into existence—as is the actual situation. But, when our entities become manifest and we—who are among the created possible things—come to inhabit designated places *to a named term* [31:29] while we are among the forms of the cosmos, we name this homestead "the abode of this world," that is, the near abode that we inhabit when we first have *wujūd* for our entities. But the cosmos might have come to be without us.
>
> However, God appointed for us in our inhabiting this abode terms at which we come to an end. Then we are transferred to another homestead which is called a "last world" and within which is found what is in the abode of this world. However, it is distinct through the abode, just as it is distinct here through the state. God did not appoint for our stay in the last abode a term at which the period of our stay would come to an end. He made that abode a locus of engendering perpetually and endlessly ad infinitum. He alters the attribute of the abode of this world, and through this alteration it becomes a last world. But the entity subsists. (III 506.7)

Ibn al-ʿArabī calls Chapter 356 "On the true knowledge of three secreted mysteries, of the Arabic mystery in the divine courtesy, and of the revelation through the self and nature." In the first half of the chapter, he describes the transmutation of all things through the renewal of creation at each instant. He begins by explaining how this world is transmuted into the last world, and how parts of the last world are transmuted into this. Then he turns to our experience of the world of imagination through dreams, where the perception of transmutation is especially strong.

> I freely gave up myself for myself,
> that I might win Him
> who was at me,
> though I was unaware of His site
> until I saw that He had a shape
> similar to me,
> so in it I became absent
> at the Lawgiver's command.
> Was that for bliss in it, or the assumption
> of the traits of the names?
> Consider the states
> of its Innovator.
> Should the All-Merciful address you
> from scripture
> with His wisdom's mystery,
> be present so as to contain it.
>
> Know—God confirm you—that when God caused the Void to be inhabited by all the cosmos, it became filled with it. He created within it movement, so that parts of it would be transmuted into other parts and the forms would be diverse through the transmutations, because of the nature of the Void, which is filled with that into which the cosmos is transmuted. The cosmos never ceases undergoing transmutation perpetually. This is the *new creation* concerning which most people are *uncertain* [50:15] and doubtful. Those of the Folk of God who know this—those whom God has caused to witness it in entity in their secret hearts—know

the transmutation of this world into the last world and the transmutation of parts of the last world into other parts, just as parts of it were transmuted into this world. For example, a report has come that the Nile, the Euphrates, the Pyramus, and the Sarus are among the rivers of the Garden that have been transmuted, so in this world they have become manifest in a form different from the form that they have in the last world.[12] Another example is the Prophet's words, "Between my grave and my pulpit is one of the gardenplots of the Garden," so it had been transmuted into a plot in this world within a determined, known area. So also is the riverbed of Muḥassir, which is a riverbed of the Fire that has been transmuted into this world.

Adam, Eve, and Iblis belong to the world of the last abode, but they were transmuted into this world. Then they will be transmuted back into the last world. Forms change over them in keeping with what is given by the nature of the imagined place to which movement transfers them. This nature leaves its traces within them, whether they be spirits or bodies, whether spatially confined or non-spatially confined. God keeps them in movement perpetually.

If not for us, the last world would not have become distinct from this world, since, in this ascription, God takes into account from the cosmos only the human species and the jinn. He appointed manifestation for the human beings, from His name the Manifest, and He appointed nonmanifestation for the jinn, from His name the Nonmanifest. Everything else is subjected to these two, just as, in actual fact, some human beings are subjected to others, because of the degrees within which God has placed them. The degrees give them the forms into which they are transmuted when the divine movement transfers them into them. Since these become manifest to our entities only here, this abode is named the abode of "this world" or the "first abode," and it is called "the life of this world." Then, when we are transmuted into the *barzakh* and, from the *barzakh*, we are transmuted into the forms within which will be the Upstirring and the Uprising, that is called "the last world." The affair in the last world never ceases to be a new creation. Within it the folk of the Garden are in the Garden and the folk of the Fire in the Fire, ad infinitum. In the last world we will witness nothing but a new creation in one entity, so the cosmos is finite/infinite.

Since this is the situation, human beings, while sleeping, may see themselves in the Garden, or at the resurrection, or in other than their own place or land, whether or not they recognize it. They may be in other than their own form and other than their own state. Through the movement by which they were transferred from waking to sleep, they have been transmuted within themselves into forms sometimes familiar and sometimes unfamiliar and into praiseworthy and beautiful states that make them happy, or into blameworthy and ugly states through which they suffer pain. Then transmutation comes quickly to them and they return to wakefulness.

They may wake up because they have fully achieved the meaning into which they were transmuted in sleep, so nothing remains for them to be given from that specific transmutation. Such is the case of the person who wakes up without any occasion, and this is "natural awakening," because the soul has taken for its eye its *ḥaqq* from sleep, within which is its ease.

If the person is transferred from sleep to wakefulness by an occasion, whether from the direction of the sensory domain, or from some frightening affair or disturbing movement that appeared from him in the state of his sleep, then he awakens. If that conforms to the eye's full achievement of the natural sleep that is its *ḥaqq*, so be it. But if it does not conform to it, and something of the eye's *ḥaqq* remains that would have been achieved had that occasion not intervened, then it achieves it in another sleep. That is why, at times, the sleep of some sleepers becomes long. The occasion of its length is what we mentioned.

As for the curtailment of sleep, that derives from one of two affairs—and that is what we mentioned. Either some occasion awakens the person, or the eye achieves fully its *ḥaqq* in that specific sleep according to the person's constitution. After all, the constitution of the weary person and that of a person at ease are not equal. The weary person seeks the ease that will take away the weariness, so sleep immerses him completely and becomes drawn out, for he loves the full achievement of ease. Nothing awakens him before its full achievement save one of three things, or all of them, or some of them, according to what happens. First he may see something in a dream that disturbs him. Second, he may be awakened by someone who is awake, either intentionally or through a great noise or a movement, or through other such occasions in the world of sensation, whether it is intended to awaken him, or that is not the intention, but it happens by chance. The third affair is that the soul is attached to the thought of accomplishing some business that it loves to do, so it sleeps with that thought and is attached to that affair. This agitates the person and he wakes up before fully accomplishing his *ḥaqq* of sleep.

My intention in mentioning all this is only to instruct you that the cosmos is not empty of transmutation at every breath. If the entity of the substance of him who receives this transmutation in himself were not one and fixed such that, in respect of the substance, the entity does not undergo transmutation, then he would not know, when he is transmuted into another affair, what his state was before the transmutation. Nonetheless, some transmutations may be hidden and delicate. Some are manifest so that the soul senses them, like the transmutation of the soul's thoughts, outward movements, and states. Others are delicate and hidden, like its transmutation in its knowledges and faculties, or like the colors of colored things in the renewal of their likenesses. None perceives this affair save one of the folk of unveiling, for he perceives it, and unveiling removes from him the uncertainty that blinds others from perceiving this affair.

You might ask: What is this form into which the substances of the cosmos are transmuted?

I would reply: The possible things, nothing else. They are in the thingness of their fixity. God refers to them in the verse, *Our only word to a thing, when We desire it [is to say to it "Be!," so it comes to be*] [16:40]. Since the thing becomes manifest through the word *Be*, that is not the thingness of *wujūd*. Thus God says, *I created you aforetime, when you were not a thing* [19:9], that is, "I determined you when you did not possess the thingness of *wujūd*," which, in reality, is the thingness of manifestation—manifestation of the thing to its own entity. Although in the thingness of its fixity it was manifest and distinct from others through its reality, this was to its Lord, not to itself. It did not become manifest to itself until after the divine command in His word *Be* became connected to its manifestation. Then it acquired manifestation to itself, knew itself, and witnessed its own entity. So it was transmuted from the thingness of its fixity into the thingness of its *wujūd*. If you want, you can say that in its own self, it was transmuted from not being manifest to itself into a state through which it was manifest to itself, through *the determination of the Exalted, the Knowing* [6:96].

The whole cosmos is rising/setting, a turning sphere, a floating star. It is manifest between sunrise and sunset from a divine revelation—which is the command that is turned toward it to become manifest or hidden—and a revelation of self, which is what the Real seeks from it and what it seeks from the Real. So the servant reveals to the Real just as the Real reveals to him. At one moment the Real acts in accordance with what His servant reveals to Him, but at another moment He may not act in that way. So also, when the Real reveals to the servant and commands him to do something or avoid something, at one moment he may obey Him and at another moment he may disobey Him. Thus the Real becomes manifest to the one for whom the Law is prescribed in his form in giving and refusing, so the servant sees nothing in the Real save his own form. So "Let him blame none but himself" when he calls upon the Real in an affair and He does not respond.

Do you not see that since the angels do not disobey God when He calls them to an act—as has been reported about them [66:6]—they do not call to Him in anything without His responding to them? For they are not in a form that prevents that to which the Real calls them. And the cosmos witnesses nothing of the Real save the form that it has.

This is why the Prophet said, concerning him who says Amen after reciting the Fātiḥa, "When someone's saying Amen coincides with the angels' saying Amen, he will be forgiven," since the angels' saying Amen is accepted by God and responded to by Him. So this coincides with the time of response to the angels. Thus he gains the response by way of following along, unless it be that his moment is the moment of response to him as a recompense for his observance of the Real's command in some other moment.

But the root in the cosmos is the acceptance of the divine command in engendering. Disobedience is an accidental affair that occurs for it relatively. In reality, no one disobeys God, and no one obeys Him, because the whole affair belongs to God. That is His words, *To Him the whole affair is returned* [11:123]. So the servants' acts are a creation of God, and the servant is the locus of that creation. (III 253.9)[13]

One of the important Koranic expressions within which the Shaykh finds reference to continual creation is *term* (*ajal*), which the Koran often pairs with the adjective *musammā*, which means "named" or "designated." Thus a person's life has a term named with God, and when this named term arrives, nothing can prevent death. *It is He who created you of clay, then decreed a term, and a term is named with Him* (6:2). *Every community has a term; when their term comes, they shall not put it back by an hour, nor put it forward* (10:49). *He subjected the sun and the moon; each runs to a named term* (13:2, 31:29, 35:13, 39:5).

The Shaykh reads the verse, *Each runs to a named term,* as an allusion to a universal principle that governs everything in *wujūd.* From one point of view, the named term of each thing is the second moment of its *wujūd,* when it disappears, to be replaced by something similar. The entity remains fixed, while the states that define the entity's *wujūd* undergo endless transmutations.

Ibn al-ʿArabī calls Chapter 382 of the *Futūḥāt* "On the true knowledge of the conclusions, the number of the divine wedding feasts, and the non-Arabic mysteries." *Khātima* or "conclusion" derives from the same root as *khātam* or "seal" as in *Seal of the prophets* (33:40). As the Shaykh points out, one is able to perceive conclusions when one conceptualizes terms or extreme limits. The opposite of *khātima* is *sābiqa,* which means that which precedes or comes first, a "precedent."

> Conclusions are entified by terms. If not for terms, nothing would have a conclusion, for the conclusion of a thing is for it to come to an end. Every conclusion has a precedent, but not the reverse.
>
> Those who consider the perpetuity and ceaselessness of the descent of the divine command will say that there is no conclusion, but those who consider the separating factors among things in the descent will say that things do indeed have conclusions, because the likenesses clarify the separations. However, all this is within the world of division and composition.
>
> For example, when you consider the Koran between two words, two verses, or two surahs, you may maintain that there is a separation that distinguishes between two affairs. If the separation falls between two words, the conclusion of the first is a designated letter. If you consider two verses, then the conclusion of the first is a designated word. If you consider two surahs, then the conclusion of the first is a designated verse.
>
> When a newly arrived affair is considered, it is said that its term in this world is such and such, since everything in this world *runs to a named term* [13:2], so its period comes to an end through the term. Thus the "conclusion" of that thing is that at which its ruling property comes to an end.
>
> The breaths of a living thing come to an end at its last breath, when it is transferred to the *barzakh.* Its period in the *barzakh* comes to an end at the separation between the *barzakh* and the Uprising. The period in the resurrection comes to an end at the separation between the resurrection and the entrance into the two abodes. The period in the Fire comes to an end—for those of the folk of the Garden who are within it—at the separation between staying within it and emerging from it through intercession and gratuitous favor. The period of chastisement for the folk of the Fire who do not emerge from it comes to an end at the separation between the state of chastisement and gaining the ruling property of the *mercy* that *embraces everything* [7:156]. Hence, they become blissful in the Fire through the diversity of their constitutions, as we have mentioned.
>
> After this no term remains that becomes manifest through period. However, there are hidden, delicate terms. This is that one of the characteristics of a newly arrived thing, perpetual in entity, is the fluctuation of forms over it so that it will remain perpetually inseparable from poverty toward the perpetuity of its *wujūd.* Its state never becomes separate from terms, so it never ceases to dwell in its states between a precedent and a conclusion. (III 512.7)

The constant renewal of creation, which demands that every movement be a new self-disclosure, throws the folk of unveiling into perplexity and bewilderment. They have no lack of certainty concerning the new creation, but they are confused by their recognition of their own ignorance. All things, inasmuch as they are God, are unknowable, but, inasmuch as they are other than God, they display nothing real to be known. Bewilderment (*ḥayra*), then, is one of the highest stages of knowledge. It is the realization of the incapacity to know that is referred to in Abū Bakr's often quoted saying, "The incapacity to attain perception is itself perception."

> You know that it is not possible for anything of His creation to be like Him, even though the interrelation that ties your *wujūd* to His *wujūd* and your entity to His Entity is rationally un-

derstood. In the same way, the *wujūd* of your knowledge of Him is tied to your knowledge of you in the Prophet's words, "He who knows himself knows his Lord." So the creature most knowledgeable of creation is the most knowledgeable of God.

You also know the difference between the unity of the One and the unity of the many; the restriction of *wujūd* to the Eternal and the newly arrived, and how it becomes restricted; the distinction between the Eternal and the newly arrived, and through what they are distinct; what names and properties are ascribed to the beginningless Eternal, and what names and attributes are ascribed to the created, newly arrived thing.

But to what does the entity of the cosmos go back, and what of the Real is witnessed when He discloses Himself to you and you see Him? To what do the diversity and difference of the self-disclosure go back? Does this go back to your differing perception in the One Entity? Then your vision in the self-disclosure would be diverse, though it does not undergo variation in itself. Or does the variation in the self-disclosure go back to the relation, not to you or to Him? In the view of the Folk of God, it is impossible for it to go back to Him. There remains nothing but going back to one of the two affairs, or to both together—either to you, or to another affair that is neither He nor you. This is how you witness Him, so not everyone who sees knows what he sees.

The Folk of Bewilderment have not become bewildered for nothing. The affair is magnificent, the matter grave, the locus of witnessing all-inclusive, *wujūd* superabundant, perfection already there, knowledge demarcating, the ruling property descending, and renewal rationally understood in the engendered things breath by breath. What is said about the Real is transmitted, while it stands between the intelligible and the non-intelligible. No one perceives these depths save the Folk of Mysteries and Lights and the Possessors of Insights and Eyesights. Those who possess only mystery without light, or light without mystery, or insight without eyesight, or eyesight without insight, or manifest without nonmanifest, or nonmanifest without manifest, belong to that which they possess. They do not achieve perfection, even if they are described by it and are complete in that with which they are busy.

What is sought is perfection, not completion, for completion lies in creation, but perfection lies in the benefits that the complete acquires and bestows. Someone may not gain this degree, despite his completion—for God *has given each thing its creation*, and thereby it has been completed, *then guided* [20:50] to the acquisition of perfection. He who is guided reaches perfection, but he who stops with his completion has been deprived. May God provide us and you with winning and reaching the station of incapacity! Surely He is the Friend, the Beneficent. (III 404.26)

From Chapter 558: The Presence of Bringing Back

God is He-Who-Brings-Back (*al-mu*ʿ*īd*). Like the Koranic verses that refer to the new creation, this name has typically been understood to refer to God's bringing people back at the resurrection, which is the "Place of being brought back" (*ma*ʿ*ād*), a term that is used for the third principle of Islamic faith, after *tawḥīd* and prophecy. The Shaykh objects to the usual understanding because it implies that things leave existence for a time and then are brought back into existence in the last world. On the contrary, he says, God does not "bring back" something that is no longer there. He brings back His own self-disclosure in each successive instant, and this self-disclosure appears as the never-repeating states of the things. What God brings back, perpetually and forever, is not the thing, but the bestowal of *wujūd*.

Bringing back is like
  the origin in the forms,
    and nothing of alteration
      joins with it.
It adds to the first
  because it has
    a shield through which
      it fends off what is known as "harm."
If not for bringing back,
  we would not seek
    when we stand up
      from the graves and the pits,
for His most beautiful names
  will demand from us
    what He had brought to us
      in the truthful report.
We are not kings, that *faces*
  should be *humbled* [20:111] to us
    at the manifestation of the angels
      and the mortals.

The companion of this Presence is called "The servant of Him-Who-Brings-Back," for *He originates and brings back* [85:13]. Hence the origin and the bringing back are two properties that belong to Him. He does not bring back a thing after it goes except that, by giving existence to its likenesses, He comes back to giving existence. So He brings back, but He does not bring back exactly what went. That cannot be, for He is more all-embracing than that. Hence He brings back the state by which He was described.

There is no existent thing to which the Real gives existence without finishing with giving it existence. Then that existent thing considers God and sees that He has come back to giving existence to another entity. So it continues perpetually and endlessly. Hence He is "the Originator and He-Who-Brings-Back"—the originator of everything and He-Who-Brings-Back His own task. He is like a ruler who issues a ruling in some affair. When the ruling itself comes to an end in its object, he has finished with it by having looked at it, and he goes back to a ruling in another affair. Thus he has the property of bringing back. So understand!

The property of the Originator is otherwise, for He originates everything as a creature. Then He brings it back, which is to say that the property—which is the fact that He creates—comes back to Him. This is indicated by His words, *It is He who originates creation, then He brings it back* [30:27], that is, He brings back creation. In other words, in the entity that He desires to bring into existence He does what He has done in that which He has already brought into existence, and this can only be bringing into existence.

After all, in some places by the word *creation,* He means the created thing, as in His words, *This is God's creation* [31:11]. In other places, He means by it the act, as in His words, *I did not give them to witness the creation of the heavens* [18:51]. Here He means the act, without doubt, for the created thing has no act whatsoever. Hence in its essence it has no reality through which to witness the act of God. This is because the created thing has no act, and it witnesses from God only what it has in itself. And "creation" can also be mentioned meaning the created thing—as we explained—not the act.

Hence I have taken His words, *It is He who originates creation, then He brings it back,* as meaning here the act, not the created thing, because the entity of the created thing—I mean the essence that abides through itself—does not disappear from *wujūd.* Rather, it is transferred from this world to the *barzakh,* just as it is transferred from the *barzakh* to the Mustering and then to the Garden or the Fire. But in respect of its substance, it is it. It does not cease to exist and then come back into existence, so that bringing back would pertain to it. Hence there is a transferal from a *wujūd* to a *wujūd,* from a station to a station, from an abode to an abode, for the configuration according to which it is created in the last world is not similar to the configuration of this world save in the name *configuration,* for the configuration of the last world is a beginning.

Were this configuration to come back, its property would come back along with it, for the property of each configuration belongs to its own entity. But its property does not come back, so it does not come back. The substance itself, nothing other than it, exists from when God created it. It does not cease to exist, for God preserves its *wujūd* through what He creates within it that allows it to subsist.

Hence the bringing back is only the fact that the Real comes back to giving existence—in respect of the property of that of this created thing to which He has finished giving existence. *Then We configured him as another creation* [23:14]. God does not mention bringing back save to say that if He willed, He would do it, as when He says, *Then if He wills, He will stir him up* [80:22]. But He does not will.

As often as He finishes with origination, He comes back to the property of origination. This is a divine property that does not disappear. So the property of bringing back does not emerge from the Real, for its property is in Him, not in the creation that is the created thing.

So the cosmos, after its *wujūd,* is transferred into new states that God creates for it; the Real never ceases creating and coming back to creation so as to create. There is no god but He, and *He is powerful over everything* [5:120] through giving existence. (IV 288.33)

Infinity

The Arabic expression for "infinity" is *mā lā nihāya lah* (that which has no end) or *mā lā yatanāhā* (that which does not end). Ibn al-ʿArabī uses this term to refer both to the fixed entities and to *wujūd.* The fixed entities are infinite in their nonexistence, which is to say that the possibilities of the Real's self-disclosure have no end. Once an entity "enters into *wujūd*" (*dakhala fi'l-wujūd*) it becomes an existent entity. The existent entities are finite, because in the state of their existence things have limits and bounds that define their identities, making them some things rather than other things. Moreover, the *wujūd* of each thing instantly reaches an end, but each end reached by a thing—each "named term"—is simply the beginning of a new self-disclosure, and these self-disclosures never cease. Each entity continues to experience the self-disclosures of *wujūd* endlessly, which is to say that each is "infinite" in that "it has no end" (*lā nihāya lah*).

Wujūd is infinite in itself, and "It is impossible for the infinite to enter into *wujūd*" (II 282.35), that is, it is impossible for *wujūd* as such, the Necessary *Wujūd* that cannot not be found, to enter into the delimited and bound *wujūd* that is the cosmos, the possible *wujūd* that may or may not be found. Sheer *wujūd*—God in His Essence—has no limits, but *wujūd* inasmuch as it discloses its own characteristics through the entities is subject to binding and constraint.

> In God's knowledge, all objects of knowledge are as they are, for He knows Himself and He knows other than Himself. But His *wujūd* is not qualified by finitude. What does not enter into *wujūd* is not qualified by finitude. (III 419.21)

One of the Koranic verses that the Shaykh sees as referring to the infinity of *wujūd* and the endless renewal of self-disclosure is *Each day He is upon some task* (55:29). This is the "day" of the Essence, which is the present moment, and at each moment God's task—His act—is new. "The 'tasks' of the Real are the diverse, contrary, and similar states that belong to the cosmos" (*ʿAbādila* 212). The root of this constant renewal is the fact that it is impossible for all entities to come into existence at once. Infinity cannot fit into the limitations of the cosmos. Hence, there is a never-ending outflow of divine acts, and these become manifest as the things and their activities.

> A Mystery
> *The task is in the task.*
>
> The "task" is what we are in,
> and He creates it.
> He creates nothing
> that He does not know.
> The Book of God came
> to teach us this,
> so he who reflects upon it
> will understand.
> God has specified this knowledge
> for whomever He will.
> When its mystery appears to him
> in his state, it rules over him.
>
> What has come in God's Book is His words, *Shall He not know—He who created?* [67:14].
>
> He says: The "task" in His words, *Each day He is upon some task*, is nothing other than the act, which is what He brings into existence "each day," which is the shortest of days—the solitary time that cannot be divided.[14]
>
> As for the act, if the Actor does not act by Essence—which is to say that things are acted upon by Him because of His Essence—then, when He brings the object of activity into existence, He must be in a guise, and that is the act itself.
>
> If God is the Actor by Essence, this does not necessitate the procession of the cosmos from Him all at once, for the possible things are infinite, and the infinite does not enter into *wujūd* except according to order, for such entrance is impossible in itself. When something is impossible in itself, the actor that acts according to the order is not qualified by the incapacity to make all of it appear, since it has no "all," for that is impossible in itself, and realities do not change.
>
> The possible thing gives rise by itself to the order that occurs, and the Real gives it *wujūd* by His Essence. This is none other than the possible thing's entity falling upon the light of self-disclosure, so it sees itself. That over which the light is deployed is called "a *wujūd*."
>
> Rational consideration has no ruling property in this. Or rather, it has a property in some of what we mentioned, and the rational person will assent to the rest.
>
> So the Real is upon His tasks, He acts by His Essence, and the order belongs to the tasks. (IV 425.7)

The nonexistent entities enter into *wujūd* only after they have become the objects of

God's desire to give them *wujūd* and His power to do so. In God's knowledge these entities are infinite and they never cease becoming the objects over which He exercises power, so His power is also infinite. This leads to a paradox that helps keep the knowers bewildered—the fact that one infinity is greater than another.

> Although power becomes connected to infinite possible things, you do not doubt that knowledge has a greater compass, because it is connected to power and to the possible things, the necessary things, the impossible things, the engendered things, and the non-engendered things, even though proofs make known that the infinite cannot be greater than the infinite. (II 501.9)

Ibn al-ᶜArabī dedicates Chapter 190 to "The true knowledge of the traveler [*musāfir*]," whom he defines as "a person whose wayfaring shows to him affairs that are his goal and others that are not. He is the one who travels through reflection, deeds, and belief" (II 382.18). The Shaykh describes how the traveler journeys through reflective thought to knowledge of his Maker's *wujūd.* As he continues his journey, he comes to know *wujūd*'s necessity, its *tawḥīd,* the *wujūd* of the cosmos, the order of the divine names, the necessity of prophecy, and the truthfulness of the prophets.[15] Having recognized that the prophet sent to him has spoken the truth, he follows the practices that are prescribed for him, and God comes to love him. *Say: "If you love God, follow me, and God will love you"* (3:31). Then God becomes his hearing and his eyesight and He unveils for him the mysteries. At this point he comes to understand that the journey has no end—that it is "infinite."

> When God loves him, He unveils for him his heart, and he examines the marvels of the Sovereignty. Everything in the cosmos becomes imprinted in the substance of his own self. He flees to God, traveling away from everything that keeps him distant from Him and veils him from Him. Finally he sees Him in each thing. When he sees Him in each thing, he desires to throw down the staff of the journey and to remove from himself the name "traveler." Then his Lord instructs him that the actual affair has no end, whether in this world or the last world:
>
> "You will never cease being a traveler as you are now. You will never reach a place of rest, just as you never ceased traveling from *wujūd* to *wujūd* in the stages of the cosmos as far as the Presence of *Am I not your Lord?* [7:172]. You never ceased undergoing transferal from waystation to waystation until you came to dwell in this alien, elemental body. You will travel through this body each day and night, crossing waystations of your lifespan until a waystation named 'death.' Then you will not stop traveling, crossing the waystations of the *barzakh*s until you each a waystation called 'the Uprising.' Then you will mount on an eminent mount that will carry you to the abode of your felicity. There you will never cease going back and forth, traveling between it and the Dune of White Musk ad infinitum.[16] This is your journey in your bodily frame. As for your travel in your true knowledges, it is the like of that.
>
> "In the same way, you will never cease traveling through bodily deeds and through breaths, from deed to deed, as long as the prescription of the Law remains. When the period of prescription comes to an end, you will never cease traveling an essential journey in which you worship Him for His Essence, not by His command." (II 383.10)

The Shaykh often tells us that the gnostics can never be satisfied with any created things. Instead they follow the Prophet, who was told to pray, *My Lord, increase me in knowledge!* (20:114).[17] Like Muhammad, they constantly strive for increase. How is it then that the Koran can speak of mutual satisfaction and good-pleasure in the verse *God is well pleased with them and they are well pleased with Him* (5:119, 9:100, 58:22, 98:8)? The answer is that God bestows bounty upon the servants to the limit of their finite capacity, but this capacity never ceases undergoing transformation and renewal, ad infinitum.

> Through its essence the soul seeks much good, because the root is such. After all, God sought only the possible things, which are infinite, and there is nothing more than the infinite. But the infinite does not enter into *wujūd* at once. Rather, it enters little by little, without end.
>
> When the fact that the soul seeks much is ascribed to someone, and then he is pleased to

have of it the insignificant and the gradual, this is because he knows that the infinite cannot be gained in *wujūd,* so he is pleased with the measure of it that enters. Thus good-pleasure can only attach itself to the small amount. No created thing has a greater measure than its Creator. Given that good-pleasure is the attribute of the Real, it is even more appropriate for the servant.

What is at God is infinite, and the servant seeks from God what is at Him. But it is impossible for this to enter into *wujūd* save little by little, ad infinitum. So the servant is pleased with this measure, even though it is little relative to what he knows to be at God. So he is *well pleased with* the Real, and the Real is *well pleased with* him. (II 482.25)

Everything of good and blessing that the Real gives you in this world and in the last world is little in relation to what is at Him, for what is at Him has no end, but everything that you gain is finite through its being there in *wujūd.* The relation of the finite to the infinite is the smallest of the small, as Khaḍir said to Moses when the bird dipped its beak into the sea to drink of its water. He declared it similar to what they had of knowledge and to God's knowledge.[18]

Thus God says, *God is well pleased with them* for an insignificant deed, *and they are well pleased with Him* [5:119] for an insignificant reward, because the infinite cannot be gained in *wujūd,* since it has no end. Hence we say that good-pleasure attaches itself to the insignificant—it is to be pleased with the existent thing. The person is pleased with it from God, and with God for it.

God gave priority to His own good-pleasure with the servants for the insignificant deeds that He has prescribed for them and accepts from them only so that they will be pleased with the insignificant reward, for they know that at Him is more than what has reached them. It reaches them instant by instant in state after state forever and ever without being cut off, even though their deeds prescribed by the Shariah will be cut off.

Although their deeds will be cut off, their worship will not be cut off. When the limit of beautiful and ugly deeds comes to an end for the folk of the Garden and the folk of the Fire, their recompense remains—the recompense for worship among the felicitous and the recompense for servanthood among the folk of the Fire. This is a recompense that will never be cut off, for it is bestowed upon them by the all-embracingness and all-envelopment of mercy.

After all, the sinners will never cease witnessing their servanthood. Even if they claim lordliness, they know from what they find in themselves that they are liars. Hence making claims disappears with the disappearance of its appropriate moment, and the relation of servanthood that they had possessed both in the state of making claims and before making claims remains for them.

Then they will pluck the fruit of their words [at the Covenant of Alast], *Yes, [we bear witness]* [7:172]. They are like those who become Muslims again after apostasy. The authority of *Yes* rules over everything. It finally gives them felicity after the wretchedness that had touched them in the measure of what they did at the time of making claims. Hence the property of *Yes* never ceases to accompany them from its own moment ad infinitum, in this world, in the *barzakh,* and in the last world. (II 212.31)

From Chapter 198: The All-Merciful Breath

The most explicit Koranic references to *wujūd*'s never-ending self-disclosure are probably the verses that say that God's words will never run out. For the Shaykh, these are the words articulated in the Breath of the All-Merciful, ceaselessly uttered without repetition for all eternity. He explains this in the first of the fifty sections found in Chapter 198, "On the true knowledge of the Breath." He calls this section, "On God's mention of Himself by 'Breath of the All-Merciful.'" The word translated here as "mention," *dhikr,* I usually translate as "remember," or sometimes, as "formula of remembrance," when it refers to a divine name or Koranic verse that is mentioned repeatedly as a practice in the path to God. *Dhikr* is also the attribute of the Koran and other scriptures, and in this sense it is often translated as "reminder"—God mentions Himself so that human beings will remember Him and come to understand their own situation.

According to a hadith, which is sound on the basis of unveiling but not affirmed by way of transmission from God's Messenger, God said something whose meaning is this: "I was a Treasure but was not known, so I loved to be known. Then I created the creatures and made Myself known to them, so they came to know Me." Since He mentioned "love," we come to know something of love's reality and its concomitants that the lover finds in himself. We have already explained that love attaches itself only to a nonexistent thing whose *wujūd* is correct, but which is nonexistent in the state.[19]

The cosmos is a newly arrived thing, while "God was, and nothing was with Him." He knew the cosmos from His knowledge of Himself, so He made nothing manifest in engendered existence save what He is in Himself. It is as if He were nonmanifest and became manifest through the cosmos.

The Breath of the All-Merciful made the cosmos manifest so as to take away the property of love and to relieve what the Lover was finding. Thus He knew Himself by witnessing the manifest, and He mentioned Himself through what He made manifest—a mention through knowledge and cognition. This is the mention of the Cloud that is ascribed to the Lord before He created the creatures. It is the mention of the all-inclusive and the undifferentiated and the fact that all the words of the cosmos are undifferentiated within this All-Merciful Breath, though their differentiations are infinite.

It is from here that some people maintain that the body can be divided rationally ad infinitum, even though it has entered into *wujūd*. Everything that enters into *wujūd* is finite, but division has not entered into *wujūd*, so it is not qualified by finitude. They are those who deny the solitary substance, which is the indivisible part [i.e., the atom].

In the same way, although the Cloud is an existent thing, the differentiations of the forms of the cosmos in keeping with an order in this world and the last world are infinite in differentiation. This is because the All-Merciful Breath takes replenishment from the name Nonmanifest perpetually and mentions in undifferentiation perpetually. Thus the Breath in the cosmos is like Adam among mortal men.

Given that *He taught Adam the names, all of them* [2:31], He thereby let us know that the Cloud—in respect of the fact that it is an All-Merciful Breath receptive to the forms of the letters and words of the cosmos—carries *the names, all of them*. And *the words of God* do *not run out* [31:27]. Hence God's mentioning is never cut off. The All-Merciful mentions God by His names, and the All-Merciful is also named by them. So *to Him belong the most beautiful names* [17:110], and He mentions Himself in respect of being a speaker and a differentiator.

So the All-Merciful's mentioning is undifferentiated, but God's mentioning is differentiated. (II 399.31)

Chapter 524: God's Infinite Words

Ibn al-ʿArabī calls this chapter "On the true knowledge of the state of the Pole whose waystation is, *Say: If the sea were ink for the Words of my Lord, the sea would run out before the Words of my Lord run out, though We brought replenishment the like of it* [18:109]." Once things enter into *wujūd,* they are finite, yet *wujūd* continues to disclose itself to them forever. A key term in the chapter is *murūr,* "to pass." *Wujūd* passes over the entities for all eternity, so the entities are "infinite" in that they have no end. Nevertheless, they are finite in that they are confined by their own realities. In discussing infinity, the Shaykh refers to the paradoxes that arise when we come to understand that some infinities are greater than others, even though this is rationally impossible. Towards the end of the chapter, he reminds us what kind of "thing" is meant when, for example, God says *when you were not a thing* (19:9). The negation of thingness can only pertain to the thingness of *wujūd,* since all things remain things forever in fixity. Realities never change.

Were the oceans Our ink
  and the trees of the earth Our pens,
busy scratching on the Tablet
  while We made you listen to that,
The words of my Lord would not *run out*
    for it
  and the depths would be equal to the
    heights in splendor.

God says, *Though all the trees in the earth were pens, and the sea and seven seas after it supplied the ink, yet the words of God would not run out* [31:27]. God also says, *[Jesus was] His word that He cast to Mary, and a spirit from Him* [4:171]. God's "words" are nothing other than the forms of the possible things, and they are infinite. What is infinite does not run out, nor does *wujūd* restrict it. So in respect of its fixity it does not run out, for the storehouse of fixity does not allow for restriction. Its all-embracingness has no perceivable end. As often as you reach a furthest end for its all-embracingness in your imagination, it is beyond that furthest end.

From this storehouse the words of God become manifest in *wujūd* consecutively and successively, individuals after individuals, words on the trace of words. As often as the first of them becomes manifest, others follow through *wujūd*.

The *seas* and the *pens* are also among the words. So, *If the seas were ink* [18:109], with them would be written nothing but themselves, and the pens and the words already in *wujūd* would remain without anything with which to write, even though they are finite through their entrance into *wujūd*. So, what about the individual possible things that *wujūd* does not restrict? This is the property of the possible things, so what do you suppose about the objects of [God's] knowledge, of which the possible things are a part?

This is one of the most marvelous questions the part and the portion are judged to be equal to the whole in their infinitude, even though it is rationally understood that there is a ranking in degrees of greatness between the objects of knowledge and the possible things. Moreover, there is no individual object of knowledge or possible thing that does not continue to pass by ad infinitum. Nonetheless, some are posterior to those that are prior, so they fall short of those that are prior to them, and the prior ones are greater than they. But neither [the prior nor the posterior] is described by finitude in its continuing passage, so being greater and falling short both may occur in that which is infinite.

The Real does not have *wujūd* through passage that He might be qualified by finitude or infinitude, for He is the entity of *wujūd*. It is the existent thing that is qualified by [*wujūd*'s] passage over it. When passage over something continues without end, while it is finite in its own entity in respect of being an existent thing—because in its own entity it has a reality, through which it is distinct from everything that does not have this reality that makes it it, and this is nothing but the entity of its it-ness—this is the existent thing, and it is not described by finitude, but it is also not described as being infinite, because of its *wujūd*. So in respect of being finite, it is infinite.

The property of the newly arrived things in this is otherwise. No one knows what the newly arrived things are save he who knows what a rainbow is. The diversity of its colors is like the diversity of the forms of the newly arrived things. You know that no colored thing is there, nor any color, even though you witness it like that. So also is your witnessing of the forms of the newly arrived things in the *wujūd* of the Real, which is *wujūd*. Thus you say, "There is there what is not there."

After all, you cannot deny what you witness while you are witnessing it, just as you cannot be ignorant of what you know while you are knowing it. But, in this question, the object of knowledge is different from the object of witnessing. Eyesight says, "It is there," while insight says, "It is not there." Neither of them is lying in what it reports. So where are the *words of God* that do *not run out* [31:27]? For nothing is there but God. He who stands between witnessing and knowledge is bewildered, because he wavers between the two. But he who is devoted to one of the two is not bewildered and has retired with that to which he is devoted, whichever it may be.

The Real gives this and He gives that,
  so through Him take both this and that,
and when He gives some thing to you,
  hold not yourself back from it.
He who recognizes "this"
  will be a great imam,
But no one who says "this"
  can escape from saying "that."
Between the two appears what
  turns him far from this and that.
Some believe in this,
  some believe in that.
Just so you should know
  the truth of things—just so.

Wujūd is all letters, words, chapters, and verses. Hence it is the Great Koran, *to which the unreal comes not from before it nor from behind it* [41:42], so it is preserved in entity. It does not become qualified by nonexistence, because nonexistence is the negation of thingness, but thingness is intelligible both in *wujūd* and in fixity, and there is no third level.

When you hear negation of thingness, the negator is saying specifically that the thingness of fixity has no thingness of *wujūd*. For the thingness of *wujūd* does not negate the thingness of fixity. Hence, God's words, *when you were not a thing* [19:9], mean the thingness of *wujūd*, because He brought the word *were*, which is a vocable that demands *wujūd*. Thus He negated this *wujūd* with *not*. So also [is the meaning of the verse], *he was not a thing remembered* [76:1]. Remembrance is a *wujūd*. So know this! *And God speaks the* **ḥaqq**, *and He guides on the path* [33:4]. (IV 166.30)

The One Entity

Ibn al-ᶜArabī usually contrasts *wujūd* with the nonexistent, fixed entities. God alone has true *wujūd*, while the fixed entities acquire *wujūd* from God and can then be called "existent entities." Sometimes he uses the term *entity* to refer to *wujūd* itself, most often in the expression, *One Entity* (*ᶜayn wāḥida*). When he does so, typically he wants to contrast the oneness of *wujūd* with the manyness of the things, as in the sentence, "Although the cosmos is a multiplicity, it goes back to One Entity" (III 306.7).

Ibn al-ᶜArabī explains how the Entity can be one while the entities are many in numerous contexts. His basic point is that *wujūd* belongs only to the One Entity, or rather, that it is identical with the One Entity. "The essential definition of the *wujūd* entity is nothing other than that it is existent, because its *wujūd* is identical with its reality" (III 227.23). Hence the diversity of properties that appear in the cosmos pertains not to the oneness of the Entity but to the multiplicity of the things, which are nonexistent in themselves, but which exist inasmuch as God bestows *wujūd* upon them. "There is no actor but the creator of the act, and that is the Real. Creation is an activity, and within it activity becomes manifest" (III 169.11). From another standpoint, the entities can be considered forever nonexistent, and what becomes manifest is their traces and properties within the One Entity. In the first passage cited below, Ibn al-ᶜArabī mentions the phrase "one in *wujūd*" (*wāḥida fi'l-wujūd*), and thereby he comes about as close as he ever does to the expression *waḥdat al-wujūd*.

I and my peers see One Essence, not two essences, and the diversity is assigned to the relations and the points of view. The Entity is one in *wujūd*, but the relations pertain to nonexistence, and in them the diversity occurs. Hence the One Essence accepts two opposites in respect of two diverse relations. (III 566.9)

I said to Him who creates what He creates,
"What is it with You that nothing You create subsists?"
He said to me, "The locus
that I create is constricted in itself.
Otherwise, it would not accept engendering,
so be silent, the door is not locked.
The Entity is nothing but one perpetually.
Be not concerned—It is unbound.
I renew the engendering in itself
but the people are *uncertain* [50:15], so speak not!
Their eyesights are behind the veil of the likenesses,
so imagination has already reached them.
Smell the aroma of their accidental qualities,
for it is the musk whose fragrance lingers!
Consider Him who gives existence to their entities.
He is not 'other.' Realize this!
Everything whose building is seen
is suspended from a form in Our Essence.
Their spirits are the food of their bodies,
and their spirits eat of My fruit." (III 227.10)

Change and renewal are properties of created things. The One Entity does not change, but everything that appears from it experiences fluctuation and diversity. All change in the cosmos is attributable not to *wujūd* itself, but to the properties of the entities that become manifest through and in *wujūd*.

The highest divine relation there can be is that the Real be identical with the *wujūd* that the possible things acquire. Hence there is nothing but the *wujūd* of the Real's Entity, nothing else. The changes that become manifest in this Entity are the properties of the entities of the possible things. Were it not for the Entity, no property would become manifest, and were it not for the possible thing, no change would become manifest. (III 211.27)

Given that the properties of *wujūd* are the properties of God's own speech, the cosmos is the Great Koran. God's words in the cosmos have the same properties as His words in the scriptures. "The property of God's [Koranic] words is the property of God's creatures" (III 247.3). Like the creatures, His words are diverse in meaning, but in the end they signify One Entity. This explains, among other things, the diversity of religion and belief.

> The Real descends in His address to the understanding of those who are addressed. All of His address is *ḥaqq*, even if it is contradictory and even if contrariety becomes manifest within it. For there is One Entity that brings it all together. In the same way, white and black are contrary opposites brought together by color, and colors are diverse realities brought together by accidentality. (III 247.1)

The relation between the One Entity of *wujūd* and the many entities of the nonexistent things is replicated in the relation between the unities and multiplicities that are found in the cosmos. A human being, for example, is one entity made up of many entities. In respect of the manyness, diverse relations are established with other entities. In the same way, every "growing thing" (*nabāt*) is one entity with many diverse properties. This term is Koranic, and it is usually understood to refer to plants, but Ibn al-ʿArabī applies it to every living thing, as is done in Islamic cosmology in general. The Koran provides precedent for this usage in such verses as *God brought you out of the earth as growing things* (71:17) and *We made her [Mary] grow up as a beautiful growing thing* (3:37).

> There is no growing thing that is not a remedy and a malady. In other words, within it are found benefit and harm in keeping with the receptivity of bodily constitutions and their preparednesses. What harms one constitution is the same as what benefits another constitution. If this belonged to the entity itself, the property would not differ. It belongs rather to the receptacle. The receptacle is a growing thing, and the other is a growing thing. Hence the growing thing receives traces to its own harm or benefit only in itself in respect of its being a growing thing, even if its individuals are many and they are distinct through their individualities.
>
> Through this we call attention only to the entities of the individuals of the cosmos and the way in which some display traces in others. The entity is one in the essential definition, but many through the accidental forms. I have already informed you in more than one place who is the entity of the manifest cosmos and that He is unchanging in substance, and to whom belongs the property through which change becomes manifest in this entity. This is like the manifestation of change in the forms of a mirror due to the change in the guise of the viewer. Or it belongs to the changes in the selves of those things that disclose themselves, and the mirror is the locus for the manifestation of that to the eye of the viewer. So the Cloud, which is the Divine Breath, is the receptacle for these forms, all of them. (II 465.3)

Among the many analogies the Shaykh offers to illustrate the relation between the One Entity and the created things is the relation between Adam and his children.

> Consider the Prophet's words, "Your Lord is one, just as your father is one." Your father is none other than the one from whom you derive. If you know from whom you derive, you know your father. The Prophet did not mention that our parents are two, as has occurred in the manifest domain because we derive from Adam and Eve. This would have been like God's words, *He lifted his two parents onto the throne* [12:100].
>
> However, Eve is identical with Adam, because she is identical with his rib, so there is nothing but one father in two diverse forms, as in self-disclosure. So Eve is identical with Adam. Just as the right hand is separate from the left hand, but both are identical with Zayd, so also Eve is separate from Adam, but she is identical with him. Hence there is no second father, so we have proceeded from one only.
>
> In the same way, all the cosmos has proceeded only from One God. So the Entity is one, many in relations. Were the affair not of this sort, no *wujūd* would have become manifest to us, we would have no *wujūd* of entity, and we would not bring any property into existence.
>
> Just as He brought us into existence in entity, we brought the property into existence for Him, *as an appropriate recompense* [78:26]—if you understand. For us, He gives existence to an entity, and for Him, we give existence to a Lord.[20]

If not for the Real,
wujūd would not be,
and if not for engendered existence,
the God would not be.
This is a recompense
through which the Real desires
the questions of the questioners,
"Who?" and "What is He?"
"What is He" is for the commoners,
no doubt,
but among the elect,
He is and He is not. (III 503.6)

Ibn al-ʿArabī often remarks that the divine names are relations that are grasped as soon as we see that there is One Entity and many entities. In one respect, the names and attributes belong to the things, because they can only be conceptualized in terms of the limits that are assumed by *wujūd* in its self-revelation through the cosmos. Without the fixed entities, there would be no things and therefore no attributes by which they could be described. However, Muslim theologians were especially careful to ascribe all attributes that carried the slightest whiff of blameworthiness to the creatures. In contrast, the Shaykh is not embarrassed to ascribe every attribute to *wujūd*, because it is the sole root. And, as he remarks in typical fashion in the following, no one should refrain from doing so, because God Himself does not refrain. The passage is from Chapter 72, "On the hajj and its mysteries." He is in the process of explaining the significance of some of the rites of the *ʿumra*, the pilgrimage to Mecca outside the season of the hajj. Through these rites, the servant comes to embody the station wherein God makes him into a light, in keeping with the Prophet's supplication, "Make me into a light!" In other words, the Light of the heavens and the earth becomes his hearing and his eyesight.

If he is one whom God has made a light or for whom the Real is his hearing and his eyesight, then he will freely act where he freely acts only through a lordly attribute.

The divine attributes are of two sorts: divine attributes that require *tanzīh*, such as the Great and the High, and divine attributes that require *tashbīh*, such as the Self-Great, the Self-High, and everything by which the Real describes Himself and by which the servant is also qualified.

Those who make [attributes of the latter sort] a descent from the Real to us have made the root belong to the servant, but those who make this belong to the Real as a divine attribute whose relation to Him is not rationally understood because of our ignorance of Him [are saying] that through being qualified by the attributes, the servant is described by a lordly attribute in the state of his servanthood. Thus all the attributes of the servant concerning which we say that they do not require *tanzīh* are attributes of the Real, no one else. However, when the servant becomes clothed in them, the tongue of being worthy for the servant is applied to them, though the affair is otherwise.

This is what pleases the Realizers among the folk of our path. Nevertheless, I have never seen anyone state this plainly, realize it, or bring it out as I have done. But it is near to the understanding, if one is fair. It is as follows:

The servant does not deduce the attribute, nor does the Real describe Himself by it from the beginning. Rather, the Real describes Himself by it in accordance with what His messengers convey and what He unveils to His friends. We were knowing these attributes only as belonging to ourselves, not to Him, by virtue of rational proof. Then, when the shariahs come with that—and He had been, while we had not been—we come to know that these attributes belonged to Him by virtue of the root, and then their property permeated us from Him. Hence they belong to Him in reality, and to us metaphorically. For He was when we were not.

Thus the actual situation, in the manner in which we have cleared the way to it, is easy to grasp and near for the taking. Do not let it alarm you, for the Real speaks of it, and you are the listener.

If someone speaks against you on this, you should answer the protester as follows: "I did not say that—He said it about Himself. He knows better what He has ascribed to Himself. We have faith in it according to His knowledge of it."

This is the safest of beliefs. When the Real unveils the form of that relation to someone, he will have knowledge of it from God through tasting and drinking.

Were it not for this commingling, it would not be correct for human beings and animals to derive *from a sperm-drop, a mixing* [76:2].[21] He made everything manifest through everything and multiplied everything by everything.

So through Him we became manifest to Him and to us. In one respect we are through Him, but He is not through us, since He is the Manifest, and we remain with our own root, even if we bestow—through our preparedness in our entities—certain affairs that belong to our entities and even if we are named by names that the veiled person supposes are our names, such as Throne, Footstool, Intellect, Soul, nature, sphere, body, earth, heaven, water, air, fire, inanimate object, plant, animal, and jinn. All this belongs to One Entity, nothing else.

So glory be to the Highest who is singled out for the most beautiful names and the highest attributes! He knows who is most entitled to the attribute of the last and the first, for *He is the First and the Last and the Manifest and the Nonmanifest, and He has knowledge of everything* [57:3].

The human being is *a great wrongdoer* inasmuch as he usurps these attributes by ascribing them to himself in reality, and *very ignorant* [33:72] of Him to whom they belong and of the fact that they are a usurpation in his hand. If someone wants to eliminate the attribute of wrongdoing and ignorance from himself, let him give back the trust to its Owner and the usurped affair to its Owner.[22] The situation here is exceedingly easy. The common people suppose that it is difficult, but it is not so. (I 690.35)

If the Real is one entity with many properties, so also is the cosmos, created in His form. The philosophers asserted that "Nothing proceeds from the One but one." In the following passage, Ibn al-ᶜArabī understands this to mean that the one entity of the cosmos becomes manifest from the One Entity of *wujūd*. The converse of the maxim, "Nothing proceeds from the many but many," means that the many divine names give rise to universal multiplicity.

Since the entities in *wujūd* are joined with some entities and separate from others, God made this a mark for those who have no unveiling that the cosmos has a suprasensory joining with God in one respect and a separation from Him in another respect.

In respect of the reality of His Essence, His Divinity, and His activeness, God is joined/separate in a single respect. That respect is His Entity, for He does not become many, even if His properties, His names, and what is rationally understood from His names are many.

His "joinedness" [*ittiṣāl*] is the fact that He created us with His two hands—*What prevented you from prostrating yourself to him whom I created with My own two hands?* [38:75]. *We have created for them cattle from what Our hands worked, so they are their owners* [36:71].

His "separateness" [*infiṣāl*] is the separateness of Divinity from servitude.

There is no god but He, the Exalted in His separateness, *the Wise* [3:6] in His joinedness.

However, the cosmos engenders things only through His joinedness, not His separateness. The cosmos engenders the acts of worship that God prescribes for it. That is why He ascribes these deeds to the servant, and He commands him to seek help from God in that [1:4], just as the servant is a tool of the Real in certain acts. Tools help the artisan in that which cannot be made without tools.

The cosmos is separate from God in its definition and reality. Hence it is separate and joined in one entity. For it does not become many in its entity, even if its properties become many. These are nonexistent but known relations and attributions.

So the cosmos emerges in the form of the Real, for "Nothing proceeds from the One but one." This "one" is the entity of the possible thing. But manyness—I mean, the properties of the possible things—proceeds only from manyness, that is, from the properties ascribed to the Real and known as "the names and attributes."

Those who consider the cosmos in respect of its entity will speak of its unity, but those who consider it in respect of its properties and relations will speak of manyness in one entity. So also will be their consideration of the Real, for He is the One/Many, just as *Nothing is as His likeness, and He is the Seeing, the Hearing* [42:11]. What does *tanzīh* have to do with *tashbīh*? Yet the verse is one, and it is His speech about Himself for the sake of instructing us about what He is in His Essence, so He separated through *Nothing is* and He affirmed through *He is.*

As for His calling to the cosmos and the cosmos's calling to Him, this is in respect of the separateness. He calls, "O people!," and we call, "Our Lord!" Thus He separated Himself from us, just as we separate ourselves from Him, so we become distinct.

What does this station have to do with the station of joinedness when He loves us and is our hearing, our eyesight, and all our faculties? He assigned that when He reported that the lover is joined with the beloved. He ascribed love to Him, and we are the objects of love. There is no hiding the difference between the properties and waystation of the lover and those of the beloved. Thus we are lifted up through Him, and He descends through us. This is so that *wujūd* will not be equal, for equality is impossible within it. Within it there is no escape from descent and uplifting, and there is nothing but us and Him. When the property of one is descent, the property of the other is uplifting and highness. Every lover descends, and every beloved is high. And none of us there is but lover and beloved, so *None of us there is but has a known station* [37:164], so none of us there is but descending/high. These are diverse properties in One Entity.

"O you with faith, be wary!"
"Our Lord, of what should we be wary?"
He called, and I called, asking,
but I did not know who has gone, and who remains.
He assigned my property to His judgment—
either *wretched* or *felicitous* [11:105].
He is pleased or wrathful in His judgment,
and He gives wretchedness and felicity when we are wary.
So which is the crown and which His foot?
Which the shoes and which the topknot?
In this and that His likeness appears
that the servants may meet what they meet.
Since what I have said is so,
the servants know of what they should be wary. (III 324.35)

From Chapter 360: The Ninth Deputyship

Human beings possess every attribute that they possess only inasmuch as they are God's vicegerents (*khalīfa*). In effect, God has entrusted certain affairs to human beings, and they are expected to act accordingly. Having entrusted these affairs to people, God then asks them to entrust their affairs to Him. The Koran commands people to take God as their Trustee (*wakīl*) and it repeatedly calls upon them to have trust (*tawakkul*) in Him. In the Shaykh's way of looking at things, trusteeship is circular (*dawrī*), since God takes people as His trustees by making them His vicegerents, and they take Him as their Trustee by observing His commands. Hence this discussion of "trust in God," presented largely in moral terms in the Koran, is rooted in an ontological issue—the intimate interrelationship between the One Entity and the many things and, more particularly, the peculiar human role in the cosmos that allows people to reach perfection. This topic of human perfection is perhaps more central to Ibn al-ʿArabī's cosmology than any other, but, in effect, everything else needs to be explained before its role becomes completely clear, because only perfect human beings bring together the Real and creation in a grand synthesis. Nevertheless, the topic constantly crops up and cannot be ignored. A passage from Chapter 360, which the Shaykh calls "On the true knowledge of the waystation of the praiseworthy darknesses and the witnessed lights," can serve to illustrate how human perfection is connected with the One Entity. Among the praiseworthy darknesses that the Shaykh discusses are the perfect human beings, who are the shadows of God. In explaining this, he has in view the verse, *At Him are the keys to the absent—none knows them but He* (6:59).

Know that God made the human being appear from the darkness of the absent domain within which he was—and he is the first among the keys to the absent that *none knows but He*. God alone has knowledge of these keys, and He negated their knowledge from everything other than He. Thus, through this verse, He affirms you and lets you know that you are not He. Were you He, as you suppose, you would know the keys to the absent through your essence. When you know something only through a standpoint, you are not identical with the standpoint.

All possible things—and by the word *all* I distinguish them from the impossible and the necessary, not that *all* restricts their entities, since that would be impossible—are in the darkness of the absent domain, so no state of *wujūd* is known for them. Each of these possible things has a key that none knows but God, for there is no existence-giver but God. *He is the creator of each thing* [6:109], that is, its existence-giver.

The first key through which opening occurs is the key to the absent domain of the perfect human being, who is the shadow of God in everything other than God. (III 279.14)

The Shaykh continues the discussion of the perfect human being by explaining that, from a certain point of view, the infinite possible things can be divided into ten things, which are Aristotle's ten categories (*al-maqūlāt al-ʿashr*).[23] These ten are all found in the perfect human being, who is the all-comprehensive engendered thing, "singled out for the all-inclusiveness of the All-Merciful Breath" (III 279.34). As God's vicegerent, the perfect human being substitutes for the Real in creation. From the standpoint of the station of praiseworthy darknesses, he has ten deputyships (*niyāba*), one for each category. In explaining the ninth deputyship, the Shaykh cites in witness the Koranic verse that commands people to take God as their trustee. He begins by referring to the fact that the perfect human being is God's "likeness" (*mithl*), created in His form.

The ninth deputyship is manifestation in the intelligible *barzakh* between the two likenesses, a *barzakh* that is the separation between the Real and the perfect human being. This separation necessitates the distinction of the Real from creation, so that the one who is more deserving is gazed upon.

If we strike likenesses, the perfect human being's site is that of the shadow within the person from whom an extended shadow extends. The shadow that abides through him—between the person and the extended shadow that is separate from him—is the *barzakh*, and it cleaves more to the standing person, so he has more of a right to it.

Creation is distinguished from the Real through the Real; the Real is not distinguished from creation through creation. After all, creation is clothed in the descriptions of the Real; the Real is not clothed with creation. So creation becomes manifest through the Real; the Real does not become manifest through creation, since the Real is always manifest to Himself. Hence He does not become qualified by poverty toward anything in His manifestation, but creation becomes qualified by poverty toward the Real for its manifestation to its entity in its entity.

Here by "creation" we mean the human being who has the attribute of being His likeness, none other, for this separation occurs between two likenesses. Separation has the property of the two likenesses, without doubt, because the separation stands counter to each likeness through its own essence. Were it not for the separation, the likeness would not have become distinct from its likeness.

Your being a likeness of Him is His words, *Expend of that in which He has made you vicegerents* [57:7]; His words, *It is He who appointed you vicegerents in the earth and has lifted some of you above others in degrees* [6:165]; [*He has lifted some of them above others in degrees*], *that some of them may take others in subjection* [43:32] through the bestowal of the perfection of humanity—the [divine] form—on some of them. They are the ones whom God has lifted up. Those above whom they have been lifted are the animal human beings.

His being a likeness of you is that He has made Himself your trustee in that which is your *ḥaqq*. Hence He acts freely in it on your behalf in accordance with the absolute, authorized, circular trusteeship. For the trusteeship of the Real cannot escape being circular, as a solicitude by God toward His servants. This is because God created the servant as a companion of heedless moments and forgetfulness. Heedlessness and forgetfulness are states that overtake the human configuration, and states have a property in absolutely everything qualified by *wujūd*. I do not exclude any existent thing.[24]

When a human being is heedless in one of his movements and acts freely in it through his own self, this free acting by himself dismisses the Real from trusteeship. But since the trusteeship is circular, whenever he dismisses the Real from it through free activity, He takes charge of the affair, so none has free activity save God. After all, He has commanded you to take Him as a trustee in Sūrat al-Muzammal. This is the benefit of the circular trusteeship, and it derives from His command to His servant. He made it pertain to *tawḥīd*, for He says, *Lord of the east and the west, there is no god but He, so take Him as a trustee* [73:9]. Here there is an allusion to free activity in the directions, of which He mentioned only *the east*, which is the manifest domain, and *the west*, which is the nonmanifest domain.

The one entity, which is the sun when it rises, gives new arrival to the name *east* [i.e., "rising place," *mashriq*], and when it sets, it gives new arrival to the name *west* [i.e., "setting place," *maghrib*]. The human being has a manifest and a nonmanifest domain. *There is no god but He, so take Him as a trustee* in your manifest domain and your nonmanifest domain, for He is *Lord of the east and the west.* So consider how marvelous is the Koran!

All the deputyships that I have mentioned and will mention are deputyships of *tawḥīd*, nothing else. If you become manifest, the manifest is nothing but He. If you do not become manifest, then He is He, since the One does not become divided in Itself except through ruling property and relation. He possesses many names, so He possesses relations and properties. His unity through us is the unity of manyness, but the Entity is one. This is why the manifestation is sometimes ascribed to us and sometimes to Him; it is correlated with Him in one property and with us in another property.

Thus it has been clarified for you that the human being abides in exactly what the Real abides, between a manifest and a nonmanifest. When either of the two is manifest, the other is nonmanifest. The manifest has the deputyship for what is nonmanifest, and the nonmanifest has the deputyship for what is manifest in that within which it is nonmanifest.

Hence the property of vicegerency and trusteeship—which is a vicegerency and a deputyship—never ceases to be perpetual and endless in this world and the last world. After all, the Real *Each day*—the "days" being the breaths—*is upon some task* [55:29] in which you have made Him your trustee, since for your sake He acts freely and for your sake He takes control of that in which He has taken you as vicegerent. Hence you act freely by command of your trustee, so you are the vicegerent of your vicegerent, just as He is the King of the Kingdom through trusteeship.

This is *wujūd*'s exact situation. There is no difference between me and the people in this in actual fact except that I know and they do not know. This is because of the coverings that are on the eye of their insight and the shelters over their hearts and the locks upon them. (III 286.32)

From Chapter 198: The Twenty-First Tawḥīd

We have already quoted from this chapter, "On the true knowledge of the Breath." In its ninth section, Ibn al-ʿArabī investigates the thirty-six Koranic verses that employ the formula of *tawḥīd* in its various permutations, such as "There is no god but God," "There is no god but He," or "There is no god but I." In the Shaykh's view, each of these verses brings out a different implication of *tawḥīd.* The twenty-first instance is found in the verse, *Then high exalted is God, the King, the Real! There is no god but He, the Lord of the noble Throne* (23:116). In explaining the significance of this verse, he shows the clear correlation between the Breath of the All-Merciful, also called "the Real Through Which Creation Occurs," and the One Entity. He compares the All-Merciful Breath to wood from which all things are shaped. Despite the diversity of the forms, they are one in their woodenness. By mentioning "two sides and a middle," he is referring to the three basic worlds of the cosmos—spirits, bodies, and the world of images between the two. Through the differentiation of these worlds, things become diverse in their levels.

This is the *tawḥīd* of the Real, which is the *tawḥīd* of the He-ness. God says, *We created not the heavens and the earth and all that between them is, in play* [21:116]. This is the same in meaning as His words, *What, do you think that We created you only for sport?* [23:115]. So *There is no god but He* is a description of the Real.

The affair within which the *wujūd* of the cosmos has become manifest is the Real. It has become manifest only in the Breath of the All-Merciful, which is the Cloud. So the Real, *the Lord of the Throne* [23:116], gave the Throne its all-encompassing shape, because *He encompasses everything* [4:126]. Hence the root within which the forms of the cosmos become manifest *encompasses everything* in the world of corporeal bodies. This is nothing other than the Real Through Which Creation Occurs. It is as if, because of this reception [of all forms], this Real is like a container from which appears the *wujūd* of everything it encloses, layer out from layer, entity after entity, in a wise order. It makes what had been absent within it appear, so as to witness it.

God declares the unity [of the Real Through Which Creation Occurs] despite the fact that it proceeds from Him. People are bewildered because it pluralizes Him, for there is nothing but He. Although He declares its unity, yet its entity is seen not to be He, for He gave existence to two sides and a middle so that the entities would become distinct within the One

Entity. Hence the forms became plural, but the woodenness did not become plural. The woodenness remained in its own reality in every form without splitting, yet this form is not the same as that form, and there is nothing added to the woodenness, so it is said, "There is nothing there." So God says, *We created not heaven and earth and what between them is, for the unreal* [38:27]. *We created the two of them only through the Real* [44:39].

It is said, "So, where is He?" The reply is given, "In the distinction itself, for I am not able to deny the distinction, and I am not able to affirm other than One Entity, for *There is no god but He, the Lord of the Noble Throne* [23:116]." (II 415.18)

Bewilderment in the Many and the One

When Ibn al-ʿArabī embarks on long and dry disquisitions in the manner of the masters of the Islamic rational sciences, it is easy to forget that unveiling is the source of his knowledge. But he frequently reminds us why he is so confident that, as just quoted, "There is no difference between me and the people in this in actual fact except that I know and they do not know" (III 287.23). The word here for "know" is the same word employed in the saying, "He who knows himself knows his Lord." From it we have *al-ʿārifūn,* those who truly know, a word I translate as "gnostics" (not, of course, to allude to a heretical sect of the past, but to suggest that there is something special about the knowledge). The gnostics are those who know through unveiling and witnessing, not rational investigation.[25] In the rest of this chapter, I provide a few examples of explicit references to the gnostic vision of the One Entity's self-disclosure.

Chapter 507: Shame

One of the important technical terms of the Islamic sciences is *ḥadd,* which means, among others, edge, border, boundary, borderline, terminus. As often as possible and in the present discussion, I translate it as "limit." In jurisprudence, the term is applied both to a legal ruling or statute, which defines the limits of right and wrong activity, and to the penalty that is meted out for transgressing the limits. The same term is used in the intellectual sciences to mean "definition," that is, a statement that establishes the limits of a thing's identity for the rational mind. In Chapter 507, "On the true knowledge of the state of the Pole whose waystation is *Does he not know that God sees?* [96:14]," the Shaykh explains that limits are established precisely by *wujūd*'s self-disclosure, which can do nothing but bind, confine, limit, and constrict. This specific verse is one of the constant invocations of the Folk of God, whom Ibn al-ʿArabī often identifies with the "Folk of the Remembrance" mentioned in the Koran: *So ask the Folk of the Remembrance if you do not know* (16:43 and 21:7). He finds a reference to them in the *ḥadīth qudsī,* "I am the sitting companion [*jalīs*] of him who remembers Me." "Remembrance" (*dhikr*), as already mentioned, is one of the names that the Koran gives to itself, and it is the most general term for the means whereby the faithful are expected to return to God. As a specific practice, remembrance is the mention of a name or names of God, often embedded in standard formulae such as "There is no god but God."

Do you *not know*
that from us
God sees us, and that
wujūd witnesses us?
We should have shame,
lest He see us
in what He has forbidden,
while we have borne witness to Him.
For me, this is one
of the most wondrous of things—
He commands us, but
He does what He desires [2:253].
He says to me, *Go straight* [11:112]
and He desires from me
an opposition
that *wujūd* confirms.
O my people, hear what I say
concerning Him,
for He is the Patron,
and we are His servants.

He desires the command,
  not what is commanded, so consider
    a ruling that whitens
      the hair of a youth![26]

The Messenger of God said, "Have shame before God as is the *ḥaqq* of shame." God says, *Does he not know that God sees?*, and He instructed thereby His servants only because the folk of rational consideration disagree over the two paths—that He sees us, and that we see Him.

In any case, from this instruction, the faithful know that God sees them. God instructed them only so that they would cling to shame toward Him in the transgression of His limits.

When someone remembers God with this formula of remembrance, God discloses Himself to him in this abode just as He disclosed Himself to the mountain of Moses. However, He does not make him crumble to dust. The occasion of this is his persistence in this remembrance, for it bequeaths the servant strength. This strength derives from the fact that he who remembers never ceases remembering God, and "God is the sitting companion of him who remembers Him," even if he is unaware of Him.

The first thing that God opens up to everyone who remembers Him in his own self is true knowledge of Him who remembers God through him, so the rememberer of God sees nothing from Him save by the He-ness of the Real. Then he remembers Him in his hearing in the same way. He witnesses that no one hears the remembrance of God from him save God. Once he sees himself as all Real, the self-disclosure that occurred to Moses' mountain and to Moses occurs to him, but he does not crumble to dust or become thunderstruck. Even if he undergoes annihilation, it is the beauty of the object of witnessing that annihilates him, for "God is beautiful and He loves beauty." Inescapably, God drapes the servant's nonmanifest domain with beauty, since He discloses Himself to him only out of love for the specific beauty that becomes bound through him and manifest within him and that cannot become manifest save in this specific locus.

Every locus has a beauty that is specific to it and belongs to nothing else. God gazes upon the cosmos only after beautifying and proportioning it so that it will receive what He brings to it in His self-disclosure in the measure of the beauty of its preparedness. The self-disclosure drapes it in beauty upon beauty, so it remains forever in a new beauty in each self-disclosure, just as in itself it remains forever in a new creation. So transmutation belongs to it perpetually in its nonmanifest and manifest domains—whenever God unveils for someone the covering of his blindness from his insight.

Know also that limits have been established in the cosmos. I mean the limits of the Shariah that the Real has commanded us not to transgress, and the limits that He has set down in the Shariah to be enacted against us when we do transgress them. All this is so that we may recognize that the affair is all limit—in us and in Him, in this world and the last world. For distinction occurs through limits, and knowledge comes to be through distinction. Were it not for the separating factor, no entity would become distinct from any other entity, and there would be no knowledge of anything whatsoever.

But He has become distinct for us, through us, and from us, just as we have become distinct for Him, through Him, and from Him. So we have come to know who we are and who He is. If a state overcomes us, that state says with its own tongue [in the words of al-Ḥallāj],

I am the one I love,
  and the one I love is I.

It is sufficient for him, in respect to the strength of the trace of the limits, to differentiate between "I" and "the one I love," even if he loves himself. Thus his state of loving, while he is the actor, is not the same as his state of being loved, while he is the one acted upon. Thus the limits have clarified the states, just as they clarify the entities.

This is a knowledge that expression does not reach in the unity of the Entity. The unity of the state cannot be declared; in no way is this possible. Concerning knowledge of God, the best way to convey the affair and the greatest in unity is to say that the *wujūd* of the cosmos is identical with the *wujūd* of the Real, nothing else. But the diversity of both the forms of the cosmos and the divine names is known. This clear diversity has no meaning other than the knowledge that, were it not for the limits, there would be no distinction. Although *wujūd* is one entity—that is, the Real *Wujūd*—the existent things and the intelligible things are diverse.

"God has cursed," on the tongue of His Messenger, "those who alter the boundary marks of the earth," which are the limits. This is because, when mutual similarity is extremely obscured, it throws into bewilderment, and the limits are hidden within it. After all, the individuals of a single last species are mutually similar through limit, and distinct through the individual. There is no escape from a separating factor in mutually similar things through the limit. It is sufficient for you that you make it a likeness, not the same entity.

The limit accompanies everything in knowledge
and delimitation accompanies the limit in consideration. (IV 145.27)

Chapter 542: Blindness

Ibn al-ʿArabī calls this chapter "On the true knowledge of the state of the Pole whose waystation is *Whosoever is blind in this world shall be blind in the last world and more misguided on a path* [17:72]." Koran commentators typically understand the term *ḍalāl*—translated here as "misguidance"—as something blameworthy, but it is a synonym for *ḥayra* (bewilderment), so the Shaykh recognizes that it can also have a praiseworthy sense. He begins this chapter by pointing out that blindness can be a good thing as well as a bad thing. Having explained that even the person who follows right guidance is bewildered, the Shaykh then needs to explain how it is that the Prophet and his followers can call people to God, as indicated in the verse, *Say: "This is my way. I call to God upon insight—I and whoever follows me"* (12:108). In fact, they are not calling to knowledge, but to the felicity that is assured through nearness to God.

The chapter begins with a reference to and then citation of Koran 22:46, which is usually understood to mean, *It is not the eyesights that are blind, but blind are the hearts in the breasts.* The word translated as "breasts," *ṣudūr*, is the plural of *ṣadr*. However, the same word can also be a gerund, in which case it means "to proceed," or "to come forth." In this case, the second clause of the verse would be translated, *But blind are the hearts in the coming forth.* In other words, the hearts are not blind, except when they come forth to see God. The Shaykh plays with the double meaning in the poetry, then refers explicitly to the "two senses" of the word in the first paragraph.

Blind only *are* those *hearts*
in the coming forth
that are enclosed
by *the breasts.*
This judgment concerns
the hearts from which
affairs come forth
after they have arrived.
He who comes forth from Him
through Him is not blind—
How can he be blind who possesses
manifestation itself?

God says, *But blind are the hearts in the* ***ṣudūr*** [22:46] in two senses. One of the senses refers to restriction and the other to the return [to Him].

Know that blindness is a bewilderment, and the greatest blindness is bewilderment in knowledge of God.

Knowledge of God has two paths. One path is reflective consideration. When the companions of this path achieve fully the *ḥaqq* of consideration, they never leave bewilderment before death, for they have no proof that does not have against it a misgiving and an obfuscation, because of the all-embracingness of the world of imagination. The reflective faculty has no free activity save in the imaginal Presence, either through what this faculty has acquired from the sensory faculties, or through what has been given form by the form-giving faculty. When a companion of this consideration *is blind*, that is, bewildered, *in this world*, and he dies—and human beings die only as they have lived, and this one has lived only in bewilderment—then he will bring that bewilderment along with him *in the last world*. When unveiling occurs for him there, his bewilderment will increase, because of the diversity of the forms that come over him. So he is *more misguided* than he was in this world, because in this world he had hoped that, if things were unveiled to him, bewilderment would leave him.

As for the second path in knowledge of God, it is knowledge from self-disclosure. The Real does not disclose Himself in a form twice, so the companion of this knowledge is bewildered in God because of the diversity of self-disclosure's forms that come over him, just like the bewilderment of the first person in the last world. What the former has in the last world, the latter has in this world.

As for the *insight* [12:108] and the *clear sign* [11:17] possessed by the one who calls to God, that is only in that to which he calls, which is the path to felicity, not the path to knowledge. After all, even when he calls to knowledge, he is calling only to bewilderment *upon insight* that there is nothing but bewilderment in God. For the actual situation is magnificent, and He to whom he calls does not accept restriction and cannot be tied down, so there is nothing of Him at hand. He is nothing but what you see in each self-disclosure.

The perfect one is he who sees the diversity of self-disclosures in the One Entity, which is like a chameleon. He who does not know God as he knows the chameleon has not become settled in affirming the Entity.

The knowledge of the last world has been hastened to the companions of self-disclosure. Hence they are *blind* in this world *and more misguided on a path* than the companions of consideration, for there is nothing to be sought in knowledge of God beyond self-disclosure, and nothing to be conceived of. This allusion is sufficient for those who are intelligent. *And God speaks the **ḥaqq**, and He guides on the path* [33:4]. (IV 185.29)

Chapter 391: The Quick-Flowing Course

The bewilderment of the Folk of God arises from the puzzle of the relation between the One Entity and the diverse cosmic entities. No final explanation of this relation can be given, since the Essence from which the entities and relations arise is unknowable in Itself. The gnostics look upon the things and describe the situation as they see it. Their descriptions are diverse, yet each is correct. Typically the Shaykh enumerates two, or sometimes three, fundamental perspectives on *wujūd* and the entities. In Chapter 391, "On the true knowledge of the mutual waystation of the quick flowing course, in which the feet of the inquiring Men do not become firm," he offers two basic views.

I saw the Real in the entities, in truth,
and in the names, so I did not see Him
apart from myself.
I make not this judgment by myself—
that is His judgment in every viewer.
For those who affirm otherwise,
He is the viewer and we are His mirrors.

God says, *You did not slay them, but God slew them* [8:17]. He also says, *Slay them wherever you find them* [4:89]. Thus He makes manifest a commander, a command, and someone commanded in this prescriptive address. When the command is observed and slaying becomes manifest as an act among the entities of the newly arrived things, He says, "It is not you who have slain them. On the contrary, I have slain them. You are to Us as a sword is to you, or any instrument that is used for slaying. The slaying occurs for the slain through the instrument, but no one says that the instrument was the slayer. On the contrary, it is said that the one who struck the blow is the slayer. So also, the one who strikes the blow is in relation to Us like the sword in relation to him."

It is not said concerning him for whom the Shariah is prescribed that he is the slayer. Rather, God is the slayer through him and through the sword. The one for whom prescription is made stands in the station of the hand that strikes with the sword. In the same way, the Black Stone is the right hand of God in swearing allegiance through kissing it and touching it, as in greeting between two individuals.

The exposition of this mutual waystation is the true knowledge of those affairs that necessitate properties. Do these affairs have entities of *wujūd*, or are they relations demanded by the properties so that they become intelligible through their properties?

There remains knowledge of the locus within which these properties become manifest. What is it? Is it the entity of the possible thing, while the relations belong to the Preponderator? That would be like His words, *You did not slay them, but God slew them* [8:17] and His words, *God created you and what you do* [37:96]. Or is the locus the *wujūd* of the Real, while the properties are the trace of the possible things in the *wujūd* of the Real? Then this trace is the forms that become manifest within Him. Each form witnesses a form, and the forms are the traces of the possible things in the *wujūd* of the Real. Thus Zayd sees the form of Khālid in a *wujūd* of the Real, and Khālid sees the form of Zayd in a *wujūd* of the Real. So also every state in which the form is seen is exactly like the form.

Each of these two affairs has been the view of a group of the Folk of God. In whatever manner someone may hold the two views, he will not be able to stay firm in one affair. That through which he affirms the judgment for one affair is exactly the same as that through which he affirms it for the other and negates it from the first. Thus he negates the former and affirms the latter. It makes no difference which of the two affairs he begins with—the judgment will be the same in both views.

This is like God's words, *You did not throw,* so He negated, *when you threw,* so He affirmed the throwing in him from whom He negated it. But then He did not stay firm in the affirmation. On the contrary, He followed the affirmation with a negation, just as He followed the negation with an affirmation, for He said, *but God threw* [8:17]. So how quickly He negated and how quickly He affirmed for one entity!

This is why this mutual waystation is called the "quick-flowing course"—because of its similarity with the flow of water that does not become firm in anything in its course, except in the measure that it passes over it. Hence the feet of the Men are not firm in anything in its entity, because this is what the station bestows. This is the same as God's words, *Each day He is upon some task* [55:29]. The length of the day is the solitary time.

So also are His words, *Be not as those who say, "We hear," but they hear not* [8:21], even though they hear. Consider this blaming—how similar it is to the furthest limit of praise bestowed on the one whose hearing and eyesight are the Real! When the Real is someone's hearing, he necessarily hears, for he does not hear except through his Lord. So he hears not through himself. But it is not correct for him to be a locus for the He-ness of his Lord, so his entity is the *wujūd* of the Real, and the property belongs to the possible thing, for that is its trace.

If God had known of any good in them, He would have made them hear [8:23], and *wujūd* is the good, so they would have been qualified by *wujūd*. *And if He had made them hear* when He gave them existence, *they would have turned away* [8:23] toward their own essences and they would have known that they had not heard. God alluded to this as *swerving aside* [8:23], since it is the Real who hears, and they are to Him as ears are to us—instruments through which we hear the sounds of those who make sounds and the speech of speakers. Hence He addresses and is addressed; He is the listening speaker.

O you who have faith, that is, who have acknowledged the truthfulness of what We say, *respond to God and to the Messenger when He calls you* [8:24]. Note that He made the caller one after mentioning two. Thus we come to know that the actual situation is one. We hear no speaker but the Messenger with sensory hearing, but we hear the speech of the Real through the hearing of the Real with suprasensory hearing. Thus *God* and *the Messenger* are two names for the Speaker, for the speech belongs to God, as God says. But the witnessed speaker is identical with the tongue of Muhammad. *Whosoever obeys the Messenger has thereby obeyed God* [4:80].

My entity is nothing but He,
 so I do not refuse Him.
Whoever witnesses with the eye
 of *wujūd* witnesses Him.
In Him we are equal—
 as He sees me, I see Him.

Thus have I mentioned the main point of this chapter with brief sufficiency. *And God speaks the **ḥaqq**, and He guides on the path* [33:4]. (III 549.20)

Chapter 430: Bewilderment in Arrival

The folk of self-disclosure see God as He discloses Himself within the limits of the created things. Inasmuch as they know the self-disclosure for what it is, the limits serve to increase them in the bewilderment that is one of the highest stages of knowledge. The Shaykh explains this in a chapter called "On the true knowledge of the mutual waystation of 'Your bewilderment will allow you to arrive at Me.'"

Whoever is bewildered arrives,
 whoever is guided stays apart.
This is a fixed description
 of Him who is exalted and majestic.
It is a description gained
 by a servant who has understood.
When a young man says that
 he is guided, he is heedless.
You will see him putting on airs
 in jewelry and raiments—
as the proverb puts it—
 displaying his private parts.

The proverb is the Prophet's words, "Many a well-dressed woman is naked."

God says, *God would not misguide a people after He had guided them, until He makes clear to them that toward which they should be godwary* [9:115]. Apropos of bewilderment He says, *God created you and what you do* [37:96]; *You did not throw when you threw* [8:17]. In the same way, *You did not slay them, but God slew them* [8:17], though slaying is witnessed only from created things. Thus He negated something concerning which there is self-evident knowledge in the sensory domain.

In this mutual waystation God's Messenger said, "I count not Thy laudations before Thee." This is the station of the exaltation of bewilderment. [He continued by saying] "Thou art as Thou hast lauded Thyself." This is the state of arrival.

In this mutual waystation al-Ṣiddīq said, "The incapacity to attain perception is itself perception." Thus he was bewildered, so he arrived.

Arrival at bewilderment in the Real is itself arrival at God. Bewilderment is the most magnificent thing that belongs to the folk of self-disclosure, because the forms are diverse for them in the One Entity. The limits are diverse because of the diversity of the forms, but limit does not apply to the Entity. The Entity is not witnessed, just as It is not known. Those who stop with the limits that follow upon the forms are bewildered, but those who know that there is an Entity that fluctuates through forms in the eyes of the viewers but not in Itself know that there is an Unknown Essence that is not known and not witnessed.

From this you grasp that the knowers of God are four sorts: One sort has no knowledge of God save by way of reflective consideration. It is they who speak of negation.

Another sort has no knowledge of God save by way of self-disclosure. It is they who speak of affirmation and limits.

For the third sort knowledge of God arrives newly between witnessing and consideration. Hence they do not remain with the forms in the self-disclosure, nor do they arrive at the knowledge of the Essence that is manifest to the eyes of the viewers through these forms.

The fourth sort is not one of these three, nor is it outside them altogether. It is they who know that God receives every belief, whatever the belief may be. This sort is divided into two sorts. One sort says that the Entity of the Real is He who discloses Himself in the forms of the possible things. The other sort says that the properties of the possible things are the forms manifest in the entity of the Real *Wujūd*.

Each of these sorts speaks of the situation as it is. From here bewilderment is configured in the bewildered, and it is identical with guidance in everyone who is bewildered. He who halts with bewilderment is bewildered, but he who halts with the fact that bewilderment is guidance arrives. *And God speaks the **ḥaqq**, and He guides on the path* [33:4]. (IV 42.34)

From Chapter 369: Annihilation and Subsistence

Ibn al-ʿArabī devotes the seventeenth subchapter of this chapter, which deals with the keys to the storehouses of munificence, to a saying by one of the early Sufis to the effect that annihilation (*fanāʾ*) is "the annihilation of him who was not," whereas subsistence (*baqāʾ*) is "the subsistence of Him who has always been." In the process, he describes again two basic perspectives on *wujūd* and the entities, and he mentions an analogy as a third view.

One of the masters said concerning this storehouse that it comprises the annihilation of him who was not and the subsistence of Him who has always been.

This is an issue in which become agitated those whose unveiling has not been consolidated and whose witnessing has not reached realization. After all, sometimes a flash of the object of people's seeking lights up for them, and they remain satisfied with it short of the full achievement and consummation of the state. Then they judge this station through what they have witnessed of it, with either the conjecture or the certitude that they have achieved it fully.

I have seen some of the Men with this attribute. Something of this sort overtook Sahl ibn ʿAbdallāh al-Tustarī—who was outstanding in this task—in the knowledge of the *barzakh*. A glimmer passed over him, and he came to encompass in knowledge the situation of the people in the *barzakh*. But he did not halt so as to see if its folk underwent any change into diverse states in what he saw, or if they continued on in one state. Hence he judged that they subsist in a single state, as he saw them. So his vision was sound and truthful, but his judgment that they would stay permanently as he saw them until the day of the Uprising was not sound.

As for those whom I have seen who are the folk of this attribute, I saw that when they are taken from themselves, they return quickly and do not remain fixed. I asked one of them, "What is it that brings you back so quickly?"

He said to me, "I fear that my entity will become nonexistent through what I see."[27]

Thus he feared for himself. Those who have this state will not possess a firm footing in the realization of any affair and they will not be among the firmly rooted in it. If they were to confine themselves to what they view eye-to-eye and refrain from making judgments, that would be more appropriate for them.

When the outsider hears the like of this from a truthful person, and he hears that things are not fixed in a single state in the *barzakh,* then he imagines that the Tribe disagree among themselves in the like of this. But this is not a disagreement. He who is firmly rooted upholds what he witnesses, and that is his extent in knowledge. He who is not firmly rooted also upholds what he witnesses, but he adds to what he maintains the judgment that things stay fixed. Had he stood in the station for a while, he would have seen the change and alteration in the *barzakh,* just as occurs in this world, for *each day*—which is the solitary time—God is *upon some task.* He says, *All those in the heavens and the earth ask of Him; each day He is upon some task* [55:29].

Creation is new wherever it may be—in this world, in the last world, and in the *barzakh.* Hence it is impossible for a state to subsist in an entity for two breaths or two times, because of the divine all-embracingness and the subsistence of the cosmos's poverty toward God. Hence change is necessary for it in each breath, and God is Creator within it in each breath. States are renewed for the entities breath by breath, and the property of the entities, in keeping with their realities, bestows within the One Entity that, were it correct for the entities to have *wujūd,* it would be through these states.

Among our companions, some see that the Entity of *wujūd* is that for which the states of the possible, fixed entities are preserved. They have no *wujūd* whatsoever—on the contrary, they have fixity and properties in the Manifest Entity, which is the True *Wujūd.*

Others among our companions see that the entities become qualified by *wujūd* and by its acquisition from the Real. The entities are one through substance, even if they become many. The Real drapes them with states breath by breath, since they have no subsistence except through the states. Hence the Real renews the states in the entities at each time.

The words "the annihilation of him who was not" accord with the first view. No trace of him remains in the entity of *wujūd.* Hence he is stripped of descriptions. This is the state of *tanzīh.*

He "who has always been" subsists as He is in His Entity, and He is the *Independent of the worlds* [3:97]. The cosmos is nothing but the possible things, and He is independent of their signifying Him, since there is nothing—as we have said—seeking to be signified. After all, the possible things in their fixed entities are witnessed by the Real, and the Real is witnessed by the possible entities through their fixed—not existent—eyes and eyesight. Hence He witnesses them as fixity, and they witness Him as *wujūd.*

According to the other view—which sees the *wujūd* of the entities of the possible things, the traces of the divine names within them, and the Real's replenishing them through those traces so that they may subsist—the traces and the entities that receive them are annihilated for the companion of this witnessing in his state. But the situation in itself exists as it was. In itself, nothing is annihilated—it is annihilated for the one who holds this view. Hence no object of witnessing subsists for him save God, and the existent things are enwrapped in the *wujūd* of the Real and become absent from the gaze of the companion of this station. In the same way, the entities of the stars become absent from the gazer with the rising of the greatest lamp, which is the sun. Then he holds that their entities have been annihilated from *wujūd,* but in actual fact they have not been annihilated. On the contrary, they are in their state of possibility in their spheres, according to their properties and their courses. Both these views have been known from the Tribe.

Some of the companions of this station make creation's situation with the Real like that of the moon with the sun in respect to the light that becomes manifest in the moon. The moon has no light in respect of its essence, nor is the sun or the light of the sun within it. However, eyesight perceives it like that. So the light that is in the moon is nothing other than the sun. So also is the *wujūd* that belongs to the possible things. It is nothing other than the *wujūd* of the Real, like a form in a mirror. The sun is not in the moon, but the light that the moon deploys upon the earth at night when the sun's light is absent is not other than the sun's light, though it is ascribed to the moon. In the same way, it is said concerning the Speech of God, *It is the words of a noble messenger* [69:40]. And it is said concerning the words of the Messenger when he recites that Speech—and the words of every reciter of the Koran—"It is the speech of God."

Each of these doctrines has a correct sense, and unveiling may occur in everything we have mentioned. So, for the Folk of God, disagreement is agreement, because they shoot from a single bow.

The affair goes back and forth between the annihilation of an entity and the annihilation of a state. Nothing in the cosmos brings together the opposites save the Folk of God specifically, because He whom they have realized is He who brings together opposites, and through Him the gnostics know. For *He is the First and the Last and the Manifest and the Nonmanifest* [57:3] in respect of One Entity and one relation, not in respect of two diverse relations. Hence they have departed from what is rationally understood, and rational faculties do not bind them. Rather, they are the divine ones, the Realizers. The Real has given them realization in what He has given them to witness, so they are and they are not. *You did not throw when you threw, but God threw* [8:17], so He affirmed and He negated. *God is sufficient for us* [3:173] and enough.

In this task, Shaykh Abu'l-ᶜAbbās ibn al-ᶜArīf al-Ṣanhājī was the imam. He used to say, "The Real becomes clear when the tracing dissolves."[28]

Shaykh Abū Madyan used to say, "There is no escape from the subsistence of the tracings of servanthood so that taking pleasure in the witnessing of Lordship may occur."[29]

Al-Qāsim ibn al-Qāsim, one of the shaykhs of al-Qushayrī's *Risāla*, used to say, "The witnessing of the Real is an annihilation within which there is no pleasure."[30]

Each of these speakers has spoken the truth. After all, I have already explained in this book that no two individuals will ever come together in one self-disclosure and that the Real never repeats self-disclosure to an individual in one form. We have already said that His self-disclosures are diverse, because they include all suprasensory, spiritual, angelic, natural, and elemental forms. Thus, in whatever form He wills, He becomes manifest, just as *in whatever form He wills He mounted you* [82:8], and, in the path, *in whatever form He wills*, He gives you a station. The mounts are diverse, but the rider is one.

When He discloses Himself to someone in suprasensory forms, he will maintain that the tracings are annihilated. When He discloses Himself to someone in natural and elemental forms, he will maintain that he takes pleasure in the witnessing. When someone maintains that there is no pleasure in the witnessing, then to him the self-disclosure was in spiritual forms. All are truthful and speak of what they have witnessed. But which witnessing is highest? In this I put your own tasting in charge so that you may know from it what I know.

From this subchapter you will come to know the separate, the non-separate, who separates, and who does not separate. From it you will know who is *upon a clear sign from his Lord* [11:17] and what a clear sign is. You will know the varieties of purity for everything described by purity. You will know the praiseworthy inclination and the blameworthy inclination. You will know what is shared in the religion and what is abrogated, such that no two messengers come together in it. You will know which of the created things is created from an existent thing and which is created not from an existent thing, and the levels of the cosmos in this. You will know that whenever the Real seeks that the creatures interact with Him through something, He interacts with them through it. This includes each and every ruling of the Shariah. He has made it the ruling property of Himself, just as He has made it rule over His creatures. And [you will know] that the noble character traits in the engendered things are the divine character traits. (III 395.20)

Chapter 473: Your God is One God

In this chapter, "On the state of the Pole whose waystation is *And your God is one God* [2:163]," Ibn al-ᶜArabī brings out some of the implications of the gnostic's bewilderment. It is passages like this, in which Ibn al-ᶜArabī allows bewilderment to touch even the doctrine of *tawḥīd*, that his critics would cite when they wanted to call his Islamic affiliation into question. He begins by pointing out that those who associate others with God—the cardinal sin of *shirk*—do so on a sound basis, as the Koran makes clear. Note that he reads the verse, *Thy Lord has decreed that you worship none but Him* (17:23), not as a prescriptive command, but rather as an engendering command. In other words, God has decreed that this be the actual situation, so it is impossible to worship others.[31] Nevertheless, reaching felicity depends upon worshiping God in the manner that He has commanded. The associators have not gone astray by associating others with God, because in fact there are no others, but rather by disobeying God's prescriptive command to perform specific acts of worship.

One group upholds
the *tawḥīd* of the God,
but the *tawḥīd* of the many
is *wujūd*.
From His most beautiful names
we come to know
that God *does*
what He desires [2:253].
Through us He is the God,
and in Him we are we.
He is the Patron,
and we are His servants.

Know—God confirm us and you with a spirit from Him—that God has commanded us to assert His *tawḥīd* in His divinity, for there is no god but He, just as He has forbidden us to reflect upon His Essence. The folk of consideration among those who supposed that they were the Folk of God disobeyed Him in that. Such, for example, were the ancients and others among the Kalām authorities, and some of the Sufis, like Abū Ḥāmid [al-Ghazālī] and others. Abū Ḥāmid did that in his *Maḍnūn* and other works.[32] They argued for affairs that went against them, not for them. After going to great lengths in their consideration, they confessed their incapacity. If there had been rightful and truthful knowledge and faith, that would have happened at the first step.

Thus they transgressed God's limits, which are the greatest of limits, and they made that transgression a means of nearness to Him. They did not know that it was identical with distance from Him. When the covering is unveiled, He who bestows and he to whom bestowal is made will become manifest.

You will see, when the dust clears,
if beneath you is a horse or a donkey.

The form is the form of a horse, but the experience is of a donkey.

This formula of remembrance bestows upon the rememberer a magnificent hope and *a clear opening* [48:1]. This is because, in this verse, God addresses both the Muslims and those who worship other than God as a means of nearness to God, so they worship none but God. When they say, *We only worship them that they should bring us nigh in nearness to God* [39:3], they confirm this and they mention the cause.

God says to us, *And your god* and the god to whom the associator seeks nearness by worshiping those that he has associated with Him are one, just as if you did not disagree on His unity. He says, *And your god,* thereby bringing us and them together through the plural, *is one god.* They associated others with Him only because of Him, according to what their consideration gave them.

When someone is intended for the sake of something else, in reality the other thing is the intended object, not that which appears to be the intended. Thus it is said that when someone becomes your companion or loves you for the sake of something else, he will turn away when the thing is achieved. That is why God mentions that they disown their associates on the day of resurrection.[33]

God takes them to task only because they [associated others with Him] from themselves, not that they were ignorant of God's measure in that. Do you not see how the Real, when He comes to know this from them, says, *And your god is one god*? He admonishes them, for He says, *[They ascribe associates to God.] Say: Name them!* [13:33], so they mention them by their names, which are different from the names of God. Then He describes them by saying that, in giving Him associates, they have *been misguided with a far* and clear *misguidance* [4:116], for they have thrown themselves into bewilderment because they have *worshiped* what they have *carved* [37:95] with their own hands, while they know that it *neither hears nor sees, nor avails* them *anything* [19:42] with God. This is God's witnessing as to the inadequacy of their consideration and their rational faculties.

Then God reported to us that He *has decreed that* we *worship none but Him* [17:23] because of the divinity that they have ascribed to the associates. In other words, they have made them like God's deputies and viziers, as if God had appointed them vicegerents. When someone is a vicegerent, it is the habit of the one over whom he is given vicegerency to see him in the level of the one who has appointed him. This explains why they ascribed divinity to the associates at the outset, without considering Him who appointed them.

Those who say, *What, has he made the gods one God?* [38:5], say so only because they believe, concerning the ones they worship, that they are *gods apart from God* [37:86], God to whom they bore witness as possessing magnificence over all. Hence these words are similar to what has been affirmed in the sound Shariah concerning the diversity of forms in self-disclosure. It is known to those who witness this that one form is not the same as another form, but the witnesser of each form has no escape from saying that it is God. However, since this is from God, while in other cases it is from themselves, He denied that they have ruling control in that, as is affirmed in His words, *Wherever you turn, there is the face of God* [2:115]. This is a reality. So God's face is found in any direction toward which anyone turns. Nevertheless, if a person turns toward other than the Kaabah in his *ṣalāt*, while he knows the direction of the Kaabah, his *ṣalāt* will not be accepted, because God has set down as Shariah for him only facing this specific house through this specific worship. If he turns [away from the Kaabah] in other than this specific worship—which is correct only through the designation of this specific direction—then God will accept that turning. In the same way, if he believed that the face of God is not in every direction toward which he turns, then he would be an unbeliever or ignorant. Nevertheless, it is not permissible for him to transgress the deeds that God has set down in the Shariah.

This explains why shariahs are diverse. What is forbidden in one shariah is permitted by God in another shariah. He has abrogated the first ruling about something through another ruling about exactly the same thing. God says, *To each of you We have appointed a shariah and a way* [5:48].

When something is abrogated from a shariah and then someone follows it after its abrogation, this is called "the soul's caprice." Concerning it, God says to His vicegerent David, *We have placed thee in the earth as a vicegerent, so judge among people through the* ***ḥaqq,*** that is, the *ḥaqq* that I have sent down upon you, *and follow not caprice,* that is, whatever disagrees with your shariah, *lest it misguide you from the path of God* [38:26], that is, the shariah that God has set down for you specifically.

Once you have come to know this and it has become settled for you, you will know that God is one God in entity in every shariah, but He is many in form and in engendered existence, for rational proofs make Him many through their diversity concerning Him; all of them are *ḥaqq,* and what they prove is truth. Self-disclosure in forms also makes Him many through the diversity of the forms, but the Entity is one.

Since this is the situation, what should you do? How is it correct for me to consider a speaker mistaken? This is why no one can be mistaken concerning Him. The mistake occurs only in affirming the other, that is, in professing an associate. This is to profess nonexistence, because there is no associate. This is why God does not "forgive" the associate—forgiveness is [literally] curtaining, and no one is curtained save that which has *wujūd.* But the associate is a nonexistence, so it is not curtained, for it is a word of realization that *God does not forgive that He be given an associate* [4:48], since He does not find it. Were He to find it, it would be correct [for Him to forgive], and forgiveness would have an entity to which it could be attached.

There is nothing in *wujūd* that receives opposites except the cosmos in respect of the fact that it is one. The opposites become manifest in this one, and they are nothing but the properties of the entities of the possible things in the entity of *wujūd.* Through the manifestation of these properties, you will know the opposing divine names and their likes. When you come to know this, then say whatever you wish—either that the manyness of the names makes manifest the manyness of the properties, or that the manyness of the properties makes manifest the manyness of the names. This is an affair that is denied neither by reason nor by the Shariah, for *wujūd* gives witness to it.

There remains only what we mentioned: To whom should the property be attributed? To the divine names or to the engendered possible things? The two are intertied and judged to have properties in One Entity.

What a loss for the ignorant!
Look at what escapes them,
and look at what escapes
those who call them ignorant!
I said this, then that,
and because of what
I said about them,
I am one of them!

He who declares God's Unity has not been fair, and he who gives Him an associate is not correct. He is One, but not through the *tawḥīd* that people voice, nor through His *tawḥīd* of Himself, since He is One in Himself. His Unity is not assigned to Him, nor is the unity of His manyness unknown.

There is nothing but a nonexistence and a *wujūd*. The *wujūd* belongs to Him, but the nonexistence does not belong to Him. However, to Him belongs making nonexistent. It is not said that nonexistence belongs to what is other than He, for then you would be affirming what you negate and using metaphorical language.

Between *wujūd* and nonexistence is that which is qualified neither by *wujūd* nor nonexistence, that is, the cosmos. It gives properties to the entity of *wujūd*, forms to the eye of witnessing, and things proved by the proofs of the knottings. So there is *a witnesser and a witnessed* [85:3], a knotter and a knotted, an existence-giver and an existent thing. There is nothing lost.

Thereby have the limits become distinct, or rather, I have distinguished every limited thing. And there is nothing but a limited thing for those who know nonexistence and *wujūd*. *And God speaks the* **ḥaqq***, and He guides on the path* [33:4]. (IV 106.9)

From Chapter 72: Trotting around the Kaabah

When pilgrims first reach Mecca, they often perform "the circumambulation of arrival," which involves circling seven times around the House of God. They walk the first circuit, then move at a quicker pace for the second, between a walk and a run, then walk the third, and so on. Four of the circuits are made walking and three trotting. In explaining the significance of these circumambulations, Ibn al-ʿArabī is led to compare the One Entity and the many things to a moving spark that appears as a single line.

According to one view, the circumambulation of arrival is a sunnah, so an animal sacrifice is incumbent upon anyone who does not perform it. Another view holds that it is an act of merit, so not performing it does not make anything incumbent.

"Trotting" is to move speedily in the good itself to the good, so it is a good in a good. This is because of the wisdom of hastening to perceive the knowledge of the divine command, for God says, *Our command is but one, like a glance of the eyesight* [54:50]. After all, nothing is speedier than eyesight, for the time of an eye's glance is the time of its connection to its object, no matter what the distance. The most distant things in sensation are the fixed stars, which are in the sphere of the waystations. When you look at them, the glance attaches itself to them. This is the speed of sensation, so what do you think about the speed of the penetration of meanings that are disengaged from binding? Speed has a ruling property in things that is possessed by nothing else.

From here you will come to know the Real's word to the thing, *"Be!," so it comes to be* [16:40]. The state of the divine *Be* is [identical with] the state of the engendered, created thing. The grammatical particle that best expresses this quickness is the *so* of outcome, so He brought it as the response to the command.

If you desire to know the form of the configuring and manifestation of the cosmos, the speed of the penetration of the divine command within it, and what of this is perceived by eyesight and insight, look at what arrives newly in the air from the speed of a spark of fire's movement in its mover's hand when he makes it turn. In the eye of the viewer, the speed causes the new arrival of a circle, or a straight line if the mover takes it straight with the movement, or whatever shape he wills. You do not doubt that you have seen a circle of fire, but you do not doubt that no circle is there and what has configured it in your view is the speed of the movement. This is His words, *Our command*, which is His word "Be," *is but one*, as is the spark, *like a glance of the eyesight* [54:50], which is the perception of the circle, though it is not a circle.

This is the same as the created form that is manifest to the eye's perception. You judge, in respect of your looking with your eyesight, your insight, and your reflection, that it is a creation; but through your knowledge and your unveiling, you judge that it is a Real Through Which Creation Occurs. Nothing becomes manifest to your eye that is not He. So this is a nonexistence within the entity of a *wujūd*.

Consider how subtle is this perception, even though sensation is a locus for its manifestation, with all its binding, density, and inadequacy. What do you think about the actual situation in relation to the side of the Real? So glory be to Him who speaks to Himself through Himself in the entities of His creation, just as He has said: *Grant him sanctuary until he hears the speech of God* [9:6]. "God says on the tongue of His servant, 'God hears him who praises Him.'" He is the speaker and the one who says, *There is no god but He, the Exalted, the Wise* [3:6].

Realize, my brother, your looking at the speed of lightning when it flashes, for the flashing of the lightning when it flashes is the occasion of the air's becoming colored by it. The air's becoming colored by it is the occasion of the manifestation of the entities of the sensory things through it. The manifestation of the entities of the sensory things through it is the occasion of the connection of eyesight's perception to it. In all this the time is one, even though you understand rationally the priority of each occasion over what it occasions. So the time of the lighting up of the lightning is the same as the time of the air's becoming colored by it, which is the same as the time of the manifestation of the sensory things through it, which is the same as the time of eyesight's perception of what becomes manifest through it. So glory be to Him who strikes likenesses and sets up semblances so that the speaker may say, "There is, and there is not," or "There is not, and there is"!

By the exaltation of Him who possesses exaltation, majesty, and greatness, there is nothing but God, the Necessary in *wujūd*, the One through His Essence, the Many through His names and His properties, the Powerful over the impossible—so what about possibility and the possible thing, since these two derive from His ruling property? So, by God, it is nothing but God, for from Him *and to Him the whole affair is returned* [11:123].

This is why the Lawgiver set down as a sunnah trotting three times—no more and no less. The first is for Him, the third for what becomes manifest, and the second—between the first and the third—is the occasion of the manifestation of what becomes manifest from Him. There is no escape from this.

When you realize what you have seen, you will see that there is what you have not seen.

Reason's perception of intelligible affairs emerges in this form, as threefold. These are the premises that are compounded of three to yield the conclusion that is sought.[34] Sensation is similar—sensation, the sensory object, and the attachment of sensation to the sensory object. It is not known if sensation attaches itself to the object, or if the object is imprinted in sensation.

Reason is inadequate—by God—reflection recedes, imagination is bewildered, and understanding is effaced. The affair is magnificent and the matter grave, the Shariah descending and reason receiving, the command penetrating and events newly arriving, the faculties abiding and the scales set up, and the *words [. . .] not running out* [18:109] and the engendered things not being taken away. But there is nothing there, despite the plurality of what is known—given that the Entity is one, and the command is one.

Bewilderment is bewildered with itself, because it finds no one through whom to be bewildered. The bewilderment by which the cosmos is imagined to be described is not as you imagine. Rather, that is the bewilderment of bewilderment, for there is nothing but He and bewilderment. Tongues, by God, are too weak to express what hearts know, and hearts, by God, are too weak to understand the actual situation. They do not know if they are bewildered or not. Bewilderment exists, but no locus is known within which it abides. For whom does it exist and in whom does its property become manifest? For there is none but God.

There is none but God,
none other than He—
There is no "there,"
for the Entity is one.
This is why we say that the essences,
though not there,
prostrate themselves to God
through God. (I 702.17)

3. *The Face of God*

Viewed in terms of *tashbīh,* the cosmos is the locus of God's self-disclosure. In other words, God is present in the world such that, in the last analysis, the world is God's presence. Among the many Koranic proof texts that the Shaykh cites to support this idea is the verse, *He is with you wherever you are* (57:4). More important are the several Koranic mentions of God's face (*wajh*), in particular *Wherever you turn, there is the face of God* (2:115) and *Each thing is perishing except His face* (28:88). Closely connected to the face is the veil (*ḥijāb*), which keeps the face hidden.

The Face

The Arabic-English dictionaries provide several meanings for the word *wajh.* Besides face, it can mean, among others, front, facade, surface, exterior, look(s), guise, side, direction, intention, purpose, goal, objective, course, method, means, sense, significance, purport, outset, aspect, viewpoint. The basic meaning—face—is relatively concrete, while the other meanings indicate the various relatively abstract senses in which the term may be used. Ibn al-ʿArabī prefers the literal sense, but when he does explain the term's figurative meaning, he understands it as a synonym for *dhāt* (essence) and *ḥaqīqa* (reality), both of which can be equivalents for the word *nafs* or self. On the human level, identifying a person's "face" with the person's self, essence, or reality follows upon the fact that for the observer, human identity lies primarily in the face. A headless body has no immediately recognizable identity, in contrast to a bodiless head. The face is the physical side of the person that the observer identifies most intimately with the person. Hence the face of a person, on the concrete level, expresses most clearly the person's self and reality.

A thing is known only through its face, that is, its reality. Everything without which a thing cannot be known is its face. (I 83.29)

The face is the most eminent thing in the manifest domain of the human being, because it is the Presence of all the nonmanifest and manifest faculties. The "face" of anything is its essence.

The Messenger of God passed by a man who was beating the face of his slaveboy. The Messenger of God said, "Beware of the face, for God created Adam in His form." The face is the locus of turning toward God, apart from the other directions. It is the most magnificent direction. (II 684.2)

God says concerning the folk of felicity, *Faces on that day shall be radiant, gazing upon their Lord* [75:22–23]. Then He says concerning the folk of wretchedness, by way of parallelism, *and faces on that day shall be scowling, thinking that a calamity will be worked upon them* [75:24–25]. Here the "faces" are the human selves, because the face of a thing is its reality, its essence, and its entity. The faces bound by eyesight are not meant, because they are not qualified by thoughts, and the general tenor of the verse tells us that here the faces are the essences of those who are mentioned. (II 266.27)

God says, *They encompass nothing of His knowledge save such as He wills* [2:255]. God has made clear to you in this verse that He gives knowledge to reason and others only such as He wills and that this is why He says, *And faces are humbled* [20:111], right after His words, *They encompass Him not in knowledge* [20:110]. In other words, when they recognize that *they encompass Him not in knowledge,* they become meek and abased, and from Him they seek increase in knowledge of that about which they have no knowledge. The "faces" here are the entities of the essences, or the realities of the existent things, since the face of anything is its essence.

God created everything of the cosmos that He created only in its perfection in itself. This perfection is its face. God says, *He gave each thing its creation,* so He has perfected it, *then guided*

[20:50]. So He has also given guidance—which here is clarification—its creation. Thus He clarified the affair to His servants in the most perfect of its faces, according to both reason and the Shariah. He was not obscure, nor did He employ tokens or riddles. *It is only a remembrance and a clear Koran* [36:69], *that thou mayest make clear to the people what was sent down to them* [16:44]. (II 671.32)

If the face of a thing is its reality, God's face cannot be known, since God's reality is His Essence, and God's Essence lies beyond human knowledge. It follows that, although *Wherever you turn, there is the face of God* (2:115), the divine face that we find and recognize is not the reality that is the Essence, but the reality that is God's self-disclosure. It is God inasmuch as He displays Himself to us, the God that we know and we worship, the "god of belief."[1] Ibn al-ᶜArabī refers to this while discussing the divine name Form-Giver (*muṣawwir*). As a human attribute, the word *muṣawwir* is commonly used to mean "painter," which helps explain the Shaykh's remarks in the second paragraph, in which he refers to the Shariah's prohibition of depicting living things.

Among people, the "form-giver" is he who goes about creating a creation like God's creation. Though he is not a creator, he is a creator, for God says, *When you create from clay as the guise of a bird* [5:110]. Thus He named Jesus a "creator," but he had nothing save the guise of a bird. The "guise" is its form.

Whenever a form receives the manifestation of sensory life, God has blamed and threatened the "form-giver," because he does not perfect its configuration, since part of the perfection of its configuration is the manifestation of its life to sensation, but he has no power over that. This is different from his giving form to that which does not possess the manifestation of sensory life, like plants, minerals, the form of the spheres, and diverse shapes.

The "form" is nothing but the entity of the shape, and "form-giving" is nothing but taking shape in the mind.

Know also that since "God created Adam in His form," we come to know here that the *form* modified by the pronoun *His*, which goes back to God, is the form of the belief concerning God that the human being creates in himself through his consideration or his fantasy and imagination. He says, "This is my Lord," and then worships Him, for God has given him the faculty of form-giving.

This is why God created the human being as bringing together all the realities of the cosmos. In whatever form he may believe in his Lord and worship Him, he does not emerge from the form that he himself possesses in respect of bringing together the realities of the cosmos. Inescapably, his humanity will assume form in the Real to perfection, or something of his humanity [will assume form].

If he asserts His *tanzīh*, he has hardly asserted His *tanzīh*. The furthest limit of those who assert His *tanzīh* is limitation. He who limits his Creator has made Him stand in a limit like himself. This is why God undid his binding for him on the tongue of His Messenger—"Worship God as if you see Him." He placed in this seeing the *as if* of *tashbīh* and declaring likeness. The Prophet said to him, "God is in the kiblah of the person who performs the *ṣalāt*." God says, *Wherever you turn, there is the face of God* [2:115], and the face of a thing is its essence and its reality. Hence, in whatever form God makes His servant stand, that is a site toward which he turns, so within it is the face of God—if you understand. Thus the Real has affirmed for you what your reason negates with its proofs. And the Real is more worthy of being followed.

So the human being configures a form within himself that he worships. He is the form-giver, and he is the created, configured thing that God configured as a servant who worships what he configures. (IV 212.29)

Perishment

In the context of the discussion of *wujūd* and the fixed entities, the most important Koranic verse concerning the face is 28:88, which the Shaykh reads in two basic ways, depending on the lesson he wishes to draw. If he understands the word *face* to mean God's face, then he reads it as *Each thing is perishing except His face*, which is to say that God alone has *wujūd*, and all things dwell in nonexistence, or that *wujūd*'s self-disclosure never ceases, and every existent entity constantly perishes, only to be given *wujūd* in the next instant through the next self-disclosure.

More commonly, the Shaykh reads the verse as *Each thing is perishing except its face.* Grammatically, this reading is more appropriate than the first, given that a pronoun should refer back to the nearest noun. Hence the pronoun translated as *its,* which is third person masculine in Arabic, should go back to the nearest masculine noun, which is *thing.* Then the verse can mean that all things in the manifest universe perish, but their faces, which are their realities—that is, their fixed entities known to God—never perish.

Within the Cloud, God gave existence to all the forms of the cosmos. Concerning them He said that each of them *is perishing,* that is, in respect of its forms, *except its face* [28:88], that is, except in respect of its reality, for that is not perishing. The *its* in "its face" goes back to *thing.* Hence, *each thing*—that is, all the forms of the cosmos—*is perishing,* but not the things' realities. Hence each thing is not perishing and cannot possibly perish.

An approximate image of this is as follows: When the form of the human being has perished and no trace of him remains in *wujūd,* his reality has not perished. This reality is distinguished by his limit, which is his own definition. Thus we say, "The human being is a rationally speaking animal." We do not remark upon whether he is existent or nonexistent, for this reality does not disappear from him, even if he has no form in *wujūd.* After all, the object of knowledge does not disappear from knowledge, since knowledge is the container of the objects of knowledge. (III 420.7)

Know that the realities are not qualified by perishment, and the "face" of a thing is its reality. The only things that are qualified by perishment are affairs that are accidental to realities through the relation of some of them to others. The reality of these accidental affairs is that they should be accidents, so their face does not perish from being accidents.

When something is qualified by an accidental relation and then this relation disappears from it when it gains another relation, the disappearance of this accidental relation is named "perishment," and the locus to which the accident was related is named "perishing" through this disappearance.

There are nothing but realities, so there are nothing but non-perishing faces. And there are nothing but relations, so there is nothing but what perishes.

Consider as you wish, and speak in keeping with your own consideration.

This is why the "face" has been specified for the impossibility of qualification by perishment—the reality does not perish. (II 100.9)

A Mystery
Emergence from Congruence
through Setting up Layers

The states of the creatures
are the same as the tasks of the Real.
Among their states are their entities,
so among their tasks are their engendered qualities.
Why is it that you have no faith in what you see
when you *know that God sees* [96:14]?
He sees you in the state of your nonexistence
and the fixity of your eternity.
You belong to yourself, and He to Himself.
You are not with Him like His full moon with His sun,
but you are with Him.
Thus He calls attention to this with His words, *Each thing is perishing.*
Reflect upon what He is saying to you—
you will know who perishes.
Does anything of the full moon perish but its light? Not its entity,
for its essence and engendered existence subsist.
The place of falling into obfuscation
is in His words, *except its face.*
The moon possessed light, then became dark,
and the things became curtained when it put on its wrap.
He said, while knowing the report,
The moon is eclipsed [75:8],
but the entity of the moon is manifest in the two eclipses
and disclosing itself in the two *wujūds.*
So the servant is the manifest,
and He is the loci of manifestation. (IV 390.33)

Ibn al-ʿArabī devotes the fourth section of Chapter 369, "On the true knowledge of the waystation of the keys to the storehouses of munificence," to the issue of God's independence. He tells us that one of the things that people should know through tasting is the difference between that through which they are independent and that from which they have no independence. The discussion focuses mainly on human poverty toward God and the exalted station of servanthood. The last third of the section provides a commentary on the face that does not perish.

There is nothing in suprasensory, sensory, and imaginal *wujūd* save a *ḥaqq,* for everything comes into *wujūd* from a *ḥaqq,* and the Real brings nothing into *wujūd* but the *ḥaqq.* That is why the Prophet said in his supplication, addressing his Lord, "The good, all of it, is in Thy hands, but the evil does not go back to Thee."

Evil is the opposite of good, but nothing proceeds from the good save the good. Evil is only the nonexistence of good. Hence, the good, all of it, is *wujūd,* but evil, all of it, is nonexistence. After all, evil is the manifestation of that which has no entity in reality. Hence it is a property, and properties are relations. I say "manifestation" only because this is [a meaning of *sharr* ("evil") in] Arabic lexicography. [The poet] Imru'l-Qays says, "Were they to make my murder *sharr,*" that is, manifest.[2]

This is why the Real says concerning Himself, *He knows the mystery,* which is the concealing of that which has an entity, *and the more hidden* [20:7], which is making manifest that which has no entity so that people imagine it is real. But God knows that it has no *wujūd* in entity despite the property itself. Hence *He knows the mystery and the more hidden,* that is, what is more manifest in hiddenness than the mystery. In a similar way He says, *[God is not ashamed to strike a likeness of] a gnat, or aught above it* [2:26], that is, above it in tininess. So also, the *more hidden* is more manifest in hiddenness than the mystery. Moreover, the "hidden" may be the "manifest," as has been related in lexicography.[3]

God says, confirming what we have mentioned, *Each thing is perishing except His face* [28:88]. Hence no existent thing that we witness through sensation and know through reason is perishing, because everything is His face, and the face of a thing is its reality. There is nothing in *wujūd* but God, so there is nothing in *wujūd* but the good, even if the forms undergo variation. After all, the Messenger of God has reported to us that the divine self-disclosure undergoes variation, and God has reported to us that *Each day He is upon some task* [55:29], employing the indefinite. This is nothing but the diversity of what He is busy with, so everything that becomes manifest is nothing but He, and it becomes manifest to Him. Nothing witnesses Him and no "other" makes Him many.

This is why He says [in the continuation of the verse of perishment], *To Him belongs the ruling property and to Him you shall be returned* [28:88]. In other words, some people believe that We have made *Each thing* to be *perishing* and they do not know what We have intended. When they see that the thing does not perish and they witness the subsistence of its entity in this world and the last world, they will come to know what We mean by the "perishing thing" and that each thing that is not qualified by perishment is My face. They will know that the things are not other than My face, for the things do not perish. Hence they will restore them to their ruling property. This is the meaning of His words, *To Him you shall be returned.*

This is a subtle meaning that is hidden from those who have not had the Koran rooted in their memory.[4]

Since the "independent" is the one that has this attribute, and "independence" is this attribute, "There is none independent but God," and independence is His attribute. But we are speaking only of the servant, not of the Real.

The servant has an absolute poverty toward his Master, and the Real has absolute independence from the cosmos. Hence the cosmos never ceases being lost in entity and perishing in essence in the Presence of its possibility. Through its properties, the Real becomes manifest to Himself inasmuch as He gazes in respect of the reality of another possible property. Hence the cosmos, through its essence, replenishes the existent things that become manifest in engendered existence, and these are nothing but the Real, none other.

So realize this subchapter, my friend, for it is a marvelous subchapter! Its property is creation in a *ḥaqq* through a *ḥaqq,* while there is no creation in the entity itself, despite the *wujūd* of the ruling property and the Real's reception of creation's ruling property. This is *wujūd*'s reception of the ruling property of nonexistence. Nothing but this can be. Were this not the case, no entity would become manifest for manyness, but there is nothing but manyness, despite the unity of the Entity. There is no escape from the manifestation of the properties of the many, and it is nothing but the cosmos, for it is the many, the plural, while the Real is One in Entity, not many.

Thus have I thrown you onto the path so that you may know what the situation is. Thereby you will know who you are and who the Real is so that the Real may be distinguished from the servant. (III 373.26)

In respect of *tanzīh,* the servant is distinct from the Real, but in respect of *tashbīh,* he is identical with the Real. From the first standpoint, the thing's face is its nonexistent fixed entity, so the face is distinct from *wujūd;* from the second standpoint, the existent thing discloses God's face, which is *wujūd.* Nothing other than the reality of *wujūd* appears and is seen, so God's face appears in every self-disclosure. Hence, *Wherever you turn, there is the face of God* (2:115). When the servants turn toward themselves and come to know themselves, they come to know their own Lord, who is the face of the Real.

The face of God is you, so you are the kiblah wherever you may be. Do not turn your face except toward yourself. The vicegerent becomes manifest only in the form of the one who appoints him as vicegerent. You are the *vicegerent in the earth* [2:30], and He is "the vicegerent in the family."[5] (IV 406.17)

A Mystery
What the Companion of the Journey Gains from Every Sect

He says: To journey from the engendered things to God is to be ignorant of Him. If he were to see the face of the Real in each thing, he would know His words, *Each has his direction [wijha] to which he turns* [2:148], and His words, *Wherever you turn, there is the face of God,* and His words, *To each of you We have appointed a shariah and a way* [5:48]—according to both interpretations in His word *a way.*[6]

He says: Darkness signifies knowledge of the absent, and light signifies knowledge of the witnessed. So *night* is *a garment* [25:47] and you are the night. Daytime belongs to movement, so it is the tasks of the Real.

Movement is life, so it pertains to the Real, and stillness is death, so it pertains to creation. Nonetheless, to Him belongs what is still in the two respects—stillness and fixedness. And to you belongs what moves in the two respects—"from" and "to." But no heed should be taken of night or daytime, for to Him belongs the property of giving existence that is within them, and to you belongs the taking benefit that is within them. Sleep is bodily ease and absent unveilings of the eye.

He says: The bestowal of blessings one after another and their uninterruptedness are the Real's support and conferral for the servants. He who is wary of God in them will reach felicity, and he who is not wary of God in them will be wretched.

He says: There is no interdiction in the Real's gifts, so do not say, "Why did You give?," for the Real will say, "Why did you take?" The proof is the prescription of the Law that has reached us. It was said to you, "Do not do it," but you did it, and "Do it," but you did not do it. Such is the affair.[7] (IV 403.15)

Seeing the face of God in things is a function of imagination, which perceives in terms of *tashbīh.* In contrast, reason perceives from the standpoint of *tanzīh,* though it can understand the logical necessity for the presence of God's face. Without God's face—the self-disclosure of *wujūd*—the things could not exist. To see the things and then claim that God's face is not present within them is tantamount to claiming that they are independent of God. The proper course for rational understanding, when confronted with Koranic statements about God's presence in things, is to follow the path of safety (*salāma*), which is to accept God at His word. The worst thing the rational thinker can do is try to explain away what God is saying, that is, to "interpret" (*ta'wīl*) the text in keeping with his own incapacity.

Reason asserts God's *tanzīh* and eliminates correspondence [between Him and creation] in every respect. The Real comes and declares it truthful in that with *Nothing is as His likeness* [42:11]. He says to us: "Reason speaks the truth, since it has given what is within its own capacity. It knows nothing other than that. For I have *given each thing its creation* [20:50], and reason is one of the things, so We have given it its creation."

Then He completed the verse with His words, *Then guided* [20:50], that is, clarified. He clarified something not given by reason nor by any of the other faculties. He mentioned for Himself various properties that He has and that are not accepted by reason except through faith or through an interpretation that will restore those properties to reason's compass. There is no escape from this.

The path of safety for those who are not *upon insight* [12:108] from God is not to interpret. They should concede this to God according to His knowledge of it. This is the path of salvation.

So the Real declares the truthfulness of each faculty in what it bestows, since it has given full due to everything God has bestowed upon it.

There remains for the Real another tasting from the side of the Real. It is known by the Folk of God, who are the Folk of the Koran—God's Folk and His elect. They tie the knot of every belief concerning Him, for no face in anything is ever empty of Him, and He is the *ḥaqq* of that face. Were this not the situation, He would not be a God, and the cosmos would be independent through itself, apart from Him. But this is impossible. Hence, it is impossible for anything in the cosmos to be empty of the face of the Real.

This is an exalted knowledge, for it gives rise to the lifting of absolute error from the cosmos. But relative error—which is put into relation with its contrary—is not lifted, for that is an error through the contrariety. Without the contrariety, it is not an error.

The perfect among the Folk of God are those who consider each affair separately in order to see its creation that God has given to it and that He has given fully. Then they see God's clarification for His servants outside the creation of each thing. Thus they put the clarification in His words, *and then guided,* in its proper place, and so also they situate every creature in accordance with what its Creator has given it. People like this do not make any errors, nor do they make any errors in applying the roots and the branches. So "Every *mujtahid* is correct"—if you understand—in the roots and the branches. This is a view that people hold.[8] (II 299.13)

Chapter 165: Realization

There can be no error (*khaṭaʾ*) in *wujūd,* because everything that occurs in *wujūd* occurs exactly as God intended it to occur, given that *He has given each thing its creation* (20:50). But human beings, who are addressed by the Shariah, can commit errors that pertain precisely to this Shari'ite address, that is, the prescriptive command—not to the engendering command. According to Ibn al-ʿArabī, when someone reaches the true understanding that everything is just as it must be, he has achieved the station of realization (*taḥqīq*), which is one of the highest stations of the Folk of God, if not the highest of all stations. The Realizer realizes (*taḥaqquq*) the Real (*ḥaqq*) and sees the face of God in everything; he alone is able to observe completely and fully the prophetic dictum, "Give to each that has a *ḥaqq* its *ḥaqq.*" The *ḥaqq* of a thing—its "rightful due"—is precisely the "real" of a thing, that is, the demands that the thing makes on the servant because it is the Real's face. The Shaykh explains something of the Realizer's vision and the way he goes about giving each thing its *ḥaqq* in a chapter called "On the true knowledge of the station of realization and the Realizers."

In respect to nature the Real
  is like a mirage you see as a garden.
You think it is water
  and you come to the water's source so as not to lose it.
Consider, and realize what you see,
  for there may be deceit!
Such are the forms of self-disclosure—
  in them the Real is like a deposit.
Texts of the Shariah have brought these forms
  in denial and confession.
Pay no heed to the lowland
  but consider your own high waystations.
You will find the riddle disclosing itself
  from behind wondrous curtains,
Not in any shape, no,
  nor in forms put together by nature.
When you see the Real, return
  and cling to avoiding excuses.
Speak about Him with the repugnant words
  with which speak the hadiths.
When a dear one contends with you,
  say to her, "Be obedient,
"Be reticent, do not
  gossip among your companions.
"When you are called by such as this,
  be the responder and the listener.
"Beautify your deeds in acceptance,
  for you will be recompensed for deeds."

Know—God confirm you—that realization is the station that accepts no detracting obfuscation. The companion of this description is the Realizer.

"Realization" is true knowledge of the *ḥaqq* that is demanded by the essence of each thing. The person gives it its full due in knowledge. If it happens that he also puts it into practice as a state, he is the one over whom the authority of realization prevails. If it does not prevail over him, then he knows that he is in error. But this error does not detract from his realization, since he sees himself and that through which he has erred, for he has erred by self-exertion.

Here there is a divine mystery, which is that God is the absolutely Wise. It is He who puts the things in their places, and it is He who has *given each thing its creation* [20:50]. So there is no error in engendered existence relative to the order on God's part. The lord of this realization—he who has realized it—knows that this is the situation, but he may also know that he himself is in error. However, he is in error in relation to what he has been commanded to do, not in relation to the actual situation in respect of the fact that God has put him in the locus where the act is called an "error." Hence the companion of realization earns a wage in his error, which is to say that he is lauded by God, just like the *mujtahid*, who does not err in actual fact, for his ruling is affirmed. His error is only in relation to others, when his proof does not coincide with their proof. But all is shariah, and all is *ḥaqq*. So also is the waystation of realization and the Realizers.

One precondition for the companion of this station is that the Real should be his hearing, his eyesight, his hand, his leg, and all the faculties that he puts to use. Hence he has free activity only through a *ḥaqq*, in a *ḥaqq*, and for a *ḥaqq*. This description belongs only to a beloved. He is not beloved until he is given nearness, and he will not be given nearness save through performing the supererogatory good works. He cannot perform the supererogatory good works until after the perfection of the obligatory works. The obligatory works will be perfected only through giving them fully their *ḥaqq*s. This is what prevents me from considering a supererogatory work correct for any specific person unless through a [divine] report-giving or a witnessing.[9]

This is because the obligatory works absorb the supererogatory works by being perfected by them. It has come in the *Ṣaḥīḥ* that God will say on the day of resurrection, "'Look at the *ṣalāt* of My servant. Has he completed it or left it incomplete?' If it is complete, it will be written for him as complete. But if anything of it is incomplete, He will say, 'Look and see if My servant has a voluntary work.' If he has a voluntary work," that is, a supererogatory work, "He says, 'Perfect My servant's obligatory work through his voluntary work.'" The Messenger of God said, "Then all the deeds will be taken in the same way."

God did not give witness to the supererogatory work of anyone save God's Messenger. He says, *And as for the night, keep vigil a part of it, as a supererogatory work for thee. It may be that thy Lord will raise thee to a praiseworthy station* [17:79]. This is the station of nearness and mastership that is witnessed by engendered existence.

When the Real is someone's hearing, no obfuscation enters in upon him in what he hears. Rather, he knows what he hears, who hears, through whom is heard, and what is required by the thing heard. Hence he acts in keeping with that, for his hearing does not err. In the same way, when the Real is his eyesight, he knows through whom he sees and what he sees. Hence no obfuscation enters into his consideration, no mistake into his sensation, and no bewilderment into his rational faculty, for he belongs to God through God. So also is the case of all his movements and stillnesses—a Realizer's movements that derive from realization. In this he does not consider those who count him in error, for it is utterly impossible for there to be in *wujūd* an affair that would conform to the personal desires of everyone, since God created their gazes disparate.

However, in actual fact, He did not place any disparity in His existent things. He says, *Who created seven heavens as layers—you see not in the creation of the All-Merciful any disparity. Return your eyesight. Do you see any fissure?* [67:3]. Thus He forbade that there be any disparity here. Rather, He shows the Realizer the affairs as established by the divine wisdom. He who has been given this knowledge has been given what is necessary for each of God's creatures.

This is an exalted station. Seldom will you see anyone who tastes it, unless you yourself possess it. The mark of the companion of this station is that there is for him, in everything that is named "error" in *wujūd*, a face toward the Real. He knows it, and he will make it known to the one who asks him about it if he knows that he will accept it from him. This is his mark. He is the one who sees his Lord through every belief, through every eye, and in every form. This belongs only to the companion of this station.

If someone claims this station, and if something happens in the world that is censured while the claimant does not have any way out to a *ḥaqq*, then his claim in this station is absurd. For the companion of this station knows where the face of the Real is to be found in the affair that is accompanied by censure. This happens mainly in articles of belief and in Shari'ite matters. Other than these two sites, it is easy to find the Real in that within which accidental censure occurs.

It is not necessary that making manifest the *ḥaqq* of the affair should come about through the tongue of praise. This is not what is sought. On the contrary, the thing may be, for example, blameworthy, although it is a *ḥaqq*. After all, not every *ḥaqq* is praiseworthy according to the Shariah and reason. What is desired from realization is knowledge of what is rightly demanded by each affair, whether it is nonexistent or existent. The realizer even gives the unreal its *ḥaqq* and does not take it beyond its locus. A person who has this description is the *Clear Imam* [36:12] and he is the locus of disclosure for the worlds. *And God speaks the* ***ḥaqq****, and He guides on the path* [33:4]. (II 267.17)

From Chapter 73: The Ninety-Seventh Question

Ibn al-ʿArabī provides one of his more detailed analyses of the relation between the face and what perishes in answering one of al-Ḥakīm al-Tirmidhī's questions:

Question: What share do the faithful have in His words, *Each thing is perishing except its/His face*?

Answer: A "person of faith" is the one we mentioned whose insight's eye has no light save the light of faith. In his view, *Each thing is perishing* from its own thingness—both the thingness of its fixity and the thingness of its *wujūd*—*except its face*. A thing's "face" is its essence and its reality, and its "face" is its locus of manifestation, that is, its manifestation in the entities. As for the thingness of its essence, this is covered by the exception—there is no escape from this. And as for its face in the locus of manifestation, some of our companions include this in *each thing is perishing*, while some of our companions do not include it there. Those who include it in the perishment take into account a specific locus of manifestation, while those who do not include it in the perishment take into account the fact that it always has some locus of manifestation.

As for us, we do not affirm the ascription of the word *thing* to the Essence of the Real, since this has not come down to us, nor have we been addressed by it, and courtesy is to be preferred. Here it is preferable that *its face* be like the ascription of the former [i.e., the word *thing*]—He means the locus of manifestation, not His He-ness. But the locus of manifestation has a certain correspondence with the face that is manifest within it, which is why the exception is correct. God says, *Our only word to a thing, when We desire it* [16:40]—so He names it a "thing" in the state of its perishment.

So *each thing* is described by perishment, since *is perishing* is the predicate of the subject, which is *each thing*. In other words: Everything to which the name *thing* can be ascribed is perishing. If it is a locus of manifestation, in its state of being a locus of manifestation it dwells in the thingness of its entity, which is perishing. Hence it is perishing in its state of being qualified by *wujūd*, just as it is perishing in the state of its being qualified by perishment, which is nonexistence.

After all, nonexistence is essential to the possible thing, which is to say that the reality of its essence demands that it be nonexistent. When things require certain affairs by their essences, it is impossible for these affairs to disappear. Hence it is impossible for the property of nonexistence to disappear from the possible entity, whether or not it is qualified by *wujūd*, for what is qualified by *wujūd* is not the entity of the possible thing. Rather it is the Manifest in the entity of the possible thing through which the possible thing comes to be called a "locus of manifestation for the *wujūd* of the Real." Hence *each thing is perishing*. That is why we negate the ascription of the word *thing* to the Real. Here, the exception is a "severed exception," like His words, *So the angels prostrated themselves, all of them together, except Iblis* [15:30].[10]

Do you not see that, since the Real rightfully demands *wujūd* by His Essence, nonexistence is impossible for Him? In the same way, since nonexistence belongs rightfully to the possible thing by its essence, *wujūd* is impossible for it. This is why we have made it a "locus of manifestation."

We said in *Kitāb al-maʿrifa*[11] that the possible thing does not rightfully demand nonexistence by its essence, as some people say. Rather, what the possible thing rightfully demands by its essence is the priority of its qualification by nonexistence over its qualification by *wujūd*, rather than nonexistence, so it receives *wujūd* through preponderation. Hence, the nonexistence over which *wujūd* is given preponderance is not the same as the nonexistence that is prior to its *wujūd*. It is rather the nonexistence that is the contrary of the thing's *wujūd* in the state of its *wujūd* such that, were there not *wujūd*, there would be nonexistence. This is the nonexistence over which *wujūd* is given preponderance in the entity of the possible thing. This is what is required by rational consideration.

As for our own position, it is that it is "possible" for the possible entity only to be a locus of manifestation, not to receive qualification by *wujūd* such that *wujūd* would then be identical with it. Hence, in the possible thing, *wujūd* is not identical with the existent thing. Rather, it is a state of the possible thing's entity, through which the possible thing is named an "existent thing" metaphorically, not in reality, since reality refuses to allow the possible thing to become an existent thing.

So *each thing* will be *perishing* forever, as each always has been. None of its descriptions will change, and none of *wujūd*'s descriptions will change, for *wujūd* is *wujūd* and nonexistence is nonexistence. What is described as being an existent thing is an existent thing, and what is described as being a nonexistent thing is a nonexistent thing.

This is the breath of the Folk of Realization among the folk of unveiling and finding.

Then, in this question, there enters the "face" that possesses the front. It is the face that is bound by the gaze, through which it is distinguished from the back. When the individual sees behind himself just as he sees in front of himself, all of him is a face without a nape.[12] He who has this attribute will not perish, because he sees in every direction, so he will not perish, for the eye preserves him through its gaze. From whatever direction comes the one who desires to make him perish, he finds no path to him, because he is unveiled to him—just as the companion of the bound face is wary of those who come from the front. (II 99.16)

Discerning the Face

One of the common errors of seekers is to conclude from an understanding of the presence of God's face in all things that there is no error in *wujūd* in any respect. It is true that, from the standpoint of unveiling, everything comes into existence just as it must, since everything has been put in its proper place by the engendering command that created it. But reason and the Shariah follow other scales. The travelers may indeed see God's face in everything, but they still must observe God's prescriptive command, which distinguishes between right and wrong and informs them of the modalities of praiseworthiness and blameworthiness made manifest by the face. If they fail to have the necessary discernment, they will have fallen under the sway of the divine deception (*makr*) and misguidance (*iḍlāl*).

Even in Ibn al-ʿArabī's day seekers on the Sufi path sometimes thought that their perception of the presence of God in all things absolved them from observing the Shariah. Otherwise, the Shaykh would not have devoted many passages in the *Futūḥāt* to refuting this idea. Ironically, in later times, short-sighted critics often attacked Ibn al-ʿArabī for believing that the Shariah was unnecessary. No doubt, the more sophisticated critics knew that they were not in fact attacking the Shaykh's own teachings, but rather the misunderstandings to which the doctrine of *waḥdat al-wujūd* could easily give rise. In effect, Sufis who grasped part of the teaching but not the whole claimed that they had seen God in everything, whether good or evil. They concluded that good and evil were both God, so moral distinctions were meaningless, and observance of the Shariah was a veil and a delusion. The Shaykh, however, constantly reminds his readers that they must observe God's scale (*mīzān*), that is, the Shariah, which provides them standards by which to distinguish right from wrong and offers the only means to achieve felicity in the next stages of existence.

From Chapter 351: Yielding

The Shaykh illustrates the necessity of observing the scale by pointing out that even the most perfect individual among the Folk of God, the prophet Muhammad, was sometimes scolded by God for not observing it. He cites the beginning of Surah 80, in which God chides the Prophet for turning away from a blind man who wanted to speak to him while he was talking with one of the powerful members of the Quraysh tribe. The Shaykh reads this as the Prophet's magnifying (*taᶜẓīm*) the divine attributes of self-greatness (*takabbur*) and domination (*jabr*), attributes that are manifest outwardly in the conduct of powerful and influential people. But in this situation, this was an inappropriate scale of judgment.

This passage is one of sixteen subchapters found in Chapter 351, "On the true knowledge of the waystation of the sharing of attributes by souls and spirits." Among these shared attributes is *khuḍūᶜ*, which means to yield and to be humble, lowly, and submissive. The more relevant of the two Koranic usages of words from the same root is the verse, *If We will, We will send down on them out of heaven a sign, so their necks will stay yielded to it* (26:4). Yielding before the Real is a praiseworthy attribute, but yielding before anything else is blameworthy. In order to know when to yield in the appropriate manner, one must be able to distinguish exactly what each successive self-disclosure of the Real demands from the human receptacle. One must recognize that each thing has a *ḥaqq* that needs to be observed and put into effect.

To yield during the Real's self-disclosure and while whispering with Him is praiseworthy, but in other than this it is blameworthy. Blame joins to anyone in whom yielding becomes manifest, except those who see the Real in all things in respect of the divine face that the things possess. However, this must accord with a realized scale that they do not transgress, because God has set up a scale for us in the earth. He says, *And heaven—He raised it up, and He set up the scale* [55:6–7].

People must employ the scale in accordance with the setting up of the Real. Even if they witness Him in each thing, He does not desire that they interact with Him in the same manner in each thing. On the contrary, they should praise Him and turn toward Him in the sites that seek praise from them, and they should turn away from Him in the sites in which He seeks that they turn away from Him. They should not transgress the scale that He seeks from them.

In this locus of witnessing, deception is hidden, and nothing can remove it save knowledge of the divine scale designated by the Shariah. Those who know it and halt at it and who model their own courtesy on God's rules of courtesy that He has taught to the messengers have won and possessed the degree of knowledge of God.

God says, teaching him who magnified the attribute of God without a scale and instructing him in courtesy, *He frowned and turned away that the blind man came to him. And what would make thee know that he*, that is, the dominating man, *will purify himself?* [80:1–3].

In the absent domain God is with those whose hearts are broken[13] and who have suffered maladies, but in the manifest entity He is with the dominating and self-great. Manifestation has a stronger property. God's Messenger eagerly desired that people should have faith in God's unity and that their blindness should be removed. When the man who was blind in the manifest domain but seeing in the nonmanifest domain came to him, such that the nonmanifest quality of the dominating man [i.e., blindness] was the manifest quality of the blind man, there happened to the mortal soul [of the Prophet] what happened.

The Prophet was witnessing no object save the Real's attribute wherever it became manifest from the engendered things. When he saw it, he would use stratagems so as to strip it from the engendered thing that had taken it in other than its scale and made it manifest in other than its homestead. He was jealous.[14]

It was said to him, *As for him who considers himself independent, to him dost thou attend* [80:5–6]. God is saying that since the Prophet has witnessed the attribute of the Real—that is, His independence of the cosmos—he is attending to it, out of eager desire to purify the person through whom the attribute has become manifest. Hence it was said to him, *It is nothing to thee if he does not purify himself* [80:7]. To you belongs only what you intend and its property. Were he to purify himself, nothing would escape you. It is the same whether or not he purifies himself.

And he who comes to thee striving and in fear, to him thou payest no heed [80:8–10] because he is blind. In other words, "Do not take it as an ill omen," for He forbade him from taking ill omens. That is why "He loved good omens, and he disliked ill omens." Ill omens have a share in the reprehensible, but good omens have a share and a portion of good. (III 219.27)

Now the Shaykh turns to Koran 18:28–29, where reference is made to a similar episode: Some of the leaders of Quraysh had said that they would like to sit and talk with Muhammad but were prevented from doing so because he was always surrounded by former slaves and other such riff-raff. Muhammad desired to meet with the leaders in order that they might accept Islam, so he told the slaves to leave when any of these men approached. God then revealed these two verses, scolding Muhammad and teaching him the proper scale.[15]

It was also said to him, *Be thyself patient with those who call upon their Lord at morning and evening, desiring His face*: Gaze upon the attribute of the Real in them, for it is the object of your seeking in engendered existence. After all, I call My servants *at morning and evening* and at every moment, desiring their face—that is, their essence—so that they may hear My call and return to Me. *And let not thine eyes pass by them,* for they have become manifest through My attribute, as I have informed you, *desiring the ornament of the life of this world,* for this ornament is also in them, just as it is in the life of this world, so here also is the object of your seeking.

And do not obey, for [the leaders of Quraysh] had sought from him that he designate a session for them apart from the others. None of them would be present there save a servant *whose heart We have made heedless of Our remembrance* [18:28]. In other words, We put his heart in a sheath, so We veiled him from remembering Us. After all, were he to remember Us, he would know that mastership belongs to Us and that he is a servant. Then this greatness that he has made manifest would disappear from him. It is this that you have magnified, because it is My attribute, and you have wished to remove it from their manifest selves. I know that I have *set a seal on every heart of the self-great and dominating* [40:35], so no greatness enters into that heart, even if he makes it manifest.

He follows his own caprice, that is, his personal desire that he has made manifest, *and his affair,* that is, what he has raised up before his eyes and witnesses, *has become all excess* [18:28], so he does not turn his gaze away from it toward what the Real says to him on the tongue of His Messenger and toward what He desires from him. *And say: "The **ḥaqq** is from your Lord; so let whoever* God *wills have faith, and let whoever* God *wills disbelieve"* [18:29], for they *will not will unless God wills, the Lord of the worlds* [81:29].

When these people came to him, the Messenger of God used to say, "Welcome to those concerning whom my Lord scolded me!" He would restrain himself before them in the session until they left. Then these remained his character traits until he died. Whenever he encountered anyone with whom he spoke after that, he would stand with him until that person was the one who turned away. In the same way, when an individual shook hands with him, he would leave his hand in the other's hand until that person withdrew it. Such has been transmitted to us concerning his character traits.

Our vision of the divine description
has a scale, when things
become manifest within it
to the Possessor of the Eye.
The learned and mindful man
deals with it according to
the Shariah and the Koran
brought by God's Messenger.
This in truth is *islām*, so act
in keeping with its ruling!
So also is it faith [*īmān*], and so also
doing the beautiful [*iḥsān*].[16]

(III 220.7)

Chapter 527: Desiring the Face

The full title of this chapter is "On the true knowledge of the state of the Pole whose waystation is *Be thyself patient with those who call upon their Lord at morning and evening, desiring His face, and let not thine eyes pass by them* [18:28]." Here the Shaykh refers once again to God's scolding the Prophet. Then he clarifies how the divine face can be found in created things.

God has a tribe who have fulfilled
that for which they were created,
and none of their generations passes
without another appearing.
So be thyself patient with this Tribe,
and you will be grateful
when you are provided
with the like of what they received—
Dejection, abasement,
misery, within which are whiffs of musk,
spread by
clinging perfume.
"Let not My attributes deceive thee!
For they have
homesteads, of which the tribes
have spoken."

Know—God confirm us and you with the holy spirit with which He has confirmed them—that God has servants whose states and acts are a remembrance through which they draw near to God and which results in a knowledge of God that is known only by those who taste it. He who restrains himself with this formula of remembrance will join them. After all, everything to which God commanded His Prophet and from which He prohibited him is identical with those servants' states and acts. At the same time, this group, in whom the Koran descended, are among the Companions of the Messenger, so they reached what they reached only by following him, and from him they understood what they understood.

With all this, God scolded His Prophet concerning these servants. When the Messenger of God met one of them or sat in a session where they were, he would not cease restraining himself with them as long as they were seated, until they were the ones who turned away. Then God's Messenger would turn away. When they were present, his *eyes* would *not pass by them*. When they came to him or he encountered them, he would say, "Welcome to those concerning whom God scolded me!" When they recognized that from him, they lessened their sitting and speaking with God's Messenger, because they knew that he was binding himself by them and was patient in himself with them.

When someone clings to this formula of remembrance, the result will be that he gains knowledge of the face of the Real in each thing. Hence he will see nothing without seeing the face of the Real within it. For they *call upon their Lord at morning and evening,* and this is the time when those provided with provision gain it, just as He has said: *They shall have their provision in [the Garden] at dawn and evening* [19:62]. Hence the provision of these *at morning and evening* is the knowledge that they gain of the face that is the object of their desire, for He says that they are *desiring His face* [18:28], that is, through calling upon the face of the Real *at morning and evening.* For they know that *Each thing is perishing except His face* [28:88], so they seek what subsists and they prefer it over what becomes annihilated.[17]

When the face of the Real discloses itself in the things to them and to those who remember with this remembrance, their *eyes* do *not pass by* this face, and their eyes are not able to pass by it, because, through its own essence, the face binds anyone who gazes upon it. (IV 169.35)

By this last clause, Ibn al-ᶜArabī seems to be saying that anyone who sees God's face and knows what he is seeing will keep on gazing upon it, because, after all, it is the Real, and everything else is unreal. Thus the face fixes and "binds" (*taqyīd*) the viewers' gaze, so they do not pass by the face. The Shaykh goes on to explain that since this verse refers to those who see God's face, the light of the face is reflected back upon them, and seeing such people leads others to remember God.

God brought a prohibition in this remembrance [with His words, *let not thine eyes pass by them*] only because they are not identical with the face. Rather, they are the witnessers of the face. Those who are among them have gained the self-disclosure of the face while this remembrance remains with them, for they desire only the subsistence of the witnessing of the face perpetually, because of what they know about the state of the possible thing and the courtesy toward God demanded by His majesty—in other words, that they should make no judgments about Him, and inescapably so, even if God makes that judgment about Himself. This is the divine courtesy.

After this, if the sought face does not appear to someone, he should seek the face that he desires through calling upon Him.

In any case, the *eyes* of God's Messenger *did not pass by them* to others as long as they were present. This is why God's Messenger said concerning the attribute of God's friends, "When they are seen, God is remembered," because of the light of the face that they have gained, the face that is the object of their desire. After all,

> when this face discloses itself to someone, inescapably there will be within him a trace that is known to him. The trace may be disclosed such that others see it from him, or it may be hidden such that only the folk of unveiling see it in him. Or it may be that no one sees it—and this is the most hidden—but it is disclosed to him in himself, because he is the companion of witnessing. (IV 170.17)

Those friends of God who see God's face in all things remain "bound" by the face and never turn away from it. But the prophets have a different function. Although they see the face in everything, they do not become bound by it—saying, for example, that they see nothing but God and nothing but good. On the contrary, their function in the cosmos is guidance, which is to lead people to felicity. Hence they must teach them how to differentiate between what is approved and what is disapproved.

> The property of non-prophets in such affairs is different from the property of prophets. Although the prophets witness these servants in the state of their witnessing the face that they desire from God through their calling upon Him, they were sent for the sake of the servants' means to wholesomeness, so in this respect they do not become bound by the servants in an absolute sense. Rather, they are bound by the means to wholesomeness because of which they were sent as prophets. Thus, sometimes they are scolded, even though they are busy with a means to wholesomeness. An example is the verse just mentioned. (IV 170.24)

The idea that the function of the prophets is to establish the means to wholesomeness (*maṣlaḥa*) of society is a standard Islamic teaching, firmly rooted in the Koranic concepts of wholesomeness (*ṣalāḥ*) and corruption (*fasād*). Ibn al-ʿArabī's point may be based on the idea that doing something for the *maṣlaḥa*—the means to wholesomeness that one sees in a situation—is not the same as doing it *desiring His face* (18:28). The prophet needs to exercise a certain judgment in deciding what the appropriate means is in a given situation, and he may be mistaken, if he uses the wrong scale with which to make his judgment.

> Another example is the verse of the blind man concerning whom was sent down *He frowned and turned away* [80:1]. When God's Messenger turned away from the blind man concerning whom the Real scolded him, he did so only out of eager desire and wishing for the Islam of someone whose Islam would bring about the Islam of many others and through whom God could confirm the religion. Nevertheless, he was scolded because of another reality, not in this respect. This includes His words, *As for him who considers himself independent, to him dost thou attend* [80:5–6]. Here He mentions the attribute, not the individual. Independence is a divine attribute. Hence the eye of God's Messenger turned only toward a divine attribute, because he had gained the realization of poverty.
>
> The Real desired to alert him to the divine all-encompassingness, since no attribute binds Him rather than any other attribute. Hence, for the Prophet to witness the Real's independence, as in His words, *God is independent of the worlds* [3:97], was not more appropriate than for him to witness the Real's seeking, as in His words, *I created jinn and mankind only to worship Me* [51:56]. What does the station of independence have to do with this seeking? God also says, *Lend to God a beautiful loan* [5.12].
>
> So the Prophet was jealous for God lest one attribute bind Him rather than another. Rather, he would make friendliness manifest to these people as was appropriate for them, and he would make cheerfulness manifest to the blind man in the measure that would be a means to wholesomeness for these dominating people. After all, humility and friendliness are lovable in essence from everyone, for they are among the noble character traits.
>
> God never ceased teaching courtesy to His Prophet until he realized the divine courtesy. He said, "God taught me courtesy, so He made my courtesy beautiful." For God has a relation with the rich and independent just as He has a relation with the poor and needy. The gnostic must not let anything of the Real escape him in anything.
>
> How beautiful is God's teaching of His servants! When God opens the eyes of our insights and our understandings, we come to know, in God's teaching His Prophet the acts of courtesy in the levels, that we also are meant by the teaching. We should consider the Prophet in keeping with the well-known proverb, "I mean you, so listen, O neighbor!" Though God intends him for the courtesy, we also are intended for emulation and following. *You have a beau-*

> *tiful model in the Messenger of God* [33:21]. Hence, we share in every address by which God addresses His Prophet so as to teach him courtesy—there is no escape from this.
>
> So, my friend, consider the great good that results from this formula of remembrance! *And God speaks the **ḥaqq**, and He guides on the path* [33:4]. (IV 170.26)

The Veil

A veil (*ḥijāb*) is something that prevents seeing the face. Inasmuch as everything in the cosmos prevents seeing God's face, everything is a veil, but inasmuch as everything discloses *wujūd*, everything is identical with His face. Even the divine names are veils: "The names are veils over the Named, just as they are signifiers of Him" (*ʿAbādila* 101). The veil remains an ever-present *barzakh* between the entities and *wujūd*, reminding us of *tanzīh* in the midst of *tashbīh*. It is synonymous with the term *curtain* (*sitr*), whose gerund form, "curtaining" (*satr*), is the conceptual opposite of self-disclosure, as the Shaykh makes clear when he speaks about "the science of the absent and the witnessed and the science of curtaining and self-disclosure" (II 276.2; cf. II 471.7).

> Some creatures are curtains over other creatures. Although curtains are signifiers, they are signifiers by way of undifferentiation, for the cosmos, or rather, all of *wujūd*, is a curtain, a curtained, and a curtainer. (IV 214.30)

Given that a veil is anything that prevents seeing something's face or reality, the ever-renewed likenesses (*amthāl*) that fill the cosmos are veils that prevent us from seeing the renewal of creation at each instant.

> The veil is nothing but mutual similarity and mutual likeness. Were it not for this, no one would remain uncertain about the new creation that belongs to God in the cosmos at every breath through each task. (IV 22.6)

Every created thing in this world is a veil, but the situation will be different in the last world, because there all the faithful will witness God's self-disclosure through the things.

> This world is the locus of the veil, except for the gnostics, for they have the station of the last world in this world. They possess unveiling and witnessing. These are two affairs given by the eye of certainty, which is the most complete means of perceiving knowledge. (II 654.4)

Although Ibn al-ʿArabī contrasts curtaining and disclosure and discusses veils as those things that prevent us from seeing the Real, his doctrine of He/not He or simultaneous *tashbīh* and *tanzīh* demands that, in respect of the He, the veils be nothing but the Real. From this standpoint, the problem is not the veils, but human failure to recognize God in His self-disclosure. People think that God is nonmanifest, so they fail to see the Real before their eyes.

> A Mystery
> *When someone's affair is hidden, his measure is unknown.*
>
> He says: *They measured not God with the **ḥaqq** of His measure* [6:91] in those attributes by which He qualified Himself and which He mentioned in His Book and upon the tongue of His Messenger.
>
> He says: There is no veil and no curtain. Nothing hides Him save His manifestation.
>
> He says: Were souls to halt with what has become manifest, they would know the situation as it is in itself. However, they seek something that is absent from them, so their seeking is identical with their veil. Hence *they measured not* what has become manifest *with the **ḥaqq** of its measure*, because they are busy with what they imagine to be nonmanifest to them.
>
> He says: Nothing is nonmanifest. The lack of knowledge has made it nonmanifest. There is nothing nonmanifest in the case of the Real, for He has addressed us by saying that He is *the Manifest and the Nonmanifest*, and *the First and the Last* [57:3]. In other words, what you seek in the nonmanifest is manifest, so do not weary yourself. (IV 407.21)

In one respect, being veiled from God is a rare attribute in the cosmos. The Shaykh often explains that everything other than human beings and jinn acknowledges God's Lordship because it sees Him present. Only these two creatures fail to perceive God and deny His reality or, having recognized it, commit the sin of *shirk*, associating others with God. Even *shirk* of course, has divine roots, and in the context of the following passage, the divine root of *shirk* is that the entities, in the state of their nonexistence, witness the Real and obey His commands through their very essences. Once they enter into *wujūd*, they continue to obey what they witness, for this a concomitant of their innate disposition (*fiṭra*).

> The cosmos never ceases to be in the state of its nonexistence, witnessing the Necessary *Wujūd*, for its nonexistence never ceases to be given preponderance, while it stays fixed in entity. In the state of its nonexistence, the Real has described it as having hearing and obedience, so it is not impossible to ascribe witnessing to it. This is why none of the possible things denies Him in the state of its *wujūd*, with the single exception, in the whole cosmos, of the human existent.
>
> Those human beings who are overcome by the veil of nature associate others with Him. At root, they are not in the habit of hearing, obeying, and worshiping any but a Lord that they witness. But the veil of nature has made that object of worship absent to them. Hence they take what they take among the existent things that they witness and see—whether from the heavenly world, such as stars, or from the lower world, such as the elements and what is born from them—as a lord that they worship in keeping with the witnessing to which they have become habituated, and their souls reach stillness in this lord. (III 308.20)

Although human beings may suffer by being veiled from God, He created the universe for mercy, so the veils manifest His mercy. The most basic mercy is *wujūd* itself, which is His generous bestowal of reality upon the creatures, a bestowal through which they gain everything that they have. In fact, the blessings that reach the creatures are precisely the veils, and without them the cosmos would not exist. The veils are nothing but self-disclosures draped over the Essence of the Real.

> Beware—the curtains and cloaks
> have not been let down
> save for a magnificent affair,
> all of it momentous.
> If what they curtain
> appeared to our eyes
> no tenets or sects
> would remain among us.
> Nothing impermanent would appear,
> within it an illness—
> no remedies, no medicine,
> and no infirmities.
> Nothing new would have come
> for the soul to wear,
> no mediation from Him, no,
> and no rest.
> The form of the curtains
> is seen by the eyes,
> but no boredom
> comes over them in that.
> The eyes of engendered existence
> gaze from behind the curtain,
> and the veils see
> what the eyes do not see. (III 257.10)

Of the seven Koranic mentions of the word *veil*, the Shaykh cites most often the verse, *It belongs not to any mortal that God should speak to him, except by revelation, or from behind a veil* (42:51). He cites a few of the relevant proof-texts in referring to the diversity of veils:

> Veils are of various sorts:
>
> Among them are engendered veils between the engendered things, as in His words, *Ask them from behind a veil* [33:53].
>
> Among them are veils through which creatures are veiled from God, as in His words, *They say, "Our hearts are in shelters"* [41:5].
>
> Among them are veils through which God is veiled from His creatures, as in the Prophet's words, "God will disclose Himself on the day of resurrection with nothing between them save the mantle of greatness on His face," or, in another version, "with three veils between Him and His creatures," or however he put it.
>
> Among them is *It belongs not to any mortal that God should speak to him, except by revelation, or from behind a veil* [42:51], as He spoke to Moses from behind the veils of *the*

fire, the tree, the right bank of the watercourse, the side of the Mount, and *the blessed hollow* [28:29–30]. In the same way, He says, *Grant him sanctuary until he hears the speech of God* [9:6]. Thus God spoke to the one to whom sanctuary was granted from behind the veil of Muhammad, since he was identical with the veil. (III 211.2)

Veils are inescapable, yet people need to recognize the face of God within them and beyond them. The test of their humanity is tied to knowledge, discernment, recognizing things for what they are, giving things their *ḥaqq*s, and putting things in their proper places. Among the veils that may be especially thick for followers of revealed religions are the messengers and scriptures, which can easily be given an absolute value so that the Real is perceived only in these specific forms. Those jurists and theologians of the Shaykh's day who were scandalized by Sufi claims to direct knowledge of God were, in his view, guilty of missing God because of the veil. The Koran itself says that God gives knowledge to whom He wills. It does not say that the knowledge must be given through the intermediary of the Koran and the Hadith—though veils in one form or another remain forever draped over the Essence. In explaining this, the Shaykh alludes to the fact that the transmission of Hadith was an oral process, and that Muslim scholars would go to great lengths to gain access to transmitters with the least number of intermediaries between themselves and the Prophet. The term "veil-keeper" (*ḥājib*) was employed for high-ranking officials who controlled access to kings or caliphs.

A Mystery
The veil-keepers are a veil.

He says: The king's veil-keepers are his veil so that he may see whether the subjects turn their eyes to the veil-keepers or go beyond them in search of the vision of the king. Hence veil-keepers are a trial from God.

He says: The messengers are veil-keepers. They call to God, not to themselves.

He says: The angels are veil-keepers between God and the messengers, so our line of ascription has become distant. In transmitting hadiths, the goal is for the line of ascription to be "high"; the fewer links it has, the higher it is. God has instructed about this. He says, *[Say: "This is my way.] I call to God upon insight,"* so the angel disappears, *"I and whoever follows me"* [12:108], so the Messenger disappears. Abū Yazīd said, "My heart narrated to me from my Lord, so I take the text of the Book from Him, O denier!"

He says: *It belongs not to any mortal that God should speak to him, except by revelation* through what God casts [into the heart] by lifting the intermediaries, *or from behind the veil* of that through which He speaks to you in the form of self-disclosure, wherever it may be, *or that He should send a messenger* [42:51] of your own kind, or not of your own kind. (IV 412.22)

Although veils are inescapable, people should aspire to go beyond them. The veils, after all, are established by *tashbīh,* whereas the first duty of the servant is to recognize *tanzīh.* Although God's face appears in every veil, the veil is not God's face. The Shaykh discusses this point while meditating upon the well-known hadith concerning paradise, "I have prepared for My wholesome servant what no eye has seen, what no ear has heard, and what has never passed into the heart of any mortal." He keeps in view the etymological sense of the word *janna* or "Garden," which comes from a root meaning to conceal, to veil. He speaks from the point of view not of the normal "exegesis" (*tafsīr*) of the term, but rather its metaphorical interpretation, the "passing over" (*iʿtibār*) from the external and obvious meaning to a more hidden and internal meaning.

His words are correct that there is "what no eye has seen" in the "Garden," that is, in the "curtain"—on the basis of the metaphorical interpretation, not exegesis. Were an eye to see it, it would not be curtained. Were someone to see it, he would speak about it and it would be "heard." Were it heard, it would be limited. Were it limited, it would pass into his heart and be known.

This is an affair that veils us from Him through a veil that is not known, for He is in the curtain called "the Garden."[18] Since His Entity is identical with the curtain, nothing veils us save the fact that we make what we see a curtain, so our aspiration attaches itself to what is behind the curtain, that is, the curtained. This comes to us from us, and nothing makes us do it save *tanzīh.* Hence along with *tanzīh* the prophets brought the attributes of *tashbīh,* so that these might make the affair nearer to the people and call the attention of those who are nearest to God—those who are in nearness itself along with the veil of the actual situation. Thus, in this calling attention through *tashbīh* is the lifting of the coverings from the eyesight, and the eyesight comes to be qualified as "piercing," just as does the eyesight of the person near death. God says, *We have unveiled from you your covering, so your eyesight today is piercing* [50:22]. The person near death sees what those who sit with him do not. He reports to his sitting companions what he sees and perceives and he reports truthfully, but those present see nothing, just as they do not see the angels and spirituals who are with them in the same session. (III 541.20)

The Koranic verse tell us that God does not speak to any mortal save from behind a veil, but the Prophet said that after death God may speak to a person "directly" (*kifāḥ*[an]). According to the lexicographers, this word means "without anything intervening between them." The Shaykh understands it to refer to the vision of God's self-disclosing veil, a vision that occurs when God loves His servant and is "his hearing through which he hears and his eyesight through which he sees." Having explained this point, he goes on to distinguish between the self-disclosure of God and that of certain other beings, such as angels, jinn, and some of the Folk of God. His regular readers will know that such beings have the power to disclose themselves in any imaginal form that they desire.[19] Moreover, they are able to display themselves in forms endlessly because, once having entered into *wujūd,* they never leave it. What then is the difference between them and God in this respect? The basic difference is of course that God is the Necessary *Wujūd* and His self-disclosure belongs to Himself. In contrast, others receive *wujūd* and the ability to disclose themselves from God.

The veils remain forever hung down. They are the entities of these forms. Hence He is not seen except *from behind a veil,* just as He does not speak except *from behind a veil.* If the viewer is to see Him "directly," he will not see Him until the Real is his eyesight. It is He who sees Himself through His eyesight in the form of His servant. Thus the form gives him direct encounter, since it carries the eyesight and all the faculties. Hence you witness Him in entity and directly within the form through the name Manifest, since He is your eyesight. But you witness Him in knowledge through the name Nonmanifest, since He is the eyesight of the instrument through which you perceive what you perceive. I say "directly" because of the prophetic report recorded by al-Tirmidhī and others employing this very word.

When the companion of a dream-vision sees his Lord directly while dreaming, in whatever form he may have seen Him, he says, "I saw my Lord in the form of such and such." He speaks the truth, and the truth of what he says is acknowledged, even though God says, *Nothing is as His likeness* [42:11], thereby negating mutual likeness from Him in His reception of self-disclosure by Himself in all the forms, which are infinite. After all, none of those other than God who possess self-disclosure in forms disclose themselves in any of them by themselves. On the contrary, they disclose themselves in them through their Creator's will and engendering. He says *Be!* to the form in which those who have this attribute disclose themselves, so the form comes to be, and the creature who has this reception [of self-disclosure] becomes manifest through it. Such are the spirits and, among human beings, the spiritualized, such as Qaḍīb al-Bān and his similars.[20] God says, *in whatever form He willed He mounted you* [82:8]. Thus *He proportioned* him and *balanced* him [82:7] in a constitution that receives every form when the Real wills, but He made this mounting belong to God, not to him. (IV 19.12)

God speaks from behind the veils in a diversity of modes, and these help explain the diverse reactions of the gnostics to visionary experience. Why, for example, did the Prophet sometimes remain unruffled when Gabriel appeared to him, but at other times he was knocked unconscious? According to Ibn al-ʿArabī, the basic reason for this is that when God discloses Himself in familiar and habituated forms, this produces one reaction; but if the forms are unfamiliar and without precedent, then the experience overwhelms the recipient.

It belongs not to any mortal that God should speak to him, except by revelation, or from behind a veil, or that He should send a messenger [42:51] who will be His deputy in speech, that is, His spokesman. God says, *Grant him sanctuary until he hears the speech of God* [9:6]. He means, "on the tongue of the spokesman, who is the Messenger of God."

I heard one of the shaykhs saying, "As long as he has his mortal nature, speech belongs to him *from behind a veil,* but when he departs from his mortal nature, the veil will be lifted." This Shaykh was ʿAbd al-ʿAzīz ibn Abī Bakr al-Mahdawī, known as Ibn al-Karih.[21] I heard this from him in his house in Tunis. He was correct in that, and he erred.

He was correct in his affirmation and stipulation that speech is *from behind the veil* and that speech cannot be brought together with witnessing. He erred in saying, without qualification, that the veil will be lifted. One should say rather that the veil of the servant's mortal nature will be lifted, because, without doubt, there are other veils behind the veil of mortal nature. Thus this veil of mortal nature may be lifted for him, but then God will speak to him from behind another veil.

The highest of veils, the nearest to God, and the most distant from the created things are the divine loci of manifestation within which self-disclosure occurs. When the witnessing of these loci of manifestation is limited and habitual, such as the manifestation of the angel in the form of a man, then He speaks to the servant in the equilibrium that belongs to the habit and the limit.

But it may happen that He discloses himself to the servant having blocked the horizon.[22] Then the servant swoons because he lacks the habitual, even if he finds the limit. So what about someone who sees no limit and has not become habituated? For the loci of manifestation may be unlimited and nonhabitual, or they may be limited and nonhabitual, or limited and habitual. The states of the witnessers are diverse in each of these Presences. (II 601.31)

Chapter 254: The Curtain

Ibn al-ʿArabī summarizes his understanding of the significance of veils in a chapter called "On the true knowledge of the curtain, which is what curtains you from what annihilates you." In the title, he alludes to the basic ontological role of the veils: the fact that existence depends upon them, or the fact that the cosmos is nothing other than a series of veils. In the title, and in the first sentence of the chapter, he repeats the definition of "curtain" that he provides in his *Iṣṭilāḥāt* (9; II 132.9). Toward the end of the chapter, he comments on the famous "veils hadith": "God has seventy veils of light and darkness; were He to lift them, the glories of His face would burn away everything that the eyesight of His creatures perceives." Several more interpretations of this hadith will be provided shortly.

God lets down the curtains and cloaks
 only for the sake of the eyes' good fortune.
This may be a warning against investigation
 or against what nature and boredom
  require—
Consider the lessons they carry
 as the foundation of motives and nations.
If the curtains did not hide special qualities,
 still unknown, I would not desire or hope
  for them.
God sends down the curtains and cloaks
 only for a magnificent and momentous
  affair.

The curtain is the covering of engendered existence, or halting with habits and with the results of deeds. We have given you the knowledge that the occasions are divine veils that cannot be lifted save through themselves. Lifting them is identical with letting them down, and the reality of obliterating them is to affirm them.

The curtain is an all-inclusive divine mercy for the common people, because of the opposition to His commands that He has determined for them. They have no escape from opposition's stains, though it would never occur along with unveiling and self-disclosure. So there is no escape from the curtain.

This is why interdictions have been lifted from the folk of unveiling in knowledge, such that for them no interdiction remains. On the contrary, for them has been made licit whatever they will in their free activity. After all, it has come in the sound report that God says to the one who has sinned, but he knows that he has a Lord who forgives sins and takes to task for sins, "Do what you will, for I have forgiven you." Thus He has made licit for the person with this attribute what He has interdicted for others. It is impossible that He command him to bring that whose bringing He has interdicted, for *God does not command indecency* [7:28], so He lets down the curtains before the folk of interdiction.

This is the curtain's ruling property in the common people. As for the elect, it is the words of the poet,[23]

You veil the heart
from its absent mystery.
If not for you,
it would have no seal.

So He has made you identical with His curtain over you. If not for this curtain, you would not seek increase in knowledge of Him. You are spoken to and addressed from behind the curtain of the form from which He speaks to you. Consider your mortal humanity. You will find it identical with your curtain from behind which He speaks to you. For He says, *It belongs not to any mortal that God should speak to him, except by revelation, or from behind a veil* [42:51]. Hence, He may speak to you from you, since you veil yourself from you, and you are His curtain over you.

It is impossible for you to cease being a mortal, for you are mortal by your very essence. Even if you become absent from yourself or are annihilated by a state that overtakes you, your mortal humanity will abide in entity. Hence the curtain is let down, and the eye will fall upon nothing but a curtain, since it falls upon nothing but a form.

All this is because of what is required by the Divinity in respect of jealousy and mercy. As for "jealousy" [*ghayra*], He is jealous lest some "other" [*ghayr*] perceive Him and He be encompassed by him who perceives Him. But He *encompasses everything* [4:126], so He is not encompassed by him whom He encompasses.

As for mercy, this is because He knows that newly arrived things cannot subsist along with the glories of His face. On the contrary, they would be burned away by them, so out of mercy toward them He curtains them so that their entities may subsist.

Then God lets down upon the worlds the curtains of the results of their deeds through His words, "Do such and such, and it will result in such and such for its doer." Hence the doer halts with the result. But, if he is one of the folk of the elect, he has no longing for the result. Those [among the elect] who do long for it long for it only so that through it and through witnessing it the deed that their Master has prescribed for them will be correct.

As for the common people, they long for the result and are enamored of it.

Since God appointed marks that signify the correctness of deeds among the doers, the elect long for witnessing the results of the deeds so as to be *upon insight* [12:108] in their affairs. After all, their object of seeking and their concern is to abide in the *ḥaqq*s that He has given them to witness. These *ḥaqq*s are nothing other than the deeds that He has prescribed for them.

He may have let down the curtain in fear of the penetration of the eye and its being correct. In this is included letting down the veils because of the facial glories that burn away the entities of the possible things. This is for the sake of some people, those who do not have this entrance into knowledge of God. They do not know that with each breath God has a self-disclosure that does not take the form of the first self-disclosure. When this perception is absent from them, they may become the constant companion of a self-disclosure, and its witnessing may become lasting for them, while nature seeks it through its reality. Then boredom seizes them, but boredom in this station is irreverence toward the Divine Side. For *They are uncertain of a new creation* [50:15] at each breath. They imagine that the affair is not changing, so a curtain is let down over them because of the boredom that leads to irreverence, because God has deprived them of knowledge of themselves and of Him. So they imagine that they are they, breath by breath; and indeed they are they in respect of their substantiality, but not in respect of that by which they are described.

Do not say that the affair is not like this! This is among the divine mysteries whose perception God has veiled from many creatures among the Folk of God, the Lords of the Opening of Unveiling—so what about the state of others in this!?

There is no escape from the curtain, for there is no escape from you. So understand! *And God speaks the* **ḥaqq**, *and He guides on the path* [33:4]. (II 553.26)

Revelation

God speaks to no mortal *except by revelation, or from behind a veil* (42:51). As we have already seen, Ibn al-ʿArabī considers the very fact of being a "mortal" (*bashar*) the most basic of veils. So also, he considers "revelation" (*waḥy*) as a sort of veil, since it is one sort of disclosure of God's face in the form of a veil. What is revealed undergoes limitation, confinement, binding, and restriction by the very fact of the revelation. To reveal is also to re-veil, or to present the Real from behind a different veil.

Revelation can be defined as a specific form of divine self-disclosure in which God addresses certain creatures from behind a veil with a message directed toward their specific situation. In the narrow sense of the term, it belongs exclusively to the prophets.[24] The veils that separate a prophet from God during the revelatory act may be many or few, thick or thin. The differing reality of the revelatory veils helps explain the diverse reactions of the prophets to the experience of revelation. In the following, the Shaykh explains this in order to clarify the difference between certain revelations given to Moses and Muhammad. Muslims consider Muhammad the greatest of the prophets, but when the angel came to him, he would sometimes swoon and froth at the mouth. In contrast, God spoke directly to Moses at the Burning Bush, but Moses carried on the conversation as if nothing special were happening.

One of the most marvelous things that happens in *wujūd* is what I want to speak of—that the angels are thunderstruck when God speaks to them through revelation "like a chain across pebbles." When revelation came down upon the Messenger of God "like a chain across pebbles," he was thunderstruck, and that was the most intense revelation for him. Gabriel *brought it down upon* his *heart* [26:193–94], and the Prophet would be annihilated from the world of sensation. He would froth, and they would cover him until he regained his composure. Sometimes revelation would descend upon him on an intensely cold day, and his sides would drip with perspiration.

As for Moses, *God spoke directly* [4:164] to him while lifting the intermediaries, yet he was not thunderstruck, nor did he depart from sensation. He spoke, and he was spoken to. And this station is greater than the station of revelation through the intermediary of the angel. So here is an angel thunderstruck by speech, and here is the most noble mortal thunderstruck by the descent of the Spirit with revelation, and here is Moses who was not thunderstruck, and nothing happened to him, even though the intermediaries had been lifted. Yet the mountain was thunderstruck by that.

You should know that all this derives from the traces of the veils, for the ruling property belongs to them wherever they become manifest. Since God created them as veils, it is impossible for them to do anything but veil—there is no escape from this. If they did not veil, they would not be veils.

God created two sorts of veils—suprasensory and material. He created the material veils as dense, subtle, or translucent. Eyesight sees nothing but the dense. As for the subtle, eyesight sees what is within them and behind them. And as for the translucent, eyesight sees what is behind them, but it becomes uncertain if it perceives what is within them. Thus it has been said [by Ṣāḥib ibn ʿAbbād],

The glass is transparent,
  the wine transparent—
    the two are similar,
      the affair confused.
There seems to be wine
  and no glass,
    or glass
      and no wine.

As for mirrors and polished bodies, neither the site of the forms within them nor anything behind them is perceived. Rather, forms that are absent from the eye of their perceiver and are not within the object are perceived. Thus the seen forms are a veil between eyesight and the polished object. It is not said that these forms are subtle or dense, but eyesight witnesses them as dense. Their shapes change with the change in the shape of the polished object. When it is wavy, they are wavy. When the thing whose form they are moves in the outside world, they move, and when it remains still, they remain still, unless the shiny object is moved. For example, when water is wavy, the eye sees the form moving, even though the object whose form it is remains still. Thus the form has two movements—one derived from the movement of the object whose form it is, and the other derived from the movement of the polished object.

There is nothing in *wujūd* but veils hung down. Acts of perception attach themselves only to the veils, which leave traces in the companion of the eye that perceives them. The greatest of the veils are two—a suprasensory veil, which is ignorance; and a sensory veil, which is you over yourself.

As for the greatest suprasensory veil, that is indicated by the words of God's Messenger when he was taken on a night journey in a tree, within which were two bird nests. Gabriel sat in one nest, and God's Messenger sat in the other. When they reached the closest heaven, something like a cushion of pearls and rubies came down to them. It was one sort of the Real's self-disclosure. The Prophet said, "As for Gabriel, he swooned at that," because of his knowledge of what had come down upon him. But the Messenger of God "remained in his state," because he did not know what it was, so it had no ruling authority over him. When Gabriel regained consciousness, he reported to the Prophet that it had been the Real. Then the Prophet said, "So I came to know his excellence over me in knowledge," that is, the excellence of Gabriel. Thus knowledge had caused Gabriel to be thunderstruck, and the lack of knowledge had kept the Prophet in his state, even though both of them had the vision. Thus ignorance is the greatest of suprasensory veils.

As for the fact that you are a veil upon yourself and that this is the densest of sensory veils, this is the poet's words,[25]

A mystery has appeared to you
that has long been kept secret,
A morning has dawned
whose darkness is you.
You veil the heart
from its absent mystery.
If not for you,
it would have no seal.
If you absent yourself from the heart,
a dweller will come
whose tents will be pitched
on the guarded plain of unveiling.
Words will arrive
that you will never tire of hearing—
Their prose and poetry
will meet our desires.

So He placed no veil over you save yourself.

Now let us return to our problem. As for Moses, he was exerting himself fully in seeking fire for his folk. It is this that brought him out striving for his family, as he was commanded to do. The prophets are the most severe of all people in making demands upon themselves to undertake the commands of the Real. So there was nothing in Moses' soul save that for which he had come. When he saw his need—the fire that was shining from the tree *from the right side of the Mountain* [19:52]—God called to him from his need itself as was appropriate to the moment: *I am thy Lord, so put off thy two shoes; thou art in the holy riverbed Ṭuwā. I Myself have chosen thee, so listen to what is revealed.* He did not say, "to what I reveal." *Verily I am God* [20:12–14].

He made Moses firm through the first address, which was the calling, for he had come to borrow a firebrand or to find guidance at the fire. That is Moses' words, *I may bring you news from it* [28:29], that is, someone who would lead him to his need. Thus he was expecting the call. He had prepared his hearing and his eyesight—[his eyesight] for the vision of the fire, and his hearing for someone who would lead him to his need. Hence, when the call came to him with something appropriate, he did not deny it and he remained firm.

When Moses came to know that the caller was his Lord, while he was already secure in his firmness, and when the call came to him from outside, not from himself, he remained firm in order to give courtesy its full due while he was listening. After all, every sort of self-disclosure has a ruling property, and the ruling property of the call of this self-disclosure is to be prepared for listening to what it brings. So he was not thunderstruck, and he did not become absent from witnessing, for this was an address that underwent binding for the sake of what is heard by the ears, and it was a differentiated address.

That which keeps human beings firm in their sensation and in witnessing sensory objects is their heart that governs their body. But this divine speech to Moses had no face turned toward the heart, so here the heart had nothing but what it received from its hearing, eyesight, and faculties according to habit. Thus, for Moses the state did not transgress its ruling property.

As for the situation of Muhammad, that was a descent on the heart and an undifferentiated address, "like a chain across pebbles." So turn your attention to this simile. The heart was occupied with what descended upon it so as to receive it, so it became absent from the governing of its body. This is called "swooning" and "being thunderstruck." The same is true of the angels. (III 214.9)

Ibn al-ʿArabī provides some clarification as to what he understands from the expression "like a chain across pebbles" in Chapter 310, which he calls, "On the true knowledge of the waystation of the spiritual clanging." The word *clanging* refers to a hadith in which the Prophet was asked how revelation came to him. He replied, "Sometimes it comes to me in the likeness of a bell's clanging, and that is the most difficult for me. Then it breaks away from me, but I have retained it in my memory. Sometimes the angel comes to me in the likeness of a man's form, and I retain in memory what he says." According to the Shaykh, it is this clanging that is "like a chain across pebbles," and it was the most difficult form of revelation for the Prophet because "it used to annihilate him from himself, that is, from his sensation" (*Dhakhā'ir* 190). The knowledge that the Prophet gained from it was similar both to the knowledge that he gained when "God struck His palm between my shoulders, and I came to know the knowledge of the first and the last folk," and to the knowledge gained through rational consideration, no doubt because the Koranic revelation embraces both knowledge of *tanzīh* and knowledge of *tashbīh*, that is, both rational and imaginal knowledge. In telling us that he himself has received knowledge by way of this sort of revelation, the Shaykh alludes once again to the rationale for naming his book "The Meccan *Openings*."

> When God speaks through revelation, it is like a chain across pebbles. Spirits are thunderstruck when they hear it. The knowledge that they gain during this clanging is like the knowledge that is gained from the striking between the shoulders, or like the knowledge that is gained from consideration, through question and answer. This is the acquisition of many knowledges simply by a striking or a consideration.
>
> I have seen all this—praise belongs to God—from myself, so I have no doubt about it. I consider it similar only to locked doors. When the doors are opened and what is behind them is disclosed to you, you encompass it in knowledge with one look. In a similar way, someone opens his eye and with one glance perceives everything from the earth to the sphere of the constellations.[26]
>
> The companion of this affair finds the snow of certainty's coldness in a measure that cannot be measured. Because of the heat we have mentioned that is found when the angel casts [revelation into the heart], God's messenger used to say at the opening of every *ṣalāt* and in most states, "O God, wash us with snow," "with cold water," or "with hail."[27] All three of these are cold things through which the heat of revelation is counterbalanced, for it burns. Were it not for the strength that the heart gains through this coldness, it would perish. (III 39.29)

Chapter 384: Mutual Waystations

Among Ibn al-ʿArabī's critics, it was often said that he claimed to be a prophet or, even worse, that he claimed that the friends of God—the saints—possessed a higher station than the prophets and that he himself, as the self-proclaimed "seal of the friends," in effect claimed to be higher than all the prophets, not just the friends. The Shaykh's defenders have answered these charges by citing specific texts where he clarifies exactly what he is saying, and these make clear that such criticisms have little ground to stand on.[28]

Nonetheless, Ibn al-ʿArabī offers plenty of ammunition to his critics on the issue of revelation. He does indeed claim that God has spoken to him, as He has spoken to the prophets and many of His friends. He even "reveals" to His friends, but so also does He "reveal"—as stated explicitly in the Koran—to the heaven and the earth, the mountains, the bees, and others. But "revelation" in this general sense is not what differentiates prophets from friends or other creatures. Rather, the differentiating factor has to do with the contents of the revelation. The prophets bring legal "rulings" (*aḥkām*), either by establishing shariahs or modifying pre-existent shariahs. In the rulings, God's friends can only follow (*tābiʿ*) the prophets, for God does not reveal rulings to them. What He does reveal to whomsoever He wills is "reports" (*akhbār*), that is, knowledge concerning anything whatsoever, including, for example, the rationale for the rulings.

One of the specific terms that the Shaykh employs to refer to this divine report-giving (*ikhbār*) or knowledge-giving (*iʿlām*) is *address* (*khiṭāb*). As usual, the term is Koranic, the root being employed a dozen times. The specific verse that the Shaykh usually has in mind when he employs the term is God's words concerning David: *We strengthened his kingdom and We gave him wisdom and the differentiation of address* (38:20). The expression *the differentiation of address* (*faṣl al-khiṭāb*) has been rendered by Koran translators with phrases such as "decisive address" (Palmer), "a clear judgment" (Muhammad Ali), and "decisive speech" (Pickthall, Arberry). It is usually understood to mean that God gave David the power of clear articulation in his speech, but the Shaykh stresses the fact that this is a divine speaking that David heard. In hearing God's speech, David heard God's own articulation of divine wisdom, along with all its details. That the address is God's own speech is implied even if we read the expression as referring to David's power of speech. From whence did David's clear articulation come if not from God? And if its content is not the divinely revealed knowledge that he possesses, why should God have given it to him?

A second verse that mentions address is also relevant to the Shaykh's understanding of what it implies: *Lord of the heavens and the earth and what is between them, the All-Merciful—they possess no address from Him* (78:37). Typically, this verse is understood to mean that people cannot address God, or speak about God, or speak with Him, but it can also mean that they have no claim upon His speaking to them. This fits in nicely with the standard Islamic teaching, often repeated by Ibn al-ᶜArabī, that prophecy (and, by extension, true knowledge of God) derives from *ikhtiṣāṣ*, specification, not from *iktisāb*, earning. People have no claim on prophecy and, by extension, revelation, because they cannot earn it. It is a sheer gift.

In short, when Ibn al-ᶜArabī claims that he has been addressed by God, he is saying something that many of the ulama would consider near to unbelief, because it implies—according to their definition of prophecy—that he is a prophet. But the Shaykh's own definition of prophecy is much more precise and accords better with Koranic teachings, as he frequently illustrates in his discussions of unveiling and witnessing. By his definition, in no sense is he claiming prophecy, at least not the prophecy of law-giving (*tashrīᶜ*). Rather, he is simply saying that God has specified him and singled him out for a knowledge that He has not given to others—just as He has specified the bees and the mountains for their own special revelations.

All this is to suggest some of the implications of the title of Chapter 384, "On the true knowledge of the mutual waystations of address." This chapter is especially significant because it introduces Part Five of the *Futūḥāt*, which deals with "mutual waystations" (*munāzalāt*). These are stations of unveiling and divine bestowal of knowledge in which God descends to the servant, and the servant ascends to God. The Shaykh devotes seventy-seven of the seventy-eight chapters of Part Five to explaining God's addresses to him in these mutual waystations. In most of these, God uttered an enigmatic saying, and the chapter explains its significance.

In this first chapter of Part Five, the Shaykh remarks immediately after the title and before the initial poem that this part of the book derives from the mystery of God's words, *It belongs not to any mortal that God should speak to him, except by revelation, or from behind a veil* (42:51) and that the whole of Part Five pertains to the Muhammadan Presence, which is to say that it is an inheritance from the Prophet Muhammad. Hence this Part deals with how God addresses the servant *from behind a veil*, so it provides a good deal of clarification concerning the Shaykh's understanding of the veil that prevents creatures from seeing God. One of the points that should become obvious in the chapter is that the discussion of the veil is intimately connected with imagination. The realms in which the revelatory veils are perceived by the Folk of God are precisely the *barzakh*s, the in-between worlds, the domains that are neither this nor that. All the mutual waystations have to do with the meeting between God and man, the commingling of the divine and the human, the ambiguity and wavering that prevent us from seeing clearly what is what. In other words, they all have to do with the actual situation in which we find ourselves in the cosmos, even if we would prefer to think that things are clear for us.

At the beginning of the chapter, Ibn al-ʿArabī explains why he employs the term *munāzala,* and from this we see that "mutual waystation" may not be the best translation, though it suggests what he has in mind and can be employed without a good deal of explanation. Literally, the term means "mutual descent." It derives from the root *n.z.l.,* from which we have *nuzūl* and *tanazzul,* both of which are usually translated as "descent." *Nuzūl* may also mean getting down from one's mount, and this implies stopping at a dwelling to rest. Hence the term *manzil* or "waystation" is the place where one descends from one's mount to rest during a journey. In a "mutual waystation," both God and the servant "descend" in order to meet each other, as travelers might descend from their horses in order to meet in a camp. The descent of the servants to God, then, is connected to the idea that when they rise up to Him through a *miʿrāj,* they travel on their own Burāq—the steed that took Muhammad on his *miʿrāj*—and then "descend" from their Burāq to meet with God.

The mutual waystations of the knowledges
 bring out the realities of the Real and the
  servants
without excess or conflict,
 without dispute or obstinacy.
So say, "I fall short in my reason, but
  tradition
 provides guidance as to transgression and
  right conduct.
"All my remembrance takes to
  wholesomeness,
 and some of my reflective thought to
  corruption.
"The most beneficial knowledge is that of my
  poverty
 toward the Bestowing, Munificent Master."

Know—God confirm you and us—that here a "mutual waystation" is the act of two actors. Each of the two descends seeking the other so that each may descend at the other or through the other—say what you wish. Hence they come together in the path in a designated site, and this is named a "mutual" waystation because of the seeking of both.

In reality, on the part of the servant, this "descent" is a rising up. We name it a "descent" only because he seeks through this rising up to descend at the Real. God says, *To Him climb up the pleasant words, and the wholesome deed—He uplifts it* [35:10]. This is his Burāq upon which he travels to Him by night and through which he descends at Him. God says concerning Himself, as God's Messenger mentioned on His behalf, "Our Lord descends to the closest heaven every night," and so on to the end of the hadith. Thus he described Him as descending to us. This is the descent of a Real to a creature, and on our part there is the descent of a creature to a Real, because we are not able to have highness, greatness, and independence from Him. So we have the attribute of smallness and poverty toward Him, and He has the attribute of independence and greatness.

Each of us is poor toward Him,
 each before Him small,
Each of us looks at Him as other,
 and He is Independent of us, the Great—
Except for me, for I see Him
 as my own entity, and I am the
  experienced.
After I came to know this, I said,
 "I am a servant, poor toward His
  independence."

In reality, through us we descend to Him, and through us He descends to us. Were it not for that, we would not know what He says to us in His address to us, for *He is the Independent, the Praiseworthy* [35:15]. But, in the reality of the reality, through Him we descend to Him, and through Him He descends to us. Whether it is a mutual waystation or a complete descent such that He is the speaker and the listener, He knows what He says. After all, He hears him who has this station, so none hears his speech save He.

Since He is the root, we are only through Him. After all, the branch emerges in the form of the root, and within the branches the fruit becomes manifest and benefits are gained. So also, the branches are the locus of needs. So there is nothing there but He.

Had I to You a path,
 I would have nothing to signify You.
So You are an exalted Lord
 and I the abased slave.
I marvel at a God and a servant
 in a high waystation that terrifies.
This is a correlation, for my words imply
 that He and we are equal.
God said it—no engendered thing said it.
 I said it because He said it.

Of the same sort is this:

> This is the affair that
>   is inescapable and sufficient.
> Act according to my words,
>   if you have taken on His qualities!
> When the one who gazes upon you
>   is the Real, treat Him fairly,
> For if you oppose Him,
>   you will be *on the brink [of a pit of the Fire]* [3:103].

> Know that the Real does not speak to His servants or address them save *from behind the veil* [42:51] of the form within which He discloses Himself to them. This form is a veil over Him and a signifier of Him, like the manifest, corporeous form of the human being. When the rationally speaking soul desires to speak to another soul, it speaks to it *from behind the veil* of its body's form in the form's tongue and language. Although the soul is a created thing, its affair is as we described. So what about the Creator?
>
> When a person descends into mutual waystations of address, he witnesses nothing but forms. From them he takes the realities and mysteries for which these forms act as spokesmen to him. These are "the tongues of the elocution." (III 523.18)

The rare term *elocution*, Arabic *fahwāniyya*, needs some explanation. It seems to be specific to Ibn al-ᶜArabī's teachings. Suᶜād al-Ḥakīm, in her dictionary of the Shaykh's technical terminology, tells us that it derives from the root *f.w.h.*, which means to mouth, to utter, to pronounce.[29] In *Iṣṭilāḥāt al-ṣūfiyya* Ibn al-ᶜArabī defines it as "The address of the Real, by way of direct encounter, in the world of imagination" (17). In the *Futūḥāt* version of the same work, the Shaykh adds, "And this is the Prophet's words concerning doing the beautiful [*iḥsān*]: 'It is to worship God as if you see Him'" (II 128.34). He frequently cites this hadith to show the importance of imagination in communicating with God. He also employs the term *elocution* to refer to the "word of the Presence," i.e., *Be*, with which the Real addresses the fixed entities in the state of their fixity (as in *Tajalliyyāt* 13). In short, he is telling us here that the mutual waystations are situations in which God addresses the servant, "directly," yet from behind the veil of imagination. They are visionary encounters in which the servant actually meets God—not God in His Essence, of course, but God in His self-disclosures.[30]

In continuing his introductory remarks about mutual waystations, Ibn al-ᶜArabī first situates them cosmologically between the Cloud, which is the Breath of the All-Merciful or the Divine Spirit that God blows into the human clay, and the earth, which is the world proper to this clay. Thus the realm of these imaginal encounters is the "space" between the unbounded Spirit, or the unarticulated Breath, and the earth, which is the dense and dark realm of the elements.

> The limit of the mutual waystations is from the Cloud to the earth and everything in between. When the form parts from the Cloud, and when the nonmanifest human form parts from the earth, and when the two meet, this is the mutual waystation. If the human form reaches the Cloud, or if the command comes to it in the earth, this is a "descent," not a mutual waystation, and the locus in which the two come together is a "waystation" [*manzil*].
>
> The Presence from which occurs the divine address to whichever of His servants that He wills is called "the Presence of Grandiloquence." (III 524.15)

"Grandiloquence" (*lasan*) is another relatively rare expression. The Shaykh defines it as "That through which divine clear-speaking falls into the ears of the gnostics, and it is the Word of the Presence. If you ask what the Word of the Presence is, we will reply, the word *Be*. *Be* is not said save to the possessor of vision, that he may know through witnessing who says *Be* to him" (II 129.1; cf. *Iṣṭilāḥāt* 17). Thus, what the gnostic hears is the engendering command *Be* itself, which presumably means that he witnesses the interchange between God and the fixed entities, the moment by moment process whereby God gives existence to the things. Naturally, he witnesses this in his own context, since the divine self-disclosure is always conditioned by the preparedness of the receptacle.

From this Presence *God spoke directly to Moses* [4:164]. Do you not see that He disclosed Himself to him in the form of his need?

From this Presence God's Messenger was given the All-Comprehensive Words, so within it all the forms of the cosmos were brought together for him. Hence the knowledge of the names of these forms is Adam's knowledge, but their entities belong to Muhammad, along with their names that were given to Adam. For Adam is among the "first" whose knowledge God gave to Muhammad, since he said concerning himself that God gave him "the knowledge of the first and the last folk."

From this Presence God gave David *wisdom and the differentiation of address* [38:20].

All the scriptures and the sent down books proceed from this Presence. From it God dictates to the Highest Pen what it should write in the Preserved Tablet. The speech of the whole cosmos, both the absent of it and the witnessed, derives from this Presence—and all is the speech of God—for this is the First Presence.

The first thing the possible things have from God when He brings them into existence is the word *Be*. This address unstitches the hearing of the possible things. And *the last of their supplication* in the Garden—*Praise belongs to God, Lord of the worlds* [10:10]—occurs when God says to the folk of the Garden, "I am pleased with you and I will never be angry with you." Were it not for the Breath of the All-Merciful, the entities of the possible things—the words—would not have become manifest.

Know also that movements—whatever they may be—come to be only from something that moves in something on the basis of the intention of the mover, whether the mover is the thing itself or something else. So forms arrive newly from the thing's movement, or rather, from its undergoing movement within that in which it undergoes movement, according to its intention. The forms take shape in keeping with the homestead and according to the intention that comes to be from the mover.

Take, for example, letters in the breath that emerges from the human being. When a person intends to make manifest a designated letter so as to give existence to its entity in the homestead that belongs to it, the form of the letter is opened up in that homestead. He designates for that letter a name specific to it through which it is distinguished from other letters when it is mentioned. In the same way, the letter's form differs from the form of other letters when it is made present, and this takes place in keeping with the extension of the breath.

When the person intends to make manifest a word in its entity, then, while making manifest the entities of the letters in his breath, he intends to manifest designated letters, and he does not manifest any others. Some are heard as joined to others, and a word arrives newly to the hearing. The word is the relation of the joining of those letters. It is nothing superadded to the letters, only the relation of their coming together. This fact of coming together bestows a form that the letters could not bestow without the relation that brings them together. Such is the composition of the entities of the cosmos—which is compounded from the noncompound things within it.

The eye witnesses nothing but something compounded from noncompound things. The compound thing is nothing superadded to its noncompound things save the relation of the coming together of these noncompound things. We mention this only so that you will know what the eye witnesses.

Compoundedness in the entities of these letters is infinite. That is why *The words of God* will *not run out* [31:27]. So the forms of the words arrive newly—that is, become manifest—perpetually. Hence *wujūd* and giving existence remain perpetually.

So know, O compound thing, who you are! From what have you been compounded? How is it that you do not become manifest to your own eye in your noncompound parts, but you do become manifest to your eye in your compoundedness? No affair of *wujūd* occurs except a relation of compoundedness that you judge to be other than it was before the compoundedness. So understand!

God configured the form of *Be* from the Breath, then the engendered things from *Be*. He made nothing manifest save words, all of them from *Be*. It is the vocable of a command pertaining to *wujūd*, so nothing becomes manifest from it except what corresponds to it—compound letters that come together with *Be* in that they are words. This means that His command is but one, and it is His word *Be*. God says, *Our command is but one* [54:50]. And He says, *Our only word to a thing, when We desire it, is to say to it "Be!," so* the thing *comes to be* [16:40] in its entity. Hence the thing that comes to be is now qualified by *wujūd* after it had been described as not existent, though it had been fixed and inserted in the Breath and not existent through letters.

The root mutual waystation bestows new arrival on the engendered things and makes manifest the forms of the possible things within the entities. He who knows what we say knows the cosmos—what it is and who it is. So glory be to Him who has hidden these mysteries in their manifestation and made them manifest in their hiddenness! They are the manifest and the nonmanifest and the first and the last, *for a people who reason* [2:164].

The Entity is One,
the property belongs to the relations;
the Entity is manifest,
coming to be belongs to the occasion.

God says, *You did not throw,* so He negated, *when you threw,* so He affirmed exactly what He negated, *but God threw* [8:17], so He negated exactly what He affirmed. Hence the affirmation of the throwing turns out to be a middle between the two sides of a negation. The first negation is identical with the latter negation, so it is impossible to affirm the entity of the middle between the two negations, since it is restricted, so the restriction governs over it. This is especially true because the latter negation adds to the first negation by affirming that the throwing belongs to Him, not to the middle.

In the domain of sensory witnessing, the throwing was affirmed as belonging to Muhammad through the affirmation of Muhammad in the word of the Real. Just as he is a thrower/not thrower, so also, in the divine word, he is Muhammad/not Muhammad. For, if he were Muhammad, as his form gives witness, he would be a thrower, as his throwing gives witness. Since the divine report negates the throwing from him, his entity is negated, because there is no difference between his entity and his throwing. The same is the case with *You did not slay them, but God slew them* [8:17].

This is the "insight" upon which are those who call to God. They know who calls to God and who is called to God. Thus, the perception is one, but when the actual situation is perceived through it, the perception is named "insight," because it is a realized knowledge. And when the relation of what becomes manifest in the domain of sensation is perceived through it, the perception is named "eyesight." The bynames that name it are diverse because of the diversity of the homestead.

In the same way, the property of a particle is diverse, even if it is one in form, since it is diverse through the diversity of the homesteads. Take the particle *mā*. There is no doubt that it is one entity. In one homestead, it is negative, like His words, ***None** knows its interpretation save God* [3:7]. In another homestead, it indicates exclamation, like His words, ***How** patiently they shall endure the Fire!* [2:175]. In another homestead, it is preparatory, like His words, *It **may** be that the disbelievers will wish* [15:2]. In another homestead, it is a pronoun, like His words, ***What** Thou didst command me* [5:117]. And so it goes, for it can also act as a gerund, indicate a question, be extraneous, and so on, depending on the homesteads. So this is one entity, and upon it the homesteads exercise diverse ruling properties.

In the same way, the forms of self-disclosure play the role of ruling properties for him who understands what he sees. God clarified for us through what He mentioned in the verse [of the throwing] that what we thought was a sensory reality was only an imaginalized thing seen by the eye's seeing. The situation in itself is different from what the eye witnesses. This pervades all the corporeal and spiritual faculties, for the whole cosmos is in the forms of raised-up images, since the *Wujūd* Presence is only the Presence of Imagination. Then the forms that you see become divided into "sensory" and "imaginalized," but all are imaginalized.

No one holds this view save him who has been given to witness this locus of witnessing. The philosopher tosses it away, as do all the companions of rational proofs. The folk of the manifest domain do not accept it, to be sure, nor do they accept the meanings for the sake of which these forms have come.

No one comes near this locus of witnessing save the Sophists. However, the difference between us and them is that they say that all this has no reality, but we do not say that. On the contrary, we say that it is a reality. Thus we part from all the tribes—may God allow us and His Messenger to conform to that concerning which He has given us knowledge and which is beyond what He has given us to witness!

We know what we witness. Witnessing is a solicitude from God bestowed upon us by the light of faith through which God has illumined our insights.

He who knows what we have explained knows the knowledge of the earth created from the leftover ferment of Adam's clay. He knows that the whole cosmos, or rather, the existent things, are the inhabitants of that earth. None is rid of that earth save the Real, its Creator and Configurer, in respect of His He-ness, since to Him belongs *wujūd* when that earth is not.[31]

Were the affair not what we have mentioned, mutual waystations between us and the Real would not be correct, nor would it be correct for the Real to descend to the closest heaven or to sit upon the Throne, nor for there to be a Cloud within which was our Lord "before He created His creatures."

Were it not for the property of the name Manifest, this Presence would not have appeared and the cosmos would not have become manifest through the [divine] form. And were it not for the name Nonmanifest, we would not have known that the thrower is God in the Muhammadan form and in other forms.

God says, *It belongs not to any mortal that God should speak to him* while he is a mortal *except by revelation*—this being like His words, *God threw,* so the thrower is God, but eyesight witnesses Muhammad—*or from behind the veil* of a mortal form, so that there may be a correspondence between the two forms through the address, *or that He should send a messenger* [42:51], who is the Real's spokesman in the servant's heart. *The Faithful Spirit has brought it down upon thy heart* [26:193–94].

When God reveals to the mortal messenger through the specific face[32] by lifting the intermediaries, and when the messenger casts it to us, this is the Real's speech *from behind the veil* of the form that is named a "messenger," if he is sent to us, or a "prophet." This level may also belong to some of God's friends.[33]

When the mortal covering is unveiled from the eye of the heart, it perceives all the forms of all the existent things in this manner, some of them addressing others, and some of them hearing from others. Thus become unified the speaking, the hearing, the holding, the running, the sensing, the imagining, the form-giving, the remembering, and all the faculties attributed to mortal man. So all mutual waystations are *barzakhī* between *the First and the Last and the Manifest and the Nonmanifest* [57:3], and between the forms of the cosmos and the forms of self-disclosure.

Grant him sanctuary until he hears the speech of God [9:6], so the spokesman is the speaker, for we have come to know that the heard speech is the speech of God, not his speech.

So consider what He brings in His *barzakhī* address! Open the eye of understanding so it may perceive! Be in accordance with that through which He addresses you! Hear not the speech of God save through the hearing of God, nor the speech of the form save through the hearing of the form! But the Hearer is "from behind" the hearing, the Speaker is "from behind" the speech, *And God is from behind them, encompassing. Nay, but it is a splendorous Koran, in a Tablet Preserved* [85:20–22] from alteration and change. [The speech] is either what signifies *tawḥīd*, or an attribute of *tanzīh*, or an attribute of an act, or what requires sharing, or *tashbīh*, or rulings, or narratives, or admonition through stirring up longing or dread, or the signification of something signified. It is restricted to firm [*muḥkam*] and ambiguous [*mutashābih*]—every address in the cosmos. (III 524.17)

At this point in the text, the Shaykh abruptly turns to commenting on a Koranic passage that he takes, in the present context, as referring to the situation of the self in a mutual waystation: *By the mount and a book inscribed on a parchment unrolled! By the inhabited house and the uplifted roof and the burning sea! Surely thy Lord's chastisement is about to fall; there is none to avert it* (52:1–8). The first sentence of the passage is usually understood to be a reference to Moses and the tablets he received at Mount Sinai. Ibn al-ʿArabī, however, offers an explanation of the type that is often called *taʾwīl*, or "esoteric interpretation," since he takes the verse as a reference to the human relation with God established through the mutual waystation. However, he would not call this a *taʾwīl*, but rather an "allusion" (*ishāra*), which he contrasts with simple "exegesis" (*tafsīr*), a point of which he reminds the reader in the third paragraph.[34]

By the mount—the body, because of the natural inclination within it,[35] since it is not independent through itself in its *wujūd*.

And a book inscribed from a divine dictation and a right hand writing with a pen of potency.

On a parchment, that is, your own entity—by way of allusion, not exegesis.

Unrolled, manifest, not rolled up, so it is not curtained.

By the inhabited house, that is, the heart that embraces the Real, so He is its inhabitant.

And the uplifted roof—the sensory and suprasensory faculties in the head.

And the burning sea, that is, nature kindled with the ruling fire that necessitates movement.

Surely thy Lord's chastisement is about to fall. In other words, something from which the animal self, the command spirit,[36] and the high intellect take refuge but which derives from the self's nurturing Master, who makes its affair wholesome, is about to fall and come down upon it. For the self possesses the low waystations absolutely in respect to its possibility and relatively in respect to its nature.

There is none to avert it, because there is only what I have mentioned. What we have is receiving His coming down and climbing up to His approach. Between these two properties become manifest the *barzakhs,* which possess towering splendor and firmly-rooted knowledge.

A mutual waystation may occur between the divine names, such as a mutual waystation in a battle over a human individual who has opposed the command of God. He is sought by the Relenter, the Forgiving, and the All-Merciful, and he is also sought by the Avenger, the Harmer, the Abaser, and the like. In this regard a hadith has come—God's words, "I never waver in anything I do the way I waver in taking the soul of a man of faith who dislikes death, while I dislike doing ill to him, but he must encounter Me." This is one sort of mutual waystation.

I have tasted this unveiling. I saw it from God in the slaying of al-Dajjāl, when the Messenger of God was present with me in the unveiling.[37] From here was opened up to me the door to the outspreading of mercy over God's servants. I came to know that His *mercy embraces everything* [7:156], so its ruling property has no escape from penetrating into all things. I also came to know the wisdom in the fact that accidents become nonexistent to themselves in the second time after the time of their *wujūd,* and God creates likenesses or opposites in the locus. Were the accident to become fixed as its locus is fixed—so long as its locus is not a meaning like it, that is, another accident, similar to it in its accidentality—it would subsist just as the substance subsists, and its state would not undergo alteration for the substance. It would either be perpetually wretched from the first point of its creation, or perpetually felicitous. Then God's mercy would fall short of certain specific entities, just as it is attained through necessity by a people described by a specific description. As for those who do not attain it through a binding attribute of necessity, mercy reaches them by way of gratuitous favor, just as it reaches those who are worthy of it and for whom it is necessary through the attribute that it gives to them and by which it becomes qualified, so mercy becomes necessary for them.[38] So, by way of gratuitous favor everything reaches mercy, and mercy reaches everything. There is nothing but the divine gratuitous favor in root and branch.

Then the mutual waystation pervades the two fingers of the All-Merciful in the heart, within the playing field of desire. If He causes the heart to swerve,[39] an All-Merciful has caused it to swerve, and if He sets it straight, an All-Merciful has set it straight. There is no ruling property save His, since it is He who sits upon the Throne, so ruling properties exercise their influence only from this name.

Then the mutual waystation between the angel and the satan becomes manifest over the heart through the two suggestions. Those for whom the Law is prescribed find these two in their hearts. If the Law is not prescribed for them and they find wavering in the heart, they are either in an abode of religious prescription, or they are not. If they are in an abode of prescription, wavering derives only from the angelic suggestion and the satanic suggestion.[40] Each of these, for the sake of that within which their suggestions exercise influence, seeks that the person prescribed for by the Law have access to aiding in corruption, so that sin [*ithm*] will be permissible for him.

Take, for example, two children who have not yet reached the degree of religious prescription and who strike each other at the satanic suggestion that has overcome each of them. Their parents come, or two of their relatives, or their neighbors, or whoever is present. They intervene between the two of them without a Shari'ite scale, but rather with the zeal of personal desire. This may give rise to their earning a sin in what they strive to do for the sake of the two children. Thus the movement of the child to evil derives from the suggestion of the satan. So understand, and recognize the homesteads, so that you may become settled in the more complete knowledge.

If prescription has not been made for the person, if he is not in an abode of prescription, and if he finds wavering in an affair between two acts, then there is no fault in him, whichever of the two he does. This wavering and this mutual waystation between two thoughts is like the divine wavering. However, in the case of the servant, it is for the sake of seeking the more appropriate and the higher, like a person for whom the Law is prescribed who wavers over which of two acts of obedience he should perform. This is a divine wavering and does not derive from the two suggestions. Rather, two personal desires, or a single personal desire, become connected to two affairs either equally, or in order to clarify a preference required by the moment. He is not prescribed for by the Law, nor is he in an abode of prescription. After all, were there no prescription, no satan would ever come near a human being to lead him astray, for that would be useless, and the Real does nothing useless, for all is His act *and to Him the whole affair is returned* [11:123].

The companion of the knowledge of mutual waystations has no escape from coming to understand all of this and its similars. This is the root of each and every wavering in the cosmos. As for the divine wavering, or the two fingers, or the two suggestions, that is another thing and it has something of a property here. But the root is the divine wavering and what is given by the realities of the contrary divine names. *And God speaks the **ḥaqq**, and He guides on the path* [33:4].

So let us mention in this Part a few of the divine gnostic sciences that we have gained in the mutual waystations, for they are more than can be enumerated. (III 526.12)

4. *Veils of Light*

Knowing the cosmos for what it is depends upon deciphering the signs, and deciphering the signs depends upon knowing oneself. We have already seen in a number of places that Ibn al-ʿArabī considers knowledge of the cosmos subsidiary to knowledge of self. In the context of his writings, the point is obvious, and perhaps there is no need to belabor it. But the idea that it is possible to achieve objective knowledge by ignoring the input and perspective of the subject is so thoroughly drummed into the modern psyche, or at least its popular version, that it may be useful to devote more space to investigating the necessary connection between the self and the cosmos.

For Ibn al-ʿArabī, what we would call "objective" knowledge of the true nature of things is impossible to achieve, and the idea that we have achieved it can only be an illusion, one that is damaging not only to those who have the idea, but also to the "objective" world itself, which people rule as divinely appointed vicegerents. Self-knowledge is an absolutely necessary precondition for any real knowledge, that is, any knowledge of the Real. But the cosmos is full of veils, and the greatest of veils, even greater than the quest for objectivity, is the self that knows. Hence the most pressing of all tasks, if we are to know anything of lasting significance, is to acknowledge the need to lift the veil that prevents the self from seeing itself and others. Nevertheless, the veil is the self, and the self is the face. The glories of the divine face that burn away all creaturely attributes, by this act of burning away, re-establish and re-affirm the burnt-away attributes.

The Veil of Self

In a passage already quoted, the Shaykh says that the self is the greatest of the sensory veils and that God "placed no veil over you save yourself" (III 215.3). In other words, "There is no escape from the curtain, for there is no escape from you" (II 554.21). The fact that the self is the veil helps explain one of the meanings of the saying, "He who knows himself knows his Lord." Once people are able to lift the veil and see instead the Real's self-disclosure, they will know that the veil is identical with the divine face and that curtaining is the same as self-disclosure. But this knowledge cannot be achieved theoretically. The ignorance to be overcome is ontological, having to do with the very forgetfulness (*nisyān*) and heedlessness (*ghafla*) that are woven into created nature. Only a perfectly balanced vision with "two eyes"—the eye of reason and the eye of imagination, or the eye that sees *tanzīh* and the eye that sees *tashbīh*—makes possible a knowledge of things for what they truly are.

> When God opens the door to the two mercies and "Morning becomes clear for the possessor of the two eyes," the Real brings whomsoever He will of His servants to a halt before His two hands. He addresses him, reporting to him what belongs to him and what he is.
>
> He says to him, "If you are not wary of God, you will be ignorant of Him, and if you are wary of Him, you will be more ignorant of Him. You have no escape from one of the two qualities. Hence I created heedlessness and forgetfulness for you, so that you may be naked of the property of the two opposites, for without heedlessness, the property of one of the two will become manifest. So give thanks to God for heedlessness and forgetfulness!"
>
> Then it is said to him, "Be cautious of the folk of the curtains lest they lead you on step by step to the curtains. They are the folk of deceit and deception. Is there a curtain over Him who, in relation to you, is *nearer than the jugular vein* [50:16]? He is curtained from you only through you, so you are identical with His curtain over you. Were you to see your own nonmanifest side, you would see Him." (III 229.8)

The problem is ignorance, the solution is knowledge. There is no change in the actual situation of *wujūd* and the entities.

> The servant's veil is from himself,
> but he knows not
> that his *wujūd*
> is the same as the veil.
> O my people, listen to my words
> and attain
> what He has said
> in the Mother of the Book:
> The word *we ask for help* [1:4]
> has made us manifest,
> but my acts and entity
> dwell in loss.
> We wander aimlessly
> in every wasteland,
> we stand waiting
> at every gate. (IV 43.18)

The self is the veil that keeps us wandering aimlessly. The way to lift the veil is to know oneself and thereby to know one's Lord. In other words, knowledge is the root of felicity. In the hereafter, people will be felicitous to the degree that they know themselves in this world. The quickest way to self-knowledge is to eliminate the veil, which is precisely the selfhood with which we normally identify. The route to this knowledge, however, is not necessarily an easy one to follow, and reaching various degrees of this knowledge does not preclude backsliding and retrogression.

> Know that those who suppose nowadays that knowledge is felicity have spoken the truth, and I say the same thing. However, they have missed what is perceived by the folk of unveiling, and that is this: When God desires the wretchedness of the servant, He makes knowledge disappear from him. For knowledge does not belong to him by essence. On the contrary, he has acquired it. When something is acquired, it is permissible for it to disappear. Then He drapes him in the robe of ignorance, because taking away knowledge is the same as ignorance. No knowledge remains for him save the knowledge that knowledge was taken away from him. If God did not leave for him the knowledge that knowledge was taken away, he would not suffer chastisement. After all, the ignorant person who does not know that he is ignorant is joyful and happy, because he does not know what has escaped him. If he knew that great good has escaped him, he would not be joyful in his state and he would immediately suffer pain. So he suffers pain only because of his knowledge of what has escaped him, or what he had possessed that was stripped from him.
>
> Once I was afflicted by a pain in my arm. I returned to God through complaint—the return of Job—out of courtesy toward God, so that I would not resist the divine subjugation, as is done by the folk of ignorance of God. In doing so, they claim to be the folk of surrender, of entrusting the affair to God, and of making no protest. Hence they bring together two ignorances.
>
> When I realized what God caused me to realize through that suffering, I said,
>
> I complained to Him about my arm
> because of my narrowed endurance.
> I said to the soul, "Call upon Him!
> Where is your calling when I am
> expanded?"
> She said, "I will complain to Him for you,
> for my loss is the same as my gain."

If not for complaint about what I undergo,
I would have emerged from it and from my nature.
This is an ignorance known to a heart
that is a companion of a state through following the prophets.
Had I not strayed from Him through my ignorance,
no caller would have called me to Him.
I said to Him who called me, "At your service!"
He said, "I desire nothing but delight.
Eagerness has been expended, so take advantage!
Reaching Me is the same as being cut off!"
So I was relieved of what I had been finding,
and what I had witnessed became absent from me.

If not for the Intellect's *wujūd,*
I would not know Him,
if not for the Tablet's *wujūd,*
I would not take His dictation.
If not for witnessing engendered existence,
I would not discharge my duty to Him,
if not for gaining knowledge,
I would not put it into practice.
He who says that creation
knows His Being
has no knowledge
of His *ḥaqq* in himself.
This is enough for him—
this much ignorance
of reality's actual situation—
this is enough for him.

When the realities are unveiled so that there is no doubt and no untruth, and their "Morning becomes clear to the possessor of the two eyes," he is given to see, contention is removed, and hearing is gained. However, between you and this state are perilous deserts, thirst-inducing wilderness, obliterated roads, and effaced tracks within which even the skillful are bewildered. No one crosses over them but the one who causes to live and to die, not the one who lives and dies. So what is the state of the one who undergoes these hardships and travels these narrow passes? Yet, in the measure of the pains will be the bliss through the varieties of ease.

But there is no wilderness and no desert save you, for you are your own veil upon yourself. So withdraw, and the affair will be easy.

He who knows creation knows the Real, but he who is ignorant of the part of this task is ignorant of its whole, for within itself, in a respect that it does not know, the part has the whole itself. Were he to know the part in all its faces, he would know the whole, for one of its faces in being the part is knowledge of the whole.

This waystation is among the waystations whose signs are many and whose signifiers are lucid, but eyesights stay in the property of their covering, hearts remain in their shelters, and rational faculties keep themselves busy warring against capricious winds, so none of them empties itself for the gaze that is sought from it. (III 245.33)

Among the veils that prevent people from recognizing the face of God in their own selves are blameworthy character traits, which cloud the mirror of the heart. The Shaykh provides an example in Chapter 427, "On the true knowledge of the mutual waystation of those whose wage falls upon God." He divides these wage-takers into three sorts on the basis of various Koranic verses. The first two are God's messengers and those who emigrate in God's path. The third are those who display various noble character traits (*makārim al-akhlāq*), such as pardoning and making wholesome, as mentioned in the verse, *And the recompense of an ugly act is an ugly act the like of it, but whoso pardons and makes wholesome, his wage falls upon God* (42:40). "Making wholesome" (*iṣlāḥ*) is the opposite of "working corruption" (*ifsād*), and an "ugly act" (*sayʾiyya*) is contrasted with a "beautiful act" (*ḥasana*). The Koran often praises the "wholesome" (*ṣāliḥūn*)—those who have achieved wholesomeness in themselves by making things wholesome and performing "wholesome deeds" (*ṣāliḥāt*). In this passage, the Shaykh explains that pardoning and overlooking the offenses of others establishes wholesomeness and is a form of "doing the beautiful" (*iḥsān*). The divine root of this character trait is God's overlooking and forgiving the sins of His servants.

The third sort whose wage falls upon God are those *who pardon* someone who does an ugly act toward them *and makes wholesome,* that is, they "make wholesome" the state of the one who did an ugly act toward them through doing the beautiful. Thus they make wholesome what would necessitate that they perform an ugly act toward that person. Here, by "making wholesome," God means nothing but this.

No one gains this station except those who have a high aspiration. After all, God has made it permissible for people to recompense the ugly-doer with an ugly deed of the same weight, but they disdain being themselves a locus qualified by what the Real has called an "ugly act."

The self of a noble man
  is noble in everything
    that the winds and decrees
      bring his way.
God judges selves
  through their measure,
    and He it is
      who has choice in His judgment.
Then the mindful man,
  whose rational faculty is authorized,
    judges differently from the noble self
      and is bewildered.

In this station God says, *Repel with that which is more beautiful*—referring here to His words *he makes* the ugly act *wholesome—and behold, he between whom and thee is enmity shall be as if he were a loyal friend. Yet none shall receive it*, that is, this attribute, *except those who are patient* [41:34] and restrain themselves from recompensing the ugly-doer with ugly-doing for his ugly-doing.

Were the people to know the measure of that to which we are calling attention in this question, they would never recompense someone who performs ugly acts toward them with ugly-doing, and you would not see anyone in the cosmos save those who pardon and make wholesome. However, the veils upon the eyes of insight are dense, and these are nothing but personal desires and the wish to hurry revenge and retribution.

This person should consider his own ugly-doing toward God in rejecting what He has prescribed for him and in mounting upon danger in this, and he should consider the Real's giving him respite in this and His passing over him in this abode. This is true even if he exposes himself to the penalty that needs to be enacted against him, and if he throws himself into perils. Thus the Prophet said, "God has curtained that for him—if he would curtain it for himself," concerning him who confessed to fornication. Moreover, the writing angels do not write against the servant any of his ugly acts until he speaks of them, as indicated by His words, *Not a word he utters, but by him is a watcher ready* [50:18], which is the writing angel. Although *They know whatever you do* [82:12], God did not say that they write it down.

Concerning God's generous nobility, unveiling bestows and a report has come that when the servant does an ugly deed, the angel asks his companion, from whom the Real has commanded him to take permission before he writes anything down, "Should I write it down?"

He replies, "Do not write it down, but wait six hours from the time of the ugly deed. If he repents and asks forgiveness, do not write it down. But if six hours pass without his asking forgiveness, then write it down as one ugly act. And do not write it down until he speaks of it by saying, 'I did such and such,' or if the ugly act was in speaking. Then write it down after this amount of time has gone by." But which person of faith would allow six hours to go by without asking forgiveness from God for it?

This sort has a wage that falls upon God in two respects. First is God's wage for pardoning, and this wage is "many," because the word *pardoning* has opposite meanings.[1] Second is the wage of making wholesome, which is doing the beautiful toward the person, thereby effacing the factor that brought about the ugly-doing. *And God loves those who do the beautiful* [3:134]. If their doing the beautiful—which is called "making wholesome"—entailed nothing but gaining for themselves God's love, that would be great, for nothing is equal to God's love. So the wage of those who have this attribute—the wage that falls upon God—is the Lover's wage to His beloved, and that is sufficient, because of what is given by the waystation of love. No one is able to measure the wage that the Lover gives to His beloved.

Thus, in the briefest terms, seeking conciseness, I have given intimations concerning those whose wage falls upon God, for the station is magnificent and the mutual waystation great. (IV 24.11)

Occasions

One of the several terms that Ibn al-ᶜArabī employs to refer to veils is secondary cause or "occasion" (*sabab*).[2] An occasion is anything that causes something else. Broadly, it is applied to both God and everything other than God, though most often it refers to a created thing inasmuch as there is some sort of causal connection between it and another created thing. Thus, if we perceive a thing or an event or a situation and then explain it without taking the Real into account, our discussion takes place on the level of its secondary causes or occasions, that is, other things, events, and situations. If we recognize the face of the Real in the things, then we are dealing directly with the Occasioner of the occasions (*musabbib al-asbāb*), what the philosophers call the First Cause or the Cause of Causes. In the first case we are involved with veils, for "Occasions are curtains and veils" (II 553.11), so "If not for the occasions, the traces would become manifest from their Existence-Giver" (*ʿAbādila* 63). In the second case, we are dealing with God's face, or His self-disclosure in the things. In the first case, we need to think of a thing's relation to God in terms of an orderly hierarchy of causal connections, so this perspective is dominated by *tanzīh*, the assertion of God's incomparability and distance. In the second case, we find that God is present in the thing without any intermediaries, so the perspective is that of *tashbīh*.

The face of a thing is its essence or reality, but in common language, the face is that which looks. Employing the word *face* to refer to a thing's reality suggests that a thing looks in keeping with the demands of its own essence, its own specific characteristics. When something looks, its face is turned in one of two directions—either the occasions or the divine face, either *tanzīh* or *tashbīh*. Ibn al-ʿArabī sometimes expresses this idea by saying that things have two faces. One face looks at God, the other at the occasions. He explains this in a letter addressed to the famous theologian and Koran commentator, Fakhr al-Dīn Rāzī (d. 606/1209). He is attempting to clarify the difference between the unveiled knowledge of God's prophets and friends and the rational knowledge of scholars and theologians. He explains that the divine names—"the divine realities"—are God's faces, in contradistinction to the divine Essence, which is God's Face.

> You should know, my friend—God give you success—that everything existent at an occasion that is newly arrived like itself has two faces. Through one face, it looks at its occasion, and through the other, it looks at its Existence-Giver, who is God.
>
> All people look at the faces of their own occasions, including all the sages, the philosophers, and others—but not the Realizers from among the Folk of God, such as the prophets, the friends, and the angels. Although they have knowledge of the occasion, they look from the other face at their Existence-Giver.
>
> Among them is he who looks at his Lord from the face of his occasion, not from his own face. He says, "My heart narrated to me from my Lord." Another—and this is the perfect—says, "My Lord narrated to me." To this alludes our companion, the gnostic [Abū Yazīd], with his words, "You take your knowledge" of the tracings "dead from the dead, but we take our knowledge from the Living who does not die."
>
> When someone's *wujūd* is acquired from another, his property—in our view—is that of a non-thing. So the gnostic has no one whatsoever that he relies upon except God.
>
> Then you should know, my friend, that the Real, though He is one, has many diverse faces turned toward us, so you should be careful about the places of divine arrival and about the self-disclosures of the faces.
>
> In this regard, the Real's property with you in respect of His being Lord is not the same as His property in respect of His being Guardian, or Compassionate, or Avenger. And such is the case with all the names.
>
> You should also know that the divine face, which is "God," is a name for all the names, like Lord, Powerful, Grateful, and the rest, just like the Essence that brings together all the attributes within Itself. (*Rāzī* 4–5)

The basic meaning of *sabab*, "occasion," is rope and cord. Hence it is something that ties two things together, or one thing that leads to something else. The Koran employs the term in nine verses in the sense of a tie, a bond, or a causal connection among things. Thus, when those who had been taken as false gods in this world come to disown their followers on the day of resurrection, the followers will suddenly see the chastisement that has been prepared for them, and *their ropes will be cut asunder* (2:166). In other words, all the ties and bonds with which they had held together their illusory world will be broken. In another sense, of course, the occasions tie all things to God, since He is their

Occasioner. Thus, in explaining the Koranic name of God *al-ṣamad*, the "Everlasting Refuge" or the "Recourse," Ibn al-ᶜArabī writes that people have recourse to Him only through the occasions that He has placed in the cosmos, so these are cords that tie things back to Him.

> [God is] *the Everlasting Refuge* [112:2], which is to say that in Him refuge is sought or recourse is had in affairs. Recourse is had to all the occasions that have been established in the cosmos. That is why they are named "occasions," because everything they occasion reaches all the way back to the First, the Everlasting Refuge, to whom the occasions have recourse. (III 181.32)

Ibn al-ᶜArabī classifies occasions into various sorts after having mentioned that the Universal Soul is the first occasioned thing in the cosmos, because God gave it existence through the intermediary of the First Intellect, which itself was created directly, without occasions.

> Know that some occasions are creaturely, and some are suprasensory and relational.
>
> An example of a creaturely occasion is the *wujūd* of a created thing that depends upon the prior *wujūd* of another created thing because it has some relation to its *wujūd*, in whatever respect it may be—whether a relation of activity, or a relation of some inescapable characteristic. Then the thing is an occasion. Otherwise, it is not.
>
> [The occasion] may leave its trace in something that is not created, as in His words, *I respond to the call of the caller* [2:186]. Thus the asking is an occasion of the *wujūd* of the response, whatever the responder may be. From this reality descended His words, *No remembrance comes to them from their Lord newly arrived, [but they listen to it yet playing, diverted their hearts]* [21:2]. This is to say that some of these affairs [mentioned in the Koran] were given new arrival by questions.
>
> As for suprasensory occasions, these are in respect of the occasioned thing and the occasioner. In respect of the occasioned thing, the occasion is the thing's preparedness to receive the trace within itself. If it had no preparedness, the trace would not occur within it. This preparedness is stronger in preventing [traces] than the impossible thing itself, which cannot come to be, yet has the preparedness to accept that it be supposed. Thus in certain issues we suppose the impossible. Even though it does not accept *wujūd*, we derive from the supposition a knowledge that had not been with us. Were it not for the impossible thing's preparedness to receive supposition, reason could not have supposed it. So the possible thing is even more receptive to the entity of *wujūd*.
>
> In respect of the occasioner, the occasion is what God mentions: *Our only word to a thing*, so He affirms His Entity and His word, *when We desire it* [16:40], so He affirms desire and its connection with the object of desire. He who is of this sort has no escape from being Knowing and Alive and from having power over what He desires to engender. All of these are relational, suprasensory preparednesses, except for the Entity who is the Occasioner, for He is an occasion pertaining to *wujūd*. He is not a "cause," but He is inescapably a "condition." (II 427.32)

This last sentence reminds us that Ibn al-ᶜArabī typically rejects the philosophical idea that God is the cause of the cosmos, even though he often uses the terms *cause* and *occasion* as virtual synonyms. He explains some of the rationale for differentiating between the two terms in Chapter 207, "On the state of the cause." The chapter allows us to understand why he defines "cause" in his glossary of Sufi terminology as "the Real's alerting His servant through an occasion, or without one" (*Iṣṭilāḥāt* 8; II 132.17). Note once again that "cause" (*ᶜilla*) and "effect" (*maᶜlūl*) mean also "infirmity" and "infirm." Here the Shaykh takes care to differentiate the two senses of the term and to show how both senses are implied in the Sufi definition.

> The infirm lean
> on the physician
> whenever they sense
> an *ᶜilla* in themselves.
> You see them worshiping him,
> though he is not their Lord,
> as a precaution lest they take up
> an abode in their graves.
> I asked, "What is the occasion
> of this reliance?" Someone said,
> "Only the fact that he is
> the same kind as they."

Know that in the view of the Tribe the *ʿilla* is an alerting by the Real. Among His acts of alerting is His saying on the tongue of His Prophet, "God created Adam in His form." Another version, considered sound by unveiling though not affirmed among the companions of transmission, reads "in the form of the All-Merciful," so the difficulty is removed.[3] Thus He is the Healer of this *ʿilla*. He says, *[We have sent down to thee the Remembrance] that thou mayest make clear to the people what was sent down to them* [16:44]. Thus we come to know that every version that removes the difficulty is sound, even if it is weak for the folk of transmission.

Since God is the Healer and the Reliever, He is the physician, just as [Abū Bakr] al-Ṣiddīq said: "The Physician has made me ill." So the occasion that brings about the longing of the companion of the infirmity for the Physician is what we mentioned in the poetry, that is, His creating him in His form.[4]

This report and this unveiled consideration is confirmed by God's words, "I was ill, but you did not visit Me." When He explained, He said, "So-and-so was ill," so He placed Himself in what afflicted so-and-so as a solicitude from Him to so-and-so.

All of these are *ʿilla*s for those who understand from God. The *ʿilla* affirms the occasion, and the Real is identical with the occasion, since, were it not for Him, the cosmos would not be, for He is *the Creator, the Author, the Form-Giver* [59:24], the Healer.

Since He is identical with the *ʿilla* in the Prophet's words *from Thee*—in his saying, "I seek refuge in Thee from Thee"—He heals people only of Himself, for there is no healer but God, so it is He that heals every *ʿilla*, since God has established the occasions. No one can remove them when God has established their ruling properties, and none can possibly repel them when He is the Occasioner of the occasions. So He created the malady and the remedy.

He assigned the healing only to Him specifically. Hence the healing is the *ʿilla* of the removal of the illness, but every *ʿilla* is not a healing. Thus every occasioner is an occasion, but not every occasion is an occasioner. But it may be an occasioner of the property, not an occasioner of the entity. Take, for example, His words, *I respond to the call of the caller when he calls to Me* [2:186].

Thus when *ʿilla* means "occasion," it has a property, and when it means "illness," it has a property. When it means illness, it is a malady, but when it means occasion, it is a wisdom. In either case, the *ʿilla* is for the Real to alert His servants.

Sometimes He alerts them to the slumber of their heedlessness through something that He sends down, and this is the "malady" and the "illness." When the person lacks health, he senses pain, so he knows that an affliction has come down upon him. God sets down as Shariah that he should say, *Surely we belong to God, and to Him we return* [2:156]. No one returns save he who has emerged.

At other times He alerts the servants to the slumber of their heedlessness through a wisdom that becomes manifest to them in their own self without their having an illness of the self. Since the Real is identical with their *ʿilla*, this comes about only through a divine self-disclosure suddenly. After all, God has sudden comings upon the hearts of His servants that arrive without having been called for and without the priority of any occasion known exactly by them. Although there is an occasion in actual fact, they have no knowledge of it.

However, the Tribe turned to this name, which is *ʿilla*, only because they saw that the cause is intertied with its effect, and the effect is tied to its cause. They knew that the cosmos is a kingdom belonging to God, that the reality of the kingdom's *wujūd* as a kingdom is tied to the king, and that the king is God. The king is not a king over himself, so he is tied to the kingdom. Once the correlation became manifest—that the cosmos is a vassal and a king's slave—they turned to the name *ʿilla*, not to the name *occasion*, nor to the name *condition*.

Moreover, since some divine alertings are pains and calamities that souls dislike by nature, they turned to a name that would bring together all the alertings, so they turned to *ʿilla*. After all, illness is named an *ʿilla*, and it is one of the strongest alertings for the return to God, because of the weakness it entails. Then God made the occasions veils over God, and souls leaned upon them. God was forgotten in them, and the reliance of the creatures was transferred to them.

Although *ʿilla* means the same as occasion, the difference of the name has a property. Thus *ʿilla* is contrasted with occasion because it alerts to God through its essence, so the name *ʿilla* is more appropriate for the alerter. Any occasion that does not turn you back to God, alert you to Him, and make Him present with you is not an *ʿilla*.

My malady is the chronic malady,
for it alerts me of my own self in every state.

My ᶜ*illa* is not other than I, and my ᶜ*illa* is
not I;
I possess no specific difference, no genus.
I stand on no knowledge, for I recognize
who I am,
nor do I stand on ignorance of my essence,
nor uncertainty.
I am not the one you mean, nor any other.
In likeness, I am the foundation. (II 490.3)

From Chapter 198: The Twenty-Fifth Tawḥīd

Given that all things, including the self, are veils and occasions, true *tawḥīd* demands that people turn away from the first face of things to the second face, that is, from the veil to the self-disclosure. Ibn al-ᶜArabī explains this while discussing the significance of the twenty-fifth instance in which the Koran employs the formula of *tawḥīd*: *Is there any creator other than God, who provides for you from the heaven and the earth? There is no god but He* (35:3). The Shaykh calls this instance "the *tawḥīd* of the cause," because of the reference to the heaven and the earth, which are the occasions for the provisions that reach the creatures. "It pertains to the *tawḥīd* of the He-ness" because of the mention of "He" rather than "God" in the formula.

> This is the *tawḥīd* of the cause, and it pertains to the *tawḥīd* of the He-ness. Were His unity not declared through the cause, just as it is declared through other than it, He would not be a God, since it is characteristic of the God that a thing's *wujūd* not go outside of Him. If it did go outside, He would have no ruling property in that thing, but He has said, *To Him the whole affair is returned* [11:123]. So there is no escape from His having the *tawḥīd* of the cause, which is that He is worshiped through this *tawḥīd* for the sake of an occasion. After all, the worshiper, at the root of his engendered existence, is poor toward an occasion, and he never emerges from his own reality. His occasion is his provision, through which his entity subsists.
>
> Those who are veiled imagine that God is within the occasions that have been established. This is a correct imagining—that He is within the established occasions. However, this derives from the property of "making" [*ja*ᶜ*l*], not from the property of their essence, for it is God who has "made" the occasions a provision, since He *provides for you from the heaven* by means of the spirits' provisions that descend from it, *and the earth* by means of the bodies' provisions that emerge from it. Hence He is the Provider in whose hand is this provision.
>
> However, God has let down veils upon the eyes of some of His servants, and they perceive nothing but what is named "provision"—not what is named "Provider." They say "This." Then it is said to them, "It is not 'this.' It has been made to be 'in this' by Him who created you. Just as He has created you, so also He provides for you. Do not consider Him equal with what belongs to Him and comes from Him. You and the things you rely upon are the same. You should not rely upon your own likenesses. If you do, you will be relying upon manyness, and reliance upon manyness results in failure to gain that for the sake of which one has had reliance, for each of the many says, 'Someone other than I will undertake that for him,' so it undertakes nothing for him."
>
> The correct state calls a person to empty himself and disengage himself for One, while the One knows that the person has disengaged himself for His sake and emptied himself of everything other than He. Then it becomes incumbent upon Him to undertake that for him. In the case of some people, this results in gaining the sought object *from behind a veil* [42:51], and in the case of others it results in witnessing and unveiling—these are the Folk of God and His elect. (II 417.22)

From Chapter 198: The Thirty-Second Tawḥīd

The thirty-second formula of *tawḥīd* is found in the passage, *How shall they have their Reminder? Know thou therefore that there is no god but God, and ask forgiveness for thy sin, and for the faithful, men and women. And God knows your going to and fro, and your lodging* (47:18–19). The Shaykh explains that unveiling allows the gnostic to see the face as the veil, or the veil as the face. He finds a reference in this verse to veiling in the mention of the word *forgiveness* (*ghafr*) which, in its etymological sense, means the covering and concealing (of sins).

This is the *tawḥīd* of the Reminder, and it is the *tawḥīd* of God.

Know that, since God made human beings naturally disposed to heedless moments as a mercy for them, they are heedless of God's *tawḥīd* through the witnessing of the occasions which they examine at every while and at which engendering becomes manifest. There is no perception through which they could witness the entity of the Real's face in the occasions from which engendering occurs. This is because heedlessness and the covering have gained mastership over them, so they imagine that engendering derives from the entity of the occasions.

When the Reminder comes to them, in any manner that it comes, they know through its coming that through its very essence it signifies that *there is no god but God* and that, were the face of the divine command not in these occasions, or were the occasions not identical with the divine command, nothing whatsoever would be engendered from them.

Since this *tawḥīd* occurs after a curtain that the Reminder lifts, its result is that they ask God to curtain the faithful men and women. After all, the lifting of the curtain and the finding of unveiling at this lifting, or of the knowledge that the lifting is identical with the curtain, not other than it, has a pleasure that cannot be measured, so it is one of God's favors to His servant. (II 419.35)

The Identity of the Veil and the Face

Ibn al-ʿArabī explains the difference between those who understand that the face of God is identical with the veil and those who stay curtained by the occasions in Chapter 390, which he calls, "On the true knowledge of the mutual waystation of 'The time of a thing is its *wujūd*, except for Me, since I have no time, and except for you, since you have no time; hence you are My time, and I am your time.'" The discussion circles around the relation between the words *aeon* (*dahr*) and *time* (*zamān*). The first means an enormously long period of time, or the whole of time, and it was often understood by the ancient Arabs to mean something like Fate. Thus the term *dahriyyūn* or "Aeonists" came to be used for those who saw no transcendent reality outside the cosmos, but simply the impersonal workings of a grand cosmic system. In a similar way, the word *ṭabīʿiyyūn* or "Naturalists" was applied to those who saw no reality governing the universe save nature itself. As for *time*, it is the generic term applied to the sequence of events perceived in the cosmos.

God says, narrating the words of a people who are the speakers, *Nothing makes us perish save the aeon* [45:24]. They speak the truth, because it has been affirmed that God's Messenger said, "God is the aeon." Hence nothing makes them perish save God, and this is the actual situation.

Know that "time" is a relation that has no *wujūd* in its entity. People have spoken at length about its whatness. The gist of their words is what we have mentioned—that time is a relation and that it arrives newly at the question, "When?" Various names arrive newly for it through the new arrival of the question, such as *ḥīn*, *idh*, and *idhā*. All the conditional particles [in grammar] are names of time, but the named thing is an affair of nonexistence. These particles are like the word *nonexistence*, which is a name that names no object that has an entity, even though its property is rationally understood. Let us provide examples so that what we have mentioned may be understood:

It is said, "When [*matā*] did Zayd come?" The answer is, for example, "While [*ḥīn*] the sun was rising" or "When [*idhā*] the sun was rising."

"When will the sun rise from its setting place?" [The answer is] "While God permits it to do so," or "When God permits it." "Whenever God permits it, it will do so." These are answers to, "Will the sun rise from its setting place, so that the setting place becomes a rising place?" From these and similar answers, time is rationally understood.

"If Zayd comes, I will honor you." The meaning is, "When Zayd comes, I will honor you." This means that the time of Zayd's coming is the time when it is incumbent upon me to honor you, given that I have made it incumbent upon myself to honor you with Zayd's coming.

In respect to newly arrived things, this is "time," but in respect to the Eternal, it is "eternity without beginning." What the rational faculty understands from time is something imagined, extended, and lacking the two sides. We judge that what has passed away within it is "the past," we judge that what will come in it is "the future," and we judge that what is within it is "the [present] state" [*ḥāl*]. This last is called "the instant" [*al-ān*]. Although the instant is a time, it is a limit for what is past in time and what is future. It is like a point that we suppose upon the circumference of a circle. Wherever we suppose the point to be, origin and end are designated for the circumference.

"Eternity without beginning" and "eternity without end" are the nonexistence of time's two sides, for it has no first and no last. Rather, it has perpetuity [*dawām*], and perpetuity is the time of the [present] state, while the state possesses perpetuity. Hence the cosmos never ceases to be under the ruling property of the time of the [present] state, and God's ruling property in the cosmos never ceases to be in the ruling property of time. That of it which is past and future never cease to be in the ruling property of the [present] state.

Do you not see that the Speech of God reports to us concerning affairs that have come to an end with the expression of past time, concerning affairs that are coming with the expression of future time, and concerning affairs that are being engendered with the expression of the [present] state? As for the state, He says, *Each day He is upon some task* [55:29]; as for the past, *I created you aforetime, when you were not a thing* [19:9]; and as for the future, *[Our only word to a thing,] when We desire it, is to say to it "Be!," so it comes to be* [16:40]; *I shall turn away from My signs those who claim greatness* [7:146]; and *I shall show you My signs, so do not hurry Me* [21:37].

At all of this, we seek an entity of *wujūd* within which all of it would be, an entity that would be like its container. We do not find such an entity in reason or sensation, but rather in a containing imagination. This container is itself the contents of an infinite, imagined container that is judged to be so only by imagination. Hence—if you have understood—nothing is understood by imagination, reason, or sensation save the Real *Wujūd* that supports us in our *wujūd*.

Because of this relation, God named Himself for us as "the Aeon." He did so in order that the ruling property would belong only to Him, not to the property of time that is imagined, for there is none that displays properties save God. In Him the entities of things become manifest through their properties.

He is perpetual *wujūd*, and the entities of the possible things become manifest through their properties from behind the veil of His *wujūd*, because of its subtlety. We see the entities of the possible things—which are our entities—from behind the veil of His *wujūd*, but we do not see Him. In the same way, we see the stars from behind the veils of the heavens, but we do not see the heavens, even if we understand that between us and the stars there are heavens. However, they have such subtlety that they do not veil what is behind them.

God is Subtle to His servants [42:19]. Part of God's subtlety is that it is He who comes to them in everything in which they are, but the servants' eyes fall only upon the occasions that they witness, so they attribute what they are in to these occasions. Thus the Real becomes manifest by being veiled, so He is the Manifest/the Veiled. He is the Nonmanifest because of the veil, not because of you, and He is the Manifest because of both you and the veil. So glory be to Him who veils Himself in His manifestation and becomes manifest in His veil! No eye witnesses anything other than He, and no veils are lifted from Him. (III 546.24)

If no eye witnesses anything other than God, one may ask, why do certain people disobey God's commandments when the prophets bring them? The basic answer is the well-known distinction between the engendering command and the prescriptive command. God's command to His creatures to enter into existence cannot be disobeyed, but His command brought by the prophets can be disobeyed. In the present context, one can understand this to mean that people always see God and obey God. However, for some of them, God's engendering command coincides with the commandments delivered by the prophets, and such people are known as the "obedient." For others, God's engendering command does not coincide with the prophetic commandments, so they are known as the "disobedient."

Ibn al-ʿArabī continues the above passage by explaining that God commands us in two ways. The first is the engendering command and the second the prescriptive command, which he calls here "the elocution of likenesses and semblances." By employing the term *elocution* (*fahwāniyya*), a word discussed earlier (p. 115), he may be referring to the fact that the prophetic messages arrive through the intermediary of the world of imagination. More likely, he is reminding us that the whole cosmos is the World of Unbounded Imagination, so every address of the Real that comes to us through the second face—the occasions—appears as a likeness and an image of a suprasensory meaning. This is true also of the messengers themselves.

Those people who recognize that the messengers are the occasions for guidance from the Real accept their messages and follow them. These are the "obedient." But these messengers are no different from us in being likenesses (*amthāl*), so some of us feel envy (*ḥasad*) toward them because they have been chosen to speak on the Real's behalf. It is this moral shortcoming that prevents the disobedient from acknowledging the prophets.[5]

> He never ceases being a Lord, and we never cease being His servants in the state of our nonexistence and our *wujūd*. Whatever He commands, *We hear and we obey* [2:285] in the state of our nonexistence and our *wujūd*, so long as He does not address us through the elocution of likenesses and semblances. However, when He addresses us through the elocution of likenesses, semblances, and the tongues of sending messages, those of us who witness what is behind the veil that is the likeness and the messenger hear and obey immediately. In contrast, those who witness the likeness necessarily hear, but they do not obey, because of the envy created within them toward their own likenesses that are given priority over them. In this manner the obedient and the disobedient become manifest. The "disobedient" disobey their likeness because God's command does not influence them to obey, but they do not disobey God.
>
> This explains why someone[6] has said as follows: God veils Himself from His servants in this world because He has precedent knowledge that He has prescribed for them, commanded them, and prohibited them, but He has also determined for them that they will sometimes oppose His command and sometimes conform with it. So there is no escape from the manifestation of opposition and conformity. Hence He addresses them on the tongues of the messengers and veils His Essence from them within the form of the messenger, for He says, *Whosoever obeys the Messenger has thereby obeyed God* [4:80], and *Grant him sanctuary until he hears the speech of God* [9:6]. Were not the Messenger His manifest, witnessed form, these sayings would be incorrect. So the opposer shows opposition through the precedent measuring out and the ruling property of the decree. He would not be able to oppose God's command along with unveiling.
>
> Thus God has become veiled by sending messengers just as He has become veiled through the occasions. The blame falls upon the occasions, for they shield the All-Merciful. Hence no one has opposed God, and no one but God has been opposed. Occasions never cease being witnessed by those who are veiled, and the Real never ceases being witnessed by the gnostics, even though they have a rational understanding of the veils in the case of those who are veiled. For the veiled, the subtle has become dense, and for the gnostics through God, the dense has become subtle.
>
> Reason knows what eyesight never witnesses
> and eyesight witnesses what reflection
> throws away.
>
> The gnostics bring together reason and eyesight, for *they have hearts through which* they *understand, and they have eyes through which* they *see, and they have ears through which* they *hear* [7:179].
>
> Those who are veiled are of two sorts: One sort has a *heart through which* he does *not understand* and an *eye through which* he does *not see* [7:179]. Another sort has a *heart through which* he *understands*, but an *eye through which* he does *not see*. The latter are the faithful, for they know, but they do not witness, and those apart from them neither know nor witness.
>
> The Folk of God both know and witness. Hence, when He addresses them, they hear, obey, and witness their own essences as a locus for what God creates within them and for what He judges as being an opposition or a conformity. They are obedient and ready to receive what comes to be engendered within them, like the womb of the woman, which is ready to receive what comes to be engendered within it and does not prevent it. So the servant who has this quality is a branch of his Existence-Giver, who is All-Merciful in the cosmos, Compassionate to the faithful.[7] (III 547.13)

Ibn al-ʿArabī now directs the discussion back to the original topic, the mutual waystation in which God said to him, "You are

My time, and I am your time." This statement turns out to be a version of his well-known teaching that a Lord (*rabb*) demands a vassal (*marbūb*) and a God (*ilāh*) a divine thrall (*ma'lūh*). This is only true, however, in respect of the attributes that are ascribed to the two sides. It does not mean that the entity of God demands the entity of the cosmos, since God is Independent of the worlds. However, as soon as one of the two sides is mentioned, it can only be understood and conceptualized in terms of the other.

So the Lord's time is the vassal, and the vassal's time is the Lord, since the property through which the ruling properties of either is determined is not affirmed without the other. In respect of the fact that the verse *Nothing is as His likeness* [42:11] is ascribed to both, neither of them is a time for the other, because the relations are lifted. But this is so only in view of each one's entity, not its property. When you shift to considering the property, for which the Real depends upon the cosmos and the cosmos depends upon the Real, then it is correct that the property of each is a time for the other, as in the case of two correlatives.

"When" does fatherhood become correct for Zayd in relation to ʿAmr? Or, it is said, "while" it is correct that sonship belongs to ʿAmr in relation to Zayd. Hence the time of Zayd's fatherhood is ʿAmr's sonship, and the time of ʿAmr's sonship is the time of Zayd's fatherhood. Thus the father's time is the son, and the son's time is the father.

So also are king and kingdom, owner and possession, powerful and object of power, desirer and desired, knower and known. However, the entity of the knower and the known may be one, since the knower may know himself. Then he would be the known to himself and the knower of himself. Thus, in respect to himself, he is the knower/known. Desirer and desired are otherwise, since the desired object can only be nonexistent, and the desirer can only be existent.

So also is the case with powerful and object of power—the object of power can never be anything but nonexistent. When it comes into existence, nothing makes it nonexistent after its *wujūd* save itself, or the withholding of the condition for its subsistence, that is, the subsistence of *wujūd* for it. Other than this cannot be. By His words, *If He wills, He will take you away* [4:133], He means holding back the condition that makes correct for you the subsistence of your *wujūd*. So you become nonexistent when He does not bring you into existence, for He has the choice whether to bring each possible thing into existence or to leave it in its own state, which is for it to be qualified by nonexistence.

Once you have come to know what time is through what we have mentioned, after that, enter along with the people into that which they enter, that is, saying that time is night and daytime, or the days; or that time is an imagined period demarcated by the movements of the spheres; or that time is the juxtaposition of one newly arrived thing with another newly arrived thing and is asked about by "when" and such words. Holding any of these views will not harm you, for they have come to be settled upon, and they are correct in temporal relations.

And God determines the night and the daytime [73:20] through making to enter, covering, and wrapping[8] so as to bring into existence the properties and entities concerning which He has precedent knowledge that He will make them manifest in the elemental world. Hence we are the children of the night and the daytime. When something arrives newly in the daytime, daytime is its mother and night its father, for the two of them have given birth to it. When something is born in the night, night is its mother and daytime its father, for the two of them have given birth to it. This state never ceases in this world as long as night and daytime continue to cover each other. So we are the children of the mother and father who belong to those born along with us in our day or in our night specifically. Those who are born in the second night or the second daytime are our likenesses, not our siblings, for the night and the daytime are new, so our parents have become nonexistent, and these two are their likenesses, not their entities. Though they are similar, this is the similarity of likenesses.

When the last world arrives, night will be in the abode of Gehenna and daytime in the abode of the Garden, so the two will not come together, even though birth will be found in the Fire and the Gardens through the new arrival of engendering within them. This is like Eve being born from Adam, or like Jesus from Mary. This is the birth of the last world. God has struck likenesses for us through Jesus and Mary, and Adam and Eve, for what comes to be engendered in the last world.

Giving birth to engendered things in the last world does not derive from a temporal marriage through the night's entering into the daytime and the daytime's entering into the night, for night and daytime are each other's likeness in time, which is the day that brings them together.

In the last world, God apportions daytime and night between the Garden and the Fire. He gives the darkness of the night to the Fire and the light of the daytime to the Garden. The "day" then comes to be from both together. This is the day of the last world, for it brings together the two abodes. (III 547.31)

From Chapter 370: The Path of Exaltation

Ibn al-ᶜArabī calls this chapter "On the true knowledge of the waystation of increase and a mystery and two mysteries among the mysteries of *wujūd* and constant change." He devotes it mainly to the perfect human beings and their connection to the various *ṣirāṭ*s or "paths" mentioned in the Koran. The Fātiḥa includes the verse, *Guide us on the straight path* (1:5), and the Shaykh asserts that altogether the Koran mentions five different paths employing this word *ṣirāṭ*. These include the path of "God," upon which all creatures walk; the path of "the Lord," which allows the vassal to embrace the diverse divine names through observing the prescription of one of the shariahs; the path of "the Blessing-Giver," which leads to felicity and is brought by all the prophets; and the path of "Muhammad," which is set down by the Koran and the Sunnah. It also includes the path of the divine name *ᶜazīz*, the Exalted. As the Shaykh often explains, God's exaltation means that He is lifted far beyond the creatures, so much so that, in this respect, He is inaccessible and unreachable; in his *Lexicon*, Lane offers "unattainable" as one of the meanings of the word *ᶜazīz*. In this chapter, Ibn al-ᶜArabī tells us that the "Path of the Exalted" is God's own path of manifesting His presence in the cosmos. It is ascribed to this name because no created thing can attain the exact manner in which God is found in the things or understand how the face and the veil are identical. Much of the discussion circles around the idea, mentioned in the verse that refers to the Path of the Exalted and elsewhere in the Koran, that God's goal in guiding His servants is to bring them out from the diverse sorts of cosmic darkness into the divine light. In the present context, the Shaykh interprets this as a reference to the emergence of the entities from the darkness of fixity into the light of *wujūd*. Once the servants find themselves in the luminous clarity of *wujūd*, the perfect among them are guided to another kind of darkness which, in fact, is the highest stage of knowledge. This is bewilderment, or the knowledge that they know nothing, or the understanding that the veil is nothing other than the face. This path is God's own path, and hence it is exalted beyond all created things. Nonetheless, it is the path followed by the perfect human beings, because, in the last analysis, they are God's very self, identical with Him because created in His form. Here again we meet the mystery of simultaneous identity and difference, the bewilderment of He/not He.

The path of exaltation is His words, *[A Book We have sent down to thee that thou mayest bring forth the people from the darknesses into the light, by the leave of their Lord,] to the path of the Exalted, the Praiseworthy* [14:1].

Know that this is the path of *tanzīh*, so it cannot be reached through tasting except by him who declares himself incomparable with being a lord or a master in one respect, or in any respect. This is exalted, for the human being is heedless, neglectful, and forgetful. He says "I," and at the moment of his heedlessness he sees that he has the level of mastership relative to other servants.

Since there is no escape from this, he should struggle to be, at death, a sheer servant within whom there is no mastership above any of the created things. He should see himself as poor toward everything in the cosmos in respect of the fact that each is identical with the Real from behind the veil of the name concerning which God said to those who had no knowledge of the affair, *Say: "Name them!"* [13:33].

Since human beings are poor by essence, God veiled Himself from them through the occasions. He made His servants gaze at these occasions, though He is behind them. Hence He affirmed the occasions in entity, but He negated them in property, as, for example, in His words to Muhammad: *You did not throw when you threw, but God threw* [8:17]. Then He followed this verse with His words, *That He might try the faithful with a beautiful trial* [8:17]. Thus He made it a "trial," that is, a test.

This is the Exalted Path into whose knowledge no created thing has any entrance, for it is the path of God upon which He descends to create us. Upon it *He is with* us *wherever* we *are* [57:4]. Upon it He descends from the Throne to the closest heaven and to the earth; this is His words, *He is God in the heavens and the earth* [6:3]. Upon it He comes near to His servant much more than His servant comes near to Him when he strives toward Him on the road that He has set down as Shariah for him, for He rushes toward him when He sees him coming so as to welcome him,[9] attaching importance to His servant and honoring him, but on the path of exaltation.

This is a path of descent on which no created thing has any ascent. If any created thing could travel on this path, it would not be exalted. But He does not descend upon us save through us, so the attribute belongs to us, not to Him. Hence we are identical with this path. That is why He described it through the word *ḥamīd* [usually translated as "Praiseworthy"], that is, the Praiser/the Praised, because [the form] *faʿīl* [which is the form taken by *ḥamīd*], when employed, demands both the active and the passive participle. Either it gives both, as in this case, or it gives one of the two, according to the context. And He has lauded Himself, so He is the Praiser/the Praised.

In our view the greatest laudation by which He has lauded Himself is that He created Adam in His form and named him by the mothers of the names, under the compass of which every name is included. That is why the Prophet said, "Thou art as Thou hast lauded Thy self." Thus he ascribed the perfect self to Him, as an ascription of ownership and bestowing honor, for he said, "He who knows himself knows his Lord." Hence every laudation through which God has lauded the perfect human being—who is His self, for He has brought him into existence in His form—is itself a laudation of God, by the testimony and instruction of God's Messenger to us in his words, "Thou art as Thou hast lauded Thy self." In other words, "Everything by which You have lauded Your creature whom You have created in Your form is Your laudation of You."

Since the perfect human being is *the path of the Exalted, the Praiseworthy,* this path cannot be traveled upon, nor is it qualified by traveling. That is why He named it "exalted," that is, forbidden in itself. Thus the Real is specified for descent within it, just as He has reported about Himself that He "descends" and "rushes." But the gnostic servant, in reality, travels only in God, so God is his path, and that is his Shariah.

In Him is our hostel,
  and in us His hostel,
    for He is my path,
      and I am His path.
Consider my words,
  for they are truthful,
    confirmed and realized
      in their source.
He is my Friend,
  and through Him am I,
    for my heart has embraced Him,
      so I am His tent.
He is exalted, so our *eyesights*
  perceive Him not [6:103]
    because of His nearness,
      so His carpet is rolled up.
He is distant because of His nearness,
  that is all there is—
    what I have said
      brings this out plainly.

He is on an exalted path because He is the Creator, and no created thing has any entrance in upon Him. *Show me what those apart from Him have created!*—you will never find it, neither in knowledge nor in entity. *Nay, but the wrongdoers are in clear misguidance* [31:11], because everything known has become clear.

God has *brought* us *forth from the darkness* of nonexistence *into the light* of *wujūd,* so we are light, *by the leave of* our *Lord, to the path of the Exalted, the Praiseworthy* [14:1]. Thus He transferred us from the light into the darkness of bewilderment. That is why, when we hear Him lauding Himself, we see that [lauded object] in ourselves, and when He lauds us, we see that His every laudation of us is His praise of His own self.

Then He distinguished us from Him and distinguished His self from us through *Nothing is as His likeness* [42:11]; and through what He knows, of which we are ignorant; and through the abasement that we have, while He is high beyond this description in Himself. Hence we say, "We are He/we are not He," after we had said, when He *brought* us *forth from the darknesses into the light,* "He is He, and we are we," thus becoming distinct.

When He brought laudation after our *wujūd*—His laudation of Himself and us—and when He prescribed for us laudation of Him, He threw us into bewilderment: If we laud Him through us, we have bound Him. If we declare Him unbounded—as in the Prophet's words, "I count not Thy laudations before Thee"—then we have bound Him by unboundedness, so we have made Him distinct. But anything that is bound is not described by independence, for the binding ties it down, since the newly arrived thing would have perceived His unboundedness. But He has said about Himself that He is *independent of the worlds* [3:97]. Hence we become bewildered, for we do not know what He is, nor what we are.

I think—and God knows best—that He commanded us to know Him and turned us over to ourselves in gaining this knowledge only because He knew that we do not perceive and do not know the reality of ourselves and that we are incapable of knowing ourselves. Hence we come to know that we are even more incapable of knowing Him. This is knowledge of Him/not knowledge.

Other than this cannot be,
  for it is manifest and clear.
Hear our word and find knowledge,
  then certainty will come to you.

So ignorance is an essential attribute of the servant, and the whole cosmos is a servant. But knowledge is an essential attribute of God.

Take the whole of what I have alluded to in this, and you will find that it is the exalted path. (III 411.27)

Chapter 514: Trust in God

The Shaykh calls this chapter "On the true knowledge of the state of the Pole whose waystation is *And whoever puts his trust in God, He suffices him* [65:3]." Here again he discusses occasions as veils and the mystery of the simultaneous identity and difference of Lord and servant.

If someone trusts in his Lord,
  mankind's God suffices him.
When his Lord sees Him through him
  in all his states without cease,
Then he is the friend of God who stays
  in what is desired from his heart.

Know—God confirm us and you with a spirit from Him—that this formula of remembrance gives its companion the fact that he is He, since he is content only with Him, for the Prophet said, "There is no target behind God." Whatever veil there is can only be between you and Him, not behind Him, for He is the First and you are the last. He is your kiblah, so nothing of you belongs to Him save face-to-face encounter.

Then He let down between you and Him the veils of the occasions, the relations, and the habits. He made them forms of Him in a respect of which you are unaware. Hence, whoever says, "They are He," has spoken the truth. But if someone should say, "They are not He," this is because of the diversity that he sees within them, so he also has spoken the truth, for the diversity of forms has veiled him from knowledge of Him. Just as he is certain that this form is not that form—that is, this occasion is not that occasion—so also he is certain that it is not He. But he has neglected the reality of the veil, which is the fact that this reality, though it is diverse, is one through occasioning or through veilness. So also, it is identical with Him, though it is diverse.

Were this not the situation, it would not be correct for there to be face-to-face encounter. Do you not see that when you encounter a blind man face-to-face and directly, his blindness and the fact that he does not see you while you see him do not detract from the property of the face-to-face encounter between the two of you? This is true even though the blind man sees darkness, without doubt, and you are at him in that very darkness that he sees. Hence he sees you as darkness, because he meets you face-to-face. Then he says, "I saw so-and-so today in a face-to-face meeting," and he speaks the truth, even though he is blind.

So, "There is no target behind God," and He has no target behind you, because the divine form reaches perfection through you and is witnessed within you. He *suffices you* [8:64], just as you suffice Him. This is why you are the last existent thing but the first intended thing.

Had you not been a nonexistent thing, you would not have been an intended thing. So your new arrival is correct. And had your knowledge of Him not been nonexistent, it would not have been correct for you to desire knowledge of Him.

This is one of the most marvelous things in *wujūd*: He who gives you knowledge of Himself does not know Himself except through you, because through themselves the possible things give knowledge of themselves to the Real, though none of them knows itself save through the Real. This is why He *suffices you,* for He is the furthest limit that you will finally reach. And you suffice Him, for there is nothing after Him save you, and from you He knows you.

The possible things are nothing but the impossible, which is identical with sheer nonexistence, in whose shadow you have become clothed, just as you have become clothed in light through the brightness of *wujūd.* Thus you are the counterpart of the two sides through your own essence.

If nonexistence is related to you, this relation is not impossible for you, because of its darkness upon you. If *wujūd* is related to you, this is not impossible, because of its brightness within you through which you become manifest to you. Thus it is not said about you that you are an existent thing, for the shadow of nonexistence within you prevents you, in respect of this ascription, from having a rightful demand on *wujūd* like the rightful demand of that which does not accept nonexistence. And it is not said about you that you are nonexistent, because the brightness of *wujūd* within you prevents you, in respect of this ascription, from having a rightful demand on nonexistence like the rightful demand of that which does not accept *wujūd.*

Hence you have been given the name *possible thing* and *permissible thing* because of an intelligible reality that is named "possibility" and "permissibility." The Necessary through Essence has gained the name *Existent* because of a reality that is called "*wujūd.*" This reality is identical with the Existent, just as possibility is identical with the possible thing in respect of its being a possible thing, not in respect of its being a certain possible thing. The impossible thing has gained the name *nonexistent,* which is what does not accept *wujūd* by its essence because of a reality that is called "absolute nonexistence," that is, impossibility.

Thus you bring together the two sides; you are the locus of manifestation for the two forms and the carrier of the two properties. If not for you, the impossible would leave traces in the Necessary, and the Necessary would leave traces in the impossible. So you are the barrier that is never pierced and never broken.

If nonexistence had a tongue, it would say that you are in its form, for it sees nothing of you but its own shadow. In the same way *wujūd,* which does have speech, said that you are in its form, for it sees its form within you. Hence your knowledge of you derives from *wujūd*'s light, and your ignorance of absolute nonexistence derives from its shadow.

So you are the known/the unknown, and as well the form of the Real. You are known in respect of your level, not in respect of your form. For, if you were known in respect of your form, the Real would be known, but the Real is not known, so you are not known in respect of your form. Hence knowledge of you is an undifferentiated summary, not a differentiated exposition.

Thus have I instructed you in the knowledge of God that this formula of remembrance bestows upon you—if you have understood. *And God speaks the **ḥaqq**, and He guides on the path* [33:4], and He is the Guide of *whom He will to a straight path* [2:213]. (IV 153.35)

The Specific Face

Every created thing has two faces. With one face it looks at the occasions, with the other it looks at the Real. The occasions are intermediaries (*wasāʾiṭ*) between the thing and the Real. If a given human being were to look at his first face and enumerate his own occasions in historical terms, he might list his ancestors going back to Adam, who was in turn shaped by God's two hands. If he were to enumerate his occasions in atemporal, vertical terms, he might speak of the various levels of existent things that are preconditions for human existence at any given moment, such as animals, plants, minerals, elements, heavens, Footstool, Throne, Nature, Universal Soul, and First Intellect. However one traces back the occasions, they eventually lead to God.

If the first face of a thing looks at occasions, the second looks at *wujūd.* From the viewpoint of this second face, there are no intermediaries between God and the thing. Ibn al-ʿArabī often calls this "the specific face" (*al-wajh al-khāṣṣ*), that is, the specific face of God that is turned toward the thing to give it existence, and this is identical with the specific face of the thing that is turned only toward *wujūd.* The specific face is the very essence and reality of a thing, the face of *wujūd* within it that never perishes, precisely because it is *wujūd*. In respect of this face, all things are poor and needy toward God, but in respect of the first face, they are poor and needy toward their causes and occasions.

> The *wujūd* that we have mentioned in the divine relation is the specific face possessed by every possible thing from God, whether or not there is an established occasion. So to God belongs giving existence in every state and through every face, whether in the high or the low worlds. (III 516.28)

> In each existent thing God has a specific face through which He casts to it from Him what He wills and what does not belong to any of the other faces. In respect of this face, every existent thing is poor toward Him, even if it derives from an occasion. (II 423.10)

While speaking of a special kind of knowledge given to Jesus, the Shaykh declares that it "derives from the specific divine face that is outside the habitual way in natural science, which requires the relational order that was established through the specific order" (II 275.1). By "specific order" he means the series of existent things that stand between us and God, that is, the chain of occasions—the causes and effects that can be followed back until we eventually reach the First Cause or the First Occasion. He alludes to this chain of occasions while explaining that everything other than God, with the sole exception of the First Intellect, was created with intermediaries and therefore has two faces—the specific face, and the face turned toward the occasions. In the case of the Universal Soul, there is but a single occasion—the First Intellect, the only thing that stands between it and God. In the case of everything else, there are two or more occasions.

> The Soul and everything that exists through an occasion receive the knowledges that they possess in accordance with two faces. Things are diverse in this through the diversity of the varieties of occasions.
>
> The first face: When any existent thing receives knowledge at an occasion from its own specific face, this occurs only through a divine self-disclosure, whether or not the locus of the self-disclosure knows it. If he knows it, then he is one of the knowers of God. If he does not know it, he is one of the folk of solicitude, but he is unaware that solicitude has been shown to him. After all, most people do not know the story of this specific face, nor do they recognize it, since it is a specific knowledge that God bestows upon those of His servants whom He has specified and employed for Himself.
>
> As for the other face of reception, that is what is acquired from the occasion. Its roads are innumerable, for occasions are diverse. What does the First Intellect's occasioning in what it makes manifest to the Soul, through its turning its face toward it and through the Soul's reception, have to do with the heaven's occasioning in the plants that it makes manifest in the earth through its turning its face toward it? It does so by casting rain into the earth, and the earth receives it along with every movement of the spheres, gaze of the planets in the high world, and replenishment by nature. All these are occasions of the *wujūd* of a flower that becomes manifest on the face of the earth. What does this have to do with the face-turning of the Intellect's occasioning? This is why we say that the thing's occasions cannot be restricted, even though, in actual fact, they are restricted. From the Soul to the last element in the cosmos and to some of the progeny between the Soul and the last element—such as the spheres, the planets, and the movements—everything has a trace and a property in the *wujūd* of the entity of that flower and leaf, from a divine command, which may or may not be known by the newly arrived occasion. All of these are "essential occasions."
>
> There are also "accidental occasions," such as a schoolmaster dictating a lesson to a group. This is one of the accidental occasions, which are all occasions within which there is a desire. Everything else is essential.
>
> The connection between the occasions and the occasioned things is never broken. It is preserved by the fact that one is the occasion and the other the occasioned. (II 428.27)

If we look at the corporeal world from the point of view of the occasions, we see minerals, plants, and animals. In Islamic thought these are known as the "things to which birth has been given" or the "progeny" (*muwalladāt*). The parents of the progeny are sometimes called the "high fathers" (*al-ābā' al-ʿulwiyya*) and the "low mothers" (*al-ummahāt al-sufliyya*), that is, the seven heavens and the four elements, the latter of which are also called the "pillars" (*arkān*). These occasions had been discussed widely in texts on philosophy and the natural sciences, and Ibn al-ʿArabī was in complete agreement with the philosophers on their importance for grasping the structure and order of the cosmos. Nonetheless, when we look at the corporeal world while recognizing that each thing has a specific face, the occasions are seen to be of no account. For Ibn al-ʿArabī, this standpoint justifies the position of the Ash'arite theologians, who rejected causal connections, though they did not speak of "specific faces," since this is his technical term. In short, Ibn al-ʿArabī's doctrine of the two faces allows him both to affirm and to deny causality, thereby acknowledging the legitimacy of both the philosophical and the Ash'arite perspectives, though this is not to claim that his purpose in offering this teaching was to harmonize the two schools. Rather, in his way of looking at things, affirming the faces of causation allows us to understand that everything is "not He," while affirming the specific faces grants us insight into the assertion that all things are "He." The first standpoint is dominated by a vision of the manyness of the realities, the second by a vision of the oneness of *wujūd*; the first stresses *tanzīh*, the second *tashbīh*.

Reproduction and procreation never cease in any species of the progeny in this world so long as they are in this world, and in the last world ad infinitum, even if the states of reproduction are various, as appears in this world in Eve, Jesus, and the children of Adam. As for Adam, he came to be through the two hands and the pillars. Reproduction assumes a great variety in plants as well, in their cultivation and their seeds, and so also in minerals. So consider how wisely God has set up His wisdom in His creation!

When God gave us an overview of the specific face that belongs to each existent thing, we could no longer ascribe any reproduction whatsoever to ourselves. Rather, we ascribe everything that becomes manifest in engendered existence to Him. That is His words, *Our command*—and we are His command—*is but one* [54:50]. So there is no existence-giver but God for every face. Those who know this know it, and those who do not do not.

In the same way, the Naturalists uphold the unity of nature in the existent natural things. Whatever existent natural thing becomes manifest, they say that it comes from nature. Hence they voiced the *tawḥīd* of the affair, just as we voice the *tawḥīd* of the God in His creation. So there is nothing but God, and He is what these people call "nature," but they do not know. In the same way, the Aeonists call Him the "Aeon," but they do not know. However, God has named Himself "Aeon" for us, but He has not named Himself "nature." (III 503.16)

To speak of the specific face is another manner of discussing "withness" (*maʿiyya*), the fact that God is present with all things through *wujūd*'s oneness. Inasmuch as God is with the thing, the thing is one through God's oneness, but inasmuch as the thing has qualities and characteristics of its own entity that unfold moment by moment through the new creation, it is many. The philosophers claimed that "Nothing proceeds from the One but one," and the Shaykh typically disagrees with them. However, he finds a certain truth in this saying because of the specific face.

God is with all things. Nothing is prior to Him, and nothing is posterior to Him. This property does not belong to other than God. That is why He has a specific face toward each existent thing, for He is the occasion of each existent thing. Each existent thing is one and cannot be two. He also is One, so nothing proceeds from Him but one, for He is in the unity of every one thing. If manyness is found, this is in respect to the unity of time, which is the container. After all, in this manyness the *wujūd* of the Real is in the unity of every one. So nothing becomes manifest from Him but one. This is the meaning of "Nothing proceeds from the One but one." Were the whole cosmos to proceed from Him, nothing would proceed from Him save one, since He is with each one in respect of His unity. But no one perceives this save the Folk of God. The philosophers maintain it in another sense, and it is among the issues in which they are mistaken. (II 434.17)

The fact that every created thing has a specific divine face known to no other creature explains why God commanded the Prophet—the most perfect of all human beings—to consult with his companions and why, with even greater reason, other people also need to consult among themselves. Each person has a unique knowledge from God that is given to no one else.

When a human being keeps to himself in his reflection and reflective thinking, he has a property, and when he governs with others, he has a property that is called, in the human world, "consultation." God says to His Prophet, *Consult with them in the affair; and when thou art resolved, put thy trust in God* [3:159].

The property of the governance through which people govern their provinces has various sorts, whether they govern alone or they seek partnership by virtue of consultation. The occasion that necessitates consultation is the fact that the Real has a specific face in every existent thing that is not possessed by any other existent thing. So, in a certain affair, God may cast to someone something that He does not cast to someone higher than he in grade, like the knowledge of the names that belonged to Adam, even though the Higher Plenum was more eminent than he with God. Nevertheless, Adam had something that they did not have. (II 423.1)

Given that the specific face looks directly upon *wujūd*, it bypasses the other face, which looks upon causes and occasions. When the gnostics reach the station of seeing things by way of their own specific faces, then their knowledge reaches them from God without intermediaries. Only gnostics at this stage of the path have truly passed beyond bondage to the occasions and causes. Ibn al-ʿArabī refers to this point toward the beginning of Chapter 291, "On the true knowledge of the breast of time, which is the fourth sphere." The word breast, *ṣadr*, is employed to refer to the front part of things in general, and hence to the origin, the source, the beginning. The verbal form of the word, *ṣudūr*, means to come forth, to appear, and "to proceed" in a philosophical sense ("Nothing proceeds from the One but one"). Ibn al-ʿArabī begins the chapter by explaining that everything has a breast, that is, a front or a beginning. Among the examples he cites is the divine name Knower, which is the "breast" of those divine names that leave their traces in the universe. In other words, the first of these names is Knower, since God creates the universe on the basis of His knowledge of the things. Other examples include the Footstool, which is the breast of the spheres; water, which is the breast of the elements; animals, which are the breast of the progeny; and the existence of Adam, which is the breast of this world. Having mentioned a series of diverse and apparently unrelated things, Ibn al-ʿArabī turns the discussion in another direction, and this allows us to see that he does indeed mean the term *breast*, not an abstract expression such as "beginning" or "origin." He alludes to the Koranic verse, *It is not the eyesights that are blind, but blind are the hearts within the breasts* (22:46), and he reads this as a universal principle, referring to all the breasts that he has just mentioned. The breasts are the occasions, while the hearts are the specific faces. If people are blind to God, it is not because their eyes do not function, but because "hearts" are surrounded by "breasts," so this veils them from seeing the face of God in themselves and in all things.

Know that every breast has a heart. As long as the heart is within the breast, it is blind, because the breast is a veil over it. When God desires to make the heart seeing, it comes forth from its breast and it sees.

The "occasions" are the breasts of the existent things, and the existent things are like the hearts. As long as the existent thing continues to look at the occasion from which it has proceeded, it will be blind to the witnessing of God, who gave it existence. When God desires to make him see, he abandons looking at the occasion at which God gave him existence and looks from the specific face that His Lord has turned toward him in giving him existence, and He makes him see.

All occasions are darknesses on the eyes of the occasioned things. In these occasions have perished those people who have perished. The gnostics affirm them, but they do not witness them. They give them their *ḥaqq*, but they do not worship them. Other than the gnostics deal with them conversely—they worship them and do not give them their *ḥaqq*. On the contrary, they rob them of the servanthood that is worthy of them and that is their *ḥaqq*. They witness the servanthood, but they do not affirm it.

You will hear none of the people saying anything but "There is nothing but God," thereby negating the occasions. Then, when you take them at their words, or when a mishap befalls them, they witness the occasion, become blind toward Him whom they had affirmed, disbelieve in Him, and have faith in what they had negated.

Sometimes it happens that the mishap is not removed when people have recourse to the occasion, and thereby the occasions are cut off from them. Then they disbelieve in the occasions and return to God, the Creator of the occasions. They do not know what it is in which they disbelieved, nor what it is in which they had faith. They do not know what the meaning of the occasion is, nor the meaning of anything else.

Were they to know that nothing can come from the occasion save what it occasions, they would know that the occasion to which they had recourse in removing this mishap was not its occasion in any respect for, if it had been its occasion, it would have removed it. Rather, the occasion that prevented them from removing the mishap was an occasion for their returning to God so that God might remove it. Thus, in meaning, they remain forever influenced by the traces of the occasions.

After all, it is impossible to lift the occasions. How can the servant lift that which God has affirmed? He cannot do that. However, ignorance pervades the people, so it makes them blind, bewilders them, and does not guide them. *But God guides whom He will to a straight path* [2:213] through the spirit that is revealed from God's command. So *He guides by it whom He will of His servants* [6:88]. Thus God has affirmed guidance by the spirit, and this is the establishment of the occasion [of guidance] in the cosmos. So, halting at occasions does not negate reliance upon God.

This is why God made the occasions to be occasioned by other occasions, from the lowest until they reach as far as God, who is the First Occasion, not from any occasion. Indeed, the occasion of engendered existence is the Level, not the Essence, and the occasion of the Level is engendered existence. Thus the occasion of engendered existence in existence-giving is the Level, while the occasion of the Level in true knowledge is engendered existence. So understand! (II 652.35)

From Chapter 198: Depending on What Falls Short

The Shaykh calls section 42 of the chapter on the Breath of the All-Merciful "On relying on and inclining toward what falls short." In it he explains that the occasions play an important role in *wujūd*, but this should not prevent us from seeing that God has a specific face in all things. The word *nāqiṣ*, translated here as "what falls short," is the opposite of *kāmil* (perfect), and hence it can also be translated as "deficient" or "imperfect."

This is the chapter of reliance on all the occasions save the occasion that is the perfect human being, since those who rely on him have not relied on what falls short, for he has become manifest in the [divine] form. Every other occasion falls short of this level.

In the same way, the woman falls short of the man through the degree that is between the two.[10] Even if the woman has become perfect, her perfection is not the perfection of the man, because of the degree. Some people say that the degree is the fact that Eve came into existence from Adam, so she has no manifestation save through him. Thus, he has the degree of being her occasion, so she will never join him in that degree. But this is the case of a certain entity, and we would counterbalance it with Mary in the *wujūd* of Jesus. Hence the "degree" is not the fact that the man was the occasion of the woman's manifestation.

The fact is that the woman is the locus of receiving activity, but the man is not like that. The locus of receiving activity does not possess the level of activity, so she falls short, but, despite the falling short, upon her is relied and toward her is inclined, because she accepts the reception of activity within herself and at herself.

God did not establish the occasions aimlessly, only so that we would accept them and rely upon them through a divine reliance. The divine wisdom bestows this when we consider the face in every object that it acts upon, whether or not the occasion is aware of that face. The divine and courteous sage is he who places the occasions where God has placed them.

Those who witness the specific face in each object that is acted upon will say that God acts "at" the occasions, not "through" them, but those who do not witness the specific face will say that God acts upon the things "through" the occasions. Thus they consider the occasions like the tool. They affirm them, but they do not ascribe the things to them. For example, a carpenter is not able to work on the form of a coffin or a chair without tools—the adz, the saw, and others. His activity is not completed except "through" them—not "at" them. Thus we affirm the tools, but the artisanry of the coffin is not attributed to them. Rather, it is only affirmed for the carpenter, the possessor of governance and knowledge, because of what becomes manifest from him. *And God speaks the **ḥaqq**, and He guides on the path* [33:4]. (II 471.19)

Witnessing the Specific Face

The doctrine of the specific divine face provides a metaphysical grounding for one of Ibn al-ʿArabī's most basic themes—that all things take knowledge directly from God. What differentiates the prophets and God's friends from ordinary people is not so much the source of their knowledge as the fact that they know what they know and where the knowledge comes from. This self-aware knowledge also explains their nearness to God and the fact that they stand in the station of "freedom" (*ḥurriyya*).[11] Creatures can never, of course, be free of God, nor can they be free of their actual situation at the present moment, that is, their "state" (*ḥāl*), but they can be free of bondage to the occasions, if they are able to see the specific face. The way to find that face is through remembering God and turning away from everything else, through waiting at His door until He opens it—and that door is nothing but the specific face. Having explained that there are three kinds of servitude (*ʿubūda*)[12]—servitude to God, servitude to the creature, and servitude to the (present) state—the Shaykh writes,

There is no emancipation from any of these save from servitude to the creature. It is of two sorts:

The first is servitude in freedom. This is the servants' servanthood to the occasions, so they are "the servants of the occasions," even though they are free.

The second is the servanthood of ownership. This is the slavehood, well-known to everyone, in which there is buying and selling. Emancipation enters here, and through it the servant emerges from the ownership of the created thing.

There remains bewilderment in ownership by the occasions. Does the servant emerge from enslavement by the occasions or not? Those who see that the occasions rule over the servant without any escape and that it is impossible for him to emerge from them except through fantasy—not in the actual situation—will say that there cannot be emancipation from slavery to the occasions.

Those who speak of the specific face, which is that within which there is no sharing, will speak of emancipation from slavery to the occasions. The servant's emancipation is his true knowledge of the specific face. When he knows it, he emerges from slavery to the occasions.

As for servitude to God and the servitude of servanthood—which is servitude to the state—there can be no emancipation from them whatsoever. (IV 199.22)

Ibn al-ʿArabī devotes Chapter 352 to three talismans that have been given control over human beings and prevent them from seeing things the way they are—reflection, imagination, and habits. He explains that people cannot overcome the rule of habits without knowing their own specific faces, and they cannot know their own specific faces without constant perseverance in the remembrance of God. One must accept nothing but what God Himself gives through the door to the human house, which is the specific face. In this passage the Shaykh also tells us that no one achieves this station except the Blameworthy—who are the highest ranking gnostics, unknown to the common people or the elect. They alone stand in the Station of No Station.[13]

As for the third talisman, it is the talisman of habits that rule over the rationally speaking selves because the selves have become familiar with them. The benefits and the means to wholesomeness always depend on the habits, so this talisman is not lifted. When an individual desires to lift the property of this talisman while he knows that it will not be lifted—for the familiar occasions are divine establishments that cannot possibly be lifted or repelled—he should return to gazing upon the face specific to him, within which the occasion leaves no trace. It is extremely hidden, so he should repair to its door so that he may open it. He should keep on clinging to the door and he should sense that the occasions are attracting him away from it so that he may take from them the trusts that they have in their hands for him. But he should not act and should not accept what they bring.

A thought may come to him saying, "This is a discourtesy toward God, *so take what* He has bestowed upon *you and be among the grateful* [7:144]. It is impossible to lift these occasions, so do not annul God's wisdom in your case, *lest you be among the ignorant* [11:46]."

He should not give ear to this scolding or this knowledge, for it is a thought from the self, not a thought from God. He should stay fixed in his clinging to the specific door and should say to that teacher, "God has forbidden that you come *to the houses by their backs.* If you were from God, you would have come *to the houses by their doors* [2:189], and I am a house." He should add nothing to this.

When the Real desires him for this station, He lets in that occasion along with the trust it has for him by the door of the specific face that this servant is facing and clinging to. This is the door of his house. When this occasion gives to him what it gives, he accepts it from it, because it has come to him from the door of the face from which he was seeking the affair, so this occasion has come to the house by its door. This is what is called "breaking the habits within the habits." (III 235.16)

After all, the world witnesses nothing from the companion of this station save someone taking from the occasions. Hence they do not make a distinction between themselves and him. He alone knows how he has taken [from the specific face]. This station belongs only to the Blameworthy, who are the highest of the tribes, for in habit-breaking they are within the habit itself. In this station, between them and the people lies what is between the witnesser and the veiled, but the people are not aware.

The companions of the manifest habit-breaking do not possess this station. They do not smell any whiff of it whatsoever. They are the ones who take from the occasions, for the occasions have not disappeared from them and will not disappear, though they are hidden. After all, the companion of the manifest breaking of habit cannot escape a sensory movement that is the occasion of the *wujūd* of the sought object. Thus he scoops or grasps with his hand in the air, and he opens it to show the grasped gold or whatever. So the gold comes to be only through the occasion of his hand's moving and grasping. Thus he does not emerge from the occasion, but this is not the habitual occasion as a whole. Nevertheless, the grasping is habitual, the movement of the hand is habitual, and the gaining of what he has gained—but in other ways—is habitual. Only gaining in this way is not habitual. Thus it is said concerning him that he has broken a habit. So know this!

Whoever desires to lift the ruling property of the talisman of habits should put himself to work in what we mentioned. Then habits will not rule over him while he remains within the habits, unrecognized by the common people and the elect. (III 235.26)

"Breaking the habit" (*kharq al-ᶜāda*) is the standard term for a miracle that appears from a friend of God.[14] By adding "within the habits" (*fi'l-ᶜādāt*) to the expression, the Shaykh is differentiating the unintended miracles of the Blameworthy from the miracles that are consciously induced by lower-ranking friends of God. Elsewhere he distinguishes between the Blameworthy and the "Sufis" by saying that the former are outwardly the same as other people, but the Sufis like to show off their charismatic gifts so as to attract people to God.[15] He explains the difference between these two sorts of habit-breaking in the continuation of the above passage:

The root *kh.ṣ.ṣ.*, from which comes the word *khāṣṣ* or "specific," is used only four times in the Koran, though it is an everyday word in later Arabic and a technical term in the sciences (as the opposite of *ᶜāmm*, "general"). One of the Koranic verses that certainly influenced Ibn al-ᶜArabī to employ the term in the expression *specific face* uses the verb *to specify*: *God specifies for His mercy whomsoever He will* (2:105). This term *specification* (*ikhtiṣāṣ*) plays an important role in the discussion of how prophets reach the station whereby they become worthy of prophethood. The general Islamic teaching is that no one can earn (*iktisāb*) this station. Rather, God *specifies* for it whomsoever He will, which is to say, in terms of this Koranic verse, that He singles the prophets out for His bounty and mercy in keeping with His desire and choice, not their desire. Muslim philosophers were often criticized for claiming, or seeming to claim, that prophecy can be earned, and the Shaykh rejects this position in several passages.

In the following "Mystery," which epitomizes Chapter 289, Ibn al-ᶜArabī makes the connection between specification and the specific face rather clear. The "inheritor" (*wārith*), it should be remembered, is the friend of God, who inherits his knowledge, stations, and states from the prophets. In contrast, the "Folk of Specification" receive their knowledge—or the knowledge in question, at least—outside every chain of intermediaries and occasions, because God Himself singles them out for this mercy and gives it to no one else. This is the station of the "unlettered" (*ummī*) friends of God, those whose knowledge is "God-given" (*ladunī*).[16] The Koranic example of such knowledge is provided primarily by Khaḍir, concerning whom God says, *They found one of Our servants whom We had given mercy from Us and whom We had taught knowledge from Us* (18:65). Ibn al-ᶜArabī alludes to this Koranic story beginning with his mention below of knowledge from Him (*min ladunhu*) and mercy from Him (*min ᶜindahu*). The "Solitaries" (*afrād*), typified by Khaḍir, are a group of God's friends who, in contrast to all other human beings, stand outside the authority of the Pole of the time, because they deal directly with God. Cosmologically, they have a station analogous to that of the Cherubim (also known as the "Enraptured Spirits"), angels who look directly upon God without the intermediary of the First Intellect. According to Ibn al-ᶜArabī, Muhammad was a Solitary before the Koran was revealed to him.[17]

A Mystery
The Knowledge of the Unlettered Prophet

The inheritor's messenger is the prophet,
and the prophet's messenger is the angelic spirit.
The Folk of Specification
possess divine revelation from the specific face.
It is found in everyone,
but understandings do not reach it.
There is no individual whom the Real does not address through it,
and to him He speaks from it.
So he says, "Such and such occurred to me,"
but he does not know from where,
because he is ignorant of the Entity.
The Folk of God have won only its witnessing [*shuhūd*],
not its *wujūd*.
All knowledge is one,
though the sources are diverse and the goals various.
The Real has taught whom He will of His servants
knowledge from Him,
and He gives him mercy from Him,
so the mercy bestows on him a property.
The back becomes the intermediary
and exercises its property over the lifeblood.
The follower denies him, undoes what he has tied,
and effaces what he has stipulated,
ignoring his dignity
and not knowing his lineage.
Indeed, he knows that through which he came to live,
but he forgets and is forgotten.
The waystations of the Solitaries
are found in the breaking of the habitual,
so their affairs lie outside
the ruling properties of the messengers and incline
away from the paths that they have prescribed,
while they follow the paths,
like Khaḍir and Moses, God's speaking companion,
and the words of Hūd, *Surely my Lord is on a straight path* [11:56]. (IV 388.33)

The Shaykh often speaks of the knowledge possessed by all things in the cosmos, a knowledge through which, for example, everything in the heavens and the earth glorifies God. Things receive this knowledge through the specific face. In Chapter 357, called "On the true knowledge of the waystation of the dumb beasts [*bahā'im*]," he explains something of the interrelationship between the heavens and the earth, or the high world and the low world, and describes the "tenuities" (*raqā'iq*)—the subtle lines of influence deriving from the divine names and tying all things together.[18] He identifies these with the specific faces, and tells us that the Koranic verse, *We are nearer to him than the jugular vein* (50:16), is a reference to these faces in human beings. From the specific faces derive the knowledge of specification—also known as "tasting" (*dhawq*)—that is possessed not only by the gnostics but also by everything else. It is these faces that help explain why paradise is divided into three basic realms—the Garden of Deeds, the Garden of Specification, and the Garden of Inheritance.[19]

> Between these high celestial forms and the low elemental forms extend tenuities that belong to the divine names and the lordly realities. These are the specific faces belonging to each possible thing that has proceeded from Him—from the word *Be* through the divine face-turning of desire. The occasioned thing does not know the specific face belonging to anything else, even though he has a specific face in himself, whether or not he knows it.
>
> From this face everything is poor toward God, not toward its engendered occasion. This is the divine occasion that is nearer than the engendered occasion, for the engendered occasion is separate from the creature, but this occasion is qualified neither by separation from it nor by proximate joining, even if, in the case of the human being, it is *nearer than the jugular vein* [50:16]—so its nearness is nearer than that.
>
> God bestows as He wills, upon every high and low form, from the knowledges of specification through which He is known by no one other than the recipient specifically. These are the knowledges of the tastings that are neither communicated nor told. No one knows them but he who has tasted them. It is not within the realm of possibility for him who has tasted them to convey them to him who has not tasted them. In this the creatures are ranked in excellence in an unknown manner. It is impossible for the entity of that through which they are ranked in excellence to be known. And since there is this specification in knowledge, there are Gardens of Specification. (III 260.27)

In respect of the fact that God is with all things through the specific face, all things are one and indistinguishable. The specification received by the great human beings arrives through the specific face, not through their greatness. They are great because God has bestowed upon them the rank of greatness. The Shaykh explains this after pointing out that nobility or "eminence" (*sharaf*) is not innate to human nature, or else everyone would be eminent. At the end of the passage, he changes his standpoint and considers eminence as deriving from the specific face. From that point of view—the fact that God is with us wherever we are—all things are equally eminent.

> People have disagreed concerning the eminence of the human being. Does it belong to him essentially, or does he possess it rather through a level that he reaches after he becomes manifest in his entity and comes to be proportioned perfectly in his humanity, whether through knowledge or through vicegerency and imamate?
>
> Those who say that the human being is eminent by his essence consider God's creation of him with His two hands, since He did not bring together the two hands in any other created thing. Moreover, they say, He created him in His form. This is the argument of those who say that his eminence is essential.
>
> Those who disagree with this view say that, were he eminent by his essence, we would know his eminence as soon as we saw his essence, but this is not the situation. Great and eminent human beings would not be distinct from other people through their knowledge and character, given that the essential definition brings the two sorts together. This proves that the eminence of human beings derives from an accidental affair known as "waystation" or "level." It is the waystation that is eminent, and the individual described by it reaches eminence as a consequence, like the levels of messengerhood, prophecy, vicegerency, and kingship. God says, *Will not the human being remember that We created him aforetime, when he was not a thing?* [19:67]. He also says, *Did there come upon man*—that is, indeed there did come upon him—*a while of the aeon when he was not a thing remembered?* [76:1]. Moreover, the angels said about him what they said about him in respect of his essence—and they spoke the truth.[20]
>
> Thus the human being's eminence is known only through the knowledge and vicegerency that God gave to him, so no created thing has

any eminence over others from his essence, only through God's giving eminence to him.

The most uplifted waystation with God is that God should preserve for His servant the witnessing of his own servanthood perpetually, whether or not He has conferred upon him any of the lordly robes. This is the most eminent waystation that is given to a servant. It is indicated in His words to Moses, *I have employed thee for Myself* [20:41]. It is also indicated in His words, *Glory be to Him who carried His servant by night* [17:1], so He linked him to His *tanzīh*.[21] In this station, one of the lovers said,

Address me not save with "O her servant!,"
for that is the most eminent of my names.

No artisanry has a higher eminence than ascription to its artisan. That is why a created thing has no eminence save through the specific face that it has from the Real, not from the direction of its occasion, which is a created thing like it. In this eminence, the first existent thing—which is the Pen or the Intellect or whatever you name it—and the lowest of existent things are equal in level, since the relation is one in giving existence, and the reality is one in everything in respect of possibility. (III 32.1)

The Shaykh discusses the specific face most commonly in terms of the special knowledge that it bestows upon those who are aware of it. For example, in one passage he differentiates between revelation (*waḥy*) in the specific sense—that is, the knowledge given to prophets through the intermediary of the angel—and two kinds of inspiration (*ilhām*), one with intermediaries and one without. Usually, as in the following, he does not differentiate between inspiration and unveiling.

Know that people have inspiration from God, but not revelation, because the way of revelation was cut off with the death of God's Messenger. There was revelation before him, but no divine report has come that there would be revelation after him. Thus God says, *Revelation was given to thee and to those before thee* [39:65], but He does not mention revelation after him, even if this is not compelling. Moreover, the truthful prophetic report has come concerning Jesus—who was among those to whom revelation was given before God's Messenger—saying, "He will lead us only from among us," that is, through our Sunnah. Hence, when he descends [at the end of time], he will have unveiling and inspiration, just as this community has it.

It should not be imagined that inspiration is not a divine report. The affair is not like that. Rather, it is a divine report and a report-giving from God to the servant on the hand of an angel made absent to its recipient. He may also be inspired by way of the specific face. The messenger and the prophet witness the angel and see him with the vision of eyesight when he reveals to them. Others sense the angel's trace, but they do not see him with the vision of eyesight. Thereby God inspires them with what He wills to inspire, or He bestows upon them from the specific face by lifting the intermediaries. This is the most majestic and eminent casting, and it is this in which the messenger and the friend come together. The "fingers of the All-Merciful" pertain to the specific face, while the "suggestion" of the angel pertains to the shared face. For the most part, there is no intermediary in divine inspiration. He who knows it knows how he takes it. (III 238.30)

The term *shared face* (*al-wajh al-mushtarak*) in the foregoing passage is not common, but its meaning is clear from the context. The Shaykh is connecting the specific face, which is the exclusive domain of God, with the Fingers of the All-Merciful, and hence with the hadith, "The heart is between two of the fingers of the All-Merciful." In contrast, he links the shared face with the suggestion of the angel, and, as noted in the previous chapter, the angel shares with the satan the attribute of casting suggestions into the heart.

Ibn al-ʿArabī devotes several passages in the *Futūḥāt* to classifying the friends of God according to various schemes. Much of Chapter 73, the second longest chapter of the book (after Chapter 69, on *ṣalāt*) deals with the Men of Number (*rijāl al-ʿadad*), who stand in a series of hierarchical stations and whose number never changes. Thus, at any given time, the universe is supported by one Pole, two Imams, four Pegs, seven Substitutes, and so on. These Men represent a chain of intermediaries and occasions that God employs to bring knowledge and blessings into the world. But God's friends may also receive knowledge and blessings through the specific face, which bypasses the hierarchy. The Shaykh makes this clear in explaining a saying of Muḥammad ibn Qā᾿id al-Awānī, a disciple of ᶜAbd al-Qādir al-Jīlānī.[22] Ibn Qā᾿id reported that he left everything in the universe behind and arrived at God, but then he saw someone's footprints before him. He became jealous, and his mind was stilled only after he was told that the footprints belonged to the prophet Muhammad. In the long version of his *Iṣṭilāḥāt al-ṣūfiyya*, while defining the term *chamber* (*mukhdaᶜ*), Ibn al-ᶜArabī explains how Ibn Qā᾿id could indeed have reached this station and not seen his master ᶜAbd al-Qādir—who was the Pole of the time—before him. In the second passage cited below, the Shaykh ties this discussion into the specific face.

> The "chamber" is the site where the Pole is curtained from the Solitaries when they arrive and robes are conferred upon them. It is the storehouse of conferral, and the storekeeper is the Pole. Muḥammad ibn Qā᾿id al-Awānī said, "I ascended until I saw before me nothing save the footprints of one person, so I became jealous. It was said to me, 'That is the footprints of your Prophet,' so my agitation was stilled."
>
> He was one of the Solitaries, and he imagined that there was no one above him save his Prophet and that no one had priority over him. And he spoke the truth, for he witnessed only his own path, and no one else had traveled his path save his Prophet. It was said to him, "Did you see ᶜAbd al-Qādir?"
>
> He replied, "I did not see ᶜAbd al-Qādir in the Presence."
>
> When ᶜAbd al-Qādir was told about this, he said, "Ibn Qā᾿id spoke the truth. I saw him there when he said it."
>
> It was said to him, "Where were you, master?"
>
> He replied, "I was in the chamber, and from me emerged the favor to him," and then he named it. Ibn Qā᾿id was asked what the favor was, and he said the like of what ᶜAbd al-Qādir said. (II 130.15).

> Ibn Qā᾿id supposed that there he saw before him nothing save the footprints of his Prophet. This pertains only to the Solitaries of the moment. If someone is not one of the Solitaries, inescapably he will see the footprints of the Pole of his moment before him, in addition to the footprints of his Prophet—if he is an Imam. If he is a Peg, he will see before him three sets of footprints, and if a Substitute, four sets, and so on.
>
> Nevertheless, he must have a station in the Presence of following. If he is standing in the Presences of following and has been taken aside to the right hand of the path—between the chamber and the path—then he will see no footprints before him. This is the path of the specific face from the Real toward every existent thing. It is from this specific face that are unveiled to the friends the knowledges for which they are censured and through which they are considered heretics. Those who call them heretics and unbelievers are those who have faith in these knowledges when they come to them from the messengers. These knowledges are identical with those. (I 201.22)

In the following passage, Ibn al-ᶜArabī calls those who knowingly take inspiration from the specific face the "gnostics" and then goes on to imply, through the attributes that he ascribes to them, something that he says explicitly in a passage quoted earlier they are the same as the "Blameworthy," those perfect human beings who stand in the Station of No Station and remain unknown and denied. "Command" and "creation" are standard terms for the two worlds—the worlds of the unseen and the visible, or the absent and the witnessed. The Shaykh says that the angels "ascend" to creation because, as he explains elsewhere, they turn their gaze only toward the face of God in things, so they always move toward Him, and He is "up" in relation to everything else. "In respect of their gaze on that to which they are descending, it is said that the angels descend, but in respect of the fact that they are gazing on the Real in that thing and that He possesses the level of highness, it is said that the angels ascend" (III 54.14). In this quality the angels are similar to the highest Pole, who "sees nothing of the things except the face of the Real within them" (II 573.26).

At the end of the passage, Ibn al-ᶜArabī offers an explanation for the meaning of the six Koranic verses that command people with the words, *sabbiḥ bi-ḥamdi rabbika,* which is typically understood to mean, "Proclaim thy

Lord's praise" or "Celebrate the praise of thy Lord" or "Glorify thy Lord's praise." The Shaykh, however, says that it should be understood to mean "Glorify through the praise of thy Lord," that is, when you glorify God, you should use the words that He has used in praising Himself. The Shaykh's reading, as usual, is perfectly plausible.

God did not assign wings to any of the spirits except those among them who are angels, for they are the emissaries from the Presence of the Command to His creation, so they must have occasions through which they descend and ascend. What has been established by wisdom demands this. Thus He assigned to them "wings" in the measure of their levels in the Presence of the Real through which they travel and in the Presence of Creation to which they ascend. Hence they go back and forth between the creation and the command. That is why they say, *We descend not save through the command of thy Lord* [19:64]. So know this!

When these emissaries descend upon hearts and find them pure and receptive toward good, they give them the knowledge that they have brought in the measure embraced by the hearts' preparedness. If they see them as unclean hearts without any good, they prohibit them from remaining in that state and command them to purify themselves through what the Lawgiver has plainly stated. If this concerns knowledge of God, then it is through what is demanded by reflection and has been brought by the prophetic report from God; if it concerns the engendered things, then it is through knowledge of the rulings and their beliefs in this.

The angels' ruling property concerning that stays with the person when they find the hearts. But if they do not find the hearts, as in the case of the hearts of the gnostics, who dwell in *Nothing is as His likeness* [42:11], then they do not know where the hearts have gone. It is they who take their states from God by means of the specific face. Hence they are unknown, and people take them to task for what they bring from this face. It was from here that Khaḍir took his knowledge. It is these who are censured, but they censure no one except with the tongue of the Shariah. It is the Shariah that censures, not they.[23]

They are like those who "glorify through God's praise," so it is God who lauds Himself for what He knows Himself to be. If someone meddles and deduces for Him a laudation whose words were not brought by a divine address, then he has not glorified Him through His praise, but rather through what he has deduced on his own, so he falls short of the degree that is appropriate. Hence you should say what He has said about Himself. Do not add to what has been related, even if it is beautiful!

Thus have I clarified for you something. If you put it into practice, you will be one of the Folk of the Real. (III 385.14)

From Chapter 379: The Servant of the Praiseworthy

Among the reasons for human inability to praise God in an appropriate manner is that He deserves praise for everything in existence, and this is unknowable in its details. Moreover, each thing praises (*ḥamd*) and lauds (*thanāʾ*) God by its own mode of existence, as is suggested by the several Koranic verses that say that everything in the heavens and earth glorifies God. In the Shaykh's view, the specific act of praise that pertains uniquely to each thing occurs through the specific divine face, known only to the thing itself. In order to make up for our inability to praise God as He is worthy, the Prophet instituted certain specific formulae of supplication. One is a supplication that he taught to Juwayriya, the daughter of al-Ḥārith. He instructed her to utter each sentence three times before moving on to the next: "Glory be to God in the number of His creatures; glory be to God through His own good-pleasure; glory be to God to the weight of the Throne; glory be to God through the ink of His words." The Shaykh comments on this supplication in Chapter 379, "On the true knowledge of the waystation of undoing and knotting, honoring and disdaining, and the configuration of supplication in the form of the reports." He begins by explaining that the numbers from one to twelve are the simple, noncompound numbers (*basāʾiṭ min al-aʿdād*). Each possesses a property not possessed by the others, and each has "a Man from among God's servants who possesses the property of that number" (III 493.34). The first eleven numbers are associated with the eleven-cycle *witr* prayer performed by the Prophet, while the twelfth brings the totality of this prayer to perfection. The Shaykh explains that each cycle gives rise to various attributes that are "a spiritual, intelligible configuration. If this configuration becomes embodied [in the imaginal world], it will be in the form of a human being who has the attribute by which he is called" (III 494.24). The Man who pertains to a specific cycle (and who may be a woman)[24] is called by one of God's names. Thus the twelfth, who perfects the whole prayer, is called ʿAbd Allāh, "Servant of God." The person who performs the third cycle is called "ʿAbd al-Ḥamīd," the Servant of the Praiseworthy. In other words, his spiritual configuration will have as its predominant characteristic the attribute of rendering praise.

> The configuration of the form of the third cycle of the *witr*:
>
> From this cycle is configured one of the Men of God who is called "Servant of the Praiseworthy."
>
> Know that laudation of God is of two sorts—unbounded and bound. There can only be the unbounded sort if there is also incapacity, as in the Prophet's words, "I count not Thy laudations before Thee—Thou art as Thou hast lauded Thyself." Their poet says,
>
> When we praise you
> with a wholesome word
> you are what we praise
> and beyond what we praise.
>
> It is impossible for any created thing to encompass the laudations that are proper to God, because it is impossible for all possible things to enter into *wujūd*. Each possible thing has a specific face toward God from which God brings it into existence and through which it knows Him. From this face it lauds Him with a laudation known only to the companion of the face. It is impossible for anyone else to know it, and it cannot be signified by words or allusions. This is the unbounded laudation of God through every tongue that has been and will be.
>
> This explains why it is inconceivable that the reward of him who says, "Glory be to God in the number of His creatures," should occur in *wujūd*. Rather, its reward never ceases coming into *wujūd* as state after state, perpetually and ad infinitum. This also explains why the Shariah has brought this statement three-fold: The servant should say it three times so that through it he may gain the sensory reward, the imaginal reward, and the suprasensory reward. Thus he will be blessed in sensation, imagination, and reason, just as he remembers in sensation, imagination, and reason, and just as he worships in sensation, imagination, and reason. A similar thing is true of the servant's mention of the "ink of the divine words" and "the weight of the Throne"—given that the "Throne" is the whole cosmos, through that which sets up its limits.
>
> So also is the case with "His own good-pleasure" in what is done by the folk of the Garden and the folk of the Fire. They do deeds and act freely only in the objects of the divine good-pleasure, for this is required by the homestead, in contrast to the homestead of this world and religious prescription. In the homestead of this world, they act freely both in that which pleases God and that which angers Him. This is because God has made the Fire the abode of those with whom He is angry. Hence, in the abode of this world, its folk have no escape from moving about in that which angers God. But, when they take up residence in the abode of the Fire and make it their habitation, it becomes impossible for them to move about save in God's good-pleasure. That is why the final issue of its folk will be with the ruling property of the *mercy* that *embraces everything* [7:156], even if the Fire is an abode of wretchedness.
>
> In the same way, it is said concerning the messenger whose messengerhood has come to an end, such that he has finished with it and gone back to God, that he is God's messenger even if, in that state, he is not a messenger. So also, concerning the abode of wretchedness, we say that it is an abode of wretchedness, even if the wretchedness has disappeared from its folk who are within it.
>
> As for the bound laudation, the philosophers bind Him with the attribute of *tanzīh*, nothing else. If they laud Him with the attribute of acts, that is by virtue of the whole or the root, not the individual instance.[25]
>
> As for other than the philosophers, they bind laudation of God with both the attributes of the acts and the attributes of *tanzīh*. They are the perfect, for they share with the philosophers in what they know, but they exceed them in what the philosophers ignore and do not know because of the inadequacy of their aspirations, since obfuscation abides in them and exercises

its ruling property over them. This obfuscation is that "Nothing proceeds" from God save only the mentioned "one" and that it is not permissible to ascribe to Him that by which He describes Himself in His Book. After all, their consideration does not affirm any revealed book or sent individual in the manner that corresponds with the actual situation and in the way in which this is affirmed by the folk of unveiling, by unmixed faith, and by the rational faculties of some of the considerative thinkers, like the Kalām authorities and others who uphold this from the direction of rational consideration.

The property of the forms of these cycles of the Prophet's *witr* prayer pervades the whole cosmos from the moment that "I was a prophet when Adam was between water and clay" to the day of resurrection. (III 495.13)

Chapter 265: The Arriver

Ibn al-ʿArabī devotes Part Three of the *Futūḥāt* to elucidating the states (*aḥwāl*) that were often discussed in earlier works on Sufism. These are the passing psychological and spiritual gifts that come upon the travelers in their journeys to God. They are contrasted with the "stations" (*maqāmāt*), which are character traits and divine attributes that become permanent acquisitions.[26] In the chapter called "On the true knowledge of the Arriver [*wārid*]," the Shaykh tells us that praiseworthy states share in the fact that all of them "arrive" (*wurūd*) at the servant, but they come from a variety of sources. They may be eternal (*qadīm*) or newly arrived (*muḥdath*), and they may derive from occasions or from the specific face. The correlative of "arrival" is "procession" (*ṣudūr*), as in the philosophical maxim, "Nothing proceeds from the One but one." Elsewhere I have translated the term *wārid* as "inrush," but the use of the term in the present context shows that the more literal term *arriver* is better suited to the nuances of the idea.

The Arriver fell in love with the Proceeder,
my pair fell in love with the One.
All His names arrived in a rush
to hide themselves from the watcher.
Through their traces they give an Aspiration
to every heart that intends to reach them.

In the view of the Tribe and in our own view, the "Arriver" is that which arrives in the heart from any divine name. The discussion here is about the fact that it arrives, not what it arrives with. It may arrive with sobriety or intoxication, contraction or expansion, awe or intimacy, or innumerable other affairs. All of these are Arrivers. However, the Tribe have taken this as a technical term for the praiseworthy passing thoughts among those we mentioned.

You should know, my brother, that the Arriver, as Arriver, is bound neither by new arrival nor by eternity, for God has described Himself, despite His eternity, as "coming." Arrival is a coming, and the Arriver may have diverse states in its coming. It may arrive suddenly, like the "intrusion" or the "befallers,"[27] or it may not arrive suddenly, but rather along with the awareness of the one upon whom it arrives through the marks and the contexts of the states that signify the arrival of a designated affair, sought by the preparedness of the locus.

Every divine Arriver brings only benefit. There is nothing but a divine Arriver, whether or not it is engendered. The benefit that pervades every Arriver is the knowledge gained from its arrival by the person upon whom it arrives. There is no stipulation here as to whether it yields happiness or hurt, since this does not pertain to the property of the Arriver. The property of the Arriver is only the knowledge that is gained by means of it. Anything beyond this pertains to that with which it arrives, not to itself.

On the day of resurrection, God will come so as to differentiate and decree among the people. Among the people will be those for whom He decrees what brings their felicity, and among them will be those for whom He decrees what brings their wretchedness. The coming is one, the decree is one, but what is decreed is diverse.

The Arriver may be qualified by procession in the state of its arrival. Then it is an "Arriver" in respect of the one in whom it arrives, and a "Proceeder" in respect of Him from whom it proceeds. Inescapably, this Arriver is a newly arrived thing from God.

If the Arriver is not qualified by procession in the state of its arrival, then it is an eternal Arriver, and the arrival is a relation that arrives newly for it within the servant in whom it arrives.

The former is a Proceeder/an Arriver, and the latter is an Arriver, nothing else.

There is nothing eternal that arrives save the divine names. If they arrive in respect of the Entity, they are not diverse in the arrival. If they arrive in respect of the property, they are diverse through the diversity of the properties. After all, they are diverse in the realities, save in their signifying the Entity such that they are not diverse.

Whether the Arriver is eternal or newly arrived, that with which it arrives cannot escape from being newly arrived. This is what subsists with the person to whom the Arriver has come when the Arriver goes away, and it must go away. The occasion of this is the subsistence of reverence in the individual, for there is no escape from the arrival of another Arriver in him, so he would have to receive it and turn away from the one that is there. That would be to fail to observe full reverence toward the first Arriver. That is why it departs after delivering that with which it arrived. When the second Arriver arrives, it finds him free for it. So he welcomes it, and there is no thought to attract him away from it through his attachment to it. Then every Arriver proceeds away from him with his reverence and respect for it, so it lauds him with good at God. This laudation is then his felicity. (II 566.12)

At this point, the Shaykh turns to explaining how these Arrivers appear in their actual manifestation. He associates them with the "breaths" (*anfās*) of the person who experiences them. "Breaths" are the human analogue of the Breath of the All-Merciful, since they give life to words and bodily things just as the All-Merciful Breath gives life to the whole cosmos. One might say that human breaths are individual instances of the All-Merciful Breath, and for those who have eyes to see, they are, in respect of *tashbīh*, identical with that Breath. When the Shaykh says, "The breaths pertain to the All-Merciful" (III 505.8), he seems to include all breathing and even all of manifest *wujūd*, for he also says that the breaths are "manifest in the cosmos through mercy" and within them "all creatures are included" (III 274.4). He speaks of "the world of the breaths" meaning "The Men of God in this path" (II 6.20). In some passages, he identifies the breaths with the world that is unveiled during God's self-disclosures.[28] In the present context, he explains that the Arrivers experienced by the gnostics are carried by their breaths. Another passage that speaks of the breaths as Arrivers helps explain what he has in mind here, and, in particular, the connection between breaths and the just-mentioned reverence (*ḥurma*) and respect (*ḥishma*) that are due to them, though he speaks rather of courtesy (*adab*).

In this waystation is found the knowledge of the *ḥaqq* due to the guest who arrives at someone. The "breaths" are the Arrivers of the Real upon the servant, and they have a *ḥaqq*. They return to Him from whom they arrived. So the servant should consider how he welcomes them when they arrive, the courtesy that is due to them in his taking what they arrive with, and what he should confer on them when they leave him, returning to the Real. (III 461.26)

Chapter 265 continues as follows:

In reality, if the Arrivers are newly arrived, they are nothing but identical with the breaths. The affairs and properties with which the breaths arrive are what the Folk of the Path recognize as "Arrivers," for the breaths are the carriers of the forms of these Arrivers. So the newly arrived Arrivers do not abide through themselves; rather, the Arrivers are the forms of the breaths. These forms are diverse through the diversity of the properties of the divine names within them. Thus the Arriver in relation to the breaths is like spatial confinement for an accident by virtue of its subordination to substance. The substance is the spatially confined thing, not the accident. So also the breath arrives, not the form.

The benefit in the form is like the message in the messenger. Thus there is an Arriver with a knowledge, an Arriver with a deed, and an Arriver with what brings these two together; an Arriver with a state, an Arriver with a knowledge and a state, an Arriver with a deed and a state, and an Arriver with a knowledge, a deed, and a state. This last is like the Arriver of sobriety and intoxication and their likes, and it is the strongest of Arrivers.

If the Arriver is not newly arrived, it is called "lifting the intermediaries between God and His servant." This is a self-disclosure from the specific face that belongs to every created thing. What it gives the creature and what he gains in it cannot be communicated. Few of the Folk of

God have this, and none of the Arrivers is like it. *And God speaks the* ***ḥaqq****, and He guides on the path* [33:4]. (II 566.32)

Chapter 396: The Veils of Knowledge

In Ibn al-ʿArabī's way of looking at things, real knowledge—knowledge that allows people to recognize the face of the Real in all things and to understand how the signs in the self and the cosmos signify God—comes only through God's teaching. All knowledge does in fact point to God in His self-disclosure, but only those taught by God come to understand how this is so. Khaḍir is the best-known Koranic model for those who come to know God through this sort of teaching and, as indicated already, the Shaykh maintains that Khaḍir received his knowledge through the specific face. He explains these points in Chapter 396, which seems to be his most thorough discussion of the specific face in the *Futūḥāt*. It is called, "On the true knowledge of the mutual waystation of 'When someone brings together the sciences and knowledges, they veil him from Me.'"

Surely unto God all affairs
come home [42:53].
O this world of mine,
you are naught but delusion!
The folk of godwariness
are not secure from her guile
despite the godwariness—
so what of the folk of depravity?
She has the attributes of the Real
in her deception,
and of His deception
we are unaware.
If they were fair to her
in her state,
how fine a herald and warner
she would be!
Part of her truthfulness
in her state is that
she shows death's millstone
turning upon us.
I see in her
and in all things with her
an admonition reminding
the experienced.
Through her in her engendered existence
the servant will reach
the Real's perfect description
on the Day of Upstirring.
They have treated her fairly
who pass her by,
but he who denies this
has wandered astray.
Her scale has been set up
along with her,
and he who knows it
is the knowing, the powerful,
like Aḥmad al-Sabtī
in his acts
when God assigned to him
the reins of affairs.[29]
The servant becomes manifest
in His names
only through her,
for He clarifies and forgives.

Know—God confirm us and you with the spirit of holiness—that in Himself, God is far higher and far more majestic than that His servant should know Him. That is impossible. There remains no object of knowledge for us to seek save relations specifically, or the entities of the possible things and what is attributed to them. Gnosis attaches itself, among the possible things, to the entities of the essences, while the knowledges attach themselves to everything that is ascribed to these entities.

You come to know the essences and entities self-evidently, without any reflection or consideration. Or rather, the self perceives them through what God has planted within it. Then you come to know the relations to them, and this is the knowledge of what is reported about them, that is, their descriptions, the judgments made about them by considerative proofs, and the inerrant report-giving [of the prophets]. There is no other way to reach knowledge of them.

The judgments and reports are infinite in their manyness. Hence the person who considers them becomes dispersed and is not able to bring them together. The Real desires to bring His servants together in Him, not in the pursuit of this manyness so as to know it. Or rather, He has made permissible for some of His servants the knowledge of this manyness that will allow them to bring things together in Him. This is indicated by His words concerning the consideration of such things, *[We shall show them Our signs upon the horizons and in themselves,] until it is clear to them that it is the Real* [41:53].

When someone becomes dispersed in himself while bringing together knowledges that are not considered in respect of the fact that they signify the Real, these have veiled him from the site of signifying the Real that these knowledges have in themselves. Such, for example, are the sciences of arithmetic and geometry, the prepatory sciences and logic, and natural science. But none of these is a knowledge that does not have within it a signifying of, or a path to, knowledge of God. However, most people do not consider this knowledge in the respect that it seeks the face that signifies God. Hence it is blamed, and it veils the fact of signifying.

Then God alerts some people to seek for the site in which every known thing signifies God. After all, God has dispersed such a person among the objects of knowledge, even if what he seeks from them is their signifying God. So we have no doubt that when someone brings together what he knows in the locus of his consideration, this veils him from God, that is, from the face in respect of which it is proper for the recipient to know from God to the extent of his own capacity.

He has no path to this save to remove everything he knows and the whole cosmos from his thoughts and to sit empty-hearted with God through presence, watchfulness, tranquillity, and divine remembrance with the name *God*—a remembrance of the heart. He must not consider signifiers that would allow him to arrive at his knowledge of God. When he clings to the door and devotes himself to knocking with the remembrance—and this is the mercy that God gives from Himself, I mean His giving success and His inspiration to do what I mentioned—then God takes charge of teaching him through witnessing, just as He took charge of the Folk of God, such as Khaḍir and others. Then He teaches him knowledge from Himself. He says, *whom We had given mercy from Us and whom We had taught knowledge from Us* [18:65] from the specific face that is between him and God. It belongs to every created thing, since it is impossible for occasions to have traces in the occasioned things. That is the tongue of the outward situation. Thus God says concerning Jesus, *And you blow into it, and it is a bird, by My leave* [5:110], not by your blowing. The blowing is the occasion of the engendering in the outward situation, but in reality the engendering occurs only by the divine leave.

This is a face of which no servant gains an overview, whether "prophet sent out or angel brought near."[30] The furthest limit of the divine solicitude to the individual—whether angel, messenger, or friend of God—is that God acquaint him with the face specific to himself, not the face of anyone else. Thus Khaḍir said to Moses, "I have a knowledge that God has taught me and that you do not know," because it derived from the specific face from God that His servant has. No one gains an overview of this face save its companion, when God shows him solicitude.

There is no created thing that does not have this specific face. From it, God teaches it many affairs. However, some of the servants do not know that He has given them this knowledge from this face. This is every self-evident knowledge that they find which is not preceded by their reflection or pondering. The companion of solicitude knows that God has given him the knowledge from that face. Then Khaḍir also said to Moses, "And you have a knowledge that God has taught you and that I do not know." If Moses knew his own specific face, then he knew the knowledge coming to him from that face. But if he did not know it, then Khaḍir alerted him to it so that he might ask God about it.

When someone knows things, all of them, from this face, then he keeps constant company with this witnessing. The divine tasks and the things are engendered from God while he gazes upon them and they do not distract him, despite the manyness of the engendered things that he witnesses in the cosmos. Such was the station of al-Ṣiddīq in his words, "I have never seen anything without seeing God before it." This is because of what we mentioned—he witnessed the things proceeding from God through engendering. He was in perpetual witnessing while the engenderings arrived newly. No newly arrived thing arrived newly from God unless God was the object of his witnessing before that thing. According to what has reached me, no one has called attention to this face and what is engendered from it in the heart of him who has withdrawn into witnessing Him save Abū Bakr al-Ṣiddīq.

However, I did not take it from Abū Bakr's calling attention, because I had not understood what he meant, nor did I reflect upon it. Rather, God showed solicitude to me in that, so knowledge of it came upon me suddenly at the beginning. I did not recognize it and I denied it. I said, "Where did this come from?" Then God opened the door between me and Him. Then I knew what I had from the Real specific to me. I came to know that this is the specific face from God that every engendered thing has from Him. So I clung to it and took my ease.

The mark of him who claims the specific face is clinging to Shari'ite courtesy. If an act of disobedience should occur from him through the divine determination, from whose penetrating power there is no escape, then, if he sees it as an act of disobedience and an opposition to the Shari'ite command, he should know that he is one of the folk of this face. But if he believes other than this, then we know that God has not given him any overview whatsoever of this specific face, that he has no opening in it, and that he is an individual whom God in no way esteems. This is because there is no one who has greater courtesy toward the Shariah or true belief that it is the Real—exactly as the common man knows it—than the folk of this face, for they know affairs as they actually are. They know that their share of this Shari'ite command and prescription, the share of him who brought it—that is, the Messenger—and the share of the common people who are also addressed by it are exactly the same. None of them has any excellence over anyone else within it, for it has come for its own essence, not for anything else. Hence, when someone declares something generally unlawful for one person on the basis of the Shari'ite address, he thereby includes all those for whom prescription is made, without specification—so much so that, were he to say that a thing is lawful only for one person, who is being blamed because of the outward situation, then everyone would consider him an unbeliever. He would be a liar in his claim to be one of the folk of this face, for the most characteristic knowledges of this face are everything brought by the shariahs.

That is why, when God's Messenger addressed the people concerning ʿAlī ibn Abī Ṭālib after he had been told that he had asked for the daughter of Abū Jahl in marriage in addition to the Prophet's daughter Fāṭima, he said, "Fāṭima is part of me. What hurts her hurts me, and what makes her happy makes me happy. It is not for me to make unlawful what God has made lawful, nor to make lawful what God has made unlawful." Thus, his knowledge of the specific divine face allowed him only to keep the unlawful in its unlawfulness and the lawful in its lawfulness. He did not make it unlawful for ʿAlī to marry the daughter of Abū Jahl, since that was lawful for him. However, he said, "If he desires that, he should divorce my daughter, for, by God, the daughter of God's enemy and the daughter of God's Messenger shall not come together under one man." Then he lauded his other daughter's spouse with good. So ʿAlī refrained from that.

If that face bestowed what this disputer supposes it bestows, then God's Messenger would have been the most appropriate for that, but he did no such thing. Yet he had the most complete unveiling, the most inclusive judgment, and the most bounteous share, for he is the greatest master.

Every individual must have a specific description that belongs solely to him and that God gives to him through this face. Through it, God will give felicity in the final issue to those concerning whom it is said that they will not become felicitous nor be reached by the *mercy* of God that *embraces everything* [7:156]. For this mercy proceeds from the faces of specification. Hence it pervades the knower and the ignorant, the obedient and the disobedient. May God place us among those who reach it in all their states! So he will encounter God, and no tongue of blame will apply to him after he comes to know this face.

The rulings of the *mujtahid*s and all the shariahs proceed from this specific face. The interpretation of dreams through innate capacity and without considering books or seeking proofs also derives from this specific face. Those who desire to gain it should cling to what we stipulated. *And God speaks the* ***ḥaqq****, and He guides on the path* [33:4]. (III 558.5)

From Chapter 369: The Storehouse of Teaching

Ibn al-ʿArabī calls the nineteenth section of Chapter 369, which deals with the keys to the storehouses of munificence, "The storehouse of teaching, the elevation of the teacher over the student, and the courtesy that the student must observe toward his mentor." His basic goal is to show that God's munificent giving through bestowal of *wujūd* and manifesting the signs is the divine root of all knowledge-giving and all teaching. Because teaching is grounded in the divine, it permeates the whole of existence, from the First Intellect down to the human world. In the same way, the courtesy (*adab*) or correct behavior that students should observe toward their teachers is divinely rooted. One sort of knowledge-giving is that which comes through the specific face. For Muslims, the primary paradigm of this knowledge-giving can only be the instruction given to the

Prophet. The Shaykh maintains that the Koran itself was given to the Prophet through the specific face. Here he is providing his own explanation of the common idea that the Prophet had received the whole Koran toward the beginning of his prophetic career, during the "Night of Power," but then Gabriel revealed its individual verses according to the appropriate occasions. Thus in receiving the Koran from Gabriel, Muhammad had a peculiar situation, because he already knew what his teacher was teaching him (a point that is supported by the two Koranic verses that the Shaykh cites). Nevertheless, God made sure that both Gabriel and Muhammad observed the courtesy appropriate to the teacher-student relationship.

Know that in reality, the teacher is God, and the whole cosmos is a taker of benefits, a seeker, poor, and needy. This is its perfection. When these are not the attributes of people, they are ignorant of themselves. He who is ignorant of himself is ignorant of his Lord. He who is ignorant of anything at all has not given it its *ḥaqq*. He who has not given something its *ḥaqq* has been unjust toward it in his judgment and is naked of the clothing of knowledge.

Thus it has become clear to you that all eminence is found only in knowledge and in those who put it into practice in accord with it. If it bestows a practice on the side of the Real, they practice it, and if it bestows a practice on the side of creation, they practice it. Thus they walk in the white path of purity and openhandedness, in which is seen no crookedness or unevenness.

The first student that accepted knowledge through learning, not essence, was the First Intellect. It came to understand from God what He taught it. He commanded it to write what He taught it in the Preserved Tablet that He created from it, so He named it a "Pen." Included in His knowledge that He taught it was that it said to Him out of courtesy to the teacher, "What shall I write?" Shall I write what You have taught me or shall I write what You dictate to me? This pertains to the courtesy of the student when the teacher speaks to him summary words that seek a differentiated exposition.

God replied to it, "Write what has been," or what I have taught, "and what will be," or what I will dictate to you, which is My knowledge concerning My creation "until the day of resurrection," nothing else.

Thus the Pen wrote its knowledge concerning what had been. It wrote the Cloud, within which was the Real "before He created His creation," and the realities enclosed by the Cloud, which we have mentioned in the chapter of this book on the Breath. It wrote the *wujūd* of the enraptured spirits, what enraptures them, their states, and what they are busy with—all of this so that it might know it. It wrote the displaying of traces by His names within these spirits. It wrote itself, its *wujūd*, the form of its *wujūd*, and the knowledges that it encloses; and it wrote the Tablet. When it finished with all this, the Real dictated to it what would come to be from Him until the day of resurrection, for the entrance of the infinite into *wujūd* is impossible, so it cannot be written. Writing, after all, is an affair of *wujūd*, so it cannot escape being finite.

The Real dictated to the Pen and it wrote, head turned down, out of courtesy toward the Teacher. For eyesight has no connection with dictation. On the contrary, what is connected to eyesight is the thing on which is written. It is the Pen's hearing that is connected to what the Real dictates to it. The reality of hearing is that what is heard does not become bound to a designated direction, in contrast to sensory eyesight, for it becomes bound, either by a specific, designated direction, or by all the directions.[31] But hearing is not like that, for the object to which it becomes connected is speech. If the speaker possesses a direction or is in a direction, that goes back to him. If he is not in a direction or does not possess a direction, that goes back to him, not to the listener. Hence hearing is better than eyesight at signifying *tanzīh*, further removed from binding, and more all-embracing and clearer in unboundedness.

So the first mentor in the cosmos is the First Intellect. The first learner who takes from a created mentor is the Preserved Tablet. This nomenclature is Shari'ite. For the rational thinkers, the name of the Preserved Tablet is the "Universal Soul." It is the first raised-up existent thing that is acted upon by the Intellect. In relation to the Intellect, it is like Eve in relation to Adam. It was created from it, and it was coupled with it. Thus it became two, just as *wujūd* became two through the newly arrived thing, and knowledge became two through the newly arrived Pen.

Then God put creation in order through giving existence, until the turn and the divine order reached the manifestation of this human, Adamic configuration. He configured it *in the most beautiful stature* [95:4]. Then *He blew into* Adam *of His spirit* [32:9] and He commanded the angels to prostrate themselves before him. They fell before him in prostration at the divine command to do so. So He made him a kiblah for His angels. Then He instructed them about his vicegerency in the earth. They did not know on whose behalf Adam would be vicegerent. Perhaps they thought that he was to be vicegerent on behalf of those who went before him in keeping the earth populated. So they protested because of the contrariety of the natures that they saw in his configuration. They knew that haste would quickly come to him and that, if the things from which his body was compounded were to become mutually contrary, this would result in contention and leave the trace of *corruption* in the earth and the *shedding* of *blood* [2:30].

God let the angels know that He had created Adam in His form and had *taught* him *the names, all of them* [2:31], those names whose faces were turned toward bringing both the elemental world and the higher worlds into existence. Then He displayed the named things to the angels and said, *Tell Me the names of these* [2:31], that is, the things toward which the names had turned their faces to give them existence. "Do you glorify Me and call Me holy by them? For you suppose that you *glorify* Me *in praise and call* Me *holy* [2:30]."

The angels replied, *We have no knowledge* [2:32]. Then He said to Adam, *Tell them their names* [2:33]. So He made Adam a mentor for them and Adam taught them all the names. At that they came to know that he was the vicegerent of God in His earth, not a vicegerent of those who had gone before.

The perfect human beings never ceased receiving the names from one another until the names finally reached the Greatest Master, Muhammad, him to whose perfection witness has been given and who was known through his prophecy "when Adam was between water and clay." The "water" was for the sake of the children's *wujūd*, and the "clay" was Adam's *wujūd*. Muhammad was given "the all-comprehensive words," just as Adam was given all the names. Then God taught him the names that He had taught Adam, so he came to know "the knowledge of the first and the last." Hence Muhammad was the most magnificent vicegerent and the greatest imam, and his community was *the best community brought forth to the people* [3:110].

God placed Muhammad's inheritors in the waystations of the prophets and the messengers, for He permitted *ijtihād* to them in the rulings. This is a law-giving on the basis of the report of the lawgiver. "Every *mujtahid* is correct," just as every prophet is preserved from error. God made the *mujtahids* His servants in this so that this community might gain a share of law-giving and within it their feet might become firm. No one has priority over them in this save their Prophet. Thus the ulama of this community will be mustered as preservers of the Muhammadan Shariah in the rows of the prophets, not in the rows of the communities, for they are *witnesses against the people* [2:143]. This is a plain text concerning their rectitude. There will be no messenger [at the resurrection] without one of the ulama of this community at his side—or two, or three, or whatever the case may be.

Each of the ulama has the degree of mastership in the knowledge of the tracings,[32] the states, the stations, the waystations, and the mutual waystations, until the affair in this finally reaches the Seal of the Friends, the Seal of the Muhammadan *Mujtahids*; and until it finally reaches the General Seal, who is [Jesus,] God's spirit and His word. He is the last learner, and he is the last mentor for those who take from him. He will die along with his companions from Muhammad's community in one breath through "a pleasant wind that will take them beneath the armpits." They will find that it brings a pleasure like the pleasure of drowsiness for the person wearied by wakefulness when sleep comes to him in the period before daybreak. The Lawgiver called this "the honeydrop" because of its sweetness. Thus they will find that death has an immeasurable pleasure. Then the rabble will remain, like the scum on a flood, similar to the dumb beasts. "Over them will occur the resurrection."

The faithful spirit, Gabriel, was the teacher and mentor of the messengers. When he was revealing to Muhammad, Muhammad used to *hasten with the Koran before its revelation had been accomplished unto* him [20:114]. Through this state God gave knowledge that He had undertaken to teach it by way of the specific face of which the angel has no awareness. God made the angel that descends with the revelation a veiling form. Then God commanded the Prophet concerning what was revealed to him, *Move not thy tongue with it to hasten it* [75:16], out of courtesy to his mentor, for the Prophet said, "God taught me courtesy, so He made my courtesy beautiful." This is one of the things that confirms that God undertook to teach the Koran Himself. Then He said, also confirming this, *Ours is to gather it and to recite it. So when We recite it, follow thou its recitation. Then Ours it is to explain it* [75:17–19]. Thus He mentioned only Himself and ascribed it only to Himself. In this instruction, no mention is made of any but God. So also were the words of the Prophet in his saying, "God taught me courtesy, so He made my courtesy beautiful." He mentioned only God. He did not remark upon any intermediary or angel.

Thus did God instruct us. Then we found that this pervades his inheritors among the ulama of every group—I mean both the ulama of the tracings and the ulama of the hearts. Thus teaching, whether with intermediary or without, goes back to the Lord. That is why the angel says, *We descend not save through the command of thy Lord* [19:64].

Through this section, the form of teaching has been made clear to you.

Then God set down as shariah for every mentor that he not see himself as possessing any superiority over his student and that the level of mastership not make him absent from his knowledge of himself and his own servanthood. This is the root to which everything goes back. *And God speaks the **ḥaqq**, and He guides on the path* [33:4]. (III 399.11)

Glories

Closely connected with God's face and His veils are the "glories" (*subuḥāt*), which are the lights of God's face that burn away the eyesight of anyone who sees beyond the veils. According to the already quoted hadith, "God has seventy veils of light and darkness; were He to lift them, the glories of His face would burn away everything that the eyesight of His creatures perceives."

The word *subuḥāt* or *glories* derives from the same root as *tasbīḥ*, "glorification," which, in one basic meaning, is to utter the Koranic formula "Glory be to God" (*subḥāna'llāh*). The Koran associates glorification specifically with the angels, who tell us, *We are the glorifiers* (37:166). More generally, *Everything in the heavens and the earth glorifies God* (57:1). All things glorify God through their own created nature or through the knowledge given to them by their own specific faces. It is the duty of human beings to add to their own innate glorification, which they are compelled to utter by their very nature, a voluntary glorification, and hence the Koran commands them to glorify God in many verses. Ibn al-ʿArabī usually discusses glorification as the acknowledgment and assertion of God's incomparability, *tanzīh*. Hence the "glories of the face" have to do primarily with God's incomparability, exaltation, and majesty, the fact that God is so brilliant and splendorous that creatures are blinded by His light. When God does disclose His face, He discloses it in terms of similarity and beauty, not incomparability and majesty. "The burning facial glories belong to the Presence of Majesty, so God never discloses Himself in His majesty. On the contrary, He discloses Himself to His servants in the majesty of His beauty" (II 542.3).[33]

If the glories pertain to incomparability, majesty, and wrath, the veils that conceal the burning glories pertain more to similarity, beauty, and mercy.

> The curtains may be let down out of mercy toward those upon whom they are let down, like the divine veils between the cosmos and God that allow the creatures to subsist, lest they be burned away by the facial glories. (III 179.22)

> He veils Himself only out of mercy toward us, for the sake of the subsistence of our entities. After all, in the subsistence of engendered existence lies the manifestation of the Divine Presence and its most beautiful names, and this is the beauty of engendered existence. Were it to go, you would not be known, for through tracings and bodily things, knowledges are spread, understandings become distinct, and the names the Living, the Self-Abiding become manifest. So glory be to Him who sends down His mercy as all-pervading to His creation and engendered existence so that its attribute and its entity may be witnessed! (*Dhakhāʾir* 144)

The glories of the face are the rays of light that emerge from the divine Light. These rays blind those who look upon them, but they also make the cosmos manifest. They blind the creatures to God's Essence, so they establish *tanzīh*, but they allow the vision of the traces of God's names in His self-disclosures, so they establish *tashbīh*. Hence the glories can be looked upon as the creative power that establishes the *wujūd* of the entities. But once the things come into existence, they act as veils, preventing the vision of the glories.

The glories of the face are the rays of the Essence. When they are deployed, the entities of the possible things become manifest, so the possible things are the veil between us and the glories. (II 488.10)

Although the glories blind, they also bestow a type of unveiling that the Shaykh in one place calls "the glance of the eyesight." The term is derived from the verse, *Our command is but one, like a glance of the eyesight* (54:50). Those who are allowed to see the glories are "the lords of the glances."

A Mystery
The glories belong to the lords of the glances.

He says: No signifier is better at signifying a thing than itself. If someones does not affirm Him when He becomes manifest to him, the shortcoming is his, even though He has given what is due. If someone's reality is incapacity and he shows his incapacity, he has given what is due. Hence giving what is due belongs to both sides.

He says: The "glance of the eyesight" is like lightning. It strikes, becomes manifest, makes manifest, and disappears. Were it to remain, it would cause to perish.

He says: The glories of the face burn away only your claims that you are you. Nothing subsists but He, for there is nothing but He. Hence this is a clarification, not a burning away.

He says: The face of a thing is its reality, and *Each thing is perishing save its face* [28:88]. So *thing* here is what occurs accidentally to the essence. If the accident has a face, it does not perish in itself. It perishes only in its relation to that to which it occurs. The pronoun that modifies "face" goes back to "thing" and it also goes back to the Real. You accord with that in which you stand, for you are the companion of a [present] moment [*waqt*]. (IV 417.14)

The hadith of the glories mentions veils of both light and darkness. The two sorts of veils can be understood as references to the two faces of each thing, or to the fact that everything other than Real *Wujūd* is luminous inasmuch as it manifests *wujūd* and dark inasmuch as it displays its own nonexistence. The glories are then the lights that emerge from Light, or the *wujūd* of the things inasmuch as it is identical with the *wujūd* of the Real. Only the light that is *wujūd* itself can burn away the veils that are the entities and bring about the perception of Light, which is to say that only *wujūd* can know *wujūd*. Things see God inasmuch as they are *mawjūd* or existent, not inasmuch as they are *maʿdūm* or nonexistent. "Not He" knows nothing of "He;" only He knows Himself as He.

God is independent of the worlds [3:97] because nothing signifies Him but Himself, for He has described Himself through independence. That which is other than *wujūd*—the newly arrived thing—does not know Him through the knowledge of new arrival. The possible thing is not qualified by *wujūd* until the Real is identical with its *wujūd*. When it knows Him in respect of being an existent thing, then nothing knows Him but He. So He is *independent of the worlds*, but the cosmos is not independent of Him in any respect, for it is a possible thing, and the possible thing is poor toward the Preponderator.

The dark and luminous veils through which the Real is veiled from the cosmos are only the light and darkness by which the possible thing becomes qualified in its reality because it is a middle. It looks only upon itself, so it looks only upon the veil. Were the veils to be lifted from the possible thing, possibility would be lifted, and the Necessary and the impossible would be lifted through its being lifted. So the veils will remain forever hung down, and nothing else is possible.

Consider the Prophet's words concerning the lifting of the veils and what he mentioned about the glories of the face burning away "everything that the eyesight of His creatures perceives." Nevertheless, God has described Himself by saying that the creatures will see Him and will not be burnt away.[34] This proves that the veils will not be lifted when there is vision. Hence vision is through the veil, and inescapably so.

In this hadith it is as if He is saying that the eyesight of His creatures will not perceive Him. There is no doubt that God perceives us today through His eyesight and that the glories of His face exist. Were the veils His Entity, they would not be lifted. Were they a creation, the glories would burn them away, for the glories would then be perceived by the eyesight of his creatures without veil. Were the veils burned away, we would be burned away and would not be. But we are, without doubt. Hence the veils are hung down.

If the people understood the meaning of this report, they would know themselves. Were they to know themselves, they would know the Real. Were they to know the Real, they would content themselves with Him, so they would look only at Him, not at the sovereignty of the heavens and the earth. After all, were the affair to be unveiled for them, they would know that He is identical with the sovereignty of the heavens and the earth. (III 276.15)

In another passage, the Shaykh reads the hadith of the burning glories as asserting the identity of all things with *wujūd,* because it affirms the Essence and negates the relations through which the cosmos and all things come into existence. If only *wujūd* is found, then everything found—every *mawjūd*—is identical with *wujūd.*

The divine face has burning glories. Were it not for the veils, the glories would burn away the cosmos. The veils may derive from the cosmos. Without doubt, if the glories were not deployed upon the veils, the veils would not veil them. But, if the glories required burning, the veils would have been burnt away.

The veils must be either dense or subtle. If they were subtle, they would not veil, just as air does not veil the ray of the sun from joining with the earthly bodies. But if they were dense, like walls and things of that sort, then it is obvious that the wall would become warm through the sun's ray, as long as its parts were solidly compressed and not loose.

Darkness does not veil light, because light dispels it, so the two do not come together. However, darkness is light's neighbor behind the veil that gives existence to the darkness that makes contact with the light. So darkness is the neighbor of the ray, and what gives existence to the darkness receives the deployment of the ray upon it. Hence, from this standpoint, darkness is not a veil. However, it has been affirmed that it is a veil and that light is also a veil upon the light of the face. But light becomes strengthened by light, not veiled.

So understand the reality of the face's glories and that they are the signifiers of the Essence. When they become manifest, they burn away relations, not entities. Thus it becomes clear that the glories are identical with those entities, which are the face. Thus ignorance disappears—the ignorance that concludes that the cosmos is not identical with the face. Hence the cosmos subsists in His form. The glories do not take it away. On the contrary, they affirm it and they clarify what the Real's face is. So the veil is suprasensory, and the relation is burnt away. (II 459.35)

The glories of the face can be said to be identical with the existent things inasmuch as the things manifest *wujūd.* The *wujūd* that is displayed as existent things demonstrates God's reality and the things' nonexistence, because nothing is found save *wujūd* itself. The cosmos is poor and needy, since, through its very essence, it is a possible thing in need of a Preponderator. And God is rich and Independent because there is nothing toward which He can be poor. He creates the cosmos not out of need for the creatures, but out of His own inherent generosity, or the fact that Light shines by definition. None knows *wujūd* but *wujūd,* so God alone sees the Hidden Treasure deployed in the infinite diversity that is the cosmos. Hence the veils that prevent the things from being burnt away are the things' nonexistent realities. They are not burnt away because there is nothing there to be burnt.

The lights of the Essence are nothing but the existent things, and they are "the glories of the face," because they are identical with the signification of Him for us. That is why the Prophet said, "He who knows himself knows his Lord." Thus he made the self of the knower, when he knows it, a signifier of knowledge of God.

Light signifies both itself and what makes it manifest to the eye, so through the light of the existent things, the existent things become manifest, and their Existence-Giver becomes manifest to them. Hence they know Him only from them, so He is what they seek. Seeking announces poverty on the part of the newly arrived things, but He is the sought, so He is the Independent. Since He is sought by them, it is correct for them to be poor toward Him and for Him to be independent from them, so His reception of them is a reception of munificence and generosity. Thus the facial glories are spread over the entities of the possible things and are reflected, so He perceives Himself. The lights of the thing do not burn it away—in the state of its nonexistence the possible thing does not accept burning. Were it to be qualified by *wujūd*, its *wujūd* would be burnt away, because the *wujūd* would return to Him who possesses *wujūd*.

Thus the possible things subsist in the reality of their fixed thingness, and the manyness of the possible things becomes manifest through the facial glories in the mirror of the Real. The Real perceives them in His own Essence through His light as appropriate to the realities of the possible things. This is the manifestation of the cosmos and its subsistence. (III 289.32)

All things have two faces. Through one face they look upon themselves and see nonexistence, darkness, and loss; through the other they look upon God and see *wujūd*, light, and gain. Even the light of God, inasmuch as it is other than God, has these two faces, one luminous and one dark, and this explains why it bestows *wujūd* on the things and also burns it away. The two faces explain not only the ontological situation of the things, but also the existential and moral situation, since the light of *wujūd* is also the light of prophetic guidance and human felicity. Just as things exist only through the face of *wujūd*, so also human beings benefit fully from their *wujūd* only through following the prophets in the direction of *wujūd*'s luminous face.

In this waystation is found the knowledge of the two faces in things. There is nothing without a benefit through one face and a harm through another. Whatever the thing may be, when you take it into account and weigh it, you will find the affair as we said, for nothing whatsoever in *wujūd* has only one face.

The most magnificent and elevated of the things is the light of God, through which the things become manifest from behind the veils. Were the veils to lift, the lights would burn away everything they have brought into existence. So the lights give existence and nonexistence.

In the same way, the descent of the Koran has a face of benefit for the person of faith, for it *increases* his *faith*, but it has a face of harm for the unbeliever, for it *increases abomination to* his *abomination* [9:124–25]. God says, *Thereby He misguides many, and thereby He guides many.* Then, out of His mercy toward His creatures, He adds, *but thereby He misguides only the ungodly* [2:26]. Thus He gives us the mark. He who finds within himself this mark knows that he is one of the folk of misguidance. (III 174.25)

Chapter 458: The Facial Glories

The Shaykh calls this Chapter "On the true knowledge of the mutual waystation of the perception of the facial glories." In this waystation, the traveler comes to understand that the "burning away" brought about by the facial glories is analogous to the disappearance of the light of the stars when the sun rises. When God is recognized in all *wujūd* through the eye of unveiling, both the light of the rational faculty and the darkness of habit and nature disappear. It is this vision that results in sayings such as Abū Yazīd's "I am God."

The glories of the face overtake us,
and thereby they make us nonexistent
out of jealousy for His sake—
does any of you understand?
What is the situation in Him?
You will meet no existent thing to tell us.

God says, *God is the light of the heavens and the earth* [24:35]. Concerning the divine veils that are sent down between God and His creatures the Prophet said, "Were He to lift them, the glories of the face would burn away everything that the eyesight of His creatures perceives." It was said to him, "Hast thou seen thy Lord?" He replied, "He is a light, how should I see Him?"

If these veils are created, how do they subsist before the glories? For they are not veiled from them. Nonetheless, you should know that there is a mystery that God has hidden from His servants, and His hiding it is named "the luminous and dark veils." Of these, the "luminous" are the reflective knowledges of Him through which He is veiled, while the "dark" are the natural, habitual affairs through which He is veiled. Were these veils to be lifted from the insights of His servants, "The glories of His face would burn away everything that the eyesight of his creatures perceives."

This "burning away" is the inclusion of the lower light within which they are—or rather, which is they—in a higher light, like the inclusion of the light of the stars in the light of the sun. Thus, when a star comes under the sun's rays, it is said that it was burnt away, even though the light continues to exist in the essence of the star. So by "burning away" is not meant nonexistence, but rather the change of one entity's state as seen by the viewer. Hence its name passes away from it through the passage of the property. The wood was wood, but when it was burnt away, it was called "coals," though the substance is one. It is known that the stars keep their brightness in themselves, but we do not perceive it because of the weakness of perception.

If He were to lift the veils in the case of the knowers, they would see themselves as identical with Him, and the affair would be one. But He did lift the veils from them, so they saw their essences as one essence. They said what has been recounted from them, such as "I am God" and "Glory be to me." As for the common people, the veils are not lifted from them, so they do not witness the affair as it is. *So they contended with one another about their affair, and* the gnostics *kept the discussion secret* [20:62] out of courtesy toward God, for they are the Courteous.

The Prophet said, "Do not bestow wisdom on other than its folk, lest you wrong it, and do not hold it back from its folk, lest you wrong them." The Lawgiver gave no more arduous prescription to the gnostics than this ruling, because thereby he commanded them to be watchful over each individual. They are watchful over the world because of this hadith, for they are the folk of wisdom. When they see someone with worthiness, they bestow wisdom upon him, lest they be qualified by wrongdoing toward his *ḥaqq*. When they do not see the worthiness within him, they do not bestow it upon him, lest they be qualified by wrongdoing toward its *ḥaqq*. Hence they remain watchful over the world perpetually and endlessly. This is their portion of His words, *And God is watchful over everything* [33:52].

When someone is watchful with God's eye, no task distracts him from any other task. He acts freely in everything through his very essence, for he is divine in locus of witnessing, while reception occurs on the part of that in which he freely acts. Hence, in this respect, the one who acts freely is at ease. In contrast, when someone is watchful through his own eye from behind the veil of his essence, he dwells in the furthest limit of effort and weariness. He never leaves hardship so long as he has this attribute.

Through light
  you perceive His lights
    and through light
      He perceives what He perceives.
When someone dwells in a description
  that is his *ḥaqq*,
    he owns through essence
      and is not owned.

This measure of allusion in this mutual waystation is sufficient for those who understand. *And God speaks the* ***ḥaqq****, and He guides on the path* [33:4]. (IV 72.20)

From Chapter 558: The Presence of Light

Ibn al-ʿArabī again discusses the meaning of the hadith of the glories in his commentary on the divine name Light. He focuses on the two basic sorts of light that are mentioned in the Koran, the light that is God Himself, and the light that God assigns to the creatures. The word translated here as "assigns" is *jaʿl*, which the Koran employs in well over three hundred verses. Translations of the Koran render the term in a variety of ways depending on the context, such as make, render, appoint, place, put, create. The basic sense is "to make," often in the sense of making something the way it is. In a handful of Koran verses, the word *light* is the direct object of the verb *jaʿl*, and this usage helps clarify the distinction between the two kinds of light. Thus, when the Koran says, *Praise belongs to God who created the heavens and the earth and* ***assigned*** *the darknesses and the light* (6:1), this suggests that God makes certain things possessors of light, while He places others under the domination of darkness. The light that is "assigned" is not the light of *wujūd* itself, but rather the light that pertains to human happiness and felicity, that is, the light of knowledge and good works. This same light is mentioned in the several Koranic verses that say that God brings the faithful out from the darknesses into the light.

The Shaykh sees the clearest Koranic reference to the two kinds of light in the words *a light upon a light* (24:35) from the famous "light verse" of the Koran. The second light is *wujūd* itself, or God, who is *the light of the heavens and the earth* (24:35). To this ontological light that underlies all things, God assigns a secondary light that is the light of guidance. The distinction between the two lights parallels the distinction that Ibn al-ᶜArabī often draws between two kinds of mercy—that of gratuitous favor (i.e., *wujūd*) and that of necessity (i.e., the felicity that He has made necessary for the faithful through His assertions that He will reward them). It also parallels the distinction between the engendering command, through which God creates the universe, and the prescriptive command, through which He guides His servants to felicity.

Light is two lights:
the light of knowledge and deeds
and the light
of our beginningless Existence-Giver.
I sought a person
whose vision I might enjoy
from my own Presence
up to the Cause of causes.
I ascended to none of the engendered
things that I passed by
out of love,
nor was any of them my hope,
until I passed on to a person
whom I did not know,
but with whom I found intimacy,
and still do.
I said, "What is that?" They said, "The Real."
I said to them,
"This is what I and all the sects
have been seeking."

The companion of this Presence is called "the Servant of the Light."

God says, *God is the light of the heavens and the earth* [24:35]. He also says, exposing gratuitous favors, *[Why, is he who was dead, and We gave him life,] and assigned to him a light whereby he walks among the people [like the one whose likeness is in the darknesses, and he comes not forth from them]?* [6:122]. This person walks only through himself, so his own self may be identical with his light, since his *wujūd* is nothing other than the Real *Wujūd,* and that is Light. Hence he walks among the people through his Lord, but they are unaware. In the same way, the Prophet said, "When God loves a servant, He is his hearing through which he hears," mentioning in this report all the servant's faculties and limbs, until he says, "and his leg through which he runs." In his state of walking through his Lord, he *walks among the people* only through his legs, so he is the Real, nothing else. Hence He eliminates through His light the darkness of the newly arrived, engendered thing. After all, nothing has arrived newly, because the entity of the possible thing never leaves the thingness of its fixity—it has no *wujūd.* Rather, there is only the property of its entity in the Real *Wujūd.*

God said to His Prophet, *Say: Are they equal—those who know and those who know not?* [39:9]. This is the same as His words concerning him who does not know, *like the one whose likeness is in the darknesses, and he comes not forth from them* [6:122]. This is everything of the possible thing that remains in the thingness of fixity without any ruling property in the Real *Wujūd,* and inescapably something of it must remain without any ruling property in the Real *Wujūd,* because the affair is infinite, so it will never be finished. Whenever an entity has a ruling property manifest in the Real *Wujūd,* another entity has no property manifest in the Real *Wujūd,* so this entity is *in the darknesses* until it becomes manifest, while others remain. So also is the one who does not know until he comes to know and thereby joins the companions of the light—inescapably, some who do not know remain. Thus the light of *wujūd* dispels the darkness of nonexistence, and the light of knowledge dispels the darkness of ignorance.

You should also know that, although lights come together in giving illumination and dispelling darkness, they have degrees in excellence, just as they have sensory entities, like the sun, the moon, the star, the lamp, the fire, the lightning, and every sensory light or illumined thing. They also have intelligible entities, like the light of knowledge and the light of unveiling. These are the lights of insight and eyesight.

The sensory and suprasensory lights are ranked in layers, some of which are more excellent than others. Thus we say, "knowledgeable" and "more knowledgeable" or "perceptive" and "more perceptive." In the same way, concerning sensory lights you say, "luminous" and "more luminous." What does the light of the sun have to do with the light of a lamp? In the same way, lights are ranked in excellence in their ability to burn, for illumination burns and takes away in the measure of the strength or weakness of the light.

The hadith of the burning glories has reached us. The "glories" are the facial lights. Here we say that through the glories it is said, "This is the cosmos." When the veils are lifted, the glories of the face shine forth and the name *cosmos* disappears. Then it is said, "This is the Real." But the veils can never be lifted in all cases, so the name *cosmos* can never be lifted. However, this name can be lifted specifically for some people, though it can never be lifted perpetually for mortal man, because of the fact that he brings together all of *wujūd*. It can only be lifted for *the high ones* [38:75], who are the enraptured ones, the cherubim.[35] For mortal man, this can happen at certain moments.

If the servant's entity is there,
the servant is nonmanifest,
if the Real's hearing is there,
the Real it is who hears.
The affair lies between an obligation
and its supererogation—[36]
you and the Entity of the Real
bring everything together.
The Real will never cease,
nor will creation;
now He gives *wujūd* to the entity,
now He holds it back.
If the servant's entity is there,
your state is the night,
if the Real's entity is there,
the light is brilliant.
You stand only between
an east and a west—
your sun in a west,
your full moon rising.

As for "the light that is upon the light," that is the light that is assigned upon the essential light. This light upon the light is His words, *A light upon a light.* So *God guides to His light whom He will* [24:35] is one of the two lights.

One of the two lights is assigned when God assigns it upon the other light. Hence it exercises ruling properties over it. The light upon which this light is assigned is clothed and contained within it. Hence nothing has a ruling property save the assigned light, and it is the manifest. This is the ruling of the Shariah's light over the light of reason.

Reason may only surrender to the Shariah
and do what the Shariah decides.
If you interpret it, from it you will have no share
of a knowledge at the Resurrection pleasing to you.

You will be mustered in the darkness of your ignorance. You will not have *a light whereby* you *walk* [6:122], nor any *light running before* you [66:8] that you may see where to put your feet. *And to whomsoever God assigns no light, no light has he* [24:40]. *We assigned it*—that is, the revealed Shariah—*as a light whereby We guide whom We will of Our servants* [42:52]. That is His words, *and assigned for him a light whereby he walks among the people* [6:122]. May God assign us among the folk of the assigned lights! Amen. (IV 312.12)

Chapter 100: The Station of Fear

The Shaykh provides still another interpretation of the hadith of the glories in Chapters 100 and 101, which he dedicates to fear (*khawf*) and abandoning fear (*tark al-khawf*). Just as the hadith of the glories can be read as asserting either the otherness or the sameness of the face and the veils, so also fear of God is fear of both otherness and sameness. People fear being other than God, for then they would be utterly unreal, but they also fear sameness with God, for then they would be effaced in the One. Hence fear is a station on the path to God that prefigures bewilderment, the vision of the continual evanescence of all things in the affirmation of He/not He. As for abandoning fear, it comes about when the servant realizes that the light of his own specific face is included in the light of the divine Face, so he can never disappear.

Fear God, poor man,
if you have faith,
when the contender's authority
comes in the affair.[37]
If they incline to peace, do thou also incline to it [8:61] and thereby
reach the levels of highness
in the World of the Command.
I do not say this, God says it,
giving knowledge
as it has come in the Koran,
in the firm text of the Remembrance.

Know—God confirm you and preserve you from error—that fear is the station of the divine ones. To it pertains the name God, for it is contradictory in property, since the servant fears the veil, and he fears the lifting of the veil.

As for his fear of the veil, this is because it entails ignorance of the one from whom he is veiled. And as for his fear of the lifting of the veil, this is because his entity disappears with its lifting, so benefit and taking pleasure in absolute Beauty cease.

The verse of the veiled one is His words, *No indeed, but upon that day they shall be veiled from their Lord* [83:15], by way of blame. As for the Hadith, that is the Prophet's words concerning the veils: "Were He to lift them, the glories of His face would burn away everything perceived by the eyesight of his creatures." How similar is this station to the words of the poet!

The night when she joins me
is like the night when she's gone—
I complain of the length
as I complain of the shortness.

The station of fear is the station of bewilderment and halting. No preference becomes designated for [its companion], because a witness [to this station] arises for him from every direction. If someone emerges from this [unbounded] fear to the fear of some object, this is a fear, but it is not a station. No other fear has this property. After all, the "station" is that which has a footing deeply rooted in the divinity. Anything without this is not a station but rather a state—it arrives and then disappears with the disappearance of the property of its connection and its object, whether through good news or something else.

The fear that is a station is the constant companion of the knowers of God who know what is there. He who does not know this is accompanied by fear only until the first step that he takes from the Narrow Path into the Garden or among its dwellers.

The fearful one is he who knows what self-disclosure is and what it is that is seen on the day of resurrection. It is he who knows that the folk of the Fire have a self-disclosure that increases their chastisement, just as the folk of the Garden have a self-disclosure that increases their bliss, a self-disclosure from which the folk of the Fire are veiled. That is why He says *veiled from their Lord*, that is, from the Lord of the folk of the Fire. The "Lord" is he who nurtures and makes wholesome.

The door to knowledge of God apart from everything else is locked in respect of His Essence, but this door is what is sought through self-disclosure. The creatures dwell in plain ignorance of what we have mentioned *save him upon whom God has mercy* [44:42].

The Mu'tazilites are correct in their denial of the vision [of God], but not in their proofs of that. If they had not mentioned their proofs, we would have imagined that they know the actual situation just as the Folk of God know it. In providing proofs they are like the man who related to his companion something that delighted and moved him. Then he cited the saying's source, and the companion's joy disappeared. He said, "You ruined it by citing the source."

He who does not know God in this manner does not know Him through the knowledge that is sought from him. (II 184.7)

Chapter 101: The Station of Abandoning Fear

Since knowledge of fear attaches itself
to nonexistence,
I dread it not, for we have reached
Eternity's level.
I am *wujūd*,
so no fear accompanies me,
for my opposite
is ascribed to nonexistence.
What you feared
had no *wujūd*,
so leave fear of it like meat
on the butcher's block!

The Prophet said in his supplication, "Make me into a light." God says, *God is the light of the heavens and the earth* [24:35].

The "glories" are lights, and light is not burned away by light. Rather, it is included within it, that is, it coheres with it because of the congeneity. This is "conjunction" and "unification."

Here there is a magnificent mystery. It is what is added to the light of the Self-Discloser from the light of the recipient of self-disclosure when the latter is ascribed to the former and included within it.

When the Prophet halted at the above-mentioned station of fear, it led him to seek to be a light. It is as if he is saying, "Make me into Yourself, so that I may see You through You. Do not take away my entity through Your vision, but let me be included in You." In the same way, al-Nābigha said,

You are the sun, and the kings are stars—
when you rise, none of the stars appears.

No entity of theirs has gone, but no entity of theirs is manifest. So they are seen and not seen, because they are behind the veil of the Most Magnificent Light, which has the ruling property in the manifest affair. But the lights of the stars possess the ruling property in the nonmanifest affair that is included in the Most Magnificent Light.

This is known by the lords of the science of the astronomical teachings, so they are the most felicitous people through this station. This is a majestic prophetic station. The Real forbade it to the faithful only as a mercy to them, for ignorance of the realities of affairs has overcome the cosmos, and the knowers are solitaries. So God had mercy upon them through that of this which He forbade to them. As for the knowers of God, they have no fault in this, for they know how to ascribe. How should they not know? After all, God says, *He revealed in each heaven its command* [41:12]. This is the traces in the cosmos that He gives to each heaven. In the same way, each tool gives to the artisan who uses it what it does for him, and the artisanry is ascribed to the artisan, not to the tool. So know this, and be as your capacity gives to you—and that is all!

Our companions have disagreed concerning the companion of this station. Is he secure from the divine deception or not?[38] If the good news is with him, then he is secure, and inescapably so. I mean by "good news" that the good news of security from God's deception should have come. But I am not able to expand on this station more than I have mentioned at this time, because of certain occasions. I will not be explicit concerning our position in this save in the measure that we have mentioned concerning the good news, for this is a realized affair that is proven both by rational faculties and the Shariah. It is that if the Garden has been hurried to the companion of this station in some manner, this cannot be changed for him, so security has been gained, and this station is correct for him. If he does not have this state, then God knows best. (II 184.26)

II

The Order of the Worlds

5. *The Roots of Order*

Wujūd is one entity. In itself it is infinite, and its self-disclosures are never-ending. However, everything "in" *wujūd*—that is, everything found in the spiritual, imaginal, and corporeal worlds—is finite, because each is limited and bound by specific modalities of self-disclosure. These modalities are determined by the fixed entities, which designate *wujūd*'s infinite possibilities of manifestation.

Wujūd discloses itself in keeping with a specific order and arrangement that is determined by itself. The roots of that order can be discerned by examining the relations, also known as the divine names. Inasmuch as the divine names are limited in number—e.g., the ninety-nine most beautiful names of God—it is possible to examine each of them in turn; in the 130 pages of Chapter 558, the third longest chapter of the *Futūḥāt*, Ibn al-ʿArabī does just that. But, inasmuch as the divine names are beyond enumeration—because every entity in the cosmos is a name of God—it is impossible to do anything more than give a summary account of relations. Ibn al-ʿArabī's teachings on the nature of the cosmos are nothing more than a summary account, and he tells us repeatedly that he is only touching on his topics.

Even on the level of the basic underlying principles of cosmology, the Shaykh does not attempt to provide a comprehensive, systematic exposition. Rather, he explains what he sees when he stands in a specific station of knowledge. When he changes his standpoint, the principles and the details may change. From the highest standpoint—the Station of No Station—every explanation has its rights, and all standpoints are legitimate. The Realizer recognizes the *ḥaqq* of each.

Diverse patterns, arrangements, and hierarchies are found in the cosmos. Like everything else in *wujūd*, they have their divine roots. Before turning to actual structures and specific orders and hierarchies, we need to look at a few of the properties of *wujūd* that give rise to orderliness.

The Unity of Manyness

Order and arrangement only make sense in the context of a multiplicity of interrelating things. *Wujūd* is one, so multiplicity is rooted in oneness, and so also is order. We have discussed in some detail how the one *wujūd* demands the many things. Another way to approach this issue is to analyze the concept of unity (*aḥadiyya*), which is what Muslims ascribe to God in their profession of faith. *Tawḥīd*, the first principle of faith, means to assert that God is one, or to acknowledge God's unity by bearing witness that "There is no god but God." Hence, the issue of how the many things arise from the one God, or how differentiation, order, and hierarchy grow up from simplicity and uniformity, is central to the theoretical exposition of Islamic faith. One of the ways in which the Shaykh deals with this issue is by analyzing the concept of unity and showing that it demands two different modalities, which he sometimes calls the "unity of the one" and the "unity of the many."

The word *aḥadiyya* or "unity" derives from the word *aḥad* or "one," as in the Koranic verse, *Say: He is God, One* (112:1). God is also called *wāḥid*, another word that means one, and theologians have often discussed whether or not these two words mean exactly the same thing. When Ibn al-ʿArabī differentiates between the two words, the basic difference he seems to see is that *aḥad* designates God's unity in respect of *tanzīh*, while *wāḥid* designates it in terms of *tashbīh*. Hence God has no relation with the cosmos in respect of the name *aḥad*, but He brings every engendered oneness into existence in respect of the name *wāḥid*. Everything, through its very thingness, possesses a certain oneness. In other words, inasmuch as God is *aḥad*, all multiplicity is negated from Him and no positive quality is affirmed. "Nondual" might be a more appropriate translation than "one." However, inasmuch as He is *wāḥid*, others can be envisaged in relation to Him. Each of these others is a one that is similar to God in possessing a unity that gives it its specific identity. But each of them is uniquely itself, so it must be differentiated from the One and from others, and it can be assigned various rankings. If we want to rank things in relation to God and if we call God "one," then we can say, for example, that the First Intellect has the property of two, the Universal Soul is three, and so on; but each of them retains its own unity, which defines its own identity. Thus, in respect of the unity of each of these realities, the cosmos is nothing but the replication of the original one.

> The *aḥad* does not accept association, and no worship is directed toward it. On the contrary, worship belongs to the Lord, so pay attention to giving the station of Lordship its full due and leaving unity in the *tanzīh* to which we have alluded. The *aḥad* is exalted, forbidden through its unreachability, and it remains forever in obscurity. There can never be any self-disclosure through it, for its reality forbids that. It is the "face" that possesses the "burning glories." What is it like?! So, my brothers, never hope to lift this veil! . . .
>
> The *wāḥid* is not made two by any other than itself. Number and manyness become manifest through its free activity in levels that are intelligible but not existent. So everything in *wujūd* is a *wāḥid*. Were a thing not a *wāḥid*, it could not affirm that oneness belongs to God, for it can only affirm for its Existence-Giver what it has itself. Thus it has been said,
>
> In each thing He has a sign
> signifying that He is one.
>
> This sign that is found in each thing signifying God's oneness is the thing's oneness, nothing else. There is nothing in *wujūd*, whether inanimate object or anything else, high or low, that does not recognize the unity of its Creator, so it is *wāḥid*, inescapably.
>
> Do not imagine that he who associates others with God does not uphold the *wāḥid*. He does, but *from a far place* [34:52]. Hence he becomes wretched, because of the distance. As for the person of faith, he upholds the *wāḥid* from a near place, and hence he reaches felicity through the nearness. (*Alif* 3–4)

Ibn al-ʿArabī refers to God's unity in respect of incomparability by expressions such as the "Unity of the One" (*aḥadiyyat al-aḥad*) or the "Unity of the Entity" (*aḥadiyyat al-ʿayn*), while he calls His unity in respect of similarity the "Unity of Manyness" (*aḥadiyyat al-kathra*). God possesses the Unity of the One in Himself, while He possesses the Unity of Manyness in respect to His many names. The name One/Many (*al-wāḥid al-kathīr*) that the Shaykh sometimes applies to God refers to these two sorts of divine unity.

Given that the first unity is based on the declaration of God's incomparability, it is accessible to reason, which is to say that it determines the *tawḥīd* of the theologians and philosophers qua rational thinkers. The second kind of unity establishes God's similarity, so its full significance cannot be grasped by employing rational categories. Nevertheless, it is affirmed by God's own descriptions of Himself. Hence it pertains to faith, as does the first kind of unity, which is affirmed by Koranic declarations of incomparability. Thus faith accepts both kinds of unity, but rational consideration can only grasp the first kind.

The person of faith is he who acknowledges the Unity of the Divine Manyness because of what it has of the most beautiful names and the diverse properties in the respect that each name signifies the Essence along with a meaning that is not the same as the meaning signified by any other name. God possesses the Unity of the Entity, so the person of faith also has faith in the Unity of the Entity, just as he has faith in the Unity of Manyness. (IV 176.8)

As for the unity of the Essence in Itself, no whatness is known for It, so properties cannot be ascribed to It, for It is not similar to anything in the cosmos, and nothing is similar to It. No intelligent person undertakes to speak about His Essence except through a report from Him. And despite the coming of the report, we are ignorant of the relation of the property to Him because we are ignorant of Him. Or rather, we have faith in it as He has uttered it and as He knows it, for, according to both the Shariah and reason, proofs can be offered only to negate *tashbīh*.

This is a near path that most of the considerative ulama follow. However, there are also those who declare Unity through the light of faith over and above the light of reason. The light of faith bestows felicity, and in no way can it be gained through proofs. It derives only from a divine solicitude toward the one at whom it is found. The object of this faith is the truthfulness of the report-giver in what he reports from himself specifically. The object of faith is no more than this. If the object of the report is unveiled, that takes place through another light that is not the light of faith, but which is never separate from the light of faith.

It is this second light that unveils to people their own unity and the unity of each existent thing through which it becomes distinct from others, whether or not there is an attribute that is shared. There is no escape from a unity, specific to each thing, through which it is distinct from others.

When this light unveils the unity of the existent things to the servant, through it he knows for certain that God has a unity that is specific to Him. This unity must be either His own Entity—so that the Unitary in Essence is the Unitary in Level, such that they are identical—or it must be the unity of the Level. Hence unveiling conforms to the considerative proof, and the servant knows for certain that the Essence has a unity that is specific to It and is identical with It. This is the meaning of the words of Abu'l-ʿAtāhiyya:

In each thing He has a sign
signifying that He is one.

That "sign" is the unity of every object of knowledge, whether it is many or not many. After all, to manyness belongs the unity of manyness, and to nothing else, of course. (II 289.25)

According to the philosophical axiom, "Nothing proceeds from the One but one." We have already noted that Ibn al-ʿArabī rejects this axiom in some senses, but accepts it in others. In the following he explains that it is true inasmuch as both the One and the many possess a unity.

The philosophers have said that nothing comes into existence from the One save one. But the cosmos is many, so it has come into existence from the many, and this manyness is nothing other than the divine names. Thus He is one through the Unity of Manyness—the unity that the cosmos demands through its essence.

Despite what they say about the one that proceeds from the One, when the philosophers saw that manyness proceeds from the One—although they had said that it was one in its procession—they were forced to take into account plural faces, which derive from this One and through which the manyness proceeds. Thus the relation of the faces to this proceeding one is the relation of the divine names to God. So why not let the manyness proceed from Him, just as it does in actual fact?!

Just as manyness has a unity that is named the "unity of manyness," so also the one has a manyness that is named the "manyness of the one," and it is this that we mentioned. Hence He is the One/the Many and the Many/the One. This is the most lucid exposition that can be mentioned in this question. (IV 231.31)

New readers of the Koran are usually struck by the inconsistent use of pronouns that refer to God. Why for example, does God sometimes say "I" and sometimes "We"? In the Shaykh's view, this has nothing to do with the idea that "We" expresses God's imperial grandeur. Rather, when God says "I," He is referring to the Unity of the One, and when He says "We," He is referring to the Unity of His Manyness. He explains this at the beginning of Chapter

386, "On the true knowledge of the mutual waystation of the jugular vein and the whereness of the withness."

I am with the servant wherever he is—
in the future, in the past, in the present,
binding, unbinding, declaring incomparable,
asserting holiness, passing by a place.
He who says in yearning that his eye desires
to see Us has turned away from Us.
"Where am I in respect to you, O eyelids!
You will not see now or in time."
How could they see My majesty?
Those who have seen Us have seen the thunderstroke.

God says, *We are nearer to him than the jugular vein* [50:16], and He says, *He is with you wherever you are* [57:4]. So through His He-ness He is with us, and through His names He is nearer to us than we are, for when the Real makes Himself plural despite His Unity, this belongs to His names in respect of the fact that they signify diverse realities. What they signify is nothing but He, for they and the objects that they signify are His Entity and His names. Inescapably this must be intimated, in the world of utterances and words, through plurals, such as "We." For example, He says, *Surely We have created everything in measure* [54:49], and He says, *It is We who have sent down the Remembrance, and We are the preservers of it* [15:9]. But He uses the singular when He means His He-ness, not His names, like His words, *Verily, I am God; there is no god but I* [20:14]. What does "We" have to do with "I"?

There is no meaning to the words of those who say that "We" intimates magnificence. On the contrary, it expresses manyness. And there is no manyness save that signified on His part by His most beautiful names or that which is identical with the entities of the existent things.[1] The forms are diverse because of the diversity of the realities of the compound possible things, for He has said about His He-ness that it is all the faculties of the forms. In other words, when He loves an individual among His servants, He unveils Himself to him through him, so he comes to know that he is He, for he sees Him through Him, even though the entity of the possible thing is fixed and the faculty that is identical with Him is ascribed to the servant. Thus He says, "I am his hearing," so the pronoun in His words *his hearing* is the servant's entity, while the hearing is the Entity of the Real. But the servant is not a servant save through his hearing. Otherwise, who is it that says, when he is called, *We hear and we obey* [2:285]? Is it any other than he who is commanded at his engendering and in his free acting? Were he not hearing, *Be* would not have been said to him, nor would he have come to be if he were not obedient to his Lord in His commanding him. And the Real is his hearing, no one else, in every state, so He unveils that for him.

Since the affair is as He Himself has mentioned and as is given by witnessing and unveiling, the plural in the words *Surely We* and *We* is correct. And since none is identical with the faculties and existent things save He, the singular is correct in *Verily, I am God* and in the *He*, the *Thou*, and the second person singular of address, as in *Thee alone we worship* [1:4] and the like.

He made Himself singular in our plurality, for He said, *He is with you* [57:4], and He made Himself plural in our unity with His words, *We are nearer to him* [50:16], thereby using a singular pronoun referring to the human being. So none is plural save through us, and none is one in entity save through Him.

Wherever creation may be, the Real accompanies it in respect of His name All-Merciful, because the womb is a branch of this name, and all people are womb relatives, for they are children of one father and one mother. After all, *He created* us *from one soul,* who is Adam, *and He scattered abroad from* Adam and Eve *many men and women* [4:1]. So we are womb relatives in respect of the fact that "The womb is a branch of the All-Merciful," so kinship is correct. And God commanded the "joining of the womb relatives." He said, *And the womb relatives are nearer to one another in the Book of God* [8:75]. He commanded us to join the womb relatives, and He is more worthy of this description than us. So the womb must have a joining, for it is a branch of the All-Merciful. God has cursed—and "cursing" [*la ͨna*] is [etymologically] distance—him who traces his lineage to other than his father and traces his origin to other than his patrons. In other words, he should not trace himself back to other than his womb. So we, in respect of the womb, are near kin, but in respect of the level, servants. So we trace our lineage to none but Him and we trace our origin to no one else. (III 530.35)

Unity and Totality

Ibn al-ʿArabī employs several terms to explain the relation between the two sorts of divine Unity. Among these is *jam ͨ*, a term that I translated in the grammatical context of the previous passage as "plural." From the same root we have the active participle *jāmiᶜ*, a divine name that I have translated as "All-Comprehensive." However, for present purposes, it can perhaps better be translated as "He-who-brings-together." *Jāmiᶜ* is also used as an adjective for the name *God* (*Allāh*), which is called *al-ism al-jāmiᶜ*, "the all-comprehensive name." The name *God* designates *wujūd* along with all its attributes, so it "brings together" every divine and cosmic quality. It signifies what all the other names signify together. The Shaykh applies the same adjective *jāmiᶜ* to the perfect human being, who is *al-kawn al-jāmiᶜ*, "the all-comprehensive engendered thing," because he brings together all divine and cosmic attributes in a single created locus.

In short, *jamᶜ*, "bringing together" or "all-comprehensiveness" is a quality that belongs to God and to the perfect human being. The term presupposes multiplicity. There must be at least two before there can be any bringing together. The passive participle of the word, *majmūᶜ*, means "that which has been brought together" or "totality." The Shaykh sometimes refers to the unity of manyness as *aḥadiyyat al-majmūᶜ*, the "unity of what has been brought together," or the "unity of the totality." "What has been brought together" is then the indefinitely differentiated attributes of *wujūd* and hence also of the myriad creatures. All attributes together comprise a unity that is the unity of *wujūd*. This then is one of the senses of the famous term *waḥdat al-wujūd*, though, as mentioned, this specific expression is never employed by the Shaykh. The following passage is from Chapter 347, "On the true knowledge of the waystation of the divine at-ness and the first row at God." One of the several Koranic verses that mention that things are "at" God is the already discussed *There is no thing whose storehouses are not at Us* (15:21).

> There is no unity in engendered existence—if you are a knower—save the unity of the totality. For He has always been a God and will always be a God. No property that He did not possess comes newly upon Him, nor does any name arrive newly by which He had not been named. For He is the Named Itself, and no description abides through Him by which He was not formerly described. On the contrary, to Him *belongs the affair, before and after* [30:4].
>
> He possesses the most beautiful names and the highest attributes. He is the God who remains forever in the Cloud, the All-Merciful who described Himself as sitting [on the Throne], and the Lord who descends every night to heaven in the last third of the night. *And He is with* us *wherever* we *are* [57:4]. *There is no whispering* by any designated number without His making that number even or odd; so He is *the fourth* of three, *the sixth* of five, or *more* than that or *fewer* [58:7].
>
> Have you seen, or has there come to you from the Real, anything in His revelation but the unity of the totality? For only one God has come, and *There is no god but He, Knower of the absent and the witnessed, and He is the All-Merciful, the Compassionate. He is God, there is no god but He, the King, the Holy, Peace, the Faithful, the Guardian, the Exalted, the All-Dominating, the Self-Great [. . .], the Creator, the Author, the Form-Giver* [59:23–24]. You know—if you are among the folk of understanding from God—that, although these names are applied, one after another, to a Named Object that is one in respect of His Essence, they signify diverse meanings. *Say: Call upon God, or call upon the All-Merciful; whichever you call upon, to Him belong the most beautiful names* [17:110]. So we call upon nothing but one God, who has these names that are diverse in their realities and in what they signify.
>
> These names have never ceased belonging to Him from eternity without beginning. They are the divine storehouses, within which are the storehouses of the possibilities, within which are stored the things. So bringing together is the counterpart of bringing together, manyness manyness, and number number, despite the unity of the Entity. And this is the unity of bringing together.
>
> "Everyone who performs the *ṣalāt* is whispering with his Lord" in seclusion with Him, and God puts His wing over him.[2] So He is the Unbounded/the Bound, the All-Inclusive in the specific/the Specific in the all-inclusive.
>
> Know also that God has assigned to us two homesteads to stand in rows that He has not assigned to any other created things—the rows in the homestead of the *ṣalāt*, and the rows in the homestead of jihad. [Concerning the second,] God says, *God loves those who fight in His path in rows, as though they were a solid*

> *building* [61:4]. And He commanded us to make our rows solid in the *ṣalāt*.[3] He mentioned that the angels make their rows solid at their Lord. He made our rows like the rows of the angels, and no other communities have that.[4] *When thy Lord comes, and the angels, row upon row* [89:22]. *On the day when the Spirit,* who is the Imam, *and the angels stand in rows* [78:38]. So the Imam is a row by himself, because he is a totality. His unity is the unity of the totality, so he is a row by himself.
>
> The Real discloses Himself to the folk of the rows in the Totality of Unity, not in the Unity of the Totality. Each individual in the rows whispers with that of the Real that is given by his own presence, what corresponds to his intention, and the knowledge he has of his Lord. That is why He discloses Himself to them in the Totality of Unity, for the totality already belongs to them. He ascribes it to unity so that they will not associate anyone with God in their worship, despite the diversity of their goals, their beliefs, their states, their constitutions, and their correspondences. Because of this, their requests are diverse and multiple.
>
> Were the Real to disclose Himself to them in the Unity of the Totality, they would not be able to look at the totality, given the priority of the unity. Were this the case, their goals would be one goal, their requests would be one request, their states in presence would be one state, and their knowledge of God would be one knowledge. But what actually happens is not like that. This proves that the self-disclosure is in the Totality of Unity, and *To Him the whole affair is returned* [11:123]. Hence the totality is returned to the One and ascribed to Him, lest it be imagined that the totality is the *wujūd* of entities, while it is the *wujūd* of properties. (III 193.23)

Everything in the universe is one inasmuch as it reflects God's oneness. In this respect, God is present in all things—God as *wujūd* manifests Himself in each thing and through each thing. What becomes manifest is simply the One. Here the Shaykh often employs the formula 1 x 1 = 1. *Wujūd* multiplied by the entity of the thing in respect of the thing's unity equals one reality, which is the reality of the Real. However, if the one *wujūd* is related to the thing in respect of the thing's multiplicity, we see multiplicity and not unity. In either case, *wujūd* is present as *wujūd*. In the first case, we see the things in respect of *tashbīh*, so we see the One in each. In the second, we see them in respect of *tanzīh*, so God alone sees one, and we see many.

In Chapter 212, "On variegation," the Shaykh takes up the theme of multiplication by one after discussing the renewal of creation at each instant. Most Sufis have held that variegation (*talwīn*), which is constant transferal from one color (*lawn*) to another color or one state to another state, is an imperfection. They maintain that the traveler should strive to establish its opposite, which is stability (*tamkīn*). The Shaykh, however, does not agree. In his view, "Variegation is a mark that its companion is a realizing, perfect, divine realizer, the one who is pleasing to God" (II 499.28). Thus, he says, real perfection is found in *al-tamkīn fi'l-talwīn*, "stability in variegation," which is the constant witnessing of the renewal of creation at each instant, direct vision of the fact that *Each day He is upon some task* (55:29). Then he turns to the question of finding unity in this never-ceasing change. If God's self-disclosure never repeats itself, how can we speak of the presence of the One? The answer is 1 × 1 = 1.

> When someone knows that the Divine All-Embracingness demands that nothing in *wujūd* be repeated, he knows that variegation is correct in engendered existence, for it is a signifier of the Divine All-Embracingness. He who does not come to understand from himself and from others that at every breath the traces of the Real are diverse has no knowledge of God, nor is he one of the folk of this station. On the contrary, he is among the folk of ignorance of God, of himself, and of the cosmos, so let him weep for himself, for he has lost his life!
>
> Nothing bequeaths people this ignorance except mutual similarity, for the separating factor may be so hidden that they are not aware of it. At least they should know that there is something of which they are unaware. Then they will know that they undergo variegation in themselves, but that they do not recognize that in which they undergo variegation or that which arrives upon them. God says, *They are given it in similarity* [2:25], that is, some of it is similar to others of it. It is imagined that the second is identical with the first, but this is not the case. Rather, the one is the likeness of the other. What separates two likenesses in things is difficult to perceive through witnessing, save for those who

witness the Real or have realized the witnessing of the chameleon. There is no animal that signifies more clearly the Real's description of *Each day He is upon some task* than the chameleon, for no attribute and no state in the cosmos remains for two times, nor does any form become manifest twice. Knowledge is the companion of the first and the last, for *He is the First and the Last and the Manifest and the Nonmanifest* [57:3]. So He has declared variegation and voiced the *tawḥīd* of the He-ness in manyness!

Those who are not able to explain oneness in manyness have made these attributes "relations" and "correlations" because of diverse faces. This is the position of the considerative thinkers. As for the Tribe, they confess the He-ness and the Oneness, but they make the face in respect to which He is First identical with the face in respect to which He is Last, Manifest, and Nonmanifest. This was made explicit by Abū Saᶜīd al-Kharrāz.[5]

The Men of God affirm for the Real only their own situation, and they affirm in engendered existence and all created things only the Real's situation. Thus the all is identical with the all and the one is multiplied by the one, but it does not become multiple. Rather, it stays exactly the same. In the same way, when one is multiplied by something, or something is multiplied by one, whether the something be a one or a manyness, nothing becomes multiple. Rather, they stay exactly the same. Such is the affair.

Thus "variegation" is multiplying the One by manyness. Nothing becomes manifest save that very manyness that was multiplied by the One, or by which the One was multiplied. The Real is one, without doubt. And to "multiply" a thing by a thing is to relate it with the other. We are many from One Entity—majestic and high is It! It is related to us by bringing us into existence, and we are related to It by a *wujūd*. So "He who knows himself" as a creature and an existent thing "knows" the Real as a creator and a giver of existence.

When you consider the unity of the cosmos, you have multiplied the one by the one, but when you consider the cosmos, you have multiplied the one by the many.

The cosmos is the trace of His names. The "trace," as we have explained, is the form of the name in flashes [*lawāʾiḥ*]. The Unity of the Real is multiplied only by the forms of His names, so it does not depart from Him. Nothing emerges after the multiplication save He, but the names are many. Thus the divine report has come concerning the ninety-nine names. And beyond that are names that are known and unknown. The Entity is One, and the colors are the levels. "Variegation" is an attribution to Him. If you say "One," you have spoken the truth, and if you say "Many," you have spoken the truth, for God's names are many because of diverse meanings. (II 500.1)

The Even and the Odd

Unity is of two sorts: the absolute unity of the Essence, to which none has access but God; and the unity of manyness, which is established by the fact that God possesses a multiplicity of faces and attributes through His relations with the cosmos. In the same way, each creature has a uniqueness or unity that establishes its specific identity, and a unity through which its diverse attributes and qualities are gathered together. Cosmologically, the Shaykh frequently discusses the two modes of unity possessed by each existent thing in terms of the thing's two faces—the face turned toward the occasions, which establishes the multiplicity of aspects of each thing; and the face turned toward God Himself, which is God's specific face turned toward the thing. This specific face makes each thing one and unique.

If unity, the most fundamental attribute of God, is itself two, what about the cosmos that arises from this unity? For the Shaykh, duality is utterly fundamental to reality. Real *wujūd* already demands duality in its two modes of unity, and every level on which *wujūd* is envisaged has two aspects or faces. A good deal of material on the Shaykh's views concerning this divine duality is already available in English,[6] so I will not attempt a detailed explanation. Instead I will review the basic concepts and imagery and provide a few representative texts.

The divine twoness appears most obviously in the many pairs of divine names that are contrary or complementary in meaning. The Shaykh sometimes classifies these names into two broad groups, the names of *tanzīh* and those of *tashbīh* (even though he is perfectly aware that every name can fit into either category, depending on the standpoint).

Probably the Shaykh's favorite Koranic verse referring to the divine twoness is that in which God asks Iblis why he did not prostrate himself when God commanded him to do so before Adam, *whom I created with My own two hands* (38:75). One of the meanings of this verse is that God placed in Adam the traces of all the divine names, both those of *tanzīh* and those of *tashbīh*. So also, when human beings reach the human perfection of which Adam is the first model, they realize the full range of complementary divine attributes and come to see God with "two eyes," the eye of reason that understands His incomparability and absence, and the eye of imagination that perceives His similarity and presence.

Another important Koranic text relevant to the divine duality is 39:67, which mentions that on the day of resurrection, God will roll up the heavens in His right hand and hold the earth in His "grip" (*qabḍa*), presumably the grip of the left hand. The root meaning of the term *grip* is tightness and constriction. From the same root we have the divine name Gripper (*qābiḍ*), which is paired with Outspreader (*bāsiṭ*). These two divine attributes give us the well-known Sufi states of "contraction" (*qabḍa*) and "expansion" (*basṭ*), which refer to the soul's constriction and tightness on the one hand and its opening and elation on the other. The Shaykh's frequent references to God's "two grips" usually have in view the two basic categories of human beings in the next world: "The 'two grips' are the two worlds, the world of felicity and the world of wretchedness" (III 75.14).

> The resurrection is exactly in the form of this world, except that what exercises the ruling property there is the One through the lifting of the intermediaries, and what exercises the ruling property here is the same One, but through the intermediaries. Thus He differentiated the two abodes, just as He differentiated between the two grips through the Garden and the Fire. (III 180.19)

In the context of the two grips, the Shaykh frequently quotes a hadith according to which God struck Adam's shoulders and his children emerged, one group of them white like pearls and the other black like coals. Then God said, "These are for the Garden, and it is no concern of Mine. Those are for the Fire, and it is no concern of Mine."

> These are the two grips. One is for the Fire, and it is no concern of His, and the other is for the Garden, and it is no concern of His. The final issue of both is at mercy, which is why He is not concerned about them. If the affair of "having no concern" were as is imagined by those who have no knowledge, people would not be taken to task for their crimes and God would not have described Himself by wrath, nor would His *assault* be *terrible* [85:12]. All of this derives from concern. (III 463.14)

A Mystery

What are the occasions of God's taking charge?

We are His occasions and His equipment,
and among us are His enemies and His beloved friends.
He who emerges under constraint
and whose face is gloomy
is the *clear enemy* [2:168],
and when he arrives newly, he lies.
But he who emerges pleasant in soul and obedient
possesses the whole affair,
for he is the *secure land* [95:3],
created *in the most beautiful stature* [95:4],
and manifest in the form of the Eternal.
This is the occasion of the arrival of the cosmos in the two grips,
the creation of the two abodes,
and the designation of *the two highways* [90:10],
whether [human beings] be thankful or *ungrateful* [76:3],
displeased and irritated, or pleased and patient.
God took charge of the cosmos to make manifest His kingdom
and to string it on His thread.
He took charge of it with His most beautiful names,
He made it dwell in the highest locus,
and He made its nearness to Him *two bows' length away, or closer* [53:9].
This is the furthest limit of the creature's nearness to the Real.
He made His nearness to the servants
nearer than the jugular vein [50:16].

This is the furthest limit of the Real's
nearness to the creature.
So the affair stands between the two
nearnesses.
And God has not assigned to any man two hearts within his breast [33:4],
but He has assigned to each heart two faces,
because He has created *of everything two, a couple* [11:40].
Hence He built bringing together on the
even,
for His oddness is none save the oddness of
the many,
and of this has spoken the light-giving
Book,
so none has born witness to it save He
and none of the created things has violated
His stronghold,
for that is not appropriate,
since *everything* other than His face *is perishing* [28:88].
But there is no other
that you should speak of equality.
The Entity is One,
and the properties are subtracted and
added.
Seek that to which I have alluded
and you will gain benefit,
for these are mysteries,
or rather, they are lights.
There is upon them no dust,
even if eyesights are blind to them.
They rise high beyond the perception of
taking heed
and the ruling property of the "others."
To this is the allusion in *How blessed the Ultimate Abode!* [13:24]—
You are the abode,
and around you is the circling. (IV 359.5)

The term *even* (*shafᶜ*) is contrasted with the term *odd* (*witr*). Both are found in the Koranic verse, *By the even and the odd* (89:3). Ibn al-ᶜArabī finds much to meditate upon in this divine oath, especially when it is taken in conjunction with the hadith, "God has ninety-nine names, one hundred less one. No one memorizes them without entering the Garden. He is odd, and He loves the odd."

God says, *By the even and the odd* [89:3]. We have already explained that evenness is the reality of the servant, for oddness is appropriate for God alone in respect of His Essence. The *tawḥīd* of His Level, that is, the level of the God, is appropriate only for God, without any association. (I 489.32)

There is no escape from a Lord and a servant. Thus bringing together has been affirmed and the even has been designated. (IV 361.33)

Closely connected to the even is the term *couple* (*zawj*), which also can mean spouse or one of a couple; the Koran often makes the term's twoness completely explicit by using it in the dual (*zawjān*). Coupleness (*zawjiyya*) can be looked upon as the root of all relations. When two things are related in some manner, they are a couple. Then, in terms of this specific relation, one is active and the other receptive, one is male, the other female. This relation is established first between God and His two forms, the macrocosm and the microcosm.

Of everything in *wujūd* there is a couple, for the perfect human being, and the cosmos through the perfect human being, are in the form of the Real. The couple are the male and the female, hence an actor and one acted upon. Thus the Real is the actor and the cosmos is something He acts upon, for it is the locus within which the reception of activity becomes manifest through the forms of the engendered qualities that come upon it one after another, such as movement and stillness, or coming together and becoming separate, or such as the forms of the colors, the attributes, and the relations. (IV 132.17)

Although twoness, pairs, and couples are mentioned explicitly only in a relatively small number of Koranic verses, the Koran's rhetorical structure presupposes duality throughout. The Shaykh reminds us of this point in his "Treatise on Majesty [*jalāl*] and Beauty [*jamāl*]." These two terms are typically employed in Islamic texts to designate the two categories of contrary divine attributes. Though the two are usually used to emphasize the contrast between the two categories, the Shaykh stresses the relativity of the concepts. Each sort of attribute is found in the other. However, all things considered, beauty predominates, just as mercy rules. Hence the "majesty" that we find in the cosmos is in fact the majesty of beauty, not pure and simple majesty, for the latter would demand the annihilation of everything other than God.

Know that the Koran contains both the majesty of beauty and beauty. As for absolute majesty, no created thing has access to knowledge or witnessing of that. The Real possesses it alone. It is the Presence in which the Real sees Himself as He is. If we had access to it, we would encompass God and what is at Him in knowledge, and that is impossible.

Know, my brother, that since God has two realities and He described Himself by "two hands" and gave us knowledge of the "two grips," *wujūd* emerged in this limit. There is nothing in *wujūd* unless its own contrary is also in it. What I mean by the fact that they are contraries goes back specifically to majesty and beauty. I mean by "majesty" the majesty of beauty, as mentioned. Nothing in the speech transmitted from those who report from God signifies majesty without there being within it the beauty that is its contrary. The same is the case with the revealed books and with everything.

In the same way, there is no verse of the Koran comprising mercy that does not have a sister comprising vengeance as its contrary. For example, God's words *Forgiver of sins, Accepter of repentance* are the contrary of *Terrible in retribution* [40:3]. His words *Tell My servants that I am the Forgiving, the Compassionate* are the contrary of *And that My chastisement is the painful chastisement* [15:49–50]. His words *The Companions of the Right Hand, what of the Companions of the Right Hand! Amidst thornless lote-trees* and so on [56:27 ff.] are the contrary of *The Companions of the Left Hand, what of the Companions of the Left Hand! Amidst burning winds and boiling water* and so on [56:41 ff.]. His words *Faces on that day shall be radiant* [75:22] are the contrary of *Faces on that day shall be scowling* [75:24]. His words *Faces on that day are whitened* are the contrary of *Faces on that day are blackened* [3:106]. His words *Faces on that day humbled, laboring, toilworn, roasting at a scorching fire* and so on [88:2–4] are the contrary of *Faces on that day blissful, with their striving well pleased* [88:8–9]. His words *Faces on that day shall shine, laughing, joyous* [80:38] are the contrary of *Faces on that day shall be dusty, overspread with grime* [80:40].

When you go deeply into the Koran, you will find all of it of this sort and this limit. All this is for the sake of the two divine watchers[7] [alluded to] in His words [*Whosoever desires this hasty life . . . ; and whosoever desires the last world . . .*] *all We assist, these and those* [17:20], and in His words, *[By the soul and That which proportioned it] and inspired it with its lewdness and godwariness* [91:8]. So also are His words concerning the acknowledging bestower, *We shall surely ease him to the Easing* [92:7], which are the contrary of His words concerning the denying miser, *We shall surely ease him to the Hardship* [92:10].

So know this! Such are the verses of majesty and beauty in the Book of God. (*Jalāl* 4)

If the Shaykh finds duality in the rhetorical structure of the Koran, he also finds it in the grammatical subtleties that God employs. Nouns in Arabic are either masculine or feminine, there being no neuter. However, some nouns can be both masculine and feminine. When God chooses to make such nouns either masculine or feminine as indicated by the gender of the verbs or adjectives that are employed along with them, He must have a reason for doing so. This is especially true when He is inconsistent. In one Koranic verse, the Shaykh ascribes God's inconsistency in designating grammatical gender to the relativity of gender relations. His basic point is that the Koran expresses the deepest reality of *wujūd* even in the seemingly accidental features of its signs, such as the grammatical gender of nouns.

Part of what is connected to this chapter is the light of the *tawḥīd* of the Essence. Know that, since the strength of the One includes in itself the unity of every existent thing, object of knowledge, and numbered thing, each thing that becomes manifest in the cosmos—whether it be a totality or a solitary thing—as well as each thing that becomes manifest in the knower as a rational classification of the objects of knowledge, becomes manifest with a unity specific to it. This is bestowed by the unity of the Essence, which gives *wujūd* to everything that exists and knowledge about every object of knowledge that comes to be known. So unity becomes manifest in the units, but it is hidden in the totality. The unity of the Essence lies in the units and the noncompound things, while the unity of totality lies in the compound things. In the divine things, the latter are called "names" by the Shariah, "relations" by sound rational faculties, and "attributes" by inadequate rational faculties.

The clearest thing within which the property of the One becomes manifest is number, because through one, number becomes manifest and is configured in the natural order, from two ad infinitum. When "one" disappears from number, number disappears. Were it not for the cause, no entity would become manifest for the effect. Were it not for God, the cosmos would not exist in its entity.

God gave the name *Essence* to Himself and the name *self* to that which carries the name *self*, whether masculine or feminine. Thus God says, *Lest any self should say, "Alas for me that I neglected the side of God"* [39:56], using the feminine form [in the verb *say*]. Then He says to the self, *Yes indeed, My signs did come to thee*, using the feminine form of the second person pronoun, *but thou*—using the masculine form—*hast cried them lies* [39:59].[8] But the entity is one. This is because the Arabs sometimes make the words *self* and *entity* masculine and sometimes feminine, because of the procreation that occurs between male and female.

This is why, concerning the divine existence-giving, the Koran has come with "word," which is masculine, and "desire," which is feminine, for God gave existence to the cosmos from a word and a desire. Thus it became manifest from a masculine and a feminine noun. He says, *Our only word to a thing*—"thing" being the most indefinite of the indefinites, while "word" is masculine—*when We desire it*—"desire" being feminine—*is to say to it "Be!," so it comes to be* [16:40]. Thus engendering becomes manifest in the desire from the word, but the Entity is one, without doubt.

Thus, through the light of the *tawḥīd* of the Essence, all newly arrived things become manifest—high and low, sensory and suprasensory, compound and solitary. Thus unity permeates everything, for there is nothing but One. No affair becomes manifest save through Him, from Him, and in Him—"in Him" in respect of the femininity that belongs to the self, "through Him" in respect of both the masculinity and the femininity that belong to the self, and "from Him" in respect of the masculinity that belongs to the self.

Thus one entity is both actor and acted upon. Reception of activity is that which becomes manifest in the entities, both the existent things and the intelligible objects of knowledge, even though no entities come into existence for them.

Then God placed reproduction in the animals—or rather, in everything that receives birth—in three sorts. *He gives to whom He will females*, taking into account the locus of engendering; *and He gives to whom He will males*, taking into account the one who casts; *and He couples them as males and as females*, taking into account the totality. If He couples them as females, or as males, or as male and female, this is because of the *wujūd* of the coming together, which gives news of what is in the Root, that is, the bringing together of relations. *And He makes whom He will barren* [42:49–50] and belonging to those who do not accept birth, like the names of *tanzīh*.

So there is no unity in *wujūd* save the unity of manyness, and that is nothing but the Essence. As for the Divinity, it is a description of the very self of the Essence, for in its very essence it is He, and *To Him belong the most beautiful names* [17:110]. So understand! Thus we say, "the unity of the totality" or "the unity of manyness."

You may say that *God is independent of the worlds* [3:97]. We would reply: This does not detract from the unity of manyness. The fact that He is an Essence is not the same as the fact that He is Independent, so what is understood by "Essence" is different from what is understood by the Essence's description as "Independent." In this objection, you are affirming what you desire to negate, so you have strengthened my words. (III 289.1)

One of the Koranic allusions to God's two hands is found in Surah 56, which contrasts the Companions of the Right Hand and the Companions of the Left Hand. In commenting on these two groups of people, the Shaykh also explains the attributes of the third group mentioned in the same surah, "the Preceders," also called "those brought near" to God.

God reported about Himself that He undergoes transmutation in forms [at the resurrection], while all these properties are affirmed. So we judge Him through that with which He rules over the forms within which He discloses Himself to His servants, whatever these forms may be. For there is nothing other than He, especially in the homestead whose reality is known to be such that no one other than God can possibly claim Divinity. So we strike no likenesses for Him.

For He is identical
  with the likeness—
    Glory be to Him,
      exalted and majestic is He!
All of us,
  in relation to Him,
    when you realize,
      stand in dread,
except him whom He has given
  the good news
    of security from Him
      and honor.

God does what is demanded by the homestead, so the knower of affairs never adds in manifestation to the property of what is demanded by the moment. That is why the Tribe has said concerning the Sufi that he is the "son of his moment." This is the property of the perfect among the Men. Thus God's Messenger, who is clement and compassionate, will say concerning a tribe on the day of resurrection, "Far away with you, far away with you!" Then, when that state disappears, he will be gentle in this question and intercede for those who have been blown down by the wind, which is the strength of the self's caprice to rule over a far-away place.

In one state the Real abides through the attributes of wrath and good-pleasure, mercy and chastisement, because of the property of the Manifest and the Nonmanifest and the Exalter and the Abaser. He is, as it were, a *barzakh* between His two attributes, for He has two grips and two hands. Each hand has a property, and within each grip is a people.

This is like the "two books" with which the Messenger of God came out to his Companions. He reported that in one of them were "the names of the folk of the Garden and the names of their fathers, families, and tribes" from the time that God created people until the day of resurrection. In the other book were "the names of the folk of the Fire and the names of their fathers, families, and tribes" from the time God created people to the day of resurrection. If these books had been written with the customary writing, a city could not embrace their pages. So how could two books in the two hands of the Messenger encompass that? This pertains to the knowledge of the inclusion of the all-embracing in the constricted without the constricted becoming all-embracing or the all-embracing becoming constricted.

When a person witnesses these affairs directly and gains tasting, then he is the knower of God and of the actual situation in itself and in its entity. For the fact is that a thing is not perceived save through itself. There is no conclusive signifier of it save itself. Eyesight has witnessing, and reason has acceptance. But when someone seeks knowledge of affairs through alien signifiers that are not identical with what is sought, it is impossible for him to gain anything of use. His hands will seize only loss.

As for "those brought near," they stand before God as the counterpart of the Essence described by the two hands, for their task is to put into effect the divine commands concerning creation in every abode.

The "folk of the right hand" do not have this free activity. Rather, they are the folk of safety and exoneration because of what they had and still have of the strength to rule over themselves and curb their caprice by following the Real.

The folk of the other hand, concerning whom it is said that they are the "Companions of the Left," bow their heads. Among them are those whose heads are masked and whose glance does not return to them, since they have been rendered speechless by the magnificence of what they have seen.

None of these three groups sees anything other than what is given to them by their station, their waystation, and their place. Each group witnesses of God something different from what the others witness. But the Real is one. Were the affair not the One of manyness, their witnessing would not be diverse. If not for the manyness in the One, the affair would be only one and it would not have accepted division. But it did accept division, so the Root is like it.

This then is the occasion of the *wujūd* of the two abodes in the last world, the two pans of the Scales, the mercy bound by necessity and the unbounded mercy through gratuitous favor, and the ranking in levels of excellence found in the ascending degrees of the Gardens and the descending degrees of the Fire.

He is nothing but the One/the Many—
  to the like of this do all affairs give
    witness. (III 485.6)

From Chapter 558: The Presence of Bringing Together

In the Shaykh's discussion of the name *jāmi*ʿ, the All-Comprehensive or He-Who-Brings-

Together, he points out that this name designates a bringing together in God Himself, and that any bringing together presupposes at least two. The word *jamʿ* or "bringing together" is used in mathematics to mean "sum" and in grammar to mean "plural." God's bringing together is the root of all summing and all plurality. Hence it is also the root of the vision of two or more, a vision which, in theology, is known as *shirk*, or associating others with God. This, of course, is the opposite of *tawḥīd*, and it is the one sin that, in Koranic terms, will not be forgiven. But God Himself establishes *shirk* in the cosmos through creating those who are associated with Him. The Shaykh reads this as good news for the people of *shirk*, for it means that God's mercy will not allow them to suffer except to the degree that they themselves have assumed responsibility for their *shirk*. Hence they will find mercy in the midst of hell.

Bringing together is only a *wujūd*—
in bringing together nothing comes apart.
The separation He has within it
is through us a coinciding.
In His ruling property over us
He has a derivation from our *wujūd*.
And we have a ruling property over Him
in which unboundedness binds Him.

The companion of this Presence is called "the servant of Him-Who-Brings-Together." God says that God is *He-who-brings-together the people for a day within which there is no doubt* [3:9]. So in Himself, He it is whose knowledge of the cosmos brings together His knowledge of Himself, so the cosmos emerges in His form. That is why we say that the Real is identical with *wujūd*.

From this Presence, He brought together the whole cosmos in its glorification of His praise and in prostration toward Him, except for *many* people, *against whom the chastisement is realized* [22:18], for they prostrate themselves to God in a form not set down by a shariah. They are taken to account for this, even though, in meaning, they prostrated themselves only to God. So understand!

From this Presence the genus of the genera becomes manifest. It is the "object of knowledge," then the "mentioned object," then the "thing," for the "genus of the genera" is the most inclusive genus, from which is excluded no object of knowledge whatsoever, whether creation or Real, whether possible, necessary, or impossible. Then the most inclusive genus is divided into various species. These are a species for what is above them, but a genus for the species that are below them. Finally the species reach the last species, after which there is no species, except through attributes. Here the entities of the individuals become manifest. All of this is a bringing together below a bringing together, and it derives from this Presence.

The least of the bringing togethers is two, and then everything beyond that. Were the affair not a bringing together, no property would have become manifest for the manyness of the names, the attributes, the relations, the correlations, and number—even though unity accompanies every bringing together. So there is no escape in the One from bringing together, and there is no escape in bringing together from the One, for each is through its companion.

From this Presence God says, *He is with you wherever you are* [57:4]. Withness is a companionship, and companionship is a bringing together. He also says, *There is no whispering between three, but He is the fourth of them, neither five, but He is the sixth of them, neither fewer than that,* which is one, *neither more* ad infinitum, *but He is with them* [58:7]. If there is one, He is its second, for He is with it. Thus bringing together becomes manifest through Him, so He is "He-Who-Brings-Together." As for what is greater than one, He is with the totality, but without this being voiced. In other words, it is not said that He is *the third of three* [5:73].[9] Rather, it is said that He is "the third of two," "the fourth of three," and "the fifth of four." After all, He is not of the same kind as that to which He is being ascribed in any sense, for *Nothing is as His likeness, and He is the Hearing, the Seeing* [42:11].

This Presence possesses perpetuity in bringing together and is not understood save as bringing together, so it has no trace save bringing together, and it separates only to bring together.

You have come to know that the signifier is the opposite of the signified and that those who look at the signifier when it is brought together in them and with them is not with the signified. Your signifier of the Real is yourself and the cosmos, as He has said: *We shall show them Our signs,* that is, that which signifies Us, *upon the horizons and in themselves* [41:53]. The Prophet said, "He who knows himself knows his Lord," so he made you a signifier of Him.

He brought you together with you and He separated you from Him in the state of bringing you together with you. Then He said to Abū Yazīd, "Leave aside yourself and come!" So He separated you from you that you might come together with Him. But you will not come together with Him until you look at the signifier through Him, not through you. Then you will know that you have always been brought together with Him in the state of your looking at the signifier, for He is your hearing and your eyesight. Thus you and He have come together in the state of your seeking Him. So whom are you seeking? Or, whom is He seeking? For you have not ceased being brought together with Him. And He it is who brings Himself together with you because of His love for you. This is one of the most marvelous of states—seeking while already having gained!

The [present] state is only a playground
in which we have a place to run.
He is our playing field
in whom we play and sport.[10]
Through Him we marry virgin girls,
through Him we pour and drink—
look at His art, all of you,
and marvel at Him, marvel!
We have nothing to seek from Him,
but He has something to seek from me.

Since perpetuity belongs to the Real's withness with the cosmos, the property of bringing together never ceases in *wujūd* and nonexistence. For He is with the possible thing in the state of its nonexistence, just as He is with it in the state of its *wujūd*. Wherever we are, God is with us. Thus *tawḥīd* is intelligible, but not existent, while bringing together is both existent and intelligible. *The men have a degree above [the women]* [2:228], and that is nothing but the degree of *wujūd*.

If He had desired *tawḥīd*, He would not have given existence to the cosmos knowing that, when He gave existence to it, others would be associated with Him. Then He commanded it to profess His *tawḥīd*. Nothing went back to Him save His own act, for "He was, and nothing was" qualified by *wujūd* "with Him." So He was "the first to lay down the sunnah" of associating others with Him,[11] for He associated the cosmos with Himself in *wujūd*. The cosmos never opened its eye and never saw itself save as an associate in *wujūd*, so it has no tasting of *tawḥīd*. From whence does it know *tawḥīd*? When it was said to it, "Voice the *tawḥīd* of your Creator!," it did not understand the address. The command was repeated and confirmed. It was said, "You have proceeded from the One."

The cosmos replied, "I do not know what you are talking about. I understand nothing but association. It is not correct for me to have proceeded from One Essence with which I have no relation. He must also have a relation of knowledge or a relation of power—there is no escape from that. If He is powerful, there is no escape from a second association, which is that, by my own essence, I possess the reception of His power and, by my own *wujūd*, the displaying of His traces. I cannot have proceeded from a One, but rather from an Essence that is powerful over something that is receptive to the trace of Its power; or, in the view of the Companions of the Causes, I have proceeded from the property of a cause and the receptivity of an effect. Hence I know no flavor for oneness in *wujūd*."

I want to be alone with the *tawḥīd*
of my Creator,
but my reception prevents
what I want.
I wish I knew—will He be put
in a locus of witnessing?
I wish I knew—will I see who it is
that puts Him?
I want something
that has no path to reach it—
His tracings prevent
arriving there.

Do you not see how He calls attention to the fact that the affair is a bringing together and that He it is who brings together? That is His words, *And of each thing We created a couple* [51:49]. He knew that His own self was a "thing," so He created Adam in His form. Hence Adam was a couple.

Then He created Eve from Adam, not from anything else, so that Adam might know the root of his own creation and know who made him a couple and who it is with whom he is a couple. Thus, when God created Eve from him, He did not increase the coupleness that Adam possessed through the form in which he was created. His coupled form made Eve manifest, so she was the first thing born from this coupleness. In the same way, God created Adam with His own two hands, so he came to be from the coupleness of the hand of power and the hand of reception. Through the two, Adam became manifest.

He was alone and then became
  one of a couple—
    in him rose up the waves
      of giving birth.
He was in the depths
  of nature's lowland,
    but he reached the heights
      through the blowing into him.
"He made me stand as a master,
  so His delegations
    come to me
      troop after troop."

O you who voice *tawḥīd*! Where are going? You voice *tawḥīd*, but your *tawḥīd* gives witness that you have associated others with Him. There cannot be *tawḥīd* without the one who declares unity and the one for whom it is declared. There is no escape from bringing together, so there is no escape from association. Hence the associator supports himself with a strong pillar. That is why his final issue will be at mercy in an abode whose essence demands chastisement—so that the stronger authority of mercy may become manifest, for the abode of bliss will assist it. The poet says,

Sweeter than security
  for the frightened and timorous!

He who is a companion of security does not know its flavor through tasting. No one knows its measure save the one at whom it arrives while he is in the state of fear. He finds its flavor through its arrival.

This is why the bliss of the Garden is renewed at each breath, as also the bliss of this world. However, in the last world, those for whom it is renewed sense it, and they witness the creation of the likenesses within themselves, but in this world they do not witness the creation of the likenesses within themselves, nor do they sense it. *No indeed, but they are uncertain of a new creation* [50:15].

The pleasure of the Companions of the Blaze is magnificent, for they witness the abode, while security is one of its properties. There is no surprise if roses are found in rose gardens. Surprise comes from roses in the pit of the Fire. God's bosom friend Abraham was in bliss and pleasure in the midst of the fire, even if he only dwelt in protection from its reaching him. The enemies saw it in their eyes as a blazing fire, but he found it, through God's command to it, *coolness and safety* [21:69], for the enemies were looking at him but were unable to attack him.

Consider how "The Garden is encircled with detestable things"! Did God make it like that other than to double the bliss for the folk of the Garden? After all, the bliss of salvation and escape is among the greatest of blisses.

Human beings were created only for bliss,
  they were given to witness only to know
that the Real's *wujūd* is a deposit in creation.
  Is this *wujūd* anything but a gracious
    bestowal?
Within the Fire a group will be blissful
    through the chastisement—
  if not for witnessing the opposite, they
    would not be safe.

And God speaks the ***ḥaqq*** *and He guides on the path* [33:4]. (IV 306.20)

Ranking in Excellence

When two things are compared, the purpose may to provide a qualitative evaluation, and it may be concluded that one is better than the other. This sort of ranking is frequently discussed with words derived from the term *faḍl*, which means excess, superabundance, superiority, excellence, free gift, bounty, favor, benefit. The Koran mentions the *faḍl* or "bounty" of God in over eighty verses. Theologians often divided the divine attributes into two categories, those of bounty and those of justice (*ᶜadl*). These are the same two categories that are more likely to be called the names of "beauty and majesty," or "mercy and wrath," or "gentleness and subjugation." The Koran often associates God's *faḍl* with mercy. God gives the creatures a bounty and a mercy to which they have no inherent right, and this comprises everything that they are. In Ibn al-ᶜArabī's terms, God's bounty is the *wujūd* that He bestows upon them so that they can find themselves and others.

More significant for present purposes are the seventeen instances in which the Koran employs the second verbal form of *faḍl*, the word *tafḍīl*. As Lane's *Lexicon* tells us, this word means to attribute an excess or an excellence to something through which it is then distinguished from other things; or to make one thing more excellent than another thing. In the Koranic context, it typically means that God makes one thing exceed another thing, or that He gives more bounty to some creatures than to others. For example, the Koran says, *God made some of you exceed others in provision* (16:71).

Ibn al-ʿArabī employs the third and sixth verbal forms of the word *faḍl* (*mufāḍala* and *tafāḍul*) to refer to the fact that different things in the cosmos have been given different qualities or diverse degrees of the same quality. I translate these terms as "ranking (in excellence)," and, to maintain consistency, I translate the Koranic expression *tafḍīl* as "to rank (in excellence)." Thus, in the context of this discussion, I render the just-cited Koranic verse as *God ranks some of you above others in excellence of provision.*

From a certain point of view, there is no such thing as ranking in degrees of excellence. Inasmuch as each thing is a word spoken by God, an articulation of the All-Merciful Breath, each signifies the Real. All things are He, there is nothing in *wujūd* but God. This is the standpoint of *waḥdat al-wujūd,* and it depends on seeing everything as a specific face of God and ignoring the chains of intermediaries and occasions that structure the cosmos.

> When you ascribe affairs to the Real, they do not become ranked in excellence according to eminence. But, when you ascribe them to you, they are ranked in excellence for you. (I 699.20)

> Just as God turns His face toward the existent thing that is highest in rank—that is, the Highest Pen, which is the First Intellect—through the knowledge and felicity that He bestows upon it, so also He turns His face to the same limit toward the existent things that are the lowest in rank and the most wretched and meanest in waystation at God. For in respect of God's Essence, there is no ranking in excellence in Him, because He is not described as being the "whole" so that a "part" could be realized within Him.
>
> There is no solitary substance in the whole cosmos—the high of it and the low of it—that is not intertied with a divine reality, and there is no ranking in excellence in that most exalted and unreachable Side, for He is seated on His Highest Throne, and "If you let down a rope, it will fall upon God." (I 506.15)

Unboundedness (*iṭlāq*) belongs to *wujūd* alone. Everything other than *wujūd* binds *wujūd*'s radiance. Inasmuch as things are themselves, they constrict *wujūd*'s self-disclosure and can be ranked in excellence in keeping with the degree to which they manifest *wujūd*'s properties. Any given entity discloses the divine names and attributes in the measure in which it allows the absolute and unbounded perfection of *wujūd* to shine through. Just as the divine names differ in scope, so also the entities differ in capacity or preparedness (*istiʿdād*). Those with the greatest preparedness display the perfections of *wujūd* in the fullest measure, while those with more limited capacity disclose *wujūd*'s perfections in accordance with their own limitations.

> When diverse traces become manifest from something that is one in entity, that is in respect of the receptacles, not its entity. (II 458.18)

> Through their preparednesses, the loci of manifestation give to Him who is Manifest within them the forms through which He becomes manifest. (II 378.19)

> Know that knowledge of the origin is an exalted knowledge, for it cannot be bound [by expression]. The nearest that one can come to expressing it is to say that the origin is the opening up of the *wujūd* of the possible things consecutively and successively because the Essence that gives existence to them demands this without any binding by time, for time is one of the corporeal possible things. So nothing can be conceived of but the intertying of a possible thing with one that is Necessary by its Essence.
>
> Thus, as the counterpart of the *wujūd* of the Real are fixed entities described by nonexistence from eternity without beginning. This is the "being" that nothing has along with God [mentioned in the hadith, "God *is,* and nothing is with Him"]. However, His *wujūd* is effused upon these entities in keeping with what their own preparednesses require, so they come to be for their own entities, not for Him, without any in-betweenness that can be rationally understood or imagined. Bewilderment occurs in

conceptualizing these entities in keeping with either path—the path of unveiling or the path of reflective proof. Rational speech about what unveiling witnesses so as to clarify its meaning is impossible, for the affair cannot be imagined. It cannot be communicated, nor can it fit more clearly into the molds of words than as we have mentioned. The occasion of its exaltation is ignorance of the First Occasion, which is the Essence of the Real. (II 55.1)

Ranking in degrees of excellence is found in everything other than *wujūd* itself, because all things are diverse in preparedness. "We do not doubt that God has assigned ranking in excellence to all things" (IV 23.19). Everything other than *wujūd* itself—that is, everything in *wujūd*—is both *fāḍil* and *mafḍūl*, ranked in excellence above and below others. This ranking in degrees is found in the divine names inasmuch as they are understood as denoting specific realities and relations. Thus Ibn al-ᶜArabī often speaks of the "compass" (*iḥāṭa*) of the divine names, the fact that some names designate relations that embrace a greater range of entities than others. For example, the Knowing is all-encompassing, since God knows all things. The name Desiring has a smaller compass, because God does not desire to bring into existence everything that He knows.

Ranking in excellence becomes manifest in all things, even in the divine names. (III 510.7)

The Real alone possesses the perfection that does not accept ranking in excellence, but everything other than God is not like that. Even the divine names, which are the highest things, accept ranking in excellence. (I 668.12)

The divine names are ranked in excellence according to inclusiveness and degrees of compass. Both the Knower and the Knowing encompass, but the compass of the Knowing is more than that of the Knower. The compass of the Experienced is more than that of others. So also is the name Desiring, [whose compass is less] than Knower, and the name Powerful in respect to the Desiring and the Knower. (IV 99.4)

Were the affair not as we have mentioned it, no prophet or messenger would have loved wife or child or preferred one person over another. This is because the signs are ranked in excellence. The fluctuations of the cosmos are identical with the signs, and they are nothing but the "tasks" upon which is the Real. *He has lifted some of them above others in degrees* [43:32] because, through that form, He has become manifest in His names, for we know that some of the names are ranked in excellence above others in respect of inclusivity and specificity. *He is Independent of the worlds* [3:97], but He is also the speaker who says, *I created jinn and mankind only to worship Me* [51:56]. What does the Creator have to do with the Independent, and what do the Gripper and the Withholder have to do with it? What does the compass of the Knower have to do with that of the Powerful and the Subjugating? Is not all of this exactly what happens in the cosmos? (III 450.3)

To understand how a thing is situated in respect to something else, we need to rank the two things in terms of specific attributes. Each thing that is situated below other things in respect of some attributes may be ranked above the same things in respect of other attributes.

Ranking in excellence among known things takes place in various respects. The most inclusive of these respects is leaving traces. Everything that leaves traces is more excellent than that within which the trace is left—in respect of the leaving of the trace specifically, for that which is ranked lower in excellence may be higher in another respect. The same can be said for the excellence of the cause over its effect, of the condition over what is conditioned by it, of the reality over what is realized, and of the signifier over what is signified in the respect that the latter is signified, not in respect of its entity. The excellence may also be that something which attaches itself more inclusively is more excellent than something which attaches itself more specifically, as for example, Knowing and Powerful. (III 447.12)

In continuing this passage, Ibn al-ᶜArabī turns to the previously mentioned standpoint of identity with *wujūd*. Although things are ranked differently in terms of attributes and relations, they are identical in respect of the fact that a face of *wujūd* is found in each. Those who see things in this respect see all things as He.

Since all of *wujūd* is ranked higher and lower in excellence, this gives rise to equality and to the statement that there is nothing ranked higher and nothing ranked lower and that, on the contrary, there is an eminent, perfect, complete *wujūd,* without any imperfection. This is especially so because there is nothing among the created things, with all their diversity, that is not supported by a divine reality and relation, and there is no ranking in excellence within God, because a thing cannot be more excellent than itself. Hence, in this respect, there is no ranking in excellence in the cosmos, for it is He to whom *the affair* is returned *before and after* [30:4]. On this depend the Folk of Bringing Together and Finding. They are called the "Folk of Bringing Together" because they are the folk of the One Entity. Thus God has said, *Our affair is but one* [54:50]. (III 447.15)

For things to be ranked in degrees of excellence, they must be of the same kind or genus (*jins*). It follows that certain realities cannot be ranked in excellence, because they have no common measure, or no common genus of which both are species. For example, inasmuch as God and the cosmos have no common measure, it is not correct to say that He is more excellent than it. In a similar way, if we understand evil to be the lack of good, and good to be *wujūd,* then "There is no ranking in excellence between good and evil" (I 322.23), because *wujūd* and nonexistence have no common measure.

Opposites are ranked in excellence, like ranking in excellence between black and white. This is because color brings the two together, so ranking in excellence occurs. Every ranking in excellence in *wujūd* must have something that brings the two together, that is, a something through which everything in *wujūd* comes together. (III 273.21)

In this waystation is found the knowledge of the interrelation that comprises the whole cosmos and the fact that it is one genus. Hence ranking in excellence is correct among the species and individuals that come under it. After all, the Imam Abu'l-Qāsim ibn Qasī, author of *Khalᶜ al-naᶜlayn,* considered this impossible, for he took into account other than what we have taken into account.[12] Hence he is correct in what he took into account, but he is mistaken in respect of what we have taken into account. There is nothing but real and more real, perfect and more perfect, since ranking in excellence pervades the species of the genus because of the ranking among the names due to the compass [of each name] and the fact that one name exceeds another in something, such as Knowing and Powerful, or Powerful and Subjugating. (III 326.17)

When the Real is contrasted with creation, nothing brings the two together. This seems to be what Ibn al-ᶜArabī has in mind in the following passage:

Ranking in excellence occurs only in interrelation, not in entities, since there is no ranking in excellence in entities, because there is no ranking in excellence between the servant and the Master, the Lord and the vassal, the Creator and the created. (III 494.33)

The Shaykh makes clear that nothing brings the Creator together with creation while discussing the Koranic notion of poverty, which he takes as equivalent to the philosophical term *possibility.* God is the Necessary *wujūd,* and hence He is *Independent of the worlds,* because, whether or not the worlds are taken into account, He cannot not find Himself and cannot not be found.

It is not said that independence is more excellent than poverty or that poverty is more excellent than independence, because poverty is the attribute of creation, but independence is the attribute of the Real. Ranking in excellence is correct only in those who are brought together by a single genus, but nothing brings together the Real and creation, so there is no ranking in excellence between independence and poverty.

Concerning independence, God says, *God is independent of the worlds* [3:97], and concerning poverty, He says, *O people, you are the poor toward God, and God—He is the Independent, the Praiseworthy* [35:15]. If someone comes to know this and then says that independence is more excellent than poverty, or that poverty is more excellent than independence—as when someone says, "Who is more excellent, God or the creatures?"—this is sufficient to show the speaker's ignorance. (II 654.26)

Ibn al-ʿArabī continues this passage by answering an objection. Someone may claim that certain creatures possess the attribute of independence and are thereby more excellent than those who are poor. The Shaykh points out that the word *independence*, when attributed to created things, does not designate real independence, and hence it might as well be called "poverty." Note here that the Arabic term also means wealth or riches. The wealthy are "independent" inasmuch as they have no need for others, but in fact, they have need of their wealth, so they are poor in the midst of their independence.[13]

> As for that which is in the hands of the people and which they name "independence," how can that be independence when you are poor toward it? In your independence, you are not without need for your independence. So your independence is the same as your poverty. In reality, this is not named "independence." How can there be ranking in excellence between that which has true *wujūd*, which is the Independent, and that which has no true *wujūd*, which is your independence?
>
> When a human being is called "independent," that consists of the *wujūd* of the occasion that allows him to display traces in that toward which he has a personal desire at the moment. The occasion makes him independent in that thing toward which he is poor, because it comes to exist through the occasion. Hence he is essentially poor in his accidental independence. When the occasion that displays a trace in that toward which he is poor does not exist at him, then he is called "poor," without any independence. Hence poverty belongs to him in both states, because his own essence belongs to him in both states.
>
> Given that the affair is like this, searching for ranking in excellence is to be ignorant of the difference between the true description and the relative and accidental description. (II 654.29)

The poverty and need that people have toward various realities of the cosmos set up distinctions among the things. At any given moment, people need some things and not others. But all things are occasions, so all things are needed by other things in some respect. What differentiates the Real from the things is that He is needed by all things in an absolute sense, but the things are needed by other things in certain limited and relative senses. Hence all things need God forever and always, and there is no distinction to be made among the things in this need. Ibn al-ʿArabī finds a Koranic reference to this idea in the just-cited verse, *O people, you are the poor toward God, and God—He is the Independent, the Praiseworthy* (35:15). He reads this to mean that in fact and at root, people need only God, because God alone is real.[14] Most people, of course, do not understand this, and they think that they need the occasions. But through their need for the occasions, they acknowledge their need for the Occasioner of all occasions. In the following passage, the Shaykh refers both to ranking in degrees of excellence and to God's transcendence of all ranking.

> God has placed the cosmos in levels and degrees, some of which are poor toward others. He *has lifted some of them above others in degrees, that some of them may take others in subjection* [43:32]. Hence He ranked the cosmos higher and lower in excellence.
>
> Given that the real situation is as God apprised Abū Yazīd [when He said to him, "Come near to Me through what I do not possess—abasement and poverty"], we are alerted thereby to knowledge of His words, *O people, you are the poor toward God, and God—He is the Independent, the Praiseworthy* [35:15]. In other words, He is lauded by everything that is poor toward Him.
>
> Hence the whole cosmos is His most beautiful names and His highest attributes. The Real never ceases disclosing and manifesting Himself perpetually to the eyesights of His servants in diverse forms when any human being is poor toward one of these forms. When someone ceases to have need of the form, then, for the one who has no need, it is a creation. When his need for the form returns to him, then it is a *ḥaqq*, and its name is the name of the Real, though in the manifest appearance the name belongs to the form.
>
> The one who is veiled imagines that he is poor toward the form, and he becomes abased because of his need for it. But he has no poverty and abasement save toward God, *in whose hand is the sovereignty of each thing* [36:83]. Hence the people stand in one riverbed, and the knowers of God in another.
>
> As for the ranking in excellence that becomes manifest in the cosmos, some people are ignorant

of it and others know about it. Some are mistaken concerning it and others correct. It is that God apportioned the cosmos in *wujūd* between absent and witnessed, manifest and nonmanifest, first and last. Then He made the nonmanifest, the last, and the absent one sort, and He made the first, the manifest, and the witnessed another sort.

Among the people, some accord excellence to the sort in which there is firstness, some accord excellence to the sort in which there is lastness, some make them equal in an absolute sense, and some make this relative. The last are the Folk of God specifically. They say that the sort in which there is lastness is better for the felicitous, but it is not better for the wretched. (III 405.14)

God's Choices

In a theological context, one might ask why God ranks things in degrees. An obvious answer is that He wills or chooses to do so. To investigate the issue of God's will (*mashī*ʾ*a*) in any detail would necessitate a separate chapter, but it may nevertheless be useful to look at the divine attribute of (free) choice (*ikhtiyār*). This term is often contrasted either with constraint (*iḍṭirār*) or compulsion (*jabr*). In Islamic thought in general, God is said to have choice and not to be constrained or compelled. Concerning human beings, there is a debate. It is obvious that human beings are constrained and compelled to some degree, if not totally, but it is also obvious that they possess a certain freedom and power of choice. Is this freedom real or illusory? Thus the issue of free will and predestination is often discussed in terms of choice and compulsion.

In Ibn al-ʿArabī's view, *wujūd* follows the law of its own nature, which is to say that God exercises His power of choice in terms of wisdom, justice, mercy, and other attributes. But God is all-knowing, and He is all-knowing always and forever. The choices He makes are based on the realities of the entities, which are fixed in His knowledge. His choices follow what He knows about the entities, because knowledge follows the known. Hence, God Himself is constrained and compelled by His own reality—His own knowledge, wisdom, compassion, and mercy—to make certain choices. Human beings, created in His form, have even more reason to be constrained and compelled. Hence human choice is illusory, but so also is human existence. In the midst of the illusion of free choice, human beings are compelled by their own fixed entities to act in certain ways. God bestows existence upon them in keeping with His knowledge of them in their fixity. Nonetheless, despite this compulsion, they are addressed by the Law and given responsibility for their actions. Their responsibility is as real as their freedom, and their freedom is as real as their existence. As usual with the Shaykh's discussions, we are left with a contradictory picture—simultaneous choice and compulsion, *wujūd* and nonexistence, *tashbīh* and *tanzīh*, He/not He, utter bewilderment.

The Koran attributes choice to God in four verses, the most general of which is this: *Thy Lord creates whatever He wills and chooses; they have not the choice* (28:68). The first thing to note is that, in typical Koranic fashion, the attribute of choice is affirmed for God and negated from the creatures. God is the Real, the creatures are the unreal. His choice is real, theirs unreal. "There is no god but God" means that there is no choice but God's choice—He alone possesses the true power of choice. Nonetheless, in the Shaykh's view, this does not mean that God possesses choice in the way that we understand—commonsensically—that we possess choice.

In the Koran God says, *Our command is but one, like a glance of the eyesight* (54:50). This one command is the word *Be*, through which the universe comes into *wujūd*. God does not say "Be a star, be a tree, be an ant!" On the contrary, He simply says *Be* to the nonexistent but fixed stars, trees, and ants and they come to be in *wujūd* as they are in fixity. He does not "make" (*ja*ʿ*l*) them what they are, since they are what they are with immutable fixity. He simply makes *wujūd* manifest, and *wujūd* displays the traces of the entities. God's "choice" is only to give the things *wujūd*. In other words, the Necessary *Wujūd* "gives preponderance" (*tarjīḥ*) to the existence of the possible things over their nonexistence. The diversity of the things depends upon the things themselves. When God says in the Koran, *If We had willed, We would have given every soul its guidance* (32:13), He is saying, in the Shaykh's reading, that He did not will because this is not a matter of will or choice; on the contrary, it belongs to the very essence of a given creature to be guided or misguided. As Ibn al-ʿArabī often points out, following the classical grammarians, the particle *law* or "if" at the beginning of such sentences indicates a thing's impossibility.

Toward the beginning of the *Futūḥāt*, the Shaykh offers a rather dense theological observation concerning the attribution of choice to God. He points out that the term suggests a multiplicity of choices, so it contradicts the fact that God's will is one. Moreover, God says in a number of verses that His Word is "realized" (*ḥaqq*), a term that the Shaykh seems to understand to mean something like "carries the weight of the Real," that is, exercises determining power over the creatures. Moreover, God's word never changes, for it is essentially one. In the passage he refers to the "mystery of the measuring out" (*sirr al-qadar*), which he clearly understands to be the fact that the creatures determine their own destiny, or the fact that God's knowledge follows the objects of knowledge, this being God's "conclusive argument." Thus, by giving *wujūd* to the things, God simply makes the realities of the things known to them. He does not make their realities what they are, since their realities are what they are always and forever. "Realities do not change" as Ibn al-ʿArabī often tells us.[15] If they did, they would not be realities.

> As for our knowledge that God possesses choice:
>
> Choice contradicts the unity of the will, so its ascription to the Real, when He is described by it, is in respect to the situation of the possible things, not in respect of the Real's situation. He says, *[If We had willed, We would have given every soul its guidance.] However, My Word is realized* [32:13]. He says, *He against whom the word of chastisement is realized* [39:19]. He says, *The word is not changed with Me*; and how beautiful is the way He finishes this verse: *And I do not wrong My servants* [50:29].
>
> Here He calls attention to the mystery of the measuring out, through which God has the conclusive argument against His creatures. It is this that is proper for the side of the Real. As for what goes back to engendered existence, that is *If We had willed, We would have given every soul its guidance*, but We did not will. *However [My Word is realized]* is an emendation for the sake of making the point that the possible thing is receptive to guidance and misguidance in respect of its reality, so it is the site of division, and it becomes divided. But in actual fact, God has nothing in it save one command, and this command is known to God from the direction of the possible thing's state. (I 162.35)

Is God compelled? The answer is, "Not from outside Himself." However, if we mean, "Does He do what He does because it is demanded by His own reality?," then it must be said that He is compelled. But in actual fact, God is beyond choice and compulsion in the way that we normally understand these words. Thus Ibn al-ʿArabī writes,

> None has any act save God, and no act occurs in *wujūd* by choice, for the choices known in the cosmos derive from compulsion itself, so all are compelled in their choices. In the true act there is no compulsion and no choice, because it is required by the Essence. (II 70.28)

On God's part, His own reality makes certain demands upon Him. On our part, it is also His reality that makes the demands, because all other realities depend upon Him. He is, and we are not. Thus we are compelled by His *wujūd* (even if, from another point of view our realities—which are nonexistent in themselves—compel us to be what we are). Both God's autonomy and our being ruled by Him might be called "compulsion," but the term has radically different meanings in the two cases.

> The Real is not described by compulsion, while the possible thing is described by compulsion. At the same time, we know that *The Word is not changed with Me* [50:29]. God either does a deed that He knew beforehand He would do, or He refrains from something that He knew beforehand He would refrain from. "Compulsion" is nothing other than this, except that,

here, what compels Him is identical with the object of compulsion. Nothing compels Him but His knowledge, His knowledge is His attribute, and His attribute is His Essence. In the case of the possible thing, compulsion is that another thing should compel it, not its own entity. If it should strive to do other than what it is compelled to do, it is not able. Thus it is compelled by a subjugation and it chooses with regard to its essence. In the first case, there is compulsion with regard to His Essence, and He chooses with regard to the deed in respect of the one for whom it is done. (III 167.29)

Given the fact that the Real is compelled in His choices, it follows that people also are compelled in their choices, which is to say both that they are compelled to make choices and that they choose what they are compelled to choose. In most of his mentions of choice in the *Futūḥāt*, the Shaykh refers to this paradoxical situation. These are three of many:

The servant is compelled in his choosing. (II 444.1)

The servant's choosing is the greatest and densest of veils. He who witnesses compulsion in choice knows that the chooser is compelled in his choosing. (IV 208.12)

God has a hidden subjugation of which the cosmos is not aware. It is that He compels them in their choosing. He also has a disclosed subjugation. It is that they are ruled over by things in which they have no choice. Hence the Men of God watch for the hidden subjugation, for it is this concerning which God will question and hold responsible. If you witness the compulsion in your choosing, then you will be one of those who witness the disclosed compulsion, so the witnessing will lift responsibility from you. However, people who witness this are rare. I have seen few of the folk of this tongue and state. Or rather, I have seen only one, in Syria, and I was joyful through him. (III 229.31)

One of the happy results of the servants' compulsion is that it provides an excuse before God and opens the door to His precedent mercy. "The excuse of the whole cosmos is accepted in actual fact, because they are compelled in their choosing. That is why God made the final issue of everyone at mercy" (III 433.4). "Make no protest against the servant, for he is compelled in his choosing through My will" (IV 46.32).

There is no escape from the ruling property of mercy over everyone. Sufficient as instruction are the Lawgiver's words, "As for the folk of the Fire, those who are its folk," for he did not say "the folk of the chastisement." It is not necessary that those who are the folk of the Fire, those who inhabit it, be chastised by it. After all, among its folk and those who inhabit it are Mālik and its keepers, who are angels; and the crawling things, serpents, and other animals within it that are raised up on the day of resurrection. But the Fire is not a chastisement for any of these. In the same way, those who remain in it "will neither die therein nor live."

Everyone who is familiar with his own homestead is happy with it. The most intense chastisement is separation from the homeland. Were the Fire's folk to become separate from it, they would suffer chastisement through their exile from that for which they had been made the folk. God created them in a configuration that is familiar with that homestead.

The two abodes will be populated, and mercy will take precedence over wrath and *embrace everything* [7:156], including Gehenna and everyone within it.

God is *the Most Merciful of the merciful* [12:64], as He said about Himself. We have found in ourselves, who are among those whom God has disposed naturally toward mercy, that we have mercy on all God's servants, even if God has decreed in His creating them that the attribute of chastisement will remain forever with them in the cosmos. This is because the ruling property of mercy has taken possession of our hearts. The companion of this attribute is I and my peers, and we are creatures, companions of caprices and personal desires. But God has said about Himself that He is *the Most Merciful of the merciful*. So we have no doubt that He is more merciful than we are toward His creatures, while we have known from our own selves this extravagant mercy. So how could chastisement be everlasting for them when He has this all-inclusive attribute of mercy? God is nobler than that.

This is all the more true because rational proofs have been affirmed that the Author is neither benefited by acts of obedience nor

> harmed by acts of opposition; that everything flows in accordance with His decree, His measuring out, and His judgment; and that the creatures are compelled in their choosing. (III 25.14)

The issue of choice and compulsion is one of many that illustrate the primacy of human beings in the cosmos, the fact that the cosmos was created for their sake, and the fact that everything in the macrocosm—the "horizons"—exists only for the sake of the microcosm, the "selves."

> God created the cosmos outside of the human being only as the striking of a likeness for the human being, that he might know that everything that becomes manifest in the cosmos is within himself and that the human being is the Intended Entity. He is the totality of the wisdoms, and for his sake were created the Garden and the Fire, this world and the last world, all the states, and the hownesses. Within him becomes manifest the totality of the divine names and their traces. So he is the blessed and the chastised, the object of mercy and the punished.
>
> Then He assigned for him that he should chastise and bless, have mercy and punish. He is the choosing for whom the Law is prescribed and the compelled in his choice. To him the Real discloses Himself through judgment, decree, and decision. Around him the whole cosmos revolves, for his sake the resurrection occurs, through him the jinn are called to account, and for him is *subjected what is in the heavens and what is in the earth* [31:20]. The whole cosmos moves out of need for him, in both the high and the low realms, in this world and the last. (III 417.24)

In Chapter 90, Ibn al-ʿArabī mentions God's choosing as the divine root of the fact that the servant has a certain choice in his own affairs. This human power of choice obligates people to choose what God has chosen for them when He prescribed the Shariah. Having said this, the Shaykh looks specifically at some of the choices God has made, basing himself on various hadiths and Koranic verses. Although few of these divine choices have direct relevance to cosmology, the chapter illustrates how Ibn al-ʿArabī relates all things, cosmological or not, back to their divine roots. Since all have a common origin, all need to be understood in terms of the same principles. Only from an especially limited, human standpoint, can we justify separating ethics, for example, from natural science, given that both are rooted in the nature of things. For the Shaykh and for Islamic thinking in general, all things fit under the rubric of *tawḥīd*. At the beginning of the explanation of why God chose various things over others, the Shaykh provides the following list, enumerating God's specific choices in a variety of categories (II 169.5):

CATEGORY	CHOICE
divine names	God
people	messengers
wherenesses	the Cloud[16]
servants	angels
spheres	the Throne
elements	water
months	Ramadan
acts of worship	fasting
generations	the generation of the Prophet
days of the week	Friday
nights	the Night of Power
deeds	obligatory works
numbers	ninety-nine
abodes	the Garden
states of felicity in the Garden	vision
states	good-pleasure
formulas of remembrance	"There is no god but God"
speech	the Koran
surahs of the Koran	Yāsīn (36)
verses of the Koran	the Footstool Verse (2:255)
short surahs	Unity (112)
supplications for various times	the supplication for the Day of ʿArafa
mounts	Burāq
angels	the Spirit
colors	white
engendered qualities	coming together
the human being	the heart
stones	the Black Stone
houses	the Inhabited House
trees	the Lote Tree
women	Mary and Āsiya
men	Muhammad
stars	the sun
movements	straight movement

CATEGORY	CHOICE
laws	the revealed Shariah
demonstrations	the ontological demonstration
forms	the Adamic form
lights	that which accompanies looking
the two contradictories	affirmation
the two opposites	*wujūd*[17]
acts of the *ṣalāt*	prostration
words of the *ṣalāt*	the remembrance of God
varieties of volitional acts	intention

Part of the Shaykh's purpose in mentioning these divine choices seems to be to bring out, once again, the necessity for revealed knowledge if human beings are to grasp the actual situation of things. After explaining the rationale for these divine choices on the basis of the revealed sources, he explains that rational thought is limited in its ability to classify and rank things; it is impossible, without God's instruction, to know how things are ranked in God's own view of things, which is nothing but the situation of *wujūd* as it is in itself.

> There is a relational sort of differentiation that reason is able to grasp on its own, and this is the ranking in excellence among things, some above others. This is based on distinguishing the levels and on the fact that some are acted upon by others, some display traces in others, and some depend on others. However, the ranking in excellence of divine nearness by way of solicitude toward things—not by way of what is given by their realities—cannot be known save by God's instructing us concerning it through the sciences of inspiration that He bestows upon our hearts or through what He has conveyed to us in the revealed books and the prophetic reports. As for a route other than this, there is none. (II 174.33)

From Chapter 73: The Fifty-First Question

Ibn al-ᶜArabī addresses the issue of God's choice in answering one of the questions that had been posed by al-Ḥakīm al-Tirmidhī: "Where are the storehouses of favors?" The term *favors* (pl. of *minna*) can be understood as a reference to various Koranic verses in which God is said to bestow favors and benefits upon His creatures, such as *God confers favors upon whomsoever He will of His servants* (14:11). Notice that this verse connects God's favors to His will, which the Shaykh often takes as a synonym for His choice. But we have already seen that God's "choice" depends upon the situation of the creatures, and the situation of the creatures is fixed, so He has no choice but to give them existence as they are in themselves. Hence Ibn al-ᶜArabī says that favors, whether divine or human, reside in a choice that is *mutawahham*, "imagined" or "illusory." Having explained this, he turns to the issue of what it might mean to ask "where" God's storehouses are, given that "whereness" (*ayniyya*) and "place" (*makān*) cannot be attributed to God in respect of His *tanzīh*.

> Question: Where are the storehouses of favors?
>
> Answer: In the imagined choice that is attributed to Him and to you, for you are compelled in your choosing, so where is choice? He is not compelled, but His command is one. So where is the choice? *If God had willed* [2:20]—but He did not will. And *If He wills, He will take you away* [4:133], but He is not the locus of newly arrived things. On the contrary, the entities are the locus of newly arrived things, and He is identical with the newly arrived things in them, for they are the loci of His manifestation.
>
> *No remembrance comes to them from their Lord newly arrived [. . .]* [21:2]. The "remembrance" is His speech, and it is this that arrives newly at them. His speech is His knowledge, and His knowledge is His Essence, so it is He who arrives newly at them. Hence, He is the storehouses of favors, and the favors are the manifestation in them of what arrives newly at them. But He has no "where," so the storehouses of favors have no whereness.
>
> Since the favors are numerous, each relation itself sought a storehouse from Him. Thus the storehouses became numerous through the numerousness of the favors, though they are one. *Nay, but God confers a favor upon you in that He has guided you to faith, if it be that you are truthful* [49:17] in saying that you have faith. So this is two favors—the favor of guidance and the favor of faith. All of His manifest and nonmanifest blessings are His favors.

Since He is the favor itself, you are the storehouse. Hence, the cosmos is the storehouses of the divine favors, and within us have been stored His favors, so He is not a where for us, but we are a where for Him. So he who has no whereness is we, for our entities are a where for His manifestation. Thus the reality of place does not accept place.

Pay no attention to those who say, "The thing emplaced in the place is a place for its place." Thereby they suppose that the emplacement and the place have two opposing movements that bestow on each of them the reality of placeness. But whoever says this has imagined it because of his own doctrine. The reality is what we have stipulated—place does not receive place, so the where of him who has a where has no where.

All this is within the natural loci of manifestation. As for the meanings disengaged from any matter, they are the holy loci of manifestation for the names that do not accept the relations of *tashbīh*. Knowledge of them is that they are not known, as has been related from al-Ṣiddīq, who said concerning the like of what we have mentioned, "The incapacity to attain perception is itself perception."

So *tanzīh* from the where is turned over to Him who accepts *tashbīh*. Hence there is no *tashbīh* in the cosmos and no *tanzīh*, since a thing is not declared incomparable with itself nor similar with itself.

Thus the levels have been clarified and the meaning of the relations has come to be known. And praise belongs to God alone that He has taught His servant! (II 74.28)

From Chapter 72: Eating the Forbidden

The issue of constraint versus choice often comes up in the Shariah, as, for example, in discussion of unlawful food. Thus the Koran forbids carrion, blood, swine, and what has been hallowed to other than God, but it adds, *Yet whoso is constrained, not desiring nor transgressing, no sin shall be on him* (2:173). In his chapter on the hajj, Ibn al-ʿArabī addresses a disputed issue concerning the pilgrims and then turns to the theological roots of choice and constraint. The juridical discussion focuses on the verse, *O you with faith! Slay not the game while you are consecrated for the pilgrimage; whoever among you slays it intentionally, there shall be recompense* (5:95). The question is: Suppose someone has nothing to eat during the hajj except carrion or swine. Should he eat that, given that it is permitted to him because he is constrained? Or should he hunt game, though it is forbidden, and pay the recompense?

Should the constrained person who is consecrated for the hajj eat carrion or game?

Some people say that he should eat carrion and swine, but not game. Others say that he should hunt game and eat that, but he must pay a recompense.

I maintain the first view. However, if he is constrained to hunt, then he should hunt, but he must pay a recompense, because he does this intentionally. God did not single out the constrained from the non-constrained [in paying the recompense].

Every created thing is accompanied by constraint perpetually, since that is its reality. Despite the constraint, the Law may be prescribed for someone. Then it will behoove him to halt with what has been prescribed for him, for absolute constraint will never be lifted from him. The only thing that will be lifted from him is a specific constraint to such and such. All the movements of engendered existence, in respect of the reality, are constrained and compelled. If choice existed in the engendered realm, you would know it.

Nevertheless, there is another knowledge through which we know that he who has choice is compelled in his choosing. Or rather, the realities demand that no one have choice, because we see that the chooser's choice is by constraint, which is to say that he has no escape from choosing. Hence constraint is a fixed, unavoidable root that accompanies choice, but choice does not rule over constraint, for all of *wujūd* dwells in essential compulsion. This is not to say that it is compelled by a compulsion from something else. After all, what compels the compelled person—who, were it not for this compulsion, would have choice—is compelled in its choosing for the compelled person.

Creation is compelled, especially since
 the Root is compelled, so where is choice?
Every created thing is in His shape
 in the state of compulsion and constraint.
The creature is distinguished from its Root
 in its abasement and poverty.
So be with the Real through His attributes
 between perpetual compulsion and choice!

And God speaks the **ḥaqq**, *and He guides on the path* [33:4]. (I 687.23)

From Chapter 198: The Twenty-Third Tawḥīd

The twenty-third of the thirty-six Koranic mentions of the first Shahadah in its various forms is the verse *And He is God; there is no god but He. His is the praise in the first and the last. His too is the ruling property, and to Him you shall be returned* (28:70). The Shaykh interprets this verse to refer to God's choosing some things over other things and His arranging the cosmos in a hierarchical order. No one has true choice in these matters but God. As he writes elsewhere, "Excellence becomes manifest in the cosmos so that it may be known that the Real shows solicitude toward some of His servants and abandons others; and so that it may be known that the possible thing never leaves its possibility, and He who gives preponderance to it has a specific gaze toward whatsoever He will" (II 281.20). In explaining this *tawḥīd* of choice, the Shaykh describes a vision that he experienced while writing the passage, thereby suggesting how the power of imagination represents the abstractions of rational thinking in appropriate forms.

This is the *tawḥīd* of choice, and it is one of the *tawḥīds* of the He-ness.

Since the cosmos is the words of God, the relation of these words to the All-Merciful Breath in which they become manifest is one relation. This provides a proof that there is no ranking in excellence within the cosmos, nor is anyone chosen because of an excellence with God over others.

However, we see that the affair has emerged otherwise in *wujūd* for all existent things. God says, *And We have honored the children of Adam, and We carried them on land and sea, and We provided them with the good things, and We have ranked them with a clear ranking in excellence over many of those We created* [17:70]. God says, *And those messengers, some We have ranked in excellence over others* [2:253]. He says, *And We have ranked some prophets in excellence over others* [17:55]. He says, *And some [plants] We have ranked in excellence of produce over others,* even though they are *watered with one water* [13:4]. There is no verse more appropriate for the ranking in excellence that actually occurs in *wujūd* than this last verse, in respect of the fact that He says *watered with one water*. Thus diversity of flavor becomes manifest from the one by way of ranking in excellence.

Verses of this sort occur often in the Koran, thereby showing the excellence of some of each kind above others. Even the Koran itself—and it is the speech of God—is more excellent than other revealed books, though they are all the speech of God. Moreover, parts of the Koran itself are more excellent than other parts, though all of it is ascribed to God in that it is His speech, without doubt. Thus the Footstool Verse is the master of the verses of the Koran, yet it is Koran, and the Religion Verse is Koran.[18] How marvelous is this mystery!

From this we come to know that the wisdom required by rational consideration is not correct, and that God's wisdom in affairs is the correct wisdom. God's wisdom is not perceived by reason. Though it is not known, people are not ignorant of it. However, it does not become designated through reflection alone, nor through consideration. On the contrary, *He gives wisdom to whomsoever He will; he who has been given wisdom has been given much good* [2:269].

While I was recording this *tawḥīd* that bestows ranking in excellence, I saw a marvelous Incident. I was given an unrolled parchment. Its width as given by eyesight was more than twenty cubits. As for its length, I did not realize it. Its shape was as pictured in the diagram [figure 5.1].

It was a single skin, a sheepskin. When you looked at it, you saw it as white when reading it. But when you looked at it when not reading it, you saw it as green. When you read it, you saw it as a skin, but when you did not read, you saw it as a piece of cloth. I do not know if it was silk or cotton. It was the marriage contract of my wife.

It was said to me, "This is a divine marriage contract for your wife."

I did not ask about the spouse, and I did not know that she was outside the preserve of marriage with me. I was happy with this affair, extremely joyful.

Then a piece of fine green silk was brought, a piece that arose from the writing as if it were part of it. Within it came to be one thousand dinars of gold coin. Each dinar was heavy, but I did not know the weight. It was said, "Divide it among its folk—five dinars to each individual." As soon as I took the first five dinars, upon them was a brilliant light, greater than the light of the brightest star in heaven and possessing a ray.

I saw that the writing itself was identical with my wife. Its writing was nothing other than

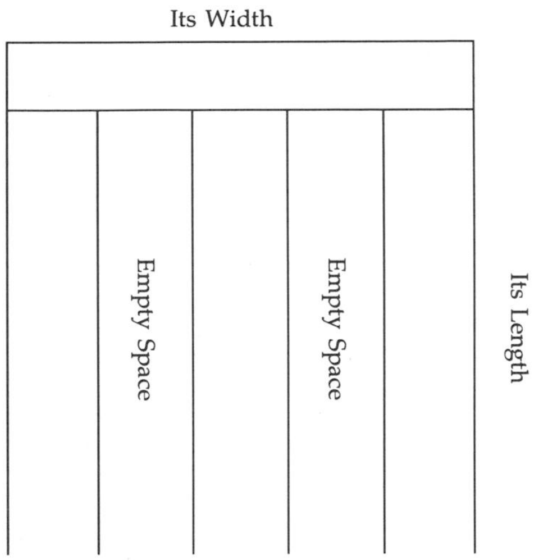

FIGURE 5.1

she. With my whole body I was lying upon her and supporting myself. I was looking at the letters of that writing and I found that it was in the handwriting of Zayn al-Dīn ʿAbd Allāh ibn al-Shaykh ʿAbd al-Raḥmān, known as Ibn al-Ustādh, the judge of the city of Aleppo. He wrote it at the dictation of the great judge Bahāʾ al-Dīn ibn Shaddād.[19]

From its beginning to its end, the marriage contract was written in rhymed prose with a single rhyme, consisting of *rah*. After the *basmala*, I retained the following:

Praise belongs to God who made His Koran,
 Furqān, Torah, Gospel, and Psalms
 the letters of this *hidden book* [56:78] and
 its lines,
who deposited within it every verse of the
 Books and every sura,
who made it manifest in *wujūd* in the most
 beautiful form,
who in the high and low worlds made its
 signposts famous,
 its verses without end or restriction,
 and its words by every tongue mentioned
 in every time and non-time.

So it continued until the end—if it had an end—in a script like sprinkles of gold. When I came back to sensation, I found that I was writing this section of the sections on *tawḥīd*, and that it was the *tawḥīd* of choice. I came to know that [the vision] was this section itself, and that my wife had the ampler share and the greater portion of this section.

When we see that ranking in excellence and choice occur in the cosmos, even in the Shari'ite formulae of remembering God—as we mentioned—we come to know that there is an intelligible affair that is not identical with the Breath and not other than the Breath within which come to be the words, which are the entities of the engendered things. When, through that, He designates His will, within the words this ranking in excellence becomes manifest in the One, as does the ranking in excellence in that which is equal. But the One is not qualified by ranking in excellence, nor is the equal described by ranking in excellence.

Thus we come to know that the mystery of God is unknown. None knows it but He. Hence we find this as the *tawḥīd* of choice in the Presence of the Mystery.

There is no god but He. His is the praise in the first, which is the praise of undifferentiation, *and the last,* which is the praise of differentiation. Thus the praises become distinct in the One Entity. So Its praise is Itself. How marvelous is the station of this *tawḥīd* for him who witnesses it!

In the Incident, I marveled at the name of my wife, which is Mary. The meaning of this name is known in the language in which Mary was named. She is "the consecrated to God," the carrier of the spirit of God, the locus of the word of God, the lauded by the speech of God. She is exonerated by the dates that fell when she shook *the trunk of the* dried *palm tree* [19:25] and by the rational speech of her son in the cradle, saying that he is *the servant of God* [19:30]. These are two just witnesses with God. Hence all of her is for God, through God, and from God. That is why God's prophet Zachariah wished for what she was, for he requested the like of her from God. Hence He gave him John, who was chaste like her. He *gave* John *no namesake aforetime* [19:7] among the prophets of God. Thus He specified him for firstness among the names of God. So consider the blessing of this name in God's *wujūd* among God's servants!

None of this happened save through God's choice. *Thy Lord creates whatever He wills and chooses; they have not the choice* [28:68]; rather, it belongs to God, and God *does whatever He desires* [11:107]. (II 416.6)

Order

When things are viewed with regard to excellence, they can be ranked in levels, some higher and some lower. The levels are determined by relations. For example, we saw that *divinity* designates the level of the Real when He is envisaged in relation to the cosmos. In contrast, *Essence* denotes the Real in Himself, without regard to relations, which is to say that the Essence as such has no level. Hence the Essence remains unknown, but "God" is known in respect of His level. In a similar way, we have nothing to say about any existent thing except in respect of relations and attributions, since it is precisely these that allow us to ascribe attributes and descriptions to things.

> In respect of His Essence, He belongs to His Essence, but in respect of what is named "God," He seeks the cosmos. The cosmos knows nothing of the Real save the Level, that is, the fact that He is a God, a Lord. So the cosmos has nothing to say about Him except concerning these relations and attributions. (II 67.22)

The Arabic word for *level* (*rutba* or *martaba*) is derived from the same root as the term *tartīb*, which I translate here as "order," though I translated it in SPK as "hierarchy." Literally, *tartīb* means to make something firm and steady, to arrange, to put into steps or levels. When God ranks things in terms of excellence (*tafḍīl*), He gives them order. Order is unavoidable, because the divine names, which are the roots of all cosmic properties and attributes, are themselves ranked in degrees. One of the most obvious domains in which we see the necessity of order is in the temporality that pertains to all things, or the priority (*taqaddum*) and posteriority (*taʾakhkhur*) that appear as soon as we consider relations in time (*zamān*).[20]

> In this waystation, I saw the knowledge of the variation of the properties because of the times, since it is impossible for something to occur in the cosmos except through a temporal order, a priority, a posteriority, and a ranking in excellence. For God gave me to witness His names, and I saw that they were ranked in excellence, for they share in certain affairs and are distinct in other affairs, despite the sharing. Whenever a name does not share with another name, there is no ranking in excellence between the two. So know this, for it is an exalted knowledge. (III 351.23)

Although the entities follow an order in *wujūd*, they have no order inasmuch as they are fixed entities in God's knowledge. The order that they acquire derives from their coming into existence under the sway of the divine names, which are ordered in certain respects.

> In the state of their nonexistence, the possible things stand before the Real. He looks upon them and distinguishes them from each other in keeping with their own realities within the thingness of their fixity. He looks upon them with the eye of His most beautiful names, like the Knower and the Preserver. The latter name, through the light of His *wujūd*, preserves them in the thingness of their fixity, lest impossibility strip them of thingness. Hence He spreads over them the mercy through which He opens *wujūd*. After all, the order of giving existence to the possible things demands that some of them have priority over others. This cannot be denied, for this is what happens. So entrance into the thingness of *wujūd* happens only in order.
>
> The affair of the things in the thingness of fixity is otherwise, because none of them is ordered. After all, their "fixity" is described by eternity without beginning, and there is no order in eternity without beginning, no priority, and no posteriority.
>
> However, among the divine names, some are inclusive and some more inclusive; some are specific and some more specific. Hence priority, posteriority, and order are correct among the divine names. Through this, the thingnesses of *wujūd* are given order. (III 280.26)

Cosmic order manifests the reality of Not He since, inasmuch as all things are He, no distinction can be drawn among them. Some gnostics may achieve a vision of *waḥdat al-wujūd* through which all distinction is erased, but this is not the final word. In effect, they see only with the eye of *tashbīh* and fail to see with the eye of *tanzīh*. They see the specific face, but they fail to see the chain of intermediaries and occasions. The perfection of human understanding demands seeing things as they actually are, as both incomparable with God and similar to Him. This is *taḥqīq*—realization, or giving each thing its *ḥaqq* and recognizing the specific face of the Real manifested by each and every creature.

Even though Ibn al-ʿArabī himself repeatedly tells us that "There is nothing in *wujūd* but God," he frequently criticizes those who claim to see only God. In fact, *wujūd* discloses itself through the levels, and correct human understanding demands perceiving the levels and giving them their *ḥaqq*. In one section of the *Futūḥāt*, he recounts the words of God to the gnostic who has come to see His face in all things. God warns him not to be misled and tells him not to mix (*ikhtilāṭ*), which is the shortcoming of those who fail to perceive the levels.

"Do not mix affairs. Place each thing where its reality places it. Do not say, 'There is nothing but God,' even if that is the case—and it is the case. Have not the intelligible levels distinguished between 'He is like this' and 'He is like that'? The Entity is one, as you say, but, in respect of one thing, He is such and such, and in respect of another thing, He is something else.

"I see you sensing pain and fleeing from it. What has called you to that from which you flee? I see you sensing pleasure and I see you lacking what you seek. In this measure, affirm your own entity and know where you are.

"Whatever the case may be, manyness exists and 'others' are witnessed—along with knower and ignorant, command and commanded, judge and judged and that through which and in which judgment is made, desirer and desired, choice and compulsion, separator and separated, joiner and joined, near and nearer, promise and threat. The benefit lies in the one who addresses, the one who is addressed, the address, and that by which he is addressed.

"The human being is one in his whole, but his organs are distinct and his faculties are numerous. Yet he is he, none other. Whenever something of him suffers pain, the pain pervades all of him. But you see one person who suffers pain, another who is happy with his pain, and still another who sorrows because of it. Were the affair one as it is in the human being, pain would pervade the whole cosmos when anyone suffered pain. So the affair is not as you imagine it. When the covering is unveiled, you will know what I say. So counsel yourself, if you desire to join the knowers of God, those to whom God has given felicity.

"The manifest and the nonmanifest that belong to God are like the spirit and the body. Just as the latter two are not separate, so also the former two are not separate. The affair is nothing but a servant and a Lord, so it is nothing but you and He. Hence the obedient are guided, and the disobedient are bewildered between what is desired from them and what they are commanded to do." (III 231.3)

Perhaps the worst way to mix levels is to ascribe the level in which one dwells to oneself. Levels are established by relations, and relations have no existence as such. One person stands on higher ground than another, so he has the attribute of highness. It would be stupid indeed for the person to consider himself a "high" person because he stands on a hill. One person is a king and another a subject. The attribute of kingship is not an essential attribute of the person. Inasmuch as it is borrowed, it must be attributed to its rightful owner, who can only be God. One person is knowledgeable and another ignorant, but, "There is no knower but God," and all human knowledge is on loan from Him. All attributes are of the same sort, and understanding things in this way is a sure antidote for pride.

There is no disagreement among the intelligent that anyone who pretends to magnificence because of someone else's eminence is stupid and ignorant, since he is not eminent through himself—the affair is otherwise.

The intelligent witnesser, present with God, sees no eminence belonging to himself through which he could boast over his peers. Do you not see that the Prophet said, "I will be the master of the people on the day of resurrection, without boasting"? Hence he negated any intention to boast in that. Then he mentioned the level, to which belongs the boasting, for which he is the spokesman, and in whose tongue he speaks, since he mentioned the level of "intercession" and the *Praiseworthy Station* [17:79]. Hence the boasting belongs to the level, not to us. No one ever perished who knew his own measure. I have—praise belongs to God!—a firmly rooted footing in this station.

The levels are relations of nonexistence. Nothing boasts by essence but God alone. Since our boasting belongs to the levels, and the levels are relations of nonexistence, we have nothing to boast about save nonexistence. What a marvel—he who boasts of nonexistence! (III 226.2)

The servant's perfection, then, is to recognize his own nonexistence. This is part of giving things their *ḥaqq*. In order to do so, people must know the things for what they are. But this sort of knowledge is inaccessible to reason without the intervention of God. Revelation provides the scales through which the levels of things can be discerned.

> God distinguished the levels, clarified them for us, became manifest through His names in their entities, and disclosed Himself to us through them only so that we might place Him in each of the levels into which we see Him descend. Then we will judge Him through that by which He judges Himself. This is the most complete knowledge of God—that we know Him through Himself, not through our consideration, and not through our placing. High indeed is God the Creator beyond that we should judge Him by means of what He has created without His becoming manifest to it as He has judged it! Thus He is the judge of Himself, not I.
>
> This is the meaning of the saying of the ulama that the Real is named only by that by which He names Himself, whether in His Book or on the tongue of His messenger in respect of the fact that he is His spokesman.
>
> When God makes someone stand in the station of spokesmanship for Him by lifting the intermediaries or by the intermediary of the luminous spirits, and when he brings a name by which he names Him, then we may name Him with this name. It makes no difference whether or not the spokesman is setting down a Shariah for us. There is no condition in this save spokesmanship for Him, so that we do not judge Him save through Him. After all, it is He who says, *If you are wary of God, He will assign you a discrimination* [8:29], through which you will distinguish Him and differentiate between what is appropriate for Him and what is appropriate for you. He "gives each that has a *ḥaqq* its *ḥaqq*." So *He has* the *keys* [39:63] and He opens with them and without them. We open with them, but we do not have them. On the contrary, they are in His hand. Anything in His hand does not go outside of Him, for there is nowhere to go, since He is the Giver and the Taker, for "Alms fall to the hand of the All-Merciful." (III 166.8)

From Chapter 360: The Sixth Deputyship

When God speaks, the cosmos is born from the Breath of the All-Merciful. Just as human speech is understandable only because of the arrangement of letters and words, so also the cosmos is intelligible only because of the arrangement and order of the divine words that are the entities. The Shaykh explains this while discussing the sixth of the ten deputyships that are possessed by the perfect human being.

> As for the sixth deputyship:
>
> God described Himself by saying that He has "words," so He made them many. Hence, there is no escape from something that differentiates the units of this manyness. Moreover, God takes one of these words and makes it many, for He says, *Our only word to a thing, when We desire it, is to say to it "Be!"* [*kun*] [16:40]. Thus He brought three letters, two of which are manifest—the *kāf* and the *nūn*—and one of which [the *wāw*] is nonmanifest and hidden, because of an accidental affair, that is, the fact that it and the *nūn* are unvowelled. Thus its entity has disappeared from the manifest domain, because of the meeting of two unvowelled letters.
>
> In this level, the perfect human being assumes the deputyship of the Real in differentiating between the prior word and the one that follows it. God speaks within this human configuration and within everyone who becomes manifest in its form through the letters articulated in the form's breath. The *wujūd* of the letter in each point of articulation is its being engendered. If no one engenders it here, then who engenders it? Inescapably, the one who engenders it is between every two words or letters so as to give existence to the second word or the second letter and to attach it to the first.
>
> There is no escape from this in the divine words, which are the entities of the existent things. Thus He said that Jesus is *His word that He cast to Mary* [4:171]. He also said concerning her, *She acknowledged the words of her Lord* [66:12], and these were nothing but Jesus. God designated him as "words" for her because he is many in respect of his manifest and nonmanifest configuration. So, each part of him, whether manifest or nonmanifest, is a word. Hence God said concerning him, *She acknowledged the words of her Lord*, for Jesus is the spirit of God in respect of his whole. In respect of the unity of his manyness are His words, *His word that He cast to Mary*.
>
> A human being speaks through letters, which are the parts of each word intended by the speaker, who is the human being. He desires to give existence to these letters so that through

them what is within himself may be understood. In the same way, the existent things that become manifest allow us to understand from God the desire in the Self of the Real for the *wujūd* of the entities that become manifest.

In speech there is no escape from priority, posteriority, and order. So also, in the existent things, which are the entities of the divine words, there is priority, posteriority, and order. This is made manifest by the Aeon, and the Aeon is God, according to an explicit text. The Prophet said, "Do not curse the Aeon, for God is the Aeon." Within the Aeon, order, priority, and posteriority become manifest in the *wujūd* of the cosmos.

It makes no difference whether the speech is spoken or it abides through the self. If it is in the self, letters must be found in it within the *wujūd* of imagination. If this is not the case, it is not speech. Thus the Arab says,

Speech is in the heart, and the tongue
has been made only the signifier of the heart.

He means, "the signifier of what is in the heart." If the one who expresses himself does not place in his expression what is in the heart by way of exact correspondence, then this is not a signifier. But manyness will be found in the expression along with priority and posteriority. So there is no escape from order in the heart's speech in keeping with this form, and that [speech] is nothing but the imagination specifically.

God says, *Grant him sanctuary until he hears the speech of God* [9:6]. So He ascribed the speech to God and made it heard by the Arab whose sense of hearing is addressed. Hence he perceived it only as demarcated, prior, and posterior.

Those who do not attribute this speech called "the Koran" to God have refused what God has sent down and are ignorant of the realities.

In keeping with what we have said, when the deputy speaks, he has no escape from ascribing the speech to Him and differentiating through his own essence between every two letters and every two words. Thereby the second comes into existence and is attached to the first. Thus, for the sake of a means to wholesomeness [*maṣlaḥa*] that he knows, he arranges what he desires to make manifest. Through his speech, he signifies what is in himself. But not everyone who hears with his ears understands all or some of what the speaker desires—only the one whose insight has been illumined by God.

A listener's share of the speech of a speaker may be the order of its letters, without understanding what the speaker desires through what he speaks. This becomes manifest in the listener when the speaker speaks to him in other than his own dialect and language. Then the listener understands only the order of the letters that become connected to his ears. This is a general connection that belongs to every listener, but such a person does not know what is desired from the words.

In the same way, the whole world knows nothing of the existent things, which are the words of God, save the *wujūd* of their entities specifically. No one knows what is desired from these existent things save the folk of understanding from God. Understanding is something that is superadded to a thing's being heard.

The perfect, rationally speaking servant acts as God's deputy in bringing into existence that of which he speaks by differentiating between his words, since, had he no *wujūd* here, it would not be correct for the entity of the word and the letter to have *wujūd*. In the same way, he also acts as the deputy of the Real in understanding. This is in His words, *And We shall assuredly try you until We know [those of you who struggle and are steadfast]* [47:31]. Thus He described Himself as trying them that He may know something that had not yet occurred.

All this is a deputyship of unity, not a deputyship of other than unity, in respect of the fact that unity has the attribute of standing over the entities of the existent things through the earning that the existent things possess. For *He stands over every soul for what it earns* [13:33]. And *every soul is a pawn to what it has earned* [74:38], which is to say that its earning has bound it.

Were it not for the Real, the existent things would not become distinct from one another and the affair would be one entity, as it is in another respect. The image of this is that human beings, in respect of their definition that envelops all of them, are one in entity, for each of them is one entity in respect of the humanity, even though we know that Zayd is not identical with ʿAmr, nor with any other human individual. Hence the very fact of the Real's making them distinct is their *wujūd*, but the very fact that they are distinct from one another belongs to themselves.

This is why the Word of the Presence adds nothing to the word *Be* in anything engendered from it. On the contrary, *Be* itself, nothing else, is applied to every engendered thing. Were we to halt with *Be*, we would see nothing but one entity. But we halt only with the traces of this word, and these are the engendered things. So they become many, numerous, and distinct through their individuals.

Once the things come together in their own definitions, we know that the word of the Real, which is the word *Be*, is found in this reality. *Be* is a command of *wujūd*. Nothing is known from it except giving existence and *wujūd*. That is why it is not said to an existent thing, "Be a nonexistence!," nor is it said to it, "Be a nonexistent thing!," because this is absurd.

Nonexistence pertains to the very self of some existent things, and for others it follows upon the nonexistence of the condition that would make their *wujūd* sound. Through this reality God is Ever-Creating perpetually and the Preserver perpetually. If He were as is mentioned by the opponents of the Folk of the Real—those who uphold the subsistence of accidents—it would not be correct for the Real to be Ever-Creating perpetually or Preserver of the *wujūd* of some existent things. But since He never ceases to be a creator perpetually, He never ceases to be with each created thing. *He is with you wherever you are* [57:4], and *you are* is an affair of *wujūd*, without doubt.

So there is nothing more delicate than the deputyship of differentiating between words for him who truly knows what we have mentioned. (III 283.15)

From Chapter 369: The Storehouse of the Servant's Posteriority

The root of priority and posteriority can be found in the relation between *wujūd* and the entities. Through *wujūd*, God "precedes" the existent things, and hence He is "prior" to them, while they are posterior to Him. Ibn al-ᶜArabī explains the cosmic order that is established through this relation in the seventh section of his chapter on the keys to the storehouses of munificence.

Within this storehouse is the necessity for the servant to be posterior to the level of his Master and the delivery of his servanthood purely over to God and to no others, for he confessed this when Adam's offspring were taken in God's grip [on the Day of Alast]. The Real desires that this confession should be the servant's constant companion in his life in this world, the site of the veil and the curtain.

After all, the Real has priority over creation through *wujūd* in all respects, as also through placement and level. He was, and there was no created thing. This is the priority of *wujūd*. He measured out, decreed, judged, and exercised an influence that could not be rejected or brought to an end. This is the priority of level. So, *You will not will unless God wills* [76:30] that you should will. This necessitates posteriority to the level of the Real in all respects.

The servant was given manyness so that Unity would belong to Him alone. Every created thing was also given the unity of distinction so that it would have unity as a tasting and know that there is a unity. Thereby it may come to know the Divine Unity in order to give witness that it belongs to God. If a created thing had no tasting of a unity through which it is distinguished from others, it would not know that God has a Unity whereby He is distinguished from His creation. Hence there is no escape from this unity. Manyness possesses the unity of manyness, and every number has a unity that does not belong to any other number, like two, three, and everything beyond, ad infinitum in intellective *wujūd*. Thus every manyness has a unity specific to it.

In any case, the Real necessitated that His servant be posterior to the level of his Creator. In the same way, He made our knowledge of Him posterior to our knowledge of ourselves. The *wujūd* of newly arrived knowledge of Him is posterior through *wujūd* to the *wujūd* of newly arrived knowledge of ourselves.

He ranked parts of the cosmos in excellence over other parts so that we might know ranking in excellence through tasting from ourselves. Through this we come to know that the Real has excellence over us, even if our knowledge of Him is posterior to our knowledge of ourselves. Thereby we come to know that we know ourselves only so that this may signify our knowledge of Him. Thus we know that we are sought for Him, not for ourselves and our entities, since the signifier is sought for what it signifies, not for itself. Therefore the signifier and the object signified are never brought together, so creation and the Real are never brought together in any respect. Hence the servant is a servant for himself, and the Lord is a Lord for Himself.

Servanthood is correct only for the one who knows it. Thereby he knows that in it there is nothing of lordship. Lordship also is correct only for him who knows it. Thereby he knows that in it there is nothing of servanthood. He made posteriority to His lordship necessary for His servants, so He prescribed as shariah for His servant the *ṣalāt* that he might be named the *muṣallī*, that is, the one who is "posterior" to the level of his Lord. He also ascribed the *ṣalāt* to Himself, so that it might be known that the affair bestows the posteriority of the newly arrived knowledge of Him to the newly arrived knowledge of the created thing. Thus He said, *It is He who does* ***ṣalāt*** *over you, and His angels* [33:43]. He also said, *Do* ***ṣalāt*** *for thy Lord* [108:2]. (III 377.35)

Etymologically, the word *ṣalāt* or ritual prayer can be understood to mean back or behind. In the same way, the word *muṣallī*, "he who does the *ṣalāt*," also means "he who lags behind" and is used in this sense in horse racing. With this meaning of the words in mind, we can translate the Koranic verses just cited as *It is He who lags behind you* and *Lag behind thy Lord*.[21] Hence the verses can be read as statements of God's posteriority to the servants (through their knowledge of Him) and the servants' posteriority to God (through their *wujūd*).

Once we come to know that something posterior to something else is cut off from it, then we know that each one [i.e., the Real and creation] is distinct from the other in level, without doubt, even if what is ascribed to the one is ascribed to the other, and even if it is imagined that they share something in common. In fact, there is no sharing, for the level has made each distinct. Each of them accepts the ascription in keeping with what is given by the level through which it is distinct.

For example, we know for certain that the divine names that we have are ascribed to God and to us. And we know for certain through our knowledge of our own level and our knowledge of the Real's level that the attribution of those names—which outwardly share words in common—to God is different from their attribution to us. So He becomes differentiated from us only through His Lordship, and we become differentiated from Him only through our servanthood. Therefore whoever among us clings to his level will not have sinned against himself. On the contrary, he will have given the affair its *ḥaqq*.

Thus the Real has become clear to you
and thus creation has become clear to you.
Say what you will, or name Him,
for each of His words is true.
In His being is no falsehood,
and in our being no truthfulness.

The words of Labīd make the same point: "Is not everything other than God unreal?" The Messenger of God said concerning this line, "The truest verse," that is, this hemistich, "spoken by the Arabs is the words of Labīd."

We say: This is a level that God has specified for and lauded in no one but the rememberer. This is because the rememberer is the one who has knowledge of something, then forgets it, because of the forgetfulness to which human beings are naturally disposed. Thus God says, *They forgot God, so He forgot them* [9:67]. The form of their forgetfulness is that they imagine, because of the deeds, possessions, and ownership that God ascribes to them, that they have a portion in lordship, or that God has appointed a share of it for them through His words, *What your right hands own* [4:3].

Once God has shown solicitude to him among them to whom He shows solicitude and *has given him mercy from Him* [11:28], then he remembers the name of his Lord. God says, "I am the sitting companion of him who remembers Me."

The rememberers are the sitting companions of the Real. Remembrance has bequeathed them the sitting companionship of the Real, and this companionship has bequeathed them witnessing the Real and seeing Him in the things. Al-Ṣiddīq said, "I have never seen anything without seeing God before it," ʿUmar said, "with it," someone else said, "after it," and someone else "in it." Still another said, "I have never seen anything without an intertying with something else."

The vision of the Real bequeaths posteriority to what someone had been imagining—that God had appointed for him a share in lordship, that lordship is one of his descriptions, and that he has an entrance into it in a certain respect. Thus he becomes posterior to this through remembrance. God says, *He remembers the name of his Lord, so he does* ***ṣalāt*** [87:15], that is, he falls back to the posterior station of servitude and ascribes lordship solely to God. Thus *he is prosperous* [87:14] in all his respects, and this attribute is witnessed only by the rememberer. So the rememberer is a servant delivered over purely to God.

Do you not see what He said concerning him who was qualified by the contradictory of this state when his Lord's remembrance—the Koran—came to him, reminding him of his self and his Lord? *He did not acknowledge the truthfulness* of him who brought it, when he said that it was from his Lord, *and he did not do the **ṣalāt*** [75:31]. God is saying that he did not fall back from his making claims and his pretense of greatness, even though he had heard God's word, the *ḥaqq*. Even if the *ḥaqq* does not come from God, it behooves the intelligent person when he hears it from whomsoever he hears it to return to it and uphold it, so that he may be one of its folk. He who rejects the *ḥaqq* has not acknowledged the truthfulness of that speech—no matter who has said it—in what it signifies.

Thus God blames him and says, *but*—introducing a supplement, to complete the story—*he cried lies* [75:32] to him who brought it to him, that is, the Messenger. He also cried lies to the *ḥaqq*, either through his ignorance, such that he did not know that it was the *ḥaqq*, or through his obstinacy, while he knew for certain that it was *ḥaqq* in actual fact. Thus he sought to throw himself into error, because this Messenger had brought it. God says in the case of those who had this attribute, *They denied [Our signs]—though their souls were convinced of them—wrongfully and claiming highness* [27:14].

Then God says, *and he turned away* [75:32] after crying lies to the *ḥaqq* and to him who brought it. So *he turned away* from the *ḥaqq*.

Then he went to his folk while strutting [75:33], which is the business of a person who pretends greatness, whose thoughts are occupied, who reflects and is bewildered, and who is made negligent by what he hears. After all, the apparent sense is that he knows that it is the *ḥaqq*, since God does not bring a miracle save to those whom He knows have the strength to accept it through what He has mounted within them. This is why the proofs are diverse for every prophet and in the case of every group. If the prophet came to them with a sign that was not in their capacity to accept because of their ignorance, God would not take them to task for turning their backs or for turning away from it.

God is knowing, wise, and just. He who delays the *ḥaqq* of others because of what he rightfully demands in himself has been fair to himself, and the person who has a *ḥaqq* against him has nothing to claim from him. Such a person has come to possess the good with both hands, so God has acquainted him with the all-comprehensive good, all of it. After all, *He who has been given wisdom has been given much good* [2:269]. For the "wise" is he who places the thing in its level and "gives to each that has a *ḥaqq* its *ḥaqq*." So he has the conclusive argument and the brain-crushing word. His witnessing is not cut off and the divine help does not fall behind assisting him in his worship. For we have supposed that he is a servant of a master, not that he is something owned. Being owned may be in him in whom servanthood is understood, and it may be in him in whom it is not understood. The state of the servant is hearing and obeying his master. Everything other than the servant is something owned, in which the owner acts freely as he wills without any laudation accruing to the thing when it does not prevent the free activity within it.

The person in whom servanthood is understood is otherwise, for when the Real acts freely in the servant and he stands in the station of possessions, God lauds him for this, because God has specified for him in his configuration the capacity to prevent and reject the word of the Real, and He has given him the ability to obey and disobey in that for which He seeks to put him to use. Hence he is lauded for this, just as God has lauded the angels with His words, *They disobey God not in what He commands them, and they do what they are commanded* [66:6]. If they did not have in their capacity and configuration both what requires rejecting God's command and what requires accepting it, God would not have lauded them as He lauded them, that is, for not disobeying and for doing what He commands them. After all, there is no laudation for someone under compulsion.

Do you not see that when the person who does the *ṣalāt* stands before his Lord in his *ṣalāt* while placing one hand over the other, the abased servant is occupying himself before his Master with the state of whispered prayers?[22] The Sunnah has brought this [holding of the hands], and it is more beautiful than letting the hands drop down to the sides. This is because God has "divided the *ṣalāt* into two halves between Him and His servant." One part is delivered purely over to Him, from the outset of the Fātiḥa to His words, *day of judgment* [1:3]. This corresponds to the servant's right hand, since *The strength altogether belongs to God* [2:165], so we have given Him the right hand. The other part is delivered over purely to the servant, from His words *Guide us* [1:5] to the end of the surah. This part corresponds to the left hand, since this is the weaker side, and this is the servant's level, for he was *created of weakness* at the beginning and will be returned to *weakness* [30:54] at the end. Still another part is between God and His servant. So this part brings God together with His servant. It is His words, *Thee alone we worship, and Thee alone we ask for help* [1:4].

Because of this bringing together, the servant brings together his two hands in the *ṣalāt* when he stands in the prayer. Thus the *ṣalāt* of the servant is perfected through his bringing together his two hands. The form of this placing one hand on the other is that he puts the right hand on the left hand, just as we have stipulated that the right hand belongs to God, so it possesses highness over the left. Its form is that he places the nonmanifest side of his right palm on the back of the left palm, the wrist, and the forearm so that it will bring together, through encompassing, the whole hand that God has commanded the servant to purify completely in the ablution before the *ṣalāt*. Thus he holds the wrist and the palm and forearm that are adjacent to it. So consider this wisdom! How beautifully displayed it is for the Possessor of Two Eyes!

Then the Prophet prohibited the servant from lifting up his eyes to heaven in his *ṣalāt*, for "God is in the kiblah" of the servant. Nothing is before him in his standing save the horizon, so that is his kiblah toward which he turns. Then He praised for him that he should consider the site of his prostration, for this is what alerts him to knowledge of himself and his servanthood. That is why God placed nearness in the *ṣalāt* within the state of prostration. Human beings are not preserved from Satan in anything of their *ṣalāt* save the prostration for, when they prostrate themselves, "Satan withdraws from them, weeping" for himself, "and saying, 'The son of Adam was commanded to prostrate himself, and he prostrated himself, so the Garden belongs to him. I was commanded to prostrate myself, and I refused, so the Fire belongs to me.'" (III 378.16)

6. *Divine and Cosmic Relations*

The cosmos manifests the properties of the divine names. To understand the significance of the cosmos, one needs to understand the meanings of the names. Most divine names have an obvious connection to human psycho-physiological and ethical qualities, such as Living, Knowing, Desiring, Powerful, Speaking, Hearing, Seeing, Merciful, and Compassionate. Clearly such names establish principles of ranking in degrees of excellence, since some loci manifest them more plainly or more intensely than others. However, none of the names just mentioned, in itself, calls to mind the structure of the cosmos. Among the most beautiful names, four in particular do suggest issues of cosmic order and structure, though they have no immediate connection to ethical and moral issues. The Koran mentions these four together in the verse, *He is the First and the Last and the Manifest and the Nonmanifest* (57:3).

These four attributes can be understood as designating two dimensions of cosmic order, one of which is "horizontal" or "temporal" and the other "vertical" or "spatial." First and Last call to mind a temporal order in which God is the Alpha and the Omega. The cosmos comes into existence from Him inasmuch as He is the First and returns to Him inasmuch as He is the Last. In contrast, Manifest and Nonmanifest refer to the vertical structure of the cosmos. At the lowest, manifest level stand the things that meet the eye or that can be perceived with the help of sensory faculties. At the highest, nonmanifest level—beyond seventy or seventy thousand veils of light and darkness—stands the divine Essence, which is totally and utterly hidden to all things.

Ibn al-ᶜArabī perceives many more implications in these names than those just suggested. Invariably, his discussions help clarify the various sorts of relations that can be envisaged as soon as we think in terms of cosmic order. To begin with, however, he accepts that these four names establish the basic division (*taqsīm*) of the various sorts of *wujūd*—though he offers other divisions and classifications as well.

> God says, *He is the First and the Last and the Manifest and the Nonmanifest*. Thereby He calls attention to the fact that He is *wujūd*, all of it, for this is the division of *wujūd*. (IV 70.5)

The First and the Last

God is First because His *wujūd* cannot not be. Hence He takes precedence over the possible things, which may or may not be, and which, in any case, can only come into existence once He gives them *wujūd*. God is Last because all things return to that from which they arose. "He is the First through necessity and the Last through the return of the whole affair to Him" (IV 326.4).

Ibn al-ʿArabī finds reference to the ontological order established by the names First and Last in Surah 112, called the surah of *tawḥīd*, which mentions the word *aḥad*, "one," both at the beginning and at the end of its four verses. In the first case, "one" refers to God: *Say: He is God, One*. In the second, it refers to everything else: *nor is His equal any one*. Thus, according to this surah, both God and everything else can be called *aḥad*, which, as an attribute, is *aḥadiyya* or "unity." However, God's unity is unlike creaturely unity, because His Unity is the source and origin of every other unity. His Unity pertains to the First, the origin, the ultimately prior. Other unities pertain to that which grows up from the First. The following passage derives from the already mentioned Chapter 90 of the *Futūḥāt*, in which Ibn al-ʿArabī explains why God has chosen certain things over other things.

> Among the surahs, God chose *He is God, One* [112], because it is specified for Him. None of the engendered things is mentioned, save only that the unity of each one is not similar to His unity. In this affirmation of unity in this surah there is an unusual knowledge for him to whom God opens it up, for He opens the surah with His unity and concludes it with the unity of the created things. So you should know that the engendered things are intertied with Him as the Last is intertied with the First, not as the First is intertied with the Last, for the Last seeks the First, but the First does not seek the Last. He is the *Independent of the worlds* [3:97] in respect of His Essence, but He seeks the Last in respect of that which is named "God" and described by unity.
>
> Thus have I called your attention to the sources of the knowledge that this surah comprises through the posterior unity. Although this unity is intertied with the first unity, it is not like it, for it seeks Him, but He does not seek it. *You are the poor toward God, and God—He is the Independent, the Praiseworthy* [35:15]. (II 172.11)

It should not be thought that the First and the Last pertain simply to the beginning and the end of the cosmos, such that, in the day-to-day workings of the universal order, these names have nothing to do and are "ineffectual" (*muʿaṭṭal*). Ibn al-ʿArabī often reminds us that all the divine names exhibit their traces in *wujūd* constantly and forever. Hence the First and Last must manifest themselves at the present moment. They do this through renewing creation at each instant. As the First, God is the source of the self-disclosure of *wujūd* that gives existence to the entity at each successive moment. As the Last, He establishes the "named term" (*ajal musammā*) of the specific properties and limits that define the entity and cease with each new self-disclosure, only to be replaced by new properties and limits.

> God established the occasions and the wisdoms and He set up an order within the cosmos through the *wujūd* of lights and darknesses in accordance with what is required by the Manifest and the Nonmanifest. In the same way He appointed beginnings for things and ends for their measures through named terms, and this extends ad infinitum. So there is nothing but perpetual beginnings and ends from His two names, First and Last. From these two realities derive the beginnings and the ends perpetually. So engendered existence is new perpetually, and

there is everlasting subsistence in engendering. (II 675.12)

From Chapter 558: The Presence of Firstness

In his chapter on the divine names, Ibn al-ᶜArabī refers to the First and the Last partly in connection to the fact that they establish the relation that we know as "time" (*zamān*). The Arabic adjectives *awwal* and *ākhir* have comparative as well as superlative senses, so *awwal* means both first and former, and *ākhir* means both last and latter. That which is former has priority (*taqaddum*) and that which is latter has posteriority (*taᵓakhkhur*), and these two terms, as noted in the previous chapter, are important indicators of temporal order. From the same root as *awwal* we have the word *taᵓwīl* or "interpretation," which means to take something back to its first principle. This helps explain why the Shaykh says "interpret" in the third line of the poetry.

Glory be to Him who gathered
His servants for His remembrance
on Friday,
for the First selected it.
Through it the God sealed the *wujūd*
of His servants
according to the Shariah
and reason, my friends.[1]
So interpret what I say.
I have brought
a plain wisdom disclosed by
the Most Descended Station.
When He brought Himself down
from the highness of His place
in His Essence, the lowest
hid Him from us.
He is the Guardian, I doubt not,
and He is
the Munificent toward His servants,
the Bounteous.

The companion of this Presence is called "the Servant of the First." He is usually surnamed "the Father of the Moment" because of what souls gain of the priority of the time that is named "aeon," which is differentiated by the moments. Thus the surname of the Servant of the First is "the Father of the Moment," just as the surname of Adam is "the Father of Mortal Man," for the First is a father in relation to moments, like Adam in relation to other people.

Through the Presence of Firstness every first becomes manifest among the individuals of every species, like Adam in the human species, the Garden of Eden among the Gardens, the First Intellect among the spirits, the Throne among the corporeal bodies, water among the pillars, and the circular shape among the shapes. Then the affair descends to the particular things of the cosmos, and it is said, "The first to speak of self-power [*qadar*] in Basra was Maᶜbad al-Juhanī," and "The first to shoot an arrow in the path of God was Saᶜd ibn Abī Waqqāṣ," and "The first poem recited in the human world was,

The lands and those upon them have
changed,
so the face of the earth is soiled and ugly."

This poem is attributed to Adam, after Cain slew his brother Abel. The Prophet said, "No one is slain wrongfully without Adam's son being liable for the load, for he was the first to set down the sunnah of slaying wrongfully."

I have a fascicle on "firsts," an eloquent fascicle that I wrote in Malatya, one of the cities of Anatolia, or in Mecca—God knows best.[2]

The first house established for the people as a place of worship was the Kaabah, and the first divine name in level is the name Living.

And God speaks the **ḥaqq**, *and He guides on the path* [33:4]. (IV 298.5)

From Chapter 558: The Presence of Lastness

In discussing the divine name Last, Ibn al-ᶜArabī continues explaining how the First and the Last are the principles of time. Then he turns to the issue of *khilāfa*—caliphate or vicegerency—first in its political and then in its cosmic sense. The root meaning of this term is coming behind or after, succession. The *khalīfa*—caliph or vicegerent—is he who comes after someone else and succeeds him or represents him in his function. Thus a caliph is "latter" in relation to the person whom he succeeds. The political caliphs succeeded the Prophet in his legal and governmental functions. The cosmic vicegerents stand in God's stead in ruling the cosmos, since they are His realized forms, so they are God's vicegerents and Muhammad's inheritors. Then the Shaykh turns to another discussion closely connected to the name Last, that is, the last world. The term *ākhira* or "last world," commonly translated as "next world" or "hereafter," is the feminine form of the adjective *ākhir* and is understood to be an abbreviation for *al-dār al-ākhira*, "the last abode," or *al-ḥayāt al-ākhira*, "the last life." In the same way, *dunyā* or "this world," means literally "closer" or "closest" and is short for *al-dār al-dunyā*, "the closest abode," or *al-ḥayāt al-dunyā*, "the closest life."

By God, He is the First and the Last
only to preserve the circling cosmos.
For it is incapable of preserving itself
since He has described the created thing as falling short.
Through the Last, He preserves it
so that the One may meet the Last.
Our affair is all a circle
for the First joins to the Last,
and He discloses His Essence to us
in the form of the Nonmanifest and the Manifest.

The companion of this Presence is called "the Servant of the Last."

The limit of the "last" extends downward from the second that follows the first. The second is called the "last" because it has the property of posteriority in relation to firstness, without doubt.

If a posterior thing deserves firstness, then it is posterior to the first only through some affair—the simplest and most obvious of which is time—not that worthiness exists within it in every respect. Then it is known that the property that rules over its posteriority and the priority of something else belongs to time. Take, for example, the caliphate of Abū Bakr, ʿUmar, then ʿUthmān, then ʿAlī. Every one of them was suited for priority and was worthy for the caliphate. There was no property with God that ruled for the priority of one over the others by virtue of an excellence that He knew that sought the caliphate, so there was only time: Since God knew that Abū Bakr would die before ʿUmar, that ʿUmar would die before ʿUthmān, and that ʿUthmān would die before ʿAlī, and since each possessed honor with God, He made the caliphate of the community as it happened. Hence He gave priority to the one among these four whose term preceded that of the others. Thus, in my view, the ones given priority were not given priority because they were more worthy than those who were posterior. And God knows best.

What is apparent is that this derives from the terms. After all, if allegiance had been sworn to two caliphs, one of them should have been killed, because of the plain text that has come.[3] If the people had sworn allegiance to one of the three other than Abū Bakr—and it was inescapable in God's knowledge that Abū Bakr should be a caliph and that there cannot be two caliphs—then, if one of the three was deposed and Abū Bakr was given the rule, it would have been disrespect toward the deposed person. Those who strove to depose him would have charged that the one who was deposed had destroyed the caliphate and that to him was ascribed caprice, wrongdoing, and transgression. If he had not been deposed, then Abū Bakr would have died during his days without being a caliph, but it was inescapable in God's knowledge that he would have the caliphate. So there was no escape from his priority, because of the priority of his term over that of his companion. So also was the priority of ʿUmar ibn al-Khaṭṭāb, ʿUthmān, ʿAlī, and al-Ḥasan.

None of those who were prior was prior because he had more of a *ḥaqq* than the others, and none of those who were posterior was posterior because of a lack of worthiness. But the people did not know this except after God had clarified it for them through the caliphs' terms and their deaths one after another in the caliphate. For us, in our outward view, priority occurred only because of the terms, or because of some other affair in God's knowledge that we have not come to understand, and God preserved the level for them—may God be pleased with all of them! This derives from the property of posteriority and priority.

God possesses firstness because He brings everything into existence. He also possesses lastness, for He says, *To Him the whole affair is returned* [11:123], and He says, *To Him you will be returned* [2:245], and *Surely unto God all affairs come home* [42:53]. So He is the Last, just as He is the First.

Between the First and the Last become manifest the levels of all the divine names. The Last has no property save in the return of every affair to Him.

Since God is the First, the perfect human being is the last, since he stands in the second level, which is vicegerency, and he is also the last through his natural creation, for he is the last of the progeny. When God desired the vicegerency and imamate for him, He began by giving existence to the cosmos. He readied it, *proportioned* it, *balanced* it [82:7], and gave it order as an abiding empire. Once the cosmos was prepared to receive the leadership of an imam, God configured the natural body of the human being and blew into it of the divine spirit. He created him in His form for the sake of appointing him as a vicegerent. Thus he became manifest in his body, and he came to be what is named "Adam." He placed him in the earth as a vicegerent. Part of Adam's affair and state with the angels was as God mentioned to us in His book. He placed the imamate in his children until the day of resurrection.

Thus the perfect human being is the last in relation to the divine form, and the last also in relation to the natural, engendered form. So he is last in self and in body, and he is last through the return of the affair of the cosmos to him, for he is the intended object. Through him this world is inhabited and comes to abide. When he departs from it, this world will disappear, the heaven will spin dizzily [52:9], the stars will be scattered [82:2], the sun will be darkened [81:1], *the mountains will be set in motion* [78:20], the pregnant camels will be neglected [81:4], the seas will be set boiling [81:6], and the abode of this world in its entirety will go. Inhabitation will be transferred to the last abode through the transfer of the human being. Then the Garden and the Fire will be inhabited—and after this world, there is no abode save the Garden and the Fire.

The name First belongs to "the first," which is the abode of this world, and the name Last belongs to "the last," which is the last world. God says to Muhammad, *And the last is better for thee than the first* [93:4] only because there is no target beyond the Last, for it is the furthest limit. He who gains its degree will never be transferred, for he will possess fixity, subsistence, and perpetuity. But the First is not like that, for it is transferred through the levels until it finally reaches the Last, which is the furthest limit, where it comes to a halt. That is why God says, *The last is better for thee than the first; thy Lord shall give thee, and thou shalt be well pleased* [93:4–5]. God will give him the attribute of subsistence, perpetuity, and perpetual bliss from which there is no transferal and no disappearance. This is what the property of this Presence gives to him. *And God speaks the* ***ḥaqq****, and He guides on the path* [33:4]. (IV 298.20)

The Manifest and the Nonmanifest

Far more often than he mentions the implications of the names First and Last, Ibn al-ʿArabī discusses the names Manifest and Nonmanifest. Inasmuch as *wujūd* is constantly renewed and all things have beginnings and ends, the First and the Last always display their properties. But in the Shaykh's view, the historical unfolding of time and the succession of events in the external world are only of secondary interest, since the most basic issue is the present moment, in which *wujūd* is always and forever with us. The cosmos and the self are nothing but ever-present signs, that is, the manifest Real pointing to the nonmanifest Real. When people forget this, they become like those mentioned in the Koranic verse, *They know a manifest side of the life of this world, but of the last world they are heedless* (30:7).

The attributes of manifestation and nonmanifestation belong not only to God but also to the cosmos. When this is taken into account, there are many ways of viewing the various relations that are established between God and God, God and the cosmos, and the cosmos and the cosmos. God is certainly manifest to Himself, but is He nonmanifest to Himself? God is nonmanifest to creation, but how exactly is He manifest to it? In what ways are creatures manifest to and hidden from each other, and what does this have to do with *wujūd* and the entities? The more Ibn al-ʿArabī meditates upon questions such as these, the more bewildered the reader is likely to become. And this, of course, is precisely the goal. Categorical knowledge of the situation as it is in itself (*al-amr ʿalā mā huwa ʿalayh*) is impossible, for the actual situation is defined by *wujūd*, the Essence of the Real. The various ways of envisaging the situation are all correct, but, from other points of view, each is inadequate. He/not He.

Many of the Shaykh's discussions circle around the issue of what it is that is manifest to us. Is it *wujūd* or is it the entities? The answer is simply that it depends on how you look at it.

The Entity of the Real is what is described by *wujūd*, while the properties of the entities of the cosmos are the manifest in this Entity, or, He is the Manifest through them. (III 107.28)

The cosmos stays upon its root in nonexistence, but it has a ruling property in what becomes manifest in the *wujūd* of the Real. So there is nothing there but the Real—undifferentiated and differentiated. (IV 92.21)

From one point of view, the names Manifest and Nonmanifest refer to God's relation to Himself and to the other. To Himself He is manifest, but to others He is nonmanifest. Hence nonmanifestation is a quality that can only be understood in terms of creation.

He is the Manifest, the Nonmanifest. He is manifest to Himself, so He never ceases to be Manifest, and He is nonmanifest to His creatures, so He never ceases to be Nonmanifest. Hence He will never be known. (IV 326.4)

When Ibn al-ʿArabī juxtaposes the Real with creation, He sometimes contrasts them by saying that the Real is the Nonmanifest and creation is the Real as the Manifest. Inasmuch as *wujūd* is hidden from us, God is the Nonmanifest, but inasmuch as the whole cosmos is *wujūd*'s self-disclosure, God is the Manifest.

The manifest of the Real is creation,
and the nonmanifest of creation is the Real. (IV 246.1)

The cosmos is not identical with the Real; it is only what becomes manifest within the Real *Wujūd*. (IV 316.11).

God's *tanzīh* is that He shares with nothing in *wujūd*. He is *wujūd*, nothing else. That which He calls the "cosmos" is the name Manifest, and it is His face. That of Him which is nonmanifest in relation to His Manifest is the name Nonmanifest, and that is His He-ness. So He becomes manifest to the cosmos, and He remains absent from it.

As for pains and pleasures, these derive from the contrariety and compatibility of the names. Through the names, the forms become many, for it is the names that assume shapes so that some of them perceive others. So He encompasses all of them and is incomparable with any of them, for He has curtaining from them and self-disclosure within them. (IV 87.5)

Given that God created the cosmos in His own form, He configured it in keeping with His names. Just as He is both manifest and nonmanifest, so also the cosmos is both apparent and hidden, witnessed and concealed. The fact that we know some things and are ignorant of most is demanded by *wujūd* itself, which is hidden in its Essence and revealed in its self-disclosures. The whole dynamic of our existence, with its comings and goings, its appearances and disappearances, its disclosures and curtainings, is rooted in these two names.

Since God named Himself Manifest and Nonmanifest, this requires that in relation to us the affair of *wujūd* should stand between disclosed and hidden. What He discloses to us is the disclosed, and what He curtains from us is the hidden. But all of this is disclosed to Him.

God's Messenger said in his supplication, "O God, I ask Thee by every name by which Thou hast named Thyself or taught to any one of Thy creatures." This is what is disclosed to anyone to whom God has taught it and hidden from anyone to whom He has not taught it. Then the Messenger said, "or kept to Thyself in the knowledge of Thy absent." This is what is hidden from everything other than God, so none knows it but God. After all, *He knows the mystery,* that is, what is between Him and His creatures, *and the more hidden* [20:7], that is, what none knows but He, like the *keys to the absent* that are *at Him—none knows them but He* [6:59]. So *He is the knower of the absent,* which is the hidden, *and the witnessed* [6:73], which is the disclosed. In addition, the possible things that He has brought into existence are the disclosed, and those that He has not brought into existence are the hidden.

The cosmos is never empty of these two relations in this world and the last world. When increase occurs in the cosmos to the cosmos, this derives from the hidden. Increase never ceases, for the cosmos is an increase, emerging from hiddenness to disclosure neverendingly.

The Real hears the disclosed asking of the askers by way of the name Manifest, and He hears their hidden asking by way of the name Nonmanifest. When He bestows upon the asker what he asks for, the name Nonmanifest bestows it upon the Manifest, and the Manifest bestows it upon the asker. Hence the Manifest is the veil-keeper of the Nonmanifest, and the disclosed is the veil-keeper of the hidden, just as awareness is the veil-keeper of knowledge. (III 321.21)

Looked at in terms of its overall structure, the cosmos can be divided into manifest and nonmanifest domains. Although the whole cosmos, including the spiritual world, is manifest in relation to the nonmanifest He-ness, some of its worlds are nonmanifest in relation to others and hence can be called nonmanifest in a relative sense. For example, the world of spirits and angels is nonmanifest in relation to the world of bodies.

In respect of its parts and its differentiations, the cosmos is like the limbs of the name Manifest. In respect of its meanings and the differentiations of its levels, it is like nonmanifest, spiritual faculties of the name Nonmanifest, faculties that are known only through their traces. Hence the configuration of the cosmos stands on *The Manifest and the Nonmanifest; and He is knower of each thing* [57:3]. (III 106.31)

The name Manifest has a special relation to the resurrection, where everyone will see God. As the Shaykh points out in many places, the realities that are nonmanifest in the present world will be manifest in the last world, and what is manifest in the present world will be nonmanifest there. This explains why secrets will be divulged and people will be brought face to face with their own intentions and character traits, embodied in appropriate forms, whether through the bliss of the Garden or the chastisement of the Fire.[4] But mercy wins out in the end, for the whole cosmos, whether in this world or the last world, is nothing but the words of the All-Merciful, articulated in His Breath. The following passage pertains to a section in which the Shaykh describes the "earth of the Mustering," where people will be gathered on the day of resurrection. Toward the end of the quotation, which begins with a reference to hadiths that speak of intercession (*shafā*ᶜ*a*) at the Mustering, the Shaykh reminds us that everything that happens in the cosmos is determined by the Manifest, while the Nonmanifest remains eternally unknown.

The interceders will intercede—and God will accept what He wills of their intercession, and He will reject of it what He wills—because on that day, God will deploy mercy over the hearts of the interceders. When He rejects the intercession of some, He does so not to diminish them, nor because of lack of mercy toward the one for whom intercession is made. On the contrary, through this He desires only to make the divine favor manifest to some of His servants, for He Himself undertakes their felicity and removes wretchedness from them. Among them will be those whose wretchedness will be removed by taking them out of the Fire and placing them in the Gardens.

It has reached us that God's intercession will take place when the Most Merciful of the merciful intercedes with the All-Dominating Avenger. These are the levels of the divine names, not a realized intercession. For God says concerning that day, "The angels, the prophets, and the faithful will have interceded, and there will remain the Most Merciful of the merciful." What is understood from this signifies not that He "intercedes," but that He Himself undertakes to take whomsoever He will from the Fire into the Garden and to transfer the state of the folk of the Fire from the wretchedness of pains to the felicity of the removal of pains. This is the measure of their bliss, and He has willed it.

God will fill Gehenna with His wrath that is mixed [with mercy] and His decree, and [He will fill] the Garden with His good-pleasure. Hence mercy will be all-inclusive, and bliss will be deployed. The creatures will be in the form of the Real, as they are in this world, undergoing transmutations through His transmutation. The last form into which He will transmute Himself in exercising His ruling properties over His servants is the form of good-pleasure. The Real will transmute Himself into the form of bliss, for the first to whom the Compassionate and the Pardoner will show compassion, pardon, and bliss will be Himself, through the removal of the tightness and wrath that are directed toward those who have made Him wrathful. Then this will permeate the objects of wrath.

If anyone has understood, I have given him security. He who does not understand will come to know and understand, for the final issue is at Him, and God, in respect of His knowing Himself and in His own He-ness and independence, is as He is.

All that has reached us through reports and has been given to us by unveiling is only states that become manifest, stations that become individualized, and meanings that become embodied. Thereby the Real teaches His servants the meaning of the divine name Manifest, which is what appears from all this, and the divine name Nonmanifest, which is His He-ness. For He has named Himself by these names for us. Everything in which the cosmos dwells—taking control, undergoing fluctuation, transmutation in the forms of Real and creation—derives from the property of His name Manifest. It is the extreme limit of the knowledge of the cosmos and the knowers of God.

As for the name Nonmanifest, it refers to Him, not us. We have nothing in our hands of it save *Nothing is as His likeness* [42:11] in some of its plausible senses. However, attributes of *tanzīh* have a connection with the name Nonmanifest, even if within them there is a certain assertion of limits. Nevertheless, nothing more than this is possible, for it is the furthest limit of what our preparedness gives us to understand.

As for His words, *None of us there is, but he shall arrive at [the Fire]* [19:71], this is because the path to the Garden passes over it, so there is no escape from this arrival.

When none of the folk of the Garden remains on the earth of the Mustering, all of it will turn into fire, that is, the abode of the Fire—even if, within it, there is also the Bitter Cold. Thus Gehenna will extend from the underside of the [sphere of the fixed] stars to the lowest of the low. (III 440.2)

From Chapter 558: The Presence of Manifestation

At the beginning of his discussion of the name Manifest in his chapter on the divine names, Ibn al-ʿArabī poses a few questions that arise when we think about God as Manifest and Nonmanifest. Meditating upon these questions quickly leads to bewilderment, because we realize that no one is manifest, neither He nor we. In fact, we cannot know the actual situation of the universe, so the only rational course is to accept the reports of the prophets and trust in God. Much of this passage is an assertion of the futility of merely rational attempts to come to know the cosmos, the self, and God.

Manifestation has a precondition
that confirms it;
nothing makes Him manifest
save what predominates.
The girls who glance
with their black eyes
take away tears
and kindle our hearts with flames.
If someone comes to you and says,
"They're only half,"
surely the better half
is that which has gone.
I paid them with cash
that I might win them,
and they spoke no reproach—
thus do I work in gold.
Were they to become manifest
to every eye,
their brilliance would blind,
so they stay veiled.

The companion of this Presence is called "the servant of the Manifest" and he is titled "the Manifest with God's command." This Presence belongs to God because He is manifest to Himself, but not to His creation. No one whatsoever perceives Him other than He. What this Presence gives to us is the manifestation of the properties of His most beautiful names and the manifestation of the properties of our entities in the *wujūd* of the Real. But He is behind what becomes manifest.

Our entities are not perceived by vision, the Entity of the Real is not perceived by vision, and the entities of His names are not perceived by vision. But we do not doubt that we have perceived something by vision, and that is what our eyesights witness. It is nothing but the properties that belong to our entities and have become manifest to us in the *wujūd* of the Real. Hence He is a locus of manifestation for our entities, so they become manifest just as forms become manifest in mirrors. The forms are not identical with the viewer, because they have something of the property of the locus of disclosure. Nor are they identical with the locus of disclosure, because they have something that opposes its property. There is no third, outside affair upon which perception falls. Yet perception has occurred. So what is this thing that is perceived, and who is the perceiver? Who is the cosmos? Who is the Real? Who is the Manifest? Who is the locus of manifestation? Who makes the locus manifest?

If these are relations, relations are affairs of nonexistence. However, the cause of vision is that the object seen has the preparedness to be perceived, so the nonexistent thing would have been seen. Thus we have conceded that the nonexistent thing is seen. Who then is the seer?

If the seer is also a relation, then, just as it has the preparedness to see, so also it has the preparedness to be seen. If it is not a relation and is an affair of *wujūd,* then just as it is the seer, so also it is the seen, since what we see sees us. If we say that it is a relation in respect of the fact that it is seen by us, then we will say that it is an affair of *wujūd* inasmuch as it sees us, just as we have said concerning us in respect of the fact that we perceive him.

So the affair is one, for we have become bewildered in us and in Him. Who are we? Who is He? One of us said to Him, *Show me, that I may look upon Thee!* He replied, *Thou shalt not see Me* [7:143]. He said concerning Himself, *Does he not know that God sees?* [96:14]. His report is true, and He knew that some in the cosmos know that God sees. Then He said with the particle of emendation [i.e., *but*], joining this to that, *"But behold the mountain—if it stays fast in its place, then thou shalt see Me."* Then He *disclosed Himself to the mountain* and the mountain crumbled to dust. I do not know if this was because of a vision, or because of a precursor of vision. No, rather it was because of a precursor of vision. *And Moses fell down thunderstruck* [7:143] because of that precursor.

When he recovered, he said [. . .] I repent, or I return to the state in which I was not asking vision from Thee, *and I am the first of those who have faith* [7:143], that is those who acknowledge the truthfulness of Thy statement, *Thou shalt not see Me,* for this statement descended for the first time only on me, so I am the first to have faith in it, and everyone who hears it until the day of resurrection will follow me in having faith in it.

God became manifest neither to the seeker of vision nor to the mountain, because, had the mountain or Moses seen Him, it would have stayed firm and would not have crumbled to dust and he would not have become thunderstruck. After all, He is *wujūd,* so He bestows nothing but *wujūd,* for "The good, all of it, is in His hands," and *wujūd,* all of it, is good. Since He is not seen, He leaves the trace of thunderstruckness and crumbling to dust. These are states of annihilation, and annihilation is similar to nonexistence. But the Real does not make the entities of things nonexistent.

Nevertheless, relative nonexistence comes from Him. This is "taking away" and "transferal." Thus He transfers you or takes you away from one state to another state, even though your entity exists in both states, and from one place to another place, even though your entity exists in both of them and between them. This is His words, *If He wills, He will take you away [. . .] and bring others* [4:133]. He "brings" through the attribute of power and He takes away through desire inasmuch as it is a specific taking away. These differentiations cannot come to be in that which is not differentiated, and *wujūd* is not a characteristic of the differentiated, for we differentiate the nonexistent into the "impossible" and the "possible," even though it is nonexistent.

There remains discussion of who it is that makes it differentiated. The discussion here is like the previous discussion of the seer and the seen.

So what should we say? Upon what should we rely? I saw that we should leave the affair in its state, whatever it may be. For personal desires have been made present, perceptions occur, pleasures rule, and witnessing is perpetual while bliss abides through it. Let it be whatever it may be—nonexistence or *wujūd,* Real or creation! Since nothing that we need has been taken away from us, we do not care.

If the divine report-giving occurs, talking about it and considering it as it is now neither adds to the affair nor subtracts from it. After all, once the report-giving comes, there is no escape from a hearing that becomes connected to this address—and an understanding, a signified, a speaker, a hearer. This is exactly what we are busy with, so it is better to leave all that [other discussion], and we should say what everyone says. After all, the whole affair in this is one entity in bewilderment. So all of it is truthfulness and nothing is unreal, since it occurs in the mind, in the entity, and in all the perceptions.

So "inclination to peace" is better for human beings, for, in the metaphorical interpretation and the allusions, the "they" in *if they incline to peace* [8:61] are the thoughts that lead you to consider that which you can do without. Here, the Real has put them in the place of the enemies for the folk of allusions. So *if they incline to peace*—this is reconciliation, which is to leave the affair as it is and not to plunge into it. After all, you plunge into it because it is a sign of God from Him, for He has said, *When thou seest those who plunge into Our signs, turn away from them until they plunge into some other speaking* [6:68]; which is nothing but busying themselves with "What should we eat and drink, whom should we marry, what should we do?"—that is, the Shari'ite deeds that lead to felicity in the last world.

So what are these affairs? We say: We do not know. We only act as we have been commanded, so that we might reach what has been said to us, for we have not been lied to. On the contrary, we have seen that everything that has passed is a *ḥaqq*—nothing of it was faulty. So also will be what remains.

And indeed *they* have *inclined to peace*. So God has commanded us, for He said to His Prophet, *do thou also incline to it, and trust in God* [8:61]. The intelligent person is he who believes in hearing and obeying God's command. This is a state that is granted in advance and an ease.

Manifestation is nothing but
what becomes manifest
and nonmanifestation is nothing
but what stays curtained.
Where is "taking away"
and where is "bringing"?
Where is settling down,
where a place to rest?
So from us to Him,
and from Him to us—
all this through the property
of measuring out and decree.
Weep not
for what has escaped,
for nothing has escaped,
and no joy turns bad.
There is nothing
but an object of attribution
and what is attributed to it.
So cross over and take heed!
Say "What Thou hast willed
upon whom Thou hast willed,"
for *wujūd*
has become manifest with this.

*And God speaks the **ḥaqq**, and He guides on the path* [33:4]. (IV 299.22)

From Chapter 558: The Presence of Nonmanifestation

After discussing the name Manifest, Ibn al-ʿArabī turns to the name Nonmanifest. He is especially concerned to bring out the implications of this name for the vision of God. In the third paragraph he refers to the "bellies" in order to point to the etymological sense of the term Nonmanifest. The Arabic word for "bellies" is *buṭūn* (plural of *baṭn*), which happens to be the same form taken by the Arabic word for "nonmanifestation." Thus the term *nonmanifest* can be understood to mean "that which is in the belly."

In the "mystery"
His reality is nonmanifest,
but He makes the "overt"
manifest to every eye.
If not for nonmanifestation
and His wisdom's mystery,
God would have lifted no creature
over mortal man.
Nothing gives it excellence
save only safety
from imperfections, fantasies,
and change.
Were anyone to reach Him
in respect of his configuration,
the folk of God's munificence
would reach Him through reflection.
Had not the Ever-Creating made contact
with the angel's form,
no creature among them would know
what I report.
The angels' faces are humbled
before us in prostration
because of the spirits and forms
that we contain.
That is why we fluctuate
through His states forever
in benefit—if that is the affair—
or in harm.

The companion of this Presence is called "the servant of the Nonmanifest."

God says, *He is the First and the Last and the Manifest and the Nonmanifest* [57:3]. Nonmanifestation pertains specifically to us, just as manifestation pertains specifically to Him. Although He possesses nonmanifestation, He is not nonmanifest to Himself or from Himself, just as He is not manifest to us. Hence the nonmanifestation by which He describes Himself is only in respect to us. He remains forever nonmanifest to our perception of Him, whether in the sensory or suprasensory domain. *Nothing is as His likeness* [42:11], but we perceive only likenesses, and He has forbidden us to strike these for God, since we are ignorant of the relations in respect of which they are likenesses.[5]

Since the "bellies" are the loci of engendering and birth, and since from them become manifest the entities of the progeny, the Real is described as the "Nonmanifest." He is saying that in respect of the fact that He is nonmanifest, the cosmos becomes manifest from Him. Thus we were within Him as nonmanifest things. Take this rationally, not imagistically, for if you take it rationally, sound knowledge will accept it. But if you take it as images and imagination, you will be refuted through His words, *He does not give birth* [112:3], and it is not appropriate for a rational person to begin something that will allow him to be refuted like this. But if you take it rationally without imagination, you will fall on the actual situation.

After all, we have no escape from a support by which we are supported in our *wujūd*, because of what is given by our possibility. [This support is] the *wujūd* of the Preponderator who gives preponderance to our *wujūd* over our nonexistence. However, He is nonmanifest to us, because there is no correspondence between us, since we are ruled by the property of possibility in our entities, in our undifferentiated state, and in our differentiation. If He corresponded to us in some affair and that affair was ruled by the property of possibility, then the Real would be ruled by the property of possibility. But He is necessary through Himself in respect to self, so the correspondence is removed. Since He has no correspondence with us, we have no correspondence with Him.

Thus we are supported by Him because of the lack of correspondence and, in one respect, because of the correspondence, but He has independence from the worlds, for His "love to be known" is the fact that He is not known. This is the limit of our knowledge of Him. Were He to be known, He would not be nonmanifest, but He is the Nonmanifest who does not become manifest.

So also, from another standpoint, He is the Nonmanifest in respect of the fact that He is within His faithful servant's heart that embraces Him. Thus He is nonmanifest within the servant, and the servant does not witness his own nonmanifest dimension, so he does not witness what is nonmanifest within him.

In both respects, we do not see Him.

Since He is, as He says, the faculties of the servant, his hearing and his eyesight, and since the servant sees through his eyesight, he sees through his Lord what his eyesight sees. But he sees nothing of his faculties, while the Real is all his faculties, so he does not see his Lord.

Here knowledge and vision are made distinct. After all, we know through faith and its light in our hearts that He is our faculties, but we do not witness that with eyesight. Hence we perceive Him/do not perceive Him. As for *the eyesights,* they *do not perceive Him* [6:103], so when He is our eyesight, in this state He does not perceive Himself, for He is within our veil when He is our eyesight. Since this is the affair, it is far-fetched that we should see Him.

As for His words, *Eyesights perceive Him not, but He perceives the eyesights* [6:103]—eyesight has come only to perceive, not to be perceived. Moreover, in the words *perceive Him not* He is indicated by the pronoun of the absent one [i.e., the third person]. The absent is not perceived by eyesight and witnessing. It is the Nonmanifest. After all, if it were perceived, it would not be absent or nonmanifest. Nonetheless, *He perceives the eyesights,* for absence is not necessary from both sides. If someone is absent from you, it is not necessary that you be absent from him. It may be so, and it may not be.

In what is signified by this verse there is another affair. It is that He perceives Himself through Himself because He is the eyesight of the servant through His He-ness, visual perception occurs only through eyesight, and He is identical with the eyesight ascribed to the servant. He says, *He perceives the eyesights,* while He is identical with the eyesights. Hence He has perceived Himself. This is why we say that He is manifest to Himself, but He is not nonmanifest to Himself.

Then He completed the verse by saying, *And He is the Subtle* [6:103] in respect of the fact that *eyesights perceive Him not.* The meaning of the Subtle in respect to the fact that *He perceives the eyesights* is that His perception of the eyesights is His perception of Himself, because He is identical with them. This is the furthest limit of subtlety and fineness.

[Then He says] *the Experienced* [6:103]. Here He alludes to the knowledge of tasting. In other words, this is not known except through tasting. In this there is no benefit in setting up proofs, unless the proof of it be within the self of the prover and is none other than his tasting. Then this servant whose eyesight is the Real sees himself through the Real, and he sees the Real through his eyesight, since He is identical with his eyesight. Thus he perceives both affairs.

Everything within Him is nonmanifest
  for within Him it is the back.
No one knows our words
  save a witnesser or one astute.
He will see what I see
  through his heart as a vision of thought.
Surely He it is
  who sees you from the sheltered eye.
But you do not see Him,
  except when you are not.

This last line is an allusion to the Prophet's words in the sound hadith in the book of Muslim, "If you are not, you will see Him, for He sees you."[6]

So if you are not, you will see Him,
  but if you are, you will not see Him.
He whose property is as
  I have said will see Him.
For my essence is His low ground,
  or if you like, His looking place.
When He is in my *wujūd,*
  then it is true that I have buried Him,
but if He accompanies *wujūd,*
  then He has come while I upstir Him.

The hearts of the heedless[7] are the burying grounds of the Real, just as their manifest sides are the loci of His self-disclosure. He is in the very hearts of His servants in respect of the fact that their hearts are the locus of knowledge of Him. However, they fail to observe His inviolability and halt not at His limits, so He is within them like the corpse that has no ruling property in its grave. Rather, the ruling property belongs to the grave, since it has covered the corpse and curtained it from the eyes of the viewers. So also is the ruling property of nature when it becomes manifest in opposition to the Shariah, for, in the case of such a person, the Shariah is a corpse during this time.

In this way the Real becomes manifest in dream-visions. In a dream I saw God's Messenger as a corpse in a site that I had examined in the Jāmiᶜ Mosque of Seville. I asked about that site, and I found out that it had been illegally seized. Hence, that was the death of the Shariah within it, since it was not owned in a Shari'ite manner.

Death and burial are ascribed to the Real in the hearts of the heedless, because within them He is as if He is not within them. *And God speaks the* ***ḥaqq****, and He guides on the path* [33:4]. (IV 300.34)

Chapter 256: The Shining of the Full Moon

In most contexts, Ibn al-ᶜArabī discusses the divine names Manifest and Nonmanifest to bring out their implications for various stations of knowledge achieved by the Folk of God. Although he usually does not address the structure of the cosmos per se in such passages, he does suggest some of the complexities of the relations that human beings can come to understand. Thus, for example, God discloses Himself to His friends in the absent world. Inasmuch as the absent world is nonmanifest in relation to the witnessed world, it displays the properties of the name Nonmanifest. Thus it is absent (nonmanifest) in relation to the witnessed world (manifest), and witnessed to the absent faculties of the Folk of God. In other words, "absent" things are both manifest and nonmanifest. They are manifest to God and to those to whom God reveals them, but they remain hidden to most people. Nonmanifestation in the absolute sense remains an attribute of the Essence. Ibn al-ᶜArabī brings out these points in Chapter 256, "On the true knowledge of the shining of the full moon and its mysteries." The moon here signifies the absent domains that are nonmanifest in themselves but become manifest when God discloses His light within them. It also corresponds to the perfect human being, who has no light of his own, but who manifests the full brilliance of the divine sun by being God's vicegerent, the locus of manifestation for all His names and attributes.

The chapter begins with an assertion of *wujūd*'s utter incomparability with all things. All the questions that one can ask about the *wujūd* of the things are meaningless when posed for *wujūd* in itself. Thus, in logical terms, one asks about a thing's *wujūd* by posing the question "whether" (*hal*), thereby asking whether or not it is to be found. Other questions establish a thing's quiddity or whatness (*mā*), its qualities or howness (*kayf*), and its cause or whyness (*lima*).[8] In Ibn al-ᶜArabī's view, *wujūd* cannot properly be the object of any of these questions, because each pertains to what can be limited and bound by human understanding, but

God's *tanzīh* demands that He transcend all the limits of created and temporal things. Even if one recognizes *tashbīh* through the omnipresence of *wujūd*, one must still recognize that these questions are addressed not at *wujūd* as such but at the things that appear through *wujūd*.

The full moon of the Return gazes only
on the full moon of the path—
so consider "whether," "why,"
"how," and "what."
If a *wujūd* rises high
beyond these questions,
then for it there is no difference
between going straight and error.
When relations leave no trace
in something's *tawḥīd*,
that is He in whose *tawḥīd*
the ancients were bewildered.
We have not seen that any rational faculty
in its fluctuation
has taken a step into the *tawḥīd*
of the Presence of the Essence.

Know that one does not ask about some mentioned thing *whether* or not it is an existent thing unless its *wujūd* is hidden. When the *wujūd* of something is manifest to every eye, the question *whether* is eliminated, because this is an inquiry, and an inquiry only occurs on the basis of ignorance of the affair about which inquiry is made. In a similar way, one asks *why* only about an effect, one asks *what* only about a limited thing, and one asks *how* only about something that acts as a receptacle for states. But the Real is incomparable with all the affairs that are understood from these questions, for His Essence is incomparable with these questions. Or rather, these questions are not permissible for Him—neither in the case of those who see that *wujūd* is God, nor in the case of those who do not see this.

Those who see that *wujūd* is God see that the property through which the Real becomes manifest is only the properties of the entities of the possible things. Hence, these questions fall only upon that which rightfully demands them, for each seeks the Entity of the Real only in respect of its manifestation through the property of the possible thing. Hence, the entity of the possible thing is the object of the question, but this fact is obscured for the questioner. And as for those who do not see that the entity of *wujūd* is the Real, the questions are not permissible for them.

Let us then return to the subject. We say: As for the "shining of the full moon" that God set up as an image in the cosmos for His self-disclosure through His ruling property within it, that is the divine vicegerent, who becomes manifest within the cosmos through the names and properties of God—mercy and subjugation, vengeance and pardon. In the same way, the sun becomes manifest in the essence of the moon and gives light to the whole of it. Then it is called a "full moon." Hence the sun sees itself in the mirror of the full moon's essence, for it drapes it in a light through which it is called a "full moon."

So also, the Real is seen in the essence of him whom He has taken as vicegerent, for he rules through God's ruling property in the cosmos. The Real witnesses him with the witnessing of him who has bestowed the light of knowledge upon him. He says, *I am placing in the earth a vicegerent* [2:30]. He taught him all the names, and He had the angels prostrate themselves to him, because He knew that they were prostrating themselves to Him. It is obvious that the vicegerent becomes manifest only in the attribute of the one who appointed him vicegerent, so the ruling property belongs to the one who appointed him.

Once when Abū Yazīd was in one of his placements with the Real, He said to him, "Go out to the creatures with My attribute, so that he who sees you will see Me, and he who magnifies you will magnify Me." To magnify the servants is to magnify their master, not them.

This is the mystery of "the shining of the full moon." God appointed the form of the full moon along with the sun as a likeness of the divine vicegerency and the fact that the Real sees Himself in the essence of the one whom He appoints as His vicegerent in the perfection of created nature, for he becomes manifest to Him only in His form and His measure.

Those who see that the Real is the mirror of the cosmos and that the cosmos sees itself within Him will make the cosmos like the sun and the Real like the full moon. Both likenesses are correct and do occur.

Know also that God has intended to strike likenesses for the people. He says, *Even so does God strike likenesses for those who answer their Lord* [13:18]. Hence the whole cosmos and everything within it is a striking of likenesses so that it may be known from it that He is He. He has made the cosmos a signifier of Himself and has commanded us to consider it.

Among the likenesses that God struck in the cosmos is the form of the moon in relation to the sun. The Real never ceases being manifest to the cosmos perpetually in the mode of perfection, so all the cosmos is perfect. God appointed for the cosmos two faces—one manifest and one nonmanifest. The perception of His self-disclosure that is subtracted from the manifest is taken by the nonmanifest, so He becomes manifest within it. Hence the cosmos never ceases being preserved by the entity of the Real, and this alone is proper.

The cosmos has three levels in its states with God. He becomes manifest in one level through the name Manifest, so nothing of the affair remains nonmanifest to the cosmos. This takes place in a specific homestead. For the common people, it occurs in the homestead of the resurrection.

In another level He becomes manifest within the cosmos in the Nonmanifest. Hearts witness Him, but not eyesights. Hence the affair goes back to Him, and every existent thing finds, within its own innate disposition, support by Him and confession of Him, without knowing Him and without considering any proofs. This is a property of His self-disclosure in the nonmanifest.

In a third level He discloses Himself in both the manifest and the nonmanifest. He is perceived in the manifest in the measure that He discloses Himself through it, and He is perceived in the nonmanifest in the measure that He discloses Himself through it.

So He has a perpetual, all-inclusive self-disclosure in the cosmos constantly. The levels of the cosmos are diverse in this self-disclosure because of the diversity of the levels of the cosmos in themselves, for He discloses Himself in keeping with their preparednesses. He who understands this will know that "the shining of the full moon" never ceases. So understand! *And God speaks the **ḥaqq**, and He guides on the path* [33:4]. (II 555.30)

Witnessing the Nonmanifest

Although Ibn al-ʿArabī typically says that people have no access to the name Nonmanifest except inasmuch as they understand it rationally and declare God incomparable with all things, in some contexts he maintains that the name Nonmanifest can be the object of unveiling. The friends of God may be given visions of the absent worlds, and inasmuch as these are nonmanifest to most creatures, they display the attribute of nonmanifestation. However, in the following passage, he talks rather of a visionary knowledge of the name Nonmanifest itself. This name discloses itself in the absent worlds to the seekers, and hence the nonmanifest becomes manifest. But they must not imagine that the Nonmanifest thereby gives up its property of nonmanifestation, for realities do not change. Here again we are approaching bewilderment.

All affairs are curtains, some upon others. The highest of curtains is the divine name Manifest, for it curtains the divine name Nonmanifest. "There is no target behind God," so it is a curtain upon Him.

When you are with the divine name Nonmanifest in the state of witnessing and vision, this divine name Nonmanifest—with which you are unified at this moment and which you are witnessing—is a curtain over the divine name Manifest. Do not say that the property of manifestation has been transferred to the divine name Nonmanifest and that nonmanifestation has fallen to the lot of the name Manifest. On the contrary, the Manifest remains as it was in property, bestowing forms on the whole cosmos. As for the Nonmanifest, even if it is witnessed, it remains in its state as nonmanifest, bestowing meanings that are curtained by manifest forms. So this is the highest and the most hidden of curtains, and the highest and most hidden of curtained things. (IV 214.12)

Although God is Manifest and Nonmanifest, these are relations with His creatures, and, from one point of view, they go back to the preparedness of the individual thing. Not everyone can see God in this world—only the Folk of God, who are precisely those to whom He has given the preparedness to see. Thus God is Manifest to His Folk, who see Him with the eye of imagination and unveiling, and Nonmanifest to theologians and philosophers, who push Him far away with the rational faculty, which knows only that *Nothing is as His likeness* (42:11).

At the resurrection, the Real will disclose Himself and say, "I am your Lord." They will see Him, but nevertheless they will deny Him and not acknowledge Him as their Lord, despite the *wujūd* of vision because of the lifting of the veil. When He transmutes Himself for them into the mark through which they recognize Him, they will say to Him, "Thou art our Lord." Yet He is the one whom they were denying and from whom they were seeking refuge, and He is the one whom they confessed and recognized.

What is this veil that was there with them along with witnessing? Is it an affair of *wujūd* or a property of nonexistence? For He is witnessed/veiled. However, there is no veil pertaining to *wujūd,* nor does nonexistence have any property in the existent thing. So consider how hidden this is! Nevertheless, nothing but this occurs in the cosmos in this world in all affairs, but the people are heedless of it.

In a similar way, we have faith that the angel is with us and the satan is with us, but no sensory veils are existent for us. Our eyes observe, but we do not perceive the angel or the jinni. But *he sees* us, *he and his tribe, from where* we *do not see* him [7:27]. So he and his tribe see us with a witnessing of the eyes, and we see him through faith, not with the eyes. So what is this curtain between us? After all, were it between us, it would veil them from us just as it veils us from them. Hence, a certain wisdom must have been designated in this.

So also is the case with what God mentions about Himself concerning the veils of light and darkness that are between us and Him. Through the darkness, *tanzīh* occurs, so we negate from Him the attributes of newly arrived things. Hence we do not see Him. We have placed the veils upon our own eyes through this rational consideration. As for the light, that is like His manifestation to us so that we may witness Him and deny Him. It is just as we remarked already concerning the self-disclosure at the resurrection. For the gnostics, He has this property today in this world.

The gnostics witness Him in the forms of the possible things, whose *wujūd* has newly arrived. But those who are veiled—that is, the ulama of the tracings—deny Him. Hence He is named "Manifest" in the case of those, who are the gnostics, but He is named "Nonmanifest" in the case of these, who are the veiled. Yet He is none but He—glory be to Him and high is He!

So the Folk of God, those who are His folk, never cease and will never cease, in this world and the last world, witnessing perpetually with the eyes. Although the witnessing is diverse in forms, this detracts nothing from them. (III 540.34)

The Folk of God see God's signs both outwardly and inwardly, both on the horizons and in themselves. Inasmuch as they see the outward signs, they see the Manifest, and inasmuch as they see the inward signs, they see the Nonmanifest. Ibn al-ʿArabī explains this after telling us how certain seekers move from a vision of the Real's utter difference from creation, which demands that they see things as lowly and despicable, to a vision of His utter sameness, which demands that they see all things as God's self-disclosures. In the first instance, the world and everything within it hangs heavily upon them, and they are constricted and oppressed. In the second instance, God opens up their eyes and expands their breasts, and they live in constant joy. The first vision is that of *tanzīh,* the second that of *tashbīh;* the eye that sees the first is the eye of *furqān* or discrimination, and the eye that sees the second is that of *qurʾān* or bringing together. Perfect vision, of course, demands seeing with both eyes.

Only the human being has an arrival at God and a procession from God that is identical with an arrival at God by another path, different from the first arrival. Thus he remains between approaching God to acquire benefits from Him, and proceeding from God to bestow benefits. This proceeding is identical with approaching God to acquire other benefits.

The greatest opening occurs in the procession from God in respect of its being the same as approaching God, so the person will be one of those who see the Real in creation. However, this vision of the Real in creation may be heavy upon some of the Folk of God, because of the distant correspondence between Him whose *wujūd* is necessary through the Essence and him whose *wujūd* is necessary through the Other.

When the servant tastes this witnessing, the Real shows him that the entity of what is heavy upon him is nothing but God, who alone has *wujūd,* but who is named "creature" because of the property of the possible thing in the Entity. When the servant comes to know what the existent entity is and what the property is, and that the property derives from a nonexistent entity, he has no more cares. The heaviness of engendered things that he was finding disappears from him—a heaviness because of which the jinn and mankind were named "the two heavy ones," though this is a name for every natural existent.

The pain of self and sensation that he was sensing disappear from him, and God *lifts him up to a high place* [19:57]. This is his share of the station of Idris.[9] So he is lifted up in placement and his chronic ills disappear. He praises Him who rid him of cares, and he knows what has given him his happiness. Thus the levels become distinct, the doctrinal positions are unified, the rivers and channels turn into an ocean, and the powerful, the not-powerful, and the earner all become equal.

The most magnificent and highest approach occurs for him whose approach to God is identical with his emerging breath and whose procession from God—which is the same as his approach to Him—is identical with his entering breath. He approaches God because He encompasses the emerging breath, and he approaches God in his procession through his entering breath because his heart embraces the Real. Hence he acquires benefits in every breath between a manifest divine name and a nonmanifest divine name. The breath emerges to the All-Encompassing, Manifest Real so that He can show him the Entity of the Real in the signs on the horizons, and the breath enters to the Nonmanifest Real so that He can show him the Entity of the Real in himself. He witnesses nothing that is manifest and nothing that is nonmanifest if not a *ḥaqq*. Hence, no protest remains within his essence toward any act, save with the tongue of a *ḥaqq*, so that he may put courtesy into effect. For the speaker and what is spoken are one entity in two forms through two attributions. (III 403.31)

Chapter 472: Following the Most Beautiful

God affirms in the Koran that He is both Manifest and Nonmanifest. The debates that often occurred among theologians over whether or not God can be seen has much to do with how these names are understood. For Ibn al-ʿArabī, it is obvious that both descriptions are correct and that it is impossible to make categorical statements about the vision of God. In one respect He is seen, in another respect He is not seen. Knowledge consists in grasping the respects, and vision lies in seeing Him as is proper to His majesty. The Shaykh explains this in a chapter that he calls "On the state of the Pole whose waystation is *Those who listen to the speech and follow the most beautiful of it—those are they whom God has guided. Those—they are the possessors of the kernels* [39:18]." The "most beautiful speech" that they follow is what God says about Himself in the Koran. They follow it by acknowledging the reality of He/not He, Manifest/Nonmanifest, seen/not seen.

Ibn al-ʿArabī begins the chapter by discussing the all-pervasiveness of speech and the necessity for standards to discern among the varieties of speech. There must be a means to find the "most beautiful" (*aḥsan*). Then he turns to the term *sūʾ*, which is the opposite of both "beauty" (*ḥusn*) and "happiness" (*surūr*). Lane gives the basic meaning of *sūʾ* in the first sense as "evilness, badness, abomination, foulness, or unseemliness" and in the second sense as "displeasingness, grievousness, vexatiousness." Thus *sūʾ* is "any evil, evil affection, cause of mischief or harm or injury, noxious or destructive thing, calamity, disease, or malady." In the following, I translate it as "ugly."

He who listens to the speech of Him
to whom *faces* are *humbled* [20:111]
will attain to the beauty
that comes to him in His words.
He is the Wise, so everyone
in engendered existence is His wisdom.
You are in His engendered existence,
so you are one of His wisdoms.
From you is heard—if you realize
what your ears hear—
some of His words concerning
the two levels of His feet.
The Throne possesses alone
the Address
that the Footstool divides
because of the words' eternity.
The newly arrived has a face
toward Him who makes it arrive
and another gazing upon
its own nonexistence.

God says, *No remembrance comes to them from their Lord newly arrived* [. . .] [21:2], and

He says, *No remembrance comes to them from the All-Merciful newly arrived* [. . .] [26:5].

Know that this is the Real's calling attention to the fact that every speech in the cosmos is His speech, for nothing comes to us from God save every newly arrived remembrance, since the coming in that which comes is newly arrived, without doubt, and nothing comes save that within which the newly arrived thing abides. This is nothing but the form within which He discloses Himself in the eyes of the viewers and from which He withdraws in the eyes of the viewers.

There is nothing save hearer, speaker, that which says, that for which is said, that through which is said, and that which is said. All this is beautiful. However, it stands between beautiful and more beautiful, for every speech is beautiful, but the words that conform to personal desire are more beautiful. So, all words are beautiful.

As for His words, *God does not love the overt in the ugly in words* [4:148], these negate that love should be connected to words overt in the ugly. "The ugly in words" is for someone to say that something is ugly when none should say this but God. "The overt in the ugly" may be in words and it may be in acts that are not words. He means by "the overt" in these the manifestation of indecency from the servant. Thus the Prophet said, "If any of you is afflicted with these filthy things, let him curtain them," that is, let him not make them overt.

The ugly is of two sorts: the shari'ite ugly, and the ugly that is ugly to you. If the Shariah praises the ugly and does not blame it, then the thing is ugly because it is ugly to you, not because God has ruled that it is ugly. For example, God says, *The recompense of an ugly act is an ugly act the like of it* [42:40]. The first ugly act is shari'ite, because it is a transgression, but the other ugly act is that which is ugly to the person who is recompensed with it. But recompense is not through a shari'ite ugliness, because God does not set down ugliness as shariah.

Since the common usage in the language has terms for the ugly and the beautiful, the Shariah descends from God in keeping with the common agreement. They name it "ugly" and say, "This is something ugly." So God says, *God does not love the overt in the ugly in words* [4:148]—that which you have named the "ugly" because it does not conform with your personal desires. In the same way, you have heard that "The beautiful deeds of the pious are the ugly deeds of those brought near."

In reality, there is nothing but the beautiful through relation and the ugly through relation, for everything from God is beautiful, whether that thing be ugly or bring about happiness. The affair is relative.

Then He says, *Those are they whom God has guided* to the true knowledge of the beautiful and the most beautiful. *Those—they are the possessors of the kernels* [39:18]. By "kernels" He means that they bring out the affairs' kernel that is curtained by the shell as a safeguard for it. After all, the eye falls only on the veil, while that which is veiled belongs to the possessors of the kernels. This calls attention to the veiling form within which the Real discloses Himself, then He transmutes Himself from it into another veil. In reality, there is nothing but transferal from veil to veil, since no divine self-disclosure ever repeats itself. Hence the forms must be diverse, while the Real is behind all of this.

We have nothing of Him save the name Manifest in vision and veil. As for the name Nonmanifest, it remains forever nonmanifest. It is the intelligible kernel that is perceived by the possessors of the kernels. In other words, they know that there is a kernel, and it is that over which a veil has become manifest, a veil that is nothing but the name Manifest, while it is He who is the named in both states.

Those who maintain that there is vision speak the truth, and those who negate vision speak the truth. After all, the Messenger of God affirmed vision for us with his words, "You shall see your Lord," and so on. He also negated vision, for he was asked, "Did you see your Lord?," that is, on the night of the *miʿrāj*. In surprise at the questioner, he said, "He is a light. How should I see Him?" In other words, He is a light, and light is not perceived, because newly arrived things are too weak. Light is God's essential description, and new arrival is likewise our essential description. We remain forever as we are, and He remains forever as He is.

Those firmly rooted in knowledge [3:7] are *they whom God has guided*. In other words, He Himself has undertaken to teach them. *Those—they are the possessors of the kernels* [39:18]. Included in the knowledge that He has taught them is that there is a kernel curtained by the shell. Hence those who negate and those who affirm both speak the truth.

When someone says that God is manifest, he is saying about God only what God has said about Himself. There is no benefit for a thing to be manifest except that it be witnessed. Hence He is witnessed and seen in this respect.

When someone says that God is nonmanifest, he is saying about God only what God has said about Himself. There is no benefit for a thing to be nonmanifest save that *eyesights perceive it not* [6:103]. Hence He is not witnessed and not seen in this respect.

When those who remember God through this verse follow the most beautiful speech, they perceive that there is a kernel that is curtained when someone says, "There is nothing there except what eyesight falls upon." Such a person is like the one who does not see that behind this manifest, human form is another affair that governs and controls it. He who has seen the form of Zayd has seen Zayd, without doubt. But those who recognize the kernel know that behind this form there is another affair and that the trace that is manifest from this form belongs to that nonmanifest thing, curtained within the veil. Its proof is death, when the form subsists and the property disappears.

When someone says that Zayd is identical with the governing power, not with the form, and that the form is no different from a form that we agree is his likeness made of wood or plaster, then he will say that he did not see Zayd.

But when someone says that Zayd is the totality, so he is the manifest and the nonmanifest, he will say that he saw him/did not see him. In this meaning God says, *You did not throw when you threw* [8:17]. Thus the "most beautiful saying" is to affirm the two affairs in both respects.

There is nothing witnessed and no witnesser save One—
the separation is understood through the coming together.
He who says "We have witnessed Him" has spoken the truth,
and he who says "We have not witnessed" is weak and inadequate.
When an eye is qualified by inadequacy, and this attribute
never leaves it, thereby preventing benefit,
then we depend on tradition and become *possessors of comprehension* [20:54],
and there is no knowledge in that which does not come from tradition.
When someone is preserved from error and speaks, his words
are the truth, and for certain no untruth comes to him.
So reason and Shariah are two companions that have become familiar—
so blessed is he who reasons and blessed is he who gives Shariah!

Know also that you can "follow" only that which He has limited for you within His words and His tracings. Then you will walk where He takes you walking, and you will halt where He has you halt. You should consider that concerning which He says to you, "Consider!," assent to that concerning which He says to you, "Assent!," use your reason in that concerning which He says to you, "Use your reason!," and have faith in that concerning which He tells you to have faith. After all, the divine signs that have come in the Wise Remembrance have come in great variety. Because of their variety, those addressed by them have a variety of descriptions. Among them are *signs for a people who reflect* [13:3], *signs for a people who reason* [2:164], *signs for a people who hear* [10:67], *signs for those who have faith* [45:3], *signs for the knowers* [30:22], *signs for* the *godwary* [10:6], *signs for the possessors of comprehension* [20:54], *signs for the possessors of the kernels* [3:190], and signs *for the possessors of eyesights* [3:13]. So, differentiate as He has differentiated, and do not step beyond to what has not been mentioned. On the contrary, put every sign and everything else in its own site.

Consider who is addressed by the sign and be yourself its addressee, for you are the totality of what is mentioned. After all, you are described by eyesight, comprehension, kernel, reason, reflection, knowledge, faith, hearing, and heart. So through your own consideration make manifest the attribute by which He has described you in that specific sign. Then you will be among those in whom the Koran has been brought together, so they have been brought together in keeping with it. Such a person has had it rooted in the memory, so he is one of its folk. Or rather, he is the Koran itself when he has this description, and he is among the Folk of God and His elect.

Words are all beautiful and more beautiful. There is nothing ugly save in that concerning which words are uttered, or in the speaker, not in the words.

There is nothing ugly in words and speech—
ugliness is found only in what is spoken about,

or what is said, or that through which is spoken, or that about which is spoken. So understand this!

Take all of *wujūd* as *a book inscribed* [52:2], though if you say, *[a book] written down* [83:9], that is more eloquent, for *wujūd* possesses two faces—speaking rationally *of* the Real and *for* the Real. Then you will be among those *whom God has guided,* that is, given success in the clarification that He has given them. *Those—they are the possessors of the kernels* [39:18], who dive after the hidden affairs and their realities, extract their treasures, undo their knots and their tokens, and know that upon which the allusions fall in the site where the expressions allow. *And God speaks the **ḥaqq**, and He guides on the path* [33:4]. (IV 104.20)

Chapter 400: Manifest Mercy

The relations established by the names First, Last, Manifest, and Nonmanifest allow Ibn al-ᶜArabī ample room to see the traces of the One Entity in all things. He develops a few of the implications of these relations in a chapter entitled "On the true knowledge of the mutual waystation of 'When someone becomes manifest to Me, I become nonmanifest to him, and when someone halts at My limit, I have an overview of him.'" He alludes here to the hadith, "There is no verse of the Koran that does not have a manifest sense, a nonmanifest sense, a limit, and an overview." This "overview" (*muṭṭala*ᶜ) is the face of the Real in all things. After the servant comes to know the first three, then "He gains the overview, so his eye does not fall upon the things—his eye falls only upon the face of the Real in them" (II 177.4).

In much of this chapter, the Shaykh adopts the voice of creation and speaks to God in the dialectic of disclosure and curtaining. When creation is manifest, the Real is hidden; when the Real is manifest, creation disappears. The chapter also offers a meditation on the *ḥadīth qudsī* about the ritual prayer that was cited earlier ("I have divided the *ṣalāt* into two halves . . . ").

My manifestation
is the Real's nonmanifestation
in every homestead, my limit is
the Real's *wujūd* in every overview.
If my entity is in my *wujūd,*
then He is not,
but, if He is, the All-Embracing remains
nonmanifest and constricted.

What a loss for the engendered things
if He did not come to be through them!
What felicity for them when He
rises up in their entities!
He is the lightning,
but the downpour is also He;
thunder never *glorifies* Him [13:13]
without the fall of rain.

Know—God confirm us and you—that God says concerning the He-ness, *He is the First and the Last* [57:3], but there is nothing but I and He.

He was, and nothing else. Then I came to be. At my *wujūd,* He divided the *ṣalāt* into two halves between me and Him. There is nothing but the doer of the *ṣalāt. [Have you not seen how everything in the heavens and in the earth glorifies God, and the birds spreading their wings?] Each knows its **ṣalāt** and its glorification* [24:41].

He is my hearing and my eyesight, so He gave none to hear save Himself, for *He is the First and the Last.* He is not I, for the tool has no property except through the artisan who employs it as he employs it. He exercises His artisanry in it through it and through Himself—"through it" in respect of its receptivity, and "through Himself" in respect of His self-disclosure through His address.

The entities are many,
the affair is one,
engendered things are given to witness,
and God is Witness,
for there is none but God,
there is no other.
He confesses His *tawḥīd—*
He does not renounce it.

When I become manifest through my entity by [saying in the *ṣalāt*] *Praise belongs to God, Lord of the worlds* [1:2], He remains nonmanifest in this address, but He hears my faith and says, "My servant has lauded Me." Thus He names His lastness a servant, but He is the Lord in the answer, so He returns the firstness to me. After all, He does not speak until I speak, just as I was not brought into existence until He said *Be.* So I was the first listener, and He the first speaker. Then I was the first speaker, and He the first listener.

Thus *the Nonmanifest and the Manifest* became designated, *and He is knower of each thing* [57:3] through me and through Himself. God became manifest only through me, and He remained nonmanifest only through me. Firstness was not correct except through me, and lastness was not affirmed save through me, for I am "each thing," and He is "knower" of me.

If I were not, through whom would He be Knower? Hence I give Him knowledge, and He gives me *wujūd*. Affairs become intertied between me and Him. He confessed this to me when He divided the *ṣalāt* equally between me and Him. For He knew that He belongs to Me, just as I belong to Him. So there is no escape from Him and me. There is no escape from a necessary thing and a possible thing. Were such not the case, He would be ineffectual and would not take up any abode.

I am his ornament, and He is my earth. *Surely We have appointed whatever is on the earth as an ornament for it* [18:7]. Through me become manifest His power, the influence of His ruling properties, and the authority of His will. Were I not, His ornament would not be.

Then the affair was reversed. He made me an earth, and He was an ornament for me. He invested me with the imamate, but there was no one for whom I could be an imam except Him. My imamate was the same as that with which He ornamented me, and He ornamented me with nothing but His He-ness, for He is my hearing, my eyesight, my tongue, my hand, my leg, and my supporter, and He made me into a light, all of me.[10] So He ornamented me with Him for Him, *and the earth shone with the light of its Lord* [39:69], and He is *the light of the heavens and the earth* [24:35].

He mentioned that the earth is *abased* [67:15], and is there any more abased than I, while I am under His exaltation?

When He created the creatures and He instructed me concerning what He created, He said to me, "Turn your attention and take comfort in My artisanry through My creation." Thus He prescribed, while I gazed upon that which He desired to make manifest and that concerning which I had no knowledge.

He set down the limits, but the servants overstepped them. He spoke, but His words were not heard. He commanded, but at the beginning no one observed His command, and He prohibited, but at the beginning no one observed His prohibition.

He spoke, and protest was made: How *wilt Thou place therein one who will work corruption therein* [2:30]? Thus [the angels] made their view more wholesome than His view and their knowledge more complete than His knowledge.

He said to me, "You."

I said, "You are abased, and no abasement is greater than Your abasement. Which abasement is greater than the abasement of him who is abased by the abased? This angel is protesting. You have appointed this vicegerent and given him prohibitions, and he has disobeyed. You have commanded this Accursed One to prostrate himself, and he has refused, claiming to be better than the one who is better than he."[11]

[God replied:] "Do you see with your eye anyone who does not recognize My magnificence and My effectuating power? Nevertheless, they oppose Me, protest against Me, and transgress My limit. Were My exaltation and magnificence not their state through which they have their ornament, none of this would have occurred. For they are a stony, bare earth, without any vegetation and with no ornament upon it. So the earth came to know that it comes to Me from Me and has its ornament through Me. So My ornament saw Me. They magnified Me, but nothing magnified Me save My ornament.

"The protester said, *We have no knowledge* [2:32]. He whom I forbade said, *Our Lord, we have wronged ourselves* [7:23]. He who opposed My command said, *I fear God, the Lord of the worlds* [8:48]. What does this station have to do with that station? What does the abode of Riḍwān have to do with the abode of Mālik?[12] *To Him the whole affair is returned* [11:123]. So who is the exalted, and who the abased?

"Were it not for the fact that He has an overview of those who overstepped the limits and the tracings, they would not have returned to their limits. Only someone who is uplifted has an overview, and He is the *Uplifted in degrees* [40:15]. Hence they were afraid and they recognized—as We said—their ignorance, their wronging themselves, and their fear of transgressing the limits of their Master."

Thus He says, *O My servants who have been immoderate against themselves* and have overstepped the limits of their Master, *despair not of God's mercy* [39:53], since "God created them for mercy." That is why He named Himself "All-Merciful" and through this name *sat upon the Throne* [20:5]. He sent the most perfect messenger—the most majestic in measure and the most inclusive in message—*as a mercy to the worlds* [21:107]. He did not specify one world rather than another world. Hence the disobedient and the obedient, the one who has faith and the one who gives the lie, the one who professes God's unity and the one who associates others with Him, are all included in this address and named "world."

When God gave the Prophet the station of jealousy for God's side and what it rightfully demands, he began to recite a prayer during his *ṣalāt,* for a month, in which he supplicated for the perishment of a tribe of God's servants, "the Riᶜl, the Dhakwān, and the ᶜUṣayya, who had disobeyed God and His Messenger."[13] Then God sent down upon him His revelation by means of the Faithful Spirit: "O Muhammad, God says to you, 'I have not sent thee as an imprecator and a curser. I have sent thee as a mercy.'" In other words, [I have sent you] so that you will have mercy on such as these. It is as if He is saying to him, "In place of supplicating *against* them, supplicate to Me *for* them." Then Gabriel recited to him the words of his Lord, *And We have sent thee only as a mercy to the worlds* [21:107], that is, so that you will have mercy on them. If you supplicate Me for them, perhaps I will give them the success to obey Me. Then you will find the happiness and delight of your eye in their obedience. But if you curse them and supplicate against them and if I answer your supplication concerning them, I cannot take them to task unless they increase in insolence and clear sin. All of that would have occurred because of your supplication against them, so it would be as if you had commanded them to increase the insolence for which We take them to task.

So God's Messenger called attention to that concerning which his Lord taught him courtesy. He said, "God taught me courtesy, so my courtesy is beautiful."

After that he said, "O God, guide my people, for they do not know." He stood the night until morning reciting nothing save His words, *If Thou chastisest them, they are Thy servants; and if Thou forgivest them, Thou art the Exalted, the Wise* [5:118]. These are the words of Jesus, and God had said to the Prophet, when He mentioned His messengers, *Those are they whom God has guided, so follow their guidance* [6:90].

The guidance of Jesus included this verse with which God's Messenger stood the whole night until morning. What does this station have to do with his supplication against Riᶜl and Dhakwān?

Surely God forgives all sins [39:53]. He did not specify one sin rather than another, just as He did not specify one immoderation rather than another, and just as He did not specify, in sending Muhammad, one world rather than another.

Surely He is the Forgiving, the Compassionate [39:53]—with the definite article to indicate all-envelopment, even though the two abodes will be fully inhabited.

Were it not for the fact that God has designated named terms and numbered days for all affairs, transferal to God through death would be identical with the mercy toward them that they will possess after full completion of the limits [i.e., the penalties] because of their transgressing the limits [i.e., the Shari'ite rulings]. Their transgressing the limits is what enacts limits against them in the last abode, just as it has enacted limits against some of them in the abode of this world.

None of God's creatures dies save as he was born—as a person of faith. He is taken to task only for what occurred between the two faiths, for God's *mercy embraces everything* [7:156].

Within the nonmanifest side of which is mercy [57:13]. This is why He said, "When someone becomes manifest to Me, I become nonmanifest to him," since no one becomes manifest to God until he departs from Him. If he did not depart from Him, he would not be able to distinguish himself from Him. Thus the Real becomes nonmanifest in his manifestation, and this is the wall *within the nonmanifest side of which is mercy and before the manifest side of which is chastisement* [57:13], but the people are not aware.

The subdivisions of speech in this chapter have no end, but this measure of calling attention is sufficient for what is within it, God willing, *for him who has a heart or gives ear while he is a witness* [50:37]. *And God speaks the* **ḥaqq**, *and He guides on the path* [33:4]. (III 567.2)

Chapter 394: Arrival through Courtesy

Ibn al-ᶜArabī calls this chapter "On the true knowledge of the mutual waystation of 'He who shows courtesy arrives, and he who arrives will not return, even if he is not courteous.'" Here he provides one of many expositions of the visionary knowledge acquired by the Folk of God, a knowledge that demands seeing the traces of the Nonmanifest and the Manifest in their proper places.

Were it not for witnessing
and the blessings therein,
in nonexistence I would have no hope
to be engendered.

Through Him we were in Him
until He said *Be*, and our entities
appeared, because we listened
to the engendering in the words.
Were we to open eyes
without fault,
we would be bewildered
in the darknesses, like the blind.
We were not, and light's *wujūd*
made us manifest
as a light, so we are indivisible
through an engendered existence.
Light is our entities,
and light is our Creator—
within it we run on legs
or without feet.

Know—God confirm us and you—that Unbounded *Wujūd* is sheer good, just as unbounded nonexistence is sheer evil. The possible things are between the two. Inasmuch as they receive *wujūd*, they have a share in goodness; and inasmuch as they receive nonexistence, they have a share in evil.

"Courtesy" [*adab*] is nothing but the bringing together of all good. That is why banquet was named *ma*ʾ*daba*—because people come together in it for food.

Without doubt, good becomes manifest in the cosmos as dispersed, so no possible thing is empty of some goodness. The perfect possible thing, created in the divine form and specified for the status of the imamate, has no escape from bringing together each and every good. That is why he has a rightful demand over the imamate and the deputyship in the cosmos. Hence God said concerning Adam, *He taught Adam the names, all of them* [2:31], and there is nothing but name and named.

Muhammad had gained the knowledge of the names when he said, "I came to know the knowledge of the first and the last folk." Thus we know that he had gained the knowledge of the names, for that pertains to the first knowledge, since Adam possessed firstness, because he was among the first in sensory *wujūd*.

Concerning what was specified for himself to the exclusion of others, the Prophet said that he was given the all-comprehensive words. "Words" is the plural of "word," and the words are the entities of the named things. God says, *His word that He cast to Mary* [4:171]—which was none other than Jesus. All the entities of the existent things are words of the Real, and they do *not run out* [31:27]. Thus the Prophet gained the names and the named things, so he brought together all good. Thereby he had a rightful demand over mastership of all the people. That is his words, "I will be the master of the people on the day of resurrection." There his mastership will become manifest, since the last world is the locus of the all-inclusive self-disclosure of the Real. Because of His self-disclosure, no one will be able to make any claims in what is appropriate for God or in what comes from God to those He wills among His servants.

Thus, His words [in the title of this chapter, "He who shows courtesy] arrives" mean "arrives at the gaining of sheer good." This is His words, "I am his hearing and his eyesight," and the like. This is the arrival at perpetual felicity, and it is the arrival that is sought.

There is no doubt that "He who arrives does not return," since it is impossible to return to the locus of the veil's attribute after the unveiling of the covering, for he who knows something does not become ignorant of it after his knowledge becomes connected to it.

In the case of the perfected Men of God, God unveils the coverings from their insights and their eyesights through the divine attributes that they gain and the engendered attributes that they come to understand. But all of the attributes, as already mentioned, are divine.

These are the Courteous, those who are wholesome enough for the Real's carpet. They are God's sitting companions and His Folk. They are the Folk of the Remembrance and the Koran, which is the "bringing together," which is why it was named "Koran."

As for the common people, they cannot escape the unveiling of the covering from their eyesights at death, so they will see affairs as they are. Even if they are not among the felicitous, they will see the felicitous and felicity and they will see the wretched and wretchedness. They will not become ignorant after this knowledge, even if they are wretched. This is the meaning of His words, "He who arrives will not return," even if he is not one of the Courteous, that is, he does not bring together the good.

The courteous person is called "he who brings together the good," though the good is one affair, because this one affair becomes manifest in many diverse forms that are brought together by him. Thus, in his goodness, he becomes manifest through every form of good. Hence he is named "courteous," that is, he who brings together these good forms in himself. However, in itself, good is one reality manifest in the cosmos in diverse forms.

It is not unknown for God
to bring together the cosmos in one.

Thus the courteous person is manifest in the form of a *ḥaqq* in the cosmos. He makes its undifferentiation differentiated through his forms and he makes its differentiation undifferentiated through his essence. When this attribute and faculty is not found in a man, he is not one of the Courteous.

These are those concerning whom it is said, "When they are seen, God is remembered." When God is remembered, His remembrance comprises the whole cosmos. Thus, he who remembers God with this tongue has remembered the cosmos, because the cosmos is the form of the Real. It is the name Manifest, within which differentiation occurs, and it also signifies the Real, because He is identical with the signifier of Himself.

Because of this name, He possesses the Nonmanifest, through which undifferentiation occurs, for knowledge is one, and it is in the nonmanifest. But the things to which it becomes connected are plural through the plurality of the forms of the objects of knowledge. The knower unveils the objects of knowledge with his insight in respect of encompassing their realities, though the objects of God's knowledge and power are infinite.

When the entity of the possible thing receives *wujūd,* nonexistence no longer has any share or ruling property within it, save that its possibility is rationally understood, even though it will not become nonexistent afterwards, and its nonexistence is not correct, because what is different from the object of knowledge cannot possibly occur. No nonexistence whatsoever can come from *wujūd,* since the procession of nonexistence from it is not within its reality.

As for those affairs whose nonexistence is given by proofs, when they become nonexistent, they do so only by themselves, or by the nonexistence of the precondition for their subsistence in *wujūd.* In this measure the *wujūd* of the possible thing is separate from the *wujūd* of the Real. After all, the property of possibility never disappears rationally from the existent possible thing that is newly arrived by itself, but the *wujūd* of the Real has no share in possibility whatsoever. Even if the *wujūd* of the entities never becomes nonexistent after their *wujūd,* the affair is as we maintain.

As for accidents, concerning which we said that they become nonexistent by themselves in the second time after the time of their *wujūd,* their reality is that they are occasions pertaining to nonexistence. They have intelligible, predicated properties which cannot be denied and through which no judgment is made. If accidents were entities of *wujūd,* their nonexistence would be absurd, even though the property of possibility is within them, just as it is absurd for every possible thing that abides through itself.

Now, if you should begin to differentiate the entities of the existent things through limits, you will find that in differentiation they are relations and in totality they are an affair of *wujūd* concerning which no created thing can know the form. There is no knowledge belonging to any created thing or to anything other than God—not even to the First Intellect—that can understand how relations come together such that, from their coming together, there comes to be an entity of *wujūd* that has its own manifestation but does not have its own independence, an entity that is poor through possibility and ruled by its property.

This is a knowledge that none knows but God. It is not possible for any but God to know it, nor can it be taught, for example, by God's teaching it to whom He wills of His servants. The most similar knowledge to it is knowledge of the Essence of the Real, and knowledge of the Essence of the Real cannot be gained by other than God. Thus it is impossible for anything other than God to gain knowledge of the cosmos, of the human being himself, or of the self of anything by itself.

So understand this issue! For I have not heard, nor do I know, that anyone has called attention to it. Although it has been known, it is difficult to conceptualize. Nonetheless, the stalwarts among the knowers uphold it, but they do not know that it is it. For example, Bilqīs said, *It seems to be it* [27:42], but it was it. So also is the case of those who speak of the Real in the state of their manifestation in a specific form with the Real. They witness Him and do not know that He is He. The property of this pervades the cosmos for those who consider and look carefully, but *God is independent of the worlds* [3:97] because of His manifestation through Himself. Hence nothing signifies Him save Him, since there is nothing but God. *And God speaks the* ***ḥaqq****, and He guides on the path* [33:4]. (III 555.31)

The Center and the Circumference

If we think of the cosmos in temporal terms, God is the First and the Last, and if we think in spatial terms, He is the Manifest and the

Nonmanifest. If we conceive of *wujūd* as a circle (*dāʾira*), then God is both the center point (*nuqṭa*) and the circumference (*muḥīṭ*). The center corresponds to the names First and Nonmanifest, because a circle begins with the center point, which, in itself, has no dimensions, and hence remains hidden. The circumference correlates with the Last and the Manifest, because it arises from the center point and can be plainly seen.

The Arabic word for circumference, *muḥīṭ*, is also a divine name, usually translated as the "(All-) Encompassing." The verb *iḥāṭa*, from which the word derives, means to surround, encompass, enclose, encircle. In contexts where Ibn al-ʿArabī has the geometrical sense of the term in mind, I translate it as "(encompassing) circumference."

> The Prophet said, "If you let down a rope, it will fall upon God." In other words, just as He is ascribed to highness through sitting on the Throne, so also He is on the bottom. In the same way, *He encompasses everything* [41:54] so as to preserve it, just as the circle's encompassing circumference preserves the center point's *wujūd*, or the point's relation to *wujūd*. From this center point, the relation of encompassment becomes manifest for the *wujūd* of the encompassing circle. Hence to Him belongs the top, just as to Him belongs the bottom. To Him belongs the Manifest, just as to Him belongs the Nonmanifest. (III 136.25)

Circularity (*istidāra*) pertains to the nature of things. It is demanded by the fact that God is the First and the Last, the Place of Origin (*mabdaʾ*) and the Place of Return (*maʿād*). Things do not leave God in a straight line and then suddenly turn around and go back. Rather, they go out from Him following a line that "inclines" (*māʾil*), eventually curving back on its source. Everything in the cosmos follows a circular route.

> The affair occurs [with an inclination toward circularity] because things proceed from God and return to Him. From Him it begins and to Him it goes back. In the world of shape the affair has no escape from taking the form of a circle, since it does not go back to God by the path on which it emerged from Him, but extends until it reaches its place of origin. This does not happen in a linear shape, or it would never go back to Him, but it does go back to Him. Hence there is no escape from circularity, in both the suprasensory and sensory domains. It is because He created the cosmos in His form that His creation is circular in shape. So consider God's wisdom! (III 119.31)

> The cosmos is globular in shape, so in his end the human being longs for his beginning, for we emerged from nonexistence into *wujūd* through Him, and to Him we shall return. He says, *To Him the whole affair is returned* [11:123]. He says, *Be wary of a day wherein you will be returned to God* [2:281]. He says, *To Him is the homecoming* [5:18], *and unto God is the outcome of all affairs* [31:22].
>
> Do you not see that, when you began, a circle was established? Having begun through it, you will never cease passing around it until you reach its first point, and then you will be a circle. Were the affair not like this, then, when we emerge from at Him, we would be a straight line and would not return to Him. His words, *And to Him you will be returned* [2:245], would not be a truthful statement—but He is the Truthful. Every affair and every existent thing is a circle that goes back to that from which it had its origin. (I 255.14)

> The Real has an inheritance from us, as He has said—*Surely We shall inherit the earth and all who are upon it* [19:40] in entity and property. The fact that this is in entity is indicated by His words, *and unto Us they shall be returned* [19:40], for affairs return to their roots, just as the last point of the circle curves back to its first point. Hence, what is sought from you from the first when you begin with the circle is the return to the circle's root, and that is its beginning. Ultimately you will reach it. (III 503.34)

> There is no divine name that is not between two divine names, for the divine affair is circular. That is why God's affair in the things is infinite, for a circle has no first and no last, except by way of supposition. Hence the cosmos has emerged circular in the form of the affair that He has in Himself, even in shapes. The first shape that accepted the All Body was the circular shape, that is, the celestial sphere. Since the things that come to be from God come to be at the movements of these spheres in keeping with the *determination of the Exalted, the Knowing* [6:96], wisdom bestows that their

shape be in the form of the celestial sphere, or near to it. Hence there is no animal, tree, leaf, stone, or body that has no inclination toward circularity—there is no escape from this. However, circularity is delicate in some things, while it becomes clearly manifest in other things. Turn your attention toward everything created by God, whether mountain, tree, or body. You will see within it a curving back toward circularity. That is why the globular shape is the most excellent of shapes. (I 662.35)

A MYSTERY
Limitation is between the folk of shirk *and* tawḥīd.

He says: Among God's blessings is that He placed the innate disposition [*fiṭra*] in *wujūd*, not in *tawḥīd*. This is why the final issue is at mercy, for the affair is a circle. The end of the circle curves back to its beginning and joins with it. So the end has the property of the beginning, and this is nothing but *wujūd*.

He says: Mercy takes precedence over wrath because the beginning was through mercy. Wrath is an accident, and accidents disappear.

He says: *Tawḥīd* is in the level, and the level is a manyness, so *tawḥīd* is the *tawḥīd* of manyness. Were the affair not like this, the meanings of the names would not be diverse. What does the object signified by the All-Subjugating have to do with the object signified by the All-Forgiving? What does the signification of the Exalter have to do with the signification of the Abaser? What an idea! We have won, but lost is *whosoever is blind in this world* [17:72]. There is no knowledge except in unveiling. If you are not of its folk, at least you should have faith.

He says: The sensory is sensory, so do not turn it away from its path, lest you be ignorant. So also, the intelligible is intelligible, so he who attaches the sensory to the intelligible *has been misguided with a far misguidance* [4:116]. (IV 405.6)

Chapter 410: The Circle of Mercy

God encompasses us, but we do not see Him, because He encompasses us "from behind" (*min warāʾ*): *God is from behind them, encompassing* (85:20). Ibn al-ʿArabī understands this to mean that our faces are always turned toward the center point of the circle, which is God, the First, the Origin. As we move through the stages of existence in this world, we travel backwards, because our faces remain turned toward the center. No matter how far we move away from the center, the circle's circumference stands behind us. Since *wujūd* is a circle, there is no end point that the creatures can reach; rather, they keep on moving for all eternity, though only the Muhammadans, who stand in the Station of No Station, attain a vision of the circularity of the actual situation. Nevertheless, since *wujūd* encompasses everything, there is no escape from the mercy that is its fundamental attribute. Ibn al-ʿArabī explains these points in Chapter 410, "On the true knowledge of the mutual waystation of *'Surely at thy Lord is the end point* [53:42], so be exalted through Me, and you will be felicitous.'" As a Koranic proof text of the all-embracingness of mercy, he cites the verse that refers to the wall that separates the inhabitants of hell from those of paradise: *A wall shall be set up between them, having a door within the nonmanifest side of which is mercy and before the manifest side of which is chastisement* (57:13). The word *imām* means "leader," or more literally, the one who stands in front. Thus the preposition *amāma*, written the same as *imām*, means "in front of."

"There is no target behind God"
for any shooter—
that is the Real
that cannot be coveted.
This is the station of the Real.
Do not transgress!
In this station, no station
is permitted.
When you arrive, my brothers,
return!
This is a *wujūd*
that has no elapsing.
Your return is from Him to you,
for there is nothing
save the entity of the mortals
and the Imam.
Be exalted through Him
and you will be felicitous,
for there is no exaltation
save the Imam's exaltation.

When they saw that their qualities
do not abide
and that there is no constancy
in their states, they said,
"The Real has 'put to sleep' [*anām*]
our engendered existence"—
thus the language
names them "mankind" [*anām*].

God says, *O folk of Yathrib! You have no station, so return* [33:13]. He says, *Surely at thy Lord is the end point* [53:42]. The Prophet said, "There is no target behind God." God says, *God is from behind them, encompassing* [85:20].

There is nothing but God and us, and He *is from behind* us, *encompassing*. Hence, "There is no target behind God" except sheer nonexistence, within which there is neither Real nor creation.

He encompasses us, and in every direction the "behind" of us belongs to Him. In respect of this verse, we will never see Him, because our faces are turned toward the center point of the encompassing circumference. We have emerged from that point, so we are not able to turn our faces toward any but it. It is our kiblah, and it is our Imam and that of all who have this description.

The affair is a globe, so our "behind" must belong to what encompasses us. Consider His words, *Surely at thy Lord is the end point* [53:42]. Here He means only through our backs, not our faces, for we walk to the circumference backwards, because He is *from behind* us, *encompassing*, since He is *wujūd*. Were He not "from behind" us, our end would be at nonexistence, and if we fell into nonexistence, no entity would be manifest for us. So it is impossible for us to fall into nonexistence, because God—who is sheer *wujūd*—is *from behind* us, *encompassing* us. At Him we reach our end. Hence His *wujūd* and His encompassment come between us and nonexistence.

Between His words, *Surely at thy Lord is the end point*, and His words, *God is from behind them, encompassing*, there is no contrariety preventing the two from being brought together. Or rather, the way to bring the two together is obvious: The cosmos is between the center point and the encompassing circumference. The center point is the First, and the circumference is the Last. So the divine preservation accompanies us wherever we may be. It directs us away from Him toward Him.

The affair is a circle. It has no extremity which can be witnessed or at which one can halt. This is why it is said to the Muhammadans—who have an unveiling of this sort—*You have no station*, for the affair is a circle, *so return* [33:13].

The cosmos never ceases to swim in the sphere of *wujūd* ad infinitum, for no end is there. The face of the cosmos remains forever gazing upon the name First, which brought it into existence. The back of the cosmos remains forever gazing upon the name Last, the Encompassing, at which it reaches its end through its behind, for the cosmos sees behind just as it sees in front. However, its perception is diverse according to the diversity of the states that come over it. Were it not for the diversity, no entity would become distinct, and there would be no discrimination.

Wujūd is a mill that turns around Me,
and I am an axis for it, so I will not perish.
Were I to disappear, it would not turn and be a mill,
for poverty is the description of engendered existence, so it is poor.
O ignorant of the affair, though it is witnessed!
Know that in these affairs you are experienced.
Bringing together veils his separation from His Entity,
but he is His signifier, so he sees.

It was said to a group, *Return behind you, and beg for a light* [57:13]. What was said to them is true, for *God is from behind them, encompassing*, and He is light. If the wall had not been set up between Him and them, they would have found the light for which they begged when it was said to them, *beg for a light*.

The life of this world is the locus of earning lights through the Law's prescriptions; it is the abode of Shari'ite deeds. Hence it is an abode of climbing and earning. When they turn toward the last world, this world will be behind them. Then it will be said to them, *Return behind you, and beg for a light*. In other words, no one will have any light save from his life in this world, so the wall of forbidding comes between them and the life of this world.

The wall is a circle between the center point and the encompassing circumference. The folk of the Gardens are between the wall and the circumference. Hence the light *is from behind them*, and toward them is the nonmanifest side of the wall, *within which is mercy*. The face of the wall, which is its manifest side, gazes toward the center point. As for the folk of the

Fire, they are between the center point and the manifest side of the wall, *before the manifest side of which is chastisement* [57:13] *until a named term* [31:29].

The wall comes between the two abodes, not between the two attributes, for in itself the wall is a mercy, while its own entity is identical with the separation between the two abodes, since the chastisement is *before it,* not within it. Rather, mercy is within it. Were chastisement within it, chastisement would be endless for the folk of the Fire, just as mercy is endless for the folk of the Garden. Hence the wall will not be removed, and the fact that it is mercy will not be removed. But there is no escape from the fact that what is on its nonmanifest side will prevail over what is on its manifest side. Inescapably, mercy must envelop those who are before the manifest side of the wall.

This explains why it was said to them, *and beg for a light.* Had it been said to them, "beg for a mercy," they would have found it at once from the *wujūd* of the wall.

When the folk of the Garden desire to take enjoyment from the vision of the folk of the Fire, they climb onto that wall and they are plunged in mercy. They have an overview of the folk of the Fire, and they find from the pleasure of salvation from it something that they do not find from the bliss of the Garden, since the security that arrives for a frightened person is greater in pleasure than the security that is his constant companion.

The folk of the Fire will gaze upon them after mercy has enveloped them, and they will find pleasure from being in the Fire, and they will praise God that they are not in the Garden. This is because of what is required by their constitution in that state. If they were to enter the Garden with that constitution, pain would seize them and they would suffer. So—if you have understood—bliss is nothing but the agreeable, and chastisement is nothing but the disagreeable, whatever it might be. So be wherever you are! If nothing strikes you but what is agreeable to you, you will be in bliss, and if nothing strikes you but what is disagreeable with your constitution, you will be in chastisement.

The abodes have been made lovable to their inhabitants. For the folk of the Fire, those who are its folk, the Fire is their homestead. From it they were created and to it they will be returned. And the folk of the Garden, those who are its folk, were created from the Garden, and to it they will be returned.

The pleasure of the homestead is essential to the homestead's folk. However, they may be veiled by an accidental falling short or a going too far that arises from their deeds. This causes the state to change. The illnesses that abide within them and that they have caused to enter into themselves veil them from the pleasure of the homestead.

This is true to such an extent that, if they had not done what necessitates the *wujūd* of pains and disorders for them and if they were mustered from their graves in the constitution of their homeland and were given a choice between the Garden and the Fire, they would choose the Fire, just as a fish chooses water and flees from the air through which the folk of the land have life. The folk of the land die because of what gives life to the folk of the water, and the folk of the water die because of what gives life to the folk of the land. Know this!

As for you, it is not correct for you to have subsistence with the Real perpetually, for there is no escape from it being said, "Take them back to their castles!" He did not say, "Take them back to their homes," nor "to their spouses." He brought the word *castles* only because of the meaning that is understood from it. When they are taken back to their castles and they look over their kingdom, it is impossible for them to become manifest within it as servants. They will only become manifest there as kings. So their folk will magnify them, and exaltation will stand over them in themselves. The Reality will say to them, "Let your exaltation that the homestead requires for you be through God, not through yourselves." Thus they will be exalted in their kingdom through God's exaltation, so *To God will belong the exaltation* at root, *and to His messenger, and to those who have faith* [63:8] as a divine conferral, not at root. Thus they will be felicitous through this knowledge with God, and they will find Him in the coming self-disclosures.

Nonetheless, the knowers of God never cease being in perpetual self-disclosure, because they know that the Real is identical with each form. Yet they still have the all-inclusive self-disclosure at the Dune, for that bestows another tasting that they do not find perpetually. *And God speaks the **ḥaqq**, and He guides on the path* [33:4]. (IV 13.32)

Circles of Wujūd

In Chapter 360, the Shaykh provides an explicit description of the cosmos as a circle. He begins the chapter by explaining that the

Necessary Being is sheer light, the impossible thing is sheer darkness, and the possible things stand between light and darkness, sharing in the attributes of both.[14] He refers to various ways in which people employ the terms *light* and *darkness* as metaphors (*majāz*). Then he explains how the cosmos, which is a circle, stands between light and darkness. The center point is sheer Light, the space outside the circumference is sheer darkness, and the circle itself is light mixed with darkness, He/not He.

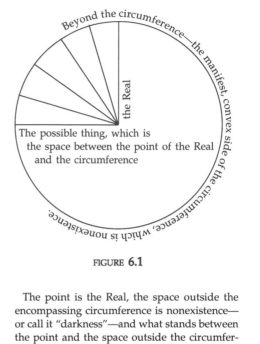

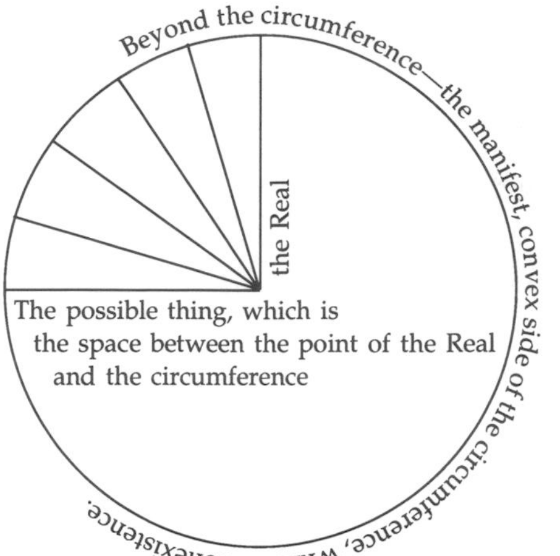

FIGURE **6.1**

> People use the names *light* and *darkness* metaphorically, so the two are well known in common language. In the manifest domain, they speak of the light ascribed to flashes of lightning, stars, lamps, and so on; of witnessed and known darknesses that are perceived in the manifest domain by sensation; of the lights of the suprasensory, nonmanifest domain, such as the light of reason, the light of faith, and the light of knowledge; of the darkness of the nonmanifest domain, such as the darkness of ignorance, associating others with God, and unintelligence. They also speak of what is neither darkness nor light, such as doubt, conjecture, bewilderment, and consideration. But in fact, none of these terms refers either to darkness or to light. All are metaphors for the realities of the Necessary, the impossible, and the possible in the common language of the possible things.
>
> The possible thing brings together in itself its own reality and the reality of its two sides. This appears most clearly in the meanings, the sensory objects, and the imaginal things that are found in the possible realm. The property of this totality is found only in the possible realm, never in the two sides.
>
> Knowledge of the possible realm is an all-embracing ocean of knowledge that has magnificent waves within which ships flounder. It is an ocean that has no shore save its two sides. About its two sides one should not imagine what is imagined by those rational faculties that fall short of perceiving this knowledge—like right and left in respect to what stands between them. The affair is not like that.
>
> On the contrary, if there is to be an imagining—and there is no escape from it—you should imagine what is nearest in relation to what we have mentioned, which is that the affair in itself is like the center point, the encompassing circumference, and what is between them.
>
> The point is the Real, the space outside the encompassing circumference is nonexistence—or call it "darkness"—and what stands between the point and the space outside the circumference is the possible thing, like the image we have drawn in the diagram [figure 6.1].
>
> We have indicated a center point because it is the root of the *wujūd* of the circle's encompassing circumference. The circle has become manifest through the point. In the same way, the possible thing becomes manifest only through the Real.
>
> When you suppose that lines extend from the circle's center point to the circumference, these reach an end only at a point. So the whole circumference has a similar relation to the point. This is God's words, *And God is behind them, encompassing* [85:20], and His words, *He encompasses everything* [41:54]. Each point of the encompassing circumference is the end of a line, and the point from which the line extends to the circumference is the beginning of the line, for *He is the First and the Last* [57:3]. He is the First of every possible thing, just as the center point is the first of every line.
>
> That which emerges from the *wujūd* of the Real and becomes manifest from the Real is the nonexistence that does not accept *wujūd*, and the lines that emerge are the possible things. From God is their beginning and to God is their end, and *To Him the whole affair is returned* [11:123], for the lines end only at the point. Hence the firstness of the line and the lastness of the line pertain to the line/do not pertain to the line—say whichever you like. Concerning

such things it can appropriately be said, "They are neither He, nor other than He," like the attributes in the view of the Ash'arites.

"He who knows himself" in this manner, "knows his Lord." This is why the Lawgiver turned you over to knowledge of yourself in knowledge of God through His words, *We shall show them Our signs*, which are the signifiers, *upon the horizons and in themselves*. Hence He did not leave aside anything of the cosmos, for everything of the cosmos that is outside of you is identical with the *horizons*, which are the regions around you. *Until it is clear to them that it is the Real* [41:53], nothing else, because there is nothing else.

This is why the line is composed of points. You will not understand it rationally except in this manner. The surface is composed of lines, so it is composed of points, and the body is composed of surfaces, so it is composed of points. The furthest limit of composition is the body, and the body is eight points.

Nothing is known of the Real except the Essence and the seven attributes.[15] "They are neither He nor other than He," so the body is not other than the points, and the points are not other than the body, nor are they identical with the body.

I say that eight points are the least of the bodies because the name *line* arises from two or more points. The root of the "surface" arises from two or more lines, so the surface may arise from four points. And the root of the "body" arises from two or more surfaces, so the body may arise from eight points.

Thus the name *length* arrives newly for the body from the line, the name *width* from the surface, and the name *depth* from the composition of two surfaces. So the body stands on triplicity, just as the configuration of proofs stands on triplicity. In the same way, the root of *wujūd*—which is the Real—becomes manifest through bringing into existence only from three realities: His He-ness, His face-turning, and His word.[16]

The cosmos becomes manifest in the form of Him who gives it existence in both sensation and meaning. It is *a light upon a light* [24:35] and a darkness above a darkness. Standing contrary to every light is a darkness, just as standing contrary to every *wujūd* is a nonexistence. If *wujūd* is necessary, the necessary nonexistence is its contrary, and if *wujūd* is possible, the possible nonexistence is its contrary. So the contrary is in the form of its contrary, like the shadow and the object. (III 275.9)

In another chapter of the *Futūḥāt*, the Shaykh provides a more complicated diagram of *wujūd* based on the relation between the center and the circumference. In this context, he sees *wujūd* not in terms of a single circle, but in terms of a series of intersecting circles and semicircles. Here he provides us with a classification of the existent entities in respect of *wujūd*. We shall return to other examples of such classifications shortly.

Every line that emerges from the center point to the encompassing circumference is equal to its companions and reaches its end at a point on the circumference. In its essence the center point does not become plural or increase, despite the manyness of the lines emerging from it toward the circumference. It is the contrary of every point on the circumference through its essence. Were it to be the contrary of one point on the circumference with other than that with which it is the contrary of another point, it would become divided and could not be one. But it is one, so it is the contrary of all the points, despite their manyness, only through its own essence. Thus manyness has become manifest from the one in entity without the one becoming many in its essence. This shows the falsity of the words of those who say, "Nothing proceeds from the One but one."

The line that emerges from the center point toward one point on the encompassing circumference is the specific face[17] that every existent thing has from its Creator. It is indicated by His words, *Our only word to a thing, when We desire it, is to say to it "Be!," so it comes to be* [16:40]. Here the "desire" is the line that we have supposed as emerging from the center point of the circle to the circumference. It is the divine face-turning that entifies the point on the circumference through giving it existence. After all, the circumference is nothing but the circle of the possible things, and the center point that entifies the points on the circumference is the Necessary *Wujūd* in Itself.

This supposed circle is the circle of the genera of the possible things. They are restricted to spatially confined substances, substances not spatially confined, engendered qualities [*akwān*], and colors [*alwān*]. That which is not restricted is the *wujūd* of the species and the individuals. This arrives newly from each point of every circle, for within the circles, the circles of the species arrive newly, and from the circles of the species, the circles of species and individuals. So know this!

The root of all this is the first point. The line that connects the center point with the entified point on the circumference extends from the circle to the points that are born from it in the outside semicircle. Perfect circles emerge from this semicircle.

The cause of this is the distinction between the Necessary *Wujūd* in Itself and the possible thing. A perfect circle cannot become manifest from the possible thing that is the circle of the genera, for then this circle would share in that through which distinction occurs, but this is impossible, so a perfect circle cannot be engendered through the genera. Thereby becomes clear the imperfection of the possible thing in face of the perfection of the Necessary *Wujūd* in Itself.

The form of the affair is represented by the diagram [figure 6.2]. This is the form of the shape of the genera and the species, without the aim of being exhaustive, for the species have species until they finally reach the last species, just as they finally reach the genus of the genera. (I 260.1)

Ibn al-ʿArabī describes the point that generates the circles of the genera, species, and individuals in Chapter 369, from which several sections have already been quoted. The chapter is called "On the true knowledge of the waystation of the keys to the storehouses of munificence." Before enumerating the individual keys, the Shaykh describes the storehouses as the various genera that contain the species and the individuals. In his long introduction to the chapter, he reviews several of his most important themes.

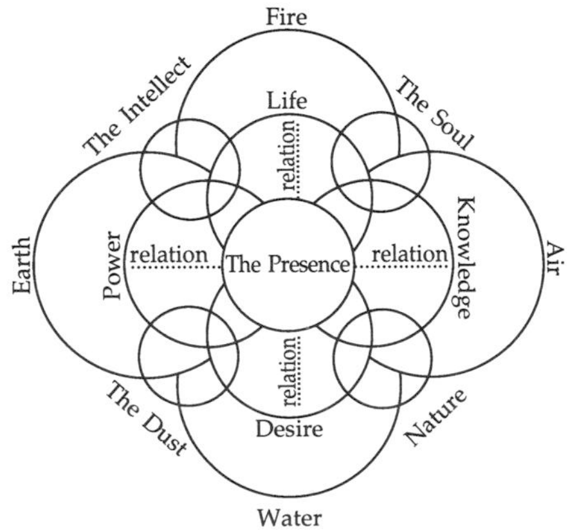

FIGURE **6.2**

The most excellent thing through which God has shown munificence to His servants is knowledge. When God bestows knowledge on someone, He has granted him the most eminent of attributes and the greatest of gifts.

Although knowledge is eminent in essence, it has another eminence that accrues to it from the object of knowledge, for it is an attribute that becomes connected to all things.

The keys are eminent in keeping with the eminence of the storehouses, and the storehouses are eminent in keeping with what has been stored within them.

The Real Existent is the greatest, most majestic, and most eminent of existent things. Hence knowledge of It is the most eminent, greatest, and most majestic of knowledges. Then the affair descends in eminence until the last object of knowledge.

Without exception, knowledge of a thing is better than ignorance of it, for the eminence of knowledge pertains to its essence, while any other eminence is earned.

The storehouses are restricted according to the restriction of the species of known things. Although the storehouses are many, they all go back to two—the storehouse of knowledge of God, and the storehouse of knowledge of the cosmos. In each of these two storehouses are many storehouses, such as knowledge of God in respect of His Essence by rational perception and in respect of His Essence by traditional [*samʿī*], Shari'ite perception; knowledge of God in respect of His names; knowledge of Him in respect of His descriptions; knowledge of Him in respect of His attributes; and knowledge of Him in respect of attributions to Him. All this is in respect both of reflective consideration and in respect of tradition. In respect of tradition He is just as He is in respect of unveiling.

The other storehouse, which is knowledge of the cosmos, also comprises many storehouses, and within each storehouse are found other storehouses. The storehouses are first, knowledge of the entities of the cosmos in respect of its possibility, in respect of its necessity, in respect of its essences that abide through themselves, in respect of its engendered qualities, in respect of its colors, in respect of its levels, and in respect of its place, time, relations, number, circumstance, displaying traces, being the locus in which traces from itself and other than itself are displayed, and so on to other knowledges. There is also knowledge of this world, the *barzakh*, the last world, and the higher and lower plenum.

The first key to these storehouses that God bestows upon the knower of God is the key to the storehouse of the knowledge of *wujūd* in an unbounded sense—without any binding by the newly arrived or the eternal—and knowledge of how *wujūd* becomes distinct. Does it become distinct through itself or through the "other," which is nonexistence? *Wujūd* is the manifestation of the Existent in Its Entity, for through that Existent all properties become manifest—negation and affirmation; necessity, possibility, and impossibility; *wujūd* and nonexistence; non-*wujūd* and non-nonexistence. None of this is affirmed and correct except from an Existent whose entity, whatness, and *wujūd* accept no multiplicity save through Its own ruling property upon Itself, for the realities that appear to It within It belong to Its own *wujūd*. Hence we say that there is manyness in Its Entity, while It is One. Each reality has a name, so It possesses names.

My names become embodied,
  so I am Many,
    and no other sees Me,
      so I am Seeing.
O you who speak of the other,
  where is its *wujūd*?
    How can there be the other?
      I am the Jealous!
Over whom is He
  high or exalted,
    when nothing is there?
      For through the Real the Real
is concealing in *wujūd*.
  By God, if not for God,
    His existence would not be
      rich, nor would the rich be poor!
Through whom and to whom
  are poverty and riches attached?
    Ask about Him through whom *wujūd*
      abides from *one experienced* [25:59].

Given that *wujūd* is the first of the storehouses of munificence, and God has bestowed upon you the key to this storehouse—like someone who makes yourself known to you so that you may come to know him—you are the first known thing, and He is the last known thing. You are the last existent thing, and He is the first existent. You have not the strength to know the nonexistent thing, for knowledge is a witnessing—if not, it is not knowledge. This is the *ḥaqq in which there is no doubt, a guidance to the godwary* [2:2].

He brought into existence from each storehouse a self-abiding entity, or an entity within an entity, or a non-entity within an entity. I mean by "non-entity within an entity" the relations, for they have no entities, but their properties rule over *wujūd*. They are not seen, and they have no *wujūd* save through ruling property.

Once He gave existence to what we have mentioned, He applied Himself to you. He gave existence to you as perfect, because the two sides of the circle reached their end. So you became manifest in your *wujūd*, even if you are a last in the form of the First. Thus the cosmos is restricted to you and to it, for He has no deliverance from the two of you, for you are not distinguished from it and it is not distinguished from you in property.

All the forms of the cosmos, which He had brought out from those storehouses, became manifest in you. They witnessed you, and you gained knowledge of them. Hence you came to know of the cosmos what it does not know of itself—its properties in its solitary individuals. He said to you, "All the infinite things that remain in the storehouses are like what you have come to know." For he who encompasses one of a genus in knowledge has encompassed the genus in knowledge, for there is nothing but likenesses.

So the two sides of the circle did not meet until the new arrival of the circumference. The circumference signifies the circle's center point. So the lines from the point to the circumference arrive newly, and they do not pass beyond the circumference, since the end of the line is at a point on the circumference. Hence it ends at that from which it emerged, so the form of its firstness is the same as the form of its lastness.

From the property of its last point, at which the line reaches its end in one circumference, it comes to another circumference, half of which is inside the first circumference and half of which is outside, because of the property of the manifest and the nonmanifest. Its two sides meet, like the meeting in the first circumference, so that the second may come to be in the form of the first. It is impossible for the second to emerge in other than the form of the first.

Then the same property becomes manifest in this circumference that became manifest in the first circumference, and so on ad infinitum. This is what appears from these storehouses, the contents of which are infinite. It is the new creation which engendered existence is in perpetually and forever. But some people, or most people, are uncertain about it, as He has said: *No indeed, but they are uncertain of a new creation* [50:15] breath by breath, but in the form we mentioned.

The center point is an occasion in the *wujūd* of the circumference, and the circumference is an occasion in gaining knowledge of the points. So the circumference is both Real and creation, and the point is both Real and creation. These two properties pervade every circle that becomes manifest from the first circle.

When the circles become manifest, as many as they may be—and they never cease becoming manifest—the first circle, which gave new arrival to these circles, becomes hidden. It is neither known nor perceived, because each circle, whether near to it or far from it, is in its form. Hence, concerning each circle, it is said, "It witnessed it/it did not witness it." This is an absent in a witnessed.

The number of the circles manifest in the first circle is equal to the number of the storehouses of the genera, whatever these may be. The number neither increases nor decreases. The circles that emerge and arrive newly from the first circle ad infinitum are the circles of the individuals of these genera, ad infinitum. The very circle of the individual signifies something that is named a "species." It is between the genus and the individual. Thus species within species arrive newly at you, though they are restricted. You recognize nothing but some of the individuals, because the species is intelligible between the most inclusive genus and the individual. Every intermediary is between two sides. If you like, you can say, "The two sides have made manifest its property of intermediacy." Or, if you like, you can say, "The intermediacy has made manifest the property of the two sides." This is the same as the knowledge of the Real through creation and of creation through the Real.

Were creation not witnessed through the
Real, it would not be,
and were the Real not witnessed through
creation, you would not be.
He who says *Be* is He whom you have
witnessed,
and there is nothing but what has come to
be through *Be*.
He who knows Him through creation
recognizes its *ḥaqq*,
and he who knows creation through the
Real is while he is not.

The circumference preserves the center point in knowledge, and the center point preserves the circumference in *wujūd*. Each of them is a preserver/a preserved, a viewer/a viewed. God says, *By a witnesser and a witnessed* [85:3]. Each is a witnessed and a witnesser, and each is ranked higher and lower. If one of the two says "I," the other says "I." If one of the two says "Thou," the other says to it "Thou." Neither becomes manifest to the other save through that through which both appear, and both sayings are correct.

O my Real, O my creation,
in whom are you annihilated, in whom do
you subsist?
I drank a drink from Him
that made my gullet choke.
There is nothing but an Entity,
so who will receive what you offer?
The one I mean said to me,
"Whenever you speak, refrain!"
For the affair is restricted
to creation and the Real.
If not for that, we would not be,
so hide the remembrance in the Real.

You, my friend, are the remembrance sent down, so you are the preserved. It was sent down only through you, so you are the preserver. Do not annihilate your entity, for, in actual fact, it is not annihilated. Your furthest limit is for you to say, "I am He." But what is signified by "He" is not signified by "I." So what you wish for will never be delivered over to you. Since He is exalted beyond such deliverance, uphold Him and uphold you; distinguish yourself from Him and distinguish Him from you. Distinguish the First from the Last and the Last from the First. Distinguish yourself from the cosmos and distinguish it from you. Distinguish the Manifest from the Nonmanifest and the Nonmanifest from the Manifest. For of the cosmos, you are the spirit of the cosmos, and the cosmos is your manifest form. The form has no meaning without a spirit, so the cosmos has no meaning apart from you.

When you distinguish your entity from the Real and from the cosmos, you will know your measure through knowledge of the Real, and you will know your waystation through knowledge of the cosmos.

Thereby are you a lord
and thereby are you a servant.
You have made a covenant
as He has made a covenant.

If you possess a kernel, deep diving,
  and astuteness,
    cling not to blame and cling not
      to praise.
When you act, do nothing
  through neglect
    and pinpoint the intention
      in your act.
You will not be such a person
  if your neglect overcomes you,
    so apply yourself with diligence
      to leaving it aside.

That to which I have called your attention is one of the keys to the storehouses of munificence, so do not waste it, for it does the work of every key, but no other key does its work. Through it every lock is opened, but nothing else opens what has been locked with this key. And *the keys to the absent—none knows them but He* [6:59], so they are not known except from Him. Do not wish to reach their knowledge through yourself. He who wishes for a thing not to be wished for has given witness against himself as to his ignorance. (III 361.16)

The Two Arcs

One of the important Koranic sources for meditations upon circularity is provided by the verses, *Then he drew close, so He came down, and he was two bows' length away, or closer* (53:8–9). The passage refers to the Prophet's *miʿrāj,* and many authorities have understood it as an allusion to the special nearness to God that the Prophet reached during this journey.[18] The word *qaws* or "bow" means "arc" in mathematics, so the "two bows" can be understood as the two arcs of a circle. Ibn al-ʿArabī reads the verse as an explicit reference to the visionary experience known as a "mutual waystation," in which God comes down and the servant rises up to meet Him.

In the Shaykh's view, the circle that is established by the two arcs is what he often calls the "totality" (*al-majmūʿ*), that is, the Real and creation. At root the two are one. Creation grows up from the Real and returns to the Real, and *wujūd* remains always a circle. Inasmuch as creation is established in contradistinction to the Real, the two arcs can be viewed as separated by a straight line bisecting the circle. The goal of the spiritual journey is to reach a point *closer* to the Real than the *two bows' length.* At that point, the traveler no longer sees the line, though its trace remains. However, the undifferentiation of the final situation is not the same as the undifferentiation of the cosmos "before" creation. At the origin of the journey, there was only the undifferentiated Real. When the journey is completed, the perfect human being is established in his station as the all-comprehensive engendered thing who has erased the distinction between Real and creation and who, at the same time, preserves it through his own *wujūd,* which is distinct from and identical with the *wujūd* of the Real. He/not He.

The term *nearness* can be ascribed to the reality of *two bows' length,* which is the measure of the line that divides the two semicircles of the circle, so it splits the circle into two portions. This is the furthest limit of the witnessed nearness. (II 132.34)

They may employ the word *nearness* and mean the *two bows,* which are the two arcs of the circle when it is bisected by the line of *or closer.* (II 558.23)

In the homesteads of the resurrection, the messengers will stand before God like guards before the king. The nearest of them in waystation will be he who is *closer* than *two bows' length away.* That is the meeting of the two semicircles of the circle. (II 84.23)

Ibn al-ʿArabī employs the imagery of the two bows in Chapter 389 while explaining the mutual waystation in which God said to him, "My *ill* is your engendered existence and your *ill* is My engendered existence." According to Lane's *Lexicon,* the word *ill,* which is not part of the Shaykh's normal technical vocabulary,[19] designates "anything which has a quality requiring it to be regarded as sacred, or inviolable; which has some right pertaining to it." More specifically, it is used to mean nearness with respect to kindred, origin, compact or covenant, Lordship, revelation, and

God. Ibn al-ʿArabī provides a definition toward the end of the quoted passage.

To me from You is drawing close at times,
  and then at times, to You from me.
I took from You knowledges as a bounty
  and You also took from me.
My I-ness is in You, O Beloved,
  when the tongue says "I."
How difficult Your words are for me
  when the heart says, "Join with me,"
even though I am not absent from Him when
    He discloses Himself—
  if it knew, it would crave in hope.

God says, *Then he drew close, so He came down*. This is precisely a mutual waystation, because both their forms left their places. Each form was *closer* to the other than *two bows' length away*. Each of the two forms has a bow that makes bending manifest. The distinguishing factor between the two forms is the line that divides the circle into two halves.

The affair was one entity. Then two affairs became manifest through the form. When the property became two affairs, one of them had a "coming down," because highness belongs to it, and, in this very coming down, a drawing close belonged to the other affair. The latter had an approach to the one who came down to it, so its drawing close was an ascent, because the coming down of the former was toward it. This lets us know that lowness is the portion of the latter.

The two approached each other only so that the affair should return to what it was—one circle with no separation between its two semicircles. Hence both are striving to remove the line that necessitates the division in the circle.

The site of the division is His words, "I have divided the *ṣalāt* into two halves between Me and My servant, so half belongs to Me and half belongs to My servant, and My servant shall have what he requests." The servant requests nothing save the removal of this division so that the affair may go back to what it was. The Real answers his request with His words, "And My servant shall have what he requests." *And to Him the whole affair is returned* [11:123].

His coming down is a drawing close,
  and our approach is an ascent.
We drew apart and came together—
  we are a *splendid couple* [22:5].
When we drew apart there arrived
  new constellations in our heaven,
and because of my coming to be they left
  clefts in our essences,
so there is a perpetual marriage act,
  an entering and an emergence.

On the same topic:

His is the coming down,
  mine the approach,
that I may see Him with my eye
  as He says—"He will see Me."

When we met out of love and yearning, He who knows best addressed me in my secret heart:

Place your hands on your liver [the seat of
    passion],
  and you will find what I find from you.
Come out seeking union
  and say to Him, "Give to me, and
    increase!"
If knowledge had no *wujūd* in him,
  no servant would remember.
If they deny this, say,
  "The Koran has come with it."

God says, *This is a message for the people,* so He specifies a designated group, *and let them be warned by it,* so He designates a different group, *and let them know that He is One God,* so He designates still another group, *and let the possessors of the kernels remember* [14:52], so He designates us. These are the ones that we mentioned, and they are the knowers of God and of the affair as it is in itself.

The line that divides the circle is none other than my distinction from Him and His distinction from me in the respect in which He is a God and I am a servant. When the distinction was realized, when separation occurred through engendering, and when the line made manifest its property; when He described us as being veiled from Him, and Himself as being veiled from us through the veils of the lights and the darknesses; when He laid down as Shariah for us what He laid down and He commanded us to turn in repentance to Him and described Himself as descending to us; then we came to understand that He desires the return of the affair to what it was.

After we came to know what we came to know and realized what we realized, He said of Himself that He is our hearing through which we hear, our eyesight through which we see, and He mentioned to us all the faculties that we find in ourselves. In this joining He affirmed our entities, so that to which the affair returns is not similar to what it was before the separation, because the property that the line affirmed does not disappear, even though the line disappears. Hence its trace subsists.

After all, we come to know that the circle was receptive to division, without doubt, but we did not know that beforehand. So, when the circle is joined, we continue to have knowledge that it possesses two portions of whatever parts you suppose to be within it, and that it accepts division, whatever the limits you suppose within it. This is because of the divine reports that have come qualifying the Real with the attributes of creation and qualifying creation with the attributes of the Real.

Thus He says, *Say: Call upon God or call upon the All-Merciful; whichever you call upon, to Him belong the most beautiful names* [17:110]. If you say "All-Merciful," you have named Him with all the most beautiful names, and if you say "God," you have named Him with all the most beautiful names. So also, you say that creation, which is the cosmos, receives the names and attributes of the Real. In the same way, the Real receives the attributes of creation, but not its names in differentiated detail. Nonetheless, He receives them in an undifferentiated manner. His reception in an undifferentiated manner is like His words, *O people, you are the poor toward God* [35:15]. As for the fact that He does not receive the names of the cosmos in differentiated detail, I mean by that the proper names. This is indicated by His words, *Name them!* [13:33], meaning the proper names. As for other than the proper names, the Real receives them in differentiated detail. After all, the Real has no proper name that does not signify a meaning other than His Essence, so all of His names are derived, but they descend to the place of proper names for Him. That is why sharing occurs in differentiated detail in the names of the Real, but it does not occur in the names of the cosmos. So realize what I have called attention to!

The greatest of our attributes that He has taken and that rational proofs show to be impossible is His words *And We shall assuredly try you until We know* [47:31]. Everything after this is easier, such as His self-transmutation in forms, and other things. But in reality, all are His descriptions. The greatest of what we have taken from Him is our knowledge of Him that rational proofs show to be impossible, and this is His words, *Nothing is as His likeness* [42:11] and the words of God's Messenger, "He who knows himself knows his Lord." Thus we take from Him, and He takes from us.

Oh the bewilderment that the realities
  of His coming to be cause to appear!
    Oh the loss for the servant
      when this escapes him!
When He gives life to someone,
  He bewilders his essence;
    when someone is not bewildered in Him,
      He has given him death toward Him.
Since creation's food
  is a realized coming to be,
    the God, the Real
      is the servant's food.

It was said to Sahl ibn ʿAbd Allāh, "What is food?" He replied, "God."[20]

Know also that the word *ill* means "God," and it is means "covenant." Hence his words, "My *ill* is your engendered existence," mean that My divinity became manifest only through you, for the divine thrall is he who places in himself the *wujūd* of the God. This is why the Prophet said, "He who knows himself knows his Lord." Your knowledge that God is your God is the fruit of your knowledge of your own essence. That is why, in knowledge of Him, God turned you over only to yourself and the cosmos. Every property that is affirmed for God is affirmed only through the cosmos. So the entity of the *ill*, in respect of its own entity, is described by these properties.

Were the cosmos to be lifted from the mind, all the divine properties would be lifted, and the Entity would remain without property. If it remained without property—even though it were the Necessary *wujūd* through its Essence—it would not be imperative for it to have the property of divinity.

Hence the *wujūd* of our entities derives from His *wujūd*, and our *wujūd* affirms knowledge of Him in our essences. Were it not for the fact that His Essence has given us our *wujūd*, it would not be correct for our entities to have *wujūd*. This is what the ulama mean when they say, "The cosmos has acquired *wujūd* from God."

As for His words, "Your *ill* is My engendered existence," this is identical with His words, "I am his hearing and his eyesight." Thus He made His He-ness identical with what is named "our hearing" and "our faculties." There is no cosmos without this property.

If I am annihilated, I am not,
but if I subsist, I am not,
for each of us belongs to each of us
and each of us comes to be from *Be!*
Take heed from us and from Him,
and you will find Him lowly in you.
So curtain Him, and make Him not manifest,
as He has come in "He is not."
In that His shining sun appeared
while He Himself did not stay still.
We have no support
and no stillness other than He.

The Real acts freely in the cosmos, and the cosmos acts freely in the Real. Do you not see that He says, *I respond to the call of the caller when he calls to Me* [2:186]? Is not response a free acting? Can response be conceived of apart from a call and a request? It is not correct for Him to exercise free acting upon Himself, so He has no free acting save in us. His free activity is His perpetual existence-giving. So entities become manifest, properties arrive newly for Him, and connections are not denied.

If you say, "We are one,"
you have spoken the truth,
and if you say, "Not one are we,"
that is no lie.

I wish I knew who is ignorant, since there is nothing there but God. Each knows what he does not know, then comes to know it. *And We shall assuredly try you until We know* [47:31]. (III 543.19)

Chapter 427: Two Bows' Length

Ibn al-ʿArabī's most detailed discussion of the circle formed by the two arcs is probably found in his chapter called "On the true knowledge of the mutual waystation of *Two Bows' Length*." He explains that the traveler who reaches this waystation finds that the center and the circumference have met and become one, and he enters with Abū Yazīd into the Station of No Station.

Two Bows' Length is nothing but a circle's diameter
distinguishing engendered existence from God.
When someone sees an Entity other than which is no entity,
that is the "closeness" of the neglectful cosmos.
It is he within whom He is *or closer*, and in Him
he has mysteries of knowledge unknown to the comprehension.
Doubt becomes manifest under the authority of *or*, for it has
the property of him brought near, the owner of authority and standing.
This verse came down in "The Star" [53]
and signifies the existence of likenesses and similars.
Whomever you reach knows Him through testing
in belief and act, in separation and union.
That is when He discloses Himself in the form of a circle,
saying, "You are the commander, the prohibiter."

God says, *He was two bows' length away, or closer* [53:9], alluding to setting up formal nearness. It has come in the prophetic report that God's Messenger said, "If you let down a rope, it will fall upon God." God says, *The All-Merciful sat upon the Throne* [20:5]. The Prophet said, "Our Lord descends to the closest heaven every night in the last third of the night," and so on. Weak rational faculties become bewildered, but rational faculties withdrawn to the door of His Presence become alerted and come to know what He desires.

Had you asked Him for increase, He would have increased. Thus He says, *Then he drew close* [53:8] in his night journey to the heavens so that He *might show him some of* His *signs* [17:1], *so He came down* [53:8]. This is an even stronger alerting and allusion to the fact that He is identical to the rope that is mentioned in the report. This signifies that the relation of rising and falling is equal in His case. Thus the report of the Companion of the Fish [Jonah] and the Companion of the Night Journey are brought together in that neither of the two is nearer to the Real than the other. So this is an allusion to the lack of spatial confinement and the fact that the Essence is unknown and not bound by a designated binding.

One of the signs that He showed him on the night of his journey was the fact that He came down in the state of his ascent. This is the same as that to which Abū Saʿīd al-Kharrāz alluded in his words concerning himself, "I knew God only by His bringing together the opposites."

Then he recited, *He is the First and the Last and the Manifest and the Nonmanifest* [57:3]. Hence, through His He-ness, He is in everything in a single state. Or rather, He is identical with the two opposites. If not for you, there would be no drawing close and no coming down.

There is no drawing close, no coming down,
no ascending and no falling—
If you consider all these
through realization, they are only lines.

In respect of your he-ness, you have no description and no attribute. It was said to Abū Yazīd, "How are you this morning?" He replied, "I have no morning and no evening. Morning and evening belong to him who is bound by attributes, but I have no attributes. For a time I wept, for a time I laughed, and today I neither laugh nor weep."

Rising and falling are descriptions, so the servant has no rising and no falling in respect of his entity and his he-ness. The one who rises is identical with the one who falls, so no one draws close save exactly the one who comes down. The coming down is to Him, and the drawing close is toward Him.

He was two bows' length away. Nothing makes the two arcs manifest from the circle save the imagined line. It is sufficient that you have said that it is "imagined," since the imagined is that which has no *wujūd* in its entity. The circle has been divided into two arcs, so the He-ness is identical with the circle, and it is nothing save the two arcs themselves. Hence the one arc is identical with the other arc in respect of the He-ness, and you are the dividing, imagined line.

The cosmos, next to the Real, is something imagined to have *wujūd*, not an existent thing. The "Existent" and the "*wujūd*" are nothing but the Entity of the Real. This is His words, *Or closer.* The "closer" is the removal of this imagined thing. When it is removed from imagination, nothing remains but a circle, and the two arcs are not entified.

When someone has a nearness to his Lord like this—I mean like the line that divides the circle—then he removes himself from the circle, no one knows the knowledge of God that he gains. This is His words, *Then He revealed to His servant what He revealed* [53:10]. He did not designate for us what He revealed in the Wise Remembrance, nor did the Messenger of God mention what He revealed to him in that nearness to Him. The reception in this homestead is an essential reception known only by him who tastes it.

None of the mutual waystations requires the meeting of the center point with the encompassing circumference save this mutual waystation. When the center meets the circumference, what is between the two disappears. This is the disappearance of the cosmos in the *wujūd* of the Real.

It is not that a center point becomes distinct from a circumference. On the contrary, the point itself in respect of being a point and the circumference itself in respect of being a circumference disappear. There subsists only a *wujūd* entity that makes its own property disappear as well as the property of that of the cosmos that is ascribed to it. This is a universal, all-inclusive disappearance, in entity and in property. *And God speaks the **ḥaqq**, and He guides on the path* [33:4]. (IV 39.24)

Modalities of Wujūd

Most of the discussion in this chapter has focused on the roots of order in terms of the divine names and certain relations implied by the names. The close attention that Ibn al-ʿArabī pays to the names places him in the context of the Koran, the Hadith, and the teachings of those Muslim authorities who grounded themselves in these sources. In contrast to these scholars, the philosophers paid relatively little attention to Koranic names of God, though divine attributes did play an important role for them, given that it is impossible to speak about God without mentioning them. But a major concern of the philosophers was to describe the order of the cosmos in terms of the modalities of *wujūd*. The most common division of these modalities—into Necessary, possible, and impossible—was made famous by Avicenna, and, as we have seen, Ibn al-ʿArabī has frequent recourse to it. He also divides *wujūd* in other ways, and these are worth investigating. His divisions are reminiscent of certain philosophical and theological discussions but, at the same time, they carry the stamp of his originality.

In the standard philosophical conceptualization of *wujūd* as Ibn al-ᶜArabī understands it, the Necessary is that which cannot not have *wujūd* because, in its own essence, it is identical with *wujūd*. The possible is that which may or may not have *wujūd*; however, its own essence demands the precedence of its nonexistence over its *wujūd*. The impossible thing cannot have *wujūd*. Once the possible thing is found in *wujūd*, it can be called "the necessary through the Other." Having seen that it exists, we know that God's precedent knowledge demanded its existence. It could not not have existed, because its *wujūd* was written in the Divine Book for all eternity. In the following, the Shaykh discusses the levels that things find in their *wujūd* in terms of position or "placement" (*makāna*), which is typically contrasted with "place" (*makān*).

> Although the levels that have entered into *wujūd* are nonexistent, they are imagined to have *wujūd*, for they are relations of nonexistence. These levels are "placement." Each thing, whether existent or nonexistent in property, dwells in its level, whether its *wujūd* is necessary through its essence or through the other, or its *wujūd* is impossible.
>
> Hence unadulterated nonexistence has a level, sheer *wujūd* has a level, and the sheer possible thing has a level. Each level is distinct from the others. Hence there is nothing that escapes from imagined and intelligible classifications. (III 419.18)

Ibn al-ᶜArabī frequently distinguishes between the *wujūd* that is eternal (*qadīm*) and that which is newly arrived (*ḥādith*, *muḥdath*), or the *wujūd* that is identical with the Real and that which is attributed to creation.

> A Mystery
> *He who* lays hold of the firmest
> handle *[31:22]*
> *will never become wretched.*
>
> He who *lays hold of the firmest handle*
> is the imam, the most godwary master.
> In its revelation the Spirit reported
> that he will be made felicitous and never
> be wretched.
>
> He says: The handle is a circle in which two semicircles are supposed, and these are separated by an imagined line. The firmest handle is you and He in respect of the circle's two semicircles. For *wujūd* is divided between you and Him, because it is divided between Lord and servant. The eternal is the Lord, the newly arrived is the servant, and *wujūd* is an affair that brings us together. "I have divided the *ṣalāt* into two halves between Me and My servant, so half belongs to Me and half belongs to My servant."
>
> In one respect this handle will break, for the arrangement of the Shariah's prescription must dissolve. Then the *ṣalāt* that is configured in this guise will disappear, and there will remain the *ṣalāt* of the essential configuration, which ties you to Him in the state of your nonexistence and your *wujūd*. This is "the firmest handle" that has no breaking. So lay hold of it!
>
> You will not be alone with Him without yourself, nor will you make Him two through yourself. Rather, He is He, and you are you. (IV 438.3)

In his chapter on the divine names, Ibn al-ᶜArabī distinguishes between the eternal and the newly arrived while looking at the names Uplifter (*rafīᶜ*) and He Who Puts Down (*khāfiḍ*) and at the Presences in which these two display their traces. He points out that uplifting is inherent to eternal *wujūd*, while putting down is inherent to temporal *wujūd*. "Uplifting belongs to Him by essence, and it belongs to the servant by accident; its property is the contradictory of the Presence of putting down, for putting down belongs to the servant at root, while uplifting belongs to the Real" (IV 227.18).

> In its own essence *wujūd* may be divided into that which has a first, that is, the newly arrived, and that which has no first, that is, the eternal. The eternal of *wujūd* is that which has priority, and that which has priority possesses uplifting. The newly arrived has posteriority, so it is put down from the uplifting that belongs rightfully to the Eternal because of priority. (IV 226.5)

Wujūd can be divided into eternal and newly arrived, but only the former is Unbounded *Wujūd*, or *wujūd* in every respect. Newly arrived things are *wujūd* in some respects and nonexistence in others. All entities are nonexistent in themselves, but existent in the respects in which God gives them existence. In one place, the Shaykh describes the possible respects as four levels of *wujūd*—existence in entity, in the mind (*dhihn*), in speech, and in writing. He is in the process of explaining that the *wujūd* of a thing depends upon attributions and relations. Things have *wujūd* "inasmuch as" they stand in one relation or another. Thus they may have *wujūd* in respect to their own existent entities, in respect to knowledge of these entities, in respect to their being spoken about, and in respect to their being written about. As for God, He has three of these relative *wujūds*, but not *wujūd* in *our* knowledge, since His Essence is infinitely beyond us.

"*Wujūd*" consists of the affirmation of the entity of a thing, and "nonexistence" consists of its negation. Once the entity of the thing is affirmed or negated, it is permissible for it to be qualified by nonexistence and *wujūd* together, but this is through relation and attribution.

Thus Zayd, who is existent in his entity, may be existent in the market and nonexistent in the house. Were nonexistence and *wujūd* descriptions that go back to the existent thing, like black or white, it would be absurd for the thing to be described by both together. In that case, if the thing were nonexistent, it would not be existent, just as, if it were black, it would not be white.

Hence it may be correct for the thing to be described by both nonexistence and *wujūd* at the same time. This is a relative *wujūd*, and a nonexistence along with the affirmation of the entity.

Since it is not correct for *wujūd* to be an attribute that simply abides without attribution in an object of sensory or intelligible description, it is affirmed that it comes unconditionally under the heading of attributions and relations, like east and west, right and left, front and behind. Thus no *wujūd* is specified for this description to the exclusion of any other *wujūd*.

It may be asked how it is correct for a thing that is nonexistent in itself to be qualified by *wujūd* in a certain world or in a certain relation, such that it would be existent in its entity but nonexistent in a certain relation. We would reply as follows:

In fact, everything in *wujūd* has four levels except God, for in relative *wujūd* He has three levels. The first level is the *wujūd* of the thing in its entity. This is the second level with regard to the Real's knowledge of the newly arrived thing. The second level is the thing's *wujūd* in knowledge. This is the first level in respect of God's knowledge of us [since He knows us first in Himself]. The third level is its *wujūd* in spoken words. The fourth level is its *wujūd* in written letters.

With regard to our knowledge [of God], the Real *Wujūd* of God has these levels, save the level of [*wujūd* in our] knowledge. (*Inshā*ʾ 7–8)

The Shaykh provides a more detailed explanation of this classification into four levels in his chapter on knowledge in the *Futūḥāt*.

You should know, brothers, that there is no known thing, whatever it may be, that has no ascription to *wujūd*, whatever kind of *wujūd* it may be. After all, *wujūd* has four sorts. Among the objects of knowledge is that which brings together all the levels of *wujūd* and among them is that which is qualified by some levels of *wujūd* and not by others. These four levels that belong to *wujūd* are as follows:

[The first level is] entified *wujūd*, which is the existent thing in itself, whatever may be the reality of its qualification by being inside, being outside, or the negation of both. In the last case, while it is an existent thing in its entity, it is neither inside the cosmos nor outside it, because it lacks the precondition for being inside or outside, which is spatial confinement. This belongs only to God specifically. As for that of the cosmos that abides through itself without spatial confinement, like rationally speaking souls, the First Intellect, the Soul, the Enraptured Spirits, nature, and the Dust—and I mean by all of these their spirits—all these are inside the cosmos. However, they are not inside the bodies of the cosmos, nor are they outside them, because they are not spatially confined.

The second level is mental *wujūd*. It is for the object of knowledge to be given form as it is in its own reality in the soul. If the assumption of form does not coincide with the reality, that object does not have *wujūd* in the mind.

The third level is speech. Objects of knowledge possess a *wujūd* in words, and this is verbal *wujūd*. Every object of knowledge enters into this *wujūd*, even the impossible and nonexistence. The impossible has verbal *wujūd*, because it is found in words, though it never accepts entified *wujūd*. As for nonexistence, if it is the nonexistence by which the possible thing is described, it accepts entified *wujūd*, but if it is the nonexistence that is the impossible thing, then it does not accept entified *wujūd*.

The fourth level is written *wujūd*, which is *wujūd* in written letters. This is the thing's relation to *wujūd* in script, figures, or writing, and for all objects of knowledge, whether impossible or not impossible, this relation is one relation. Although no entity is found for the impossible thing, it has the relation of *wujūd* in words and script.

Thus there is no object of knowledge that is not qualified by *wujūd* in some respect. The occasion of this is the strength of *wujūd*, which is the root of roots, that is, God, because through Him these levels become manifest and the realities become entified. Through His *wujūd* that which accepts all levels of *wujūd* is known as distinct from that which does not accept them.

Thus the *wujūd* of the names, whether these are spoken or written, applies to every known thing. Hence the known thing becomes qualified by one sort of *wujūd*, so there is nothing in knowledge that is nonexistent in an absolute sense, such that it should have no relation with *wujūd* whatsoever. This cannot be conceived of. So understand this root, and realize it! (II 309.21)

Ibn al-ᶜArabī often classifies things in a more detailed fashion by describing the mode in which they become manifest in *wujūd*. Some things, for example, are substances and some are accidents. The former are said to "abide through themselves" (*qāʾim bi nafsihā*), while accidents abide through substances. Bodily things are localized in space or "spatially confined" (*mutaḥayyiz*), while spirits are not. After having explained the rationale for God's choices (those listed on pp. 189–90), Ibn al-ᶜArabī provides a brief version of this sort of classification:

We do not know by way of encompassment the differentiated details of the existent things that have been created by God, even though we are able—because God has enabled us—to restrict the existent things such that everything is included. But we occupy ourselves with this only for the sake of knowing the individual things that God has chosen and selected from every kind of created thing restricted within *wujūd*. These may abide through themselves; they may or may not be spatially confined, whether or not they abide through themselves; they may be of the kind that accepts spatial confinement only through subordination; or of the kind that is or is not formed of combinations of all this. All the sorts of the cosmos and the existent things are restricted within what I just mentioned. (II 174.30)

The Shaykh expands on this way of arranging the existent things in the following passage:

Know that every object of knowledge can be classified, for it has no escape from entering into mental *wujūd*. That which enters into mental *wujūd* may accept entified *wujūd*; or, it may not accept it, like the impossible thing.

That which accepts entified *wujūd* either abides through itself—in which case it is said [that it abides] "not in any substrate [*mawḍūᶜ*]"—or it does not so abide.

The sort of *wujūd* that abides through itself is either spatially confined or not spatially confined.

The sort of *wujūd* that is neither within any substrate nor spatially confined must either be the necessary *wujūd* through its Essence, and that is God; or a necessary *wujūd* through the Other, and that is the possible thing. The possible thing is either spatially confined or not spatially confined.

As for the division of the possible things that abide through themselves, they are either

[1] not spatially confined, like the rationally speaking souls that govern the substance of the luminous, natural, and elemental worlds.
[2] or spatially confined. These are either
  [a] compound and possessing parts or
  [b] not possessing parts.
    If the thing does not possess parts, it is a solitary substance [i.e., an atom]. If it possesses parts, it is a body.

As for the sort of *wujūd* that is within a substrate, it is that which does not abide through itself, nor does it become spatially confined, save by subordination. It must be either a concomitant of the substrate, or not a concomitant in the view of the eye. As for the actual situation, nothing that abides through itself remains in the actual situation for more than the [momentary] time of its *wujūd*. However, some of it is followed by likenesses, and some of it is followed by that which is not a likeness. What is followed by likenesses is the one concerning which it is imagined that it is a concomitant, like the yellow of gold or the black of an African. As for what is not followed by likenesses, that is named an "accident," while the concomitant is named an "attribute."

The known things that have entified *wujūd* are nothing other than what we have mentioned. (II 454.1)[21]

The Shaykh employs classifications of *wujūd* in a variety of contexts. In the following, he builds on the distinction between substances and accidents to explain that in every situation the cosmos has need of God, because of its poverty or possibility. This explains why God is called the "Watchful" (*al-raqīb*). The passage is taken from a chapter on *murāqaba*, which means literally to watch, observe, guard attentively, supervise. The term also designates a type of Sufi practice, "self-watchfulness," often translated as "self-examination" or "meditation."

Murāqaba is a divine description in which we have drinking.[22] God says, *God is watchful over everything* [33:52]. This is also referred to in His words, *The preserving of those two oppresses Him not* [2:255], meaning by *those two* the heavens, which are the higher world, and the earth, which is the lower world. There is nothing but higher and lower.

[The cosmos] is of two sorts—a world that abides through itself, and a world that does not abide through itself. What abides through itself is substances and bodies. What does not abide through itself is engendered qualities and colors, which are attributes and accidents.

The worlds of bodies and substances have no subsistence save through the giving of existence to accidents within them. Whenever accidents are not given existence within them—accidents through which they have subsistence and *wujūd*—they become nonexistent.

There is no doubt that accidents become nonexistent in the time second to the time of their *wujūd*. Hence the Real never ceases "watching" over the world of the higher and lower bodies and substances. Whenever an accident through which something [in these two worlds] has *wujūd* becomes nonexistent, He creates at that time an accident like the first or opposite to it so as to preserve the thing from nonexistence at each time. So He is Ever-Creating perpetually, while the cosmos—whether the world of accidents or that of substances—is perpetually poor toward Him through an essential poverty. This then is the Real's "watching" over His creation to preserve *wujūd* for it. And these are the "tasks" concerning which He gave expression in His Book: *Each day He is upon some task* [55:29]. (II 208.24)

7. *The Worlds of the Cosmos*

Up to this point, discussion has centered on the relation between God and the cosmos in terms of *wujūd* and the divine names. Often this has brought up reference to various existent things that inhabit the cosmos and to the relations that are established among these things. These things and their interrelationships will be the focus from here on. However, given the nature of Ibn al-ʿArabī's perspective, focusing on the things within the cosmos does not mean that God can now be left out of the picture. *Wujūd* remains the fundamental issue, since nothing exists in any world save through *wujūd*'s self-disclosures.

The most salient feature of the cosmos as an existent thing is that it is God's form. Hence the names and attributes that are applied to God can also be applied to the cosmos, though not in exactly the same manner. It follows that any intradivine relations that are designated by the divine names can also be observed in the cosmos, once the appropriate adjustments have been made. Thus, for example, we have already seen that just as

God is Manifest and Nonmanifest, so also the cosmos has manifest and nonmanifest domains. Just as God is First and Last, so also the cosmos has a beginning and an end. First and Last set the stage for the division of the cosmos into two basic worlds on the horizontal or temporal level—this world and the last world. Manifest and Nonmanifest are the divine principles of two basic worlds of the cosmos when it is viewed vertically—the bodily world and the spiritual world. Both horizontal and vertical perspectives allow for indefinite subdivision. In both cases, a third world can also enter the picture, a world that is often called the *barzakh* or "isthmus." Although Ibn al-ʿArabī's teachings on the relation between the *barzakh* and the last world are extensive, what follows will concentrate instead on the vertical and atemporal picture of the cosmos. A detailed discussion of the cosmological status of the last world will have to wait for the next volume.

The basic terms that Ibn al-ʿArabī and others employ to refer to the cosmic dualities that manifest the traces of the names Manifest and Nonmanifest include command and creation, heaven and earth, sovereignty and kingdom, spirit and body, meaning and form, high and low, subtle and dense, absent and witnessed, intelligible (or suprasensory) and sensory. Each of these pairs has its own range of meanings and connotations. Although the meanings may overlap sufficiently for the pairs to be used as synonyms, the differences in nuance also need to be taken into account.

Each member of these pairs is a correlative, which is to say that each member needs to be understood in terms of the other member. Even if Ibn al-ʿArabī uses only one of the terms, the other is implied, because these terms have no independent meanings. It makes no sense to speak of heaven, for example, without earth, and vice versa. It follows that such terms do not designate discrete objects. One might think that a "body" is a thing that can be investigated without reference to "spirit," but not from Ibn al-ʿArabī's standpoint. To speak of the body is to mention, if only by implication, the spirit. Moreover, what is body from one point of view may be spirit from another point of view.

The shifting nature of labels becomes obvious as soon as we consider the intermediary world, the *barzakh* or imagination. Cosmically, the world of imagination stands between the world of spirits and the world of bodies. From the standpoint of bodily things, imagination is spiritual, but from the standpoint of spiritual things, imagination is bodily. Any attribute that belongs properly to imagination has this characteristic of ambiguity, because it cannot be understood without reference to other attributes. And since every attribute in the cosmos and God can be found in imagination, all attributes have this characteristic. Hence there are no absolutely discrete qualities or characteristics. Any attribute that is ascribed to anything in the cosmos has to be understood in the respect in which the attribute makes sense. This same attribute, from other standpoints, can be stripped from the thing to which it is ascribed. After all, every attribute is rooted in the Real, and every entity is He/not He. Inasmuch as the entity is He, real attributes will be found within it, but inasmuch as it is not He, such attributes will not be found. Although certain attributes, such as ignorance and nonexistence, do not pertain to the Real, they remain ambiguous in the creatures. Everything is ignorant when compared to God, but everything is knowledgeable when compared to nonexistence.

From the standpoint of *tanzīh*, all the dualities found in the created order point to the fact that God stands beyond any duality. Thus the Shaykh writes,

> We considered everything other than the Real and found it to be of two sorts. One sort is perceived through its very essence; it is the sensory and dense. Another sort is perceived through its activity; it is the intelligible and subtle. So the intelligible is lifted above the sensory through this waystation—the fact that it is kept free of being perceived through its essence and is perceived only through its act.
>
> Given that these are the descriptions of the created things, the Real is too holy to be perceived either through His Essence, like the sensory thing, or through His act, like the subtle or intelligible thing, for there is no correspondence whatsoever between Him and His creation. This is because His Essence is not perceived by us,

or else He would be similar to the sensory thing, nor is His act like the act of the subtle thing, or else He would be similar to the subtle thing. After all, the Real's act is to innovate the thing not from something, whereas the spiritual, subtle thing acts on the thing through things. So how can these two correspond? If it is impossible for there to be a correspondence in acts, for an even greater reason it is impossible for there to be mutual similarity in essences. (I 93.32)

Absent and Witnessed

If *tanzīh* tells us that God lies beyond all duality, *tashbīh* provides a different picture, since it alerts us to the fact that every duality in the cosmos is prefigured in the divine names. Moreover, the terms that specify dualities in God can also be employed to refer not only to dualities in the cosmos itself, but also to distinctions between God and the cosmos. Take, for example, the term *absent* (*ghayb*), which is mentioned in some fifty Koranic verses. It is a basic Islamic concept, so much so that it designates, in summary fashion, the objects of faith, much as the word *ṣalāt* designates, in summary fashion, Islamic practice. The Koran is *the Book wherein is no doubt, a guidance to the godwary, who have faith in the Absent and perform the* ***ṣalāt*** (2:2–3). Thus the term *ghayb* refers to God and the angels, not to mention everything else that is absent from the visible world, which is called the "witnessed" (*shahāda*), that which presents itself to the eyes of the viewers. In ten verses the Koran says that God is *the Knower of the absent and the witnessed.* In contrast, people cannot witness the absent with their eyes, so they must have faith in it, and through their faith they witness it in their hearts. Hence the basic act of faith—uttering the double testimony—is named by this same word *shahāda,* though in this case it needs to be translated as "witnessing." Only faith can allow the Koranic absent to become witnessed.

Like other attributes that can be applied to the Real, the term *ghayb* has two basic senses—absolute and relative. Absolute absence pertains to the divine Essence, *wujūd* itself, and relative absence pertains to everything in *wujūd.* But to say that the Essence is absolutely absent means, of course, that it is absolutely absent from every *created* thing, not from God Himself, by whom it is witnessed. From the divine point of view, nothing can be absent. Absence pertains only to a creaturely perspective.

Nothing is absent in God's case. A thing is "absent" only relatively. (III 92.17)

I mean by "absent" the absent of *wujūd,* that is, what is in *wujūd* but is made absent from some people's eyesights and insights. As for what is absent through not being existent—the key to that absent *none knows but He* [6:59]. (III 350.34)

When God created the cosmos, He appointed for it a manifest and a nonmanifest, and He made some of the cosmos absent from itself and some witnessed by itself. That of the cosmos that is absent from the cosmos is "the absent," and that of the cosmos that is witnessed by it is "the witnessed." But all of this is witnessed by God and manifest to Him. (III 303.2)

The Real is named the Manifest and the Nonmanifest—the Manifest because of the forms within which He undergoes transmutation, and the Nonmanifest because of the meaning that accepts this transmutation and manifestation in forms. Hence He is *the Knower of the absent* in respect of being the Nonmanifest *and the witnessed* [6:73] in respect of being the Manifest. (II 390.33)

You should know that knowing an affair does not entail witnessing it. This proves that the relation of your vision of the things is other than the relation of your knowledge of them. Hence the relation of knowledge attaches both to the witnessed and the absent. Hence, what is witnessed of every witnessed thing is known, but not every known thing is witnessed.

Nowhere has it come in the Shariah that God "witnesses" the absent things. It has only come that He "knows" the absent things. This is why He describes Himself by vision, for He says, *Does he not know that God sees?* [96:14]. He also describes Himself by eyesight and by knowledge. Thus He differentiated among the relations and He distinguished some from others, so that the differences might be known.

Since it is not conceivable that there be an absent in the case of God, we come to know that the "absent" is something relative to us because of what is absent from us. It is as if He who says *Thou art the Ever-Knowing of the absent things* [5:109] is saying that this is what is absent from us. So also is the case with *the Knower of the absent and the witnessed* [6:73]—that is, what is absent from us, and what we witness.

The creature may witness the thing, but witnessing it does not necessitate knowledge of its definition and reality. However, "knowing" a thing necessitates knowledge of its definition and reality, whether it be in nonexistence or in *wujūd*. Otherwise, you have not known it.

All things are witnessed by the Real in the state of their nonexistence. Were this not so, He would not have specified some of them apart from others for existence-giving, for there can be no distinction in sheer nonexistence, within which there are no fixed entities—in contrast to the nonexistence of the possible things.

The fact that knowledge distinguishes some things from others and differentiates some from others is called "His witnessing them" and "His entifying them"—that is, His seeing them through His Entity. Although they are described by nonexistence, they are not nonexistent to God, the Real, in respect of His knowledge of them. In the same way, a human being who devises things conceives of the form of what he desires to devise in himself. Then he makes it appear, so he makes its entity become manifest to itself, for it has come to be qualified by entified *wujūd*. In the state of its nonexistence, it had been described by having *wujūd* in "mental *wujūd*" in our case, and in "cognitive *wujūd*" in God's case. Hence the manifestation of the things is from a *wujūd* to a *wujūd*—from a *wujūd* of knowledge to a *wujūd* of entity.

As for the "impossible," which is sheer nonexistence, within it are no entities to become distinct. (I 538.22)

One of the many Koranic references to the absent is the already mentioned verse, *At Him are the keys to the absent—none knows them but He* (6:59). Ibn al-ʿArabī provides a number of explanations for this verse, one of which deserves to be cited in the present context. The word *miftāḥ* or "key" is derived from the same root as the word *fatḥ* or "opening." Literally, a *miftāḥ* is the means whereby opening is achieved, and "opening" is one of Ibn al-ʿArabī's favorite designations for unveiling. More broadly, opening can refer to anything that has the characteristics of a door. In the following, the Shaykh understands the term *key* to be an allusion to the entity's preparedness, which opens it up to the effusion of *wujūd* and knowledge. The passage derives from Chapter 382, which has a curious title that can perhaps best be rendered as follows: "On the true knowledge of an unknown mutual waystation. It is when the servant climbs without designating the intention of what he intends with the Real. But everything is designated at the Real. Hence he has intended from the Real, by way of the lack of designation, something that does not correspond with his intention."

As for *the keys to the absent—none knows them but He* [6:59], this is a topic that belongs to this chapter. These keys are known only by God's knowledge-giving. But, if they are known, it is not known that they are the keys to the absent. So pay attention to this!

You should know that knowledge-giving has made manifest to us that the preparednesses of the receptacles are *the keys to the absent*. This is because there is nothing but an unbounded, all-inclusive gift and an effusion of munificence. In actual fact, there is no absent domain, nor is there any witnessing. On the contrary, there are infinite objects of knowledge. Among them, some have *wujūd*, some have no *wujūd*, some have occasioning, some have no occasioning, some have the receptivity for *wujūd*, and some have no receptivity for *wujūd*.

There is a key, an opening, and something opened. When the opened thing is opened, that which had been veiled by it becomes manifest. So the key is your preparedness for learning and receiving knowledge, the opening is the teaching, and the opened thing is the door at which you come to a halt.

If you do not halt and you travel on, you will see with every step what you had not been seeing, and you will come to know *what you did not know, and God's bounty to you is ever magnificent* [4:113], for preparedness is not earned. On the contrary, it is a divine grant. This is why none knows it but God.

Hence it is known that there are keys to the absent, but the key to any specific absent domain among the individual absent domains is not known.

Once the preparedness is gained from God, the key is gained. There remains the opening so that teaching may occur. Thus He says, *The All-Merciful—He taught the Koran, He created the human being, He taught him the clarification* [55:1–4]. The teaching is identical with the opening. (III 542.28)

Ibn al-ʿArabī sometimes employs the terms *absent* and *witnessed* to help delineate various modes of visionary knowledge that the travelers achieve in their ascents to God.

The divine names have a manifestation that prevails over every *miʿrāj*. This is why at certain moments each of the groups we have mentioned [in this waystation] report about their Lord without any intermediaries. This is indicated by the Prophet's words, "I have a moment when none embraces me other than my Lord." This station belongs to every individual among the creatures. Did he not say, "Everyone who performs the *ṣalāt* is whispering with his Lord"? Where are the intermediaries in this station?

So also is the situation in the last abode at the Halting Place. The Prophet said, "There is not one of you to whom God will not speak directly, there being no spokesman between Him and him." So also is the situation right now. However, at the resurrection, everyone will know that his Lord is speaking to him, but in this world, no one knows this save the knowers of God, the companions of the marks. They recognize God's speech to them.

So glory be to Him who created us in stages and who appointed for us night and daytime as signifiers of the knowledge of the absent and the witnessed! He *obliterates the sign of the night*, because it signifies the absent, *and He makes the sign of the daytime to see* [17:12], because it signifies the world of the witnessed. Hence, among us are those to whom their Lord speaks in the absent domain, and this is the self-disclosure that is similar to the moon on the night it is full. This shining of the full moon is your own attribute. In other words, when you reach perfection, the Real speaks to you in the self-disclosure of the moon as a full moon, for He is with every existent thing through His Essence.

Among us are those to whom their Lord speaks in the witnessed domain, and this is the self-disclosure that is similar to the sun, below which is no cloud.[1] (III 56.13)

Chapter 492: Knowledge of the Absent

One sort of knowledge of the absent pertains to the prophets. They are those to whom God has given knowledge of specific absent things, such as angels or the day of resurrection. Faith in God demands faith in the absent realities concerning which God's messengers speak, and such faith is a characteristic of all the faithful. In contrast, direct knowledge of the absent is the distinguishing feature of the Folk of God, those who, as the Shaykh never tires of reminding us, possess "insight" and stand *upon a clear sign from* their *Lord* (11:17). This knowledge of the absent arrives by way of the specific face. Ibn al-ʿArabī explains this in the chapter called "On the true knowledge of the state of the Pole whose waystation is *Knower He of the absent, so He does not make His absent manifest to anyone, save only to a messenger with whom He is well-pleased* [72:26–27]."

Were the absent to appear to an eye,
  that would not be the absent, for it would be witnessed.
He does not make the World of the Absent manifest—
  no, and no one becomes manifest within it.
All existence is witnessed by Him;
  with Him nothing is absent that is not found.
The absent pertains to us, not to Him—
  through this is He solitary in *wujūd*.
Hence He said to those He witnessed, "Be!"
  So take Him, my friend, as your support.

Know—God confirm us and you with the spirit of holiness—that someone may happen upon knowledge when conjecturing that he is described by knowledge, for he is described by knowledge in actual fact. This is why God's Messenger said to the man to whom it had occurred that [the most magnificent section of the Koran] was the Fātiḥa, "So that the knowledge may benefit you," that is, in actual fact. The Prophet said to him, "So that the knowledge may benefit you" concerning what the man had mentioned about what had occurred to him, and thereby he himself gained the knowledge of the affair as it was in actual fact, and inescapably so.

Know that the "absent" is of two sorts. One sort will never be known. It is nothing but the He-ness of the Real and His relation to us—though, as for our relation with Him, it is otherwise. This absent domain is forever impossible and unknown.

The other sort is relatively absent, because what is witnessed by one thing may be absent from another. In *wujūd* nothing whatsoever is absent such that it would be witnessed by no one. The least of it is that the existent thing should witness its own self that is absent from everything save itself. Hence there is no absent thing that is not witnessed in the state of being absent from those who do not witness it.

When it is God's good-pleasure to let someone know about the absent, He gives him an overview of it through knowledge, not through conjecture or surmise. Hence the person knows only through God's knowledge-giving, or through the knowledge-giving of the one to whom, in the person's belief, God has given knowledge. No one else has any knowledge whatsoever of the absent.

The only one who is specified for this knowledge-giving is the one called the "messenger," because He did not give him knowledge of the absent so that he would keep it for himself, but rather so that he would make it known. Thereby he gains the degree of excellence over the person to whom he gives the knowledge, so that this person may come to know his placement at his Lord. This is why He calls him a "messenger."

This sort of absent comes to be only from the specific face. No angel or anyone else knows it, save the messenger specifically, whether the messenger is an angel or something else. For God has negated that *He make His absent manifest to anyone*; He says concerning the one *with whom He is well-pleased* in this that *He dispatches before him and behind him guards* [72:26–27], to protect him from detracting obfuscations. So obfuscations have no access to the companion of this knowledge. This is the companion of insight who is *upon a clear sign from his Lord* [11:17] in his knowledge.

He has a specific tasting through which he becomes distinguished and in which no one shares with him, for, if it were shared, it would not be specific. When the messenger comes with it to the one whom he teaches, this does not, for the learner, pertain to the knowledge of the absent. For God has made it manifest to the messenger, so for him it does not pertain to the knowledge of the absent that God *does not make manifest to anyone*.

This is what any knower may gain by way of the specific face. However, this does not occur now in this world, though it does occur in the last world. The occasion of this is that Muhammad knew every knowledge that human beings gain in this world—knowledge of God specifically—for he knew "the knowledge of the first and the last folk," and you are among the last folk, without doubt.

As for what concerns other than knowledge of God, a human being may be given this by way of the specific face, and no one will know it except from him. Then he is a messenger in teaching it to the one to whom he teaches it. This bestows upon him the station of Muhammad. However, no benefit accrues save in knowledge of God, for it is this knowledge through which the form of the cosmos becomes beautiful in his soul. Thus knowledge of God from the messenger is greater and more beneficial for the student than knowledge you gain from the specific face—if the object of knowledge is one of the engendered things, not God. After all, human beings have no eminence save in their knowledge of God. As for their knowledge of other than God, it is a diversion through which veiled human beings divert themselves. Those who have achieved the equitable balance have no aspiration save toward knowledge of Him.

So strive, if you are among those who take knowledge of God from the Messenger of God. Then you will be Muhammadan in witnessing. For we know for certain that today none of God's creatures knows God through an eye that is designated specifically for him.

ʿĀʾisha alluded to this in her interpretation concerning God's Messenger. She said, "Whoever supposes that Muhammad saw his Lord has committed a great calumny toward God, for God says, *Eyesights perceive Him not* [6:103]."

Here there is a mystery. Investigate it, and do not say, "I have been forbidden access completely." I have not forbidden access to you by saying, "You shall not know." Rather, I have forbidden access to you by saying, "You will not know the like of this from the Real except in the Muhammadan form." We have already explained that the greatest vision is the Muhammadan vision in the Muhammadan form. This was maintained by the imam Abu'l-Qāsim ibn Qasī in his book *Khalʿ al-naʿlayn*. It was related to us from him by his son in Tunis in the year 590 [1194].[2]

I have not seen this breath from anyone else, so we have designated him, for it has not arrived at us. It is possible that it is as I know it to be from God as a divine casting without any intermediary—I mean what Ibn Qasī knew in that. It is also possible that God gave someone other than Ibn Qasī to see that before him, after him, or in his time, but it has not reached us. God knows best.

So there is no eminence higher than the eminence of knowledge, and there is no state above the state of understanding from God. (IV 128.17)

From Chapter 369: The Storehouse of Nature

This chapter, from which five sections have already been quoted, deals with the "storehouses of munificence." The eighteenth section addresses the divine root of absence and explains how it permeates the whole of *wujūd*. In truth, everything is absent but *wujūd* itself, because all things are nonexistent entities. In this particular discussion, the Shaykh takes a rather theological approach to various issues, pointing out, for example, that the "limits" (*ḥudūd*) that define the things and make them what they are—so much so that this very word is the standard term for "definition"—all pertain to the absent domain, since none of them is anything but an affair of nonexistence. Limits display their traces by taking away *wujūd*, not by displaying it. Toward the end of the passage, Ibn al-ʿArabī focuses on how human perfection involves recognizing the divine limits established in all things and observing them as God wants them to be observed. He cites the hadith, "Give to each thing that has a *ḥaqq* its *ḥaqq*," and makes clear that a thing's *ḥaqq* is precisely what is demanded by the face of the Real in the thing. The Shariah provides the guidelines for observing the *ḥaqq*, that is, for recognized the Real in each thing and acting appropriately. Finally the Shaykh turns to a Koranic criticism of Christians inasmuch as they are "excessive" (*ghuluww*) in their religion. The Arabic term means to exceed the proper bounds, to transgress the limits. The verse in question is this: *People of the Book, be not excessive in your religion, and say not as to God but the **ḥaqq**. The Messiah, Jesus son of Mary, was only the Messenger of God, and His Word that He cast to Mary, and a Spirit from Him. So have faith in God and His messengers, and say not "Three"* (4:171).

This section entails the excellence of nature over everything else, because of its similarity to the divine names, for, it is no wonder when an existent thing leaves traces, it is only a wonder when a nonexistent thing leaves traces. Relations are all affairs of nonexistence, but they possess traces and ruling properties. Everything nonexistent in entity but manifest in property and trace is, in reality, what is called "the absent," for anything that is absent in entity is "the absent." Nature is absent in entity both from *wujūd*, because it has no entity in *wujūd*, and from fixity, because it has no entity there. Hence it is the realized world of the absent. But nature is known, just as the impossible is known, except that, although nature is like the impossible in that both *wujūd* and fixity are lifted from it, it has a trace and from it forms become manifest, but the impossible is not like that.

The keys to this *absent* are the divine names *that none knows but* God [6:59], who is the Knower of everything. The divine names are absent relations, since the key to the absent can only be absent.

From these names are understood many diverse realities of obvious diversity. The names are attributed only to the Real, for He is what is named by them, but He does not become multiple through them. If they were affairs of *wujūd*, abiding through Him, He would become multiple through them.

God knows the names in respect of the fact that He knows every object of knowledge, and we know them through the diversity of their traces within us. We name Him "such and such" because of the trace of what is found in ourselves. The traces are multiple within us, so the names are many, and the Real is named by them. Hence they are attributed to Him, but He does not become multiple in Himself through them. Thus we come to know that they are absent in entity.

Through the names, God opened up the world of the natural bodies by bringing them together after they had been separate in the absent, with a known separation within [God's] knowledge. Had they been brought together in their essence, the *wujūd* of the world of the bodies would have belonged to itself from eternity without beginning, not to God. But there is no existent thing apart from God that derives from anything other than God. There is none necessary through its Essence save God. Other than He is existent through Him, not by its essence. Thus *the mystery* is what is understood from the relations, *and the more hidden* [20:7] than they is their entities.

The trace of nature becomes manifest through the [divine] will, but nature is absent. Hence the will is the key to this absent, and the will is a divine relation that has no entity, so the key is absent. Were these relations not affirmed in knowledge, and were they something absent and nonexistent, it would not be correct for any existent thing whatsoever to have *wujūd,* and there would be no creation and no Real. So there is no escape from them.

The absent is the brilliant, all-inclusive light through which all of *wujūd* becomes manifest, but it has no manifestation in its own entity. It is the all-inclusive storehouse whose storekeeper is from itself.

If you desire to bring near to yourself the conceptualization of what I have said, consider the essential limits[3] of the limited thing through which alone the limited thing can be rationally understood and without which the known object would be nonexistent [as known object]. It is a known object only through their *wujūd* in the widest sense, even if they are not described by *wujūd.*

This would be, for example, when you undertake to define the limit of the substance—I mean the solitary substance [i.e., the atom]. You say concerning it that it is a thing, so you bring the most inclusive genus. But the thingness of things does not pertain to *wujūd*—and there is no escape from this, for included in "thing" is everything limited as a thing, whether it abides through itself or not.

When you desire to clarify it—and the objects of knowledge are only clarified through their essence, which is their essential limit—you say "existent thing." Hence you have brought a word more specific than *thing,* a word within which is included every existent thing. Through it everything that has a thingness but no *wujūd* is separated from it.

Then you say, "abiding through itself."

All these are known meanings, and for the limited object known through them, they are attributes. But the attribute does not abide through itself. From the coming together of these meanings derive entities of *wujūd* that are perceived by sensation and reason.

[Now you have] excluded from [the known object] everything that does not abide through itself. Then you say, "spatially confined." So other things share with it, while still others are thereby distinguished from it. Spatial confinement is a ruling property. It is that which has measure in area or receives place.

Then you say, "the solitary thing whose essence is not divided." Thereby body and every divisible thing is excluded.

Then you say, "receptive to accidents." So everything that is not receptive to accidents is excluded, and there enters along with it in this limit everything that receives accidents.

Through the totality of these meanings the thing comes to be named a "solitary substance."

In the same way, through combination with the other limits, "body" becomes manifest.

Since the combination of meanings has given rise to the manifestation of forms abiding through themselves along with those seeking loci through which to abide—like accidents and attributes—we come to know for certain that everything other than the Real is a vanishing accident and an object on display. Although it is qualified by *wujūd* and it has these characteristics, in itself its property is that of the nonexistent thing. Hence it must have a preserver to preserve its *wujūd,* and that is nothing but God.

If the cosmos—I mean its *wujūd*—pertained to the Essence of the Real, not to relations, the cosmos would be coextensive with the Real in *wujūd,* but this is not so. Hence the relations are a property of God from eternity without beginning, and they demand that the *wujūd* of the cosmos be posterior to the *wujūd* of the Real. Thus the new arrival of the cosmos is correct, and this pertains only to the relation of the will and the precedent knowledge of its *wujūd.* Hence the *wujūd* of the cosmos was given preponderance over its nonexistence, but the *wujūd* to which preponderance has been given is not coextensive with essential *wujūd,* which is not qualified by preponderation.

Since the manifestation of the cosmos in its entity is the totality of these meanings, all these meanings occur as accidents to this limited and intelligible thing, and it becomes manifest. In itself, it is none other than the totality of these meanings. The meanings are renewed for it, and God is the Preserver of its *wujūd* through renewing them for it. They are identical with the limited thing. Hence all limited things are in the *new creation,* concerning which *people are uncertain* [50:15].

Thus God is a creator perpetually, and the cosmos is in perpetual poverty toward Him for the preservation of its *wujūd* through His renewing it. So the cosmos is intelligible by its essence and existent through God, and thus the limits pertaining to its own self are identical with it.

It is this that called the Ḥusbāniyya to say that the entities of the cosmos are renewed perpetually at each solitary time. But they neglected the intelligibility of the cosmos in respect of its being a limited thing. It is an imaginary affair that has no *wujūd* except through imagination, but it is receptive toward these meanings. In knowledge, it is nothing other than all these meanings. An affair that was in itself a totality of intelligibles became a sensory object.

Conceptualizing this became confusing and difficult for those overcome by their imagination. They became bewildered between their knowledge and their imagination, which is the site of bewilderment.

One group said that accidents are renewed for the substance, but the substance is fixed in *wujūd*, even though it has no subsistence save through the accidents. The companion of this view did not understand what he was denying. Something remained absent from him, so he was ignorant of it, and something became manifest to him, so he came to know it.

Another group said that some accidents are renewed, and these are what are called, in their view, "accidents." Other things—even if they are accidents in reality, according to what is bestowed by knowledge—they named "concomitant attributes," like the yellow of gold and the black of an African.

All this is in the case of those who affirm them as entities of *wujūd*. But there are those who say that all of it is relations that have no *wujūd*, save in the eye of their perceiver. They have no *wujūd* in their entity. This was the position of Qāḍī Abū Bakr ibn al-Ṭayyib al-Bāqillānī,[4] according to what has reached us, though the responsibility lies with the narrator.

The folk of unveiling have been given an all-inclusive overview of all the positions, the tenets, the sects, and the doctrines concerning God. They are not ignorant of any of these. Adherents follow tenets, sects conform to specific laws, and doctrines are held concerning God or something in the engendered universe. Some of these contradict others, some disagree, and some are similar. In every case the companions of unveiling know from where the doctrine, the sect, or the creed is taken, and they ascribe it to its site. They offer an excuse for everyone who holds it and do not declare him in error. They do not consider his words to be in sport, for God *did not create* any *heaven* nor any *earth and what is between the two for the unreal* [38:27] and He did not create the human being *for sport* [23:115]. On the contrary, He created him alone to be in His form.

Hence everyone in the cosmos is ignorant of the whole and knows the part, except only the perfect human being. For God *taught* him *the names, all of them* [2:31] and gave him the all-comprehensive words, so his form became perfect. The perfect human being brings together the form of the Real and the form of the cosmos. He is a *barzakh* between the Real and the cosmos, a raised-up mirror. The Real sees His form in the mirror of the human being, and creation also see its form in him. He who gains this level has gained a level of perfection more perfect than which nothing is found in possibility.

The meaning of the vision of the Real's form in him is that all the divine names are ascribed to him, just as has come in the reports. Through the perfect human beings you are helped, but God is the Helper. Through them you are provided, but God is the Provider. Through them you are shown mercy, but God is the Merciful.

It has come in the Koran concerning him whose perfection we know and concerning whom we believe all this that he is *clement and compassionate toward those with faith* [9:128]. So also, *We have sent thee only as a mercy to the worlds* [21:107], that is, that you should show mercy to them—when he supplicated against the Riʿl, the Dhakwān, and the ʿUṣayya.

All the ulama maintain that assumption of the traits of the names takes place. Thus human beings are qualified by them and called "alive, knowing, desiring, hearing, seeing, speaking, powerful." All the divine names, whether names of *tanzīh* or names of acts, come under the encompassment of these seven names that we mentioned. Not one is outside them. Hence we do not mention them in detail. We have mentioned a full portion of them in our book named *Inshāʾ al-jadāwil wa'l-dawāʾir*.[5] Within it we have pictured the cosmos and the two Presences as imaged in shapes so that the companion of imagination may gain nearness to knowledge of them, since, despite his rational faculty, the human being never departs from the property of imagination in what he knows to be impossible. Nevertheless, he conceives of it, and the property of imagination overcomes him, since he cannot retain knowledge of this except after conceiving of it. At this point, the preserving faculty [i.e., memory] retains it, and the reminding faculty rules over him when it overcomes the preserving faculty. Thus he emerges from under its ruling property, for the reminding faculty does not go to excesses.

The object of knowledge never ceases being restricted in knowledge, and this is why knowledge's object is encompassed. God says, *He encompasses everything in knowledge* [65:12].

He who knows what we have mentioned in this section and what this storehouse contains will know himself and he will know his Lord. He will know the cosmos and what its root is. When anything of it appears to him, he will know from where it comes and to where it goes back. He will know what it rightfully demands, so he will fulfill its *ḥaqq* and he will "give to each thing that has a *ḥaqq* its *ḥaqq*," just as God *has given each thing its creation* [20:50].

That which the *Ḥaqq* alone possesses is only creation, and that of the cosmos which the perfect alone possesses is the *ḥaqq*, for he knows what every existent thing rightfully demands, so he gives it its *ḥaqq*. This is named "equitable balance" [*inṣāf*]. When you have given something its *ḥaqq*, you have achieved the equitable balance in it. If you are excessive, you will not be perfect; rather, you will be imperfect. After all, exceeding the limit is an imperfection in the limited thing. Thus the perfect does not allow anything to transgress its level.

As a teaching for us in enacting justice in things, God has blamed those who go to excesses in their religion and declare the Real incomparable with what He rightfully demands. Such people, though they intended magnification through this act of excessiveness, fell into ignorance and brought imperfection in the site of perfection. God says, *Be not excessive in your religion, and say not as to God but the* ***ḥaqq*** [4:171].

Being excessive is like attributing states to God, when these are nothing but the properties of the meanings. The *wujūd* of the meanings belongs to God. When they are found in that within which they are found, they bestow through their essence the state by which is described the locus through which the meaning abides. So this pertains to being excessive.

This is like knowing and powerful, white and black, brave and timid, moving and still. These are states, and they are the properties of the intelligible meanings, or the relations—call them what you will. These meanings are knowledge, power, whiteness, blackness, courage, timidity, movement, and stillness. He says to us, *Say not as to God but the* ***ḥaqq*** [4:171], whatever it may be. Thus they ascribed to Him a female companion and a child, they struck likenesses for Him, and they assigned peers to Him, being excessive in their religion as a magnification of their messengers. They said, "Jesus is God," and a group said, "He is the son of God." Those who were not excessive in their religion said that he is God's servant and *His word that He cast to Mary and a spirit from Him* [4:171]. Thus they did not transgress the actual situation.

He who travels in our way has traveled the path of salvation and faith. He has given faith its *ḥaqq* and has not followed reason and reflection in the *ḥaqq* of faith or in what belongs to it. *And God speaks the* ***ḥaqq*** *and He guides on the path* [33:4].

Among the knowledges found in this storehouse is the knowledge of the station of all the angels, the knowledge of the lights and the mysteries, and of temporal excellence, not excellence through place. From here the angels descend upon the hearts of the mortal messengers with Shari'ite revelation and upon the hearts of the friends with speaking and inspiration. Whenever anyone perceives this in the secret heart or the absent such that it belongs to him in the overt and the witnessed, this derives from this storehouse.

So glory be to Him who puts the affairs in order, expands the breasts, and raises up everyone in the grave through the Upstirring! There is no god but He, the Knowing, the Powerful. (III 397.3)

Command and Creation

The Koran sometimes uses the expression *al-khalq wa'l-amr*, "the creation and the command," to designate the absent and witnessed domains. The word *amr* or "command" has two basic Koranic senses, and Ibn al-ʿArabī uses it accordingly. In his more common usage, it means "affair" or "situation." For example, he frequently employs the expression *al-amr ʿalā mā huwa ʿalayh*, "the situation as it actually is," or "the actual situation." He also uses the phrase, *fī nafs al-amr*, "in the self of the situation," or "in actual fact." On the basis of this meaning of the term, the Shaykh understands the words *whole affair* (*al-amr kulluhu*) in the Koranic verse, *To Him the whole affair is returned* (11:123), to mean "that upon which is the cosmos in its entirety" (III 471.14), that is, the whole cosmos in its actual situation.

When the term *amr* is used to mean "command," two basic commands can be distinguished. These are frequently called the "engendering command" and the "prescriptive command." Through the first, God creates the universe, and through the second, He lays down rules and regulations—shariahs—for His servants to follow. The first command cannot be disobeyed, because it is the word *Be* that brings creation into existence moment by moment. Choice and free will, to the extent that they are real, pertain to the second command. The more basic of these two commands is the engendering command, which becomes manifest on various levels of the cosmos in different forms. The prescriptive command branches off from it at a certain point.[6]

Although Ibn al-ʿArabī employs the expression *creation and command* most commonly to differentiate between the two basic worlds brought into existence by the engendering command—the absent and the witnessed—he sometimes applies the distinction to questions that arise in relation to the prescriptive command, as in the following:

> Among the souls are those that do not undertake what is intended for them. Such souls are disobedient and oppose God's command when He commands them to deeds and worship. Thus worship occurs from the obedient person in the state of both constraint and choice, but if he is not obedient, then only in respect of the command to do the deed. If a soul is willing and obedient, then it wins the occurrence of what is intended for it in the creation and the command, for God's *are the creation and the command—blessed is God, Lord of the worlds* [7:54].
>
> As for the disobedient person, worship occurs for him only in the state of constraint, not in the state of choice. The form of the deed occurs from him, but not the deed that the shariah has prescribed for him. Hence he opposes the command of God and does not undertake that of the creation and the command that is intended for him. (III 123.32)

When Ibn al-ʿArabī employs "command and creation" to refer to the domains of spiritual and corporeal things, he typically cites Koran 7:54 as a supporting text, as in the passage just quoted. He makes use of this terminology in the following to suggest the difference between two divine names derived from the same root, the Potent (*muqtadir*) and the Powerful (*qādir*). The first, he says, designates God's power to create things through intermediaries and the second His power to create things without intermediaries.

> *God is powerful over each thing* [2:20]. But the property of the Potent is another property, not that of the Powerful, for potency is a property of the Powerful in the manifestation of the things through the hands of the occasions. The occasions become qualified by the acquisition of power, so they are potent, which is to say that they exert themselves in potency. This is none other than the Real, for He is the Potent over everything that He brings into existence "at" or "through" an occasion—say what you will—and this is His words, *Verily, His are the creation*. [He is also Potent] over everything that He does not bring into existence through an occasion, and this is His words, *and the command. Verily, His are the creation and the command—blessed is God, Lord of the worlds* [7:54].
>
> This is why the Folk of God have adopted "the world of creation and command" as a technical term. By "world of creation" they mean everything that God has brought into existence on the hands of the occasions. This is His words, *from what Our hands worked* [36:71]—these are nothing but the hands of the occasions. This is an attribution bestowing eminence, or rather, a realization [of the actual situation]
>
> By "world of command," they mean what He does not bring into existence at an occasion. Thus God is "Powerful" in respect of the command and "Potent" in respect of the creation, so the latter is the differentiation of the former.
>
> It is said, "The commander struck the thief" or "The commander cut off the hand of the robber." But the cutting took place at the hand of one of his guards. The command to cut issued from the commander, so the cutting is ascribed to the commander. He is the "potent." When he strikes him directly, then he is the "powerful"—so long as there is no instrument, made of iron or something else, with which he cuts off the hand.
>
> God creates with instruments and so is Potent, and He creates without instruments and so is Powerful. Thus power is more hidden than

potency, because potency is a state of the powerful, just as naming is a state of the namer. (IV 296.34)

Inasmuch as He is Powerful, God creates without occasions, which is to say that He creates through the specific faces of things. Inasmuch as He is Potent, He creates by means of occasions. In a similar way, God is Creator in terms of the chain of occasions through which He brings things into existence, and He is Innovator (*badīᶜ*) inasmuch as He is connected to things through the specific face. In the human being, these two faces of things can be called "command and creation."

What God casts into your soul from the specific divine face that is outside creation is the divine command, for *His are the creation and the command* [7:54]. What derives from this face is "the command," and what derives from other than this face is "the creation." (II 423.21)

Within the world of creation, the specific face can be differentiated from occasions, but not in the world of the command. Things in the world of creation have two faces, but in the world of the command, they have but one.

The world of the command is the face that adjoins the Real in all existent things, and that which was not created at an occasion in some existent things. The world of creation is that which comes into existence at the intermediaries, so it is ascribed to them. (*ᶜAbādila* 63).

Every possible thing in the world of creation has two faces—a face toward its occasion and a face toward God. Every veil and darkness that overtakes it derives from its occasion, while every light and unveiling derives from the side of its Real. But no possible thing in the world of command can be conceived of as veiled, since each of them has only one face, so it is sheer light. *Does not pure religion belong to God?* [39:3]. (I 46.12)

Every existent thing in the cosmos, if it pertains to the world of creation, possesses a specific face toward its Existence-Giver. But if it pertains to the world of the command, it has nothing save this specific face. God discloses Himself to each existent thing from the specific face and bestows upon it a knowledge of Himself known from Him only by this existent thing. It makes no difference whether the existent thing knows this or does not know it—I mean, that it has a specific face and that it has knowledge from God in respect of this specific face.

The Folk of God have excellence only through their knowledge of this face. Then they are ranked in excellence in this. Among them are those who know that God has a self-disclosure to the existent thing from this specific face, and among them are those who do not know this. Among those who know this are those who know the knowledge that they gain from this self-disclosure, and among them are those who do not know it—I mean exactly. (IV 222.14)

In the longer version of his *Iṣṭilāḥāt al-ṣūfiyya,* Ibn al-ᶜArabī defines creation and command while explaining the difference between the knower (*ᶜālim*) and the gnostic (*ᶜārif*). The basic distinction that he draws here—though he draws other distinctions elsewhere, and sometimes makes no distinction[7]—is that the knower witnesses God Himself. In contrast, the "gnostic" is he who has achieved the knowledge referred to in the hadith, "He who knows [*ᶜarafa*] himself knows his Lord." Hence the gnostic knows God as "Lord" rather than as "God."

If you ask, "What are the knower and knowledge?," we will reply: The knower is the one whom God gives to witness His Divinity and His Essence and over whom He does not allow any state to prevail. Knowledge is his state, but on condition of its being differentiated from gnosis and the gnostic.

If you ask, "What are gnosis and the gnostic?," we will reply: He whose locus of witnessing is the Lord, not any other divine name. States become manifest from him, and gnosis is his state. The gnostic pertains to the world of creation, just as the knower pertains to the world of command.

If you ask, "What is the world of creation and command, for God has said, *Verily, His are the creation and the command*?," we will reply: The world of the command is what comes into existence from God, not at a newly arrived occasion. The world of creation is what God brings into existence at a newly arrived occasion, so the absent is curtained within it.

If you ask, "What is the absent in your technical language?," we will reply: It is that of you that God has curtained from you, but not from Himself. (II 129.25)

God's engendering command is a single command through which He creates all things: *Our command is but one* (54:50). In contrast, His prescriptive command becomes divided into commands and prohibitions (*nahy*). The inhabitants of the world of the command, known as angels and intellects (*ʿuqūl*, pl. of *ʿaql*), have but a single face and receive only commands, not prohibitions. Human beings, who dwell in the world of the creation, encounter both commands and prohibitions, in keeping with the multiplicity of faces that they meet through the occasions. Ibn al-ʿArabī explains some of these points while discussing "those who fast" as one of the many subgroups among the friends of God, whom he classifies in Chapter 73, the second longest chapter of the *Futūḥāt*. Note that the word *ʿaql* here, "intellect," is the same term that I usually translate as "reason" or "rational faculty." But this is not the *ʿaql* of the considerative thinkers, which is subject to darkness, doubts, and obfuscations. Rather, it is the rational faculty of the gnostic, transmuted by unveiling into an illumined visionary organ. It is identical in substance with the angels, so it is pure and "disengaged" (*mujarrad*) from all the dross of the lower worlds, including imagination.

Among the friends of God are "those who fast," male and female—may God be well-pleased with them. God has befriended them through a holding back that bequeaths to them lifting up at God beyond everything from which the Real has commanded them to hold back themselves and their bodily parts. Among this is the incumbent and the recommended.

As for His words to this group, *Then complete the fast until the night* [2:187], this calls attention to the furthest limit of the moment that is fixed for holding back in the world of the witnessed, which is the daytime. The night is a realized likeness that is struck for the absent. Thus, when they reach the level of companionship with the world of the absent—which is given expression by "night"—holding back is no longer correct. Holding back the self and the bodily parts takes place only in relation to prohibited things, and these are found in the world of the witnessed. The world of the absent is a command without any prohibition. That is why it was named the "world of the command." This is because the world of the absent is disengaged intellects within whom is no appetite, so they have no prohibitions in the station of prescription. They are as God has lauded them in His exalted Book: *They disobey God not in what He commands them, and they do what they are commanded* [66:6]. He did not mention that they were prohibited anything, for their realities do not require that.

When a human being fasts and is transferred from his mortal nature to his intellect, then his daytime has been perfected and holding back has departed from him, because prohibition has departed. He has joined the world of the command through his intellect. Hence he is a sheer intellect, without appetite.

Have you not seen the words of the Prophet concerning such a person? "When the night approaches from there, when the daytime goes away over there, and when the sun goes down, then the fasting person has broken his fast." He is saying: The sun has gone down from the world of the witnessed and risen up in the world of his intellect, so the fasting person has broken his fast. In other words, he is not prevented, for the interdiction has been lifted from him because his intellect does not feed upon that from which God has commanded him to hold back, that is, the share of his nature. So know this!

When the affair reaches this limit, he gains the divine uplifting beyond the property of his own nature, and self-disclosure lifts him up beyond the property of his reflection, since reflection derives from the property of elemental nature. That is why angels do not reflect, but the human being does reflect, for he is compounded of an elemental nature and an intellect. The intellect, in respect of itself, possesses self-disclosure, so it is lifted up beyond the low reaches of the natural reflection that accompanies imagination and takes from sensation and the sensory thing.

The poet says, "When the daylight 'fasts'," that is, the daylight rises up, "and brings the midday heat."[8] He who does not have this lifting up as a result of holding back is not "the one who fasts" who is sought and named here. This is the fasting of the gnostics through God, and they are the Folk of God. (II 30.2)

Heaven and Earth

The pairs "heaven and earth" and "heavens and earth" occur repeatedly in the Koran, and Ibn al-ᶜArabī often understands them to refer to everything in the cosmos. When he says, "It is said that 'heaven' and 'earth' mean highness and lowness" (II 603.12), he is repeating a statement found in the Arabic dictionaries.

> God said that He *created the heavens*, which is every high world, *and the earth*, which is every low world. *Heaven* derives from the world of wholesomeness, while *earth* derives from the world of corruption. Hence "woodworm" [*araḍa*], which corrupts cloth, paper, and wood, is derived from the word *earth* [*arḍ*], though it is also called *sūs* and *ᶜuthth*. [The verse continues,] *and what is between them* in the cosmos *only through the Real* [15:85]. (II 285.10)

Ibn al-ᶜArabī sometimes uses *heaven and earth* to refer to the heaven and the earth that we witness with our eyes, but more commonly he uses the terms to refer to the absent and the witnessed domains.

> *From God nothing whatever is hidden in the earth*, [a word whose meaning] is well-known; the earth is also all the mysteries that are found in nature, for nature's forms are the earth of the spirits. *And the heaven* [3:5], which is also well-known; it is also all the spirits that are between nature and the Cloud. These spirits are what illuminate the earth with their lights. (IV 156.6)

When Ibn al-ᶜArabī says that the heavens are "everything that is high," this might be understood in a spatial sense. But he makes clear that, when he juxtaposes "high" and "low," he has the relation of giving and receiving in view, which is the normal relation between spirit and body.

> The high world is intertied with the low world so as to bestow benefits, while the low is intertied with the high so as to acquire benefits. The one that bestows benefits is always the "higher," and the one that acquires benefits is always the "lower." Area and highness of place have no ruling property [in the definition of the terms]. (III 197.7)

"High" is a divine name. Hence it can be considered the divine root of the heavens and everything that is high. But "low" is not a divine name, so Ibn al-ᶜArabī traces the attribute of lowness back to God indirectly. Or, we can say that the high and the low gain their properties from the fact that God is present within both the high and the low parts of the cosmos, as affirmed by the Koran.

> There is nothing but a heaven and an earth, and *To Him belongs the highest likeness [in the heavens and the earth]* [30:27]. So He has a form in every heaven and earth. *It is He who is in the heaven a God and in the earth a God* [43:84]. *He is God in the heavens and the earth; He knows your mystery*, because He is in the earth, *and your overt* [6:3], because He is in the heaven.
>
> In respect of the [human] configuration, *He knows your mystery*, because He is in the heaven, which is your meaning, whose entity is hidden from the eyesights but whose property is manifest. To Him belongs highness, so He is in the heaven and He is the Nonmanifest.
>
> He also knows *your overt*, because He is in the earth, which is your manifest domain, whose entity is manifest to the eyesights, but whose property is hidden. After all, the property of the manifest domain is in its spirit, for it is the spirit that acquires knowledges through the senses. To Him belongs descent, so He is in the earth and He is the Manifest. (III 363.11)

Although the earth is low, it gains its nourishment and adornment from God. Hence, in reality, it is high through the ornament that it receives from God, since this is the trace of the divine attributes.

> God explained that He possesses the most beautiful names. He designated those of them for us that He willed and He commanded us to call Him by them. Nonetheless, to Him belong the names of everything in the cosmos. Hence, every name in the cosmos is beautiful through this relation. From here it has been said, "All of God's acts are beautiful" and "There is no actor but God." Such is the ruling property of the names by which all the cosmos is named. This

is especially so if we accept the view of those who say that the name is the Named—and we have already explained that there is no *wujūd* but God. In the same way, if we were to say that the name is not the Named, what is signified by the name would also be the *wujūd* of the Real. In either case, there is nothing but the Real, so there is nothing debased.

Everything possesses genuine dignity and pervasive splendor and eminence. As for the *reckoning* that God threw down *from the heaven* on the garden plot of one of the two men, so that it became *a smooth plain* [18:40] and *its water sank into the earth* [18:41], the fact that it became *a smooth plain* bequeathed it eminence. By describing it as *smooth*, He bequeathed it clearing and lifting up in degree. For He made it *a plain* and eliminated various sorts of opposition from it by taking away its "trees" [etymologically, its "conflicts"]. For the *reckoning* was *from the heaven*. Hence it gave the level of heavenliness to that which was described by the earth, which curtains those within it. Hence it is named a "garden" [etymologically, a "concealment"]. Nothing brought about the appearance of what appeared from it save the munificence of heaven, which is the rain, and its munificence through the heat of the sun. Hence, from the heaven becomes manifest the earth's ornament. Thus the heaven draped the earth with its reckoning, and the heaven stripped its ornament from it through its reckoning. From the earth's ornament, its names became many, because of the various classes of fruits, trees, and flowers within it. But from its becoming stripped and cleared, its name was made one. Its names disappeared with the disappearance of its ornament. *Surely We have appointed whatever is on the earth as an ornament for it* [18:7].

In the metaphorical interpretation, the *earth* is nothing but what is called "creation," and its *ornament* is what is named "Real." Hence, through the Real it is ornamented, and through the Real it is cleared and stripped of the garments of number and it becomes manifest in the attribute of the One. (IV 250.23)

From Chapter 73: The Forty-Third Question

Heaven and earth, according to the Koran, were originally *sewn up together*, and then God *unstitched them* (21:30). One of the Koranic names of God, *fāṭir al-samāwāt wa'l-arḍ*, usually translated as "Creator of the heavens and earth," suggests rather "Separator of the heavens and earth." The word *fāṭir* along with other derivatives from the same root occurs several times in the Koran. The basic meaning of the root is to split, to cleave, and to bring forth. The etymological sense of the Koranic term suggests that creation is a separation and a bringing forth from an original unity. The word *fiṭra*, a verbal noun that designates this act of bringing forth, is especially well-known because of its occurrence in the hadith, "Every child is born in accordance with *fiṭra*; then his parents make him into a Jew, a Christian, or a Zoroastrian." In this context, translators render *fiṭra* with expressions such as "innate disposition" or "primordial nature." In answering al-Tirmidhī's question, "What is the *fiṭra*?," Ibn al-ʿArabī clearly understands the term as having to do with the splitting of the heavens from the earth and the separation of the high from the low and the luminous from the dark.

Answer: [The *fiṭra*] is the light through which the darkness of the possible things is cleft and the separation occurs among the forms. Then it is said, "This is not that," whereas it had been said, "This is the same as that" in respect of what they shared in common. Hence *Praise belongs to God, the Separator of the heavens and the earth* [35:1] is equivalent to God's words, *God is the light of the heavens and the earth* [24:35].

The cosmos, all of it, is a heaven and an earth, nothing else. Through light it became manifest. This is God's words, *With the Real We have sent it down, and with the Real it has come down* [17:105]. God has made the heavens and the earth manifest, so He is their light. Hence the manifestation that pertains to the loci of manifestation is God, so He is *the Separator of the heavens and the earth*. He separated the heaven from the earth through Him, so He is their *fiṭra* and the ***fiṭra*** *in accordance with which He separated people* [30:30], for "Every child is born in accordance with *fiṭra*." *"Am I not your Lord?" They said, "Yes"* [7:172]. Hence He separated them only in accordance with Him, and He separated them only through Him. Through Him the things became distinct, differentiated, and entified. But in their divine manifestation, the things are no-thing, for the *wujūd* is His *wujūd*, and the servants are His servants. Hence they are servants in respect of their entities, but they are the Real in respect of their *wujūd*. So their *wujūd* became distinct from their entities only through the *fiṭra*, which differentiated between the entity and their *wujūd*. This is one of the most abstruse things to which the knowledge of God's knowers becomes connected. Its unveiling is difficult, but its time is short. (II 70.7)

From Chapter 558: The Presence of the Food-Giver

In discussing the divine name Food-Giver (*muqīt*), the Shaykh explains how God supplies food (*qūt*) to everything in the cosmos—the high and the low, the heaven and the earth. The food of creation is the command, for the divine command gives sustenance to the witnessed world. In the same way, the "command" that God *revealed in each heaven* (41:12) is the heaven's food. Once food is understood in these terms, it is obvious that nothing other than God can do without its own specific food, not even the divine names, whose food is the traces and properties that they leave in the cosmos. The Food-Giver to all, then, is *wujūd* itself.

He who has determined all foods
is the Food-Giver who has prescribed the Shariah for His servant.
He it is who has determined all moments,
as provision, as creation, and as artifact, just as He made them.

"The servant of the Food-Giver" is the twin brother of "the servant of the All-Provider," for "provision" is the food of him for whom provision is made.

Food takes a specific measure that neither increases nor decreases in the case of each appetite in the Gardens, and in the case of each repulsion of pain and each appetite in this world, which is the abode of commingling and the configuration of mixing.

From this Presence comes food to everyone whose form does not subsist in *wujūd* without food.

From this Presence are designated the moments and scales of the foods. Thus God says concerning the creation of the earth, *He determined therein its foods* [41:10], that is, He bestowed the measures and scales of the moments of the foods.

These foods are identical with "revelation" in the heaven, so the food in the earth is like the command in the heaven, and the determining of food in the earth is like revelation in the heaven. It is the same as it, not other than it, for *He revealed in* the *heaven its command* [41:12], which is determining its foods, and *He determined* in the earth *its foods*.

The heaven's constellations have a strength
through which God raises up the dead of the earth.
Heaven's wisdom in the earth is its traveling
to bring together thereby all its scattered things.
For God *built it* [91:5] for us
and designated through the traveling its moments.
Its moment is a food for it,
and *He determined* in the earth *its foods*.

This [determination] is the revelation of the earth's command.

The names are diverse because of the diversity of the loci and the forms. Through "the heaven and the earth" He included what is high of the cosmos and what is low, and there is nothing in *wujūd* but a high and a low.

Among God's names are High and Uplifted of Degrees. Hence the command and the foods of the names are the entities of their traces in the possible things, for through the traces, their entities are understood. Hence the names subsist through their traces, so the name's "food" is its trace, and its "determination" is the period of its ruling property in the possible thing, whatever possible thing it may be.

From this Presence God says, *There is no thing whose storehouses are not at Us, and We send it not down but in a known measure* [15:21]. The storehouses at God are high and low. The highest of them is His Footstool, which is His knowledge, and His knowledge is His Essence.[9] The lowest of the storehouses is what reflective thoughts store up in mortal man. Everything between these two storehouses is sensory and intelligible, and all of it is at God, for He is identical with *wujūd*. So this is a Presence that brings together the entities and the relations, new arrival and eternity. Hence creature and

Creator, object of power and Powerful, possession and Owner—each is a command and a food for its companion.

His command is in His heaven, which is His highness, and His food is in His earth, which is His drawing close. For we are among the folk of the earth, and we are addressed by this address, no one else. That is why the Koran is "sent down" [*munazzal*]. Its "descent" [*nuzūl*] can only be from highness, just as an "ascent" can only be toward highness.

From a lowness to a highness is an ascent,
from a highness to a lowness a descent—
Each has come in the Sending Down
concerning us.
Whichever you say, consider what you say.

Since there is nothing in engendered existence but infirmities and the infirm [or "causes and effects"], we come to know that high and low foods are remedies for the removal of illness. There is no illness save poverty, for *None is there in the heavens and the earth that comes not to the All-Merciful as a servant* [19:93] and the heaven and the earth came to the All-Merciful *willingly* [41:11]. Every servant is poor toward his master, and "The retainer of the people is their master," because he undertakes the means to their wholesomeness. The servant is the one who undertakes to be retained by his master so that the reality of servitude may subsist for him. The master undertakes the means to his servants' wholesomeness so that the name mastership may subsist for him. If the possession were annihilated, the name *owner* would be annihilated in respect of his being an owner. Even if the entity subsisted, it would subsist stripped of ruling property. Things have benefits only through their properties, not through their entities, though the properties come to be only through the entities. So their entities are poor toward their properties, and their properties are poor toward their entities and toward the entities of those within whom they exercise ruling control. Hence there is nothing but a property and an entity, so there is nothing but something poor and that toward which it is poor. *And God's is the affair altogether* [13:31].

He knows what every soul earns [13:42]. Here He brought *every*, which is a word of all-envelopment, so it envelops every soul; He left nothing aside in this affair. *The unbeliever*—the one from whom this knowledge is curtained in this world's life—*will certainly know whose will be the ultimate abode* [13:42] in the last abode, when the covering is unveiled from the eyes. Thus he will know who was ignorant and who was ranked higher than he through his knowledge in this world's life. These are the folk of the "good news." Everyone who realizes an affair will come to be in keeping with what he has realized.

He who determines the food has
determined—
food is what is specified by the state of the
mortals.
Or rather, its property is all-pervading, so it
includes us
and Himself, so consider—you will see
what you will see!
All from which nourishment is taken abides
in His *wujūd* as a *ḥaqq*—this is no lie.

Thus food's food through which it is fed is its being put to use. He who puts it to use is a food for it, since it cannot be food until someone is fed by it. Know then who your food is and whose food you are!

We have transmitted from the knower of this affair—Sahl ibn ʿAbdallāh al-Tustarī—that he was asked about food. He replied, "God." It was said to him, "We are asking about nourishment." He replied, "God," because he was overcome by the state. "States" are the tongues of the Tribe, and they are tastings.

The questioner alerted Sahl in the measure of what his own state gave to him at the moment. He said, "O Sahl, I am asking you only about the food of bodies," or "[bodily] apparitions."

Then Sahl knew that the questioner was ignorant of what he meant. So he came down to him to answer him with another breath, different from the first breath. He knew that he had been ignorant of the state of the questioner, just as the questioner had been ignorant of his answer. Sahl said to him, "What do you have to do with them?," that is, apparitions. "Leave the houses to their Builder. If He wills, He will destroy them, and if He wills, He will make them flourish."[10]

Thus Sahl retained his first answer, but in a different form. The house flourishes through its dweller, so the food is God, just as he said the first time. However, the questioner was satisfied with the second answer, because Sahl came down from the plain text to the outward significance. So also are most answers by the gnostics. If they are in the state, they answer with plain texts, but if they are in the station, they answer with the outward significance. They accord with their moments.

This measure of calling attention to the eminence of this Presence is sufficient, God willing. *And God speaks the* ***ḥaqq****, and He guides on the path* [33:4]. (IV 248.18)

Two and Three Worlds

It was noted earlier that the word *ᶜālam* may refer to everything other than God, in which case it is translated as "cosmos," or to any domain within the cosmos, in which case it is translated as "world." Sometimes the Shaykh employs the word to refer to human beings, or to human beings and the jinn. Thus in one passage he writes, "Here I mean by 'world' the human beings and the jinn who are the inhabitants of the two abodes—the Garden and the Fire" (III 550.29). In a similar way, he understands the Koranic term "world" in the title the Koran gives to Muhammad, "mercy to the worlds" (or, as it can also be translated, "to the world's inhabitants") to refer to the various groups of people that make up the human race. In a passage already quoted, he remarks that, in giving the Prophet this title, God "did not specify one world rather than another. Hence the disobedient and the obedient, the one who has faith and the one who gives the lie, the one who professes God's unity and the one who associates others with Him, are all included in this address and named 'world'" (III 567.34).

The Shaykh commonly speaks of the cosmos as being made of up two worlds, meaning the absent and the witnessed, or the spirits and the bodies. The absent world stands between God and the witnessed world. It is nearer to the divine realm in terms of the intensity of the divine attributes, such as luminosity, knowledge, life, and power. It is the source of everything that appears in the visible realm. All movement (*ḥaraka*) derives from its giving movement (*taḥrīk*).

The high world gives movement to the world of sensation, such that the witnessed is under its subjugating force, as a wisdom from God, not that this belongs to it by right. There never becomes manifest in the world of the witnessed the property of movement or stillness, eating or drinking, speaking or silence, except from the world of the absent. This is because the living thing moves only as the result of an intention and a desire, and these two are deeds of the heart. Desire is from the world of the absent, while motion and such things are from the world of the witnessed.

The world of the witnessed is everything we habitually perceive through sensation, while the world of the absent is that which does not habitually become manifest in sensation and which we perceive through the Shari'ite report or reflective consideration.

Then we say: The world of the absent is perceived through the eye of insight, just as the world of the witnessed is perceived through the eye of eyesight. (II 240.32)[11]

Although Ibn al-ᶜArabī frequently speaks of the cosmos as two worlds, he also commonly mentions a third world—the *barzakh.* He refers to these three domains as *ᶜaql* (or *maᶜnā*), *khayāl*, and *ḥiss*; that is, intellect/intelligence/reason (or meaning), imagination, and sensation (e.g., II 73.20 [Y 12, 296.10], 390.11, 391.23). Sometimes he speaks of the world of light, fire, and dust (III 365.14), thus alluding to the prophetic and Koranic teaching that the angels are created of light, the jinn of fire, and bodily things of earth. In the following, he offers a basic description of the three worlds. "Presence," it will be remembered, denotes the sphere of influence of a specific attribute and is often employed as a synonym for "world."

The cosmos is two worlds and the Presence is two Presences, though a third Presence is born between the two from the totality. The first Presence is the Presence of the absent, and it possesses a world called the "world of the absent." The second Presence is the Presence of sensation and the witnessed; its world is called "the world of the witnessed" and it is perceived by eyesight, while the world of the absent is perceived by insight.

That which is born from the coming together of the two is a Presence and a world. The Presence is the Presence of imagination, and the world is the world of imagination. It is the manifestation of meanings in sensory molds, like knowledge in the form of milk, perseverance in religion in the form of a fetter, *islām* in the form of a pillar, faith in the form of a handle, and Gabriel in the form of Diḥya al-Kalbī and in the form of the bedouin; and *he became imaginalized* to Mary in the form of *a well-proportioned mortal* [19:17]. In a similar way, blackness appears in the body of gallnuts and vitriol when the two are brought together [in the process of making ink], though they did not possess this description when they were separate. That is why the Presence of imagination is the most all-embracing of Presences, because it brings together the two worlds—the world of the absent and the world of the witnessed. (III 42.5)[12]

The Breath of the All-Merciful is also called "the Highest Barzakh," because it stands between Unbounded *Wujūd* and absolute nonexistence. When the cosmos becomes articulated as the words of the All-Merciful, it reflects the three fundamental realities from which it emerges—*wujūd*, the Highest Barzakh, and nonexistence. Hence it has three worlds: spirits, the *barzakh*, and bodies. Just as the Highest Barzakh brings together *wujūd* and nonexistence, so also the cosmic *barzakh* brings together spirits and bodies. Through its very essence, a *barzakh* possesses the properties of the two sides.

There is no intermediary or degree between imagination and meaning, just as there is no intermediary or degree between it and the sensory object. Hence imagination is the centerpiece of the necklace. Meaning descends to it, and the sensory object is lifted up to it, for it encounters the two sides through its essence. (II 390.4)

The cosmos is restricted to highness and lowness. Its highness and lowness are relative and relational affairs. The high of it is named a "heaven," and the lower of it is named an "earth." The cosmos has these two relations only through an intermediary affair that comes to be between the two. This affair, in itself, possesses directions. What overshadows it is a heaven, and what lifts it up is its earth. If you want, speak of the "higher plenum" and the "lower plenum." Everything that comes to be from nature is the lower plenum, and everything born from light is the higher plenum.

The most perfect world is that which brings both worlds together. It is the *barzakh* that makes them distinct through its directions, or through the fact that it brings everything together. It makes them distinct through highness and lowness in respect of that which displays traces and that which receives traces. As for the Real with regard to Himself, He is not qualified by anything by which the *wujūd* of the cosmos is qualified. (III 537.16)

Looked at statically, the *barzakh* is the most perfect of worlds because it embraces the attributes of the two sides. Nevertheless, it should not be forgotten that in terms of activity and the display of traces, the meanings are the highest world, and the meanings themselves become manifest in the form of the intermediary and lowest worlds.

The meanings are the root of things. In themselves they are absent, intelligible meanings. Then they become manifest in the Presence of sensation as sensory and in the Presence of imagination as imaginal, yet they are they. However, they undergo fluctuation in each Presence in keeping with it, like a chameleon that accepts the colors it stands upon. (II 677.12)

Ibn al-ᶜArabī sometimes refers to the three worlds by employing the well-known terms *kingdom* (*mulk*), *sovereignty* (*malakūt*), and *domination* (*jabarūt*). *Mulk* and *malakūt* both derive from the root *m.l.k* (though *malakūt* is considered an Aramaic loan-word). The root conveys the sense of ownership and kingship, and both *mulk* and *malakūt* have this meaning. But when the two terms are juxtaposed, *mulk* suggests something more concrete and hence more external and manifest than *malakūt*. The Koran attributes the "kingdom of the heavens and the earth" to God in about twenty verses and attributes their "sovereignty" to Him in two verses. It also attributes the kingdom in general to Him in several verses, and in two other verses in which it mentions sovereignty, it says, *in His hand is the sovereignty of everything* (23:88, 36:83).

As for *jabarūt*, the Koran does not employ the term, but it is connected to the word *jabr* (compulsion or domination) and the divine name *jabbār* (the All-Dominating). The basic sense of the root is dominating power. Those Sufis who made it the highest of the three worlds no doubt did so because it suggests a greater strength and intensity than is suggested by either *mulk* or *malakūt,* and hence it is appropriate for it to rule over the lower worlds. For Ibn al-ᶜArabī, this same overpowering strength is appropriate for the all-embracing world of imagination, which he often calls the greatest and strongest of God's creatures, because it embraces all things. In his use of this term, he may be following al-Ghazālī, who also considered *jabarūt* the intermediary world.[13] In his glossary of Sufi terminology, the Shaykh writes:

> The World of Sovereignty is the world of the meanings and the absent. One climbs up to it from the world of the kingdom. If you ask, "What is the world of the kingdom?," we will reply: the world of the witnessed and the letter. Between the two worlds is the world of the *barzakh*. If you ask, "What is the world of the *barzakh*?," we will reply: the world of imagination. Some of the Folk of the Path call it the "world of the domination," and so it is with me. (II 129.16)

Imagination is located between the domain of sensation and the domain of meaning, so it is nearer to the spiritual domain and has greater power and strength than sensation. This is proven by the fact that imagination displays its traces in sensation, but sensation does not have the same controlling power over imagination.

> The world of the *barzakh* displays traces more intensely than the world of sensation, for it displays traces in the world of sensation in the same way that sensation does, but sensation is not able to display traces in imagination. Do you not see that the dreamer sees in his imagination that he is performing sexual intercourse, and water descends from him in the world of sensation? The dreamer sees what frightens him, and that leaves a trace in his body through a movement or a sound that proceeds from him, or words that are understood, or perspiration—all because of the strength of imagination's authority over him. Imagination makes manifest in the form of sensation that which is not in itself sensory, thus making it join with sensation. But sensation does not have the strength to turn the sensory thing itself into an imaginal thing. (II 609.17)

Sometimes the Shaykh refers to the two basic worlds as the height (*ṭūl*) and the breadth (*ᶜarḍ*) of the cosmos. Although he also refers to imagination in this context, he does not refer to it as a separate world. Instead he classifies it as one sort of body since, like bodily things, it has sensory attributes.

> This knowledge [discussed in this chapter] is connected to the height of the cosmos—I mean the spiritual world, which is the world of meanings and the command. It is also connected to the breadth of the cosmos, which is the world of creation, nature, and bodies. And all belong to God. *Verily, His are the creation and the command* [7:54]. *Say: The Spirit is from the command of my Lord* [17:85]. *Blessed is God, Lord of the worlds* [7:54].[14] (I 169.1)

> The height of the cosmos is the world of the spirits, while its breadth is the world of the bodies' forms. I say "bodies' forms" instead of "bodies" because of imaginalized bodies. Although these are true bodies in their Presence, they are not considered bodies by everyone, because of the speed of their alteration and because they go back to the eye of the viewer, not to themselves. "True bodies" are bodies to themselves, not to the eye of the viewer. Whether the viewer is existent or nonexistent, they are bodies in themselves. The others are bodies not in themselves. Hence God said, *[Moses] was made to imagine because of their sorcery that [the ropes and staffs] were sliding* [20:66]. They were bodies in their entity, but they had no property in the sliding. Hence they became manifest in the eye of Moses through the form of sliding bodies, though the affair in itself was not like that. (III 108.1)

Everything that enters into the witnessed world descends from the absent domain by way of imagination. In one passage Ibn al-ᶜArabī adds two important points to what we have already heard about the world of the absent. First, part of that world—or perhaps we should say one of the absent worlds—can enter into the witnessed world. Everything that enters into the witnessed world exists first as a potentiality of manifestation, or a meaning, within this prior absent world, which contains all possibilities of manifestation. Second, once something has descended from the absent domain, entered into the witnessed domain, and then disappeared, it enters into a second absent domain wherein are found "impossible" things. They are impossible because they can never again enter into manifestation, since "Self-disclosure never repeats itself." Ibn al-ʿArabī makes these points in Chapter 321, "On the true knowledge of the waystation of him who distinguishes the world of the witnessed from the world of the absent."

Reason has a light,
and faith has lights—
surely insights are the eyesights
of the eyesights.
Eye, hearing, and all
sensation
are aiders and helpers
of reason's acquisitions.
With the eye you will see the absent,
not with my arguments—
do not be veiled by imaginings
and reflective thoughts.
When some do not gain knowledges
of the absent through eyesight—
for these are virgin girls behind
the curtain of chastity—
They say, "Take heed, true knowledge is in
the engendered things."
The house is ignorant of its lord,
O house-sitter!

Know, dear friend, that *wujūd* is divided between worshiper and worshiped. The worshiper is everything other than God, that is, the cosmos, which is called and named "servant." The worshiped is that which is named "God."

There is nothing in *wujūd* save what we mentioned, for everything other than God is a servant of God, whether already created or to be created. In what we have mentioned are great mysteries connected to the rubric of the true knowledge of God and His *tawḥīd* and the true knowledge of the cosmos and its level. Among the knowers, there is a disagreement in this issue that will never be lifted. No fixed foot can be realized in it.

This explains why God determined felicity for His servants through faith and in knowledge of God's *tawḥīd* specifically. There is no path to felicity save these two. The faith is connected to the reports brought by the messengers from God; this is a sheer following of authority that we accept whether we know Him or not. The knowledge is that which is given by rational consideration or divine unveiling. If this knowledge is not gained as self-evident, such that no obfuscations detract from it for its knower, then it is not a knowledge.

Then we say: The cosmos is two worlds, there being no third—a world perceived by sensation, which is called "the witnessed," and a world not perceived by sensation, which is called "the world of the absent." If something is absent at one time, then becomes manifest to sensation at another time, it is not called "absent." The absent is only that which sensation cannot possibly perceive. However, the absent is known to the rational faculty, either through categorical proofs, or through truthful reports, which is perception by faith. The witnessed is perceived by sensation, which is a path to knowledge, not knowledge itself. The witnessed pertains specifically to everything other than God that is perceived by sensation, while the absent is perceived by knowledge itself. In what we have mentioned rational faculties wander aimlessly and the kernels are bewildered.

Now, when someone enters the path upon which we are traveling and desires to attain distinction among its ulama and its masters, he must not allow himself to be bound by anything but God alone. This is the essential binding to Him that allows of no disjoining from Him whatsoever. It is a servanthood that accepts no freedom in any respect, an owning [by Him] that never disappears.

The human being may bind himself only through that by which he is bound in his essence—which is, as we said, his binding through God, *who created him, then determined him, then eased the way for him* [80:20]. Since this is his level, and inescapably so, he should never allow himself to halt except in the *barzakh*. It is the imaginal station that has no *wujūd* save in imagination between the world of the witnessed and the world of the absent. The affair of the person who halts will be such that when anything at all emerges from the absent—that is, the absent that can become qualified at some moment by the witnessed, not the absent that cannot possibly be witnessed in any respect—he will know it.

When it appears in the world of the witnessed and he perceives it, then two things are possible: Either it will subsist in the world of the witnessed, or it will not subsist—as is the case with accidents. If it does not subsist, it departs from the witnessed, and when it departs from the witnessed, it enters into the absent that can never be perceived as witnessed. It can have no return after it becomes manifest to the absent from which it emerged, for the station of the absent from which it emerged is the "possible absent," while that to which it is transferred after it has been in the witnessed is the "impossible absent." Nothing ever becomes manifest from the impossible absent so as to become qualified by the witnessed. Since that to which it is transferred never becomes qualified by the witnessed in any moment or any state, it enters this absent and never returns to the absent from which it emerged.

When someone halts in this station and realizes it, the Real takes him and makes him halt between Himself and everything beside Himself, whether this be the servant's self or others. Then he sees his own self and entity, while he is outside of it in that station in which He has made him halt. He sees it along with everyone else in the cosmos, but it is his entity. In the same way, Adam saw himself and his offspring in the grip of the Real, but he was outside the Real's grip within which he saw himself in the state of his seeing himself outside of it, just as has entered in the divine report.[15]

He comes to a halt in this station, which is the most elevated of the stations of unveiling. Every other station is below it. It is the station of al-Ṣiddīq through which he possessed the excellence on the basis of which God's Messenger gave witness that he was ranked over others in excellence. The others may have been those who were present, or the community. No one knows which of these God's Messenger meant save him to whom the truthful report comes in his unveiling.

When he comes to a halt in this station, he gazes over the two absent domains—the absent from which the engendered things come into existence, and the absent to which some of the engendered things are transferred after they become qualified by the witnessed.

This is a question of majestic worth that is not known by many people. I mean these affairs that emerge from the absent to the witnessed, then are transferred to the absent. They are the engendered accidents. Are they affairs of entified *wujūd*, or are they states that are qualified neither by nonexistence nor by *wujūd*, but simply intelligible? Then they would be relations. They are among the mysteries concerning which creation is bewildered, for they are not God, nor do they have an entified *wujūd* that they should pertain to the cosmos or that which is other than God. Thus they are intelligible realities. When you ascribe them to God, He accepts them, and they are not impossible for Him. But when you ascribe them to the cosmos, it accepts them, and they are not impossible for it.

Then they are divided into two sorts in the case of God. Among them are those that cannot possibly be ascribed to God, so they are not ascribed to Him. And among them are those whose ascription to God is not impossible. Everything that is not impossible for God is accepted by the cosmos—all of it except the relation of unboundedness. The cosmos does not accept that. As for the relation of binding, the cosmos accepts it, but God does not.

These intelligible realities possess the unboundedness that does not belong to other than themselves, so the Real and the cosmos accept them. They are not from the Real, nor are they from the cosmos. They are not existent, but the rational faculty cannot deny the one who knows them. From here bewilderment occurs, the matter becomes grave, people differ, and bewilderments are bewildered.

None knows this save God and he whom God allows to see it. This is the sound absent from which nothing comes into existence to be witnessed and to which nothing is transferred after the witnessed. It is not an impossible thing such that it would be a sheer nonexistence. It is not necessary in *wujūd* such that it would be sheer *wujūd*. It is not a possible thing such that its two sides would be equal between *wujūd* and nonexistence. Nor is it unknown. On the contrary, it is a known intelligible thing. So no definition is known for it, and it is neither worshiper nor worshiped.

The ascription of "absent" to it is more appropriate than the ascription of "witnessed," because it has no entity that would permit it to be witnessed at some moment. So this is the absent that belongs to the Real alone when He says, *the knower of the absent,* not linking it with the witnessed; *so He does not make His absent manifest to anyone* [72:26]. As for the absent that He links with the witnessed, that is the absent that is the contrary of the witnessed, so the Real described Himself as knowing the two contraries, for He said, *the Knower of the absent and the witnessed* [6:73]. (III 78.4)

From Chapter 69: On the Mysteries of the Night Ṣalāt

Given that *wujūd* becomes manifest as three worlds, these must show their signs and traces not only in the cosmic and the revealed books, but also in the ritual forms of the Shariah, all the more so since the Shariah's function is to bring human beings into harmony with *wujūd* in its full deployment. Thus it is not surprising to see Ibn al-ᶜArabī explain the three basic times for the *ṣalāt*—daytime, night, and the in-between periods of morning light and evening light—in terms of the three worlds. The daytime corresponds to the world of the witnessed, the night to the world of the absent, and the in-between periods to the *barzakh*. There are two in-between periods because imagination works in two directions. It corporealizes meanings, which is to say that it brings things from the darkness of the absent into the light of the witnessed; and it subtilizes bodies, which is to say that it takes things from the light of the witnessed into the darkness of the absent. Thus the *ṣalāt*s of the various times of day leave different traces in the worshiper in keeping with the specific domains of *wujūd* to which each corresponds.

Ibn al-ᶜArabī begins the discussion of this particular section, "On the last moment for the night *ṣalāt*," by mentioning, as he does throughout his chapters on jurisprudence, various opinions of the ulama on the ruling in question. Then he turns to some of the hidden significance of the ruling. The word he uses for hidden significance is *iᶜtibār*, which means to cross over, that is to move from the outward and obvious to the inward and hidden. The word can also be translated as to take heed, to take into account. "Metaphorical interpretation" suggests something of the term's sense. Sometimes, as here, he specifies the type of crossover he has in mind, since he calls it *al-iᶜtibār fi'l-bāṭin*, crossing over into, or taking heed of, the nonmanifest and hidden dimension of the issue.

The ulama of the Shariah have disagreed on the moment of the night *ṣalāt* in two places—concerning the first of its moment and the last of its moment.

Some say the first of its moment is the absence of the red of the dusk. I agree with this view. Others say the first of its moment is the absence of the white that is after the red.

"Dusk" [*shafaq*] is two, and this is the occasion of the disagreement. The first dusk is true, and the white that follows it is the second dusk, within which doubt occurs. One may doubt because it is similar to the false dawn, [called] "the tail of the wolf," which is the "elongated" [dawn]. The Lawgiver has made [the false dawn] part of the night, and the *ṣalāt* of morning is not permissible with its appearance, nor is the person who desires to fast prevented from eating. One may also doubt because dusk is similar to the "spreading dawn," at whose appearance the morning *ṣalāt* is performed and at whose appearance it is not permitted for the faster to eat.

However, in my view, it is more obviously similar to the spreading dawn at whose appearance the morning *ṣalāt* is performed. This is because it is joined with the "red" until the rising of the sun. It is not cut off by darkness, as the false dawn is cut off.

In the same way, the white that is at the beginning of the night is joined to the red. When the red becomes absent, the white remains. If there were a short darkness between the white and the red, as there is between the elongated dawn and the red of the morning's shine, then we would connect it to the false dawn and we would annul its ruling property. This is why—and God knows best—those who observe the absence of the white at the first moment of the night are more worthy of regard.

However, since it has been affirmed that the Lawgiver performed the *ṣalāt* at the white after the absence of the red dusk, we halt at that. It is for the Lawgiver to take into account the white and the red that are at the first of the night differently from the way he takes them into account at the last of the night, even if this derives from the traces of the sun in its setting and rising.

As for God's words, *By the morning when it breathes* [81:18], in my view the most plausible sense in its exegesis is that it is the elongated dawn, because it is cut off, just as the breath of the breather is cut off. Then, after that, his breaths continue.

As for the last of its moment, some say that it is until the third of the night, some say it is until half of the night, and some say that it is until the rising of the dawn. I agree with the last. I also saw a view, but I do not know who held it or where I saw it, that the last of the moment of the night *ṣalāt* is as long as someone has not yet slept, even if he should stay awake until the rising of the dawn.

Crossing Over into the Nonmanifest Dimension in This

As for the crossing over concerning the first and the last moment of this *ṣalāt*:

Know that the Real has divided the cosmos into three levels, and the Real has also divided the moments of the *ṣalāts* into three levels.

[1] He made the world of the witnessed. That is the world of sensation and manifestation. It corresponds to the *ṣalāt* of the daytime. Hence I whisper with the Real through the signifiers of Him given by the world of the witnessed and sensation and by His names that look upon this world. Concerning something like this God's Messenger said, "God says upon the tongue of His servant, 'God hears him who praises Him'," that is, during the *ṣalāt*. Here the servant is the Real's deputy. This derives from the name Manifest, since the Real has become manifest through the form of him who says the words, "God hears him who praises Him." So also are His words to His prophet Muhammad concerning the nomad: *Grant him sanctuary until he hears the speech of God* [9:6]. He was hearing nothing but sounds and letters from the mouth of the Prophet, but God said, "That is My speech," and He attributed it to Himself. Thus the Real became manifest within the world of the witnessed in the form of the reciter of His speech. So understand!

[2] God made the world of the absent. It is the world of reason and corresponds to the *ṣalāt* of the night. Its moment is from the absence of the evening glow to the rise of the morning glow.

"He who performs the *ṣalāt* is whispering with his Lord" in this *ṣalāt* through the proofs and demonstrations of Him given by the world of the absent, reason, and reflection. This is a specific proving through a specific kind of knowledge, known by the Folk of the Night.

This is the *ṣalāt* of the lovers, the Folk of the Mysteries and the Abstruse Knowledges, those sheltered by the veils. God gives them knowledges appropriate to this moment in this world. This is the moment of the ascents of the prophets, the messengers, and the mortal human spirits so as to see the imaginal signs of God and gain spiritual nearness. It is also the moment when God descends from the station of Sitting [upon the Throne] to the heaven closest to us for the sake of those who seek forgiveness, repent, ask, and supplicate.[16] So it is an eminent moment. "When someone performs the night *ṣalāt* in a gathering, it is as if he has stood half the night." In this hadith there is a fragrance for him who maintains that the last moment for saying this *ṣalāt* is until the halfpoint of night.

[3] God made the world of imaginalization and the *barzakh*. It is the descent of meanings within sensory forms. The meanings are not of the absent world, because they have put on sensory forms, nor are they of the witnessed world, because they are disengaged meanings and their manifestation within these forms is an accidental affair that has happened to the perceiver, not to the meanings themselves. Here knowledge is seen in the form of milk, religion in the form of a fetter, and faith in the form of a handle.

Among the moments for the *ṣalāts*, the *barzakh* is the moment of the sunset and the morning *ṣalāts*, since neither of these moments belong to the night or the daytime. They are two *barzakhs* between night and daytime on the two sides, since the time of night and daytime is cyclic. That is why God says, *He wraps the night around the daytime and wraps the daytime around the night* [39:5], from the "wrapping" of the turban. Each of the two is hidden by the manifestation of the other. Thus God said, *He makes the night cover the daytime* [7:54], and in the same way He makes the daytime cover the night.

"He who performs the *ṣalāt* is whispering with his Lord" at this moment through the signifiers of God given by the world of the *barzakhs* in the self-disclosures, their constant variations, and the transmutation within forms, as has reached us in the sound reports.

However, the *barzakh* reality of the sunset *ṣalāt* is the servant's emergence from the world of the witnessed to the world of the absent. He passes by means of this odd-numbered *barzakh*,[17] and thereby he gains awareness of the mysteries of the acceptance of the witnessed world by the absent world. This corresponds to sensation when it gives a form to imagination, and imagination takes it by means of the faculty of reflection and joins it with the intelligible things. Thus imagination has subtilized the form that belonged to the thing in sensation and rid it of density. Hence the form comes to be spiritualized by means of this *barzakh*.

The occasion of this is that the sunset *ṣalāt* has an odd number of cycles, for activity belongs to the odd number. In reality, it is the odd number that subtilizes the form of the *ṣalāt* so that the absent world and reason will receive it, since reason does not receive the forms of dense things, and the absent does not receive the witnessed. Inescapably, the *barzakh* subtilizes the form of the *ṣalāt* so that the world of the absent may receive it.

The *barzakh* of the morning glow is similar. It is the world of the absent's emergence into the world of the witnessed and sensation. The servant has no escape from passing through the *barzakh* of imagination, which is the moment of the *ṣalāt* of the morning—from the rise of the morning glow to the rise of the sun. Hence the morning glow belongs neither to the world of the absent nor to the world of the witnessed. So the *barzakh*—which is imagination and is expressed as "the moment of the morning glow until sunrise"—takes the intelligible, disengaged meanings, to which belongs the night, and then imagination densifies them in its *barzakh*. Through its imaginalizing it robes the meanings in density after they had been subtle, so the meanings gain a correspondence with the world of sensation. They become manifest as dense forms in sensation after they had been spiritual, subtle, absent forms. This is one of the traces of the *barzakh*: It turns the intelligible into the sensory at the last of the night, and it turns the sensory into the intelligible at the first of the night.

The image of this is as follows: Within the rational faculty there is the form of a house—a subtle, intelligible form. When imagination looks at this form, it gives it a form through its strength. It differentiates it and densifies it, ridding it of the subtlety it has in the rational faculty. Then it directs the bodily parts to build it by collecting bricks, clay, plaster, and everything that the builder who is the architect imagines. Imagination sets up the meaning in sensation as a dense form witnessed by the eyesight, after it had been a subtle, intelligible form that took the shape of any form that it willed. In the sensory realm the meaning no longer has this strength because it has undergone binding. Hence, for the whole of the daytime it remains bound by this form, so long as daytime lasts.

If the daytime never ends, like the day of the last abode, then the duration of the form never comes to an end. If the daytime ends, then that is like the day of this world, and the days of this world are ranked in degrees. One of them fills twenty-four hours, another a month, another a year, still another thirty years, and less than that and more than that.

The form remains bound for this period—the length of its day. This is called its "lifespan to the named term." When the moment of sunset arrives, the *barzakh* subtilizes its form and transfers it from the world of sensation, turning it over to the world of reason. Thereby the form returns to the subtlety from which it came. Such is the movement of this turning wheel!

If you have understood and rationally grasped the meanings whose mysteries I have clarified for you, you have come to know the knowledge of this world, the knowledge of death, the knowledge of the last world, and the times and properties specific to each locus. May God give us and you understanding of His ruling and place us among those whose feet are firm in true knowledge of Him!

The night is three thirds, and the human being is three worlds—the world of sensation, which is the first third; the world of his imagination, which is the second; and the world of his meaning, which is the last third of the night of his configuration. Within the last the Real descends, as indicated by His words, "The heart of My servant embraces Me."

According to the Prophet's words, "God looks not at your forms," which are the first third, "nor at your deeds," which are the second third, "but He looks at your hearts," which are the last third. Thus He has included the whole of the night

Those who say that the last moment [for the night *ṣalāt*] is the first third do so from the standpoint of the third of sensation. Those who say that its last moment is until midnight—which is the middle of the second third—do so from the standpoint of the second third, which is the world of their imagination, because it is the locus of working on subtilization or densification. Those who say that its moment is until the rise of the morning glow do so from the standpoint of the human being's world of meaning.

Each group says something in keeping with what becomes manifest to them. But everyone agrees that with the rise of the morning glow, the person has emerged from the moment of the *ṣalāt* of night. So what is apparent is that the last of its moment is until the rise of the morning glow, because of the consensus and agreement on emerging from the moment at the rise of the morning glow. Our words are upheld by Ibn ʿAbbās, that is, that the last of its moment is until the rise of the morning glow. (I 394.33)

III

The Structure of the Microcosm

8. *Spirits and Bodies*

The cosmos consists of two or three basic worlds. Each is a homestead that leaves specific traces in everything that dwells within it. In other words, despite the uniqueness of each individual thing in the cosmos, general statements can be made about things in keeping with the worlds they inhabit. Spiritual things have certain characteristics that distinguish them from bodily things, and imaginal things share in the attributes of the two sides. Spirit and body are among the most basic conceptual categories of Islamic thinking in general and Ibn al-ʿArabī's teachings in particular. Everything in the universe can be classified in terms of this basic duality, and before any attempt is made to investigate the structure of the cosmos in detail, it is necessary to look closely at the manner in which these two terms are understood.

For Ibn al-ʿArabī, as for many other Muslim thinkers, the word *rūḥ* or spirit is more or less synonymous with *nafs*, self or soul, though distinctions may be drawn in specific contexts. Often the choice of terms depends on the relevance of the discussion to a Koranic verse or hadith where one of the two is employed. Other terms that are used in similar senses are "intellect" (*ʿaql*), "secret heart" or "mystery" (*sirr*), and "subtlety" (*laṭīfa*). The last is commonly employed in the expression, the "human subtlety," which is equivalent to the "rationally speaking soul" (*al-nafs al-nāṭiqa*).

The root meaning of the word *rūḥ*, similar to Latin *spiritus* and Hebrew *rūwach*, is "wind." "Soul" (*nafs*, Hebrew *nephesh*) derives from the same root as "breath" (*nafas*). A basic implication of these derivations is that the spirit or soul is invisible in itself but visible through the traces that it leaves in the body, like the wind that moves the leaves of a tree. As Ibn al-ʿArabī expresses it, "The soul is nonmanifest in entity, manifest in property" (II 563.22).

Self and Soul

The hadith "He who knows himself knows his Lord" can also be translated "He who knows his soul knows his Lord." The word *nafs* in Arabic, like *self* in English, is a reflexive pronoun that refers back to an already mentioned noun, which may be animate or inanimate. In this reflexive sense, the word is commonly employed to refer to God. The Koran does so in five separate instances, though two of these are repeated verses: *God warns you about Himself* (3:28 and 3:30), *God has made mercy a duty for Himself* (6:12 and 6:54). The final instance is placed in Jesus' mouth as he addresses God: *Thou knowest what is in my self and I know not what is in Thy self* (5:112). In all these verses, and especially the last, a case can be made for saying that the word *nafs* is not simply a reflexive pronoun, but rather designates God's own Reality or Essence. But the term is rarely if ever used as a technical term in this sense. Thus, if Ibn al-ʿArabī says *al-dhāt*, "the Essence," it clearly refers to God. But *al-nafs*, with no qualification, refers rather to the human side, "the self" or "the soul"—never to "the Self" as one might understand the parallel term in a Hindu context.

In most Western language sources on Islamic thought, including my own writings, *nafs* is commonly translated both as "soul" and "self" depending on the context. In the present book, with some hesitation, I have continued this practice, but it is important to remind the reader that, by abandoning consistency, we risk blurring an intimate connection between various dimensions of Ibn al-ʿArabī's thought. For example, when the hadith is rendered as "He who knows himself knows his Lord" and when the term *soul* is then used in contradistinction to "spirit" and "body," it is easily forgotten that this soul is precisely the self that needs to be known. Hopefully, these remarks will help avoid this problem.

In those Sufi teachings that focus on the necessity of overcoming the limitations of the human self, the term *nafs* is usually employed in a negative sense, and hence in translating *nafs* as used in some Sufi writings, the term *ego* may suggest this negative side of the *nafs*. The Muslim philosophers, in contradistinction to most Sufis, were concerned to develop a more "scientific" perspective on the self, so they tended to use the term *nafs* as a convenient designation for the object of this discussion, with no negative connotation. For them, the specific characteristic of human beings that differentiates them from other beings is their rationally speaking soul, and they analyzed this soul in terms of its relation to its own faculties, the senses, the body, and various aspects of the external world.

Chapter 267: The Soul

In this chapter, devoted to "the true knowledge of the *nafs*," Ibn al-ʿArabī refers to both ways of looking at the *nafs*—as a problem to be overcome, and as the "object" of study for those who would like to situate the human reality within the cosmos. He begins by calling the *nafs* a *barzakh*, because, however we define it, it pertains to an intermediate domain. It belongs exclusively neither to the body nor to the divine Breath, but is rather configured by the Breath inasmuch as it animates the body. Much more will be said about the soul's *barzakh* nature in what follows.

The first sentence of the chapter provides a definition for the term *nafs*, a definition that is the same as that given in *Iṣṭilāḥāt* (7; II 132.24): "The *nafs* is those attributes of the servant that are infirm" (II 568.1). The word "infirm" translates *maʿlūl*, which, as noted earlier, also means "effect" or, more literally, "caused." In explaining the servant's infirmities, Ibn al-ʿArabī takes advantage of the double meaning of the term *ʿilla* ("infirmity" and "cause") to allude once again to the fact that all created things are infirm because they depend upon causes and take their reality from others.

Although grammatically *nafs* can be treated either as masculine or feminine, most often it is considered feminine, as in the introductory poem:

The soul comes
  from the world of the *barzakh*s
    so every secret becomes
      clear from her.
Her station
  in the knowledges is lofty
    and everything difficult
      becomes easy through her.
Her spirit is deeply rooted
  in the Cloud,
    replenished through God's
      Faithful Spirit,
who deletes from her what is deleted
  through marriage,
    and whose mystery is buried
      in mortal man.
Her splendor is proud and soaring
  in its height—
    Glory be to Him, whatever He wills
      comes to be!

Know that, in their technical terminology, for the most part the Tribe mean by *soul* the attributes of the soul that are infirm. Hence, in this chapter we limit ourselves to discussing that specifically. However, they sometimes apply the term *soul* to the human subtlety. But in this chapter, we will give intimations, God willing, concerning the soul inasmuch as it is the infirmity of the thing that is infirm.

Know that in the technical terminology of the Tribe, the word *soul* derives from the world of the *barzakh*s in two senses. This is true even of the Universal Soul. A *barzakh* is only a *barzakh* when it has two faces, one each toward the two things between which it is a *barzakh*. Although there is no existent but God, He has placed the manifestation of things at occasions. So the occasioned thing can have no *wujūd* without the occasion. Hence everything that has come into existence at an occasion has a face toward its occasion and a face toward God, so it is a *barzakh* between the occasion and God.

The first of the *barzakh*s among the entities is the *wujūd* of the Universal Soul, because it comes into existence from the Intellect, though the Existence-Giver is God. Hence it has a face toward its occasion and a face toward God, so it is the first *barzakh* to become manifest.

Once you have come to know this, know also that no entity becomes manifest for the soul—which is the servant's subtlety that governs the body—except at the proportioning and balancing of the body. Then the Real *blew into him of His spirit* [32:9]. Hence the soul becomes manifest between the divine inblowing and the proportioned body; this is why the constitution displays traces in the souls and they come to be ranked according to excellence. For, in respect of the divine inblowing, there is no ranking in excellence. Ranking in excellence occurs only in the receptacles. So souls have a face toward nature and a face toward the Divine Spirit, which is why we have made them pertain to the world of the *barzakh*s.

In the same way, those attributes of the servant that are infirm derive from the world of the *barzakhs*, for the servant is blamed—in the view of the Tribe and most of the ulama—from the direction of the soul, but he is praised because he is ascribed to God in respect of the fact that he is God's act. Hence he belongs to the world of the *barzakh*s between praise and blame, not in respect of the occasion. Rather, he is blamed in respect of the occasion, not his entity.

When the servant's soul has a description in which the soul does not witness the Real at the *wujūd* of its entity, that description is infirm. This is why it is said concerning the description that it is "*nafs*"; that is, the servant witnesses nothing within it save his own *nafs*. He does not see it as deriving from the Real, as some others do, for they witness the Real within it. In the same way, when this description prevails over him because of an engendered cause [or "infirmity"] for which no connection to God is witnessed, nor is there any thought to ascribe it to God, he is caused ["infirm"] by this engendered cause that moved him such that this description came to abide in him.

For example, someone may desire one of the impermanent goods of this world such that he is moved to speak and act only through this good and his love for it, so no thought of the Real's side occurs to him. Then it is said that this movement is "infirm," that is, God has no entrance into it in your witnessing. Thus He says, *You desire the impermanent goods of this world,* that is, the ransom for the prisoners at [the Battle of] Badr, though He sent down this address generally concerning all the impermanent goods of the world; *but God desires the last world* [8:67].

The near, impermanent good is the first, manifest occasion, other than which the common people recognize nothing as an object of witnessing. But the last world's affair is absent from them and from the companions of heedlessness, because it is witnessed by the eye of faith.

It may also happen that human beings become absent for some moments from the knowledge that they have faith, because their heedlessness busies them with witnessing some affair. But, if they were to die in that state, they would die in faith, without doubt, despite their heedlessness. After all, the "heedless person" is he who, when called to presence, becomes present, but the ignorant person is not like that. He does not become present when called to presence. So know this! *And God speaks the* ***ḥaqq****, and He guides on the path* [33:4]. (II 568.3)

The Divine Spirit

The root of every soul and every spirit is the Divine Spirit (*al-rūḥ al-ilāhī*), which is sometimes called the "ascribed spirit" (*al-rūḥ al-iḍāfī* or *al-rūḥ al-muḍāf*), because God ascribes it to Himself with the pronouns "His," "My," and "Our" in several Koranic verses, especially three connected to the creation of Adam. One of these verses, which occurs twice in the Koran, is God's command to the angels to prostrate themselves before Adam: *When I have proportioned him and blown into him of My spirit, fall down before him in prostration* (15:29 and 38:72; cf. 32:9). Ibn al-ʿArabī also calls this spirit the "*yāʾī* spirit," that is, the spirit to which is attached the letter *yāʾ*, which is the pronoun "My." He identifies it with the "one soul" (*nafs wāḥida*) from which Adam, Eve, and their children were created (Koran 4:1, 6:98, 39:6). Each person manifests its properties to the extent of his own preparedness (*istiʿdād*).

> The souls were created from one quarry, as God says, *He created you from one soul* [4:1]. He says, after the preparedness of the body's creation, *I have blown into him of My spirit* [15:29]. So the mystery that was blown into the object of the blowing correctly derives from one spirit—that is, the soul. God says, *in whatever form He willed He mounted you* [82:8]. Here he means the preparednesses. So the human being comes to be according to the property of the preparedness to receive the divine command. (II 272.21)

The spirits born from the Divine Spirit are often called "partial" or "particular" (*juzʾī*) spirits, in which case the Divine Spirit may be called "the All Spirit" (*al-rūḥ al-kull*) or the "Universal Spirit" (*al-rūḥ al-kullī*) or "the All Spirit of which is blown into forms" (III 461.23). The partial spirits become differentiated when God blows something of the undifferentiated, Universal Spirit into the bodies, which receive it in keeping with their preparednesses. The All Spirit is one, but the partial spirits are many. That which "divides" the spirit is bodies, just as windows divide the light of the sun.

> The body of the cosmos came alive through the Divine Spirit. Just as the body of the cosmos comprises the bodies of its individuals, so also its spirit comprises the spirits of its individuals. *He created you from one soul* [4:1]. On this basis someone has said that the spirit is one entity in the individuals of the human species, so Zayd's spirit is the same as the spirit of ʿAmr and of all the individuals of this species. But the person who said this did not realize the affair, for just as the form of Adam's body is not the body of every individual of his offspring—even though it is the root from which we became manifest and were born—so also is the spirit that governs the body of the cosmos in its entirety.
>
> Suppose, for example, that the earth is level such that you do not see any crookedness or unevenness within it. Suppose also that the sun is spread over it and it shines with its light such that different parts of the light are not distinguished from other parts and neither the light nor the earth can be judged to be partitioned or divided. When cities and houses become manifest and the shadows of the standing objects appear, then the sunlight is divided and some parts of it become distinct from other parts, because of what overtakes it through these forms in the earth. When you take this into account, you come to know that the light specific to this dwelling is not the light specific to the next dwelling or to other dwellings.
>
> However, when you take into account the light from which this light becomes manifest and the fact that this is identical with that in respect of spreading out from it, then you will say that the spirits are one spirit. The sun becomes diverse only through the loci, like lights that are the light of one entity. However, the property of diversity in the receptacles is diverse because of the diversity of their constitutions and the forms of their shapes. (III 187.22)

According to Islamic beliefs, one of the signs of the Last Day is that the sun will rise from its setting place. Given that the human spirit is a divine light, this belief can be understood on the microcosmic level to mean that at death the soul rises from whence it has set, that is, from the bodily configuration within which it is hidden.

A Mystery
In the setting of the sun is the soul's death.

> The setting of the sun is the soul's death,
> so consider a light inserted in dust.
> That spirit is God's spirit within us,
> and at the inblowing, it starts to go back
> to the Most Majestic from whom it has
> turned away,
> so it hurries in its returning and departing.
>
> He says: The soul is like the sun. It has shone from the spirit ascribed to God and has set in

this configuration, so the atmosphere has become dark. It is said, "Night has come, and daytime has gone away." The soul's death is the fact that it is within this configuration, and the life of this configuration is through its *wujūd* within it.

This sun has no escape from rising in its own setting place. That is the day when *its faith shall not profit a soul that has not had faith before, nor earned good in its faith* [6:158], for, in its case, the time of religious prescription will have departed and expired.

The rising of the sun from its setting place is the life of the soul and the death of this configuration. This is why human deeds are cut off through death—the [divine] address falls only on the whole. So in the soul's death is its life and in its life is its death. Its affair interpenetrates, for it is in the form of its Existence-Giver. What does the great have to do with the Self-Great, and what does the high have to do with the Self-High? But he is He. If the homesteads rule over him, then he is the ruled, and in him is what is in Him [*fīhi mā fīhi*]. (IV 434.13)

When speaking of the relation between *wujūd* and the entities, Ibn al-ʿArabī often says that the entities' diversity goes back to the diversity of their preparedness for *wujūd*. So also, it can be said that the diversity of the partial spirits can be traced back to the diversity of their preparedness to receive the light of the Universal Spirit. He makes this point in the following passage, in which he is speaking about the First Intellect. At the end of the passage, he makes clear that the First Intellect is another name for the Ascribed Spirit or the Universal Spirit. The "intellects" are angelic intelligences and human rational faculties.

The realization of the affair by way of voicing the most appropriate likeness and similarity is that the form of the engendering of the intellects from the greatest Intellect is through the "first lamp," from which all wicks are lit. The lamps become numerous according to the number of wicks. The wicks receive the light of that lamp in keeping with their preparednesses. A natural wick in the furthest limit of cleanliness, limpid in oil, and ample in body will have a receptivity toward the all-embracingness of light and the magnitude of light's body that is greater and larger than a wick that has less of the attribute of cleanliness and limpidness. So the disparity among the lights accords with the preparednesses of the wicks.

With all this, nothing is decreased from the First Lamp. On the contrary, it remains in its perfection as it was, while each of these lamps conforms to it. Each says, "I am like it. How is it more excellent than I? For [light] is taken from me, just as it is taken from it." So it leaps up and speaks, but it does not see the First Lamp's excellence over itself in respect of the fact that it is the root and possesses priority. Moreover, the First Lamp is not found in any sort of matter, and there is no intermediary between it and its Lord. Nothing else has any *wujūd* save through it and the sorts of matter that receive burning from it, such that the entities of the intellects become manifest. All this is absent from the intellects, or rather, they have no tasting of it. How can that which has no *wujūd* save from a father and a mother perceive the reality of that which has *wujūd* without any intermediary?

Since the intellects are incapable of perceiving the First Intellect from which they become manifest, their incapacity to perceive the Creator of the First Intellect, who is God, is even greater. For "The first that God created was the Intellect," and it is this from which these intellects became manifest by means of these natural souls. So it is the first of the fathers. In His exalted book, God called it "the Spirit" and He ascribed it to Himself. He said concerning these natural souls, this Spirit, and the partial spirits that belong to all the natural souls, *When I have proportioned him and blown into him of My spirit* [15:29]—which is this greatest Intellect. This is why it has been called the "native" [*gharīzī*] intellect. The meaning is that this intellect is required by the natural configuration through its preparedness, which consists of the proportioning and balancing of the configuration so that it will receive this affair. (II 66.33)

Governance

The spirit's basic attribute is life (*ḥayāt*). Inasmuch as the Divine Spirit, which is the Breath of the All-Merciful, has been blown into everything in the cosmos, it is sometimes called "the sphere of life" (I 119.10).

God chose the Spirit above all the angels because it is blown into every form, whether angelic, celestial, elemental, material, or natural, and through it things have life. It is the Spirit ascribed to Him, and it is the Breath of the All-Merciful from which life comes to be. Life is bliss, bliss is pleasurable, and taking pleasure accords with the constitution. Thus we say concerning a person with a cold constitution, "He enjoys that through which a person of a hot constitution suffers chastisement." So understand! Enough for you should be the Lawgiver's calling attention with his words—if you understand—that the Fire has folk who are its folk and the Garden has folk who are its folk. He mentioned concerning the folk of the Fire that "They will neither die therein nor live," so they will be seeking bliss through the Fire because of the *wujūd* of the cold, and this is one of the properties of the constitution. (II 172.4)

Sometimes the Shaykh distinguishes between life and spirit, as when he says, "The spirit is alive, no doubt, but not every living thing is a spirit" (III 346.22). In this case, he seems to be using *spirit* to refer to the invisible and absent force that "governs" (*tadbīr*) a body. All bodies are alive and thus have spirits, but not all have governing spirits. Animals do, but minerals do not. The Shaykh makes this point in one of his many discussions of the Koranic account of how Moses asked God to show Himself. Moses saw what the mountain saw, but the difference between Moses' being "thunderstruck" and the mountain's "crumbling to dust" has to do with the difference between a body that possesses a governing spirit and one that does not. The Shaykh compares the function of the spirit to that of a king's appointed ruler (*wālī*) in a province.

When his Lord disclosed Himself to the mountain, that self-disclosure *made it crumble to dust* [7:143], but it did not make it nonexistent. Rather, it caused its loftiness and highness to disappear. Moses had looked upon it in the state of its loftiness, and the self-disclosure had occurred from the direction not adjacent to Moses. When the mountain crumbled, what made it crumble became manifest to Moses, so *Moses fell down thunderstruck* [7:143]. For Moses possessed a spirit, which has the property of maintaining the form as it is. The spirit of everything other than animals is identical with its life, nothing else. So Moses' being thunderstruck was like the mountain's crumbling, because of the diversity of the preparedness, since the mountain has no spirit to maintain its form for it. Thus the name *mountain* disappeared from the mountain, but neither the name *Moses* nor the name *human being* disappeared from Moses through his being thunderstruck. Moses regained consciousness, but the mountain did not return as a mountain after crumbling, since it had no spirit to make it abide.

After all, the property of spirits in things is not like the property of life in them, because life is perpetual in all things, while spirits are like rulers: Sometimes they are described as dismissed, sometimes as possessing rulership, and sometimes as absent while rulership remains. Rulership belongs to the spirit as long as it governs this animal body, death is its dismissal, and sleep is its absence while its rulership remains. (II 540.11)[1]

Chapter 447: Essential Governance

The spirit's attribute of governance derives from the inherent relation between spirits and bodies, high and low, heaven and earth, effuser and receptacle. In the microcosm, spirit and body are interrelated just as they are in the macrocosm, and this in turn reflects the relation of the Real with creation, or the Speaker with the words articulated within the Breath. Governance pertains to the very essence of the governing spirits. Its divine root is that creativity belongs to the Essence of the Creator. It follows that human beings cannot sever the connection between their spirits and their bodies. Sufis and philosophers often describe the goal of disciplining the soul by the term *disengagement* (*tajrīd*), literally, the "stripping" of the spirit from its attachment to the body. Ibn al-ʿArabī sometimes employs this term in the same context, but he maintains that it is impossible for the human spirit to disengage itself totally from governance of a body. Governance goes on, whether or not the spirit is aware of the governance. And when the corporeal body drops off through death, the spirit finds itself occupied with governing an imaginal body. The spirit never ceases governing a body or bodies in any world. The Shaykh discusses these points in Chapter 447, "On the true knowledge of the mutual waystation of 'Whoever enters the Presence of purification speaks on My behalf.'"

When the servant is purified of his
engendered qualities,
the tool will itself be the speaker.
Such is he who performs the *ṣalāt*: When he
stands
after bowing, he is the truth-speaker.[2]
He becomes the Real's deputy in his
speaking,
so no hindrance abides within him.
His every word is true,
his every wine is sparkling.

God says, *On the day when their tongues, their hands, and their feet witness against them for what they were doing* [24:24], that is, what they were doing through these [bodily parts]. They witness only as outsiders, for there is no escape from someone against whom they witness. If it were not as we say and if the witnesser were identical with the one against whom he witnesses, that would be "confession," not "witnessing." But God did not mention that this is a confession.

This proves that the bodily parts are intertied with the rationally speaking soul just as possessions are intertied with their owner, and so also is the affair of the root. The root is the Real. He was forever a Governor in eternity without beginning. Hence He must govern a specific object of governance in eternity without beginning. This object is none other than the entities of the possible things, which are witnessed by Him in the state of their nonexistence, since they are fixed. Hence He governs the fact that among them some are prior and some posterior in the engendering of their entities and in the forms within which they are brought into existence. This is "the mystery of the measuring out," the knowledge of which God has hidden from His creatures so that its ruling property may become manifest in the existent forms in the view of the eye.

In a similar way, when God desired to configure the governing spirits, they came to be only as governing. If they did not possess entities and forms within which their governance became manifest, then their reality would be nullified, for they govern through their very essences. Such is the affair for the folk of unveiling.

Here there is a strange and marvelous mystery, of which I shall give intimations, God willing, in the following detailed explanation. We say: God configured these corporeous forms from light, fire, dust, and vile water, in keeping with the diversity of the diverse roots of this configuration.[3] When proportioning reached its perfection in the forms, which are the locus for the governance of the governing spirits, God configured from these forms—that is, from their reception of what their Existence-Giver blew into them, which is perpetual effusion—governing spirits that abide through them according to the form of their reception. Thus the spirits are ranked in excellence because of the ranking in excellence of the configurations. They do not come to be in one level except in that they are governors. So the governing spirits become manifest only in the forms of the constitution of the receptacles. In their governance, the spirits do not transgress what is required by the governed frames.

Consider the entities of the possible things before they become manifest in entity. The Real cannot possibly become manifest within them except in the form of what they receive, so, in reality, they are not in the form of the Real. Rather, the governor is in the form of the governed, since nothing of the governor becomes manifest from the governed save in the measure of its reception—nothing else. Hence "the Real" is nothing but the situation of creation. Nothing is seen of the Real, and nothing is known, other than this. In Himself, He is as He knows, and He has in Himself that which cannot be known at all. The affair that can never be known is what He has in Himself, as indicated by His words, *God is independent of the worlds* [3:97].

I have made manifest the knowledge of God to which I have just called your attention not by my own choice; rather, compulsion has imposed it upon me. So preserve it and do not become heedless of it, for it will teach you courtesy toward God!

From this station descended God's words, *Whatever ugly thing strikes you is from your soul* [4:79]. In other words, "I bestow upon you only in the measure of your receptivity." The divine effusion is all-embracing, because He is all-embracing in bestowal. There is no shortcoming on His part. But you have nothing of Him except what your essence receives. Hence your own essence forbids you from access to the All-Embracing and puts you in the midst of constriction. The measure in which His governance occurs within you is your "Lord" whom you serve and whom alone you recognize. This is the "mark" within which He will transmute Himself to you on the day of resurrection by way of unveiling. In this world, this mark is absent from the common people. Every human being knows it from himself, but he does not know that it is known by him. Hence the common people say, "God has habituated me only to such and such."

Once you have understood this, you will know that the Real is with you in your situation, but you are not with Him. He called this to your attention in the Koran with His words, *He is with you wherever you are* [57:4]. You are not with Him, and it is not correct for anyone to be with God. So God is with everyone in the actual state of each one. So consider the individuals of the cosmos. That in which you will see each is the Entity of the Real, nothing else.

There is no unveiling beyond this unveiling
  and no description beyond this description.
So glory be to Him who appears and hides!
  To this both Shariah and common consent
    bear witness.

Disengagement from governance is not correct. If it were correct, Lordship would be nullified, but it is not nullified, so disengagement is impossible. Disengagement has no support, since you cannot rationally conceive of your God save as a Governor within you. You will not know Him save from yourself, so you must be busy with governance. Hence there is no escape from body and spirit, in this world and the last world—in each abode according to the configurations that are appropriate to it. The spirits undergo variation in accordance with the variation of these configurations in the form of creation and the Real, as has already been mentioned in this book. This is the meaning of this verse, which speaks on behalf of the Real:

Be wherever you will, for
  as you are, I will be.

Such is the actual situation in its entity. *And God speaks the **ḥaqq**, and He guides on the path* [33:4]. (IV 62.2)

The Spirit from the Command

The "world of the command" is the world of spirits. We have seen that the term *command* in this sense is employed in contradistinction to "creation," which designates the world of bodies. In several passages, the Koran employs the expression *the spirit from His command,* and here *command* seems to be used in another sense. On the basis of such passages, Ibn al-ʿArabī differentiates between the ascribed, divine spirit and the "command" (*amrī*) spirits. The first sort of spirit is "ascribed" to the personal pronouns that refer to God, while the second sort carries instructions that God addresses at specific creatures. God blows something of the first into all bodies, whereas He sends the second with messages to the prophets and the Folk of God, thereby giving them support or "confirmation" (*taʾyīd*).[4] The Shaykh often refers to the command spirit when discussing the highest stations of the spiritual journey.

Since hearts come alive through knowledge, just as the entities of all bodies come alive through spirits, God named knowledge a "spirit" that the angels bring down upon the hearts of God's servants and that He also casts and reveals without any intermediary in the case of His servants. His casting and revealing it is His words, *He casts the spirit from His command upon whomever He will of His servants* [40:15] and His words, *Even so We have revealed to thee a spirit from Our command* [42:52]. As for sending down the angels with it upon the hearts of His servants, that is His words, *He sends down the angels with the spirit from His command upon whomever He will of His servants* [16:2]. Hence these angels in the absent domain are teachers and mentors that are witnessed by those upon whom they descend.

When this spirit descends upon the heart of the servant through the sending down of the angel or the casting and revelation of God, the heart of the one to whom it is sent down comes alive. Then he is the companion of witnessing and finding, not the companion of reflection, wavering, or any knowledge that accepts misgivings such that its companion would be transferred from the degree of certitude to the state of consideration. Hence the knowing, chosen servant either ascends and sees, or he is descended upon in his site. (III 356.2)

From this waystation one comes to know the gnostic sciences that the Real sends down upon the hearts of His servants through sending the spirits down upon them. He says, *He casts the spirit from His command upon whomever He will of His servants* [40:15]. *[He sends down the angels with the spirit from His command upon whomever He will of His servants: "Warn] that there is no god but I"* [16:2]—He did not say "He." Hence the "spirit" is what is cast from God to the hearts of His servants, and God's command does the casting. The spirit [indicated in this verse] is the form of His words, *There is no god but I, so be wary of Me* [16:2].

In this waystation, the intermediary is lifted, for the sent down revelation is identical with the spirit, while the one who casts is God, none other. Hence this spirit is not the same as the "angel" [*malak*], but it is the same as the "message" [*malʾaka*]. So understand! A spirit like this is not known by the angels, for it is not of their kind. It is a spirit that is not carried, nor is it luminous, while the angel is a spirit in light. This tasting belongs to us and to all the prophets.

As for "angels," they may be those whom God has specified for the messengers. This is His words, *The Faithful Spirit has brought it down upon thy heart* [26:193], so he is the messenger to the Messenger.

As for the descent of the angelic spirits upon the hearts of the servants, these descend only with a command of God, the Lord. This does not mean that God commands them from the Presence of Address to descend. Rather, He casts to them something that is not appropriate to their station in the form of him to whom they should take it down. Thus they recognize that God has desired from them sending down and descent with the revelation that they find in themselves and that is not appropriate for them. This revelation is one of the specific characteristics of mortal man. The angels witness the form of the one to whom they are sent down within the forms whose glorification they have in themselves. O He who makes manifest the beautiful and curtains the ugly with the curtains that are let down and lifted up! They recognize from the forms the person to whom they belong in the earth, so they descend to him and cast to him what has been cast to them. What they cast is called "shariah" or "revelation." If it is ascribed to God as an attribute, it is named "Koran, Furqān, Torah, Psalms, Gospel, or Scriptures." If it is ascribed to God as an act, not as an attribute, it is called "hadith, report, view, or sunnah."

The angels may also descend with the command from the Presence of Address. (II 638.2)

Chapter 268: The Casting of Knowledge

Ibn al-ʿArabī calls this chapter, "On the true knowledge of the spirit, which is what casts knowledge of the absent into the heart in a specific respect." It is clear from his mention of "casting knowledge" in the title that he has in view the spirit from the command. He begins with a poem that differentiates the two kinds of spirit.

The spirit is two—
of the *yāʾ* and of the command—
while the ruling is affirmed
between prohibition and command.
Everything else is reports
giving news
that the engendered things stand
between mystery and overt.
The world of the Highest Barzakh
delivers him
from the grasp of imprisonment
as a solicitude to his state.

God says, *Even so We have revealed to thee a spirit from Our command* [42:52]. He says, *He casts the spirit from His command upon whomever He will of His servants* [40:15]. He says, *The Faithful Spirit has brought it down upon thy heart, that thou mayest be one of the warners* [26:193]. Here He mentions "warning," as He does in His words, *He casts the spirit from His command [. . .] that He may warn them* [40:15] and in the verse, *He sends down the angels with the spirit from His command upon whomever He will of His servants: "Warn!"* [16:2].

This spirit comes only to give knowledge. But within it is a kind of reproof, for the knowledge-giving is conveyed by the word *sending down*. Hence it is a knowledge-giving through a reproof, for it gives good news and warning, and good news comes only through knowledge-giving. In the spiritual sending down, the rubric of reproof and fear has overcome, because of the confidence that abides in the souls and necessitates the sending of messengers to let them know that they will be turned over from this world to the last world and returned from their selves to God.

As for our words, "the spirit of the *yāʾ*," by this we mean God's words, *I have blown into him of My spirit* [15:29] employing the *yāʾ* of ascription to Himself. He calls attention to the station of bestowing eminence. He is saying, "You are eminent in root, so act only in accordance with your root—do not perform the acts of the vile."

The spirit from the command is His words, *They will ask thee about the spirit*, that is, from whence it has become manifest. It was said to him, *Say: The spirit is from the command of my Lord* [17:85]. Hence, this was not a question about whatness, as some have supposed, for they did not ask, "What is the spirit?" Although it is plausible for them to question in this manner, the sense that we have maintained is supported by the answer to the question: *From the command of my Lord*. He did not say, "The spirit is such and such."

The spirits bring down the knowledges of the absent upon the hearts of the servants. Those who recognize the spirits receive them with courtesy and take from them with courtesy. But those who do not recognize them take the knowledge of the absent without knowing from whom—like soothsayers, the folk of auguries, the companions of arriving thoughts, and the folk of inspiration. They find knowledge of this in their hearts, but they do not know who brought it to them. The Folk of God witness the descent of the spirits upon their hearts, but they do not see the descending angel, unless the one upon whom it descends is a prophet or a messenger.

The friends of God witness the angels, but they do not witness them as casting to them; or, they witness the casting and they know that it comes from an angel without witnessing it. No one brings together the vision of the angel and the angel's casting except a prophet or a messenger. For the Tribe, this is how the prophet is differentiated and distinguished from the friend—that is, the prophet who is the companion of a sent-down Shariah.

God has locked the door of angelic descent with Shari'ite rulings, but He has not locked the door of descent with knowledge of these rulings into the hearts of His friends. He has made the spiritual descent with knowledge of the rulings subsist for them so that they may stand *upon insight* in their calling to God through the rulings, as do those who follow after the Messenger. Hence He says, *Say: "This is my way. I call to God upon insight, I and whoever follows after me"* [12:108]. This is a taking [of knowledge] that is not encroached upon by doubting in their view.

This is why al-Qushayrī, in lauding the knowledge of the Folk of God, says, "What do you think of a knowledge in which the ulama know doubting?" After all, the ulama other than these [Folk of God] are not *upon insight*, neither in the roots nor in the branches. As for the branches, this is because of the plausibility of interpretation. And as for the roots, this is because of the misgivings and obfuscations that find a way into the proof of the considerative thinker, who is the companion of the proof, from himself and from others. Thus his proof is doubted because of these misgivings, though he had been certain of it. But the folk of insights from God are not qualified by this in their knowledge. This knowledge is "the *ḥaqq* of certainty,"[5] which is to say that its coming to rest in the heart has been realized such that nothing can shake it from its resting place. This is enough concerning the knowledge of the casting spirit.

As for how the casting takes place, understanding this depends upon tasting, which is the "state." However, I can give you the knowledge that it occurs through correspondence. Inescapably, the heart of him who receives the casting has the preparedness for what is cast into it. Without it, there would be no reception. But preparedness does not lie in reception, since it is only a divine specification. Indeed, certain souls may walk on the path that takes them to the door from behind which, when opened, this specific casting and other kinds occur. Then, when they reach the door, they halt until they see that through which it will be opened in their case. When it is opened, the affair emerges one in entity, and they receive it from behind the door in the measure of their preparedness. They exert no effort in this. On the contrary, God specifies each of them with a preparedness. It is here that distinctions are drawn among the various groups, between followers and those who are not followers, between the prophets and the messengers, and between the messengers and those followers who are named in common language "friends."

He who has no knowledge imagines that their traveling to this door was the occasion through which they earned what was gained at the opening. Were this the case, all would be equal, but they are not equal. Hence this takes place only through the preparedness, which is not earned. It is from here that those considerative thinkers who claim that prophethood is earned fall into error.

No one says that prophethood can be earned save those who see that it does not come from God but that it is rather an effusion from the Intellect and the high spirits upon certain souls described by limpidness and delivered from the occasions of nature. Because of their limpidness, within them come to be imprinted the forms of everything in the cosmos, and this limpidness is earned. Hence what is gained by their limpidness is earned. But this is a gross error. Rather, limpidness is correct, and the imprinting of the forms of the cosmos in the soul of him who possesses the attribute of this overview is correct. However, if this individual, apart from others of the folk of limpidness like himself, is a messenger, a prophet, and the companion of a Law-giving, this is a divine specification that imprints in his soul everything within the forms of the cosmos. After all, the Preserved Tablet includes everything we have mentioned, since within it is imprinted the form of the messenger and his message, the form of the prophet and his prophethood, and the form of the friend and his friendship.

So, once the soul becomes limpid and everything in the Tablet is imprinted within it, this does not necessitate that the person will become a messenger. On the contrary, who is to be a messenger is imprinted within it, and things become distinguished for it. This disagrees with what the considerative thinkers imagine about what is gained through the limpidness of souls. What is imprinted in the soul is the levels and the companions of the levels, in both the high and the low worlds.

Then there is the property of the preparedness that receives the casting through the correspondence. The correspondence is the divine *cord* [3:103] that is gained in the heart and exists through the preparedness. When the servant joins with the Presence of the Real, the casting descends upon him, and this is the path. Then the heart is illumined through the knowledge of the absent that it gains, especially if this pertains to the knowledge of God that has no connection with engendered existence, like the knowledge that He is *Independent of the worlds* [3:97] and incomparable with attributes and that *Nothing is as His likeness* [42:11].

The image for the preparedness, the descent, and the joining cord is the likeness of a wick when fire remains within it. Something like smoke emerges from the fire and seeks by its nature to rise up above. So here we have a kindled lamp. The wick, from which the smoke emerges, is placed at the bottom of the lamp and above it such that the smoke quickly joins with the head of the wick. The wick takes fire, and the form of the illuminating lamp becomes manifest, and from this lamp light descends upon the wick. Here one should consider: Is anything diminished from the lamp, or does anything of the fire inhere within it? You will not find it so, even though you find the form as if it were so.

He who knows this mystery will know the meaning of the Prophet's words, "God created Adam in His form." He will know that when the preparedness stands receptive, when the correspondence is correct, and when the specific Aspiration attaches itself, then a descent upon him will occur in keeping with this. The small or large extent of the light gained by the wick will accord with the small or large body of the wick. The radiance will accord with the limpidness of the wick and of the oil, and the light will abide in the wick in keeping with the large or small amount of the oil, since the oil helps the light subsist.

If you have understood what I have said in this simile, you have come to know a knowledge known only by the knowers of God. You have realized how the spirit casts knowledge of the absent domain to the heart, which is the heart that receives this, and what attributes are possessed by this heart. You will also know that the Aspiration of the lower leaves its traces in the higher when it attaches itself to it. In the same way, God responds to the servant when he calls to Him. *And God speaks the **ḥaqq**, and He guides on the path* [33:4]. (II 568.30)

Bodies

To mention "spirit" is to mention by implication a locus within which the spirit manifests its traces. This locus is generally referred to as "body" (*jism, jasad, badan*), but other terms are used more or less synonymously, such as "frame" (*haykal*), "apparition" (*shabaḥ*), "mount" (*markab*), and "mold" (*qālab*). Thus the Shaykh mentions "the forms manifest in the cosmos and named *jism, jasad*, or *haykal*, whether these be luminous or non-luminous"

(II 282.8). One of the most common of the terms used interchangeably with body is "form," which is typically juxtaposed with "meaning." Thus the spirit is the body's meaning, and the body is the spirit's form. Sometimes the Shaykh refers to the body as the spirit's "matter" (*mādda*) within which it displays its traces and exercises its properties. He rarely if ever speaks of "form" as juxtaposed with "matter," as was done by the Muslim philosophers, following the Greek tradition.

The relation between spirit and body is mutual, which is to say that each leaves traces in the other. Ibn al-ʿArabī sees the archetype of this mutuality in the relation between God and the cosmos.

> In the spirit, the body has intelligible, known traces, because it bestows on the spirit knowledges of tastings and what cannot be known except through it; and in the body, the spirit has sensory traces that every living thing witnesses in itself. So also is the cosmos with the Real. In the cosmos God has manifest traces, which are the states within which the cosmos undergoes fluctuation. This is one of the properties of His name Aeon. And the Real reported that the cosmos, in respect of the prescriptions of the Law made for it, has traces which, had He not instructed us in them, we would not recognize. Thus, when we follow God's Messenger in the obedience toward God that he has brought for us, He loves us and we make Him pleased, so He is pleased with us. He reports that when we oppose Him, fail to observe His command, and disobey Him, we make Him displeased and wrathful, so He is wrathful toward us. When we call to Him, He responds to us, so calling is one of His traces [in us], and responding is one of our traces [in Him].
>
> All this is so that you might know that He has made nothing manifest save in the form in which it is He. It is impossible for the affair not to be so. Otherwise, from whence does it come, when there is nothing but He? Things give only what their capacity bestows. This is why the Real describes Himself to us with descriptions of the things which in our view are newly arrived, but which, in reality, are His descriptions that have become manifest within us. (III 315.9)

Bodies are of three basic sorts. The bodies of angels are natural and luminous (*nūrī*), but not "elemental" (*ʿunṣurī*), because not compounded of the four elements. The bodies of intermediate realities such as the jinn are imaginal, and whether or not they should be considered elemental seems to depend on how one defines the "fire" of which they are made. The bodies of the progeny—that is, the animals, plants, and minerals—are elemental and corporeal (*jismānī*). In the terminology of the Koran and the Hadith, the angels are made of light (*nūr*), the jinn of fire (*nār*), and Adam of earth (*arḍ, turāb*). Fire is an intermediate realm that combines the luminosity of light and the corporeality of earth.

> Life belongs to the spirits that govern the bodies—all of them, whether fiery, earthy, or luminous—exactly as radiance belongs to the sun. Life is an attribute of their very selves. They do not become manifest to anything without that thing's coming to life and becoming permeated by the life of the manifest spirit, just as the radiance of the sun permeates the body of the air, the face of the earth, and every site in which the sun becomes manifest. (III 65.18)

Sometimes Ibn al-ʿArabī classifies spirits by the attributes of the bodies that they govern. Thus "fiery spirits" are spirits that govern bodies of fire and "luminous spirits" are spirits that govern bodies of light.

> One of the properties of "penetrating eyesight" is that its companion perceives luminous and fiery spirits without there being any desire on the part of the spirits, any manifestation, or any assumption of form. This was the case of Ibn ʿAbbās and ʿĀʾisha, when they perceived Gabriel while he was speaking to the Messenger of God, without Gabriel's knowing and without his desiring to become manifest to them. They reported this to the Messenger of God, but they did not know that he was Gabriel. The Messenger said to her, "Did you indeed see him?" And he said to Ibn ʿAbbās, "Did you see him?" They replied, "Yes." He said, "That was Gabriel."
>
> In the same way, they perceive the Men of the Absent in the state of their desire to remain veiled. Even if they are not manifest to the eyesights, the companion of this state sees that. Also deriving from penetrating eyesight is that, when meanings become embodied for them,

they recognize them in the entity of their forms, so they know without delay what meaning it is that has become embodied. (III 332.11)

In the midst of discussing the often debated issue of whether or not angels are superior to human beings, Ibn Sawdakīn, one of the Shaykh's disciples, reports that his master divided spirits into three kinds:

> I heard the Shaykh say something whose meaning was this:
>
> People disagree concerning the ranking in excellence between angels and mortal man, but we incline in another direction. Ibn Qasī and those who agree with him maintain that ranking in degrees occurs only among things that share common genera. Thus it is said that the most excellent jewel is the ruby and the most excellent cloth is silk. However, if the genera are diverse, it is not asked, "Which is more excellent, ruby or silk?" A group agree with Ibn Qasī in this.
>
> The direction in which we incline is that no ranking in excellence occurs among spirits except through reports from God. Spirits assume three varieties: spirits that govern luminous bodies, which are the Higher Plenum; spirits that govern fiery bodies, which are the jinn; and spirits that govern earthy bodies, which are mortal man. All the spirits, as angels, are one reality, so they are one genus. If ranking in excellence occurs, it occurs from here. This is a perception that is not achieved by him who thinks that the genera are different.
>
> There remains ranking in excellence in that which the spirits govern. Everyone has looked at what should be given preponderance according to his own consideration. The realized view here is that the most excellent is the nearest to God by way of specification and nearness. When God reports to someone concerning this, he has gained complete knowledge. He who takes it from somewhere else is speaking as if from obscurity, not from certainty.
>
> If we consider the question of ranking in excellence unconditionally, then the rational faculty will maintain that the angels are more excellent. But if we consider the perfection and all-comprehensiveness of the configuration, we will judge that mortal man is more excellent. So where do we find support? If the configuration of the angels has less composition, or the configuration of mortal man is more perfect, does any of that bestow nearness to God? There is no proof of that, so nothing remains but the divine report-giving. (*Wasāʾil* 50–51)

All things have spirits, but human beings, jinn, and angels are distinguished from other creatures by their specific make-up—the combination of governing spirit and earthy, fiery, or luminous body. It is this governing spirit that may find itself veiled from the absent domains. Other creatures along with the bodily parts and faculties of these three sorts of creatures witness God's self-disclosure in all things and, on this basis, glorify Him ceaselessly.

> The whole cosmos other than human beings and the jinn is fully unveiled toward that which is absent from mortal human sensation. No human being or jinn witnesses this absent domain except at the moment when habits are broken because of a charismatic gift given to him by God or because of the specific characteristic of something that bestows the unveiling of the absent things. In the same way, every inanimate object, plant, and living thing in the whole cosmos and in the world of human beings, the jinn, the bodies of the angels, and the celestial spheres, and every form governed by a spirit—whether sensation perceives that governance in the forms whose life is manifest, or does not perceive it in those whose life is nonmanifest—such as human bodily parts, skin, and other such things, all dwell in the locus of the unveiling of the divine absent things; but these things are curtained from the spirits that govern the bodies of angels, human beings, or jinn—but from nothing else. For they are veiled from the perception of this absent divine domain except through the breaking of habit for some of them or all of them. (II 682.25)

Corporeous Bodies

Ibn al-ʿArabī employs both *jism* and *jasad* to mean body. Sometimes, however, he differentiates between the two terms by making the first pertain to the visible world and the second to the imaginal world. Both terms are translated here as "body," unless the distinction is important to the context, in which case *jism* is translated as "corporeal body" and *jasad* as "corporeous body." For example, in one passage the Shaykh divides the cosmos into three worlds by making it consist of spirits and the two sorts of bodies: "There is nothing but the worlds of corporeal bodies, corporeous bodies, and spirits" (II 335.8)

In his glossary of Sufi terminology, Ibn al-ʿArabī defines *jasad* as "any spirit or meaning that becomes manifest in a luminous or fiery body" (*Iṣṭilāḥāt* 14). Although the definition seems to imply that the spirit itself is the corporeous body, other passages that we have quoted suggest that the Shaykh means that the corporeous body is the luminous or fiery body within which the spirit appears. In the parallel passage in the *Futūḥāt*, he writes that a corporeous body is "every spirit or meaning that becomes manifest in the form of a luminous or elemental body such that it is witnessed by the other" (II 130.3). Again the passage is somewhat ambiguous, but it seems to mean that when a spirit becomes manifest in the form of an angel or a corporeal thing—such as Gabriel in the form of a bedouin—and is witnessed by "the other," which is anything other than God, then the witnessed form is called a "corporeous body." This interpretation is supported by a saying of the imaginal personage "ʿAbd Allāh ibn ʿAbd al-Haqq" that the Shaykh offers in *Kitāb al-ʿabādila*: "The corporeous bodies derive from the world of imagination and imaginalization. Most of what becomes manifest to the folk of this path has an entrance into the gate of the divine deception" (57).

The paired terms used to describe the absent and witnessed worlds—such as manifest and nonmanifest, light and darkness, meaning and form, subtle and dense—are all relative. It follows that things called "spirit" in one context may be called "body" in another. This is especially true of corporeous bodies, which are absent and spiritual in relation to corporeal bodies, but witnessed and corporeal in relation to spirits. In the same way, Ibn al-ʿArabī often calls corporeous bodies "subtle" bodies, since they do not have the same solidity and density as corporeal bodies. So also, the animal spirit can be called a "subtle body" (III 156.30). Within the corporeal world itself, corporeal bodies themselves have degrees of subtlety and density, just as the elements—which are simple and corporeous—are ranked in a scale of decreasing density and increasing subtlety. Thus the densest and least subtle is earth; then water is less dense and more subtle than earth; then air; and finally the least dense and most subtle is fire.

> "Corporeal bodies" are those bodies that are well known to everyone, whether they be subtle, translucent, or dense, seen or not seen. "Corporeous bodies" are those within which spirits become manifest. This may be in wakefulness when spirits are imaginalized in the forms of bodies, or it may be in the forms that dreamers perceive in their dreams; these are similar to the bodies in what is given by sensation, but in themselves they are not bodies. (III 186.28)

All bodies share in the ability to act as matter for the activity of spirits, which cannot display their properties unless in conjunction with bodily forms. But given that bodies are defined precisely by this receptivity toward the activity of a higher reality, spirits themselves can be called "bodies" in relation to the activity of God. Hence, just as the whole cosmos can be called "imagination," so also it can be considered a body.

A Mystery

Attainment belongs to the Folk of the Night.

The power of the Living, the Self-Abiding
  becomes manifest only in the configuring of bodies.
There is nothing but a tracing,
  so there is nothing but a body.
But bodies
  are diverse in arrangement—
among them subtle spirits,
  and among them dense apparitions.
Everything other than the Real, who is the Way,
  is a commingling and a mixing.
The attributes and the accidents are followers
  of this all-comprehensive body,
for it is compound [*murakkab*],
  and a compound thing is a mount [*markab*].

He who desires knowledge of the form of the state
should realize the knowledge of imagination,
within which power becomes manifest
and which will illumine his full moon.
He will fluctuate only in forms
and become manifest only in the station of the mortal,
but I do not mean by the "mortal" human beings,
for I bear witness against myself that I am bankrupt.
Yet I am the knower of my time,
because of my knowledge of the containers,
since there is nothing but a cup
and a full container.
So ponder,
and you will see clearly! (IV 389.18)

Just as there is nothing but body, so also, from another point of view, there is nothing but spirit. Whether things are called spirits or bodies depends on where we stand. Ibn al-ʿArabī makes this point when discussing place (*makān*)—which, along with time, is a concomitant of natural bodies—and the emplaced thing (*mutamakkin*). He differentiates between places and emplaced things in order to distinguish between "emplaced spirits" and "spirits of place," the former of which he discusses in the chapter. According to this classification, there are two sorts of things in the witnessed world—places and emplaced things. The latter can in turn be divided into two sorts—bodies or substances, which are "on" the places and hence can move to other places; and attributes or accidents, which are "in" their places and hence cannot, by themselves, move elsewhere. Thus, we have two sorts of emplaced things—bodies (or substances) and attributes (or accidents)—and both can be called either "spirits" or "bodies," depending on how we look at them.

Know—may God give you understanding—that all things other than God are pure spirits that declare the incomparability of their Existence-Giver and Creator. They can be divided into place and emplaced. Place can be divided into two sorts—a place called a "heaven" and a place called an "earth." The emplaced things of these two can be divided into two sorts—emplaced "in" the place and emplaced "on" the place. Something emplaced in the place comes to be in respect of its place, but something emplaced on the place does not come to be in respect of its place.[6] This classifies everything other than God. All of them are spirits in reality/bodies and substances in the Real Through Which Creation Occurs. (III 91.35)

When Ibn al-ʿArabī refers to "luminous" bodies, he typically means the bodies of angels. Nevertheless, given that all things can be called spirits, he points out that even corporeal and "dark" bodies are luminous at root, because all existent things come into existence from light.

The root of natural bodies is from light. Hence, when a human being comes to know how it is that all dark, dense bodies become limpid, he makes them appear as translucent to the luminosity that is their root. This is like glass—when it is purified of the turbidity of sand, it becomes translucent. The polishing of stones, crystals, and quartz is the same sort of thing. This is because the root of all existent things is God in respect of His name *Light of the heavens*, that is, everything high, *and of the earth* [24:35], that is, everything low. So think about His ascription of light to the heavens and the earth!

Were it not for the luminosity in dense bodies, it would not be correct for things that are behind walls, beneath the earth, and above the heavens to be unveiled for the unveiler. Were it not for the subtlety that is the root of bodies, it would not be correct for certain of the friends of God to pass through walls. Nor could the dead person stand in his grave, when the earth is over him or the coffin is nailed down on him with earth piled over it—yet none of this prevents him from sitting up. Although God has blinded our eyesight from seeing this, the unveiler has it unveiled for him. Concerning this many reports and accounts have come from the Wholesome.

This is why you will never see a body that God created and that has remained in its created nature as straight. It always inclines toward circularity—whether it be an inanimate thing, a plant, an animal, a heaven, an earth, a mountain, a leaf, a stone. The occasion of this is its inclination toward its root, which is light.

The first existent thing is the Intellect, which is the Pen. It is an innovated divine light. From it God brought the Soul into existence, which is the Preserved Tablet. It is below the Intellect in luminosity because of the intermediary between it and God. The things never cease becoming dense until they reach the pillars and the progeny. Inasmuch as every existent thing has a specific face toward its Creator, it is permeated by light, but inasmuch as it also has a face toward its occasion, the darkness and density within it come to be. Think about this, if you have a rational faculty!

Hence, the more the situation descends, the darker and denser it becomes. What does the station of the Intellect have to do with the station of the earth? How many intermediaries there are between these two!

You should also know that the body of the human being is the last of the progeny, so he is the last of the children, a *dry clay* compounded of *stinking mud* [15:26]. As you see, he inclines toward circularity, even if he has a straight movement, apart from dumb beasts and plants. Within him are suprasensory, sensory, and glassy lights that you will not find in the other progeny. This is because of the spiritual faculties that God has given him. Nothing receives these faculties except the luminosity that is within him. This is the correspondence that allows him to receive these perceptions.

This is why God says, *And a sign for them is the night; We pull out from it the daytime* [36:37]. Know that light is kept nonmanifest by darkness. If not for light, darkness would not be. He did not say, "We pull out from it the light," since were He to take the light from it, the *wujūd* of the darkness would turn to nonexistence—if it were a taking of nonexistence. And if it were a taking of transferal, its *wujūd* would follow it wherever it was transferred, since it is identical with its essence.

Daytime is one of the lights born from the shining of the sun. If darkness had no essential light, it would not be correct for it to be a container for the daytime, nor would it be correct for it to be perceived, but it is perceived. Nothing is perceived unless it has a light from its essence through which it is perceived, and this is identical with its *wujūd* and its preparedness to receive the perception of eyesights, through what it has of the lights that belong to it. (II 647.4)

Just as light is present in the darkest of bodies, so also life is present in all things, and along with life, spirit. As mentioned earlier, Ibn al-ʿArabī typically identifies this all-pervasive spirit with the Divine Spirit or the Breath of the All-Merciful, and he differentiates it from the partial, governing spirit, called, in the case of the human being, the "rationally speaking soul." But sometimes he takes into account the Koranic verses that attribute rationality to all creatures, such as *God. . . gave rational speech to everything* (41:21).

God blew a spirit from Him into every form that He configured, so each came to life. He made Himself known to the form through the form, so it came to know Him through an affair to which it was naturally disposed. He made Himself known to it only through itself. Hence it sees Him only in its own form.

Forms possess diverse constitutions, though they are created from one soul, like the hearts of the children of Adam. God created them *from one soul* [4:1], but they are diverse.

Among the forms are some whose life is nonmanifest, so God takes the eyesights of most people away from it. These forms are of two sorts. One sort has growth and nourishment, and another sort has growth but no nourishment. The one sort we name "plants," and the other sort "minerals" and "stones." Among the forms are also some whose life is manifest. We name them "animal" and "living."

In actual fact, all these forms are alive and possessors of rationally speaking souls. It is impossible for there to be in the cosmos a form that has no soul, no life, and no essential and commanded worship. It makes no difference if that form is among the shapes to which human beings or animals give new arrival, or if the creatures give new arrival to them intentionally or unintentionally. No matter how the form is formed or upon whose hands it becomes manifest, God clothes it in *a spirit from* His *command* [42:52] and makes Himself known to it at once. Hence it comes to know Him from itself and it witnesses Him in itself. Such perpetually is the affair, in this world and the last world, that is unveiled to the folk of unveiling. (III 437.27)

Rational speech (*nuṭq*) is normally considered the "specific difference" (*faṣl*) through which human beings are distinguished from other animals. Ibn al-ʿArabī disagrees, partly because the Koran often refers to the rational speech of inanimate objects. If all things have rational speech, this cannot be the specific difference that makes human beings unique. Elsewhere, he tells us that it is only the fact of having been created in the divine form that distinguishes human beings from others.[7]

Know that God created no engendered thing unless it be living and rationally speaking, whether it be an inanimate thing, a plant, or an animal, in the higher or the lower world. The proof text of this is His words, *There is nothing that does not glorify Him in praise, but you do not understand their glorification; surely He is clement*, so He does not rush punishment upon you, *forgiving/concealing* [17:44], that is, He curtains their glorification from your ears. Everything in the world of nature is "a sensate, self-nourishing body," so it is "a rationally speaking animal" standing between the disclosed and the hidden in each of the specific differences of this definition. When something lacks something of the definition, this "lack" is what is hidden in the case of some people. Whatever of it is manifest is what is disclosed. This is why the definitions of inanimate things, plants, animals, and human beings are diverse. However, for the folk of unveiling, all are rationally speaking animals, glorifying God in praise.

Since the affair is like this, it is permitted—or rather it happens and is correct—for the Real to address all existent things and to reveal to them, whether they be heaven, earth, mountains, trees or whatever existent thing. He described them as obeying him in what He commanded them [41:11] and refusing to accept His offer [33:72]. He made everything prostrate itself to Him, since He discloses Himself to everything, and He revealed to everything through His addressing it. He said to the heaven and the earth, *"Come willingly, or unwillingly!" They said, "We come willingly"* [41:11]. *He revealed to each heaven its command* [41:12], and so also did He reveal to the earth [99:5]. *And thy Lord revealed unto the bees* [16:68], and *We revealed unto thee*, Muhammad, by addressing you with *a spirit from Our command* [42:52]. So His revelation includes all things.

However, there remain those who obey and those who do not obey, and how it is that one listener is ranked above another listener. For among the most marvelous of things is the description of the listener by deafness, the seer by blindness, and the speaker by dumbness. Thus they did not use intelligence, nor did they return, even if they understood.[8]

Denial is an attribute of souls
  when they refuse,
    like fire that flames up
      through reception, though dead.
If not for choice
  and their compulsion within it,
    souls would not refuse
      when they refuse.

God says, *On the day when their tongues, their hands, and their feet witness against them for what they were doing* [24:24]. This is why they say to their skins, when they bear witness against them, *"Why did you witness against us?"* Their skins shall say, *"God gave us rational speech, as He gave rational speech to everything"* [41:21]. The skins made this speech all-inclusive, so they have a better knowledge of the affair than those who make rational speech a constituting specific difference only for human beings and who consider others devoid of the totality of their definition in animality and rational speech.

When witnessing has escaped someone, much knowledge has escaped him. So do not judge what you do not see! Say, "God knows better what He has created."

The earth of the human being is his body, and it bears witness to what he has done. Do you think it bears witness against him with what it does not know? Do you think it acts other than by a divine revelation that comes to it from God? In the same way, we will bear witness against the communities through what God reveals to us of the accounts of the prophets along with their communities.[9]

So the individual bears witness
  in what he does not see
    when the truthful report
      comes to him.
He through whom revelation comes
  has revealed
    to everyone, so all are
      rationally speaking.
Consider: There is nothing other than He
  in His engendered existence,
    for He is the *wujūd*
      of creation and Creator.

Since the affair is restricted to truthful report and witnessing, we come to know that the cosmos is all unveiled.

There is no curtain, nor any veil—
  no, all is manifest and clear.
The Real is known without doubt,
  but His mystery is buried in the bowels.

He reveals by saying *Be* [to the thing], *so it comes to be* [16:40] and it witnesses what He

> wills, so it sees. Its witnessing is through the truthful report, like the witnessing by eye in which there is no doubt. (III 393.23)

One of the consequences of the fact that all things glorify God by their own innate dispositions is that it is difficult to understand how opposition to God's commandments enters the cosmos. The partial spirits, after all, derive from the Divine Spirit, and the bodies are created glorifying their Lord. In some places, Ibn al-ʿArabī deals with this issue by explaining the distinction between the engendering command and the prescriptive command. In the following passage, he presents the problem, but suggests only briefly how it might be solved.

> We turn now to the knowledges possessed by the angels, by everything other than the rationally speaking souls that govern these human frames, and by the human frames themselves. All of them are knowers of God through innate disposition, not reflection or reasoning. That is why, of this configuration, the skins, ears, eyes, hands, legs, and all bodily parts bear witness against the [rationally speaking soul] that governs them for commanding them to transgress the limits of its Lord. Their bearing witness is nothing but reporting the acts of God that flowed through them, for they do not recognize transgression of limits or disobedience. This giving knowledge by designating these acts will be a bearing witness against the souls that acted freely within them through the acts. After all, everything other than the souls that are witnessed against knows only glorification through the praise of its Lord, nothing else, through what it finds in its innate disposition.
>
> No knowledge is more difficult to conceive of than this knowledge, because the rationally speaking souls are pure through the property of the root, and the bodies and their faculties are pure through that to which they are innately disposed. Then, through the coming together of the soul and the body, the human being arrives newly, the Law is prescribed, and acts of obedience and opposition become manifest.
>
> The rationally speaking souls have no share in opposition because of their own entities; the animal souls flow with the property of their nature in things, and there is no prescription of the Law for them; and the bodily parts speak in praise of God, glorifying Him. So who is it that opposes and disobeys? Who is blamed and punished?
>
> If another affair has newly arrived through the totality, because of the coming together that abides through the human being—just as the name "human being" has newly arrived—then that alone is blamed for the opposition. After all, the rational, mature human being is the one for whom the Law is prescribed, no one else. If these preconditions disappear from any member of the species, he is not the object of prescription, nor is he blamed for leaving something aside or performing a forbidden act. (III 402.26)

The Rationally Speaking Soul

A distinction has been drawn between the Universal Spirit and the partial spirits that are blown into living things. Inasmuch as living things can be divided into three levels—plants, animals, and human beings—there are three sorts of partial spirits or souls, that is, vegetal, animal, and human. Muslim psychologists differentiate among these spirits by distinguishing among their faculties. In one passage where Ibn al-ʿArabī lists many of these faculties (II 459.25), he clearly has in mind the division into three levels, though his purpose here and elsewhere is not to provide a definitive and final classification.

The vegetal soul possesses six basic faculties: growth-producing, nutritive, attractive, expulsive, digestive, and retentive. The animal soul possesses these six, plus the five senses, plus appetite, wrath, imagination, and memory. The human soul possesses all these plus reason, reflection, and form-giving. Given that the highest of these faculties, the most all-encompassing, and the nearest to God is reason or intellect, it is typically designated as the distinguishing characteristic of human beings.

> We say that God is identical with each thing in respect of His name Manifest. Here there is a hidden proof. It is that eyesight falls only upon the instrument, and this is employed by something else that outward sensation does not reach. The proof of this something else is death, when the instrument exists but the activity has been negated. Hence the instrument is not what acts, but sensation perceives only the instrument.

Those who exercise judgment know that beyond sensation is something that acts through this instrument, employs it, and is called by the ulama of rational consideration the "rational, rationally speaking, and animal soul." Thus the ulama have moved to a meaning that is not one of the objects perceived by sensation.

In a similar way, the Folk of Unveiling and Witnessing in Bringing Together and Finding perceive in the rationally speaking soul exactly what the folk of consideration perceive in the sensory instrument. Hence they recognize that beyond the rationally speaking soul is the one that acts, and He is called "God." The soul in this act plays the same role in the view of the Folk of God as the sensory instrument plays in the view of the folk of rational consideration. (III 477.31)

The distinction between the various levels of soul has many practical implications. The concept of rationally speaking soul allows us, for example, not only to differentiate between human beings and animals, but also to understand human suffering in the last world along with one of the many implications of the precedence of God's mercy over His wrath. The rationally speaking soul is at root the divine breath, which is disengaged from the animal dimension of existence. In contrast, the animal soul is so intimately tied to the body and its faculties that, in practice, it is indistinguishable from it. It follows, in Ibn al-ʿArabī's view, that the rationally speaking soul's proximity to God keeps it free of chastisement even in hell, because hell's chastisement is bodily, and bodily affairs are perceived specifically by the soul that pertains to the body, which is the animal soul.

Know—God give us and you endless felicity—that the rationally speaking soul is felicitous in this world and the last world. It has no share of wretchedness, because it does not derive from the world of wretchedness. However, God mounted it upon this bodily mount that is called the "animal soul." The animal soul is like its beast, and the rationally speaking soul is like the animal soul's rider.

The rationally speaking soul has nothing in this animal mount save walking with it on the straight path that the Real has designated for it. If the animal soul complies with this, then it is a docile, well-trained mount. If it refuses, then it is a recalcitrant beast—as often as the rider desires to bring it back to the path, it is unruly and recalcitrant. It goes right and left because of its headstrongness and the ugliness of its constitution's composition.

The animal soul does not intend opposition, nor does it disobey so as to violate the Shariah's sanctity. On the contrary, it simply follows the course of its own nature, for it has no knowledge of the Shariah. It happens to have a constitution that does not agree with its rider in what he desires from it.

The rationally speaking soul cannot possibly be in opposition, because it derives from the world of preservation from sin and of pure spirits. When punishment falls on the day of resurrection, it falls only on the animal soul. In the same way, the rider whips his beast when it is recalcitrant and leaves the path upon which he desires to make it walk.

Do you not see that the locus of the penalties for fornication, theft, armed robbery, and slander is only the animal, bodily soul? It is this soul that senses the pain of killing, cutting off the hand, and whipping the back. Thus penalties are enacted against the body, and the pain abides through the sensate, animal soul, which is shared by all animals that sense pains. Thus there is no difference between the locus of chastisement in human beings and in all the other animals, in this world or the last world.

Given its eminence, the rationally speaking soul remains with its own world in its perpetual felicity. Do you not see that the Prophet rose to his feet before the casket of a Jew? It was said to him, "That is the casket of a Jew."

He replied, "Is it not a soul?" Hence he assigned the cause only to the soul's essence. Hence he rose up to assert the majesty and greatness of the soul's eminence and its placement. How could the soul not have eminence, since it is inblown from the spirit of God? It derives from the most eminent, angelic, spiritual world, the world of purity.

So the rationally speaking soul, along with this bodily, animal soul, is no different in form from a rider on a beast, whether it be recalcitrant or docile. Thus has it been clarified for you that the rationally speaking soul does not disobey. Rather, the animal soul fails to assist it in what it seeks from it. Moreover, the animal soul is not addressed by prescription of the Law such that it could be qualified by obedience or disobedience. If it happens to be recalcitrant, this is required by the nature of its specific constitution. So know this, and know that God will include everyone in His mercy, for "God's

> mercy takes precedence over His wrath" when the two vie with each other over the human being. (III 262.34)

One of God's mercies toward people is that He purchases from them their souls and possessions, and then, having bought them, He commands people to employ them in struggle (*mujāhada, jihād*) on His path. The souls that He buys are the animal souls, and the sellers are the rationally speaking souls. Ibn al-ᶜArabī explains this in Chapter 76, "On struggle," in which he divides the strugglers into four categories in keeping with various Koranic verses.[10] This is one of many passages where *nafs* means both "soul" and "self," so it is translated accordingly.

> [The second sort] are *those who struggle in the path of God* [4:95]. This is the road to God, or to reaching Him in respect of the fact that He is a God. Thus it is a struggle to attain the knowledge of the Level from which the cosmos and its properties become manifest, and of which there come to be vicegerents in the earth.
>
> Those who struggle in these paths are stricken by the hardship by which a traveler is stricken in a fearful road, for the traveler in his road exposes himself to the destruction of his possessions and his self, the orphaning of his children, and the loss of everything familiar to him. God says, *Struggle with your possessions and your selves in the path of God* [9:41]. He says, *They fight in the path of God; they slay and they are slain* [9:111].
>
> God knew from the servants that something like this would oppress them, because of their claim that their selves and their possessions belong to them, just as the Real has affirmed that they do belong to them—and God speaks nothing but a *ḥaqq*. Hence God gave priority to buying the possessions and selves from them so that they would let go of them. The Buyer would be left to act freely with His commodities as He willed. Although the seller may love his commodities, he loves the compensation that he has been given for them—the payment—more than what he has sold. God says, *God has bought from those who have faith their selves and their possessions* [9:111].
>
> After this buying, He commands them to struggle in the path of God so that this will be easy for them, for they struggle with borrowed selves—I mean the animal souls that abide through the bodies—and with borrowed possessions. They are like those who travel on borrowed beasts with someone else's possessions, while the owner has lifted from them any fault in what they have borrowed, should the beast expire or the possessions perish. Thus their hearts are at ease, and no hardship remains in their souls if they have faith, except the hardship that the animal mount suffers because of the length of the hard journey and the trouble of the road. If they are battling the enemy, [then the hardship is] what the mount attains through the attack and retreat, the piercing with lances, the shooting of arrows, and the striking with swords.
>
> The human being is disposed toward natural pity. Hence he has pity on his mount in respect of the fact that it is an animal, not on behalf of its owner. For it may be that the borrower knows that its owner desires it to be destroyed and would love for this to happen. Thus no pity remains for him save natural pity.
>
> Hence the selves that the Real has bought in this verse are only the animal souls. He has bought them from the rationally speaking souls that have faith. The rationally speaking souls of the faithful are the sellers, the owners of the animal souls that the Real buys from them, for it is these animal souls that are visited by slaying, but they are not the locus of faith. Those that are described by faith are only the rationally speaking souls. From them the Real buys the souls of the bodies. Thus He says, *God has bought from those who have faith,* who are the rationally speaking souls described by faith, *their selves,* which are their sensory mounts. It is these that are taken out to fight and struggle. Hence the person of faith owns no self, so he has no pity on it except the essential pity that belongs to the rationally speaking soul toward every animal. (II 147.2)

The human being is the microcosm, so everything in the human configuration has its analogue in the macrocosm, also known as "the great human being" (*al-insān al-kabīr*). The analogue of the rationally speaking soul is Muhammad, while the other perfect men among the prophets and messengers correspond to the soul's spiritual faculties, such as reflection, memory, and imagination. Ibn al-ᶜArabī explains this in Chapter 346, which he calls "On the true knowledge of the way-station of a mystery concerning which one of the gnostics spoke the truth, for he saw how his light rises up from the sides of the way-

findings of Michel Chodkiewicz indicate that this waystation corresponds to Surah 38 of the Koran, which is called *Ṣād*.[11] The discussion in this chapter of the perfect human being may have to do with the fact that Surah 38 mentions that God created Adam, that is, the perfect human being, with His own "two hands," a bestowal of eminence which, in Ibn al-ᶜArabī's view, distinguishes him from all other creatures.

Know that the level of the perfect human being in relation to the cosmos is the level of the rationally speaking soul in relation to the human being. This is the perfect one more perfect than whom there is none, and he is Muhammad. The level of the perfect human beings who are below the degree of this perfection, which is the furthest limit of the cosmos, corresponds to that of the spiritual faculties in the human being, and these are the prophets. The level of those in the cosmos who are lower in perfection than the degree of the prophets corresponds to that of the sensory faculties in the human being, and these are the inheritors. Everyone else who has the form of the human being in shape is one of the animals; they correspond to the level of the animal spirit in the human being, which allows for growth and sensation.

Know also that today, the cosmos has lost the all-comprehensiveness of Muhammad in his manifestation in spirit and body, form and meaning, so it is asleep, but not dead. The cosmos's spirit, which is Muhammad, has, in relation to the cosmos, the form of the locus where the human spirit dwells in sleep [and such it will remain] until the day of the Uprising, which is like the awakening of the sleeper here.

We say precisely that Muhammad is the spirit which is the rationally speaking soul of the cosmos because of what unveiling has given, and also because of his words, "I am the master of the people." The cosmos is one of the people, since it is the human being great in size, and it has priority in proportioning and balancing, so the form of Muhammad's configuration became manifest from it. In the same way God *proportioned* the body of the human being and He *balanced* [82:7] it before the *wujūd* of his spirit. Then, *of His spirit, He blew into him* [32:9] a spirit whereby he became a complete human being and whereby God gave him his creation, which is his rationally speaking soul.

Before the manifestation of Muhammad's configuration, the cosmos was in the state of proportioning and balancing, like the embryo in its mother's belly. Its movement derived from the animal spirit within it, through which it was correct for it to have life. So polish your reflective faculty through what I have mentioned to you!

At the resurrection, the whole cosmos will come to life through the manifestation of the perfected configuration of Muhammad, fully equipped with faculties. In the humanness of the cosmos, the level of "the folk of the Fire, those who are its folk," is like the level of the human being that grows [i.e., the vegetal level], so it is qualified neither by death nor by life. Thus a plain text has reached us concerning them from God's Messenger that in the Fire "They will neither die therein nor live." God says concerning them, *Then he shall neither die therein nor live* [87:13].

The angels in respect to the whole cosmos are like the forms manifest within man's imagination, as also are the jinn. So the cosmos is a great human being only through the *wujūd* of the perfect human being, who is its rationally speaking soul. In the same way the configuration of the human being is a human being only through the rationally speaking soul. And this rationally speaking soul in the human being is perfect only through the divine form mentioned in a plain text by the Prophet. In the same way, the soul of the cosmos, who is Muhammad, achieves the degree of perfection through the completion of the divine form, in subsistence, in the constant variation in forms, and in the subsistence of the cosmos through him.

Thus it has become clear to you that the state of the cosmos before Muhammad's manifestation corresponds to the proportioned body, its state after his death corresponds to the sleeper, and its state through his uprising on the day of resurrection corresponds to alertness and wakefulness after sleep. (III 186.30)

Toward the end of the same chapter, Ibn al-ᶜArabī addresses his reader and suggests the significance of this long discussion of the perfect human being in the cosmos. He points out that the spiritual faculties, despite their apparent eminence and nobility, are utterly beholden to sensation. Hence one finds God present not on the "spiritual" level, but rather in the actual sensory experience that many pious people tend to disparage. The resurrection is "bodily" because sensation alone actually finds the presence of God.

So recognize your waystation, my friend, in respect to this human form of which Muhammad is the spirit and the rationally speaking soul. Are you one of its faculties, or one of the loci of its faculties? Which one of its faculties are you? Are you its eyesight, its hearing, its smell, its touch, its taste? I, by God, have come to know which of the faculties of this form I am—to God belongs the praise for that!

Do not suppose, my friend, that the fact that our waystation in this form has been specified as corresponding with the sensory faculties in the human being, or rather, in the animal, makes us fall short of the waystation of the spiritual faculties. Do not suppose that. On the contrary, these are the most complete faculties, because to them belongs the name the All-Bestower, for it is they that bestow upon the spiritual faculties everything within which they act freely and through which they have their cognitive life, whether the faculty be imagination, reflection, memory, form-giving, fantasy, or reason. All this derives from the various sorts of matter that belong to these sensory faculties. This is why God says concerning him among His servants whom He loves, "I am his hearing through which he hears and his eyesight through which he sees." He mentioned the sensory form, but He mentioned nothing of the spiritual faculties, nor did He put Himself in their waystation, for their waystation is poverty toward the senses, but the Real does not descend to the waystation of that which is poor toward other than He. The senses are poor toward God, not toward something other. He descends to that which is poor toward Him and does *not associate anything with Him* [72:20].

Thus has He given the senses independence, for from them and by means of them things are taken, but they do not take from the other faculties, only from God. So recognize the eminence and worth of sensation and the fact that it is identical with the Real! This explains why the configuration of the last world is not perfected save through the *wujūd* of sensation and the object of sensation, for it is not perfected save through the Real.

In reality the sensory faculties are the *vicegerents* of God *in the earth* [27:62] of this configuration. Do you not see how He has described Himself as hearing, seeing, speaking, living, knowing, powerful, desiring? All these are attributes that have traces in sensory objects, and human beings sense from themselves that these attributes abide within them. But God did not describe Himself as rational, reflective, or imagining.

The only other spiritual faculties are those that share in sensation, that is, preserving [i.e., memory] and form-giving. Sensation has a trace in preserving and form-giving. Were it not for this sharing, God would not have described Himself by these two, for He is the Preserver, the Form-Giver. These two attributes are both spiritual and sensory.

So pay attention to that to which I have called your attention! Then your heart will not be broken because God has placed you in the waystation of the sensory faculties—since sensation is contemptible in your view, and reason eminent. I have let you know that all eminence is found in sensation and that you have been ignorant of your affair and your worth. So, if you knew yourself, you would know your Lord, just as your Lord knows you and He knows the cosmos through His knowledge of Himself. You are His form, so there is no escape from your sharing with Him in this knowledge. Thus you know Him from your knowledge of yourself.

This is a fine point that became manifest from the Messenger of God when he said, "He who knows himself knows his Lord," since, in knowing the cosmos, what the Real actually knows is Himself. This is equivalent to His words, *We shall show them Our signs upon the horizons and in themselves*. Thus He mentioned the two configurations—the configuration of the form of the cosmos through His words "the horizons," and the configuration of its spirit through "in themselves"—for this is one human being, possessing two configurations. *Until it is clear to them*, i.e., the viewers, *that it is the Real* [41:53]—i.e., that the viewer in what he sees is the Real, nothing else.

So look, my friend, at how subtle God's Messenger is toward his community and how beautiful is what he has taught them and the road he has made for them! What an excellent schoolmaster and road-maker! May God place us among those who walk upon his ascending road until it joins with his degree! Amen, by His exaltation!

If you are astute, we have given you intimations of the affair as it is in itself. Or rather, we have declared it explicitly. In this we have put up with the things attributed to us by those who deny that to which we have alluded in this issue. They are the blind, those who *know a manifest side of the life of this world, but of the last world they are heedless* [30:7]. By God, were it not for this Koranic verse, we would judge that they are blind in the manifest side of both this world and the last world, just as God has judged that they do not hear while hearing, in His words while prohibiting, *Be not as those who say, "We hear," but they hear not* [8:21]. Even though they hear, He negates hearing from them. So also is the knowledge of these people concerning the manifest side of life through the sensory affairs—and nothing else—that their senses perceive, for the Real is not their hearing and their eyesight. (III 189.2)

Chapter 216: The Subtlety

Ibn al-ᶜArabī calls this chapter "On the true knowledge of the subtlety and its mysteries." It belongs to Part Three of the *Futūḥāt,* much of which is devoted to the interpretation of standard Sufi terminology. The term *subtlety* (*laṭīfa*), as he notes at the outset, was used by the Sufis in two basic senses—to refer to a concept that is difficult to express, and to refer to the human soul inasmuch as it is difficult to fathom. In explaining the second meaning of the term, the Shaykh reviews his basic understanding of the soul.

When meanings are exalted beyond explanation,
those are the All-Merciful's subtleties within us.
Through them allusions are made for us from afar,
and through their allusions we live for years.
God grants them hearts
that caprice enraptures while after while,
not the blameworthy caprice,
but the love with which He tries us.

Know—God confirm us and you with the spirit of holiness—that the Folk of God ascribe the word *subtlety* to two meanings. They ascribe it and mean by it the reality of the human being, which is the meaning for which the body is the mount, the locus of governance, and the instruments for gaining this meaning's suprasensory and sensory objects of knowledge.

They also ascribe it and mean by it every allusion of delicate meaning that shines forth in the understanding but is not embraced by expression. This pertains to the knowledges of tastings and states, so they are known but not communicated. No definitions apply to them, even if they are defined in actual fact. However, it is not necessary that something that possesses a definition and reality in actual fact be expressed. This is what the folk of understanding mean when they say that among affairs is that which is defined and among them is that which is not defined, that is, it is impossible for expression to clarify its reality and definition for the listener such that he might understand it. The knowledges of tastings are of this sort.

Then they use *subtlety* in a broader sense. They name every delicate meaning, rare in likeness—or it may be said that it is possessed only by solitaries among the Men—a "subtlety."

Among the divine names is the name Subtle. One of the properties of this divine name is conveying to the servants sensory and suprasensory provisions whose occasions are cut off such that the one provided is not aware of them. This is indicated in His words, *and He will provide for him from whence he never reckoned* [65:3]. Deriving from the divine name Subtle is the Prophet's words concerning the bliss of the Garden, "Within it is what no eye has seen, what no ear has heard, and what has never passed into the heart of any mortal."

Know then—God give you success—concerning the subtlety gained by the servant from God from whence he is not aware that when the servant conveys it through his Aspiration to his student or to whomsoever he wills among God's servants from whence that individual is not aware, by an intention of the shaykh, then it is said concerning him that he is the "companion of a subtlety." This is correct only for him who has assumed as his character trait the divine name Subtle. If there is awareness of this, he is not a companion of a subtlety. If the student or the one to whom this meaning has been conveyed understands on the basis of a realized knowledge—not a reckoning, a beautiful conjecture, or a surmise—that this has reached him from this shaykh, then the shaykh is not a companion of a subtlety in this issue. After all, one of the characteristics of the companion of this station is exaltation and the impossibility of anyone being aware that this is from him—in the details of what he has conveyed, not in summary fashion. In the same way, you know in summary fashion that the All-Provider is God, but you do not know in detail and with exactitude how the provision will be conveyed to the one who is provided for, though this is known to the Real through His name Subtle. If this is known, it is known from the ruling property of another divine name, not from the name Subtle, so this is not a subtlety. There is no escape from ignorance of the conveying.

Because of this meaning, the reality of the human being is named a "subtlety," for it becomes manifest through the inblowing, when the body is proportioned for the governance of the spirit that is ascribed to God in His words, *When I have proportioned him and blown into him of My spirit* [15:29]. This is the divine breath, concerning which there was an earlier chapter [198]. It is a subtle divine mystery that is attributed to God in summary fashion, without saying how.

When the human being's entity becomes manifest through the inblowing at the proportioning, and its manifestation is from a *wujūd*, not a nonexistence, nothing arrives newly save the attribution of rulership to it through its governance of this body. This is like the manifestation of letters from the breath of a speaker.

Within this mount the human being is given spiritual and sensory instruments for the perception of knowledges that cannot be known save through these instruments. This also derives from the fact that he is subtle. After all, according to what has appeared from certain rational thinkers among the theologians, it lies within the domain of rational possibility for the affair to be known without the intermediary of these instruments. But this is weak in rational consideration, for we mean by "instruments" only the meanings that abide through the locus. Thus we mean hearing, eyesight, and smelling, not ears, eyes, and nose. No one perceives the object of hearing save through the fact that he is the possessor of hearing—not the fact that he is the possessor of ears. So also, he perceives the object of eyesight only through the fact that he is possessor of eyesight, not possessor of pupils and eyelids. Hence it is not correct to abolish the attribution of these instruments.

There remains the question as to what the realities of the instruments go back. Do they go back to affairs that are extraneous to the entity of the subtlety, or do they go back only to the entity of the subtlety? Is it that their properties are diverse because of the diversity of the perceived objects, while the entity is one? This is the position of the Realizers among the folk of unveiling and sound rational consideration.

When the entity of this subtlety, which is the reality of the human being, becomes manifest, this is identical with its governance of the body, and this also comes under the heading of "subtleties," because it is not known how life becomes intertied with this body through the *wujūd* of this subtle spirit, for nature shares with the spirit in requiring the *wujūd* of life—which is the animal spirit—in the body. Thus a sort of sharing becomes manifest. No one knows in reality whether this bodily, animal life belongs to this subtlety that becomes manifest from the divine inblowing and is addressed with religious prescription, or it belongs to nature, or to the totality, save the folk of unveiling and finding. They know this through tasting, since they may have come to know that there is nothing in the cosmos that is not alive and rationally speaking through the glorification of its Lord with an eloquent tongue that is ascribed to it in keeping with what its reality requires for the folk of unveiling.

As for other than the folk of unveiling, they know nothing whatsoever of this. They are the folk of inanimate things, plants, and animals. They do not know that everything is alive while they are unaware, just as they are unaware of the life of the martyrs, slain in the path of God. Thus He says, *Say not of those slain in God's path, "They are dead." Rather they are living, but you are not aware* [2:154].

The governance of this body by the subtlety is for the sake of the subsistence of the companionship of the gnostic sciences and the knowledges that the subtlety acquires through companionship with this frame. This is especially so for the folk of luminous frames. Here the Folk of God are divided into two sorts:

One sort maintain that disengagement takes place at the departure from the body, for the subtlety gains from its character, knowledges, and gnostic sciences states and guises through which its sisters know it in the world of disengagement. So it seeks the degree of perfection. Although this sort are among the Folk of God, they are not among the folk of unveiling. Rather, reflection predominates in them and rational consideration rules over them.

The other sort among the Folk of God are the folk of the Real. They are not concerned with when the departure will come, because they are in an increase of knowledge forever and perpetually. They are the kings of the folk who govern over every sort of natural and elemental matter in this world, the *barzakh*, and the last world. They are the faithful who profess the resurrection of the bodies. It is they who possess sound unveiling, for the divine subtlety becomes manifest only through governance, differentiation, and a governed frame that is the root of its *wujūd* as a governor, so the subtlety never becomes disjoined from this reality.

He who realizes what he sees himself busy with in the state of sleep during dreams will recognize what we say. After all, God has struck as a likeness what the dreamer sees in his sleep, and He has struck waking from that dream as another likeness, that is, for the Mustering. The first is what the dead person goes back to after departure from the domain of this world. *But most people do not know; they know a manifest side of the life of this world, but of the last world they are heedless* [30:6–7].

Thus we are in a perpetual climb and an increase of knowledge in this world, the *barzakh*, and the last world. The instruments accompany us and, in these waystations, homesteads, and states, they do not become disjoined from this human subtlety.

For this subtlety, wretchedness is an accidental affair. It occurs to it accidentally just as illness occurs to it in this world because of the corruption of the humors through excess or deficiency. When the deficient is increased or the excessive is decreased and equilibrium is gained, then the illness disappears and health becomes manifest. So also is the wretchedness that overtakes it in the last world. Then the final issue will be to felicity, and that is the uprightness of the configuration, in whichever abode it may be, whether Garden or Fire, for it has been affirmed that "Each of the abodes shall have its fill." May God place us among those for whom soundness of constitution preserves their gnostic sciences and their knowledges!

So this is an aspect of the reality that is named the "human subtlety." Or rather, every existent thing among the corporeal bodies possesses a spiritual, divine subtlety that gazes upon it in respect of its form—there is no escape from this. The corruption of this form and guise is "death," wherever it may be.

As for their technical use of "subtlety" in the meaning of "every allusion that shines forth in the understanding but is not embraced by expression," you should know that the Folk of God have made allusion "a call from the point of distance and a display to the eye of infirmity."[12] However, in classifying allusions, a distinction becomes manifest. The allusion that is "a call from the point of distance" carries what expression does not reach, like gesturing for someone too far distant for voice, though he can see. One gestures to him concerning what one desires from him, and he understands. This is the meaning of their words, "a call from the point of distance." Thus every knowledge that expression does not embrace is like someone whom voice does not reach. He is far from the alluder, but he is not far from what is desired from him. After all, the allusion has allowed him to understand what speech gives to understanding, or voice allows to reach. And you know for certain that, when the alluder is the Real, He is far from the limit through which the servant is distinguished. This is a true distance from which there is no escape. The affair cannot be otherwise. So there is no escape from allusion, and this is the subtlety, since it is a subtle meaning of which one is not aware.

Then, if the meaning is not distant, it is "a display to the eye of infirmity." This is when the deaf person is near to the speaker, but the nearness has no benefit, because the voice does not reach him, because of the infirmity of deafness. Thus he gestures for him, despite the nearness, just as "God says on the tongue of His servant, 'God hears him who praises Him.'" This is the furthest limit of nearness along with the *wujūd* and manifestation of the infirmity. No nearness can be greater than this. After all, there are also His words, "I have divided the *ṣalāt* into two halves between Me and My servant." Thus He discriminated and separated. What does this have to do with him whose words He makes His words, indicating that He is the speaker and the sayer, not he?

This is an infirm nearness, and this is the meaning of their words, "and a display to the eye of infirmity." This is why it is named a "subtlety"—because it inserts the Lord into the servant. Thus He says, *Grant him sanctuary until he hears the speech of God* [9:6], but the speaker was Muhammad through God's speech. He also says, "I am his hearing, his eyesight, and his tongue." This is one of the subtlest ways in which a Lord may become manifest in the form of a creature on the basis of a divine knowledge-giving. No howness is known for it and in-betweenness does not leave it, for *Nothing is as His likeness, and He is the Hearing, the Seeing* [42:11].

Also pertaining to this chapter is the longing and tenderness of mothers for their children, longing for homelands, and the yearning for familiars. These are, in short, correspondences between two affairs. When an individual desires to know their causes, he is not able to, though he comes near—except for him who gains the divine instruction, since it is he who is a knower of the affair as it is. He receives it from the root of *wujūd*, or rather from *wujūd* itself, since the Real is *wujūd*, nothing else. (II 503.5)

From Chapter 373: The Wisdom of the Inheritors

Ibn al-ᶜArabī calls this chapter "On the true knowledge of the waystation of three mysteries manifest in the water of wisdom, whose level is ranked in excellence above the cosmos through solicitude, and on the subsistence of the cosmos forever and ever, even if its form is transferred." He tells us that this is a waystation that derives from the Muhammadan Presence and explains at the outset that the Koranic signs should be utilized to fathom the cosmic signs. In the process he speaks of his own activity as one of the Realizers or gnostics. Knowing all things—all the signs—in respect of God's unity, the Realizers differentiate among them in keeping with the divine wisdom. Thus they imitate God, who says in the Koran that He differentiates the signs, as in the verse, *We differentiate the signs for a people who use their intelligence* (30:28). The Shaykh then explains that the partial spirits become articulated within the Breath of the All-Merciful just as letters are written out on a parchment. The relation between the Universal Spirit and the partial spirits is that between ink and letters. Only the folk of unveiling are able to perceive the words in the ink before they are written out, and this helps explain why they possess true wisdom (*ḥikma*). In contrast, the philosophers (*falāsifa*)—who are often called the "sages" (*ḥukamāʾ*) and to whom wisdom is usually ascribed—have no share of this knowledge. The rest of the chapter covers many of the Shaykh's favorite themes, including the inheritance of knowledge from the prophets by the Folk of God, the constantly renewed transmutation of the cosmos through the divine self-disclosures, and the remembrance of God through which God's folk are His sitting companions.

Some stations stipulate
harmony
for informed,
noble spirits.[13]
I speak of them, but my sitting companion
does not know,
because light is in
the very darknesses.
Were it not for darkness,
there would be no light,
so imperfection itself
makes completion manifest.
When he who sees the ascription
comes to know it,
he becomes bound
by knotting and standing.
He sees that *wujūd*
has an end,
and that the origin becomes manifest
through the conclusion.
Between origin and end
intervenes
a *wujūd* that is never-ending
and perpetual.

Know—God support you—that the whole cosmos is *a book inscribed on a parchment unrolled* [52:2–3], and it is *wujūd*. It is manifest and spread out, not rolled up, so that it may be known through this outspreading that it was created for mercy. Through its manifestation, what is within it and what it signifies are rationally understood and known. God made it a "book" [*kitāb*] because some of its letters are joined to others—this is the order of the cosmos, in the various respects that we have mentioned[14]—and its meanings are joined to its letters. [The word *kitāb* is] derived from the "ranking" [*katība*] of troops.

We said that it was spread out for mercy only because it was sent down from mercy, as God has said: *A sending down from the All-Merciful, the Compassionate, a book whose signs have been differentiated as an Arabic Koran for a people who have intelligence* [41:2]. Concerning this God also said, *A book whose signs are made firm, and then differentiated, from One who is Wise, Experienced* [11:1]. Within the book, the making firm of the signs and their differentiation is known only to those whom God has given *wisdom and the differentiation of address* [38:20].

The form of the wisdom given by the Wise, the Experienced, to the Folk of Solicitude is knowledge of the levels of affairs and of the *ḥaqq* that is rightfully demanded by and belongs to the existent things and the objects of knowledge. This is giving to *each thing its creation* [20:50] through a divine giving so that each creature will be given its *ḥaqq* as an engendered giving through what God has given to us. Thus we know in potentiality what is rightfully demanded by every existent thing in the limits. After that, in actuality we differentiate each as signs for all those who understand rationally—just as the Experienced, the Wise, has given this to me. We place affairs in their waystations, give them their *ḥaqq*, and do not allow them to transgress their level.

The differentiation of the signs and the signifiers by the differentiator, when he puts them in their places, accords with this precondition. Not every differentiator is "wise"—signifying that he has been given wisdom and knowledge of both the properties of the signs and His mercy to the signs and the existent things, which are the Divine Book. Such a person is none but the "knower"—signifying that he has knowledge of Him who sent down the Book, who is none other than the All-Merciful, the Compassionate.

The conclusion of the affair is nothing other than the precedents of the conclusion, and its precedents are the All-Merciful, the Compassionate. From here you will come to know the levels of the cosmos and that its final issue is with unbounded mercy, even if it suffers on the way and is seized by hardship and trouble.

Among the people are those who attain to mercy and ease at the moment when they enter the waystation that they reach, and these are the folk of the Garden. Among them are those with whom remain the suffering, hardship, and diseases of the path in keeping with their constitutions. Some of these are ill and infirm for a time, then are transferred from their malady and attain to ease. These are "the folk of the Fire, those who are its folk." They are not the same as those who leave the Fire for the Garden, such that the Fire touches them in the measure of their wrongs, even though God made them die within it, for the waystation of those who leave is not the Fire, such that they would inhabit it and abide in it with their families. Rather, for these the Fire is one of the watering places at which a traveler stops in his journey before he reaches the waystation where his family resides.

This is the meaning of "wisdom" and "differentiation." After all, the affairs—I mean the possible things—are distinct in themselves in the state of their nonexistence, and God knows them as they are in themselves. He sees them, and He commands them to engendering, which is *wujūd*, so they come to be from His command. There is no undifferentiation at God, just as there is no undifferentiation in the entities of the possible things. On the contrary, the affair in itself and in God's knowledge is differentiated. Undifferentiation occurs only at us and in our case, and it becomes manifest within us.

When differentiation in the entity of undifferentiation is unveiled for someone through knowledge, eye, or *ḥaqq*,[15] he is the one whom God has given *wisdom and the differentiation of address* [38:20]. Such are the messengers and the inheritors specifically. As for the "sages"—I mean the philosophers—wisdom on their part is a borrowed thing, for they do not know differentiation in undifferentiation.

The form of this, as seen by the companion of this station—to whom God has given the wisdom that is at Him through a divine solicitude—is the entification of the partial spirits blown into the bodies, which were proportioned and balanced from elemental nature, by the All Spirit that is ascribed to Him. Hence He mentioned that He "created" them before the bodies. In other words, He determined them and entified them. Each body and form has its governing spirit, existent potentially in the All Spirit that is ascribed to Him.

For the companion of unveiling this becomes manifest in actuality, in a differentiated manner, at the inblowing, which is the "All-Merciful Breath." In the ink, which is in the inkwell, he sees all the letters and words as well as all the forms it comprises to which the scribe or designer will give form. All this is a "book." He says, "Among the forms in the ink is such and such a form." When the scribe and the designer come, or the designer without the scribe, or the scribe without the designer—in accordance with what the companion of unveiling mentions—he writes and designs with that ink everything mentioned by the unveiler, such that nothing is added to it and nothing subtracted from it. This is not perceived by those who are called "sages" according to the common language of the rational thinkers, for this is the share of the folk of unveiling. They are the ones to whom God has given *wisdom and the differentiation of address.*

God's Messenger has commanded us to "give to each that has a *ḥaqq* its *ḥaqq*." We cannot do this until we know the *ḥaqq* that each possessor of a *ḥaqq* rightfully demands from the Real. This can occur only when the Real makes it clear to us. That is why He ascribes the clarification to Himself, for He says, *We gave him wisdom* [38:20]. *He who has been given wis-*

dom has been given much good [2:269]. No one knows it save those who have been given it, for it is a bestowal from God, just as He has bestowed our entities *wujūd,* though we were *not a thing* [76:1] of *wujūd.* So divine knowledge is the knowledge whose teacher is God through inspiration, casting, and the sending down of *the Faithful Spirit upon* the person's *heart* [26:193–94].

For us, this book is of that sort. By God, I have not written a letter without a divine dictation and a lordly casting, or a spiritual inbreathing within an engendered mind. This is the whole affair, even though we are not messengers giving a shariah or prophets prescribing a Law. After all, the messengerhood of shariah-giving and the prophethood of Law-prescription was cut off at God's Messenger, Muhammad, so there is no messenger after him, nor any prophet[16] who might give a shariah or prescribe a Law. Hence this is only knowledge, wisdom, and understanding from God concerning what He has given as shariah on the tongues of His messengers and prophets and concerning the letters of the cosmos and the words of the Real that He has penned and written on the tablet of *wujūd.* So sending down does not come to an end. Rather, it is perpetual in this world and the last world.

Through folding and conferral
  God configured my body,
    so He balanced me as a creation
      and proportioned me.
For me the Real configured
  a purified spirit,
    so no other's building is
      like my building.
I recognize a spirit
  who has been descending to me
    from above the seven heavens
      with *a discrimination.*

Here I mean His words, *If you are wary of God, He will assign you a discrimination* [8:29].

In this I make no claims
  of prophetic knowledge from God—
    rather a generous giving
      through beneficence.
Between us
  and the house of prophecy
    the lock is secured
      with the bolt of faith.

I only say this lest some imaginer imagine that I and people like me claim prophethood. No, by God, nothing remains save inheritance and wayfaring on the ascending road of Muhammad, the Messenger of God, specifically. Even so, people in general, and I and those like me specifically, have what God has left for us of prophethood, such as heralding visions and noble character traits, and such as memorizing the Koran when someone has rooted it in his memory.[17] Such things are some of the inherited parts of prophethood.

This is why the first human being configured by God, that is, Adam, was a prophet. Whoever walks in his path afterwards is inescapably an inheritor through this earthy configuration. As for station, Adam and those apart from him are inheritors of Muhammad, because he was "a prophet when Adam was between water and clay," so Adam was not yet an existent thing.

Hence prophethood belongs to Muhammad but not to Adam, but the Adamic, natural, human form belongs to Adam, while Muhammad has no form—God bless him, Adam, and all the prophets and give them peace. So Adam is the father of the human bodies, and Muhammad is the father of the inheritors, from Adam to him who seals the affair among the inheritors.[18]

Thus every shariah that has become manifest along with all knowledge is a Muhammadan inheritance in every time and in every messenger and prophet, from Adam to the day of resurrection. This is why Muhammad was given "the all-comprehensive words." Among these words was that God *taught Adam the names, all of them* [2:31]. So the property of the *all* became manifest in both the Adamic form and the Muhammadan form. In Adam, these are names, but in Muhammad they are words. *The words of God* do *not run out* [31:27] and His existent things are not taken away in respect of their substance, even if their forms disappear and their properties change. So the Entity does not disappear or change. Rather, change occurs in the cosmos because of the Real's self-transmutation in forms, so if change did not become manifest in the cosmos, the cosmos would not be perfect.

There remains no divine reality unless the cosmos is supported by it. The realization of the affair for the folk of unveiling is that the changes undergone by the cosmos are identical with the divine self-transmutation in the forms. Thus, the fact that He discloses Himself in whatever He wills is the same as the fact that *He mounted you* in whatever *He wills* [82:8]. For *You will not will unless God wills* [76:30]. In reality, that is God's will, not your will, and you will through it.

[*He created death and life*]. "Life" belongs to the very substance, while "death" belongs to the change in forms. All this is *to try you,* through prescribing the Law, *which of you is more beautiful in deeds* [67:2]. He tries you only so that the attribution of the name the Experienced will be correct, for this is a knowledge through an experience, since something may be known without experience. Thus He sets up an argument against those in whom contention and denial have been created.

All this derives from the differentiation of the signs in the address and in the entities. So *He is the Wise, the Experienced* [6:18], and *He is the Exalted, the Forgiving/Concealing* [67:2]. Were He to unveil to everyone what He unveils to some of the cosmos, He would not be the Forgiving/Concealing, and no one would have any excellence over anyone else, since there is no excellence save through increase in knowledge—of whatever it may be.

The whole cosmos is ranked higher and lower in excellence. The highest of the knowers share with the lowest in knowledge of artisanry, for the cosmos is the artisanry of God. Knowledge of the artisanry of weaving is the weaver's knowledge, and it is his artisanry. Among the common people, this is the lowest of knowledges, but among the elect, knowledge of artisanry is the most elevated of knowledges, because the Real becomes manifest through artisanry in *wujūd*. Hence artisanry is the greatest signifier, the clearest road, and the most upright in word.

This explains why the ruling property of the greatest of God's elect becomes manifest in the form of the common people. Hence their level is unknown, and no one knows them but they. They have no superiority in the world's eyes. They differ from the companions of states, who are distinguished and noted among the common people because of the states that overcome them, that is, their miraculous breaking of habits. But the Folk of God are wary of that, because it is shared by other than their own kind. So the Folk of God are known through the station, but unknown and unrecognized through witnessing.

In the same way, God is known to all His folk through the innate disposition, but unknown to them through reason and witnessing. Were He to disclose Himself to one of them, he would not recognize Him. Or rather, He never ceases disclosing Himself perpetually, but He is unknown except to His folk and His elect. They are the Folk of the Koran, the Folk of the Remembrance, from whom God has commanded us to ask, for they report only about Him. He says, *So ask the Folk of the Remembrance if you do not know* [16:43], because the Folk of the Remembrance are the sitting companions of the Real.

The rememberer, concerning whose remembrance of God God Himself bears witness, reports only about his own sitting companion. Hence he reports about the affair as it is, and this is "knowledge." For he is *upon a clear sign from His Lord, and a witness from Him recites it* [11:17], this witness being his manifestation in His form. In other words, the knowledge about God that he brings is His attribute in which this individual who remembers discloses himself. In the measure of his remembrance, the Real is his perpetual sitting companion. That is why ʿĀʾisha said about the Messenger of God, "He was remembering God all the while." Hence she affirmed that he was God's sitting companion perpetually. She knew this either through unveiling, or because God's Messenger had reported it to her.

When the Prophet sat with God, God would narrate to him news of the messengers, and through that his heart would be made firm, because of the contention that he saw from his community in what he brought from God. If God had not been with him in this situation and its likes, there would be no difference between him and other mortals, for He is with them however they may be and wherever they are.

There is no escape from His being with those who remember Him—through a withness of specification. There is nothing but an increase of knowledge through which excellence becomes manifest. Any rememberer whose knowledge does not increase in remembering the remembered object is not a rememberer, even if he remembers with his tongue, because the "rememberer" is only he who is pervaded entirely by the remembrance. That is the "sitting companion" of the Real. He has no escape from gaining benefit, because the Generous Knower, in whom niggardliness is inconceivable, must bestow upon His sitting companion something that he did not have. Here there is no niggardliness that could cancel out munificence. There remains only the receptive locus, and none sits with Him who is not the possessor of a receptive locus. This then is the sitting companion of the Real.

The Real is the sitting companion of everyone in the cosmos from whence they are not aware. The furthest limit of the common people—if they have faith—is that they know that God is with them. But the benefit lies in your being with God, not in His being with you, for such is the affair in itself. He who is with the Real has no escape from witnessing the Real. That which witnesses Him is none other than the *wujūd* of knowledge within him. These knowledges are the divine grants.

Knowledge is the most eminent grant
  that He gives,
    but unveiling is the most magnificent
      and clearest way.
If you ask God, the Real,
  in seeking,
    ask Him for unveiling,
      for He will grant it.
Devote yourself to knocking,
  for the claims of engendered things
    have locked the door,
      but God's munificence opens it.

When a knowledge is not gained through an unveiling after the opening of the door—an unveiling that is bestowed, made manifest, and elucidated by the divine munificence—then it is an awareness [*shuʿūr*], not a knowledge, because it has been gained from behind the door, while the door is locked. This door is nothing but you, for you are under the ruling property of your meaning and your habitation, and that is the locking of the door.

You are aware that behind this body and manifest form there is another meaning that you do not know, even though you are aware of it. The manifest form is one leaf of the door, and the soul is the other leaf. When the door is opened, the one leaf is made distinct from the other leaf, and what is behind the door appears to you. This is knowledge. You will see it only as differentiated, for you have differentiated between the two leafs such that this has become distinct within you.

If the door consists of a Real and a creation, that is, you and your Lord, such that the affair has become confused for you, then your entity has not become distinct from your Lord. You will not distinguish Him as long as the door remains unopened. The opening itself will give you knowledge of the door and of the difference between the two leafs. Thus you will know your essence and know your Lord. This is the Prophet's words, "He who knows himself knows his Lord." So there is awareness when the door is closed, and knowledge when the door is opened.

When you see that the knower has doubts concerning what he is supposed to know, then he is not a knower. Rather, this is "awareness." When the doubts are removed in what he knows, this is "knowledge." Then he knows that the door has been opened for him and that munificence has made what is behind the door appear to him. (III 455.14)

Ibn al-ʿArabī now turns his attention to explaining the difference between *shuʿūr* or "awareness" and *ʿilm* or "knowledge." The term *shuʿūr* derives from the same root and has the same basic sense as the word *shiʿr*, but the latter is also the standard term for "poetry." Hence, when the Koran says that God has not taught Muhammad "poetry," the Shaykh takes this to mean that He has not given him "awareness," but rather, true and explicit knowledge of the actual situation. God opened the door for him—He did not simply let him know that something is behind the door.

Many people imagine that awareness is a knowledge, but this is not so. The share of awareness in knowledge is that you have a summary knowledge that something is behind the door, but you do not know what it is. That is why God says, *We have not taught him poetry* [36:69]—because of their words, *He is a poet* [21:5]. Then He says, *It is not seemly for him. Surely it*, that is, that for which We have raised him up, *is only a remembrance*, which is to say that he has taken it from the Real by way of being a sitting companion; *and a clear Koran* [36:69], that is, it is manifest and differentiated in the very fact that it brings everything together. He did not take the Koran on the basis of an "awareness." After all, everything that the companion of awareness designates concerning the object of awareness is an inference. If it happens to coincide with the affair, such that it is a knowledge, still, he is not *upon insight* [12:108] in that. It is not seemly for an intelligent person to invite to an affair until he is *upon insight* in that affair, which means that he knows it through vision and unveiling such that he has no doubt concerning it.

The messengers of God alone are not specified for this station. On the contrary, it belongs both to them and to their followers, the inheritors. No one is an inheritor until his following is perfect in word, deed, and nonmanifest state specifically, for the inheritor must curtain the manifest state, since making it manifest depends upon the incumbent divine command. In this world, the manifest state is a branch, while the root is nonmanifestation. This is why God generally veils Himself from His servants in this world, but in the last world He discloses Himself to all of them.

When He discloses Himself to him to whom He discloses Himself, it is specific to him, like His *disclosing Himself to the mountain* [7:143]. In a similar way, the [miraculous] state that becomes manifest for the messengers is to prove the messenger's truthfulness so that he may prescribe a Law for the people. The inheritor calls to what this messenger has stipulated, but he is not a Lawgiver, so he has no need to make manifest the state, in contrast to the Lawgiver's need. So the inheritor preserves the subsistence of the call in the community that follows the call. His share is only this.

Even if the inheritor were to bring a shariah—though he does not bring one, but let us suppose that he does—the community will not accept it from him. So there is no benefit in the manifestation of the state when there is to be no acceptance, as there was with the messenger. So know this!

When God makes something of the states manifest in them, this goes back to God. It does not derive from a self-exertion or an intention on the part of the servant. This is named a "charismatic gift" in the community. That for which the friend of God and His seeker struggle is only the opening of the door, so that in his states he will be in himself *upon insight* [12:108] from God, not that he should make this manifest to His creatures. *So he is upon a light from his Lord* [39:22] and fixed in his station. Nothing makes him tremble save He.

A charismatic gift of this sort is his knowledge of God and the pertinent details of His most beautiful names and His highest words. Thus *he knows what enters into the earth* of his nature, that is, the seeds that God planted within it when He proportioned it and balanced it, *and what emerges from it* [57:4], which is the verbal expressions of what is within it and the practices and artisanal acts in their levels, because what emerges from the earth is diverse in kinds. It is the earth's ornament. So what emerges from the earth of man's nature and his body is an ornament for him, such as eloquence in verbal expression and well-done artisanal acts.

In the same way, he knows *what descends from the heaven* of his intelligence through what he considers of his shariah concerning the knowledge of his Lord. This is the divine sending down upon his heart. *And what ascends into it* [57:4], that is, his pleasant words on the Burāq of wholesome deeds, which lift him up to God. Thus God says, *To Him climb up the pleasant words,* which are what emerge from the earth, *and the wholesome deed—He uplifts it* [35:10], and this also is what his earth causes to emerge. Thus, what descends from the heaven is what enters into the earth; and what emerges from the earth, which is what becomes manifest from that which entered in, is what ascends to the heaven. Hence the descender is identical with that which enters in, and the emerger is identical with the ascender. Thus the affair is male and female, a marriage act, and a birth. So there are existent entities, witnessed properties, limited terms, and intended acts, some of which are blameworthy by accident, though they are praiseworthy by essence.

Know then that differentiation becomes manifest in *wujūd* only through deeds. If the doer differentiates the deed as it is differentiated in undifferentiation—the undifferentiation of wisdom—that is "the wholesome deed." If he differentiates it otherwise in view of the differentiation of the human being within it, then this deed is unwholesome.

For the most part, unwholesome deeds are found in those who differentiate affairs through rational consideration, not through the divine knowledge-giving. That which is differentiated through the divine knowledge-giving is all wholesome deed. As for that which is differentiated through rational consideration, some of it is wholesome and some unwholesome in relation to its differentiation, nothing else. But all is a wholesome deed in relation to God. Thus one says that imperfection in *wujūd* is part of the perfection of *wujūd,* or, if you like, say "part of the perfection of the cosmos," since, were imperfection to be taken away from the cosmos, the cosmos would be imperfect.[19] So understand!

Know also that we were not speaking about "unwholesome deeds" or "corruption," out of courtesy toward the divine knowledge, and in reality. However, we saw that in the divine convention, God has warned against corruption. He says, *Seek not corruption in the earth; surely God loves not the workers of corruption* [28:77]. He says, *That is the Last Abode; We appoint it for those who desire neither highness in the earth, nor corruption* [28:83]. We saw the mention of "corruption" in the common language of the rational thinkers, or rather, in that of all people. That is why we venture to mention it. In place of "corruption," we were saying only "the manifestation of one form and the elimination of another," as is the actual situation in respect of a specific composition or the arrangement of a natural constitution. As for

God's words, *surely God loves not the workers of corruption,* what is meant is changing the divine ruling, not change of the entity, nor alteration of the form. As for His words, *highness in the earth,* that is a realized affair, since the earth does not accept highness so long as it remains an earth for those for whom it is an earth. Everything that we see as high and towering within it is a mountain and a peg with which God has weighed it down so that its shaking will be stilled.[20] Thus the mountains are not earth.

God created the earth like a globe with earthy and stony parts, some of which He joined to others. After God created the heaven, He outspread the earth so that those for whom she was created as a place could settle down upon her. That is why she shakes. If she had remained a globe, she would not shake and He would not have created the mountains.

So "He created the mountains, and He said to them, 'Upon her'" once. He surrounded the water that encompasses her with a mountain that He made like a belt for her. It is said that upon the mountain are the edges of the dome of heaven; and that the blue color which we attribute to the heaven and by which we describe it pertains to the body of heaven because of its distance from you in visual perception. In the same way, you see the mountains as blue when they are distant from you, but the blue belongs to them only because of their distance from the gaze of the eye. So also, you see the mountain that is distant from your gaze as black. Then, when you come to it, it may not be as you had seen it.

We have already explained to you that colors are of two sorts—a color that abides in the body of the colored thing, and a color that arrives newly to the eyesight when it gazes at the body because of some accidental affair that stands between the seer and the seen. One example is like this [mountain]. Another is like the colors that arrive newly in the colored object through the true color because of some guises that overtake it, so the viewer sees them in other then the color that abides in them and that he knows. This is like obfuscations in rational proofs. So they are colors/not colors. Their share of the divine realities is *You did not throw when you threw* [8:17] and "Thou/not Thou." This is also like the whole cosmos, which, in reality, is creation/not creation, or Real/not Real; or, it is like imagination—I mean what is imagined—which is sensation/not sensation and sensory/not sensory.

Earth is acted upon by water, which is acted upon by air, for, in our view, air is the root. That is why it is nearest in relation to the Cloud, which is the Breath of the All-Merciful.[21] Air brings together heat and wetness. From heat becomes manifest the pillar fire, and from wetness the pillar water. From the solidity of water earth comes to be. Thus air is the son of the Breath, which is the Cloud; fire and water are two children of air; and earth is the child of the child. It is the water that becomes solidified. That which does not become solidified remains as water in its root, and earth is upon that water.

I have seen how the Euphrates River, when it freezes in Kawānīn in the lands of the north, returns to being an earth upon which walk caravans, people, and beasts, while water is flowing beneath the ice. This water is upon air, which replenishes it through its wetness, thereby preserving its entity, while it rests upon it. After all, air makes water flow when it moves. But when it is held back and is still, the water on it stays still, so the water does not penetrate into it. We have seen this in sugar cane reeds and such things when penetrated by holes. When you fill it with water and block the reed's higher hole, nothing of the water flows out of the lower hole. When you let it go, the water flows. Thus the water supports itself only upon the still air, because it is still. This is a form that pervades the whole cosmos.

When air comes in waves, it is named "wind." Wind transfers the odors of what it passes over, whether pleasant or loathsome, to the sense of smell. In the same way, it transfers the cold and the heat of things. That is why wind is described as a "talebearer" and is described as taking reports to the listeners. The only thing that receives these affairs through which it brings its tales and reports to the listeners and smellers is the faculty of hearing and smell. The movements of the celestial bodies bring the air into movement, such that the name *wind* arrives newly for it. Air moves the celestial bodies, and within it the celestial bodies move.

As for "breaking" [*kharq*], it is only that certain things are emptied from certain spatial confines and these confines are then occupied by other things, for there is no void in what the cosmos inhabits, only transmutations of forms. There are forms that make affairs arrive newly and forms that take them away. But the substance that fills the Void is fixed in entity. It is not transmuted into anything, and nothing is transmuted into it. The divine names are connected to nothing save bestowing new arrival on these forms and their diversity. As for their going away, that occurs through themselves.

However, their going away occurs when that is required by the Essence of their Existence-Giver. This is a subtle knowledge, for it is a speech of *ḥaqq* from a *ḥaqq*, but understandings of it are diverse. God says to the forms, *If He will, He will take you away and bring a new creation* [14:19]. The meaning is that if He will, He will make you witness in each solitary time the new creation from which God *has taken away [. . .] your eyesight* [6:46], for such is the affair in itself. But concerning it, the people are *uncertain* [50:15], except the folk of unveiling and finding.

You may object, "But you have said that the entity of the substance subsists." We reply: Its subsistence does not belong to its entity but rather to the forms that arrive newly within it. Hence its poverty toward God never ceases, perpetually. The substance's poverty toward God is for subsistence, and the forms' poverty toward God is for their *wujūd*. Thus everything dwells in poverty toward God, but God is *the Independent, the Praiseworthy* [35:15] through independence, that is, lauded because of the attribute of independence from the cosmos. (III 458.10)

Chapter 397: The Soul's Ascent

Ibn al-ʿArabī calls this chapter "On the true knowledge of the mutual waystation of *To Him climb up the pleasant words, and the wholesome deed—He uplifts it* [35:10]." He begins the chapter by explaining how God appointed the rationally speaking soul to govern the body. He compares the body to a home and the soul to the homeowner, whose duty is to "govern the waystation," that is, his home (the term *tadbīr al-manzil*, "governance of the domicile," is sometimes translated as "economics"). Eventually, however, the wholesome soul understands the limitations within which it has been placed. It sees that God gave it the power of governance, but He did not tie that power to any specific locus, which is to say that the soul governs wherever it may be, in this domicile or any other. The soul now looks for a steed with which to ascend to the world of light where it will be able to exercise its full powers, and it finds that steed in its own deeds, which are its "Burāq"—the beast as quick as lightning (*barq*) that took Muhammad on the *miʿrāj*.

Next the Shaykh turns to investigating the nature of the vision of God that the soul achieves, and he tells us that the most perfect vision is to see God in the form of Muhammad. Then he describes some of those who have failed to reach the fullness of the Muhammadan vision and who, instead of standing unknown in the Station of No Station, are marked by the specific divine attributes that they realize. Finally he discusses *shaṭaḥāt*, "unruly utterances" or, as they have also been called, "theopathic locutions" (Massignon), "inspired paradoxes" (Corbin), and "words of ecstasy" (Ernst). Ibn al-ʿArabī makes the observation, surprising perhaps at first sight, that whatever God's friends say about Him is fine and truthful, because Unbounded *Wujūd* assumes every binding. However, if these utterances are directed against the friends of God, this is a discourtesy (*sūʾ al-adab*) and more worthy of blame. Although the famous Sufi ʿAbd al-Qādir al-Jīlānī (d. 561/1166) was guilty of this sort of unruly utterance, he spoke on the basis of a form from the Real. Certain others have made such utterances on the basis of visionary experience of the imaginal world, but, because of the discourtesy involved, they are of no account and have been driven from God's door.

The Men are God's Men, all of them,
as are the gnostics. But among those who are left and remain,
not one of them knows His reality,
save him who brings together the verses and surahs
and abides through the Real racing on foot,
not caring who blames or is grateful.
God has favored us in our vicegerency
through the seal of the property that He specified for no mortal.
But we mean no boasting in this, lest
a defect come over us, or He join someone else to us.

Know—God confirm us and you with a spirit from Him—that God says, *Whoso emerges from his house as an emigrant to God and His Messenger* [. . .] [4:100]. The Prophet said, "He whose emigration is to God [. . .]." Then he said, "There is no emigration after the conquest," that is, the conquest of Mecca, for there would be nowhere to go.

God made the houses of the human souls these natural bodies, which *He created*, and *proportioned*, and *balanced* [82:7], as a structure for the residence of these human souls, which are among the words of the Real.

He blew the soul into the body and gave it this residence. He gave it knowledge of what it has at God in the governance of this empire, over which God has made it king. He planted within its natural disposition the knowledge of governance without qualification. Then He designated for it in its specific and general governance the moments, measures, and directions of governance through the tongue of the Shariah, in conformity with the scale of its nature, so He praises that specific and general governance.

Whatever the folk of this situation among the knowers of nature have said, no one has said concerning the root of this knowledge anything more comprehensive and wondrous than God's Messenger when he said, "The stomach is the house of malady, practicing abstinence is the head of every cure; and the root of every malady is indigestion." He commanded concerning food, if a person must eat much, that one-third should be for food, one-third for drink, and one-third for the self. He said, "A few mouthfuls to firm up his backbone are enough for the child of Adam."

All this concerns the governance of this house. A person keeps on ruling it through God's ruling until it occurs to him in his secret heart that, although he rules it through God's ruling, in fact only God rules it through God's ruling, even though his entity is fixed at Him. When he views this eye-to-eye, he disdains to be restricted by the darkness of this frame and he seeks to keep himself free from it. Then he finds that God has readied for him from his deeds a docile, not unruly mount, a *barzakhī* beast below a mule and above a donkey that He has named a "Burāq," because it is born from the world of nature just as lightning is born in the world of the atmosphere. God has bestowed upon it speed in journeying, so it places its hoof along with its rider at the extreme limit of its gaze.

So he *emerges as an emigrant* [4:100] from the city of his body and sets off in the Sovereignty of the Higher Plenum and its signs with the eye of crossing over [*iʿtibār*], because of the knowledge of God that the signs give to him. The Real receives him when he enters in upon Him from his engendered qualities and those of the existent things. He makes him His guest in the best of waystations and instructs him in what he had not known before that—the true knowledge of a divine address and the witnessing of the [divine] will in keeping with the correspondence, so that the affair will not come suddenly upon him and unexpectedly, lest he perish at that, just as Moses was thunderstruck. After all, God discloses Himself to him only in a Muhammadan form, so he sees Him with a Muhammadan vision. This is the most perfect vision within which and through which the Real is seen. Through this He lifts him up to a waystation that is reached only by the Muhammadans. This is the waystation of the He-ness, so his locus of witnessing stays in the absent, and no trace of it is seen in the sensory domain.

This was the locus of witnessing of Abu'l-Suʿūd ibn al-Shibl in Baghdad. He was one of the most elect of the companions of ʿAbd al-Qādir al-Jīlī.[22]

When the companion of this witnessing is not the companion of a He-ness, but he witnesses Him in the Sovereignty as a king—and every witnesser must put on the form of the object of his witnessing—then the companion of this witnessing becomes manifest as a king. He becomes manifest through the name Manifest in the world of engendered existence through displaying traces, free acting, rule, broad claims, and divine strength. Such was ʿAbd al-Qādir al-Jīlī, as was Abu'l-ʿAbbās al-Sabtī in Marrakech.[23] I met the latter and conversed with him. His scale was comformative—he had been given the scale of munificence. But ʿAbd al-Qādir was given impetuosity and Aspiration, so he was more complete than al-Sabtī in his occupation.

The companions of this station are of two sorts. For some of them, the courtesy of language is preserved—like Abū Yazīd al-Basṭāmī and Sulaymān al-Danbulī.[24] But others are overcome by unruly utterances, because of their realization of the Real—like ʿAbd al-Qādir. They manifest highness toward their peers and equals and toward those who are higher than they in station. In the Path, this is considered discourtesy in respect of those toward whom courtesy is preserved.

As for those who display unruly utterances through God toward God, they show more courtesy to God than do those who make unruly utterances toward their peers. After all, God receives unruly utterances concerning Himself, because He receives all forms. But the created thing does not receive unruly utterances concerning it, because it is tied to a divine station at God that is unknown in respect of the specific face. Thus, the person whose utterance is unruly toward him might be lying without aiming and intending to. But one cannot lie concerning God—like the All Hyle that receives every form in the cosmos. Whatever form you ascribe to it or make manifest, you have spoken the truth in the ascription, and the manifestation is truthful, for the forms make the ascription manifest. As for artifactual hyle, it does not receive this. It receives only specific forms. So it is possible that someone may be ignorant in ascribing things to it, so he ascribes forms to artifactual hyle that it does not receive. So also is the affair in what we have mentioned concerning unruly utterances toward God and the Folk of God, the companions of the waystations.

ᶜAbd al-Qādir al-Jīlī was one of those who made unruly utterances toward God's friends and the prophets through the form of a *ḥaqq* in his state. Thus he was not preserved from error in his tongue.

I have seen some people making unruly utterances toward God and toward the Folk of God on the basis of a witnessing in an imaginal Presence. We have nothing to say to them, for they have been driven from the door of the Real and made distant from the Seat of Truthfulness. You will see that in most of their states they give no notice to the Shari'ite rulings, nor do they halt at God's limits, even through the rational faculty for which prescription is made is found in them.

In short, presumptuousness [*idlāl*] before God is in no way correct for the Folk of God brought near to Him. He who claims nearness along with presumptuousness knows nothing of the station of nearness, nor of the sound reality of being His folk. *And God speaks the **ḥaqq**, and He guides on the path* [33:4]. (III 559.35)

9. *The Natural Constitution*

The realm of the body is that of nature (*ṭabīᶜa*, *ṭabᶜ*), which is the domain that displays the traces of the higher worlds. In modern Islamic languages, the word *ṭabᶜ* is used to mean "printing," and nature is indeed the domain of imprints. In Ibn al-ᶜArabī's view, the word has two basic senses. In the broader sense, it refers to the Breath of the All-Merciful, which receives the imprint and articulation of all God's words. In a narrower sense, it designates the lower worlds that bear the imprint of the spiritual domain. In the latter meaning, the Shaykh typically employs the term in contradistinction to *spirit*. Both the imaginal and the corporeal worlds are "natural." "That which leaves the trace is spiritual, and that which receives the trace is natural. There is nothing that has a natural form in the cosmos that does not also have a holy spirit" (II 305.8).

In order to prepare the body's natural realm for the inblowing of the spirit, God proportions and balances the human clay, and this gives rise to the "constitution" of the body. The constitution then interacts with the inblown spirit, and this allows for a differentiation among various human types.

Spirit and Nature

Nature is composed of the "four natures"—heat, cold, dryness, and wetness. These are tendencies or relations or qualities. The first two are active, the second two acted upon by the first two. Heat produces dryness, and cold brings about wetness. When the four natures mix, they give rise to the four "pillars" (*rukn*) or elements—earth (cold and dry), water (cold and wet), air (hot and wet), and fire (hot and dry). "Nature is four-fold and understood as two active things and two things acted upon. It makes the four pillars manifest" (II 367.23).

When the four elements combine, they give birth to the three progeny (*muwalladāt*)—minerals, plants, and animals. The elements are noncompound (*basīṭ*), while the progeny are compounded (*murakkab*) of the elements. All elemental things are natural, but not all natural things are elemental. Thus the noncompound things, including the four elements themselves, are natural but not elemental. This is one criterion for distinguishing between imaginal and corporeal bodies. Both have bodily characteristics, but corporeal things are elemental, while imaginal things are natural but not elemental.

> The [three] worlds include elemental bodies—and every elemental body is natural—as well as natural, non-elemental bodies, since not every natural body is elemental. Thus the elements themselves are among the natural bodies—they cannot be called elemental bodies—as are the spheres and the angels. (II 335.9)

> God says, *The earth altogether shall be His grip* [39:67]. Spirits follow bodies; bodies do not follow spirits. When He grips the bodies, He has also gripped the spirits, since the bodies are their frames. Hence He reported that all is in His grip. Every body is an earth for its spirit, and there is nothing but body and spirit. However, bodies are of two sorts—elemental and luminous. The latter, like the former, are natural. God tied the *wujūd* of the spirits to the *wujūd* of the bodies and the subsistence of the bodies to the subsistence of the spirits. (II 115.13)

In one respect, the relation established between spirit and nature is one of leaving traces and receiving traces, or activity and receptivity. Hence the Shaykh often refers to the Divine Spirit as the "father" and to nature as the "mother." When the two marry, they give birth to the partial spirit, or the rationally speaking soul. "The partial soul is born from nature, which is its mother, but the Divine Spirit is its father" (II 189.25).

If spirit and nature relate to each other as husband and wife, this is because duality and complementarity give order to the cosmos, so the relation between spirit and nature manifests a universal principle. As Ibn al-ʿArabī puts it, the "marriage act" (*nikāḥ*) pervades every atom of existence.[1] Interrelationships between the active and the receptive, the high and the low, the father and the mother, give rise to all existent things, so everything is a child. In one chapter, the Shaykh analyzes three basic levels of marriage—divine, spiritual, and natural. On the divine level, *wujūd* is the husband who marries the fixed entities, and they give birth to the cosmos. On the spiritual level, the Divine Spirit marries the existent entities, who give birth to the partial spirits. On the natural level, animals and plants marry each other and give birth to their children.

> As for the spiritual marriage act, its Presence is nature, which is the root wife in the divine marriage act. Once a form is born from the first marriage, this form becomes the wife of the All Spirit. Then the Real marries the Spirit to her, so he goes to her. When he has had intercourse with her, a child becomes manifest from this intercourse. It is the partial spirit, and through it the form comes to life. The child abides through the wife/form, governs her, strives for her, and travels and plunges into dangers for her so that he may earn sensory and suprasensory provisions through which he can be munificent toward her on both the sensory and suprasensory levels.
>
> The marriage feast that belongs to this spiritual marriage is undertaken by the faculties, which have no manifestation save in this natural form through the *wujūd* of this marriage act. So the faculties take pleasure and rejoice in the traces that they gain because of the *wujūd* of this consummation.
>
> As for natural marriage, it is what is sought by the partial spirits that govern these forms. It is the coming together of two natural forms through the conjoining and consummation that is named in the world of sensation "a marriage act." From this marriage act are born the likenesses and the spouses among every animal and plant. So a human being becomes manifest from two human beings, and a horse becomes manifest from two horses. It may also happen that the conjoining takes place between two that are unlike, so an unusual shape is born from the two that is not similar to the entity of either spouse, like a mule from a donkey and a horse. (III 516.29)

The father/mother relation is rooted in the complementary sets of attributes that belong to God Himself and are sometimes called His "two hands." Ibn al-ᶜArabī identifies the two hands with all the basic pairs of attributes, such as majesty and beauty, wrath and mercy, subjugation and gentleness, *tanzīh* and *tashbīh*. Most generally, he understands them as a reference to the principle of He/not He.

When citing Koranic evidence for God's *tanzīh*, the Shaykh typically mentions 42:11, *Nothing is as His likeness*. Most authorities think that the "as" is redundant, and Ibn al-ᶜArabī accepts this view when he reads the verse in terms of *tanzīh*. However, sometimes he prefers to read the verse in terms of *tashbīh*. Then he insists that the "as" is not redundant, and the verse signifies that nothing is like God's likeness—His "likeness" being the perfect human being. In short, the verse signifies both *tanzīh* and *tashbīh*, depending on how it is read. In the following, the Shaykh takes both meanings into account and understands the verse to be a declaration of the fundamental complementarity of dual attributes and realities that fill the cosmos. Hence, it points to the divine root of spirit and nature, which are the father and mother of all the progeny.

In the correct understanding, the meaning of His words, *Nothing is as His likeness*, is the same as that of the Prophet's words, "God created Adam in His form," in one of the plausible senses of this report. So also it means His words, *We indeed created the human being in the most beautiful stature* [95:4], only because He created him in the form of the Real. He *restored him to the lowest of the low* [95:5], only to bring together in him the perfection of the form through the attributes that He has mentioned that He Himself possesses.

What does the negation of likeness from Him have to do with His being qualified by limit and measure, such as sitting, descending, showing tenderness, being kind in address, wrath, and good-pleasure, when all these are descriptions of the created thing? Had He not described Himself by our descriptions, we would not have known Him, and had He not declared Himself incomparable with our descriptions, we would not have known Him. It is He who is known in both states and described by both attributes.

This is why *of each thing* He *created a couple* [51:49]—so that highness will belong to one of the couple, the male; and lowness will belong to the other, the female; and so there will become manifest from between them, when they come together, the subsistence of the entities of the species. He assigned this to every species in order to teach us that the affair in our *wujūd* follows the same course, so we are between Him and the intelligibility of nature, from which He configured the natural bodies. Likewise, from the relation of His own face-turning toward the bodies, He configured the governing spirits.

Nothing other than God has any escape from being compounded [*murakkab*] from a rider [*rākib*] and a mount [*markūb*], so that the rider will be poor toward the mount, and the mount will be poor toward the rider. Thus God stands alone in the independence by which He describes Himself. He is Independent through Himself, but we are independent through Him in our very poverty toward Him because of that which we cannot do without.

Everything other than God is a governor and a thing governed by this governor. The governor, inasmuch as it is a governor, finds this in itself as a faculty that is poor toward a governed thing within which its governance can become manifest. The governed thing, inasmuch as it is a governed thing, finds this in its essence as a state through which it is poor toward that which governs its essence, so that its entity will be wholesome and subsist. Hence the poverty of each toward the other is an essential poverty.

The governor is qualified by independence of the governed only because it is poor toward something governed, but not this governed thing itself. So also, the governed is qualified by independence only because it is poor toward a governor, but not toward this governor itself. Each of them is independent of the other's entity, but not of the governance—by the other or of the other. So neither's independence is absolute.

But the Real's independence is absolute with regard to His Essence, while creation is poor absolutely, also with regard to its essence. Thus the Real is distinguished from creation. This is why he who said, *God is poor and we are the independent* [3:181], was an unbeliever, for this distinction is never lifted, since it is an essential distinction in both the Real and the creation that are described by it.

Thus there are only two thingnesses—the thingness of a Real and the thingness of a creation. Hence *No thing is as the likeness* of creation in its poverty, for there is no one but the Real, and the Real is not described by poverty. So He is not like creation, so no thing is like creation.

So also, *No thing is as the likeness* of the Real in His independence, for there is nothing but creation, and creation is not described by independence by its essence. So it is not like the Real, so no thing is like the Real because, as we said, there is no "thing" but creation and the Real.

Hence creation in respect of its entity is one essence in many, and the Real in respect of His Essence and Entity is one Essence that has many names and relations. (III 534.32)

Nature is not only spirit's opposite, it also carries within itself internal opposition, because each of the four natures is the opposite of one of the others, and this opposition also derives from the divine names. The Shaykh frequently mentions the mutually opposing names in connection with the Koranic verse that speaks of the quarrel of the Higher Plenum (38:69, cf. 3:44). Such verses prove to the Shaykh that the angels in question pertain to the world of nature, which is to say that the light of their luminous bodies is ruled by the four natures. Opposition among the names also provides the deepest reason for differences of opinion among scholars, sages, and Sufis.

In this waystation is found the knowledge of the conferences and controversies among the ulama in their sessions and the fact that all of this derives from the conferences among the divine names. This becomes manifest in the Higher Plenum when they quarrel, even though they are occupied with God and *they never fail* [21:20] in their glorification, *nor do they grow weary* [41:38]. So, is their quarreling part of their glorification, just as the Messenger of God "was remembering God all the while"? Even so, he was speaking with the Arabs in their gatherings and with his family. Was all of this remembrance of God, or was it not?

No one denies the diversity of the things created from the natures, for the natures are opposites. Everyone perceives this and no one denies contention in the world of nature, but they do deny it in what is above nature. As for the Folk of God, in no way do they deny contention in *wujūd*, for they know the divine names and that these are in the form of the cosmos. Or rather, God brought the cosmos into existence in their form, because they are the root. And among the names are contraries, opposites, compatibles, and assistants. (III 466.28)

The angels are created from the world of nature, like human beings. However, they are more subtle, just as the jinn are more subtle than human beings because they derive from fire, from its *flame* [55:15]. Fire belongs to the world of nature, yet the jinn are spirituals, assuming shapes and imaginalizing themselves. If nature did not receive this, the world of the jinn would not receive it. How can this be denied?

It is known for certain that human beings belong to the world of dense nature, and that they have of nature in themselves the storehouse of imagination in the front of the brain, through which they are able to imagine any impossible thing that they will—so what about possible things?

In the same way the angels belong to the world of nature. They are the inhabitants of the spheres and the heavens. God has instructed you that *He went straight to the heaven when it was smoke* [41:11] and then *He proportioned them as seven heavens* [2:29], making its folk [i.e., the angels] from them, which is what is meant by His words, *and He revealed in each heaven its command* [41:12]. No one denies that smoke is from nature, even if the angels are luminous bodies, just as the jinn are fiery bodies. Were light not natural, it would not possess the quality of burning, just as fire possesses the quality of drying and taking away wetness. All these are attributes of nature.

God reported that the Higher Plenum are quarreling. Quarrel derives from nature, because it is a totality of opposites. Contention and disagreement are identical with quarrel, and this takes place only between two opposites. It was in this respect that the angels said, *What, wilt Thou place therein one who will work corruption therein and shed blood?* [2:30]. This derives from their nature and their jealousy for the Divine Side. Had they halted with their spirituality, they would not have said anything like this when God said, *Surely I am placing in the earth a vicegerent* [2:30]. On the contrary, they would have answered in keeping with the divine mystery that they had within themselves, saying, "That belongs to Thee. Glory be to Thee! Thou dost what Thou wilt, and we are servants, under Thy command to obey anyone whom Thou commandest us to obey."

Through the corruption and other things that are required by the world of nature itself and that occurred from the human being, the angels fell to protesting. They saw corruption in others but they did not see it in themselves. (II 650.29)

He who puts things in their own places has given them what they rightfully demand from him. He is the wise man of his moment, for wisdom requires the putting of each thing in its place, *And God is Wise, Knowing* [4:26].

Nothing whatsoever is unbounded, for possibility does not require that, nor is it given by the realities. After all, unboundedness is itself a binding. So there is no affair that does not have a homestead that accepts it and a homestead that rejects it and does not accept it—there is no escape from this. Take, for example, natural nourishments for the natural body. There is nothing that acts as a nourishment that does not have within it a harm and a benefit. This is known by him who knows nature in the respect that it governs the body, the one who is named a "physician." The naturalist knows something of this, but the physician knows its detailed explanation. So there is no tongue of unbounded praise in the cosmos, nor any tongue of unbounded blame.

The root is the contrary divine names, for God has named Himself for us by them in respect to the fact that He is the Speaker. In the same way, He voiced *tanzīh* and *tashbīh*, He declared His oneness and He associated others with Him, and He spoke to His servants with both attributes. Then He said, *Glory be to thy Lord, the Lord of exaltation, above what they describe. Peace be upon the envoys, and praise belongs to God, Lord of the worlds* [37:180–2]. (I 664.35)

Ibn al-ʿArabī frequently identifies the natural configuration with the body. Thus, in explaining the different reactions of Moses and the mountain to God's self-disclosure, he points out that nature demands that God provide for it a governor in order for it to subsist. The chapter has to do with the divine name *qayyūm*, the Self-Abiding or Ever-Standing, as mentioned in the Footstool verse of the Koran: *God, there is no god but He, the Living, the Ever-Standing* (2:255). In this particular section of the chapter, the Shaykh is discussing various human implications of the Koranic description of God as *He who stands over every soul for what it has earned* (13:33).

The Real may disclose Himself in the attribute of all-domination to one of His servants. If the locus of the disclosure has no governor save God, like Moses' mountain, it crumbles to dust because of His self-disclosure, for there is nothing within it save itself. But if it has a governor that God has assigned to it—like the rationally speaking souls that govern their bodies—its body does not crumble to dust.

Nevertheless, the self-disclosure exercises its ruling property over people's spirits just as it does over the mountain. Hence, having "stood over" the governance of the body, the spirit ceases to do so, so the property of thunderstruckness became manifest in Moses' body. It was nothing but the disappearance of his governor's over-standing, nothing else. In the same way, the mountain ceased to have the attribute of being a peg. Thus it remained fixed in itself, but it did not make anything else fixed, for God put the mountain in place only so that the shaking of the earth would be stilled. Its property disappeared when its mountainness disappeared, just as the governance of the spirit disappeared from the body of the companion of the thunderstroke when the spirit ceased to abide through the body.

Moses regained consciousness after having been thunderstruck, but the mountain did not return to its pegness, for there was nothing there to seek the mountain, because it had been replaced by another mountain. But this specific body had no created governor save this spirit. Hence the body, through its state, sought from God its own governor, and God gave it back to it, so it regained consciousness.

Thus the natural configuration preserves governance for its governing spirit, for it has no independence from a governor to govern it. But the earth does not preserve the pegness of a designated mountain. The earth has no need for it, because it has other mountains. (III 485.34)

Chapter 225: Increases

In several places the Shaykh associates the four natures with four divine attributes, such as life, knowledge, desire, and power (or word). He is not completely consistent in these associations, but for present purposes, it is sufficient to point out that he insists that quaternity (*tarbīʿ*) pertains to *wujūd* itself, so it must become manifest on every level. In his chapter called "On the true knowledge of the increases," he makes use of the idea of the four natures to explain the meaning of the Koranic story of the four birds that Abraham placed on four mountains.

Know that "increases" in the terminology of the Sufis among the Folk of God means "increases of faith in the absent and of certainty."

When a surah descends with light
  it increases the faithful in happiness.
Knowledge of the absent is the most precious
    of all knowledge
  and best at bringing presence.
Perceiving the absent things with no signifier
  but the All-Merciful will not lead to
    destruction.
The absent has no entity at the Real
  even if He discloses Himself to you in the
    name Experienced.
He has veiled the servants and every intellect
  with *until We know* [47:31] the steadfast
    and patient.

God says, *Whenever a surah is sent down, some of them say, "Which of you has this increased in faith?" As for the faithful, it increases them in faith, and they are joyful; and as for those in whose hearts is illness, it increases them in abomination added to their abomination* [9:124–25]. So there is no escape from increases in the two separate groups. These are the "tasks" upon which and in which is the Real *each day* [55:29], that is, each breath, which is the shortest of days.

However, the word *increases* that the Folk of God have taken as a technical term means those increases that bestow a specific felicity and a knowledge of the absent that increases the servant in certainty. Take, for example, the words [of Abraham], *"My Lord, show me how Thou shalt give life to the dead." Said He, "What, dost thou not have faith?" Said he, "Yes, but so my heart may be confident"* [2:260]. He is saying: Yes, I have faith, but the modes of life-giving are many and varied, like the *wujūd* of the creatures. Among the creatures are those You brought into existence from *Be!*, among them those You brought into existence with Your hand, among them those You brought into existence with Your two hands, among them those You brought into existence at the beginning, and among them those You brought into existence by means of another creature. Thus the *wujūd* of the creatures assumes a great variety, and bringing creatures to life after death is only another *wujūd* in the last world. It may be various, or it may be one. I have sought knowledge of the affair's howness. Is it various or one? If it is one, which one is it of all these kinds? When You give knowledge to me, my heart will be at rest and confident through gaining that [specific] face and the increase of knowledge that You have commanded, for He says as a command, *Say: "My Lord, increase me in knowledge!"* [20:114].

God turned the explanation of the howness to him over to the four birds, which are the image of the four natures. Thereby He reported that the last world's *wujūd* is natural—that is, the mustering of the natural, corporeous bodies. After all, some people say that the corporeal bodies will not be mustered. Rather, [they say,] through death, the souls will be mustered to the Universal Soul as disengaged from the natural frames. So God reported to Abraham that the affair is not as they suppose. Thus He turned him over to a situation existent at him in which he acted freely, thereby giving him knowledge that if the natures were not witnessed, known, and distinct at God, they would not have become distinct. So He gave existence to the natural world only from something that was known at Him and witnessed by Him and that acted freely in that world. He brought some parts of nature together with other parts, and He made manifest the body in this specific shape. Thus, by turning Abraham over to the four birds, He clarified for him the *wujūd* of the affair that was enacted by God when He gave existence to the natural and elemental bodies, for there is no body unless natural or elemental.

The bodies of the last world's configuration are natural in the case of the felicitous, but the bodies of the folk of the Fire are elemental. *The gates of heaven shall not be opened to them* [7:40] for, were these to be opened for them, they would leave the elements by climbing up.

As for the mustering of the spirits that Abraham desired to understand from this signification that the Real turned over to him through the four birds, in the divine things it is that the cosmos in its manifestation is poor toward a God who is Powerful over existence-giving, Knowing of the differentiations of its affair, Desiring to make its entity manifest, and Alive so that these relations may be affirmed—given that they can only belong to something that is alive. So there is no escape from these four in the divine things, for the cosmos does not become manifest save from Him who has these four. This is what the birds signified for Abraham in the divine things concerning the intellects, the spirits, and that which is not a natural body. In the same way, they signified the quaternity of nature for the sake of giving existence to the natural and elemental bodies.

Then there are God's words, [*Take four birds*] *and twist them*, that is, join them, this joining being a bringing together after a separation. When some of the natures are joined to others, the bodies become manifest. *Then place [part of them] on each mountain*. This is what I mentioned about the four divine attributes. They are "mountains" because of their loftiness and fixity, for mountains are pegs. *Then call them, and they will come to you rushing* [2:260]. No one is called save him who hears and possesses a fixed entity, so He placed Abraham's calling in the station of His word *Be* in His words, *Our only word to a thing, when We desire it, is to say to it "Be!," so it comes to be* [16:40]. Thus Abraham's certainty increased him in confidence through his knowledge of the specific face among the faces of possibility.

Among the increases is *Be wary of God, and God will teach you* [2:282]. Thus you increase in a knowledge that was not at you. The Real teaches it to you as a bestowal of eminence that is granted to you by godwariness. When a wary servant makes God his protection, God veils him from seeing the occasions through himself, so he sees the things proceeding from God. This is a knowledge that had been absent from you, so He has given you a knowledge of Him as an increase of faith in the absent. Were this absent to be placed before most rational faculties, they would refute it with their demonstrations. This is the benefit of this state.

Among the increases is that you come to know that the property of the entities is not the self of the entities and that this property becomes manifest in the *wujūd* of the Real. It is attributed to the servant with a correct attribution and it is attributed to the Real with a correct attribution. Hence in respect of this property, the Real increases with a property that He did not have, and the entity increases by the ascription to it of *wujūd*, by which it was not qualified in eternity without beginning.

So consider how wonderful is the property of the increases! This is why they include the two separate groups—they increase the felicitous in faith and they increase the wretched in abomination and illness. *And God speaks the ḥaqq, and He guides on the path* [33:4]. (II 520.25)

The Light of Guidance

Just as *God is the Light of the heavens and the earth* (24:35), so also spirits are the light of bodies, and spiritual realities are the lights that become manifest through imprints in nature. Nature itself is darkness, though receptive to light. In one interpretation of the *three darknesses* mentioned in Koran 39:6, Ibn al-ʿArabī identifies two of them with the *darkness of the land and of the sea* mentioned in three Koranic verses and he understands the third to be the rationally speaking soul that is the mixture of this land and sea.

> From this the Folk of God come to understand the levels of guidance and bewilderment and of the guided and the misguided. God assigns to them a light, or rather, lights, by which they are guided in the *darknesses of the land* of their nature, in the darknesses of *the sea* of their reflective thoughts, and in the darknesses of their rationally speaking souls—both the land and the sea of these souls, because of what they possess in their configuration. For the rationally speaking souls are born between unadulterated light and sheer, unmixed, elemental nature. (III 141.31)

The spirit's light corresponds to the prophetic light of guidance. Just as spirits bestow integrity and wholeness on natural forms, so also the shariahs protect the *wujūd* of the servants in this world and the next. Those who follow the light of guidance are preserved from the destructive activity of darkness and misguidance. "Preservation (from error)" in the following renders *ʿiṣma*, a term that is commonly translated as "sinlessness" or "inerrancy." In theology, the term is employed to mean that God preserves the prophets from falling into sin. In the Shaykh's understanding, God does this through the light of guidance. Note that the protecting light bestows "shame" (*ḥayāʾ*) upon the person receptive to it. This is because shame demands awareness of God's presence and activity in keeping with *iḥsān*, which the Prophet defined as "worshiping God as if you see Him." Shame is an internal luminosity that preserves the servants from disobeying their Lord. It is closely related to "godwariness" (*taqwā*), whereby the servants protect themselves from God's displeasure by following His prophets. Thus the passage also investigates the notion of "protection" (*wiqāya*), which is sought by the godwary servant.

Lights are of two sorts—root lights, and lights that are born from the darkness of engendered existence. An example of the latter is His words, *And a sign for them is the night: We pull out from it the daytime, and they are in darkness* [36:37]. His words, *Breaker of dawn and Maker of daytime as repose* [6:96], look toward the same light. *Among His signs is that He created for you, of yourselves, spouses, that you might repose in them* [30:21] and that those born from them might be born into light.

The light that is spoken about in this waystation is the born, temporal light. This waystation pertains specifically to one of the two Imams who belong to the Pole. His name is "Servant of his Lord."[2] This light is sometimes masculine and sometimes feminine. When the night covers the daytime, that which is born from it is the desired light.[3]

This born light that we have begun discussing is, for the prophet, the light of preservation [from error] and, for the friend of God, preservation [*ḥifẓ*]. It bestows shame and complete unveiling, for it is unveiled, and through it unveiling takes place. In contrast, the root light becomes unveiled, but unveiling does not take place through it, because it overcomes the light of the eyesights. Hence it takes away the benefit for which light comes. This is why the souls of those who are gnostics through the lights and their levels have recourse to this light that is born from darkness—because of the correspondence between us and it, since our spirits are created. After all, partial spirits are born from the Universal Spirit ascribed to the Real and from the dark natural bodies after they have been proportioned, thus gaining their preparedness to receive. The partial spirit, which is the human spirit, becomes manifest between the two within the body. The spirit breaks from the body, just as the dawn breaks from the night through the *Breaker of dawn.*

Thus there occurs a correspondence between this light and the spirit of the human being. He becomes intimate with it and takes benefit from it. Suchwise has God caused the habitual situation to occur. He gave no more strength than this; if He had willed, He would have done so.

The divine loci of manifestation, called the "self-disclosures," follow the same course, for the root light is kept nonmanifest within them and absent from us, but the forms within which the self-disclosure occurs are a locus within which the loci of manifestation become manifest. Hence our vision falls upon the loci of manifestation. This is why they are loci of manifestation bound by forms—so that our perception will occur through a correct correspondence. After all, what is intended in this is to gain benefit through it and through what comes from it.

This is a high waystation, great in rank. Its knower is distinguished from the children of his own kind. It pervades all things. For just as God mentions that He is *Breaker of dawn,* so also He is *Breaker of the grain and the datestone* [6:95] through what becomes manifest from the two. No benefit accrues except through the like of this light. The prophets take it as a protection through which they warily protect themselves from the mishaps of the engendered things, which are the darknesses of the "others."

Now that the rank and waystation of this born light has become clear to you, let us clarify that against which protection is taken: Human beings need protection because of affairs that they dislike by nature or the Shariah. These are affairs that are specific to the world of creation and natural composition, not the world of command. We have explained in this book and elsewhere what we mean by the world of command and the world of creation. Both belong to God. He says, *Verily, His are the creation and the command—blessed is God, Lord of the worlds* [7:54]. He specified these for the name Lord apart from any other.

The world of creation and composition requires evil by its essence, but the world of the command is the good in which there is no evil. The world of the command saw the creation of the human being and his composition from the mutually averse natures, and [it saw] that mutual aversion is contention, and contention leads to corruption. Hence the angels said, *What, wilt Thou place therein one who will work corruption therein, and shed blood* [2:30] unless he subjects himself to the applications of the Shari'ite rulings? Then there occurred the like of what they had said. They saw that the Real says, *God loves not those who work corruption* [5:64], and He says, *God loves not corruption* [2:205], so they disliked what God disliked and loved what God loved, but God's ruling property in creation followed the course determined by the Exalted, the Knowing.

The evils that become manifest in the world of composition derive from its nature, which was mentioned by the angels. The good that becomes manifest from it derives from its divine spirit, which is the born light. Hence the angels spoke the truth. Therefore God said, *Whatever ugly thing strikes you is from your soul* [4:79]. Since the world of creation is like this, it is incumbent upon every rational person to seek preservation from error through the light mentioned in this waystation. All evils are ascribed to the world of the creation, and all good is ascribed to the world of the command.

Know also that nature underwent combination and coming together after it had been mutually averse for the sake of the manifestation of the world of creation, so as to make manifest the eminence of this light through the good that it has, even though it was born of this composition. For the light has strength, and the world of the command predominates in its configuration. So nature entered into *wujūd*, and it was named "body, animal, plant, and inanimate thing." Corruption and change exist in all this in every state. Were it not for this preserving light, the world of creation would perish totally. Hence God commanded that people should have recourse to this light in repelling all these disliked things. God confirms this spirit through the light that He gives from the name Lord, so that it can repel the harm that falls upon it from the direction of the darkness of nature. (II 575.6)

If nature is darkness and spirit is light, then ignorance and misguidance arise from immersion in nature. Most of Ibn al-ʿArabī's mentions of nature make it an obstacle in the path to perfection. Thus, for example, he explains that if nature predominates over the individual, love will be misdirected. But if spiritual love predominates, the person will be led to salvation. He makes these remarks in his long chapter on love, in the midst of which he provides a capsule description of God's lovers, mentioning over fifty of their attributes. The first nine are "slain, destroyed, journeying to Him through His names, flying, constant in vigil, concealing heartache, craving to leave this world to encounter their Beloved, weary with the companionship of anything that stands between themselves and the encounter with their Beloved, and full of sighs" (II 345.34). Later in the same chapter, he presents a twelve-page treatise in which he comments on the first forty-four of these attributes. His explanation of the lover's being "slain" (*maqtūl*) typifies the treatise's style and provides a good example of how he juxtaposes the terms *spirit* and *nature*.

The lover is described as being slain because he is compounded of nature and spirit.

The spirit is light, nature darkness—
each in its entity the other's opposite.

Opposites are averse, and things averse to each other contend. Each seeks the ruling property and the possession of the kingdom for himself.

For the lover, two things are possible: It may be that nature will predominate in him. Then his frame will be dark and he will love the Real in creation and wrap light in darkness, relying on the root in His words, *And a sign for them is the night: We pull out from it the daytime, and they are in darkness* [36:37]. Daytime is a light, so he knows that night and daytime are neighbors—even if they are opposites—and that it is permissible for one of them to be kept nonmanifest in the other: "It will not harm me to love the Real in creation in order to bring the two affairs together."

It may be that spirit will predominate in the lover. Then his frame will be illumined and he will love creation in the Real, in keeping with the Prophet's words, "Love God for blessings that come to you in the morning." "Hence," the lover says, "I love Him in His blessings at His command," for his object of witnessing is the Real.

Whenever jealousy occurs between the two opposites and each of them sees that the Sought Object may deliver Himself over completely to its own opposite, it says, "I shall slay my opposite so that it does not become manifest through him instead of me." If nature slays its opposite, the lover dies while being a lover of the engendered things. If the spirit slays its opposite, the lover is a martyr, alive at his Lord and provided for. In either case, every lover in the cosmos is slain, even if he is not aware of this. (II 350.10)

Nature is the domain of darkness and of receptivity toward the worlds of light. Those who wish to come out of the darknesses into the light must turn their attention toward their father, the Divine Spirit. Nonetheless, the body bestows great good on the soul, even if the soul has not become aware that it has a father. The Shaykh explains this while commenting upon a hadith which refers to the reward that God gives to mothers who take care of their children after their husbands have died. Umm Salma married the Prophet after the death of her first husband, by whom she had several children. The passage represents the whole of a brief section from the chapter on *zakāt* called "The true knowledge of who are the parents of the human soul."

> The governor of the body and the faculties is the partial soul, which is the human soul. It is the child of the human being's natural body, which is its mother, and the Divine Spirit, which is its father. This is why the soul says in its whispered prayers, "Our Lord, and Lord of our fathers," the high things, "and our mothers," the low things. *When I have proportioned him and blown into him of My spirit* [15:29]. *Mary [. . .], who guarded her private parts, and We blew therein of Our spirit* [66:12]. So Jesus was her child, and she was his mother. A breath was blown into the proportioned body from the spirit, so the body is a mother, and that from which the inblowing occurs is a father.
>
> However, this child is like an orphan who has no father, because his rational faculty has not become firm in gazing upon the father. Hence he is like someone who has no rational faculty. He is like a child who has no father to teach him and train him in courtesy. So his vegetal soul, which is his body, directs him through the wholesomeness of the constitution in which God created it. The nonmanifest and manifest faculties are in the furthest degree of limpidness and equilibrium, so they benefit the soul with knowledges, which correspond to the woman's charity toward her fatherless child. Thus the individual gains from the direction of his body—as a recompense for the alms he has spent on himself—a divine knowledge whose measure cannot be measured save by God.
>
> Umm Salma, the Prophet's wife, said, "Will I receive a wage for what I spend on the sons of Abū Salma? I will not abandon them in such a situation, for they are my sons." He replied, "Yes, you will have a wage for what you spend on them." Muslim recorded it in his *Ṣaḥīḥ*. (I 575.26)

Those who refuse to follow the Divine Spirit when it offers its guidance remain in the lowliness and receptivity of nature's domain. This helps explain the chastisement of hell, which is a natural world barely open to the light of the spirit. Those who fall into hell do so because they deny their servanthood to God and choose instead to serve their natural needs. In contrast, those who enter paradise do so by having freely surrendered themselves to God. Having attached themselves to God, they are released from the domination of everything other than God and, in turn, are given control over everything below themselves.

> God says, *Call upon Me and I will respond to you* [40:60]. He says, *Those who claim to be too great to worship Me shall enter Gehenna abject* [40:60]. Thus He describes them by saying that they will not emerge from servanthood and that abasement is their reality, that is, with the word *abject*.
>
> [In other words,] "He who does not desire to be My servant, as he is in actual fact, will be a servant of his nature, which is Gehenna, and he will be abased beneath its ruling authority, as he is not in actual fact. Hence he will have abandoned knowledge and become qualified by ignorance. If he possessed knowledge, he would be My servant and he would not call upon anyone else, just as he is in actual fact My servant, whether he likes it or not and whether he knows it or not. When he is My servant through calling upon Me, and when he is not too great in himself to be My servant within himself, then I will give him free activity in nature. He will be her master, take control of her, and act freely with her, though she had been his mother. So look at the exaltation and authority that has escaped him who claims to be too great to worship Me and does not call upon Me in prosperity and for the removal of harm! Occasions have made him their servant, so he is one of the ignorant." (IV 20.16)

The path to gain release from the hold of nature and to escape from the evils of the created world is set down in detail by the Shariah, or, more broadly, by "religion" (*dīn*). In Ibn al-ᶜArabī's view, the Arabic word *dīn* has three basic meanings—obedience or acquiescence (*inqiyād*), requital or recompense (*jazāʾ*), and custom or habit (*ᶜāda*).[4] In general terms, it is understood to mean doing the good (*khayr*) and avoiding the evil (*sharr*) that are designated by the Shariah. The human soul inclines naturally toward the Shariah's good, because it is born of good, since its father is the Holy Spirit, which is pure good; and its mother, which is the body, was balanced and perfected by God's own hands. All this helps Ibn al-ᶜArabī explain the meaning of the hadith, "Good is a habit" (*al-*

khayr ʿāda), which might also be translated as "Good keeps on coming back." As for evil, which is instigated by Satan, whom the Koran calls "the Comrade" (*al-qarīn*), it is, in the Prophet's words, "an obstinate persistence" (*lajājā*). Satan, who is the embodiment of obstinate persistence, coerces the soul into obeying him, but a person who is "coerced" (*mukrah*) is not held responsible by the Shariah. Hence the soul's fundamental good is still another reason for its ultimate return to mercy. Toward the end of the passage, the Shaykh comments in detail on the Koranic verse, *O My servants who have been immoderate against themselves, despair not of God's mercy. Surely God forgives all sins; surely He is the Forgiving, the Compassionate* (39:53).

Since religion is doing the good, and since religion is "habit," the Prophet mentioned that good is a habit. This mention is a good news—from a knower of the affairs, who is the Messenger—that the soul is good by essence and does not receive evil except through the obstinate persistence of the Comrade, because of that in which he is obstinately persistent against the soul. So God did not make evil pertain to the soul's essence. Hence the Prophet said, "Good is a habit, and evil is an obstinate persistence."

When the Comrade presses the soul to evil and obstinately persists, while evil is identical with opposition to God's commands and prohibitions, and when the soul's breaths are constricted by this pressing and obstinate persistence, God reveals to it; or rather, He speaks to it from the specific face that is not known by the angel. He says that it should accept the evil that the Comrade is pressing upon it. Then the Real sees that the soul is terrified and fears the divine deception. So He allows it to witness the Presence of Changing and allows it to witness that the final issue of those for whom the Law is prescribed is to mercy. He recites for the soul, *God will change their ugly deeds into beautiful deeds* [25:70], and He recites for it concerning the immoderate, *Despair not of God's mercy, surely God forgives all sins* [39:53]. So He removes its terror, and it accepts from the Comrade the evil with which he came. Thus the Comrade becomes happy because of the acceptance that occurs from the soul, because he is ignorant of the all-inclusiveness of mercy and the all-inclusiveness of pardon and forgiveness. After all, God designated pardon only for this group who receive the evil brought by Satan, the Comrade. What Satan does not know is that God has assigned to the soul, in its accepting the evil of the Comrade because of his obstinate persistence and pressing, the waystation of him who is coerced, and the coerced person is not taken to task.

The Prophet named evil an "obstinate persistence" as a divine good news, of which not everyone is aware. And he made good a "habit," for the soul is good in essence, because its father is the pure Holy Spirit, so its nature is good, nothing else. Its mother is this form proportioned from the humors. The first reception that became manifest in it was the reception of proportion and balance. This is indicated by God's words, *Then He proportioned you, then He balanced you* [82:7]. Acceptance of balance is good itself.

Through its root, this configuration received the adjacency of the opposites, which are the humors. One of the habits of an opposite is aversion to its opposite. But here [in this human configuration] mutual aversion is not found. This signifies the goodness of the root.

Then there was its reception, after the proportioning and the balancing, of the inblowing of the Holy Spirit. Thus its first reception of what was greater than its configuration was its reception of the inblowing of this good, pure, purified Spirit. Hence good is its "habit" through the nature with which it is imprinted. So the final issue is to its root, for the root has the reception of good that we mentioned. Thus mercy joins it in the final issue, just as its *wujūd* was mercy itself. So the affair is sealed with that with which it began, and the conclusion is identical with the precedent.

Among the things that confirm what we mentioned is that the first human configuration, which was the root of the human configurations, was in the furthest limit of declaring holiness and the pinnacle of eminence, for it was created in the divine form. Hence nothing became manifest from this configuration save what corresponds [to the divine form].

It was appropriate for this configuration, given the *wujūd* of the opposition that is bestowed by the contrary divine realities, not to be encroached upon by blame, for some of the names are opposed to others. So also is the opposition that becomes manifest in this human configuration. The everlastingness of chastisement will not encroach upon this configuration in the final issue, for the root will defend it from that, and the root is the [divine] form.

The human configuration is compelled in its opposition, because there is no escape from the contrariety of the divine names in him who is created in His form. After all, the Benefiter is not the Harmer, nor is the Giver the Withholder. There is no escape from the manifestation of these realities in this configuration so that the perfection of the form may be correct. Thus the obedient is contrary to the disobedient, the associator is contrary to him who voices *tawḥīd,* the divester is contrary to the affirmer, and the conformer is contrary to the opposer. All this derives from the assistance of the divine names. This is His words, *All We assist—these and those—from thy Lord's gift.* He means both the obedient and the disobedient, both the folk of good and of evil. *And the gift of thy Lord is not walled up* [17:20], that is, held back, because He gives through His Essence, and the loci—the receptacles—receive through their preparedness. Their preparedness is the trace of the divine names within them, and among the divine names are the conforming and the opposing. The conforming are like the Compassionate, the Forgiving, and their similars. The opposing are like the Exalter and the Abaser.

Inescapably, the preparedness of the locus will be under the ruling property of one of these names, so its reception of the divine ruling property accords with this, whether he is opposing or conforming. When this is someone's situation, how can essential blame be attached to him? Accidents have no fixity, so good is essential in the human being, and it is this whose ruling property remains. Evil is accidental, so it disappears, even if after a while. God says, *You shall surely know its news after a while* [38:88].

This is like His words, *O My servants* [39:53], so He ascribed them to Himself, just as He ascribed their souls to Himself in their creation, for He said, *And I have blown into him of My spirit* [15:29]. *All We assist—these and those—from thy Lord's gift* [17:20].

Then He says, *Those who are immoderate against their souls* [39:53]. "Immoderation" is a wide-ranging generosity that exceeds limit and measure. Thus He says concerning expenditure, *They are neither immoderate nor parsimonious* [25:67]. In other words, they are not openhanded beyond need, and they are not parsimonious and do not decrease from that touched by need. *Despair not of God's mercy* [39:53], for it *embraces everything* [7:156], and you are among the things.

Moreover [God says], I have instructed you how I configured you and from which things I have configured you—from a purified spirit and a nature that is conforming, receptive, and obedient; not disobedient and not opposing.

Surely God forgives all sins [39:53], so He left nothing of them. Through which thing will chastisement be everlasting for them? After all, it is only *an appropriate recompense* [78:26]. But He has forgiven, and whatever has been forgiven has no ruling property, for He who has forgiven it is *the Forgiving, the Compassionate* [39:53]. Moreover, He is the Forgiving, the Compassionate in His Essence, so He never ceases for an instant forgiving the object of forgiveness. The property of sin does not return to the object, since the Preserver is the Forgiving, the Compassionate. If these names released him and he were forgiven by other than these and their similars, it is possible that the other name would not stay fixed [in its forgiving], because there would be no preserver for him.

So pay attention to the knowledge I have given you, for it pertains to the kernel of true knowledge. (III 182.23)

From Chapter 71: Fasting on Sunday

One of the practices that God has set down for bringing the soul out of its claims to greatness and into the path of its own felicity is fasting. In the following, Ibn al-ʿArabī explains the significance of the voluntary fast on Sunday, a day that is called in Arabic, *yawm al-aḥad,* "the Day of the One." Normally, this is taken to mean that Sunday is the first day of the week, but it can also be read to mean that it pertains to the divine name *aḥad,* which, as we have seen, designates God in respect of *tanzīh.* The Shaykh begins by referring to some of what he has mentioned in the previous section of the chapter concerning fasting on Saturday. Towards the end of the section, he explains why only fasting for the sake of God deserves the Koranic appellation "fasting." If it is done for the sake of the body's health, then it should be called "zeal" (*ḥamiyya*)—a term that the Koran uses to designate the attitude of the people of the Age of Ignorance before Islam (48:26).

Those who take into account what we have mentioned of this witnessing—the fact that it is a feast day for the Christians—fast so as to oppose them.

As for those who take into account that it is the first day in which God showed concern for creating the creatures in their entities, they fast so as to show gratitude to God. They offer as the counterpart of that [incomparable act of creation] an act of worship that has no likeness.[5]

The intention of the gnostics is diverse in their fasting. Some of them fast on Sunday specifically because it is [the Day of] the One, for the One is an attribute that asserts the incomparability of the Real. In the same way, fasting is an attribute of *tanzīh* and of a level that is forbidden through its unreachability, because the faster is prohibited from taking the soul's share through eating and enjoying sexual intercourse. Moreover, he keeps himself free of blameworthy things, for the faster is prohibited from backbiting, obscenity, foolishness, or being qualified by anything that the Shariah blames in that state. Thus there is a correspondence between him and the One in the attribute of *tanzīh*. This is why he fasts on this day.

Each of them imbibes what is known to him and puts it into practice with the most eminent of attributes.

This is why fasting has, among nature's [four qualities] cold and dryness—because of the lack of nourishment. This is the opposite of what nature seeks, since it seeks heat for the sake of life, not what is produced through heat's activity [i.e., dryness], and it seeks wetness, which is produced by the activity of cold. Thus the faster counterbalances nature with the opposites, so he counterbalances it with the root and what is produced by it, for he is commanded to oppose the soul.

The soul is a sheer nature that contends with the God by its essence, because the *wujūd* of the whole world of bodies depends upon the soul. If not for the soul, no entity would become manifest for the world of bodies, so the soul becomes conceited and wanders aimlessly.

Hence it is said to the spirit that governs this elemental body and is commanded to preserve the equilibrium of the corporeous body and to look after the means to its wholesomeness, "When you see the natural soul in this station of conceit and haughtiness, hold it back from food, drink, and the enjoyment of sexual intercourse through the intention of opposing it and the intention of keeping yourself free of what nature imagines you to be poor toward in that. Let nature know that she is ruled over so that she will become abased beneath servitude and poverty toward the seeking of nourishment from the governor of this frame." This sort of governance is named "fasting."

But if the spirit holds the soul back from all this for the sake of the wholesomeness of the constitution, this is not named "fasting." This activity of the spirit pertains only to a part of the governance of nature, and this sort of thing is named "zeal," not fasting. If, through this zeal and assisting nature in what the zeal commands, the spirit intends to achieve the wholesomeness of the body's constitution for the sake of worshiping God so that it may perform all the worship that God has commanded it by way of the movements and stillnesses that do not become manifest save through the wholesomeness of the constitution, then the spirit is rewarded for the zeal, even if it is not a fasting. Thus have I clarified for you some of the mysteries of fasting on Sunday. (I 647.8)

Chapter 418: Understanding

Darkness prevents the vision of light and keeps the servant in ignorance and misguidance. Hence nature is a barrier to "understanding" (*fahm*). Ibn al-ʿArabī explains this in a chapter called "On the true knowledge of the mutual waystation of 'When someone does not understand, nothing has been conveyed to him.'"

He who understands the affair
is the one
addressed by the All-Merciful
from every entity.
He it is around whom
mortals turn,
and he it is whose property rules over
every "where."
Iyās was distinguished
from Bāqil[6]
because of the wisdom contained
in His two grips.
God has clarified His ruling property
for us
in every two groups
in engendered existence.

The opposite does not know
its opposite,
but the Real is known to us
without untruth.
The likeness has been affirmed
for Him
and then negated from me
after a time.

God says, *They say, "Our hearts are in shelters from that to which you call us"* [41:5]. Know that speech is of two sorts: First is a speech in those sorts of matter that are named "letters," and it is of two sorts: Either the letters are written and named "writing," or they are spoken and named "words" and "speech."

The second sort is a speech that is not in any sort of matter. The speech that is not in matter is known, but one does not say concerning it, "It is understood." The knowledge of a listener becomes attached to it when he does not hear through an instrument, but rather through a Real disengaged from the instrument. Thus when the speech is not in a matter, it is heard only through what corresponds to it.

"Understanding," which is a specific attachment of knowledge, becomes attached to the speech that is in a matter. When a listener knows words from the one who utters them, or when he sees writing, if he knows what the speaker means by the speech—even though, in common usage, the words comprise many meanings that are opposed to what the speaker means—this is called "understanding."

The listener may not know in detail what is meant by the speaker of the words. It may seem plausible to him that the words signify many of the senses that the words may signify, but he does not know exactly which of these senses the speaker means, or whether he means all of them, or one of them, or whatever. Despite the fact that he knows what the words signify, it is not said concerning him that he has been given "understanding" of the words. He has only been given "knowledge" of everything that they signify, since he knows the common usage. This is because the words have been spoken to a listener who is overcome by two affairs: First, inadequate knowledge of what the words signify in the language; and second, even if he knows everything that they signify, they were spoken only in a meaning required by a context.

He who understands what is meant by the speaker's words is the one who has been given understanding of them, but he who does not know this has not understood. Thus the speaker has not conveyed anything to him in that speech.

Then there is the speech of God when it descends in the tongue of a people. The folk of this tongue are diverse in their understanding from God of what He means by that word or those words, given that what they signify is diverse. All of them, even if they disagree, have understood from God what He means. For God knows all the senses. There is no sense that is not intended by God in relation to that designated individual, so long as it does not leave the tongue. But if it leaves the tongue, then he has not understand or known.

The same is true of those who take by way of allusions. Their perception of this under the rubric of allusions within the speech of God is a specific understanding of it, for it is intended by God in the case of this person to whom the allusion is made by the speech. But the speech of the created thing does not have this waystation.

He who has been given understanding from God in every respect has been given *wisdom and the differentiation of address* [38:20]. This is the differentiation of the various senses and meanings in that speech. *He who has been given wisdom has been given much good* [2:269]. God has made it "much" because of the senses.

When someone's heart is in a shelter, or a lock is upon it, or its insight is blind, or it is tarnished, or rust is upon it, then God has come between him and understanding from God, even if he interprets the speech. That is why they *have taken God's signs as mockery* [45:35] and His *religion as a diversion and a sport* [7:51]—they have not understood from God what He has addressed to His servants. Hence He said [in this mutual waystation], "When someone does not understand, nothing has been conveyed to him."

As for "rust," that is tarnish and cloudiness. It is nothing but the forms that are disclosed in the mirror of the heart and that God does not call the servant to see. These forms can be polished from the mirror through remembrance of God and recitation of the Koran.

As for the "shelter," that is like *those confined in tents* [55:72], for the heart is in the house of nature, busy with its mother. It has no news of its father, which is the spirit of God. Hence it stays in the darkness of the shelter, which is the veil of nature, so it is within two veils—a shelter and a darkness. It hears, but it does not understand. Concerning such people, God says, *Be not as those who say, "We hear," but they hear not* [8:21], that is, they do not understand.

As for the *heaviness in his ears* [31:7] or deafness, this is the weight of the occasions in this world, which turn him away from the last world.

If there is a cloudiness, that is the hardening of his heart, lest any trace be left in it by the acceptance that occurs to the soul when it prompts him to consider and listen to the Lawgiver who is calling to him. This is indicated in His words, *[The unbelievers say, "Do not give ear to this Koran,] and talk idly about it; perhaps you will overcome"* [41:26] so that you will not hear any call. They do not return, and they do not use their intelligence, for He addressed them in their tongue. *Deaf, dumb, blind—so they do not return* [2:18]. *Deaf, dumb, blind—so they do not use intelligence* [2:171]. *So* God *made them deaf, and blinded their eyes* [47:23], and He sealed their tongues, so they do not utter that to which He calls them, even if they pronounce it.

As for the "lock," that belongs to the folk who offer excuses on the day of resurrection. They will say, "We did not place locks upon our hearts. We found the locks upon them." This is part of the dispute in respect of which God says about these people, *They cite him not to thee, save to dispute. Nay, but they are a quarrelsome people* [43:58]. "We do not know who locked them. We aimed to come out, but we feared the breaking of the seal and the stamp. So we kept on waiting for the one who placed the locks upon them. Perhaps he would undertake to open them. Nothing of that was in our own hands."

One of these people was ᶜUmar ibn al-Khaṭṭāb—I mean, one of the folk of the locks. God says, *Or are there locks upon their hearts?* [47:24]. When God undertook to open the lock, he became a Muslim, and God strengthened and fortified Islam through him—God be pleased with him and make him pleased with Him. Thus have we mentioned in brief, in the measure of the moment, the occasion for not understanding from God. *And God speaks the* ***ḥaqq****, and He guides on the path* [33:4]. (IV 25.1)

From Chapter 73: The Twelfth Question

The twelfth question posed by al-Ḥakīm al-Tirmidhī is as follows: "How is the attribute of their traveling?" Ibn al-ᶜArabī takes this as a reference to "The folk of the sitting places and the speaking" (*ahl al-majālis wa'l-ḥadīth*), who are, as he has already explained, those among the Folk of God who sit with God and are addressed by Him. As Chodkiewicz has pointed out, the discussion has to do with the elevated stations that are accorded to those who perform the *ṣalāt* as it should be performed.[7] Al-Tirmidhī is asking how they are able to reach these sitting places with God. In answering the question, the Shaykh suggests something of the process whereby the soul may be purified of nature's darkness. The specific term that he discusses is *himma* or "Aspiration," which is the power of concentration through which the seeker focuses on the Real.[8]

We say in answer: [They reach the sitting places] through Aspirations that are disengaged from the "other." The expansion of this is what we will say:

It is not correct for people to "travel" so as to gain suprasensory affairs, which do not receive or delimit any sort of matter. No one can gain what derives from these suprasensory affairs through traveling distances or crossing spaces. However, material movements that are based on knowledge or faith with the condition of *tawḥīd* can be linked with Aspiration.

As for their traveling in respect of their being knowers, this is through purifying the souls from the turbidities of nature and undergoing seclusions so as to empty the hearts from the thoughts that are connected to the parts of engendered existence and gained by directing the senses toward the sensory objects; through this the storehouse of imagination becomes filled, and the form-giving faculty gives form to everything of this that it loves, so these forms come between them and gaining this divine level.

Thus they incline toward seclusions and formulas of remembrance so as to praise *Him in whose hand is the sovereignty* [36:83]. Once the soul is purified and the natural veil between it and the World of Sovereignty is lifted, there becomes impressed in the soul's mirror all the knowledges imprinted in the forms of the World of Sovereignty.

The Higher Plenum gain an overview of the soul that has this quality. They see within it what they have at themselves, so they take it as a locus of disclosure for the manifestation of what is within them. Thus the Higher Plenum also aid the person in making this limpidness last, and they come between him and what is required by the veil of nature.

This soul receives knowledge of God from the high world in the measure of its correspondence with the Higher Plenum. This knowledge leads the travelers to receive from the divine effusion, but through the intermediary of the luminous spirits. There is no escape from this. They name this a "traveling." There is no escape from the disengagement of the Aspirations in seeking this. Were it not for the fact that the Aspiration attaches itself to gaining what has been stipulated at it in an undifferentiated manner, the person would not be able to turn his face toward the Higher Plenum.

If it happens in his traveling that this Man has faith along with his knowledge, or faith without knowledge, then his Aspiration attaches itself only to God. After all, faith signifies only God for him, but knowledge signifies only the intermediaries and the order of the habitual wisdom in the cosmos.

As for the attribute of the traveling of the companions of faith, they have no path to that save through the statutes of the Shari'ite affairs in respect of their being Shari'ite. They are of two sorts.

One group has tied their Aspiration to the fact that the Messenger has come only to call attention to and to teach the path that allows one to arrive at the Side of the Real. Once the Messenger has bestowed knowledge of this, he departs from the path and leaves them alone with God. When such as these vie and *outrace each other* to good works and *in good works* [23:61], they see before themselves the footsteps of no creature, for they have made [the Messenger] disappear from themselves and they have gone on alone to the Real—like Rābiʿat al-ʿAdawiyya.[9] When they gain the sitting places and the speaking, the Real addresses them with the divine speech, without the intermediary of a designated tongue.

As for the other group, they are a people who have deemed for themselves that they have no path to Him unless the Messenger is the veil-keeper. They witness nothing from Him without seeing the Messenger's footsteps before them in their traveling. The Real addresses them only with his tongue and his language—like Muḥammad al-Awānī. He said, "I left everything behind me and I came to Him, and I saw before myself footprints. I became jealous and said, 'To whom do these belong?'—out of confidence on my part that no one had outraced me and that I was among the folk of the first squadron. It was said to me, 'These are the footprints of your Prophet,' so my mind was stilled."

The first state is that of ʿAbd al-Qādir, Abu'l-Suʿūd ibn al-Shibl, Rābiʿat al-ʿAdawiyya, and all those who follow their course.

When the companions of faith are also knowers, they bring together the two affairs. They are the most perfect of the Men, on condition that, when they travel to Him and take their sitting places with Him through suprasensory speaking, as was mentioned earlier, and the speaking of hearing, they see the all-pervasiveness of His traveling in the existent things. This derives from His words, "When someone comes near to Me by a span, I come near to him by a cubit," and from the fact that He "descends to the closest heaven," than which none is nearer, since He is *nearer than the jugular vein* [50:16]

At such a person, the world of nature joins the spiritual world, and at him all *wujūd* becomes a Higher Plenum and a Nearer Placement. No engendered thing veils him, no entity distracts him, equal for him are the "where" and the "non-where," "was" and "was not." He sees Him in the veil-keepers and the patrols, and he hears His speech and His speaking in silence and sound.

This is the attribute of their traveling according to their grades.

Among them is he who travels in Him through His names. He is the companion of travel from Him, to Him, in Him, and through Him.[10] He travels in his halting and halts in his traveling. Al-Khaḍir and the Solitaries are among the folk of this station. From here, the "delight of the Prophet's eye" was in the *ṣalāt*,[11] for he was whispering with Him despite the diversity of the states that are restricted to standing, bowing, prostrating, and sitting—and there is no more than these [four] pillars [of the *ṣalāt*]. These are the states of spiritual quaternity, so they are similar to the [four] elements in quaternity. The forms of the meanings arrive newly from the commingling of these four states, just as the forms of the corporeal, natural progeny arrive newly from the commingling of the elements. (II 48.17)

Chapter 52: Weakness

Ibn al-ʿArabī calls this chapter "On the true knowledge of the occasion because of which the unveiler flees to the world of the witnessed when he sees Him." He begins by addressing the fact of human weakness, taking inspiration from such Koranic passages as *Surely the human being was created fretful, when evil visits him, worried* (70:19–20) and *God is He that created you of weakness* (30:54). Human frailty is an ontological fact, obvious to everyone, yet people make claims (*daʿwā*). The source of these claims is the strength that comes from God through the spirit, and human problems arise precisely because they fail to attribute the strength to its owner. God prescribes the Shariah so that people will recognize their own frailty and come to understand that their strength and salvation derive only from the divine side. The significance of this chapter's title does not become clear until a section at the very end where the Shaykh describes his disciple Aḥmad al-Ḥarīrī, who would flee back to ordinary consciousness whenever he experienced unveiling.[12]

Whoever fears for his own frame
  does not see the Real overtly and openly.
You will see him, when he witnesses Him,
  returning to engendered existence, wanting
    the body.
But you will see the courageous going
    forward, seeking
  Him who frightens the timid.

Know—God confirm you with a spirit from Him—that God has given human souls the natural disposition to be anxious about the root of their configuration. Hence courage and boldness are accidental affairs for them. In human beings, anxiety is stronger than in all the animals, except the cockroach. The Arabs say, "More timid than a cockroach." The occasion of its strength in human beings is reason and reflection, through which God distinguished them from the other animals. Human beings are never courageous save through the faculty of imagination, just as, through this same faculty, they increase in timidity and anxiety in specific situations. After all, imagination [*wahm*] is a strong ruling authority.

The occasion of this is that the human subtlety is born between the Divine Spirit, which is the All-Merciful Breath, and the proportioned body, which was balanced out from the pillars, which were balanced out from nature, which God placed under the subjugation of the Universal Soul, just as He subjugated the pillars under the ruling authority of the spheres. Then the animal body is subjugated under the ruling authority of the pillars, which are the elements. Thus it is subjugated to something that is subjugated under something that is subjugated—this last being the Soul, which is subjugated under the Intellect. Thus the animal body is in the fifth degree of subjugation in one respect. Hence it is the weakest of the weak.

God says, *God is He that created you of weakness*. So weakness is its root. Then He appointed for it an accidental strength, indicated by His words, *Then He appointed after weakness strength*. Then He restores it to its root in weakness, for He says, *Then after strength He appointed weakness and gray hairs* [30:54]. The latter weakness prepares it only so that the last configuration may stand over it.

In the same way, the configuration of this world stands on weakness. *You have known the first configuration* [56:62]. This was only so that his essence would cling to abasement, poverty, seeking help, and need before his Creator. With all this, he neglects his root and wanders aimlessly by means of the strength that has come to him accidentally. He makes claims and says "I," and he indulges in the wish to confront great horrors. But when a flea bites him, he manifests anxiety because of the existence of pain, and he hastens to eliminate the harm. He does not come to rest until he finds the flea and kills it. What is a flea that he should show so much concern for it, that he should be shaken from his bed and not sleep? Where are his claims and his boldness toward great horrors? The bite of a flea or a gnat disgraces him. This is his root.

All this is so that he may know that his boldness toward great horrors is through other than himself, not himself. It is that through which God confirms him in this. Thus He says, *And We confirmed him* [2:87], that is, We strengthened him. This is why He set down as shariah *and Thee alone we ask for help* [1:4] in every cycle of the *ṣalāt*. "And there is no power and no strength save through God."

The human being may come to know that, were it not for God's *wujūd*, no entity would have become manifest for him in *wujūd*, and that his root *was not a thing remembered* [76:1]. God says, *I created you aforetime, when you were not a thing* [19:9]. Now *wujūd* has a pleasure and a sweetness, and this is the good. But in imagining nonexistence in entity, souls have a great, intense pain whose measure is known only by the knowers. Nevertheless, every soul is anxious about nonexistence, lest it join with it in its state. Hence, whenever the soul sees an affair that it imagines may make it join with the nonexistence of its entity or something near to that, it flees from it. It is frightened and fears for its own entity.

Moreover, the soul derives from the Divine Spirit, which is the Breath of the All-Merciful. Hence, God referred to the spirit with "blowing," because of the correspondence with the Breath. He said, *I have blown into him of My spirit* [15:29]. In the same way, He had Jesus blow into forms of clay *as the guise of a bird* [3:49]. So spirits become manifest only through the breaths.

However, the locus over which the breaths pass leaves a trace within them, without doubt. Do you not see that when the wind passes over something that stinks, it brings the stinking odor to your nose? And when it passes over something fragrant, it brings a pleasant odor? This is why the spirits of the people are diverse. A pleasant spirit belongs to a pleasant body; it never associates anything with God, nor does it become a locus for base character traits. Such are the spirits of the prophets, the friends, and the angels. A loathsome spirit belongs to a loathsome body; it never ceases to associate things with God or to be a locus for base character traits.

This is because certain natures—I mean humors—predominate over others in the root of the body's configuration. This is the occasion of the pleasantness of the spirit, the *wujūd* of noble or base character traits, and the loathsomeness of the spirit.

The "health" and "well-being" of the spirits are the noble character traits that they acquire from the configuration of their elemental body, so they bring every pleasant and comely thing. The "illness" of the spirits is the base and blameworthy character traits that they also acquire from the configuration of their elemental body, so they bring every loathsome and ugly thing.

Have you not seen that when the sun effuses its light on the body of green glass, the light becomes manifest on the wall—or on the body upon which it casts its rays—as green? If the glass is red, the ray is cast as red in the gaze of the eye. The viewer sees it take on the color of the locus. Because of its subtlety, it receives things quickly.

Since air is one of the strongest of things, and the spirit is a breath, which is similar to air, the spirit has strength. The root of the spirits' configuration is from this strength. They acquire weakness from the natural, bodily constitution. No entity becomes manifest for them except after the trace of the natural constitution within them. Thus they emerge weak, because they are nearer to the body in the manifestation of their entity. When they receive strength, they receive it from their root, which is the All-Merciful Breath, called "the spirit from which the inblowing occurs and which is ascribed to God." Thus spirits receive strength just as they receive weakness, both of which pertain to the property of the root. But spirits are nearer to the body, because they are more newly acquainted with it,[13] so their weakness overcomes their strength.

Were the spirits to be disengaged from matter, then their root strength—which they possess from the divine inblowing—would become manifest, and there would be nothing more arrogant than they. Hence God made them inseparable from the natural form perpetually, in this world and the *barzakh*, in sleep and after death. They will never see themselves disengaged from matter. In the last world they remain forever in their corporeous bodies. God raises them up out of the forms of the *barzakh* in the corporeous bodies that He configures for them on the day of resurrection, and through these they enter the Garden and the Fire. This is so their natural weakness will remain inseparable from them, and they will remain poor forever.

Do you not see how the spirits, in the moments of their heedlessness of themselves, intrude upon and act boldly toward the Divine Station? They claim lordship, like Pharaoh. When this state overcomes them, they say, "I am God" or "Glory be to me!," as one of the gnostics has said. This is because he was overcome by a state. Therefore words like this have never proceeded from a messenger, a prophet, or a friend who is perfect in his knowledge, his presence, his clinging to the door of the station that belongs to him, his courtesy, and his observance of the matter within which he dwells and through which he becomes manifest.

The human being is a dam overflowing with his weakness and poverty even though, in another respect, he witnesses his root in knowledge, state, and unveiling and knows his root and the station of his vicegerency. Were this to be his state, he would claim divinity, for he possesses the property of the affair that emerges at the inblowing of the Inblower in the affair's measure. Were he to claim it, he would not be claiming something impossible.

In the measure in which he has the divine strength made manifest by the inblowing, religious prescription turns its face towards him—for he is identical with the object of the prescription—and acts are attributed to him. It is said to him, "Say, '*and Thee alone we ask for help*' [1:4] and 'There is no power and no strength save through God,' for He is your root to which you go back."

Thus the Mu'tazilites spoke the truth in the attribution of the acts to the servants in one respect, through a Shari'ite proof. So also their opponents spoke the truth in the attribution of all the acts to God in another respect, also through a Shari'ite proof, as well as a rational proof. They upheld "earning" for the servants in the servants' acts, because of His words, *To it belongs what it has earned* [2:286]. Concerning form-givers [e.g., painters], He said on the tongue of His Messenger, "Where are those who go about creating, like My creation?," so He attributed creation to the servants. He said concerning Jesus, *When you create from clay* [5:110], so He attributed creation to him, and that was his giving existence to the form of the bird in clay. Then He commanded him to blow into it, and the form to which Jesus had given form stood up as a living bird. His words, *by the leave of God* [3:49], mean the affair that God had commanded for him, that is, his creating the form of the *bird*, the *blowing*, the *healing* of *the blind and the leper*, and the bringing *of the dead to life* [3:49]. Thus He reports that Jesus did not rise up to that through himself; that was only by God's command, so that it might come to be. Bringing the dead to life was one of the signs for what he was claiming.

If human beings, in respect of their reality, did not derive from the All-Merciful Breath, it would not be correct and it could not have been affirmed that from their inblowing, a bird would come to be flying with its wings. But since the reality of human beings is of this sort, God made them fear through mentioning the attributes of those who claim greatness, their final issue, and the blackening of their faces. All this is a remedy for the spirits so that they will halt with the weakness of their nearest constitution in the manifestation of their entity.

Without doubt the human being is the son of his mother in reality, for the spirit is the son of the body's nature. She is the mother that nursed him. He was configured in her womb and nourished on her blood, [so his property is her property,][14] for he cannot do without nourishment if his frame is to subsist.

A Completion. It is this then that overcomes human beings, so let us return to the unveiler who flees to the world of the witnessed when he sees what frightens him in his unveiling. One such was our companion Aḥmad al-ʿAṣṣād al-Ḥarīrī. When he was taken, he would quickly return to his senses shaking and trembling. I used to scold him and tell him not to do that, but he would say, "I am frightened and terrified that my entity will become nonexistent because of what I see." If only the poor man knew that, were he to depart from all matter, the breath would return to its resting place, and that is his entity, for everything returns to its root. However, were this to happen, the benefit for the servant in what becomes manifest would be nullified, and the affair is not like this. This is why we said, "and that is his entity," that is, the entity of the servant. The subsistence that the Real desires [for the servant] is more appropriately gained through the *wujūd* of this frame, which is elemental in this world and natural in the last world.

He who stays fixed here—I mean when the Arriver arrives [for him]—only becomes fixed when he enters as a servant. He who does not stay fixed enters with something of lordship in his soul, so he fears that here it may disappear and he flees to the *wujūd* within which his lordliness had become manifest, so there is little benefit. But he who stays fixed enters as a receptive servant through an Aspiration inflamed for his root, so that He may give him those of His gentle favors that will accustom him. Then he comes out as a light from which illumination is sought.

He who enters into that High Side with his lordship is like him who enters in with a burning lamp, while he who enters in with his servanthood is like him who enters with a wick without flame, or with a handful of smoldering twigs. When the two of them enter like this, a breath from the All-Merciful breezes against them. The lamp is extinguished by the breeze, but the twigs flame up. The companion of the lamp comes out in darkness, but the companion of the twigs comes out in a light from which illumination can be sought. So consider what his preparedness has given him!

Everyone who flees from there fears that his lamp will be extinguished. He fears that his lordship will disappear, so he flees to the locus where it is manifest. He comes out only after his lamp has been extinguished. If he came out and it was still lit, such that the breeze had left no trace in it, then the lordship would have been rightfully his, though that would still have been through God's preserving him.

He who enters as a servant has no fear. When his wick is ignited there, he knows who ignited it and he sees in that His gratuitous favor toward him. Then he comes out as an illuminated servant. Thus God says, *Glory be to Him who carried His servant by night* [17:1], that is, as a servant. But then he came back out to his community *calling unto God by His leave, and as a light-giving lamp* [33:46], just as he had entered in as an abased servant, knowing that into which he was entering and to whom he was entering.

God may give someone success, such that he clings to his servanthood in all his states. If he knows his two roots, he should prefer the root nearer to him, the side of his mother, for he derives from his mother, without doubt. Do you not see what the Sunnah says about instructing the deceased when he reaches his grave? It is said to him, "O servant of God, and O son of God's handmaid!" Thus he is attributed to his mother, as God's curtaining over him. He is attributed to his mother since she has a greater right to him, because of the manifestation of his configuration and the *wujūd* of his entity. For his father, he is a "son of the bedding,"[15] but for his mother he is a son in reality.

So understand the true knowledge of yourself that we have given you in this chapter! *And God speaks the* ***ḥaqq****, and He guides on the path* [33:4]. (I 274.32)

Constitution

In several passages mention has been made of God's "proportioning" (*taswiya*) and "balancing" (*taᶜdīl*) the body in preparation for the inblowing of the spirit. An important Koranic source for these two terms is the verse, *O Man! What deceived you as to your generous Lord? He created you, then* ***proportioned*** *you, then* ***balanced*** *you; in whatever form He willed He mounted you* (82:6–8). Proportioning and balancing give rise to a specific bodily "constitution," a limited and defined mixture of the elements and humors. Then the constitution has an effect on the manifestation of the spirit, given that it determines the preparedness of the receptacle. In a more basic sense, each of the elements has its own constitution, which is equivalent to its own specific nature (*ṭabᶜ*). In the following Ibn al-ᶜArabī explains the difference between "constitution" (*mizāj*) and "commingling" (*imtizāj*), two terms from the same root that etymologically might be considered synonymous.

Know that the "constitution" of an element differs from the "commingling" of one sort of that element with another sort or with another element. [Commingling with another element] is like the commingling of water and earth that give new arrival to the name "clay," which is neither earth nor water.

Commingling within one element is like indigo and ceruse when the two are mingled by pulverization such that the parts become so mixed and so thoroughly commingled that they cannot be separated from each other, and another color, which belongs to neither, arrives newly from the two. From this commingling another property arrives newly in natural acts. Or, it is like fresh water and salt water when the two are commingled and another flavor arrives newly between them that is neither salt nor fresh. This is what commingling gives within one element.

In the same way, when fire warms water, inasmuch as it is cold, such that it does not leave it cold and does not bring it to its own degree in heat, then it is lukewarm, neither hot nor cold. This is a commingling that is not similar to the commingling of one sort of an element with another sort, nor is it similar to the commingling of two elements.

As for "constitution," it is that through which the entity of the element has *wujūd*. It is what is called "the nature." Thus it is said that the nature of water or the constitution of water is cold and wet; that of fire is hot and dry, of air hot and wet, and of earth cold and dry. The entities of these pillars do not become manifest save through this natural constitution, so every constitution is "natural."

Commingling is not like this. In the commingling that we mentioned within the element water, we know for certain that the parts of salt water are adjacent to the parts of fresh water, and the parts of indigo are adjacent to the parts of ceruse. This is a rational adjacency that is not perceived or differentiated by sensation. However, in the commingling, a property arrives newly through these manifest forms of commingling, as in the composition of remedies. Each drug within the remedy has its own benefit. Then, when all are mingled together, it is the same, but, inescapably, the nature in the totality has its own property. When all the drugs are placed in one vessel, and one water is poured on them all, each gives to the water's substance a strength. Hence, within the water's one substance is found the strength of each of the drugs, so long as the strengths are not mutually opposite. Although this is a "commingling," it is not like the other commingling, nor does its property reach the property of the "constitution." It is a state whose rational state stands between the constitution and the commingling. It is called neither constitution nor commingling. (II 456.3)

When the Divine Spirit marries nature, the soul is born and grows up in keeping with the constitution of the body, which is its natural receptacle. The most basic faculty of the soul in the body is "growingness" (*nabātiyya*), the fact that it is a growing thing or a "plant" (*nabāt*).

If you realize the affair and follow the root in it, you will find growingness in the partial, rationally speaking soul, because it has become manifest only from this proportioned, balanced body and in the form of its constitution. Hence the body is the soul's earth from which it grows up when God causes it to grow up by blowing of His spirit into the body. So also is every spirit that governs an elemental body. (III 138.26)

The soul is a *barzakh* between spirit and nature or body. In the following passages, the Shaykh suggests that his usage of the term *soul* always has in view its *barzakh* reality.

The human being is naturally disposed to forgetfulness. The Messenger of God said, "Adam forgot, so his offspring forgot; Adam refused, so his offspring refused." This prophetic hadith is good news from the Prophet to all the people, for God had mercy on Adam, so his offspring will be shown mercy wherever they may be. God has assigned for them a mercy that is specific to them in whatever abode He places them, for the situation is relative, but the roots exercise their properties over the branches.

This will prove to you that these human souls are the result of these elemental bodies and are born from them. They did not become manifest until after these bodies were proportioned and their humors were balanced. In relation to the souls that are blown into them from the Spirit ascribed to Him, these bodies are like the places on which the sun casts its rays. Their traces are diverse in keeping with the diversity of the receptacles. What does sunlight's brightness in dense bodies have to do with it in polished bodies? That is why souls become ranked in excellence in keeping with the ranking in excellence of the constitutions. You see a soul that quickly accepts excellent qualities and knowledges, another soul is its opposite, and others are intermediate between the two. Such is the affair, if you have understood.

God says, *When I have proportioned it,* that is, the human body, *and blown into it of My spirit* [15:29]. This is why we say that forgetfulness in the human being is a natural affair that is required by his constitution. In the same way, recollection is also a natural affair in this specific constitution, as are all the other faculties ascribed to the human being. Do you not see that the activity of these faculties is little in some individuals and much in others? (I 663.11)

In most cases, the soul is ruled forever by the property of its constitution. There are few people whose soul rules over their nature and constitution. After all, motherhood belongs to the proportioned body, and sonship belongs to the soul. The human being has been commanded to do what is beautiful toward its parents, to show them loving kindness, and to observe their commands so long as neither of them commands opposition to the command of the Real. [If either commands opposition], he should not obey, as God says, *But if the two of them strive with you to make you associate with Me that whereof you have no knowledge, do not obey them. Keep them company honorably in this world, but follow the way of him who turns to Me* [31:15]. (III 138.32)

A Mystery

Breathing at ease is like the morning.

Although the soul has an uplifted
waystation,
it is bound between the All Spirit and
nature.
That is why the constitution
has mixings,
and the soul has no release
and no expansiveness.
When to it are ascribed expansiveness and a
roaming place,

this is only when it reaches the Presence of imagination.
It fluctuates in forms
just as eyesight perceives them
in what is given by its gaze,
like the variation undergone by thoughts
in this abode,
though they are encompassed by these walls.
How can the souls have a roaming place
when the extreme limit of their deeds is at al-Ḍurāḥ?[16]
In the end they go not beyond
the Lote Tree of the Extreme Limit.
Souls remain in respect of their deeds,
not in respect of their hopes
until the day of the Uprising—
then they will know what was breathed into their minds
as a knowledge of witnessing [*shuhūd*] and *wujūd*,
for there the affair is witnessed.
What faith fell upon here
will be gained there through viewing eye-to-eye.
They will find the difference between the two affairs,
for morning is not hidden from the Possessor of the Two Eyes,
who distinguishes the in-between
from the in-between.

But viewing eye-to-eye has a subtle meaning—
this is why Moses asked to view eye-to-eye. (IV 384.27)

Ibn al-ʿArabī stresses the intermediate status of the constitution in an answer he gave to Ibn Sawdakīn, who asked him, "When the traces of love appear in the servant, why does he find its intangible forms in *wujūd* in an unqualified manner?" In other words, when people love God, why does their experience of love permeate their whole being? The Shaykh replied,

When you see that love or something else is unqualified, then you should know that it is a divine affair, because the Real's relation with all things is equal. In contrast, when you see specification, then you should know that it is a property that pertains to accidents and constitution.

Know also that nature is unqualified, because it seeks an undesignated marriage act, undesignated food, and undesignated clothing. When it becomes specified and designated, this is not the property of unqualified nature. On the contrary, it is the property of the constitution that is born [of nature]. In respect of this mingled affair, God has commanded His servant to repent and ask forgiveness.

Look at how the constitution is born from the Universal Spirit and the Universal Body. The Spirit is the unqualified world of the divine command, while the body is the world of unqualified nature pertaining to the world of creation. Between them, they give rise to the constitution, and it is the caprice of the soul. This constitution demands in relation to itself something that is mingled. It does not come from the world of the divine command in an unqualified sense, nor from the world of unqualified nature, whose abiding is sought in an unqualified sense and concerning which it is said that it gives nature its *ḥaqq*. Rather, it has a mingled birth. Hence the great ones repent of the constitution, while others repent of their great sins. (*Wasāʾil* 2–3)

The constitution displays its traces in the soul, determining whether it becomes manifest in keeping with the luminous attributes of its spiritual father or the dark qualities of its natural mother. The general principle at work here is that the receptacle exercises influence on what it contains. In Junayd's words, "The water takes on the color of its cup." In a section of *Kitāb al-ʿAbādila* on the wisdom of ʿAbd Allāh ibn Ibrāhīm ibn ʿAbd al-Mubdiʿ, the Shaykh identifies the constitution with the preparedness (*istiʿdād*) and offers the analogy of sunlight and colored glass. Then he explains the "mark" (*ʿalāma*) whereby people will recognize God on the day of resurrection, according to the hadith of God's self-transmutation.

He says: The soul is inblown, so it is the breath of a pure spirit that is ascribed to Him. So from whence does infirmity overtake it? This affair comes only from the constitution, which is called the "preparedness." Reception accords with the preparedness.

He says: The light of the sun has one attribute. It strikes colored glass and is reflected, so within it become manifest to the eye's view the colors of the glass, though the light in its entity does not change. Understand this likeness, for it is majestic! So also will be the transmutation in the mark on the day of resurrection. The glass is the hearts, the colors are the beliefs, and the Real does not change, though you see Him as such. (*ʿAbādila* 199)

A Mystery
It is impossible for the state to be general.

He says: Constitutions are diverse, and souls follow the constitutions. The souls are the receptacles for the Arrivers, and the Arrivers arrive with the states. It is impossible for one state to be general. Rather, each Arriver has a state specific to it. Therefore the same thing that makes one person drunk makes another sober—neither drunkenness nor sobriety is general.

He says: The state is general in respect of the generalness of the name. These are states that become distinct through their traces in the souls, and they are perceived through reason and sensation.

He says: The divine wrath and good-pleasure are among the states. There is no one who is not qualified by the state—whether he is the object of wrath or of good-pleasure. It is said concerning the newly arrived thing that it enters under the ruling property of the state, but courtesy is necessary toward that Side.

He says: The tongue of the state sends down His words, *The word is not changed with Me*, and the tongue of the reality His words, *and I do not wrong My servants* [50:29]. (IV 416.17)

Since the constitution determines receptivity, it acts upon the soul, but this does not prevent the soul from acting upon it. Thus soul and constitution leave traces in each other. This reciprocity leads Ibn al-ʿArabī to illustrate how traces left by the higher in the lower depend upon the lower's knowledge of the higher. Only ignorance can allow us to remain unmoved by God's self-disclosure in our souls. Knowledge is the receptivity that permits the self-disclosure to leave its trace.

God proportioned the human configuration—or rather, all the natural and elemental bodies of the cosmos that He configured—and He balanced it, all according to an order that is required by wisdom for each body. He balanced and readied each for the reception of what He desired to bestow upon it in His blowing of the Divine Spirit into it. Then *He blew into him of His spirit* [32:9]. At that, there became manifest within him a soul governing the frame. It became manifest through the form of the frame's constitution, so the souls became ranked in excellence, just as the constitutions are ranked in excellence.

In the same way, sunlight strikes diverse colors in glass and gives lights that are diverse in color, whether red, yellow, blue, or something else, in keeping with the color of the glass in the view of the eye. The diversity that arrives newly in the light derives only from the locus. No part of the light becomes designated in itself as different from other parts save through the locus. Hence the locus is identical with the light, and the locus is other than it.

So also are the souls that govern the natural and elemental frames. The souls leave traces in the frames by the property of the governance, but the frames receive the governance from these souls within themselves only in the measure of their preparedness. The frames leave traces in the souls in keeping with their constitutions at the root of their manifestation when they became entified. Among the souls are the clever and the dull, in keeping with the frame's constitution. The situation between the soul and the frame is marvelous, for each leaves traces in the one who leaves traces within it.

God took away from the eyesight of most of mankind and jinn the perception of the governing, rationally speaking souls that belong to what is named "inanimate thing, plant, and animal." But He unveiled this for some people. The traditional proof for what we say is the words of God, *There are some of them*, that is, stones, *that fall down in fear of God* [2:74]. Thus He described them by fear. But people like us have no need for reports concerning this, for God has unveiled it for us in entity and given us to hear their glorification and their rational speech. Praise belongs to God for that!

So also is the crumbling of the mountain at the self-disclosure of the Lord to it. Were it not for the magnificence [sensed] in the mountain's self from its Lord, it would not have crumbled to dust at His self-disclosure to it. After all, essences do not leave traces in their likes. What leaves traces in things is only the measure and waystation of those essences in the soul of the one that receives the trace. His knowledge of the measure of the one that discloses itself leaves the trace in him. What manifests itself to him does not leave the trace. For example, when we see that a king takes on the form of the commoners and walks among the people in the market such that they do not recognize that he is the king, he has no weight in their souls. However, when someone who recognizes the king in that state encounters him, the king's magnificence and measure come to abide in the person's soul. Hence his knowledge of the king leaves a trace in him, so he honors him, shows courtesy, and prostrates himself before him.

When the people see this from this person and when they know this knower's nearness to the king and that his waystation does not allow him to manifest an act like this save with the king, they come to know that he is the king. Hence eyesights become fixed upon him and voices are lowered, and they treat him with great reverence and they attempt to see him and honor him. Does anything leave this trace in them save the knowledge that has come to abide in them? They do not honor him because of his form, for they were already witnessing his form, but they did not know that he was the king. The fact that he is a king is not the same as his form. Rather, it is a relational level given to him by his ruling control over the world that owes allegiance to him.

In *Dalāʾil al-nubuwwa,* Abū Nuʿaym al-Ḥāfiẓ has brought a report concerning one of the Prophet's night journeys. He said that one night Gabriel came to him along with a tree, within which were two bird nests. God's Messenger sat in one nest and Gabriel sat in the other. Then the tree rose up with them until it reached the heaven, and a cushion of pearls and rubies came down. Muhammad did not know what it was, so it left no trace in him. As for Gabriel, as soon as he saw it, he swooned. So the Prophet said, "So I came to know his excellence over me in knowledge." For Gabriel knew what he saw, and his knowledge of what he saw left in him the trace of swooning. But God's Messenger did not know that, so he saw no trace in himself from it.

Hence nothing leaves any traces in things save that which comes to abide through them, and that is only knowledge. (III 554.6)

Each constitution that God proportions and balances is unique, so each has a unique preparedness to receive the light of the spirit, and thereby it determines the degree of the receptacle's understanding. Since constitutions are diverse, understandings are diverse, and this leads to the diversity of doctrines and creeds both within a given religion and among different religions and ideologies. Ibn al-ʿArabī suggests how constitutions give rise to diversity of beliefs while discussing the five properties of the name Lord in his chapter on the divine names. One of these properties is the Lord's authority over those who dispute concerning God.

As for the authority of this Presence over the folk of contention concerning the Real, this is as follows: Doctrines about God are greatly diverse because of one faculty—reflection—in many individuals of diverse constitutions and mixings. There is no one to draw out the faculties save their natural constitution.

Each individual's share of nature is given to him by the constitution that he has. When nature's strength is poured into it, it gains a preparedness to receive the blowing of the spirit into it. Then there becomes manifest from the inblowing and the proportioning of the natural body a luminous, spiritual form that is a commingling of light and darkness. The form's darkness is a shadow, and its light is a radiance. Its shadow is what the "Lord" draws out, so it is lordly. *Do you not see how your Lord draws out the shadow?* [25:45]. Its light is a radiance, for the illumination of the natural body occurs only through the light of the sun, and God has mentioned that *He has made the sun a radiance and* He has made *the moon a light* [10:5]. That is why we have made its light a "radiance," because of the specific face that God has in every existent thing, or the fact of the effusion of the radiance upon the mirror of the proportioned body. Then, the sun's radiance becomes manifest in the reflection, as it becomes manifest from the moon. This is why we have named the partial spirit a "light," for God has made the moon a "light." It is a light through [God's] making [it so], just as the sun is a radiance through making. But in essence the sun is a light, and in essence the moon is an obliteration. So annihilation belongs to the moon and subsistence to the sun.

To the moon belongs annihilation
  in every respect
    and to the sun irradiation
      and subsistence.
The face that is beautiful
  with every loveliness
    grants us cheerfulness
      and encounter.

Its beauty protects us
from every eye
just as bark
protects a tree.
We came to dwell in a heaven
upon a *wujūd*
to whom belongs the Encompassing
Throne and the Cloud.
To Him belong coming
and going in us,
to Him belong splendor's property
and brilliance.
When He draws close,
His sitting place is spacious,
and if He takes us high,
ours is the laudation.
He has the property
of desire in my *wujūd*—
He is the Chooser,
He does what He wills [3:40].

Then the spiritual and sensory faculties follow the creation of this partial spirit that is inblown by way of *tawḥīd,* for He says, *I blew* [15:29]. As for the spirit of Jesus, it is inblown through bringing together and manyness, for within him are the faculties of all the names and the spirits. After all, God says, *We blew* [66:12], using the plural form *We,* for it was Gabriel as *a well-proportioned mortal* [19:17] who bestowed Jesus upon Mary, so he disclosed himself in the form of a perfect human being, who blew, and this was the inblowing of the Real. In the same way, "God says on the tongue of His servant, 'God hears him who praises Him.'"

When these faculties followed the spirit, among them was the reflective faculty, which was given to the human being so that through it he might consider the signs *upon the horizons and in* himself, *until it is clear* to him through this *that He is the Real* [41:53], but constitutions are diverse. Inescapably reception is diverse, so inescapably, there must be ranking in degrees of excellence in reflection. Inescapably, in every rational faculty consideration gives something different from what it gives in every other rational faculty, so it may become distinct in one affair, while it shares with others in another thing. This is the occasion of the diversity of doctrines.

Then the Lord judges among the companions of these doctrines through what the revealed Shariah has brought. Rational faculties remain halted in their proofs, but the diversity of their considerations concerning the Shari'ite material after they had first considered it with their rational considerations will be taken away, though this belongs specifically to the faithful among the men and the women. Those among the contentious who halt in this at the Lord's ruling are the faithful, and they possess the eye of understanding. They are diverse along with agreement. Their diversity is in what they understand from what the Lord has ruled concerning the *ḥaqq.* This is the *ḥaqq* that the Shariah has set up for the servants. We name Him with that by which He names Himself and we describe Him with that by which He describes His Essence. We do not add to what has been conveyed to us and we do not devise a name for Him from ourselves.

As for the contention of those without faith concerning the diversity of their beliefs, the Lawgiver is one of them inasmuch as, concerning the *ḥaqq,* he has tended in a direction in which they have not tended, since they do not have faith. So, what judges between the two—I mean between the Shariah and the rational thinkers without faith—is only God through the forms of self-disclosure. Through this they will be separated, but in the last abode, not here, for in the last abode the property of compulsion will become manifest, so no contentious person whatsoever will remain there, and *the kingdom* there will be *God's, the One, the All-Subjugating* [40.16]. All claims will disappear from their owners, and the faithful will remain as the masters of the halting place in relation to everyone at the halting place. (IV 198.19)

Diverse constitutions lead people not only to diverse understandings, but also to diverse perceptions with their sense organs. The Shaykh provides a concrete example in the chapter on fasting. He sets out to explain the meaning of a sound hadith: "By Him whose hand holds Muhammad's soul, on the day of resurrection the bad breath of the mouth of the fasting person will be sweeter to God than musk's fragrance is to you." What we find disgusting, God finds sweet-smelling. To suggest some of the implications of this, he first turns to his own experience. "Incident" is a technical term that is employed for certain types of visions.

I had an Incident in something of this sort. I was staying with Mūsā ibn Muḥammad al-Qabbāb in the minaret in the sacred precinct of Mecca, by the gate of Ḥazawwara, where he used to give the call to prayer.[17] He had a food whose odor tormented everyone who smelled it. I had heard the prophetic report, "The angels are tormented by everything that torments the children of Adam," and the Prophet forbade anyone from going near mosques with the odor of garlic, onions, and leeks. So I had decided and was determined to say to that man that he remove the food from the mosque for the sake of the angels.

Then I saw the Real in a dream. He said to me, "Do not speak to him about the food, for its odor with Us is not like its odor with you." Next morning, he came, as was his habit, to visit me. I reported to him what had happened. He wept and prostrated himself to God in gratitude. Then he said to me, "Nevertheless, my master, courtesy toward the Shariah is to be preferred!" So he took the food from the mosque—God have mercy on him!

Healthy natural constitutions—whether human or angelic—shun disliked and loathsome odors, because of the torment they feel from the lack of correspondence. For the face of the Real in loathsome odors is perceived by no one but God Himself and by the animal who has within it the constitution to accept it, or the human being who has the constitution of that animal—but not by any angel. That is why the Prophet said [in the hadith] "to God," for the fasting person himself, in respect of his being a human being with a healthy constitution, dislikes the bad breath of fasting in himself and others.

Does it ever happen that any creature with a healthy constitution realizes his Lord at some moment, or in some locus of witnessing, and perceives loathsome odors as pleasant in an absolute sense? I have not heard anything like that. I say "in an absolute sense" because some constitutions are tormented by the smell of musk and rose, especially people with a hot constitution. When someone with such a constitution is tormented by something, it is not pleasant for him. That is why we said, "in an absolute sense," since, for the most part, constitutions find musk, rose, and suchlike pleasant. Anyone tormented by these pleasant fragrances has a strange, that is, unusual, constitution.

I do not know whether or not God has given anyone the perception of the equality of odors such that for him, there is no loathsome smell. I have not tasted this from myself, nor has it been transmitted to me that anyone has perceived it. On the contrary, what is transmitted from the perfect human beings and the angels is that they are tormented by loathsome odors. No one but the Real perceives them only as pleasant. This is what has been transmitted. Nor do I know what the situation of animals other than the human being is in that, for the Real has never given me to abide in the form of an animal other than the human being, though He has given me to abide, at times, in the forms of the angels. And God knows best. (I 603.14)

Although the constitution exercises a pervasive influence on the soul, in the last analysis everything goes back to God. From this point of view, God alone appoints a specific spirit to a specific constitution, but then the constitution allows the spirit to manifest itself in certain ways. The spirit is like a carpenter who is given certain tools and not others. The tools he has in hand have an important determining effect on the finished product.

You should consider and reflect upon your own essence in order to recognize who brought you into existence. God turned you over to you in His words, *And in yourselves—what, do you not see?* [51:21], and in the words of His messenger, "He who knows himself knows his Lord." He turned you over to you through detailed explanation, but He hid you from you with a summary exposition, so that you would consider and seek for proofs.

By way of detailed explanation He says, *We created the human being from an extraction of clay*—meaning here Adam—*then We set him, a sperm-drop, in a secure resting place* [23:12–13], referring to the configuration of the children in the wombs, the falling places of the sperm-drops, *the dropping places of the stars* [56:75]. He intimates this with "a secure resting place." *Then We created of the sperm-drop a clot, then We created of the clot a tissue, then We created of the tissue bones, then We draped the bones with flesh* [23:14]. Thus the body was completed according to the detailed exposition, for the flesh includes veins and nerves.

In each stage there is a sign of Him
signifying that I am poor.

Then He provided a summary exposition of the creation of the rationally speaking soul, through which human beings are human, in the verse, *Then We configured him as another creature* [23:14]. Thereby the Real lets you know that the constitution leaves no trace in your subtlety. Although this is not a plain text, it is obvious. Even clearer is His words, *Then He proportioned you, then balanced you* [82:7]. This is the constant fluctuation in the stages that He mentioned in the detailed explanation. Then He says, *in whatever form He willed He mounted you* [82:8]. He connects this to the will. Thus it is obvious that if the constitution demanded a specific, designated spirit, He would not have said *in whatever form He willed.* "Whatever" is an indefinite pronoun, like "whichever," for it is applied to everything.

Thus He clarified for you that the constitution does not demand a form in its entity. However, once the form is there, it has need of this constitution and refers back to it, for the constitution is such through the faculties within it, without which the form cannot govern it. Through its faculties, the constitution belongs to the form, just as, for example, tools belong to the carpenter or builder. When the tools are readied and properly fashioned and when they are finished, they demand through their essence and state an artisan who will employ them in that for which they were made. The tools do not designate Zayd, ʿAmr, Khālid, or anyone else in his entity.

When an artisan comes, whoever he may be, the tool gives him an ability from itself—an essential giving of ability in which it is not qualified by choice. Through the tool the artisan works at his artisanry in keeping with that for which the tool was readied. Among the tools, some are perfected, and they are the *well created,* that is, the complete in creation; but some are imperfect, and they are the *not well created* [22:5]. The worker falls short in his work in the measure in which the tool falls short in excellence. This is in order that it be known that essential perfection belongs only to God.

Thus God clarified for you the level of your body and your spirit in order that you consider and reflect. Then you will take heed of the fact that God did not create you aimlessly, even if you are granted a long respite. (I 331.26)

From Chapter 558: The Presence of All-Embracingness

Just as the body leaves traces in the soul, so also the preparednesses of the fixed entities leave traces in *wujūd.* The names that are applied to the soul go back to the traces left within it by the bodily constitution. In the same way, the names that are applied to God go back to the preparedness of the entities. The Shaykh explains this in discussing the divine name All-Embracing (*wāsiʿ*).

The All-Embracing is only He
  whose creation embraces all.
But when He leaves us alone,
  His creatures contend with the Real.
He shines brightly through him
  whose horizon appears from the sun's
    splendor,
so He is with us through the sun's light
  and in that I am His *ḥaqq.*

The companion of this Presence is called "the Servant of the All-Embracing."

The angels say, *Our Lord, Thou embracest everything in mercy and knowledge* [40:7]. Thus they gave priority to mercy over knowledge, because "He loved to be known." The lover seeks mercy for himself, so the station of the divine Lover was the first object of mercy. He created creation, which is the Breath of the All-Merciful, and He said, *My mercy embraces everything* [7:156]. Thus He included every object of mercy within *every,* and there is nothing but an object of mercy. He whose knowledge of the thing is through tasting, such that it is his state, knows what is within it and the ruling property that it requires.

God's spokesman said, "He who has faith will not become perfect until he loves for his brother what he loves for himself." We have come to know that God possesses perfection, that He is the Faithful, and that the cosmos is in His form. Hence "brotherhood" is affirmed through the form and the faith, for there is nothing that does not profess Him, have faith in Him, and acknowledge His *wujūd,* for *There is nothing that does not glorify Him in praise* [17:44]. There is nothing that His mercy does not embrace, just as His glorification and His praise embrace everything, so He is the All-Embracing for everything.

Because of this all-embracingness, He repeats nothing in *wujūd,* for the possible things have no end. They are likenesses that come into existence in this world and the last world perpetually, and states that become manifest.

His Footstool, which is His knowledge, *embraces the heavens and the earth* [2:255], and His mercy embraces both His knowledge and the heavens and the earth. And there is nothing but a heaven and an earth, for there is nothing but a higher, a lower, and what is between the two. *Glorify the name of the Lord, the Highest!* [87:1], so there is none higher than He; "If you let down a rope, it will fall upon God," so there is none lower than He.

He descends to the closest highness, which is the first heaven from our direction, for it is the "closest" heaven, that is, the nearest to us. He does not descend to chastise and make wretched. On the contrary, He says, "Is there any caller so that I may respond to him? Is there any asker so that I may give to him?" Nothing is empty of asking good for its own self. "Is there any turner so that I may turn toward him?" There is nothing that does not turn back to Him through its own constraint when the occasions are cut off from it. "Is there anyone seeking forgiveness so that I may forgive him?" There is nothing that does not seek forgiveness in most of its moments from Him who is a God. He did not say that He descends to chastise His servants for whom He descended. When someone has this description and He chastises, then His chastisement is a mercy and a purification for its object, like the chastisement of the remedy for the infirm person. The physician chastises him to have mercy on him, not to take revenge.

Then there is the all-embracingness of the gift, for He gives *wujūd* first, which is pure good. Then He never ceases giving what is rightfully demanded by the existent thing—that within which is its abiding and its wholesomeness. Whatever it might be, it is a wholesomeness in its case. This is why the gnostic through Him, the spokesman for Him, the word of the Presence, the tongue of the divine station, His Messenger—God bless him and give him peace—ascribed the good to Him. He said, "The good, all of it, is in Thy hands." And he negated that evil be ascribed to Him, for he said, "but the evil does not go back to Thee."

We have clarified that there is no giver but God. Hence there is nothing but good, whether it yields happiness or hurt. Happiness is the sought object, but it may not come until after hurt has been inflicted because of what is required by the composition's constitution and by the locus's reception of the accidental qualities that occur in *wujūd*. But every accidental quality disappears.

This is why He is named Giver and Withholder, Harmer and Benefiter. His giving is all benefit, but sometimes the locus finds pain because of certain gifts, so he does not perceive the pleasure of the gift. He feels harm through the gift and does not know the divine benefit within it, so he names Him "Harmer" because of the gift. He does not know that this derives from the constitution of the receptacle, not the gift. Do you not see how things that are beneficial to certain constitutions harm other constitutions?

God says concerning honey that it is *a healing for the people* [16:69]. A man came to the messenger of God and said to him, "My brother's belly has become loose."

The Messenger said, "Give him some honey to drink." So he gave him some honey to drink and the looseness increased. He returned and reported that. The Prophet said, "Give him some honey to drink." Again the looseness increased. But the man did not know what the Messenger of God knew, which was that there were harmful excesses in the locus that could not be expelled without drinking honey. Whenever these disappeared, they would be followed by wellbeing and healing.

When the man returned to him, He said, "O Messenger of God, I gave him some honey to drink, but his looseness increased."

He replied, "God has spoken the truth and your brother's belly has lied. Give him some honey to drink for the third time." So when he gave it to him, he recovered, for he had completed the expulsion of the harmful excesses.

Another example is the person whose taste organ has been overcome by yellow bile, so he finds that honey is bitter and says, "The honey is bitter." Thus the locus has lied by ascribing bitterness to the honey, for it is ignorant that the yellow bile is in charge of the taste organ, so it perceives bitterness. It is truthful in tasting and finding, but it lies in the ascription. Thus the receptacles always possess the ruling property, for nothing comes from God except sheer good.

Part of the all-embracingness of mercy is that it embraces harm, so there is no escape from its property in the object of harm. Within mercy, harm is not harm but rather an affair of good. The proof is that when the affair itself arises in a constitution that conforms to it, the person takes pleasure in it and enjoys it. But it is it, nothing else.

The things are ascribed to God only in respect of the fact that they are entities that are existent from Him. The property of pleasure or anything else in the things goes back only to the receptacle.

If people knew the relation of wrath to God, they would know that mercy embraces all. After all, anyone who has the power to remove pain from himself will not leave it there.

The states of the creatures and the homesteads in relation to the Real stand in the station of the constitution in relation to the living thing. Thus it is said concerning the Real that He is "wrathful" when the servant makes Him wrathful, that He is "well-pleased" when the servant pleases Him. The state of the servant and the homestead pleases the Real and makes Him wrathful. This is like the constitution of the living thing. It takes pleasure in something through which another constitution suffers pain. The living thing accords with the constitution, just as the Real accords with the state and the homesteads.

Do you not see what He says when He descends to the closest heaven? For this is a descent of mercy required by the homestead. When the day of resurrection comes, the homesteads will require that He come for differentiation and decision among His servants, for this is a homestead that brings together the wrongdoer and the wronged and a homestead of ruling properties and quarrels. The ruling property in the Real belongs to the homestead and the states, and the ruling property in suffering pain and experiencing enjoyment and pleasure belongs to the constitution.

Surely thy Lord is all-embracing in forgiveness [53:32], that is, "all-embracing in curtaining," for there is nothing that is not curtained through His *wujūd,* which is the all-inclusive curtain. Were the thing not curtained, it would not say about God, "He," nor would it say, "Thou." After all, there is but One Entity, so how can there be an addressee [a second person] and someone absent [a third person]? Thus we say that *wujūd* is the all-inclusive curtain. Then there is another curtain through the agreeable and the disagreeable. So He is *all-embracing in forgiveness,* and this forgiveness is the Presence of letting down the curtains, concerning which we have already spoken in this chapter.[18]

Then [in the same verse] God says, *He knows best who is godwary.* Curtaining is a protective wariness, and forgiveness is a curtaining. The servant is wary through curtaining himself against the pain of cold and heat when he knows that his constitution is receptive toward the pain of heat and cold. Heat and cold have come only as a means toward the wholesomeness of the world, so that plants—which are the provision of the world—may be nourished. He makes plants appear so that benefit may be taken from them.

Thus the body of the living thing has a preparedness through which it may suffer harm. It says, "I am tormented by heat and cold." But when it thinks over what is intended by the two in keeping with what is given by the seasons, then he knows that they have come only for his benefit. He suffers harm from that which benefits him. Heedlessness and ignorance are the occasion of all this. *And God speaks the ḥaqq, and He guides on the path* [33:4]. (IV 256.21)

10. *The Imaginal* Barzakh

The terms *spirit* and *body* are employed to designate two extremes of cosmic manifestation—subtle and dense, light and dark, high and low. They are relative, which is to say that nothing is absolutely spiritual or absolutely bodily. What is spiritual from one point of view is bodily from another. Spirits are subtle and high in relation to everything below them, but they are dense and low in relation to God. The earth is low in relation to heaven, but high in relation to non-existence.

When looking at the cosmos, it is frequently necessary to step out of a dualistic framework and focus on the relativities and the shifting nature of relations. Ibn al-ʿArabī often employs the term *imagination* in this context. The term designates intermediate reality, everything that shares the qualities of two sides, anything that needs to be defined in terms of other things. When imagination is understood in this broad sense, nothing in the cosmos escapes its ruling property. It is synonymous with *barzakh* or isthmus, a term that is applied to any intermediary reality. As already mentioned, the expression *Unbounded Imagination* refers to the cosmos as an intermediate realm between *wujūd* and nonexistence, and the term *Highest Barzakh* has the same sense. However, the Shaykh more commonly employs the terms *imagination* and *barzakh* to refer to the domain that is intermediate between spirits and bodies, though he does not forget that spirits and bodies themselves belong to the realm of Unbounded Imagination, so they also can never escape the characteristic of intermediacy.

Imagination

Imagination in the microcosm pertains to the domain of the "soul" considered as that which brings spirit and body together. Hence, "The form of imagination is between intellect and sensation, and imagination has no locus save the soul" (IV 393.10). The word also denotes the specific faculty of the soul which embodies meanings by thinking and understanding in appropriate concepts and images and which spiritualizes the bodily and sensory realm by bringing images of concrete, external realities into the soul by way of the senses. Among the adjectives the Shaykh employs to refer to the corporeous bodies that become manifest through imagination are "imaginal" (*khayālī, mithālī*) or "imaginalized" (*mukhayyal, mumaththal*). Imagination's outstanding characteristic remains its intermediacy, the fact that it combines the attributes of the two sides, such as spiritual and bodily, absent and witnessed, intelligible and sensory, subtle and dense.

> Part of the reality of imagination is that it embodies and gives form to that which is not a body or a form, for imagination perceives only in this manner. Hence it is a sensation that is nonmanifest and bound between the intelligible and the sensory. (III 377.11)

> The world of imagination is the embodied lights that signify what is beyond them, for imagination brings intelligible meanings down into sensory molds, like knowledge in the form of milk, the Koran in the form of a cord, and religion in the form of a fetter. (*Rāzī* 3)

Through imagination, spirits establish contact with bodies. Or rather, imagination is the spirit's corporeous embodiment on the nonmanifest side of the corporeal body. No spirit can govern a body without the intermediary of imagination. The "high bodies" in the following are the luminous, imaginal, or corporeous things, just as the "low bodies" are the corporeal things.

> This waystation contains knowledge of the spirits that govern the high and low bodies and what their ruling property is in the luminous bodies; and that their property in them is specifically their taking shape in forms. In the same way, their property in the animal, human bodies is their taking shape in the imaginal faculty, along with certain other properties. For luminous bodies have no imagination. Or rather, they are identical with imagination. The forms are the fluctuations that derive from the spirits that govern them. This is a noble knowledge.
>
> Just as human imagination is not empty of form, so also the angel's essence is not empty of form. This is a noble knowledge that contains many mysteries.
>
> In the hand of these governing spirits is the designation of the affairs that the Real desires through all these bodies. For the human being knows all the Real's affairs in him in respect of his governing spirit, but he does not know that he knows. He is like the neglectful, forgetful person. The states, stations, and waystations remind him. (III 22.6)

If the whole cosmos is Unbounded Imagination, the bound imagination that is found between the spiritual and corporeal domains can be divided into two basic sorts: contiguous (*muttaṣil*) and discontiguous (*munfaṣil*). The existence of the first depends on the soul's perception, but the second is relatively independent of the soul. Most dreams pertain to contiguous imagination, but the visionary realities seen by prophets dwell in discontiguous imagination. However, as always with imagination, the lines are not clearly drawn, and Ibn al-ʿArabī seldom tells us which of the two sorts of imagination he has in view, nor does he provide clear criteria for differentiating between them.

The knowledge of imagination and of its contiguous and discontiguous worlds is a magnificent pillar among the pillars of true knowledge. It is the knowledge of the *barzakh* and the knowledge of the world of corporeous bodies within which spiritual things become manifest. It is the knowledge of the Market of the Garden and the knowledge of the divine self-disclosure at the resurrection in the forms of change. It is the knowledge of the manifestation of meanings that are not self-abiding as embodied, like death in the form of a ram. It is the knowledge of what people see in dreams and of the homestead in which creatures dwell after death and before the Uprising. It is the knowledge of forms such as those that are seen in polished bodies, like mirrors. After the knowledge of the divine names and of self-disclosure and its all-pervadingness, no pillar of knowledge is more complete, for it is the centerpiece of the necklace—the senses ascend to it and meanings descend to it, but it never leaves its homestead. *To it are collected the fruits of everything* [28:57].

Imagination owns the elixir that you place upon a meaning such that it embodies it in whatever form it desires. There is no halt to the penetration of its free activity and ruling property. The shariahs assist it and the natures affirm it. It is witnessed as possessing complete free acting. It brings meanings into conjunction with bodies and bewilders demonstrations and rational faculties. (II 309.13)

Ibn al-ᶜArabī discusses imagination allusively but relatively comprehensively in two of the mysteries of Chapter 559. He says concerning the first that it summarizes Chapter 8, which is called "On the true knowledge of the earth that was created from the leftover ferment of Adam's clay and is named 'the earth of the reality.'" This "earth of reality," about which more will be said shortly, is precisely the world of imagination.

A MYSTERY
The Manifestation of Corporeous Bodies in the Habitual Way

The spirit becomes corporealized to
eyesight through imagination,
so halt not with it, for the affair is a
misguidance.
The proof of this stood up for me through
witnessing
when Gabriel, the spirit of revelation,
descended.

The *barzakh* is that which is the counterpart
of the two sides through its essence,
clarifying, for the Possessor of Two Eyes,
those of His wondrous signs
that signify His strength,
and demonstrate the proofs of His
generosity and chivalry.
It is the fluctuating and the changing,
undergoing transmutation in every form.
The great rely upon it
while the small remain ignorant of it.
It penetrates into varieties of wisdom
and its foot is firmly rooted in "how" and
"how many."
It is quick in transmutation,
and the gnostics know its state.
In its hand are the keys to affairs,
and within it are the supports of delusion.
To it belongs the eminent divine lineage
and the lofty engendered dignity.
It becomes subtle in its density
and dense in its subtlety.
Reason invalidates it through its
demonstrations
and the Shariah justifies it through the
strength of its ruling authority.
It exercises its ruling property in every
existent thing,
and the soundness of its property is proved
by witnessing.
Both he who is ignorant of its measure and
the knower recognize it,
and no ruling thing has the power to reject
its ruling property. (IV 328.26)

A MYSTERY
The Towering Station in the Barzakh*s*

The *barzakh* is between-between,
a station between this and that,
not one of them, but the totality of the two.
It has the towering exaltation,
the lofty splendor,
and the deep-rooted station.
Knowledge of the *barzakh*s in terms of the
resurrection pertains to the Ramparts
and in terms of the names to becoming
qualified by them,
so it has come to possess the station of
equitable balance,

for it is not identical with the name, nor with the Named.
Its it-ness is unknown save to those who solve the riddle,
and equal concerning it may be the seeing and the blind.
It is the shadow between the lights and the darknesses,
the separating limit between *wujūd* and nonexistence,
and at it the near path comes to an end.
It is the limit of halting between the two stations for him who understands.
Of the times, to it belongs the clinging state [i.e., the present moment],
for it is the perpetual *wujūd*.
The *barzakh* brings together the two sides
and is the courtyard between the two knowledges.
To it belongs what lies between the center point and the circumference.
It is neither compound nor noncompound.
Its share of the rulings [of the Shariah] is the indifferent,
so it possesses choice and free roaming.
It does not become bound by what is forbidden, incumbent,
reprehensible, or recommended by any of the legal schools. (IV 337.29)

Cosmically, the cosmos is a *barzakh* between *wujūd* and nonexistence. In the same way, the cosmos that is manifest to us in the present moment is the *barzakh* between the past and the future. On the divine scale, the past is the infinite *wujūd* of God from which the cosmos is born at every moment, so it is known as "eternity without beginning" (*azal*). For the same reason, the future is the infinite *wujūd* of God that will never cease disclosing itself, so it is "eternity without end" (*abad*). Ibn al-ᶜArabī speaks of the *barzakh* in these terms in a passage where he is discussing "manifestation and hiddenness," or the fact that God is manifest through self-disclosure when He is hidden, but He is hidden through the forms that appear when He is manifest. Thus, "He becomes manifest without any doubt in that He is He, but He is hidden through the binding that He undergoes in His manifestation" (III 107.27), so He is not recognized as He.

Between each two homesteads of manifestation and hiddenness occurs a *barzakhī* self-disclosure in His words, *The All-Merciful sat upon the Throne* [20:5]. Thereby the *barzakh* may preserve the *wujūd* of the two sides, and neither side may see the ruling property of the other side, while the *barzakh* has the ruling property in both sides. It lightens the dense and densifies the light. In each homestead it has a property through which it does not become manifest in any other homestead. The properties of the world of this abode will flow in accordance with the *barzakh*, until God, the Inheritor, *inherits* the earth *and all that are upon it* [19:40].

In keeping with the reality of these homesteads, the cosmos becomes manifest in this world in the form of manifestation, which is what sensation perceives, and in the form of curtaining, which is what sensation does not perceive, including the meanings and everything curtained from the eyesights, such as angels and jinn. God says, *No! I swear by what you see*, which is what becomes manifest to us, *and by what you do not see* [69:38–39], which is what is hidden from us.

The cosmos is a *barzakh* between eternity without beginning and eternity without end. Through it the one becomes differentiated from the other. If not for it, no property would become manifest for either and the affair would be one and would not become distinct. This is like the [present] state between the past and the future. If not for the state, the past nonexistence would not become distinct from the future nonexistence. This is the property of the *barzakh*, and it never ceases in the cosmos in perpetuity. It is the tie between the two premises. If not for it, no sound knowledge would become manifest. (III 108.10)

One of Ibn al-ᶜArabī's more detailed summaries of what he understands by the *barzakh* and its imaginal properties is found in Chapter 382, which is dedicating to elucidating some of the knowledge that is bestowed by Surah 2 of the Koran.

Know that this waystation is the waystation of the true *barzakh*. After all, people employ the term broadly, but it is not as they suppose. It is only as God has instructed us in His Book with His words concerning *the two seas [that meet together], between them a* ***barzakh*** *they do not overpass* [55:19]. So the reality of the *barzakh* is that within it there be no *barzakh*. It is that which meets what is between the two by its very essence. If it were to meet one of the two with a face that is other than the face with which it meets the other, then there would have to be within itself, between its two faces, a *barzakh* that differentiates between the two faces so that the two do not meet together. If there is no such *barzakh*, then the face with which it meets one of the two affairs between which it stands is identical with the face with which it meets the other. This is the true *barzakh*. It is, through its own essence, identical with everything that it meets. Hence the separation between the things and the separating factor become manifest as one in entity. Once you come to know this, you have come to know what the *barzakh* is.

Its likeness is the whiteness of every white thing. Whiteness is in every white thing through its very essence. It is not in one white thing through one of its faces, and in another through another face. On the contrary, through its own entity it is in every white thing. The two white things may be distinct from each other, but whiteness is their counterpart only through its essence. Thus the entity of whiteness is one in the two affairs, but neither of the two affairs is identical with the other. This is the image of the true *barzakh*. So also, humanity, through its essence, is in each human being.

Hence, the "one" is the true *barzakh*. Anything that can be divided is not one. The one divides but it is not divided, which is to say that it is not divisible in itself. After all, if it receives division in its entity, then it is not one. If it is not one, then it is not the counterpart of each of the two things between which it stands through its essence. But in such a situation the one is known to be one, without doubt. The *barzakh* is known but not perceived, rationally understood but not witnessed.

People have made everything between two other things a *barzakh*, employing the term broadly. Even if the thing they name a *barzakh* is a large or a small body, they name it a *barzakh*, because it prevents the meeting of the two affairs between which it is situated.

When neither of two adjacent substances can be divided rationally or in sensation, there is no escape from a *barzakh* between the two. The adjacency of the two substances is the adjacency of their spatial confines. Between these confines there is no third confines without a substance. Between the two confines and the two substances there is an intelligible *barzakh*, without doubt, which prevents each substance from being identical with the other and each confines from being identical with the other. Thus this *barzakh* is the counterpart of each substance and each confines through its own essence.

He who knows this knows the ruling of the Lawgiver when he said that God created water pure, and "Nothing makes it impure," even when there is impurity within it without doubt. However, since the impurity is distinct from the water, the water remains pure according to its root, except that it is difficult to remove the impurity from it. That of the water within which there is impurity the Lawgiver made lawful to use, so we use it, and as for that of it which he forbade, we hold ourselves back from it, because of the Shariah's command. Nonetheless, we understand rationally that the impurity is in the water, and we understand rationally that the water is pure in its essence and that "Nothing makes it impure." So the Lawgiver did not forbid us from using water within which there is impurity because it is impure or has become impure. Rather, he forbade us from using the impure thing because we are not able to separate its parts from the parts of the pure water. For between the water and the impurity is a preventing *barzakh*, because of which the two do not meet. Were the two to meet, the water would become impure. So understand this!

Do you not see the forms that are in the Market of the Garden? All of them are *barzakhs*. The folk of the Garden come to this Market because of these forms, which are those within which the entities of the folk of the Garden undergo fluctuation. When they enter this Market, everyone who has the appetite for a form enters into it and goes back with it to his family, just as he would go back with the needed thing that he had bought from the market.

It may happen that a group will see one of these forms of the Market, and each of them will have an appetite for it. Through his very appetite for it, he becomes clothed by it. He enters into it and comes to possess it. Thus each of the group will come to possess it. He who does not have an appetite for it in his entity will halt and gaze, as each of the group enters into that form and goes back with it to his family, even though the form remains as it was in the Market, not emerging from it.

No one knows the reality of this affair which the Shariah has stated plainly and in which faith is incumbent save him who knows the configuration of the last world, the reality of the *barzakh*, and the self-disclosure of the Real in numerous forms. He transmutes Himself within them from form to form, but the Entity is one. His transmutation in forms is witnessed by eyesight, but it is known by reason that He has undergone no transmutation whatsoever. Each faculty perceives in keeping with what its essence bestows, and the Real in

Himself shows the truthfulness of reason in its judgment and of eyesight in its judgment. Nonetheless, He has a knowledge of Himself that is not identical with what reason judges concerning Him, nor is it identical with what the witnessing of the eyesight judges concerning Him, nor is it other than these two. On the contrary, He is identical with what the two judge, and He is what the Real knows of Himself that is not known by these two judgers. So glory be to the Knowing, the Powerful! He measures out, He decrees, He judges, He causes to occur, *And thy Lord has decreed that you worship none but Him* [17:23] in every object of worship. What could be clearer than His self-transmutation in the forms of the objects of worship? *But most people do not know* [7:187].

Then He set down as Shariah for us that we not worship Him in any of these forms, even if we know that He is identical with them. Whoever worships Him in these forms has disobeyed, and He has made him an associator, forbidding Himself to forgive him. Hence, taking the associator to task is incumbent, and inescapably so. Then, after that, the taking to task will be lifted, and it will only be lifted because of his ignorance of the form that the associate has with him, since that attribute will be negated from the associate in the last world. This is why he is punished, and this is why mercy is all-enveloping after the punishment, even if he does not emerge from the Fire.

He among us who knows here the form of what the associator worships is not budged from his knowledge in this world or in the last world, because in this world his eye looks upon nothing and his knowledge attaches itself to nothing save the object of worship within the form. The associator's state is not like that. His state is only the witnessing of a form, so he turns back from it in the last world, but the knower does not turn back. Were he to turn back, he would be one of the refusers, so it is not correct for him to turn back.

The associating remains,
  but no one knows it
    save him who witnesses
      the entities and the forms.
He who maintains *tawḥīd*
  is correct, but he who
    maintains association
      has shown the truth of the report.
The associate
  is a nonexistent thing that has
    no entity or trace
      in its worshiper's entity. (III 518.1)

Ibn al-ʿArabī sometimes calls imagination the most all-embracing and the most constricted thing in existence. It is all-embracing because it gives form to all things, whether or not the things exist. It is constricted because the only forms it gives are sensory. Hence imagination is both unbounded, because everything is included within it, and bound, because everything within it has assumed a limited and defined form. In the following passage, he refers to one of the divine roots of imagination—the fact that God knows all things and acts freely (*taṣarruf*) in them in keeping with His own will and desire. This is not unrelated to the idea that the cosmos, as Unbounded Imagination, is the dream of God.

God's Messenger said, "The client of a people is one of them." Imagination is one of the clients of the rationally speaking soul, so, in relation to it, it corresponds to the client in relation to the master. The client has a certain sort of ruling control within the master because of ownership since, through this and similar clients, it is correct for the master to be an owner and a king. Since the master cannot have this waystation except through the client, the client thereby has a hand that gives him a certain ruling control in the master.

Imagination's ruling control in the soul is only that it gives it any form that it wills. Although the soul has a form in itself, imagination does not leave the soul with the imaginer save in keeping with the forms it desires in its imagining.

Imagination has no strength that would bring it out of the degree of sensory things, for it was born, and its entity became manifest, only from sensation. Whenever it acts freely in nonexistent and existent things, and in things that have entities in *wujūd* or those that have none, it gives the thing a sensory form that has an entity in *wujūd*. Or, it gives form to a form whose totality has no entity in *wujūd*, but all of whose parts are sensory forms of *wujūd*. It is not able to give them form save within this limit.

Imagination possesses an all-inclusive unboundedness, similar to no other unboundedness, for it has an all-inclusive free acting in the necessary, the impossible, and the permissible. There is nothing that has the property of this unboundedness. This is the Real's free acting in the objects of knowledge by means of this faculty.

Imagination also possesses a specific, restrictive binding, for it is not able to give form to any affair save in a sensory form, whether or not this sensory form is an existent thing. However, inescapably all the parts of the imaginalized form will be existent in sensory things, as we mentioned. In other words, imagination will have taken the parts from sensation when it perceived them as dispersed, but the totality itself will not be found in *wujūd*. (III 470.5)

Imagination's chief characteristic, after its intermediacy and ambiguity, might be said to be its receptivity, and in this respect it is practically synonymous with nature. When the Breath of the All-Merciful is considered as Unbounded Imagination or Universal Nature, its attribute is to become articulated through every divine word. The words spoken by the Breath, or the shapes assumed by the Cloud, are neither God nor the cosmos, but images of both, He/not He and it/not it.

God has an all-inclusive being [*kaynūna*], for He is with the existent things in all their levels wherever they might be, as He clarified in our case with His words, *He is with you wherever you are* [57:4]. All these are relations in keeping with what is proper to His majesty, without declaring how, without *tashbīh*, and without assumption of forms—rather, as is given by His Essence and what can appropriately be ascribed to It. *There is no god but He, the Exalted,* so no one reaches the knowledge or the attainment of His Essence, *the Wise* [3:6], who descends to His servants in His words. Thus the Distant becomes near in the address, because of a wisdom that He desires.

Within the Cloud God opened up the forms of everything of the cosmos beside Himself. However, the Cloud is realized imagination. Do you not see that imagination receives the forms of all engendered things, while giving form to that which is not engendered? This is because of its all-embracingness. It is identical with the Cloud, not other than it, and within it become manifest all existent things; it is called the "Manifest" of the Real in His words, *He is the First and the Last and the Manifest and the Nonmanifest* [57:3].

That is why those who have no true knowledge of what is appropriate for God's majesty imagine His assumption of forms through contiguous imagination. If contiguous imagination exercises its ruling property over Him, what do you think about Unbounded Imagination, which is the Real's being in the Cloud?

Through this strength, contiguous imagination ties Him down. Then the Shariah comes concerning certain places that confirm what contiguous imagination has tied down, such as the being of the Real in the kiblah of him who performs the *ṣalāt* and in his face-to-face meeting with Him. So contiguous imagination receives Him, and it is one of the faces of Unbounded Imagination, which is the All-Comprehensive Presence and the All-Enveloping Level.[1] (II 310.8)

Like Unbounded Imagination, contiguous and discontiguous imagination receive all forms, because everything takes shape within them, even things that are impossible in the external world. This characteristic is related to the divine name Subtle (*al-laṭīf*). As we have already noted, the higher domains are called "subtle" in relation to the lower domains, which are then called "dense" (*kathīf*). The heavens are subtle and the earth is dense and, in a similar way, spirits are light (*khafīf*) and bodies are heavy (*thaqīl*). Thus, "The world of the spirits is lighter than the world of bodies, and because of its lightness, it hurries to undergo transmutation within forms without corruption of the entity, but the world of bodies is not like that" (III 280.20). If subtlety is understood to mean receptivity to forms, imagination might be considered even more subtle than the spirits, since it shares in the properties of both sides, being able to assume the forms of both spirits and bodies. Spirits, in contrast, cannot become embodied without imagination.

We investigated the self-disclosures and we saw that artifactual hyle receives some forms, but not all. Thus we find wood receiving the form of chairs, pulpits, planks, and doors, but we do not see it receiving the form of shirts, mantles, and pants. We see cloth receiving the forms of these, but it does not receive the form of knives and swords.

We saw that water receives the form of the color of its containers and the colored things that are disclosed within them, so it is qualified by blue, white, and red. Junayd was asked about knowledge and the knower. He replied, "The water takes on the color of its cup."

We examined the world of each of the elements and the spheres. We found that each element and each sphere receives specific forms and that some of them receive more than others. We looked at the All Hyle and found that it receives all the forms of the bodies and the shapes.

We looked at affairs and saw that the subtler they are, the more they receive many forms. We looked at the spirits and found that they are more receptive toward taking shape within forms than anything else we have mentioned. We looked at imagination and found that it receives what has a form and gives form to what has no form, so it is more all-embracing than the spirits in undergoing variation in forms.

Then we came to the absent among the self-disclosures, and we found the affair more all-embracing than what we have mentioned. We saw that He appointed that as names and that each name receives infinite forms in the self-disclosures. Then we knew that the Real is beyond all this. *Eyesights perceive Him not, but He perceives the eyesights, and He is the Subtle, the Experienced* [6:103].[2] Thus, concerning the lack of perception, He brought the name *Subtle*, since subtlety is that which is remote from sensation's perception, so it is understood rationally but not witnessed. Hence, in His being described as incomparable with perception, He is named *the Subtle, the Experienced*. In other words, He is too subtle to be perceived by newly arrived things, but it is known and understood rationally that there is something there by which things are supported. (I 285.11)

Ibn al-ʿArabī tells us repeatedly that the reality of imagination is understood most easily through dreams, which allow a glimpse into its almost infinite receptivity toward forms.

God appointed for human spirits natural instruments, such as the eye, the ear, the nose, and the palate. He placed within them faculties that He called "hearing," "eyesight," and so forth. He created for these faculties two faces, a face toward the sensory things, the world of the witnessed; and a face toward the Presence of Imagination. He made the Presence of Imagination an all-embracing locus, more all-embracing than the world of the witnessed. Within this Presence, He assigned a faculty named "imagination" to many faculties, such as form-giving, reflection, memory, fantasy, reason, and so on. Through these faculties the human soul perceives all the objects of knowledge given by the realities of these faculties.

Through eyesight's face toward the world of the witnessed, the soul perceives all sensory things and lifts them up to imagination. It preserves them in imagination through the preserving faculty [memory] after the form-giving faculty has given form to them. The form-giving faculty may take affairs from diverse existent things, all of which are sensory, and compound from them an alien shape, the totality of which the soul has never seen in the sensory domain. However, there is no part of it that it has not seen.

When human beings sleep, eyesight gazes by means of the face that it has toward the world of imagination. It sees what has been transferred there by sensation as a totality, or what has been given form by the form-giving faculty, though sensation has never fallen on its totality, only on the parts from which the form has been combined. Thus you see someone sleeping next to you, but he sees himself in chastisement or bliss, as a merchant, a king, a traveler. In his sleep, fear overtakes him in his imagination, and he cries out. But the one next to him has no knowledge of that or of what he is in. Sometimes, when the affair intensifies, a change occurs in his constitution, and in his manifest, sleeping form, this leaves the trace of a movement, a shout, words, or a nocturnal emission. All this derives from the faculty of imagination's overcoming the animal spirit such that the body changes in its form. (III 38.12)

Since dreams alert us to the nature of imagination, they also provide insight into the reality of the *barzakh* after death. The apparently impossible events that occur in dreams and the *barzakh* are among the many proofs of reason's incapacity to fathom the reality of *wujūd* and the worlds that it enfolds. The "greater death" is physical death, while the "lesser death" is sleep.

It is not within the capacity of the created thing to judge the Creator, except for him who witnesses the possible things as they are in the state of their nonexistence. He sees that through themselves they give knowledge to the Knower, so from this a whiff of judgment might be smelled.

Nevertheless, the possible things' poverty in respect of their possibility overcomes them. Hence you will see that those who negate possibility on the basis of rational proofs are heedless, in most states, of what their proofs give to them, that is, the negation of possibility in the actual situation.[3] They maintain possibility until they refer back and are alerted, and then they remember. There is no escape from some affair that has a ruling authority over this servant so that he becomes qualified by heedlessness and neglect of what his proof requires. This is nothing but the natural affair and the constitution.

Do you not see that, when he is transferred to the *barzakh* through the greater death or the lesser death, he sees in the lesser death affairs that he was considering rationally impossible in the state of wakefulness? Yet, in the *barzakh,* he perceives them as sensory things, just as, in the state of wakefulness, he perceives that to which his sensation is connected, so he does not deny it. Despite the fact that his rational faculty proves to him that a certain affair cannot have *wujūd,* he sees it existent in the *barzakh.* There is no doubt that it is an affair of *wujūd* to which sensation becomes connected in the *barzakh.* After all, the homesteads of sensation are diverse, so the properties are diverse. Were that thing's acceptance of *wujūd* impossible in itself, it would not have become qualified by *wujūd* in the *barzakh,* nor would sensation have perceived it in the *barzakh.*

What is more, the Folk of God gain a realization of this to such an extent that they perceive it in the state of their wakefulness—but in the *barzakh.* In the state of their wakefulness they have a state like the dreamer in dreaming and the dead person in death.

If you have been astute, I have tossed to you the path of knowing the inadequacy of rational consideration and the fact that it does not encompass the levels of the existent things. It does not know the how of *wujūd.* Were that thing impossible as reason judges, no *wujūd* would become manifest for it in any level. But it does become manifest. Hence the rational thinker cannot rely on what his reason proves to him in anything. (IV 99.8)

Appetite

When God blows of His own spirit into the body molded of clay, the human individual comes into existence as a microcosm, embracing spirit, soul, and body. Soul, which is the realm of the microcosm's knowledge and experience, corresponds to the realm of nature in the macrocosm. In other words, the ruling property of the realm of consciousness pertains to imagination. Human awareness of self fills the imaginal domain between the light of the spirit and the darkness of the body.

The divine attributes in the form of which Adam was created become manifest in the soul as corporeous qualities and forces, and the senses import impressions from the outside that add to the confusion. Properties that originated in the daylight of manifestation and others that derive from the night of nonmanifestation become indistinguishable in the interior domain of the soul. Tendencies that draw the soul up into the unity of the spirit or down into the dispersion of the body wear the same imaginal garment. Without the scales of the Shariah and reason, there is no way to distinguish between the conflicting forces.

The contrary tendencies of the soul manifest themselves as darkness and light, or spirit and nature, or reason and "appetite" (*shahwa*). Human beings share appetite, which is desire for food, sexual gratification, and all forms of pleasure, with other animals. This is an attribute that is not inherent to the rationally speaking soul, so it is contrasted with reason or intelligence. Unless appetite is guided by intelligence, it will lead a person far from the straight path of the Shariah. Nevertheless, appetite is a specific kind of desire, so it manifests properties of God's own desire, which is one of the primary divine attributes. Concerning desire, the Shaykh most commonly cites the verse, *Our only word to a thing, when We desire it, is to say to it "Be!," so it is* (16:40).

Know that "appetite" is a natural, qualified desire, while "desire" is a divine, spiritual, and natural attribute that attaches itself only to something that stays nonexistent.[4] Desire is more inclusive in attaching itself than appetite, for the reality of each attaches itself to certain things with which it has a correspondence. The corresponding thing is that with which it shares a common root, so appetite attaches itself only to attaining something that is natural.

If human beings should find in themselves an inclination toward an affair that is not of the natural domain—such as an inclination to perceive meanings and the high spirits, to reach perfection, or to see and know God—this inclination stems from one of two things: They may incline to all this by way of taking pleasure from formal imaginalization. This is appetite's attachment and inclination for the sake of the form, for when imagination embodies something that is not a body, this is the act of nature. The inclination may also attach itself to something other than gaining imaginalization. Rather, it leaves the meanings, the spirits, and perfection in their state of disengagement from binding and from being restricted by imagination through imaginalization. This is the inclination of desire, not the inclination of appetite, for appetite has no access to disengaged meanings.

Hence desire attaches itself to everything desired by the [rationally speaking] soul and reason, whether or not this object of desire is also the object of love. But appetite attaches itself only to that which belongs to the soul in attaining a specific pleasure. The locus of appetite is the animal soul, and the locus of desire is the rationally speaking soul. (II 192.29)

The fact that appetite becomes attached to things in the natural world does not detract from its inherent eminence and worth—if it did, there would be no appetite in paradise. Ibn al-ʿArabī repeatedly cites the Koranic verses telling us that the felicitous will be given everything for which they have appetite. After all, appetite is the soul's desire to take pleasure, and pleasure is found on the natural, bodily level. The greatest thing in which the soul takes pleasure is its own configuration in the natural realm, because it is configured in God's own form. The Shaykh writes,

Appetite is an instrument of the soul. It rises high in keeping with the highness of its object, and it falls low in keeping with its object's lowness. Appetite is the desire to take pleasure in that in which it is appropriate to take pleasure. Pleasure is of two sorts—spiritual and natural. The partial soul is born from nature, which is its mother, but the Divine Spirit is its father. Spiritual appetite is never delivered from nature.

There remains that in which pleasure is taken. Pleasure is taken only in the corresponding thing, but there is no correspondence between us and the Real save through the [divine] form. The pleasure of human beings in their perfection is the most intense of pleasures, so their pleasure in Him in whose form they are is the most intense pleasure.

The demonstration of this is that pleasure does not pervade their all, nor do they become totally annihilated in the witnessing of anything, nor do love and passion pervade the nature of their spirit, except when they fall in love with a woman or a man. The occasion of this is that they are wholly the counterpart of each of them, because they are in each other's form. But everything in the cosmos is a part of the human being, so they are its counterpart only with the corresponding part. Hence they do not become annihilated in anything they love save in their own likeness. (II 189.24)

Ibn al-ʿArabī maintains that people gain true knowledge of reality through the guidance of the prophets. To search out knowledge of *wujūd* through reason is to misuse the faculty, since its basic function is to keep appetite in check.[5] Cosmologically, reason represents the angelic or spiritual dimension of the human microcosm, while appetite pertains to the animal dimension. The spirit must rule over the body if human beings are to remember their Lord. The Shaykh refers to these points in Chapter 378, in which he discusses the true knowledge of the "community of dumb beasts" (*al-ummat al-bahīmiyya*). The word *bahīma* or "dumb beast" derives from the same root as *ibhām*, which means uncertainty and obscurity, while the word "community" refers to any group to whom God has addressed revelation. In speaking of the beasts as a community, Ibn al-ʿArabī has in mind the Koranic verse, *No crawling thing is there on the earth, no bird flying with its wings, but they are communities like you* (6:38).

The gnostics fly
  to the Named
    with the wings
      of noble angels,
to the Essence of essences,
  without description,
    and It sends them back
      with the spirits of the names.

Their essence reaches perfection
in every respect
through incomparable
states and stations.
The witness of their state
appears and decrees,
for each is a leader
on behalf of a Leader.

Know—God confirm us and you—that the dumb beasts are communities among all the communities, so they have glorifications and a *ṣalāt* specific to each genus, like those that belong to other creatures. Their glorification is what they know of their Creator's *tanzīh,* for they have a share in *Nothing is as His likeness* [42:11]. As for their *ṣalāt,* they have with the Real specific whispered prayers. God says, *And the birds spreading their wings—each knows its* **ṣalāt** *and its glorification* [24:41]. He says, *And thy Lord revealed unto the bees: "Take unto yourselves of the mountains houses, and of the trees, and of what they are building. Then eat of all manner of fruit, and travel submissively on the paths of your Lord"* [16:68–69], which are the paths God has set down as shariah for them to travel on.

Each created thing has a speech specific to it taught to it by God. It is heard by those whose hearing God opens up to its perception. All movements and artisanries that become manifest from animals and do not become manifest save from a possessor of reason, reflection, and deliberation, along with all the measures that are seen therein, signify that they have a knowledge of all this in themselves.

Certain affairs are also seen from them that signify that they do not possess the general governance possessed by human beings. Thus observers see that their affairs are incompatible, so their situation is obscure. This may be why they are called "dumb beasts," because of the "obscurity" of the affair—except for us, since it is as clear as it can be.

The obscurity that has come to some people is because of the lack of unveiling in this, so they know of the created things only in the measure of what they witness from them. In the same way, there are some who attach the dumb beasts to the degree of the gnostic sciences, knowledge of God, and that for which God has given them the aptitude. They do so only because God has unveiled to them the beasts' affair and states; or, they are truthful in their faith, and the beasts' affair has reached them from God in a Book or a Sunnah. . . .

Even though the considerative thinkers and the common people may say that something in the cosmos is neither alive nor an animal, in our view God has given every such thing, when He created it, the innate disposition to recognize and know Him. It is alive and speaks rationally in glorifying its Lord. The faithful perceive this through their faith, and the folk of unveiling perceive it in entity.

As for animals, God gave them the innate disposition to know Him and to speak rationally in glorification of their Lord. He assigned to them an appetite that is not possessed by any of the other created things just mentioned.

He gave the angels the innate disposition of knowledge and desire, but not appetite. He commanded them, and He reported that they do not disobey Him with the desire that He created for them. If not for that desire, He would not have lauded them by saying that they do not disobey Him and *they do what they are commanded* [16:50].

He gave the jinn and human beings the innate disposition of knowledge and of appetite, which is a specific attachment in desire, for appetite is a desire of the natural domain. So the human beings and jinn, unlike the angels, have no divine desire, but rather, a natural desire that is named "appetite."

God gave the human being and the jinn the innate disposition of reason, but not for the sake of acquiring knowledge. Rather, God made it an instrument for them to deter appetite in this abode specifically, not in the last abode. That is why He says to the folk of the Gardens concerning the last abode, *Therein you shall have everything for which your souls have appetite* [41:31]. Thereby He lets us know that the configuration of the last world within which He will configure us is natural, like the configuration of this world, since appetite only comes to be in natural souls, and natural souls have no share in desire.

When human beings or jinn acquire a knowledge without unveiling, this pertains to the faculty of reflection that God has placed within them. When reflection gives something to the rationally speaking soul that is in actual fact a knowledge, it derives from reflection through conformity, since knowledge in human beings belongs only to innate disposition, self-evidence, and inspiration. The unveiling that they possess occurs when the knowledge that God has placed in their innate disposition is unveiled to them, so they see the object of their knowledge. As for reflection, it is impossible to reach knowledge through it.

Someone may ask me how I know this—since it is not one of the objects perceived by sensation, nothing remains but rational consideration. I would reply: It is not as you say. On the contrary, there remain inspiration and the divine knowledge-giving. Hence the rationally speaking soul receives it from its Lord through unveiling and tasting by way of the specific face that belongs to it and to each existent thing other than God.

Sound reflection adds nothing to possibility—it yields nothing but this. But that [other knowledge] derives from God's knowledge and His knowledge-giving. It is not perceived through reflection. (III 487.32, 489.6)

Although reason's function is to keep appetite in check, appetite, within its own homestead, manifests the divine desire, so it has its rights. Ibn al-ʿArabī sometimes refers to those rationally speaking souls who disengage themselves from the world of nature and come to take on the attributes of their father, the Divine Spirit, as the "spiritualized ones" (*mutarawḥinūn*). Their characteristic is that they are completely detached from appetite, but this does not mean that they ignore it. Instead, they give it its *ḥaqq* by allowing it to achieve its objects within the limits of the Shariah.

The mark of the spiritualized ones as sons of their father is only that they stay free from natural appetites, taking from them only that through which they allow their configuration to abide. The Prophet said, "A few mouthfuls to firm up his backbone are enough for the child of Adam." Their aspiration lies in joining with their father, who is the *yāʾī*, Divine Spirit, not the command spirit. I say the "*yāʾī*" spirit only because of God's words, *I have blown into him of My spirit* [15:29], with the *yāʾ* of ascription to Himself. Thus He differentiates between the spirit of the command and the spirit of the *yāʾ* of ascription. He made the spirit of the command pertain to the confirmation that comes from Him, but He made the spirit of the *yāʾ* pertain to the *wujūd* of the spirit's entity, which is the Real's word blown into nature.

The [partial] spirit longs for its father with the longing of the child, so that it will be confirmed by God in what it seeks—witnessing the Real outside spirit and nature inasmuch as He is independent of these two, not inasmuch as He discloses Himself to the children from them, or through them, or in them. All this belongs to Him.

This is an exalted object of seeking. When someone reaches it and is strengthened through it, he comes to his appetites out of disinterested kindness toward them, as a descent from him to them. Through appetite he exercises a ruling property over appetite's objects. No appetite exercises any ruling property over him in its objects, so he bestows appetite on appetite, but others are under the ruling property of appetite. The companion of this station causes appetite itself to arrive newly within himself so as to gratify and answer the requests of those that have appetites within his own specific world. Through this appetite they attain the objects of their appetite. Thus the animal spirit takes enjoyment.

Such souls are *gazing upon their Lord* [75:23], not veiled. He has disclosed Himself to them in His name Ever-Creating and conferred this name upon them so that from them may be engendered what they desire, not what they have appetite for. These are excellent, noble souls, having become similar to Him to whom they belong. They look upon nature with the gaze of a loving child toward its mother—though they have been delivered of need for her—so as to fulfill her *ḥaqq*. (III 125.12)

Ibn al-ʿArabī usually calls appetite a "strength" or "faculty" (*quwwa*), and in this he follows the standard usage of the philosophers, who were the intellectuals most concerned with delineating the structure and faculties of the soul. Like them, he pairs appetite—a term that has often been translated in Western sources as "concupiscence"—with a second faculty called "wrath" (*ghaḍab*), which has usually been translated as "irascibility." However, it is important in the present context to connect the wrath of the animal soul with the divine attribute that is its root—the wrath that is preceded by mercy.

In some passages, the Shaykh employs the term *soul* as a virtual synonym for *faculty*. Thus, in the following, he divides the animal soul into two souls—the appetitive soul and the wrathful soul. This is probably the longest exposition of the functions of the vegetal and animal souls that he provides in the *Futūḥāt*. It derives from the beginning of Chapter 353, which is called, "On the true knowledge of the waystation of three talismanic mysteries of wisdom that point to the true knowledge of the occasion and fulfilling its *ḥaqq*." Ibn al-ʿArabī understands the Arabic word *ṭilism* (talisman) in terms of its palindrome, *musallaṭ,* which means "having been given ruling authority." The three talismanic mysteries in the chapter are the "three souls" that rule over human beings. The *ḥaqq* or rightful due of a faculty of the soul is everything of *wujūd* that pertains to it and belongs to it because *God has given each thing its creation* (20:50).

Know—God confirm you with a spirit from Him—that when God created the rationally speaking soul that governs this frame named a "human being," He gave ruling authority over it to three things within this specific constitution in the configuration of this world, making these three concomitants of the constitution's configuration. These are the vegetal soul, the appetitive soul, and the wrathful soul.

As for the vegetal and wrathful soul, they disappear in the configuration of the folk of felicity in the Gardens, and there remains in that configuration only the appetitive soul, so it is a concomitant of the two configurations, and through it the folk of bliss take enjoyment.

The vegetal soul is that which seeks nourishment to restore thereby what is diminished from the body; through it the body grows and never stops taking nourishment perpetually either from what it draws from outside, which is called "food," or from whence God wills without designation.[6] The vegetal soul has four guards—[faculties called] attractive, retentive, digestive, and expulsive.

The ruling property of the attractive is to transfer nourishment from place to place. It transfers it from the mouth to the stomach, from the stomach to the liver, from the liver to the heart and to all the veins and parts of the body. To all the parts of the body it apportions what they need to sustain their faculties.

The expulsive assists the attractive, for it expels the nourishment from its place when it sees that it has fully given its *ḥaqq* to that place and has no other business with it. It expels it so that it will not vie with others when they come, so it assists the attractive.

The retentive retains the nourishment in each place so that governance may take its *ḥaqq* from it. When it sees that governance has taken fully its *ḥaqq,* it lets the nourishment go, and the expulsive and the attractive take charge of it.

The digestive is that which changes the form of the nourishment and drapes it in another form so that it may have a different form from what it had. For it had a beautiful form with a pleasant aroma, but when it falls into digestion's hand, digestion changes its shape's form and drapes it in an altered form with an odor whose proper arrangement is dispersed. That is why it is named "digestive" [*hāḍim*], from "wrongdoing" [*ihtiḍām*]. However, wisdom is found in this wrongdoing since, without digestion, the goal for which the Nourisher intended the nourishment would not have been reached. Thus, the situation becomes manifest as corruption, but on the nonmanifest level it is wholesomeness.

The digestive never ceases transferring the nourishment from form to form, and the retentive retains it in its subsistence so that it may govern it in keeping with its knowledge and that over which it has been put in charge. When these two make full use of it in keeping with this homestead, they let it go and it is taken by the attractive and the expulsive. When they take over and transfer it to another place, they give it back to the retentive and the digestive, who do with it the like of what they did in the previous place and open up within it diverse forms. Then it is taken by the attractive and the expulsive, and they travel with those forms on designated paths that they do not transgress so long as God desires the subsistence of this natural configuration.

Were it not for these guards, the vegetal soul could not reach the object of its seeking. When God desires the perishment of this natural configuration, the vegetal soul seeks the assistance of appetite so that the governing soul will rise up and draw to itself the objects of its appetite. But appetite does not do this, and God weakens it by letting the ruling authority of heat gain mastery over its locus. Thus it weakens, just as a lamp weakens in the light of the sun. It remains without any ruling property. The vegetal soul in its reality keeps saying to its guards, "I must have something to nourish myself." Hence it nourishes itself with the body's humors and the leftovers that remain with it. It may also be that the guards have weakened, just like the vegetal soul. So the configuration stays in ever-increasing diminution. The expulsive becomes stronger and the attractive becomes weaker, and so also the retentive, until the human being dies.

Were it not for the fact that these instruments govern this configuration in this manner, no ear would hear, no eyesight would look, and none of the sensory and suprasensory faculties would have any ruling property.

As for the appetitive soul, its ruling authority in this frame is seeking what is beautiful in its view. It does not know if that will harm it or benefit it. This is so only in the human configuration. As for the other animals, they partake of nourishment only through desire, not appetite, so as to expel from themselves the pain of hunger and need. They intend only that which has benefit for them. For animals, the property of appetite remains in their seeking much nourishment such that they suffer disorder because of it. So also, human beings suffer disorder from seeking much nourishment when a small amount would be beneficial, or from partaking of what has no benefit whatsoever for them and is sought by the appetite, though the constitution suffers harm because of it. This is what distinguishes human beings from animals in partaking of nourishment.

The appetitive soul is related to the vegetal soul in the manner indicated by the poet:

When a mindful man tests this world,
 it is unveiled to him
  as an enemy in the clothing
   of a sincere friend.

The appetitive soul shows sincere friendship to the vegetal soul, because it is its assistant in nourishment and in the partaking of it. But the appetitive is the enemy since it brings in nourishments that harm the vegetal soul and do not give benefit. Its assistance to the vegetal soul is accidental, not essential, for it is the clinging enemy from whom it is impossible to depart and from whose evil there is no security.

The wrathful soul is the predatory. It seeks subjugation because of what it sees of its own superiority over other living things, since it has been given the faculties and ability to act freely. It sees the world subjected to its configuration and its own governor. It sees in *wujūd* accidental affairs that occur by chance or through occasions that become manifest, all this preventing it from reaching its personal desires. Thus it becomes wrathful because of not achieving the personal desire. If it possesses a strong ruling authority assisted by an aspiration that is active or that commands it from outside to carry out its wrath in its object, then it destroys the object and manifests vengeance from it. It does not recognize the scale of wrongdoing and justice in this vengeance and subjugation, since this does not belong to it, but rather, to reason and the law of the moment [*nāmūs al-waqt*]. That is why the poet erred who said,

Wrongdoing belongs to the soul's birthmark,
 so if you see
  a decent man, he avoids wrong
   for some cause.

If he had said "subjugating" instead of "wrongdoing," he would have spoken correctly, since no one brings wrongdoing save one addressed by a law. From such a person it is known.

The soul has nothing save subjugating—a *zeal of the Age of Ignorance* [48:26]. If this coincides with the Real, then it is a religious zeal. This is why wrath for God and in God is praised, but wrath for other than God and in other than God is blamed. This belongs to the governance of the Wise, the Real, who has ordered all affairs according to their levels and *has given each thing its creation* [20:50], that it might be a sign of Him for the possessors of the kernels and for the other folk of the signs among the world's inhabitants. For they are diverse in their taking in this, just as God has numbered them in His exalted Book *to which the unreal comes not from before it nor from behind it, a sending down from a Wise, a Praiseworthy* [41:42].

God joined all these signs together in the Book of *Wujūd*, within which there is only clarification and mercy, nothing else. Whenever something that contradicts mercy becomes manifest in the cosmos from the side of the Real or from the interaction of some of the cosmos with others of it, this is an accidental affair within the Book and is explained by the clarification wherever this accidental affair may be. It is not in the self of this Book, for in respect of its essence, the Book is all mercy and clarification. God did not make it a chastisement. God is more generously noble than that He would chastise His creatures with a chastisement whose situation does not ultimately reach a term that is comprised and designated by the Book's clarification. Then the ruling property goes back to mercy. There is no escape from this, *And God is Forgiving, Compassionate* [2:218]. (III 237.1)

Ibn al-ʿArabī often mentions the intimate correlation between appetite and imagination, since appetite is a desire that functions only on the natural level, which is precisely the level of forms, and all forms are images.

A Mystery
Partaking of Appetites in Mutual Similarities

There is no solace
 from appetite,
for it derives from the reality of the
  configuration

both here and at the final return.
In mutual similarities
is inclination in all directions.
There is no surprise that the cosmos is in the Form,
the surprise is only that someone should see it as a *barzakh* in status.
The *barzakh* is between two sides,
and there is nothing but two entities—
you and He from whom you derive,
though everything is from Him.
In our view, the *barzakh* is affirmed only in the existent entity,
because it is between the nonexistent, fixed entities and *wujūd.*
When someone observes this most towering station,
he will affirm that the cosmos, in the state of its *wujūd,* is a *barzakh.*
Were the cosmos lifted from *wujūd,*
this limited *barzakh* would disappear.
Affairs are similar through likenesses
and dense bodies are similar through shadows.
And to God prostrate themselves those in the heavens and
those in *the earth, willing or unwillingly,*
as do their shadows
in the mornings and evenings [13:15]. (IV 343.2)

Imagination and Understanding

Ibn al-ʿArabī clarifies appetite's connection to imagination in the midst of a broader discussion that points indirectly to one of the important contributions of his own perspective to Islamic thought, that is, his stress on the role of imagination in human cognition. As far as Ibn al-ʿArabī is concerned, although the Muslim philosophers theorized about imagination and understood that it has a tremendous power to control the world of forms, they never quite grasped its significance for acquiring knowledge. For them, as for the Kalām authorities, true knowledge had to come by way of reason. However, as the Shaykh demonstrates repeatedly, reason is unsuited to gain positive knowledge of the divine, because its reality is to declare God incomparable with all things and to deny His similarity. Hence it can know for certain only what He is not, not what He is.

While explaining the inadequacy of the philosophical approach to knowledge, Ibn al-ʿArabī points to the cosmic root of imagination by identifying it, on the angelic level, with possibility (or contingency), the fact that everything other than God stands halfway between *wujūd* and nonexistence. It is well to remember here that the Shaykh identifies the philosophical term *possibility* with the Koranic term *poverty.* God alone is Independent and Self-Sufficient. Everything else, including even the First Intellect, is poor and needy toward God. The essential poverty of all things puts them in the station of intermediacy between the nothingness of themselves and the *wujūd* of the Real, and intermediacy is precisely the defining characteristic of both imagination and possibility. Thus, in a broad cosmological perspective, every possible thing is precisely an imaginal thing, an image of both *wujūd* and nonexistence.

This topic [imagination] has a wide playing field, but it is of no account in the view of the ulama of the tracings, or in the view of the "sages"—those who suppose that they have come to know wisdom. But they have fallen short of knowing that this level towers over the other levels. It has no worth in their view, for none knows its worth, nor the strength of its ruling authority, save God, and then His folk, whether prophet or specified friend. Other than these two, none knows the worth of this level. Knowledge of it is the first of the stations of prophethood. This is why, when God's Messenger awoke and sat in a session with his companions, he would say to them, "Has any of you seen a dream-vision?" Thereby he would see that to which God had given new arrival in the cosmos during the night or that to which He would give new arrival in the future and had revealed to the dreamer during his sleep, either through explicit revelation or a revelation whose form is known by the dreamer, though he does not know what is meant by it. Then God's Messenger would interpret what God meant by it. All this derived from his concern for this level that is unknown to the ulama.

How beautifully does God call the attention of the possessors of the kernels and the folk of crossing over when He says, *It is He who forms you in the wombs as He will* [3:6]. Among the "wombs" is that which is imagination. God forms within it the imaginalized things as He wills on the basis of a suprasensory marriage and a suprasensory pregnancy. He opens up meanings in this womb and *in whatever form He wills He mounts* them [82:8]. He shows you Islam as a dome, the Koran as butter and honey, perseverance in religion as a fetter, and religion as a shirt—long, short, plaited, doubled, clean, dirty—in keeping with the situation of the religion of the dreamer or the one upon whom the clothing is seen. I saw such a thing for the judge of Damascus while he was in charge of the judgeship in Damascus. This was Shams al-Dīn Aḥmad ibn Muhadhdhib al-Dīn Khalīl al-Jūnī—God give him success, support him with His angels, and protect him from error in his rulings! A speaker was saying to him in the dream, "God has bestowed upon you a clean, long gown. Dirty it not and let it not shrink!" I awoke and mentioned that to him. May God make him one of those who preserve the divine admonition! Thus imagination is one of the wombs within which forms become manifest.

Since this imaginal Presence receives meanings as forms, God said concerning it, *Ornamented for the people is the love of appetites—women* [3:14], that is, appetite for women. Hence He gave love a form that He ornaments for whomsoever of His servants He wills. The servants love the form in itself, not in anything else, because He ornamented only the love of appetite for what He mentioned. So unqualified love was ornamented for them, then He attached it to appetite for what He mentioned. He also attaches it to appetite for other affairs in the case of whom He wills. God mentioned "appetite" only because it is a natural form, for imagination's Presence is nature.

Imagination rules over nature and embodies it however it wills, so it is a branch that rules over its root, because it is a noble branch. God brought nothing into existence more magnificent in waystation or more inclusive in property. Its ruling property permeates all existent and nonexistent things, including even the impossible. Hence among the things that the divine power has brought into existence, none is more magnificent in *wujūd* than imagination. Through it the divine power and the divine potency become manifest. Through it God *has written mercy* and other such things *upon Himself* [6:12] and necessitated them for all. This is the Presence of the locus of divine disclosure at the resurrection and within beliefs. It is the greatest of God's waymarks pointing to God.

The strength of the ruling property of imagination's authority causes the philosophers to make certain affirmations concerning it, even though they do not know what they are saying and do not give it its full *ḥaqq*. Thus they say that although imagination derives from nature, it has a magnificent authority over nature because of the divine strength with which God has confirmed it. Hence, when a human being wants his child to be highborn, he should set up in his soul, during intercourse with his wife, the form of any of the great ulama that he wills. If he desires to do this well, he should picture that form as it has been transmitted to him or as he has seen the person. He should mention to his wife the beauty of that form. When he pictures that form, he should picture it according to the form of the beauty of the person's knowledge and character traits, even if his sensory form was ugly when looked upon. He should picture his form only as beautiful to look upon, in the measure of the beauty of the person's knowledge and character traits, as if he is embodying those meanings. He should make that form present to his wife and himself during intercourse. They should exert themselves fully in gazing upon the form's beauty.

If the woman becomes pregnant from that intercourse, the form that the two of them imagined will leave a trace in the soul. The child will emerge in that waystation—there is no escape from this. If it does not emerge like that, this is because of something that overtook the soul of the parents during the settling of sperm in the womb, something that took them away, while they were not aware, from the witnessing of that form in imagination. The common people give expression to this as "the craving of the woman."

It may happen that by chance, during intercourse, the form of a dog, a lion, or some other animal occurs to the soul of one or both of the spouses. As a result, the child of that intercourse emerges such that its character traits take the form of the imaginalization of the animal that occurred to the spouses, even if the two of them differed. Thus there becomes manifest in the child the form of what the father or the mother imagined even in the manifest domain of sensation, in outward form or ugliness.

Despite their knowledge of imagination's ruling authority, the philosophers give it no notice in the acquisition of the divine sciences. This is because, in their ignorance, they wish for that which cannot be wished for, which is disengagement from every sort of matter. This will never happen, whether in this world or the last world. This—I mean disengagement from matter—is an affair that is rationally conceivable, but not witnessed. The considerative thinkers have no greater mistake than this, but they are not aware of their mistake. They imagine that they have gained something, but in fact they have lost. They shorten their lifespans trying to gain what they cannot gain.

No rational faculty is safe from the ruling property of fantasy and imagination, which, in the world of angels and spirits, is possibility. No spirit and no knower of God is safe from the possibility that falls to him in everything that he witnesses. After all, the reality of everything other than God, in its essence, is possibility. A thing never leaves the property of its own self, so it never sees what it sees—whether the object be eternal or newly arrived—except through itself. So possibility accompanies it constantly, and no one is aware of this save those who know the affair as it is.[7]

Through imagination the philosopher conceives rationally of disengagement, but he is unable to achieve it in himself, because there is no such thing. Here the feet of many slip, save the Folk of God, the elect. They know this through God's knowledge-giving. (III 508.10)

Ibn al-ᶜArabī again discusses reason's incapacity to grasp the reality of things without outside help in Chapter 276, which he dedicates to "True knowledge of the waystation of the pool." He identifies the pool with the natural body, within which meanings assume corporeal form at the level of imagination. The pure and lustrous water of the spirit becomes turbid, thus leaving human beings with the problem of how to discern truth from falsehood. They need the science of interpretation (*taᶜbīr*), which gives them the ability to "cross over" (*ᶜubūr*) from the turbid water to the undefiled source. Ultimately, the only knowledge that delivers from nature's turbidity is the knowledge given by God, but this cannot be found by the rational faculty's reflective thought. Only the remembrance (*dhikr*) of God can bring down the cleansing light of the spirit.

The "pool" is the waystation where
water is described as turbid,
and these are the knowledges
specific to mortal man.
In its own entity
the water is limpid, not turbid,
but its depth makes manifest
the turbidity within it.
The cause of its roiling
is the reflection that stirs it up.
So seek from knowledge
what rises beyond reflection!
When imagination comes
to someone, through reflection
it binds the knowledges to the world
of corporeous bodies and forms.
Sometimes reflection delivers them
from their forms,
but nothing protects it
from harm.
So seek Him through remembrance,
not reflection, and enjoy Him
incomparable and pure
from the stain of the others. . . .

The occasion of the manifestation of turbidities is the settling down and stillness of the water. It seeks ease from moving in other than movement's site and locus. We referred to this state with the word *pool,* because the water of a pool is settled and still. Hence I said in a ghazal, describing the incomparability of the beloved's own self,

She is the ease of whoever
burns for her,
transferring him from the levels
of mortal man
out of jealousy, lest her sparkle
be stained
by the turbidity
in the pools.[8]

What I mean by these lines is that when the lover who has this attribute falls in love, the beloved exercises a ruling property over him and transfers him to the beloved's self. The beloved drapes him in its own clothing and brings him out of the turbidities of the obfuscation required by the world of nature—this is when the beloved is knowledge. If the beloved is deeds, turbidity derives from doubts and the unlawful; if the beloved is a spirit disengaged from matter, it derives from natural appetites; if the beloved is an angel, it derives from mortal humanity; and if the beloved is God, it derives from everything other than God. Thus the truthful lover is he who is transferred to the attribute of the beloved, not he who brings the beloved down to his own attribute.

Do you not see that the Real, when He loved us, descended to us in His hidden gentlenesses through that which corresponds to us, but beyond which His majesticness and greatness are high exalted? He descended to receiving us joyfully when we come to His house intending to whisper with Him; to rejoicing at our repentance and our return to Him after our turning away from Him; to wonder at the young man who lacks sensual desire when he is in the locus of its ruling authority, even though he has that through God's giving him success; to being our deputies in our hunger, our thirst, and our illness; and to placing Himself in our waystations. When one of His servants is hungry, He says to the others, "I was hungry, but you did not feed Me." When another of His servants is thirsty, He says to another servant of His, "I was thirsty, but you did not give Me to drink." When another of His servants is ill, He says to another servant of His, "I was ill, but you did not visit Me." When these servants ask Him about all this, He replies to them, "Verily so-and-so was ill; if you had visited him, you would have found Me at him. So-and-so was hungry; if you had fed him, you would have found that at Me. So-and-so was thirsty, if you had given him to drink, you would have found that at Me." This is a sound report.

This is part of the fruit of love, when He descends to us. This is why we say that truthfulness in love makes the lover become qualified by the attribute of the beloved. So also is the case in the truthful servant's love of his Lord. He assumes the traits of His names, so he becomes qualified by "independence" from anything other than God, "exaltation" through God, "giving" through the hand of God, and "preserving" through the eye of God.

The ulama know about assuming the traits of God's names and have written many books about it. The occasion of this is that when they loved Him, they became qualified by His attributes in the measure proper to them.

Now let us return to that in whose path we were. We say, while *God speaks the **ḥaqq**, and He guides on the path* [33:4]: When the knowledges—by which I mean the known things—become manifest through their essences to knowledge, and when knowledge perceives them as they are in their essences, this is sound knowledge and complete perception within which, as a matter of course, there is no obfuscation. It makes no difference whether the known thing is a *wujūd* or a nonexistence, a negation or an affirmation, a dense or a subtle thing, a lord or a vassal, a letter or a meaning, a body or a spirit, a compound or a solitary thing, the result of a composition or a relation, a description or what is described.

Whenever anything that we have mentioned ceases to appear to knowledge in its own essence but appears to it in other than its own form, then nonexistence has appeared to it in the form of *wujūd* and vice versa, negation in the form of affirmation and vice versa, the subtle in the form of the dense and vice versa, the lord in the attribute of the vassal and the vassal in the attribute of the lord, and meanings in the forms of bodies, such as knowledge in the form of milk, perseverance in religion in the form of a fetter, faith in the form of a handle, Islam in the form of a supporting pillar, and deeds in the form of beautiful and ugly persons.

This then is the turbidity that joins with knowledge. When this becomes manifest for people, they need a divine faculty that will take them from this form to the meaning that has become manifest in this form and has troubled them.

The occasion of this is the Presence of imagination and imaginalization and the reflective faculty. Its root is this natural body, which, in this waystation, is called the "pool." The depth of the pool is the storehouse of imagination. The water's turbidity that has settled in the depth of the pool is everything that imagination and imaginalization remove from its own form. Thus, when a person considers what becomes manifest to him, obscuration overtakes him. He does not know which meaning has put on this form, so he is bewildered. He is never able to rid his consideration of bewilderment except by chance. He has no realized certainty concerning that of it which is correct except through a report-giving from God.

This explains what happened when Abū Bakr stood in this station and asked the interpretation of a dream-vision. The Prophet commanded him to interpret it. When he had finished, he asked the Prophet concerning his interpretation. Was he correct or mistaken? The Prophet replied, "You were correct in some and mistaken in some." Hence we see that Abū Bakr was not able to discern his being correct in the *ḥaqq* from his being mistaken. That is why we say that he who is correct in something like this has no certainty concerning that of it in which he is correct.

This explains why the gnostics incline away and hold themselves back from taking knowledge except from God by way of bestowal.

Among God's friends the path to bestowal is remembrance, not reflection. If they are given the meanings as disengaged and if the known things appear to them through their essences in the forms that are their realities, that is the intended goal. But, when the gnostics occupy themselves with remembrance and seeking, the Real may make the meanings appear in forms that do not belong to the meanings, so these forms keep the essences veiled from the gnostics. Then the gnostics are given the faculty and the light to penetrate into those forms to what is behind them, that is, to what is desired from those forms and has become bound through them. In any case, what the gnostics witness is the meanings that are the intended goal. In the world of letters and expressions, these meanings correspond to the plain statement and firm text within which there is no confusion or interpretation. The other corresponds to apparent words that support numerous meanings, so that he who considers does not know what their speaker has intended.

Know also that God may give these knowledges to the servant in other than their own forms and give him the knowledge of what is meant by them. Then by means of the form he comes to understand them in themselves within the form. He is similar to the pool, for he perceives the water and he perceives the turbidity that is in the depth of the pool and obscures the water. The person who looks cannot escape the color of that turbidity, whether it is red or yellow or whatever. Hence he sees the water as red, or yellow, or some other color. (II 594.22, 595.33)

Bodies Forever

In the last world, the soul experiences the constant renewal of creation. Born from a lowly mother who is the body, this child will take on the attributes of its spiritual father and enjoy the never-ending self-disclosures of the Real. Ibn al-ᶜArabī finds an allusion to the soul's destiny in the Koranic verse, *They say, "If we return to the city, the more exalted will expel the more abased from it." To God belongs the exaltation, and to His messenger, and to those who have faith* (63:8).

A MYSTERY
His Words: The more exalted
will expel the more abased
from it.

He says: The rationally speaking soul was in the Breath itself, from which the inblowing occurred, so it is identical with the breath that was blown into this elemental form. This form was configured from an abased earth, so the soul is abased through the abasement of its root, for its constitution leaves its traces within it. Thus the son is *more abased* than his mother, for he is in her service, subjected to her, and commanded to take care of her.

The *more exalted* is the Real, the soul's Creator. He swears that *the more exalted will expel the more abased from it,* which is to say that He will make the soul exalted through a province more beautiful than this city. That province is the last configuration, which is pure, purified, and assists the soul in what is desired from it—undergoing variation in forms and self-disclosure in any form that He wills, as it is in itself. That is why He says, *To God belongs the exaltation, and to His messenger, and to those with faith,* but not to those without faith. They do not possess this waystation. (IV 422.21)

Ibn al-ᶜArabī calls Chapter 355 "On the true knowledge of the waystation of the born paths and the earth of worship, of its all-embracingness, and of His words, *O My servants[. . .], surely My earth is all-embracing, so worship Me* [29:56]." The word translated here as "all-embracing" is *wāsi*ᶜ, and it would be more normal in this context to translate it as "wide" or "vast." However, it is also a divine name, and it is important to preserve the connection between this name and the use of the term in this context, for the vastness of the human reality is the mirror image of the divine vastness. If human beings are "all-embracing," it is because they were created in the form of the all-comprehensive name, and hence they bring together in their realities, at least potentially, everything in *wujūd.* In the middle of this passage, Ibn al-ᶜArabī turns to an often cited *ḥadīth qudsī* to prove that the human body is God's all-embracing earth: "Neither My heaven nor My earth embraces Me, but the heart of My servant with faith does embrace Me." Thus

God's "all-embracing earth" is the corporeal form that embraces Him by knowing Him and worshiping Him, and such an earth can only be the human body, within which is God's house, the heart. In connection with worshiping God, the Shaykh turns at the end of the passage to the famous hadith of Gabriel, which says that *iḥsān* or "doing what is beautiful" is to "*worship* God as if you see Him, for if you do not see Him, He sees you."

What is it with God's all-embracing earth?
God's heaven marries it.
All the doors are locked,
but the right hand of munificence opens them.
The dwelling of the breasts is narrow,
but He expands them with knowledge's light.
The mystery's obscurities are dark,
but the sciences of unveiling illumine them.
All the blessings given to the earth
were bestowed by the Presence of the Beneficent.
Though corruption comes to abide in it,
perhaps the All-Merciful will make it wholesome.
If it becomes violent or turns away,
the halter of guidance will rein it in.
Every claim that is not truthful
will be exposed by incapacity's tongue.
The flint of trial will kindle that claim
with every torment of the world's affliction.

God says, *But was not God's earth all-embracing? Thus you might have emigrated in it* [4:97]—He did not say "from it," nor "to it." It is God's earth, whether its dwellers worship Him or claim to be too great to worship Him. God says, *O My servants* [. . .], *surely My earth is all-embracing, so worship Me* [29:56]. . . .

You should know, dear brother, that the earth of your body is the true "all-embracing earth" in which the Real commanded you to worship Him. This is because He commanded you to worship Him in His earth only so long as your spirit dwells in the earth of your body. When your spirit departs from it, the Law's prescription will drop away from you, even though your body will continue to exist in the earth, buried within it. Thus you come to know that the "earth" is nothing other than your body. He made it "all-embracing" because of the faculties and meanings that are found only in this human, bodily earth.

As for His words, *Thus you might have emigrated in it,* this is because the body is both a locus of caprice and a locus of reason. *Thus you might have emigrated* from the earth of its caprice to the earth of its reason, while in all this you were in it—you did not emerge from it. If caprice put you to work, it ruined you and you perished. But if the rational faculty within whose hand is the lamp of the Shariah put you to work, you were saved and God gave you salvation through it. For God took the healthy rational faculty, quit of the attributes of imperfection and obfuscations, and opened the eye of its insight to perceive affairs as they are in themselves. Therefore, employ the earth in the path of rightful claims and "Give to each that has a *ḥaqq* its *ḥaqq*."

He who does not worship God in the all-embracing earth of his body has not worshiped Him in the earth from which he was created. God says, *He originated the creation of the human being from clay, then He made his descendants from an extraction of vile water,* which is the water that gushes from this bodily earth and settles in the woman's womb; *then He proportioned him* [32:7–9]. After the proportioning of the body's earth and its reception toward flaming up because of the moisture and heat that is in it, God blew into it and it flamed up. That flaming up is a spirit for it, so the spirit emerged only from the body, so the spirit was created from the body.

He made the rational faculty in this configuration the equivalent of *the moon* in the earth—*a light* from which radiance is taken but which does not possess the power to penetrate the preventing veils, which are the houses, walls, and shelters. *He made [the sun* of] the Shariah in this bodily earth *a lamp* [71:16] for this rational faculty, so the corners of this earth became radiant with the light of the lamp, since it gave to it a knowledge of what is in the earth that the light of reason—which corresponds to the moon—did not give.

Then He will return us *to it* [i.e., the body's earth], that is, in the last configuration, just as He had created us in it, *and He will bring* us *forth* [71:18] to witness Him.

Thus He created our spirits from the earth of our bodies in this world to worship Him, and He makes us dwell in the earth of our bodies in the last world to witness Him—if we are felicitous—just as we had faith in Him in the first configuration because God showed us solicitude. The state is exactly like the state in the division of the creatures in this. And so they shall be tomorrow.

Death is a *barzakhī* state between the two configurations. In it the spirits inhabit *barzakhī*, imaginal, corporeous bodies, like what they inhabit in sleep. These are corporeous bodies that are born from the earthy, corporeal bodies, for imagination is one of their faculties. Thus the spirits do not depart from the bodies or from what derives from them. Know this!

God's earth, which is a pillar, is existent, and you are buried within it. You are not commanded to worship your Lord unless you remain in the all-embracing earth of your body along with the existence of your reason and the lamp of your Shariah. Thus you are commanded to worship your Lord. In reality, this bodily earth is for you *God's all-embracing earth* in which He commanded you to worship Him until your death.

"When someone dies, his resurrection has come." This is the "partial resurrection." It is indicated by His words, *and We shall return you into it* [20:55]. Once you have understood the partial resurrection through the death of this designated individual, you will have known the general resurrection for every dead person upon the earth. For the period of the *barzakh*, in relation to the last configuration, corresponds to the woman's carrying the embryo in her belly. God configures the embryo in one configuration after another, so the stages of its configuration are diverse until it is born on the day of resurrection. This is why it is said concerning the dead person when he dies, "His resurrection has come." In other words, the manifestation of the other configuration has begun within him in the *barzakh* and until the day of the uprising from the *barzakh*. In the same way, he rose up from the belly to the earth through birth.

Thus the governance of his body's configuration in the earth is the time he is in the *barzakh*, so that He may proportion him and balance him in other than a precedent image, as is appropriate for the last abode. Thus he worships Him in it—I mean, in the earth of his configuration in the last world—through an essential worship, not a prescribed worship. After all, unveiling will prevent him from being the servant of any other than Him who has a rightful demand that he be His servant. In the same way, the Men of God attain this station here.

When God created the earth of your body, He placed within it a Kaabah, and that is your heart. He placed this heart-house, the most eminent of houses, in the person of faith, for He reported that the heavens, in which is the Inhabited House, and the earth, in which is the Kaabah, do not embrace Him and are too constricted to hold Him, but He is embraced by the heart in this configuration of the human being with faith. What is meant here by "embracing" is knowledge of God. This will prove to you that the human configuration is the "all-embracing earth" and that it is the earth of your worship.

You should worship Him "as if you see Him" in respect of your eyesight, for your heart is veiled lest your eyesight perceive Him, since He is nonmanifest to you. So "worship God as if you see Him" in your essence, in the manner proper to His majesty, while the eye of your insight witnesses Him, for He is manifest to it through a manifestation of knowledge. Thus you see Him with the eye of your insight, and it is "as if" you see Him in respect of your eyesight.

Hence you bring together in your worship the two forms—the worship that is rightfully demanded by Him in imagination and the worship that is rightfully demanded by Him in other than the homestead of imagination. You worship Him as both unbounded and bound. And this belongs to nothing other than this [human] configuration. That is why He has made this faithful configuration His sacred precinct and His magnified and honored house. I have alluded to this meaning with my words,

When someone is all *ḥaqq*,
  all of him has disappeared from him.
The *Ḥaqq* is a standing person
  and you are His shadow,
or within Him you are His shadow,
  so the affair is all *ḥaqq*.
What He makes unlawful is held sacred,
  and the lawful does not permit to Him
anything inappropriate,
  for He is greater than that.

Every creature in *wujūd* worships God as absent, except the perfect human being with faith, for He worships Him as witnessed. The servant becomes perfect only through faith, since to it belongs the brilliant light, or rather, faith is the brilliant light that takes away every darkness. When he worships Him as witnessed, he sees Him as all his faculties. Thus no one other than He undertakes to worship Him, and it is not appropriate for anyone apart from Him to do so.

There is no one who gains this station save the human being with faith, for he has no faith save in his Lord, and He is the "Faithful."[9] (III 247.13, 249.31)

When Ibn al-ʿArabī distinguishes spirits from bodies, as he usually does, he maintains that bodies are the companions of spirits forever. Without the body's specific preparedness, the spirit would be indistinguishable from the Divine Spirit. The cup gives shape and color to the water. Without the cup, the water would be reabsorbed into the ocean. The Shaykh explains this point in many contexts. For example, he calls Chapter 346 "On the true knowledge of the waystation of a mystery concerning which one of the gnostics spoke the truth, for he saw how his light rises up from the sides of the waystation." At the beginning of his explanation, he writes,

> This waystation is one of the waystations of *tawḥīd* and the lights. God made me enter into it twice.[10] In this waystation I became a light, just as the Prophet said in his supplication, "Make me into a light." From this waystation I came to know the difference between corporeal bodies and corporeous bodies. (III 186.27)

Later on in the chapter, Ibn al-ʿArabī describes some of the knowledge that was unveiled to him when God made him light. He compares the lights of the individual spirits to water in containers, and the light of the Divine Spirit to a river. When the containers are broken through death or annihilation, does the water become indistinguishable from the river? Certainly, Sufis who express this idea in poetry often leave the impression that the drop returns to the ocean and loses its individual identity, but the Shaykh disagrees.

> When I was given this waystation and made to stand in it in the year 591 [1195], I was made to see the similitude of water in a river within which no form was distinct. The water was itself, nothing else. Then some of the water was put into containers. Thereby the water of a jar became designated as different from the water of a pot, and the water of a pot as different from the water of a jug. The shape and color of the receptacle became manifest in the water. The receptacles exercised their properties over the water by dividing and shaping it, even though you know that something that did not become manifest as a shape when it was in the river was exactly the same as something that became manifest when it was not in the river.
>
> In the likeness that is struck here, the difference between the two forms is that, when the containers are gone, the water of the containers returns to the original river, whereas the lights of the waystations return to the original light. Such would be the affair in itself, if the containers and the waystations did not subsist. After all, God desired that these lights should subsist in the distinctions that they received, so He created for them corporeous, *barzakhī* bodies within which these spirits become distinct when they are transferred from their this-worldly corporeal bodies during sleep or after death. In the last world He creates for them natural, corporeal bodies, just as He assigned that for them in this world. However, the constitution is different, so He transfers them from the corporeous body of the *barzakh* to the corporeal bodies of the last world's configuration. There also they are distinct according to the property of the distinction of the forms of their corporeal bodies. It never ceases to be so, forever and ever. They never return to the oneness of entity of their first state. (III 187.31)

God joined spirits to bodies so that they would recognize their natural incapacity and poverty. He did this not because the spirits deserve or merit bodies, but because He is merciful toward the spirits. He gives them the bodies as free gifts so that they will enjoy the blessings of *wujūd* forever. Ibn al-ʿArabī clarifies this point while discussing the properties of the divine names Governor and Differentiator, which are referred to in the verse, *He governs the affair, He differentiates the signs* (13:2). He also has in mind the verse *A book whose signs are made firm, and then differentiated* (11:1). God's attribute of governance is the archetype of the governing power of the spirits. Through it He brings about the various sorts of compoundedness that are found in the cosmos, in particular the compoundedness of spirit and body. Here the Shaykh has in view, once again, the Koranic verse *in whatever form He willed He mounted you* (82:8). As previously noted, this can also be translated as "in whatever form He willed He compounded you." "Compoundedness" (*tarkīb*) is the mounting of a rider (*rākib*) on a mount (*markab*), or something carried (*maḥmūl*) on a carrier (*ḥāmil*). The discussion pertains to Chapter 343, "On the true knowledge of the waystation of two mysteries in the differentiation of revelation."

God has differentiated
  His signs
    for the mindful and
      far-seeing,
He made them firm
  for pure hearts
    that follow none
      but the paths of guidance.
He gave rational speech
  to all who keep on speaking
    to our ears,
      imploring and singing.
Their speech has bewildered our minds,
  but He brought
    the light of guidance,
      and those were guided
who saw and became manifest
  through His lights—
    to Him belong the beginning
      and the end!

Know—God confirm you—that the two divine names, the Governor and the Differentiator, are the two heads of this waystation. They bestow on him who enters into it all the divine knowledges that it carries and comprises. Some of these demand the engendered things and some pertain to God.

The Governor's property in affairs is that He makes them firm in the Presence of Bringing Together and Witnessing and gives to them everything that is rightfully theirs. This all takes place before their *wujūd* in their entities, while they exist for Him. Once He has made them firm, as we mentioned, the Differentiator takes them. This name is specific to the levels. He sends down each engendered thing and each affair into its own level and waystation, like the director of ceremonies for the sultan.

God created two mercies, and they are the first creation that God created. One mercy is noncompound, but He created the other mercy compound. Through the noncompound mercy, the Governor has mercy upon all the noncompound things that God created, and through the compound mercy, He has mercy on all the compound things that God created.

God appointed for the compound mercy three waystations, since the compound thing has two sides and a middle. The middle is identical with the *barzakh* between the two sides so that they may become distinct. Thus He has mercy on every compound object of mercy through the compound mercy in these waystations.

Through the first compound mercy He joined the parts of the bodies to each other so that their entities may become manifest as abiding forms. Through the second compound mercy, from the second waystation, He mounted meanings, attributes, character traits, and knowledges in the rationally speaking soul and in the animal soul that carries the sensory faculties. Through the third compound mercy, from the third waystation, He joined the rationally speaking souls to the governance of the bodies. This is the compounding of a spirit and a body, and this sort of compoundedness is described by death.

The Governor makes these souls appear from their bodies when the Divine Inblowing turns its face toward them through the Spirit that is ascribed to God. Thus the Governor compounds the souls with the bodies from which they were born. This is a compounding of choice. Were it a compounding of rightful demand, the soul would not depart from the body through death. Then the Governor makes the spirit govern another *barzakhī*, corporeous body, and He joins the first body to the earth. Then He configures for it another configuration in which He compounds it in the last world.

Since the mounts are diverse, we come to know that the rationally speaking soul does not govern this designated body—which is its mother from which it is born—by way of rightful demand, for its governing is transferred to another body. However, the body has a *ḥaqq* due to it from the soul that is born from it—as long as the soul governs the body, it must not move the bodily parts except in obedience to God and in the places and states that God has designated for it on the tongue of its Lawgiver. This is the body's rightful demand from the soul because of the *ḥaqq* of birth.

Among the souls are some that are loving children, so they listen to their parents and obey, and in their good-pleasure God is well pleased. He says, *Be thankful to Me*, in respect of the specific face, *and to your parents* [31:14], in respect of the face of occasioning. Also among souls are those that are recalcitrant children, so they do not listen or obey.

The body commands the soul only to the good. That is why the skin and all the bodily parts witness against the body's child on the day of resurrection, for the child has subjugated them and employed them wherever his caprice took him.

God divides the compound mercy into known parts, of which He gives six hundred parts to Gabriel, and through these He has mercy on the folk of the Garden. He places in His hand nineteen parts, through which He has mercy on the folk of the Fire, those who are its folk. Through these he fends off the angels of chastisement, who are nineteen, as God has said: *Over it are nineteen* [74:30].

Then there are the one hundred mercies that God created. He placed one of them in this world, and through it He provides for His servants, the unbelievers among them and the faithful, the disobedient among them and the obedient. Through it all the animals show tenderness toward their children, and through it people show mercy to one another and act tenderly toward each other.[11] Thus God says, *The faithful [. . .] are friends of one another* [9:71]. [He says,] *The wrongdoers are friends of one another* [45:19] and the hypocrites are friends of one another. All this is the fruit of that mercy.

When the day of resurrection comes in the last world, the one mercy will be joined with the ninety-nine mercies stored there.[12] Thereby God will have mercy on His servants gradually and in temporal order, so that He may make manifest through this delay the levels of the interceders, God's solicitude toward them, and their distinction from others.

When there remain in the Fire only its folk who have lost hope within it, those who will not emerge from it, and when the nineteen angels of chastisement desire to chastise the folk of the Fire, nineteen angels will be embodied from the compound mercy and they will come between the angels of chastisement and the folk of the Fire and halt before them. The mercy that *embraces everything* [7:156] will fortify them, for mercy will have embraced the angels of chastisement like the other things, and what embraces them will prevent them from standing up to this compound mercy. What had fortified them in the first place was God's wrath, which becomes manifest from the wraths of the opponents.

Once the session of the trial has been concluded, God will have commanded to prison those whom He commands, and that is Gehenna, as He has said, *For the unbelievers We have made Gehenna a restriction* [17:8]—that is, a prison, since the restricted one is imprisoned and prevented from coming and going. This is in contrast to the folk of the Garden, because they *dwell within* it *wherever* they *will* [39:74]. The folk of the Fire are not like that, and this is because of God's hidden kindness to His servants. Had He given them dwelling in the Fire wherever they will, they would have found no place in which to rest, seeking escape from the chastisement when they felt it, hoping that they would find ease from it in another place. But, at the moment for chastisement, there is no ease in Gehenna, so there would have remained no sort of chastisement that they did not taste. Constant chastisement is easier than chastisement that is ever-renewed, as is the bliss. This is why God will *exchange their skins* in the Fire as soon as they are *wholly burned so that they may taste the chastisement* [4:56]. A time will pass over them during which they are tasting the chastisement constantly, until their skins are wholly burned. Then a new chastisement comes to them through the exchange.

So, were they able to dwell in Gehenna wherever they will, they would not rest until their skins were wholly burned. Rather, they would taste in each site to which they moved a new chastisement until their skins were wholly burned. Hence that movement would give them a more intense chastisement. Thus God has mercy upon them from whence they are not aware, just as He deceives them from whence *they are not aware* [27:50].

These are seven hundred and nineteen mercies. Of them, one hundred are in God's hands, and with these none of God's creatures acts freely. He has specified them for Himself, and through them God has mercy on His servants by lifting the intermediaries. Or rather, these come to the object of mercy from Him specifically. They are in the number of the divine names—the ninety-nine names of enumeration. To each name belongs one of these one hundred mercies in God's hand, and no created thing has any knowledge of them. The one hundred are completed by the mercy that is attributed to Him and that *embraces everything* [7:156].

Through these one hundred mercies, He gazes on the ascending degrees of the Garden, and they are one hundred degrees. Through them also, after the expiration of the time that rightfully demands chastisement, He gazes on the descending degrees of the Fire, and these are one hundred degrees. Each descending degree is the counterpart of a degree of the Garden.

This all-embracing mercy will confirm the nineteen mercies that stand up to the angels of chastisement in the Fire, and these angels will be embraced by it. They will find in themselves a mercy toward the folk of the Fire, since they will see that God has disclosed Himself in other than the form of wrath that had been encouraging them to take vengeance for God from the enemies. Hence they will intercede with God for the folk of the Fire, those who do not emerge from it. They will be for them, after they had been against them. God will accept their intercession for the Fire's folk, and thus will have been realized the divine word that they are the inhabitants of this abode.[13] He will assign their ruling property to the *mercy* that *embraces everything.* (III 171.2)

From Chapter 360: The Tenth Deputyship

Ibn al-ʿArabī describes the soul's embodiment in the imaginal forms of the *barzakh* while explaining the tenth of the ten deputyships given to the perfect human being. At the beginning of the passage, he has in view the words of God directed to the newly deceased soul, *You were heedless of this, so We have unveiled from you your covering, so your eyesight today is piercing* (50:22). He also refers to the common distinction made among three degrees of certainty—the knowledge of certainty, the eye of certainty, and the *ḥaqq* of certainty.

The tenth deputyship is the deputyship of the *tawḥīd* of the dead. Through death, the coverings are unveiled and the Real becomes clear to everyone. However, for the common people, the unveiling at this moment does not bestow felicity, except for him among them who has knowledge of it. Then, when the covering is unveiled, he will see with the eye what he knows, so he will be felicitous.

As for the companions of witnessing, here they already have the eye, so when the covering is unveiled, the eye becomes a *ḥaqq* for them. Thus the folk of unveiling are transferred from the eye to the *ḥaqq,* while the knower is transferred from knowledge to the eye.

As for those other than these two individuals, they are transferred from blindness to seeing. Hence they witness the situation when the covering of blindness is unveiled for them, not on the basis of a prior knowledge.

No group has any escape from increase at death and the lifting of the covering. That is why one of the Companions said, "Were the covering unveiled," thus affirming for you that there is a covering, "I would not increase in certainty," that is, in what he knows when he views it eye-to-eye.[14] Hence he will not increase in certainty in knowledge, but the unveiling of the covering will give him an affair that he did not have. Thus his words, "I would not increase in certainty," are correct concerning his knowledge, if he is the possessor of knowledge, and concerning his eye, if he is the possessor of an eye. But this does not mean that the unveiling of the covering will not increase him in any affair that he did not have. Were this the case, the unveiling of the covering for him who has this attribute would be useless and empty of benefit.

But viewing eye-to-eye has a subtle
meaning—
this is why Moses asked to view eye-to-eye.

There is no covering unless beyond it is an affair of *wujūd,* not of nonexistence.

This deputyship by the servant for the Real occurs in the *barzakh,* so he undertakes to exercise a ruling property through a Real form and a deputyship in the world of imagination, so he has an authority over imagination in the abode of this world. He embodies whatever meanings he wills to the viewer.

A near portion of this authority was attained by the people of sorcery, that is, those concerning whom God says, *He,* meaning Moses, *was made to imagine because of their sorcery that [the ropes and staffs] were sliding* [20:66], but they were not sliding in actual fact, even if they were sliding in the view of Moses and those present—except the sorcerers, who saw them as ropes. If a stranger had entered, he would have seen them as the sorcerers saw them.

This is different from the situation of someone who has deputyship over the world of imagination and within its Presence—someone like Moses—for he does not see the meaning that he embodies as a corporeous body like that which the sorcerers embodied. Rather, he sees it as a meaning. This is only because the sorcerers lack strength. There is nothing between a sorcerer and the companion of this deputyship, like Moses, save the fact that the Real made Moses His deputy, and that he took Him as his trustee. *So Moses threw down his staff* [26:45] on the basis of a command of the Real, which was the command of Him whom he had taken as trustee.

God said to Moses, *Throw down your staff* [7:117], and he saw it as a serpent, so he became fearful. God reported about the sorcerers that *they threw down their ropes and their staffs* [26:44], but not on the basis of a divine command. On the contrary, they did so on the basis of the property of certain [divine] names that they had with themselves, names that had the characteristic of making the eyes of the viewers look at what the sorcerers desired to make manifest. Through those names they possessed the transformation of the viewing, not transformation of the viewed object. Through the divine command, the viewed object is transformed, and the view follows the object.

Hence, in the case of the deputy, the viewing is not transformed. The activity in the viewing and what is viewed occurs only after the casting. When the thing leaves the hold of him who casts it, God undertakes to transform the viewed object in the case of the deputy and to transform the viewing in the case of him who is not a deputy and who has knowledge of these names, which are the *sīmiyā*ʾ [Gk. *semeia*], that is, the "marks" upon what becomes manifest to the eyes of the viewers.

When the covering is unveiled for the common people through death and their transferal to the *barzakh*, there they will be exactly as they were in their bodies in this world, except that they will be transferred from Presence to Presence, or from property to property. But the gnostics—the Real's deputies—possess this property already in the life of this world.

Here the deputyship is a deputyship only of *tawḥīd* because the ruling property does not become manifest until after the casting. In other words, the affair leaves the hold of the caster, and God takes it over through the property of the trusteeship in the case of the deputy and through the property of the reality in the case of the sorcerer. This pertains to the Divine Jealousy, so that nothing will have any ruling property in things except God.

There remains for the companion of this deputyship in this Presence free acting perpetually, as we have mentioned. The common people name this "charismatic gifts," "signs," and "the breaking of habits." For the Realizers, these acts are not the "breaking of habits," but rather the bringing into existence of engendered things. In actual fact, there are no habits, since there is no repetition, so there is nothing that becomes habitual. This is God's words concerning the companions of habits, *No indeed, but they are uncertain of a new creation* [50:15]. He says: They do not know that in every blink they are in a new creation, such that what they see in the first blink is not identical with what they see in the second blink, so they are uncertain about this.

There is no return, so there is no breaking. This is how the Realizers from among the Folk of God perceive the affair, and it is nothing but as we have mentioned. After all, through this, creation is perpetually and forever poor, and the Real is Creator and Preserver of *wujūd* for this *wujūd* perpetually, because of the new creation that He brings into existence within it so that it may subsist.

Consider your sacrifice. Why have you
  brought it?
 Knowledge perceives what eyesight does
  not.
The Men of Knowledge are nearer to taking
  heed,
 the Men of the Eye nearer to looking.
The one described by reason has
 a strength that takes him out of eyesight;
the one described by unveiling has
 a form that lifts him beyond all forms.
You see him perpetually in his state
 becoming manifest from this "other" to that
  "other."

In these imaginal others the deputy acts freely as he desires and wills, but on the basis of the command of his Trustee, since he who takes a trustee is ignorant of the means to wholesomeness that are known by the trustee in the free acting. If he errs and acts freely through heedlessness, without the command of the Trustee, God will preserve him in his moment, for the trusteeship, as we mentioned, is circular.[15] However, when there is this preservation that we mentioned, the form that occurs from the free activity of heedlessness will not reach the same degree as the form that derives from the Trustee's free activity within which this deputy acts freely. This is so that the levels may become distinct, and the uplifted and the more uplifted may become known.

Know also that the level of this specific deputyship is reached only through death. Death is of two sorts: The first is death by constraint, which is well-known to everyone in common language. It is the *named term* concerning which it is said, *When their term comes, they shall not put it back by an hour, nor put it forward* [16:61].

The other death is death by choice. It is a death during the life of this world, the "decreed term" in His words, *Then He decreed a term* [6:2]. Since the moment of this decreed term is known at God and named at Him, its property in itself is the same as the property of the named term. This is indicated by His words, *Each runs to a named term* [31:29], that is, in its state. A human being does not die during his life until he has correctly reached this deputyship. Then he is dead/not dead, like the one who is slain in the path of God. God transfers him to the *barzakh*, but not because of death. The martyr is slain/not dead. When someone given this solicitude has slain his own soul in the Greater Jihad, which is the jihad against the soul, God provides him with the property of martyrdom. Thus He undertakes to give him a deputyship in the *barzakh* during his life in this world. So his death is suprasensory, and his being slain is his opposition to his soul. (III 287.24)

The Trumpet

As noted earlier, Ibn al-ʿArabī says that imagination is simultaneously the most all-embracing and the most constricted thing in existence. Hence it can be pictured as a horn. The Shaykh finds Koranic references to this horn in the ten mentions of the trumpet that the angel Seraphiel will blow to announce the imminence of the Last Day. When he blows it the first time, *Everyone in the heavens and earth will be thunderstruck* (39:68). The second time, *They will hasten from their tombs unto their Lord* (36:51).

The Arabic word for trumpet, *ṣūr*, is also a plural of the word *ṣūra*, meaning "form." As some of the early Koran commentators recognized, the repeated Koranic expression, *When the Trumpet is blown* can also be read as "When the forms are blown into." Seraphiel will blow into the *barzakhī* forms to bring about the resurrection just as God blew into Adam's clay in creating him. The Prophet said that the Trumpet is a horn of light. In the Shaykh's view, this saying refers to imagination's luminosity relative to the corporeal realm.

God created the spirits and He commanded them to govern the forms. He made them undivided, or rather, to be one essence. He distinguished some of them from others, so they became distinct. Their distinction was in keeping with the forms' receptivity toward the self-disclosure. The forms are not the wherenesses for these spirits in reality, except that the forms in relation to the spirits are like a possession in the case of elemental forms, and like loci of manifestation in the case of all forms.

Then, through another self-disclosure, God gave new arrival to the corporeous, imaginal forms between the subtleties and the forms. In these corporeous forms, luminous and fiery forms disclose themselves as manifest to the eye, and in these corporeous forms, sensory forms disclose themselves as carriers of suprasensory forms in dreams, after death, and before the Uprising.

This is the formal *barzakh*, a horn of light. Its highest point is all-embracing and its lowest point is constricted, for its highest point is the Cloud and its lowest point is the earth. These corporeous forms, within which become manifest the jinn, the angels, and the nonmanifest human domain, are manifest in dreams and in the forms of the Market of the Garden. It is these forms that populate the earth [created from the leftover of Adam's clay], concerning which we spoke in its own chapter.

Then God appointed for these forms and these spirits a nourishment through which they subsist. This is a sensory and a suprasensory provision. The suprasensory includes the nourishment of knowledges, self-disclosures, and states. The sensory nourishment is well known. It is the spiritual meanings—I mean the faculties—carried by the forms of things that are eaten and drunk.

This then is nourishment. Hence all nourishment is suprasensory, according to what we have said, even if it takes sensory forms. Each form—whether it be luminous, animal, or corporeous—takes nourishment as is appropriate for it. But to discuss this in detail would take too long. (I 149.5)

Ibn al-ʿArabī calls Chapter 8, to which he has just referred, "On the true knowledge of the earth that was created from the leftover ferment of Adam's clay, which is named 'the earth of the reality,' and on the mention of some of the marvels and wonders within it." In the chapter, he describes this earth as enormously more vast than our earth and as the locus of wonders that the rational mind cannot comprehend.[16] He mentions it elsewhere in the context of discussing the Highest Barzakh, which is Unbounded Imagination:

It is the world that is infinite and has no borders where it would reach an end. It is the inhabitant that inhabits the earth created from the leftover ferment of Adam's clay just as forms, manifest to the viewer in a polished body, inhabit it with an "inhabiting" through effusion. (III 47.2)[17]

At the end of Chapter 8, most of which is dedicated to quoting the reports of various gnostics concerning the wonders that they have witnessed in the earth of the leftover clay, the Shaykh identifies it rather clearly with the World of Imagination.[18]

Whatever reason's proofs have declared impossible to us, we have found possible and actually occurring in this earth. *God is powerful over each thing* [2:20]. Thus we came to know that rational faculties are inadequate and that God is powerful over bringing together opposites, a corporeal body's *wujūd* in two places, an accident's abiding through itself and its transferal, and a meaning's abiding within a meaning. When any hadith or Koranic verse has come to us and reason has turned aside from its manifest meaning, we have found it in this earth according to the manifest meaning. Every corporeous body in which a spiritual being—whether angel or jinn—assumes shape, and every form in which the human being sees himself in dreams, is one of the corporeous bodies of this earth. These bodies have specific sites within it, and the spiritual beings have tenuities that are drawn out into the whole cosmos.[19] Every tenuity is guarded by someone trusted. When the trusted one sees that one of the spirits is prepared for any of the forms in its hand, it clothes it in the form, like the form of Diḥya for Gabriel.

The occasion of this is that the Real drew out this earth in the *barzakh*, and within it He designated a site for the corporeous forms which are put on by the spiritual beings and to which souls are transferred during sleep and after death. We derive from part of the world of this earth. It has one side that enters into the Garden and is called the "Market."

We will explain to you an image for the form of the extension of the side of this earth that is adjacent to the world. When someone gazes at a lamp, or the sun, or the moon, and when he makes his eyelashes intervene between his gazing eye and the luminous body, he sees something like numerous lines of light coming from the luminous body to his eyes and joining the lamp to his eyes. When he lifts the eyelashes from before his gazing eye little by little, he sees those extended lines being brought in to the luminous body.

The luminous body is an image for the site that is designated for those forms in this earth. The gazing eye is an image for the world. The extension of those lines is like the forms of the corporeous bodies to which people are transferred during sleep, after death, and in the Market of the Garden. What puts on the forms is the spirits. Your intention to see those lines through that act—by letting the eyelashes intervene between the gazing eye and the luminous body—is an image for the preparedness. The rising up of those lines in this state is the rising up of the forms in the preparedness. The bringing in of the lines to the luminous body when the obstruction is removed is the return of the forms to that earth when the preparedness disappears. There is no clarification after this clarification! (I 130.26)

In Chapter 63, "On the true knowledge of people's subsistence in the *barzakh* between this world and the Uprising," the Shaykh provides more details concerning Seraphiel's Trumpet.[20]

When God grips the spirits away from the natural and elemental bodies, wherever they may be, He deposits them in corporeous forms in the totality of this luminous Horn. The human being perceives all the affairs that he perceives after death in the *barzakh* with the eye of the form within which he dwells in the Horn and through its light. This is a true perception.

Among the forms there, some are bound back from free activity and some—like the spirits of all the prophets and the spirits of the martyrs—are unbounded. Some have a gaze toward the domain of this world in this abode. Some disclose themselves to the dreamer in the Presence of imagination in which he dwells—he is the one whose dream-vision is always truthful. But all dream-visions are truthful and make no errors. When the dream-vision errs, it is no error, but the interpreter who interprets it errs, since he does not know what is meant by the form.

Do you not see what the Prophet said to Abū Bakr when he interpreted the dream vision? "You were correct in some and mistaken in some." He said the same thing to the man who saw in a dream that his neck was struck by a sword and his head fell off. Then the head began to roll while it spoke to him. The Messenger of God mentioned to him that Satan was playing with him.[21] So the Messenger knew the form of what he had seen. He did not say to him, "Your imagination is corrupt," for he saw a *ḥaqq*. However, he was mistaken in the interpretation, so the Prophet reported to him the reality of what the dreamer saw. (I 307.7)

In continuing this passage, Ibn al-ʿArabī cites a Koranic passage that he reads as referring to the chastisement in the *barzakh*: *The ugliness of the chastisement engulfed the folk of Pharaoh—the Fire, to which they shall be exposed morning and evening. And on the day the Hour comes: "Admit the folk of Pharaoh into the more intense chastisement"* (40:45–46).

Something similar is the situation of the people of Pharaoh. *They shall be exposed to* the Fire in those forms in the morning and the evening, but they will not enter into the Fire, for they are imprisoned in the Horn in that form. Then, on the day of resurrection, they shall enter *the more intense chastisement*. This is the sensory chastisement, not the imaginal chastisement that they had in the state of their death through the exposure [to the Fire].

With the eye of imagination, imaginal and sensory forms are perceived together. Thus the imaginer, who is the human being, sometimes sees imaginalized things with the eye of his imagination. Take, for example, the Prophet's words, "The Garden was imaginalized to me in the breadth of this wall." He perceived that with the eye of his sensation. I say "with the eye of his sensation" because he stepped forward when he saw the Garden to pick some fruit from it, but he stepped back when he saw the Fire, all while he was performing the *ṣalāt*. We know that he had the strength such that, had he perceived it with the eye of his imagination, not the eye of his sensation, this would not have left in his body the trace of stepping forward and coming back, for we ourselves find that, and we do not possess his strength or stand in his grade.

In the *barzakh*, all human beings will be pawns to what they have earned and imprisoned in the forms of their deeds until they are raised up from those forms on the day of resurrection in the last configuration. (I 307.16)

Chapter 302: The Spirit's Subsistence

Although Ibn al-ʿArabī repeatedly tells us that the human spirit will never be separated from bodily forms, he recognizes that many Muslim authorities disagree with him. He touches on some of their opinions in the chapter called "On the true knowledge of the waystation of the disappearance of the higher world and the *wujūd* of the lower world." The chapter "derives from the Presences of Muhammad, Moses, and Jesus" and corresponds to Surah 82, which, in its nineteen verses, describes the day of resurrection in vivid detail. At the beginning, he differentiates between the absent and the witnessed and then points out that the characteristics of witnessed things can be described in terms of Aristotle's ten categories.[22]

The waystation of imparting arguments
  is the waystation of him who has gone up,
so be not like the person who,
  when the door was opened, went away.
Persevere, and be like the person who,
  when the door was opened, entered.
He who seeks shelter with God will be
    protected,
  and he who implores will be enwrapped
in everything he asks from Him
  in constriction and relief.
This was said in the proverb,
  "Who sets off at night reaches the goal."
In the like of this, my brother,
  souls and lifebloods are annihilated.
How many a mindful person has perished
  in His ocean in the midst of the depths,
and when you see a soul perish in Him
  no fault can be held against it.

Know that the "absent" is a container for the world of the witnessed. Here by "world of the witnessed" is meant every existent thing apart from God, whether it is found, not found, or was found and then was sent back to the absent—such as forms and accidents. All this is witnessed by God, which is why we said that it is the world of the witnessed.

The Real never ceases bringing the cosmos from the absent domain—one thing after another, to an infinite number of individuals, genera, and species. Among these are those that are sent back to His absent and among them are those that are never sent back. Those that are never sent back to the absent are all the essences that abide through themselves, and these are nothing but substances specifically. Everything other than substances—the corporeal things or accidents of engendered quality and color—are sent back to the absent, and their likes appear. God brings them out from the absent to their own witnessing of themselves, since He is the *Knower of the absent and the witnessed.*

The things in the absent have no quantity, since quantity requires restriction, for it is said, "How many is such and such?" But this is not applied to the things in the absent, for they are infinite. How many, how, where, time, establishing,[23] correlation, accident, activity, and reception of activity are all relations that have no entities. Their properties become manifest through the manifestation of the substance to itself, when the Real makes it appear from His absent. Once the entities of the substances become manifest, these relations follow them.

It is asked how many entities became manifest, and the reply is given that they are ten, or more, or less.

It is asked how they are, and the reply is given that they are combined. Corporeality occurs for them, so it is correct to speak of howness through corporeality and the indwelling of engendered quality and color.

It is asked where, and the reply is given: In spatial confinement, or in place.

It is asked when, and the reply is given: While it was such and such in the form of such and such.

It is asked what his tongue is, and the reply is given that it is Persian or Arabic.

It is asked what his religion is, and the reply is given that it is the shariah of so-and-so.

It is asked if anything has become manifest from him that would be a manifestation from a father, as he became manifest from someone else. It is answered: "He is a son of so-and-so."

It is asked what he did, and it is answered that he ate.

It is asked what he received from his eating, and the reply is given that he became full.

These are all the relations that occur as accidents to substances when God brings them out from His absent. So there is nothing in newly arrived *wujūd* except the entities of the substance and the relations that follow upon the substance.

It is as if the absent, through what is within it, contains a form that coincides with its knower, since His knowledge of Himself is His knowledge of the cosmos. The cosmos appears in the form of the Knower in respect of the fact that He knows it.

In respect of substance, His form is His Essence.

In respect of how many: His names.

In respect of how: His words *Each day He is upon some task* [55:29]; *We shall surely attend to you at leisure, you two weighty ones!* [55:31]; *The All-Merciful sat upon the Throne* [20:5]. The likes of these that He has reported from Himself are many.

Where: "God was in a Cloud" and He is God *in the heaven* [43:84].

Time: God was in eternity without beginning.

Establishing: *God spoke directly to Moses* [4:164], *Grant him sanctuary until he hears the speech of God* [9:6]. So all the shariahs are His establishing.

Correlation: Creator of creation, *Owner of the kingdom* [3:26].

Activity: "In His hand is the scale; He lets down the just measure and lifts it up."

Reception of activity: People call to Him and He responds, they ask and He bestows, they seek forgiveness and He forgives.[24]

All this is the form of the Knower. Everything other than God has become manifest in the form of its Existence-Giver, so He has made none manifest save Himself. Hence the cosmos is the Real's locus of manifestation to perfection. So "There is nothing in possibility more wondrous than this cosmos," because there is nothing more perfect than the Real. Were there anything in possibility more perfect than this cosmos, there would be something more perfect than its Existence-Giver. But there is nothing but God, so there is nothing in possibility except the likeness of what has become manifest, not more perfect than it. Ponder what I have said, for it is the core of the true knowledge of God!

Then God epitomized from the cosmos a total epitome that contains all its meanings in the most perfect respects, and He named him Adam. The Prophet said that He created him in His form. So the human being is the totality of the cosmos, so he is the small human being, and the cosmos is the great human being. Or, name the human being the "small cosmos"—however you will, so long as you know the affair as it is in itself and its entity. Ascribe to him and use whatever technical term you desire.

The human being has no excellence over the cosmos through his entirety, but the cosmos is more excellent than the human being, since it adds to him one degree, which is that the human being came into existence from the macrocosm. Hence it possesses over him the degree of being the occasion, because he was born from it. God says, *The men have a degree above them* [2:228], because Eve proceeded from Adam, so that degree over her never ceases to accompany him in masculinity over femininity. Although the mother is the occasion of the *wujūd* of the son, her son exceeds her through the degree of masculinity, for he is more similar to his father in every respect.

Hence it is incumbent upon the human being to magnify his parents. His mother is the whole cosmos, and his father is well known and not disavowed. The marriage act is the face-turning, so the child emerges in the form of his parents. Since the child is claimed only for his father, he is not ascribed to his mother, for the father possesses the degree and he has highness, so the child is ascribed to the more eminent.

Since Jesus was not able to be ascribed to [Gabriel] who bestowed him upon *her as a well-proportioned mortal* [19:17], his mother was given perfection, which is the most eminent station. So Jesus was ascribed to her, and it was said "Jesus son of Mary." She has this eminence through perfection—the station of the degree by which men are given eminence over women, so that because of it the child is ascribed to its father. Mary's perfection was given witness to by God's Messenger, as also that of Āsiya, wife of Pharaoh.

As for the perfection of Āsiya, that was because of the eminence of the station claimed by Pharaoh. Because of that station, it was not appropriate for the throne upon which he sat to be described by anything but perfection. Thus Āsiya gained perfection through the eminence of the station through which Pharaoh became wretched and joined up with *clear loss* [22:11], while his wife won felicity. Because of the eminence of the station through which she gained perfection, she said, *My Lord, build for me a house in the Garden at Thee* [66:11]. Nothing made her utter *at Thee* but the strength of the station. She did not seek the neighborhood of Moses or any of the created things. That would not have been appropriate for her, since the state had overcome her. After all, the perfect will not be below the perfect, for belowness is a descent in degree. Since the perfection of Mary was through Jesus, in his being ascribed to her she did not say what Āsiya said.

Āsiya says, *Deliver me from Pharaoh and his deed, and deliver me from the people of the wrongdoers* [66:11], so that the honor of the ascription will not be violated.

Mary says, *Would that I had died before this and become utterly forgotten* [19:23], but, in actual fact, she was innocent with God. So she did not say that for God's sake, as Āsiya said *at Thee*, thereby giving Him priority and seeking His neighborhood and preservation from the hands of His enemies. But Mary said that out of shame before the people, because of what she knew of the purity of her house and her fathers. She feared that disgrace would be joined to them because of her.

We have mentioned that the cosmos was curtained in God's Absent and that the Absent corresponded to a person's shadow. If some affair were pulled out from the whole shadow, it would emerge in the shadow's form. The shadow has the form of the one that throws it, so what comes forth from it and is pulled out from it takes the form of the person. Do you not see that when *the daytime* is *pulled out* from *the night* [36:37] it becomes manifest as a light? So the things that were curtained by the night become manifest through the daytime's light. The daytime is not similar to the night, but it is similar to the light in that things become manifest through it. So the night is the light's shadow, and when the daytime is pulled out from the night, it emerges in the form of light. So also is the cosmos in its emergence from the Absent—it emerges in the form of the Knower of the absent, as we have explained.

Thus has become clarified for you from this station a knowledge of God within which is sufficiency if you recognize its worth, *So be not one of the ignorant* [6:35].

As for the question of the spirit of this cosmos's form and the spirits of the high and low worlds' forms, I will expound it for you in this question pertaining to this waystation, in its eighth degree—for this waystation comprises seventeen sorts of knowledge, and this is one of them.[25] Thus we say:

• The spirit of the macrocosm is the Absent from which the macrocosm emerged. So understand! It should suffice you to know that the cosmos is the highest and greatest locus of manifestation, if you use your intelligence and know His words, *Do you not see how your Lord draws out the shadow?* [25:45].

Now that the spirit of the macrocosm has become clear to you, there remains for you to know about the spirits of the cosmos's forms.

Do they come into existence from a form, before a form, or along with a form?

In relation to the cosmos's forms the spirits correspond to the spirits of the organs' forms found in the small human being [i.e., the microcosm]. For example, power is the spirit of the hand, hearing is the spirit of the ear, eyesight is the spirit of the eye.

Know that people disagree in this question, as we have mentioned in detail. In our view, the realization in this is that the governing spirits of the forms existed in the Presence of Undifferentiation, not differentiated to their entities, but differentiated at God in His knowledge. In the Presence of Undifferentiation they were like letters existent potentially in ink. Hence they were not distinct to themselves, even though they were distinct at God, differentiated in the state of their undifferentiation.

When the Pen wrote upon the Tablet, the forms of the letters became manifest as differentiated after they had been undifferentiated within the ink. Hence, concerning the noncompound things—that is, the spirits of the noncompound things—it was said, "This is an *a*, this a *b*, this a *c*, and this a *d*." It was also said, "This stands, this is Zayd; this emerges, this is ʿAmr"—these are the spirits of the compound bodies.

When God proportioned the forms of the cosmos—whichever cosmos He desired—the All Spirit was like the pen and the writing hand, the spirits like the ink in the pen, and the forms like the waystations of the letters in the tablet. He blew the spirit into the forms of the cosmos, so the spirits became manifest as distinct through their forms. Then it was said, "This is Zayd, this ʿAmr, this a horse, this an elephant, this a serpent," and so on with every possessor of a spirit—and there is nothing that does not possess a spirit, though it is perceived or not perceived.

Some people say that the spirits, in the root of their *wujūd*, were born from the constitution of the form. Others refuse to accept that. Both have a standpoint by which they are supported.

The middle path is the one we walk on. It is God's words, *Then We configured him as another creation* [23:14]. Then, when God had proportioned the corporeal forms, *He mounted* them *in whatever form* among the spiritual forms *He willed* [82:8]. If He willed, it was in the form of a pig, a dog, a human being, or a horse, in accordance with what the Exalted, the Knowing determined.

One individual is overcome by stupidity and dumb beastliness, so his spirit is the spirit of a donkey, and he is called this when the property of the spirit becomes manifest. It is said, "So-and-so is a donkey." In the same way, every attribute *is called forth to its book* [45:28]. It is said, "So-and-so is a dog, so-and-so is a lion, so-and-so is a human being." The last is the most perfect of attributes and the most perfect of spirits.

God says, *who created you, then proportioned you, then balanced you,* thus completing the configuration manifest to eyesight; *in whatever form He willed* among the forms of the spirits *He mounted you* [82:7–8], so you are ascribed to them, as we mentioned, and they are designated at God. Thus the spirits became distinct through their forms.

Then the spirits depart from these sorts of matter. According to a group of our companions, the spirits then wholly disengage themselves from matter and go back to their root, just as the sun's rays born from a polished body return to the sun when the body rusts. Our companions diverge here into two paths.

One group say that after their departure, spirits do not become distinct to themselves. In the same way, when pots on the bank of a river are broken, the water is not distinct, so it returns to the river. So the bodies are the pots, and the water with which they were filled from the river is like the spirits from the All Spirit.

Another group say that on the contrary, when the spirits are neighbors of the body, they earn vile or beautiful guises. Through these guises they become distinct when they depart from the bodies. In the same way, when the water is in the pots, certain affairs alter its state in color, smell, or taste. When it departs from the pots, the smell, taste, or color that it earned accompanies it in its essence. Then God preserves them in those earned guises. In this view, they agree with some of the philosophers.

Still another group say that the governing spirits never cease governing in the domain of this world. When they are transferred to the *barzakh*, they govern *barzakhī*, corporeous bodies. These are the forms in which human beings see themselves in dreams, and so also is death. They are called the "Trumpet." Then, on the day of resurrection, the spirits will be raised up in natural bodies, just as they were in this world.

Here ends the disagreement among our companions concerning the spirits after departure. As for the disagreements among other than our companions, these are many, but it is not our intention to cite the speech of those who do not belong to our path.

Know, my brother—may God take charge of you with His mercy—that the Garden that is reached in the last world by those who are its folk is witnessed by you today in respect of its locus, not in respect of its form. Within it you undergo fluctuations in your states, but you do not know that you are within it, because the form within which it discloses itself to you veils you.

The folk of unveiling, who perceive that from which the people are absent, see that locus, if it is a Garden, as a green gardenplot. If it is a Gehenna, they see it in keeping with the descriptions that are within it—its bitter cold and its burning heat—and what God has prepared within it.

Most of the folk of unveiling see this at the beginning of the path. The Shariah has called attention to this with the Prophet's words, "Between my grave and my pulpit is one of the gardenplots of the Garden." The folk of unveiling see it as a gardenplot as he said. They see the Nile, the Euphrates, the Sarus, and the Pyramus as rivers of honey, water, wine, and milk, as they are in the Garden. After all, the Prophet reported that these rivers belong to the Garden.

When God has not unveiled someone's eyesight and he remains in the blindness of his veil, he does not perceive this and is like a blind man in a rosegarden. He is not absent from it in his essence, but he does not see it. The fact that he does not see it does not necessitate that he is not within it. No, he is within it.

So also are those places which God's Messenger mentioned as being of the Fire, like Baṭn al-Muḥassir in Minā and others. This is why he prescribed for his community that they make haste in leaving it, for he saw what they did not see and he witnessed what they did not witness.[26]

Among people are those whom this witnessing accompanies constantly, and among them are those whom it does not accompany in keeping with what God means from that, because of a wisdom that He has hidden in His creation.

Do you not see that when God protects the folk of abstinence from eating something forbidden, one of its marks for them is that the food changes in their gaze to the form of something forbidden? Thus they see it as blood, or pork, for example, so they hold back from eating it. Then when they investigate how that food was earned, they find that it was earned in other than a way approved by the Shariah.[27]

The folk of God have *eyes through which they see* [. . .], *ears through which they hear* [7:195], *hearts through which they use intelligence* [22:46], and tongues with which they speak that are other than these eyes, ears, hearts, and tongues possessed by the form. Through these eyes they witness, through these ears they hear, through these hearts they use intelligence, and through these tongues they speak. Hence their speech is correct. After all, *It is not the eyesights that are blind, but blind* toward the Real and taking from Him *are the hearts within the breasts* [22:46]. *Deaf, dumb, blind—so they do not use intelligence* [2:171] from God. [*Deaf, dumb, blind—*]*so they do not return* [2:18] to God. But, by God, their eyes are in their faces, their hearing is in their ears, and their tongues are in their mouths. However, precedent solicitude has not been shown to them, nor the most beautiful.[28]

So praise belongs to God, in gratitude that He has given us life through these hearts, tongues, ears, and eyes.

A prophetic hadith has reached us that is sound for the folk of unveiling, even if its path has not been affirmed for the folk of transmission, because of the weakness of the narrator—even if he spoke the truth in it. He said that God's Messenger said, "If not for the excess in your speaking and the tumult in your hearts, you would see what I see and hear what I hear."

God says, [*We have sent down to thee the Remembrance*] *that thou mayest make clear to the people what was sent down to them* [16:44]. Nothing can be clearer than this explicit clarification. However, where is he who has emptied his locus for the traces of his Lord? Where is he who transmits what he has heard without addition? Such are truly few. And God it is who gives success.

Know also that this waystation comprises the knowledge of dissolution; the knowledge of the knowledges gained by the folk of the Fire in the Fire when they enter it; the knowledge of the divine secrets that are bestowed by the world of nature, secrets that are not known from other than it; the knowledge of the precedent and of the subsequent, which is the outcome; the knowledge of the composition of the ontological demonstrations; the knowledge of spiritual and formal existence-giving; the knowledge of the occasion that leads to wretchedness; the knowledge of that through which the arrangement of the cosmos subsists and its form is preserved; the knowledge of self-disclosure in the veil; the knowledge of the divine rulings by other than the path of the Lawgiver; the knowledge of the *tawḥīd* of acts; and the knowledge of joining the higher things to the lower things and the lower things to the higher things. This last, or near to it, is the knowledge of the conjunction of the farther things with the closer things and the closer things with the farther things. *And God speaks the **ḥaqq**, and He guides on the path* [33:4]. (III 10.26)

From Chapter 369: The Storehouse of the Final Issue

Ibn al-ʿArabī provides a survey of several of his teachings concerning the soul and its ultimate destiny in the thirteenth and fourteenth sections of Chapter 369, from which several sections have already been quoted. He begins the thirteenth section by referring to the often discussed theological issue of the benefit of repentance (*tawba*). How close to death can people be and still have their repentance accepted by God? In the Shaykh's view, as long a person has not reached the point where death is actually present (*iḥtiḍār*), repentance will have a salvific effect.

The final issue of the affair is the return from manyness to the One, whether the person be one of the faithful or a disbeliever, because [God,] the Faithful, who gives the unveiling of affairs as they are, demands it. That is His words, *We have unveiled from you your covering, so your eyesight today is piercing* [50:22]. This takes place before the person's emergence from this world. No one is taken when he is taken except with an unveiling. Thereby he inclines toward the *ḥaqq*, the *ḥaqq* being *tawḥīd* and faith in Him.

Those who gain this certainty before the presence of death will surely reach felicity. After all, certainty on the basis of sound consideration and explicit witnessing will prevent their being deflected from the *ḥaqq*. Hence they will stand *upon a clear sign* [11:17] and insight in the affair.

Those who gain this certainty only at the presence of death will remain in the [divine] will. Although the final issue will be to felicity, this will occur only after the experience of hardships in the case of those who are taken to task for their sins.

Death is "made present" only after a person witnesses the affair to which creation will be transferred. As long has he has not witnessed that, death is not present with him, and he has not been made present with death. So, if someone has faith before being made present with death by a single breath, or if he repents, that faith and repentance will benefit him at God in the last abode. His state, when his spirit is taken, will be the state of one who has no sins.

It makes no difference if the person is pushed back to that by the intensity of pain, an illness that demands that he cut off hope for this world's life, or something else. He will still be a repentant person of faith, and that will benefit him, since he has not yet been made present with death. He has had faith or repented only through a ferment which he had in his nonmanifest domain and his heart and of which he was unaware. He inclines to that to which he inclines only through an affair within himself whose property had not become manifest externally or within himself until this solitary time that came to him in the time followed by his being made present with death, and at this point the faith already there in the [divine] will becomes necessary for him.

What a difference between him
who has been judged for felicity
and him against whom
His will has decreed!
That is an exalted, sacred
deliverance
and it has a state shown to him
by his reality.
If not for it, his path
would not have become clear for him,
and one day His creatures would be
called to witness against him.

The servant is then transferred from the life of this world to the life of the Greatest Exposure.

God has placed within engendered existence two resurrections—a lesser resurrection and a greater resurrection. The lesser resurrection is the servant's transferal from the life of this world to the life of the *barzakh* in the imaginal body. The Prophet referred to it with his words, "When someone dies, his resurrection has come." All who are among the Folk of Vision will see their Lord, for God's Messenger said, when warning his community about al-Dajjāl, that no one will see God until he dies.

The greater resurrection is the resurrection of the Uprising and the Greatest Mustering, within which all people will be brought together. At the Greater Resurrection, the human being will either be questioned, or called to reckoning, or interrogated or not interrogated concerning his reckoning. The last is the *easy reckoning* [84:8];

it is the presentation of the deeds to the servants without interrogation. "Interrogation" is being questioned about the causes of the deeds.

"Questioning" is general and for everyone, even the messengers. Thus God says, *The day when God shall gather the Messengers and say, "What answer were you given?"* [5:109].

Questioning is of two sorts. The first is a questioning to stipulate blessings by way of the Real's cheerful expansiveness toward the one who is questioned, so the servant takes pleasure in the questioning. The second is questioning by way of reprimand, also to stipulate blessings, but the person is in hardship. The Prophet said to his Companions after they had eaten dates and water out of hunger, "You will be questioned about the bliss of this day." This questioning is plausibly understood as warning and good news for a specified people, that is, those who were the folk of that sitting place. But it is a calling attention to the actual situation for everyone.

Having explained this, we say: God created the cosmos only for felicity in essence. Wretchedness occurs in the case of him for whom it occurs as an accident. This is because nothing proceeds from the Sheer Good in which there is no evil—which is the *wujūd* of the Real that gave *wujūd* to the cosmos—except that which corresponds with it, and that is good specifically. Hence good belongs to the cosmos in essence. The property that rules over the cosmos is possibility, because it is alternately qualified by one of the two sides. It does not stand in the level of the *wujūd* that is Necessary because of Its Essence, so evil occurs to it accidentally.

"Evil" is failure to attain the personal desire and what is agreeable to one's nature, for the thing's possibility does not intervene between it and nonexistence. In this measure evil becomes manifest in the cosmos. Hence it becomes manifest from the direction of the possible thing, not from the direction of the Real. That is why the Prophet said in his supplication, "The good, all of it, is in Thy hands, but the evil does not go back to Thee." It goes back only to creation in respect of its possibility.

We are felicitous
  through the Real's Essence,
    and wretchedness arises
      from mankind's possibility.
Encountering the Real
  is a necessary *ḥaqq*,
    so give the good news that all good
      is found in the encounter.
From us we have
  annihilation and subsistence,
    from Him we have
      wujūd and encounter.
He is a good
  for which no opposite is seen,
    and when the good
      comes together with the good,
all that comes to be
  is good
    and evil has no place to walk,
      no occasion for meeting.

Know that the bodies are the sepulchers and the tombs of the spirits. It is they that veil the spirits from witnessing and being witnessed. Hence the spirits do not see, nor are they seen, until they depart from these graves by annihilation from them—not by separation [through death]. When they are annihilated from witnessing them, while possessing eyesight, they witness their Existence-Giver through witnessing themselves, for "He who knows himself knows his Lord," and so also, he who witnesses himself witnesses his Lord. Then he is transferred from the certainty of knowledge to the certainty of the eye. When he is sent back to his grave, he is sent back to the certainty of the *ḥaqq*, not the certainty of knowledge. From here the human being comes to know the Real's differentiating through His truthful report among the *ḥaqq* of certainty, the eye of certainty, and the knowledge of certainty. Every property becomes settled in its own level, things are no longer obscured for him, and he comes to know that the news-giving [of the prophets] does not lie to him.

He who knows God by this path has truly known Him. He has come to know the wisdom of the pearl's being engendered in the shell from sweet water in the midst of salty brine. The shell is his body and the brine his nature. That is why the property of nature prevails over his shell, for salt is whiteness, which corresponds to the light through which unveiling takes place. So realize this signifier! *And God's it is to point out the path* [16:9]. (III 388.33)

From Chapter 369: The Storehouse of Humanity

Ibn al-ʿArabī continues the above discussion in the next section, which he calls, "Listening knocks and is given enjoyment, bringing together the lowland and the hill."

Since the intended goal of the cosmos was the perfect human being, the animal human being—who is similar to the perfect human being in the natural configuration—is also found in the cosmos. The realities that were brought together by the human being were disseminated throughout the cosmos. The Real summoned them from the whole cosmos, and they came together. The human being came to be from their coming together, so he was their storehouse. The faces of the cosmos turned toward this human storehouse to see what would become manifest from God's summoning all these realities. They saw a form standing erect, moving straight, and designated in directions. No one in the cosmos had ever seen the like of this human form.

From that moment on the fiery spirits and the angels have assumed the form of the human being. This is God's words, *[Gabriel] became imaginalized to her as a well-proportioned mortal* [19:17] and in the words of God's Messenger, "Sometimes the angel becomes imaginalized to me as a man." For the spirits assume the shape only of forms that they know, and they know nothing of them without witnessing. So, before the creation of the human being, the spirits were assuming the form of every form in the cosmos except the human form. After all, although the spirits possess the assumption of forms, in contrast to the human being they do not possess the form-giving faculty, since it follows upon reflection, which is an attribute of the reflective faculty.

Assuming forms is one of the attributes of self of the spirits' essence, not a suprasensory attribute—it does not belong to a form-giving faculty that they possess. However, although the assumption of forms pertains to their essence, they assume only the forms of the natural world that they perceive. Thus the spirits above nature do not accept the assumption of forms, because they have no knowledge of the natural shapes. These spirits are only the Soul, the Intellect, and the enraptured spirits, in this world and the last world. Hence, those above nature do not witness the forms of the cosmos, even if some of them, like the Universal Soul, give replenishment to the world of nature through their very essence, without any intention, just as the sun gives its radiance by its very essence without any intention of benefit or harm. This is the meaning of "by its very essence."

The relations of knowledge and practice belong to the Soul's very essence because it knows itself, not what is above it—its cause and other things. As for its practice, it is attributed to it just as the whitening of a piece of cloth and the blackening of the face of the washerman are attributed to the sun and just as heating and burning are attributed to fire. It is said that the sun whitened this and made that manifest, and the fire burned this, cooked that, and heated this. Such is the situation in the cosmos—if you are a possessor of the kernel and astuteness.

God knows each thing [2:231] and *is powerful over each thing* [2:20]. This is why He discloses Himself in each form. The whole cosmos came out from nonexistence into *wujūd,* with the sole exception of human beings, who became manifest from a *wujūd* to a *wujūd*—that is, from a *wujūd* of separation to a *wujūd* of bringing together. Hence their state changed from a separateness to a bringing together, while the state of the cosmos changed from nonexistence to *wujūd.* What distinguishes human beings from the cosmos is what distinguishes *wujūd* from nonexistence. That is why *Nothing* of the cosmos *is as* the human being's *likeness* [42:11].

I am churned from *wujūd*
only because I come from *wujūd.*
No affair has any property of nonexistence over me
that might be carried out in my *wujūd.*
The Book has nothing like me
in tasting the pleasure of increase.
That is why my being was specified for prostration
and I came to be for prostration's sake.
The command made every engendered thing prostrate itself
to me, save the one who spoke in refusal.

When a solid thing dissolves, the forms change, so the name changes, and hence the ruling changes. When a liquid thing freezes, the form changes, so the name changes, and hence the ruling changes. The shariahs descended addressing the entities in respect of their forms, states, and names. The entity is not addressed in terms of its essence, and no ruling applies to it in respect of its reality. That is why, among the rulings of the Shariah, "indifferent" pertains to the entity. As for doing the incumbent, the recommended, the forbidden, and the reprehensible, this pertains to alien suggestions that befall the entity's *wujūd,* and these belong to what is connected to the pure and angelic spirits and the impure and satanic. So the person wavers among three rulings—his essential ruling from him concerning himself, and two rulings that have come to be connected with him. He possesses acceptance or rejection in keeping with the precedence of the Book and the decree of the Address. So, *Among them are the wretched and the felicitous* [11:105], just as, among the comrades, there is the one brought near and the one driven far. He belongs to the one he answers, and God's it is to clarify between the mistaken and the correct.

The furthest limit of the affair is that *God—at Him is the most beautiful place of return* [3:14]. God does not explicitly link any ugliness whatsoever to the place of returning to Him. Things of that sort that have come to us play the role of threats in the first understanding. *Those who do wrong shall surely know by what overturning they shall be overturned* [26:227]. Concerning God's generosity they shall surely know *what they had never reckoned with* [39:47]—before being taken to task for those who are forgiven, and after being taken to task for those from whom this will be cut off. For His mercy is all-embracing, and His blessing is abundant and all-comprehensive. The souls of the cosmos wish for His mercy, for He is generous without delimitation and unqualified in munificence, without any qualification.

This explains why the world will be mustered on the day of resurrection *like scattered moths* [101:4]. Mercy will be scattered in all the homesteads, so the world will scatter in search of it, for the world has diverse states and variegated forms. Through that scattering they will seek from God the mercy that will remove from them the form that leads to wretchedness. This is the occasion of their scattering on that day.

In a similar way, solid mountains will be *like plucked wool-tufts* [101:5] because hardness departs from them so they may become the softness that mercy gives to the servants. No one knows what I am saying but the folk of witnessing and the realizers of the realities of *wujūd*.

As for the "weightiness" that remains, God named the "two weighty ones" by this name only to distinguish them from everyone else perpetually, wherever they may be. Their spirits will never cease governing natural bodies and corporeous bodies in this world, the *barzakh*, and the last world. In a similar way, their waystations within which they dwell are of the same kind as their configuration. Hence they have no bliss save through places with shape.

As for those who uphold disengagement, they are correct, for, in reality, the rationally speaking soul is disengaged from these natural corporeal bodies and corporeous bodies. It has nothing to do with them save governance. However, they have not recognized that the governance of these bodies belongs to the souls perpetually and endlessly. Hence they are correct in this respect, if that is what they intend, and mistaken if they say that the soul becomes separated from governance.

In our view, the rationally speaking souls are contiguous [with the body] through governance and separate through essence, definition, and individual reality. Hence they are neither contiguous nor separate, while governance belongs to them essentially. They are like the sun, for the sun has an essential governance of those upon whom it deploys the lights of its essence. However, there is a difference in that by their essence, the sun, the moon, the stars, and most of the occasions in which God has placed the means for wholesomeness of the cosmos do not possess any knowledge of that. But rationally speaking souls, even though their governance belongs to their essence, know what they govern. Thus the excellent souls among them that possess unveiling are given an overview of the particularities of what they govern through their essence. Souls that are not excellent do not know the particularities of that. Or, they may know, but they do not know that they know. So also is every governing spirit.

He who governs the cosmos is the most knowledgeable concerning the particularities of the cosmos, and that is God, who knows the entified part and the whole, while possessing an essential governance other than which nothing is possible.

On the day of resurrection, the felicitous souls have as their mounts the animal souls in the most pleasurable and comfortable mode of life. They are given that by the homestead. In the same way, if they are made wretched and imprisoned in a constricted place, they will be in the most intense pain and the most constricted prison. Thus God says, *And when they are cast, coupled in fetters, into a constricted place of it,* i.e., of Gehenna, *they will call out for destruction* [25:13]. These are the states that belong to the animal souls.

The rationally speaking souls take pleasure in what they know of the diversity of the states of the mounts, for through that they have an increase of divine, corresponding knowledge.

Do you not see that even here, two individuals have a tasting, and each of them has a rationally speaking soul and an animal soul? Each is overtaken by an occasion of pain, but one of them suffers pain, and the other enjoys it. This is because, although the first has a rationally speaking soul, his animality has overcome him, so the reflective, considerative instrument is ineffectual in his rationally speaking soul. In the case of the other's rationally speaking soul, its consideration, reflection, and witnessing are not ineffectual. It knows from whence the painful affair has arisen in the animal soul, so it conveys it back to its First Occasion. It immerses itself in Him, and the animal soul follows it in that. So the pain disappears, though the occasion is found.

Both these individuals, as we said, possess rationally speaking souls and pain-inducing occasions. The pain disappears in the case of one, but it does not disappear in the case of the other. After all, the animal gains radiance through the light of the rationally speaking soul. When the rationally speaking soul turns its consideration in the direction of the Real, its light follows it, just as the light of the sun follows the sun when it sets or descends. Then the animal soul takes pleasure in what it gains through witnessing something that it had not seen before.

Nothing has pain or pleasure except the animal souls. If it is as we mentioned, this is a cognitive pleasure. But if it comes from agreement with one's nature and constitution and attainment to personal desire, then it is a sensory pleasure.

The rationally speaking soul is a disengaged knowledge that does not support pleasure or pain. He who has no knowledge of the affair as it is in itself has been overtaken by obscuration and error. He imagines that the rationally speaking soul takes pleasure in knowledges. These people have even held this doctrine concerning the Divine Side. They say that He is joyful through His perfection. So consider this, my brother! How far they are from knowledge of the realities of affairs! And how beautiful are the words of the Lawgiver, "He who knows himself knows his Lord." Thus he attributed to Him only what he attributed to himself. God is far too high for any state or locus to exercise its properties over Him! Rather, *To God belongs the affair before and after* [30:4]. May God preserve us and you from calamities, and may He take us to the highest degrees and the furthest ends! (III 390.6)

From Chapter 198: The Real Situation

After a good deal of introductory material in this chapter, which is devoted to the Breath of the All-Merciful, the Shaykh turns to a discussion of each letter of the Arabic alphabet along with the divine name and the cosmic realities that pertain to it. The first letter is the *hamza* or glottal stop, which corresponds to the divine name Innovator (*al-mubdi*ᶜ)—He who creates out of no previously existent substance. The only cosmic reality that correlates fully with this name is the First Intellect, since it was created with no intermediaries. Everything else in the universe was created through the intermediary of the Intellect. Having spent several pages on the name Innovator and the First Intellect's characteristics and concomitants, the Shaykh inserts a short section that he calls "An Eloquent Exposition of the Affair As It Is" (*ifṣāḥ bimā huwa al-amr ᶜalayh*). Here he draws a picture of God and the cosmos employing much of the terminology that has been the focus of this book. It can serve as a preview of the promised next volume, *The Breath of the All-Merciful.*

Notice that in enumerating the main cosmic levels, Ibn al-ᶜArabī begins not at the beginning, with the First Intellect, but rather at the end, with animals. Then he gradually moves back along the chain of occasions through plants, minerals, the elements, the nine heavens, the Footstool, the Throne, the All Body, the Universal Soul, and the First Intellect. In this perspective, the perfect human stands on the same level as the Intellect, because the Muhammadan Reality precedes the whole of creation. However, the Intellect and the human reality are differentiated because only the human reality comprehends all the names of God without exception.

Know that the affair is a Real and a creation. It is sheer *wujūd* without beginning and end, sheer possibility without beginning and end, and sheer nonexistence without beginning and end.

Sheer *wujūd* never receives nonexistence from eternity without beginning to eternity without end, sheer nonexistence never receives *wujūd* from eternity without beginning to eternity without end, and sheer possibility receives *wujūd* through an occasion and receives nonexistence through an occasion from eternity without beginning to eternity without end.

Sheer *wujūd* is God, nothing else. Sheer nonexistence is that whose *wujūd* is impossible, nothing else. And sheer possibility is the cosmos, nothing else. Its level is between sheer *wujūd* and sheer nonexistence. Through that of it which gazes upon nonexistence, it receives nonexistence, and through that of it which gazes upon *wujūd,* it receives *wujūd.* Some of it is darkness, and that is nature, and some of it is light, and that is the All-Merciful Breath that gives *wujūd* to the possible thing. Hence the cosmos is carrier and carried. Through that of it which is carrier, it is form, body, and active. Through that of it which is carried, it is spirit, meaning, and acted upon.

There is no sensory, imaginal, or suprasensory form that does not have a proportioning and a balancing from the side of the Real as is proper to that form, its station, and its state. This is before compoundedness—I mean its coming together with the carried that it carries.

Once the Lord proportions the form through what He wills through word, hand, two hands, or hands—and there is nothing other than these four, since *wujūd* stands on quaternity—and once He balances it, which is to give it the readiness and preparedness for compoundedness and carrying, then the All-Merciful takes charge of it. He turns His Breath toward it, and that is the Real's spirit in His words, *When I have proportioned him and blown into him of My spirit* [15:29], which is identical with this Breath.

The form receives the Breath, but the forms' receptions are diverse in keeping with the preparedness. If the form is elemental and its wick ignites through the Breath, it is named an "animal" at the igniting. If no igniting becomes manifest for it, but there does become manifest movement to the eye, while it is elemental, it is named a "plant." If neither ignition nor movement becomes manifest for it—I mean, in sensation—and it is elemental, it is named a "mineral" and an "inanimate thing."

If the form is acted upon by a movement of the spheres, it is named a "pillar," and these are ranked in four levels. Then a proportioned and balanced form is acted upon by these pillars and is named a "heaven," and these are ranked in seven layers. So the All-Merciful turns His Breath toward these forms, and they come to life with a life that sensation does not perceive but faith and the soul do not deny. This is why they do not receive igniting. Every site in these heavens that does receive igniting is named a "star." The stars become manifest, and through them their spheres come into movement. The heavens are like animals in that of them which ignites, and like plants in that of them which moves.

If the form derives from a suprasensory movement, a practical faculty, and a face-turning of the Soul, it is named "All Body, Throne, Footstool, and Sphere"—the sphere of the constellations and the sphere of the waystations. The All-Merciful turns His face toward these forms through His Breath. That among them which receives igniting is named "stars," and for the Breath these are like the pupils of the eye in the human face. That among them which does not receive igniting is named a "sphere."

If the form is intellective and is made to arise through an essential arising by a disengaged Intellect, then it seeks through its preparedness what is carried by the All-Merciful's face-turning when the form is proportioned by the proportioning of the Lord Himself. That of it which ignites is named a "light of knowledge," and that of it which moves but does not ignite is named "practice." The essence that carries these two faculties is called a "Soul."

If the form is the divine form, it must either be all-comprehensive, that is, the form of the human being, or not all-comprehensive, that is, the form of the Intellect. Once the Lord has proportioned the intellective form with His command or He has formed the human form with His two hands, the All-Merciful turns His face toward them through His Breath, and He blows into them *a spirit from His command* [16:2].

As for the form of the Intellect, in that inblowing it is made to carry all the knowledges of engendered existence until the day of resurrection. God makes its form a root for the *wujūd* of the cosmos and bestows upon the Intellect firstness in the *wujūd* of the possible domain. And as for the form of the first human being, created with the two hands, in that inblowing it comes to carry the knowledge of the divine names, but the form of the Intellect does not carry these names.

So the human being emerges in the form of the Real. Within him the ruling property of the Breath reaches its extreme limit, since nothing is more perfect than the form of the Real. The cosmos turns full circle, and the *wujūd* of the possible domain becomes manifest between light and darkness, nature and spirit, absent and witnessed, curtaining and unveiling.

Of everything that we have mentioned, what adjoins sheer *wujūd* is light and spirit, and what adjoins sheer nonexistence is darkness and body. Through the totality it is a form.

If you consider the cosmos in terms of the Breath of the All-Merciful, you will say, "It is nothing but God." If you consider the cosmos in respect of the fact that it is proportioned and balanced, you will say, "the created things." *You did not throw* in respect of your being a creature *when you threw* in respect of your being a *ḥaqq, but God threw* [8:17], because He is the *Ḥaqq*.

Through the Breath all the cosmos is breathing, and the Breath made it manifest. As belonging to the Real, the Breath is nonmanifest, and as belonging to creation, it is manifest. So the nonmanifest of the Real is the manifest of creation, and the nonmanifest of creation is the manifest of the Real. Through the totality engendered existence is realized, and through leaving aside the totality, it is said, "Real and creation."[29]

The Real belongs to sheer *wujūd* and creation belongs to sheer possibility. Everything of the cosmos which becomes nonexistent and whose form disappears belongs to what adjoins the side of nonexistence. Everything that subsists and cannot be nonexistent belongs to what adjoins the side of *wujūd*.

The two affairs never cease ruling over the cosmos perpetually, so creation is new in each breath in this world and the last world. The Breath of the All-Merciful never ceases turning its face, and nature never ceases coming to be as forms belonging to this Breath. Thus the divine command never becomes ineffectual, since ineffectuality is not correct.[30] So forms arrive newly and forms become manifest in keeping with the preparednesses to receive the Breath.

This is the clearest possible exposition of the innovation of the cosmos. *And God speaks the ḥaqq, and He guides on the path* [33:4]. (II 426.27)

APPENDIX I: IBN AL-ʿARABĪ'S VIEWS ON CERTAIN SUFIS

Ibn al-ʿArabī's accounts of past or contemporary Sufis remain to be studied carefully, though Claude Addas has cited many of them in her *Quest*. In what follows, I gather together what I have found in the *Futūḥāt* concerning three well-known figures—his contemporary Abu'l-ʿAbbās al-Sabtī, the patron saint of Marrakech; the third/ninth century woman saint and lover of God Rābiʿat al-ʿAdawiyya; and the eponym of the most widely spread of the Sufi orders, ʿAbd al-Qādir al-Jīlānī. It is interesting to note that in all three cases, Ibn al-ʿArabī agrees with the tradition in its evaluation, but he also offers certain criticisms in keeping with the perspective of *taḥqīq*, which demands that everything be given its *ḥaqq*.

1. Abu'l-ʿAbbās al-Sabtī

All accounts of Abu'l-ʿAbbās al-Sabtī (d. 601/1205) agree that he was selfless in giving charity, and Ibn al-ʿArabī calls him "the companion of charitable acts" (*ṣāḥib al-ṣadaqāt*; cf. Addas, *Quest* 176–77). The Shaykh visited him in Marrakech, and on five occasions that I have found mentions him in the *Futūḥāt*.

In Chapter 248, "On tasting," Ibn al-ʿArabī begins by defining the term, and then points out that in his own case he had the "tasting of meaning" through the vision of the One Entity, not the tasting of forms or of names, and it is this that explains the peculiar structure of the *Futūḥāt*, in which everything is interrelated in a manner similar to the Koran (for a translation of the passage, see SPK 220–21). Having mentioned that he has heard that the grammarian Rummānī is the only Koran commentator who has investigated this issue, he refers briefly to al-Sabtī as follows: "But I have seen in Marrakech, among the cities of the Maghrib, Abu'l-ʿAbbās al-Sabtī, the companion of charitable acts, who was traveling this way, and I conversed with him concerning it. He was among the companions of the scales" (II 548.20). This seems to mean that Abu'l-ʿAbbās also viewed the Koran in terms of this sort of interrelationship. As for "companions of the scales" (*aṣḥāb al-mawāzīn*), I will return to what Ibn al-ʿArabī may have in mind shortly.

In Chapter 70, which deals with the *zakāt*, Ibn al-ʿArabī explains that poverty is a more excellent situation than wealth. He offers the example of two people, each of whom has a total of ten dinars. One of them gives away nine in charity, the other gives away one. Everyone agrees that the first is more excellent, but the most profound reason for this excellence is that the person has put himself closer to poverty. Then he writes,

> No one who knows the stations and the states denies this, for the Tribe do not halt with the wages [given for acts], they halt only with the realities and the states and what is bestowed by unveiling. Through this they have excellence over the ulama of the tracings. If that person had given everything as alms and had remained in his root, having nothing, that would have been higher. He fell short in degree and tasting in the measure of what he held back. Do you not see that our shaykh Abu'l-ᶜAbbās al-Sabtī said that the dying person should bequeath one-third? After all, [according to the Shariah] the dying person owns only one-third of his possessions. [By giving away one-third] he emerges from what he owns and leaves nothing remaining. The Lawgiver permitted him to give in alms the one-third that belongs to him, so he is praiseworthy in this according to the Shariah. Thus he meets God poor, in keeping with the property of the root—just as he emerged from Him. He returns to Him empty-handed. (I 577.8)

At the end of Chapter 360, which corresponds to Sura 24, Ibn al-ᶜArabī enumerates all the sciences contained in the sura that he has not had space to explain in the chapter itself. Among these sciences, he says, is "the knowledge of the marriage that takes away poverty." Apparently, he is referring to verse 24:32: *Marry the spouseless among you, and your slaves and handmaidens who are righteous; if they are poor, God will enrich them of His bounty; God is All-Embracing, Knowing*. He writes,

> [The marriage that takes away poverty] was upheld by Abu'l-ᶜAbbās al-Sabtī, the companion of charity in Marrakech. I saw him and was on close terms with him. I saw him when a person came to him complaining of poverty. He said to him, "Take a spouse." So he took a spouse, and he complained to him of poverty. He said, "Take another spouse." So he took another spouse, and he complained to him of poverty. So he said to him, "A third time," and he did so a third time, then complained to him of poverty. He said to him, "A fourth time," so he did so a fourth time. Then the shaykh said, "Now he is complete, so he has no more needs, and God has made His provision all-embracing for him. His wives that he took have nothing of their own of this world. God has enriched him." (III 292.16)

Ibn al-ᶜArabī discusses Abu'l-ᶜAbbās once again, but this time somewhat critically, in Chapter 485, "On the true knowledge of the state of the Pole whose waystation is *Whoso desires the life of this world and its adornment, We will pay them in full for their works therein, and they shall not be defrauded in them* [11:15]." He begins the chapter by recalling that the intention (*niyya*) of an act is more important than the act itself, and that intention is a specific sort of desire. When God pays people in full for their works, they will be losers if their intention in the works had been focused on this world, "so they will have no share in the last world, which is the Garden or the bliss that is the result of works, for they will have been paid in full in this world" (IV 121.14). He then turns to a related point, which is that a person of faith who suffers pain in this world will be rewarded in the next world for his suffering. Then he says that in the case of those who desire the life of this world, God hurries up this reward and bestows it in this world. He continues:

> God did so with Abu'l-ᶜAbbās al-Sabtī in Marrakech, among the cities of the Maghrib. I saw him and I conversed with him about his situation. He reported to me concerning himself that he had asked God to hurry all of that to him in the life of this world. So God hurried that to him. Thus he was making ill and healing, giving life and giving death, appointing and dismissing, and *doing what he desired* [2:253]. All of this was through charity, and his scale in all this was "predacious" [see below].
>
> However, he mentioned something to me, saying, "With Him I have concealed for myself one-quarter dirham, specifically for my last world." So I thanked God for his faith, and I was happy with him. His situation was one of the most marvelous of things. No one would know this root from him except someone who had tasted it, or those among the outsiders with understanding who had asked him about it, and he reported it to them. Other than these two groups, no one knows anything about this.
>
> It may happen that God will give what He gave to the mentioned al-Sabtī not because someone desires that, but because God hurries it to him as an increase over what He has stored away for him in the last world, since the person did not desire to hurry what was stored away—like ᶜUmar al-Wāᶜiẓ in Andalus and

> others whom we have seen of this type. I acted in this manner myself for a time in my country at the beginning of my entrance into this path, and I saw in it marvels. This belonged to these—and to us—from God, not from their desire or our desire.
>
> Had Abu'l-ᶜAbbās al-Sabtī known himself as I knew his self from him, he would not have asked for that to be hurried, for he was in a form such that nothing else could come to be. However, he asked for that from God, and He gave it to him on the basis of his asking. Had he remained silent, he would have won both affairs in the two abodes. However, his ignorance of himself, of the nature imprinted within him, and of the form in which God had mounted him made him ask. Thus he lost while others gained, though the works are one. This is why knowledge brings rejoicing, for it is the most eminent attribute with which the servant becomes adorned. (IV 121.22)

I come back to the expression *companions of the scales,* mentioned in the first passage. "Scale" for Ibn al-ᶜArabī is the means of weighing something, and in his view, everything has a scale. Thus, for example, logic is the scale of reason, and the Shariah the scale of human acts (see SPK 172–73 and passim). In the present context, the "scales" might be the scales employed by the gnostics in judging their acts (cf. I 581.14; Y 8:430.4). Then "companions of the scales" would be those who are carefully observant of the appropriate scales. However, such observation would seem to be a general characteristic of the gnostics, so it is not clear why some among them should be singled out for it.

Ibn al-ᶜArabī also employs the word *scale* in relation to Abu'l-ᶜAbbās in two other passages. In one of these, translated on p. 302, the text says that Abu'l-ᶜAbbās was *shayāᶜī al-mīzān* (III 560.26), which might be translated "well known in scale" or "conformative in scale." In the other, which we have just seen, the text says that his scale was *subāᶜī* (IV 121.24), which means "predacious." Given that the difference between *shayāᶜī* and *subāᶜī* in the Arabic script is a matter of the placement of dots, it seems certain that these two words were originally a single word and that one of them has been corrupted by a scribal error. At first sight, it might seem that the former word makes more sense. However, I have found no other instance in which Ibn al-ᶜArabī uses this term *shayāᶜī,* though he does use the term *subāᶜī* in a relevant technical sense in a poem at the beginning of Chapter 73. There he is enumerating the ranks of the Men of Number, whose common characteristic is that their number never changes. He writes,

> Upon the heart of Abraham
> we have Men
> who are predacious,
> like the lions of the thicket. (II 2.20)

The attribute of predaciousness here does not seem to be connected to God's wrath, as one might expect (since the "predatory" [*sabᶜī*] qualities of the soul pertain to its wrath or "irascibility" [*ghaḍab*]), but rather to true manliness (as, for example, in ᶜAlī, who is "the lion of God"). Such manliness demands generosity and magnanimity. Thus, in the text of this chapter, Ibn al-ᶜArabī describes the Men of Number who have Abraham's attributes in terms of their vision of God's goodness and mercy in all things, and this might well apply to Abu'l-ᶜAbbās, especially since paradise has been "hurried to" these Men already in this world.

> Among them are seven on the heart of Abraham who neither increase nor decrease in every time. Concerning this has come a report narrated from God's Messenger. Their supplication is Abraham's supplication: *O Lord, give me judgment and link me with the Wholesome* [26:83]. Their station is safety from all disquiet and doubt. God has *stripped away* the *rancor* from their *breasts* [15:47] in this world and made people safe from ugly conjecture [*ẓann*] by them, since they have no ugly conjecture—or rather, they have no conjecture, since they are a folk of sound knowledge. After all, conjecture occurs only for those who have no knowledge concerning that in which they have no knowledge, through a sort of preponderation.
>
> These seven know nothing of the people except the good that belongs to them. God has let down a veil between them and the evils that belong to the people, and He has given them an overview of the relations that are between God and His servants and of the Real's gaze at His servants through the mercy through which

He gave them existence. Every good in creation derives from that mercy, and that is the object witnessed by them from God's servants.

I met them one day, and I have not seen any more beautiful in features than they. They are knowers, clement, *brothers* of truthfulness, *upon couches sitting face to face* [15:47]. God has hurried to them their suprasensory, spiritual Gardens in their hearts. What they witness of creation is the Real's control in respect of the fact that He is *wujūd*, not in respect of the attachment of a ruling property to *wujūd*. (II 10.25)

2. *Rābiᶜa*

Ibn al-ᶜArabī cites a few of Rābiᶜa's sayings, usually with approval. In his chapter on love, he mentions her words, "If Thou shouldst cut me limb from limb, it would increase me only in love for Thee," and then quotes the famous lines of poetry ascribed to her on the two types of love (II 359.8). In two passages he recounts that Rābiᶜa struck her head against the pillar of a wall such that blood began to flow. It was said to her, "Do you not sense the pain?" She replied, "My occupation with conforming to His desire in what happens has occupied me from sensing what you see from the witness of the state" (I 511.22; II 447.6). He tells us that Rābiᶜa had achieved already in this world the state of essential worship that is given to everyone in the next world (cf. SPK 45–46, 311–12). "In the last world, the people are with their Lord in essential worship, but in this world they are in Shari'ite worship, except those of His servants whom God specifies such that He bestows upon them in this world the state of the last world, like Rābiᶜat al-ᶜAdawiyya" (IV 432.21).

Rābiᶜa is best known for her refusal to give any regard to either paradise or hell because of her utter devotion to her Beloved. Ibn al-ᶜArabī usually refers to this standpoint with approval, but on two occasions at least he criticizes her for pushing it a bit too far. On the approval side, he quotes her as saying "What evil servants—you are servants of the wage, but I serve Him for Him" (*ᶜAbādila* 58). He also writes,

A woman from among the gnostics said to a group of the Men of God, "Do you not see that if He had created neither Garden nor Fire, He would still be worthy of worship?" This woman is alluding to the pure religion, which is this station. She was Rābiᶜat al-ᶜAdawiyya. (IV 57.31)

He approves of Rābiᶜa's standpoint once more in his chapter on *ṣalāt*, where he devotes a section to an explanation of the "face-turning" (*tawjīh*), a prayer recited at the beginning of the *ṣalāt* that begins with the words of Abraham: *"I have turned my face to Him who originated the heavens and the earth"* (6:79). During the explanation, he addresses the issue of worship (*ᶜibāda*) and brings up a saying of Rābiᶜa that God should be worshiped simply because He is worthy of worship, and he criticizes a theologian for being critical of her on this point.

[The worshiper] says, [*My* ***ṣalāt***, *my ritual sacrifice, my living, and my dying*] *belong to God, the Lord of the world's inhabitants* [6:162], which is to say that giving existence to all this belongs to God, not to me. In other words, its manifestation within me is for God's sake, not for the sake of the good that goes back to me. After all, God says, *I created jinn and mankind only to worship Me* [51:56]. Thus He made the cause go back to His side, not to me. Hence the first intention is not our good. Preference here belongs to the side of the Real, for whom preference is appropriate. This then is a teaching for us and an admonition by the Real. This is [the sense of] Rābiᶜa's words, "Is He not worthy of worship?"

The knower is he who worships God for God, while other than the knower worships God for what he hopes for from God—the shares of his soul in the worship. This is why it has been set down as Shariah for us that we say, *belong to God, the Lord of the world's inhabitants,* that is, the Master of its inhabitants, their Owner, and the one who makes them wholesome through what He has set down as Shariah for them and clarified for them, for He does not abandon them in bewilderment. Thus He says, by way of showing His favor to His servant, *Did He not find thee misguided, and He guided thee?* [93:7]. In other words, He found you bewildered and He clarified for you the path of guidance in relation to the path of misguidance. Here, the path of guidance is the knowledge of that for which you were created, so that your worship will accord with it, and so that you will be *upon a clear sign from* your *Lord* [11:17].

Then the worshiper says, *No associate has He. Even so have I been commanded, and I am the first of those who submit* [6:163]. In other words, in this site no god is intended through worship except God, who created me for worship's sake. This is to say that I do not associate my own soul in the worship through the thought of reward that occurs to it—the reward that God has promised to those who have this attribute.

One scholar has held that the worshiper should be present with the reward in the state of this worship, and he has declared anyone who does not hold this an unbeliever. But this is of no consequence—and he was one of the greatest of the Kalām authorities! However, he was not one of the knowers of God by way of tastings. On the contrary, he was one of the folk of consideration, one of the greatest of them, and he rejected what Rābiᶜa said concerning this.

But in our view, that in which the ulama of the tracings disagree with us is of no account, except in the transmission of the Shari'ite rulings, since in that, everyone is equal. Their opinion is taken into account in detracting from the path that conveys [the reports to us], or in what is understood from the Arabic tongue. (I 418.27)

Rābiᶜa holds that the worshiper should worship God for God's sake alone, but this has clearly been interpreted to mean that the worshiper should worship God in His Essence, since Ibn al-ᶜArabī criticizes her for saying as much. This he does in another section of the chapter on *ṣalāt,* while explaining the manner in which the worshiper follows the imam. He is explaining why there is a difference of opinion as to whether or not the follower should say along with the imam, "God hears him who praises Him." Ibn al-ᶜArabī maintains that it is better for the follower not to say this.

Since the imam has the status of a deputy for the Real in the case of those who follow him, it is correct for him to say "God hears him who praises Him." He is the Real's spokesman for the followers, and he is instructing them that God says this when they praise Him in their recitation and in their glorification when bowing. Thus he reports from Him who has taken him as vicegerent. If God had put the imam in His own station in that state, he would say, "I hear those who praise Me." So the imam affirms the entity of the servant with his words, "God hears him who praises Him."

Know also that the worshiper worships Him only inasmuch as He is a God, not in respect of His Essence—contrary to the words of Rābiᶜat al-ᶜAdawiyya. (I 454.22)

On one occasion, in the context of describing the good character traits of the Prophet, Ibn al-ᶜArabī criticizes a woman, who is most likely Rābiᶜa, for failing to see the limitations of her own point of view.[1] The beginning of the passage is especially interesting because of the light it throws on Ibn al-ᶜArabī's view of the role of women in his own society:

One of the Prophet's companions invited him for food. The Prophet replied, "Me and her?," and he pointed at ᶜĀʾisha. The man replied, "No," so the Prophet refused the invitation. Finally, the person favored him by asking her to come along with him, so the Prophet and ᶜĀʾisha accepted to go to the man's house.

God says, *You have a beautiful model in God's Messenger* [33:21]. Where is your faith? If nowadays you were to see a man of dignity—a judge, a preacher, a vizier, a sultan—doing something of this sort so as to follow this model, would you ascribe to him anything but base character traits? But if this attribute were not one of the noble character traits, God's Messenger—who was raised up "to complete the noble character traits"—would not have done it.

God's Messenger was preaching on Friday from the pulpit and he saw that Ḥasan and Ḥusayn were coming forward, tripping on their clothes. He did not restrain himself from descending from the pulpit, picking them up, and carrying them while he ascended the pulpit and continued with his sermon. Do you consider this an imperfection in his state? No, by God, that derived from the perfection of his knowledge! For he saw with which eye he looked and at whom he looked in a way that was absent from the blind, those who do not see. They are the ones who say concerning these sorts of acts, "Did he have no occupation with God to keep him from the like of this?" But he, by God, occupied himself only with God.

Thus, she who did not know—and would that she had conceded the fact!—said, when she heard a reciter reciting, *Today the companions of the Garden are in an occupation rejoicing* [36:55], "The poor folk of the Garden—in an occupation, they and their spouses!" You poor thing yourself! God mentioned that they were occupied, but He did not instruct you as to with whom, nor as to in whom they and their spouses are rejoicing. Why have you judged that they are occupied with other than God?

If this speaker had occupied herself with God, she would not have said these words, for she would not have ascribed to them occupation with other than God, lest she conceive in herself this state that she imagined to be in them. When she did conceive of it, her object of witnessing at that moment was only that form. So she is the poor thing, for we have realized that in that moment she was occupied with other than God. The companions of the Garden pertain to the domain of possibility [so they may or may not be occupied with God], but she bore witness against herself through a witnessing of realization that she was occupied with other than God. This is part of God's hidden deception of the gnostics—disparaging others at the first opinion and implying, concerning themselves, that they are free of that. (I 743.8)

3. ᶜAbd al-Qādir and His Circle

ᶜAbd al-Qādir al-Jīlānī died in 561/1166, the year after Ibn al-ᶜArabī's birth. Addas tells us that one line of the transmission of Ibn al-ᶜArabī's *khirqa* extends back to ᶜAbd al-Qādir through the intermediary of Jamāl al-Dīn Yūnus ibn Yaḥyā al-Hāshimī (d. 608/1211), who was also one of Ibn al-ᶜArabī's teachers in Hadith (*Quest* 214, 316). However, Ibn al-ᶜArabī has little to say about al-Hāshimī, though he does mention receiving accounts of ᶜAbd al-Qādir and his companions from two of ᶜAbd al-Qādir's disciples, Abu'l-Badr al-Tamāshikī and ᶜUmar al-Bazzāz (*Quest* 241). Ibn al-ᶜArabī's remarks about ᶜAbd al-Qādir are especially interesting because of the great respect in which ᶜAbd al-Qādir has been held by posterity and the resulting puzzlement of Western scholars. J. Spencer Trimingham writes,

> It is difficult to penetrate through the mists of legend which formed even during the lifetime of ᶜAbd al-Qādir ibn Abī Ṣāliḥ Jangīdōst and thickened rapidly after his death, and to discern why he, out of the hundreds of saintly figures of the period, survived in a unique way to become the inspirer of millions, a heavenly receiver of petitions and bestower of benefits, right up to the present day. . . . And as for his Sufi reputation there is not the slightest indication that he was a Sufi at all.[2] (*The Sufi Orders in Islam* 40–41)

Annemarie Schimmel agrees that there is something strange about the rank that has been accorded to ᶜAbd al-Qādir. She writes, "A satisfactory explanation of the transition from the sober Hanbalite preacher . . . to the prototype of saintliness venerated all over the Muslim world is still lacking" (*Mystical Dimensions of Islam* 247–48). The main problem for Western scholarship in general seems to be "the mists of legend which formed even during the lifetime of ᶜAbd al-Qādir," as Trimingham put it. What makes the accounts misty and legendary is their supernatural tenor and the fact that historical scholarship is forced by its own premises to reject them out of hand.

Whether or not we want to consider Ibn al-ᶜArabī a reliable source himself, he clearly accepted that many of the reports of ᶜAbd al-Qādir's extraordinary activities were true. As the Shaykh depicts him, his most salient feature is that he made manifest the powers that God had given him. He displayed the attributes of *taṣarruf* (free activity) and *taḥakkum* (ruling control) through the Aspiration (*himma*) that is given to some of the Folk of God (see SPK 264ff.). It is these powers that appear in what are called *karāmāt* or "charismatic gifts." Normally, Ibn al-ᶜArabī considers such displays by the Men as a defect, and he makes it clear that one of the attributes of the Blameworthy is that they do not perform them. Nevertheless, he considers ᶜAbd al-Qādir not only one of the Blameworthy (III 34.11), but also the Pole of his time (I 201.21 [Y 3, 256.5]). Because of the contradiction between ᶜAbd al-Qādir's high rank and his charismatic gifts, Ibn al-ᶜArabī often explains why he should have acted in this way. Typically, he excuses him for his spiritual rambunctiousness by saying that it must have had to do with the specific function that God had given him. In other words, these acts were not really of his own doing; rather, God commanded him to perform them.

In these discussions, Ibn al-ʿArabī frequently contrasts ʿAbd al-Qādir with the latter's disciple Abu'l-Suʿūd Aḥmad ibn Muḥammad ibn al-Shibl. According to Yahia, he died some twenty years before his master, in 540/1145–46 (*Futūḥāt* Y 3:189n), but Ibn al-ʿArabī refers to him as living on after ʿAbd al-Qādir's death (II 624.18, 627.25). In some passages, Ibn al-ʿArabī considers Abu'l-Suʿūd superior to ʿAbd al-Qādir, and generally this has to do with the fact that he also was given the power of free activity, but he did not make it manifest. On a few occasions, Ibn al-ʿArabī mentions a third disciple, Muḥammad ibn Qāʾid al-Awānī, and in one passage, he places all three among the Blameworthy (III 34.11). The *nisba* al-Awānī may in fact be al-Lawānī (in one passage, according to Yahia's edition of the *Futūḥāt*, the oldest manuscripts agree on this; the Cairo edition has al-Alwānī, II 130.16; Y 13:184.8); or it may be al-Wānī, since the text tells us that he was from Wāna, near Baghdad (Y 11: 357.4; the Cairo edition has Lawāna in place of bi-Wāna II 19.10). ʿAbd al-Qādir used to call him *muʿarbid al-ḥaḍra*, "the mischief-maker of the Presence" (II 19.11; Y 11:357.5). The following are most of the passages in the *Futūḥāt* that speak of these three figures.

Among the special gifts that God had given to ʿAbd al-Qādir was the ability to see into the inner qualities of people by sniffing, and the ability to know the future because the units of time would imaginalize themselves to him and speak to him about what they would be bringing.

> We have seen a group of the Men of the Scents. ʿAbd al-Qādir was one of them—he recognized individuals through smell. My companion Abu'l-Badr reported to me that Ibn Qāʾid al-Awānī came to ʿAbd al-Qādir, while Ibn Qāʾid was seeing that his own self had a share in the path. ʿAbd al-Qādir took to sniffing him, about three times. Then he said to him, "I do not know you." This was a training in his case. Then Ibn Qāʾid's Aspiration became high so that he might join with the Solitaries. (II 392.18)

> Abu'l-Badr narrated to us from our shaykh ʿAbd al-Qādir that he said, "The year comes to me when it begins, and it reports to me what will be, and then that happens; so also the month, the week, and the day." (II 637.3)

In Chapter 119, "On abandoning trust [*tawakkul*]," which follows the discussion of trust in Chapter 118, Ibn al-ʿArabī cites ʿAbd al-Qādir's opinion on a disputed issue. Trust, as he explains, negates the existence of the "others," which are the occasions or the creatures, since the traveler turns totally toward God and abandons reliance on anything else. As we know, however, Ibn al-ʿArabī considers negating the occasions a discourtesy and a lack of *taḥqīq*, since each thing has its *ḥaqq* that should be given to it. Hence, when one abandons trust after having achieved it, one is acknowledging the proper role that should be accorded to the occasions. Thus, he says, one group of Sufis maintain that trust annihilates all the "others" and that this annihilation is higher than seeing the subsistence of the others, but another group, including himself, ʿAbd al-Qādir, and Abu'l-Suʿūd, maintain that allowing things to subsist in the appropriate manner—according to their *ḥaqq*—is in fact the higher station.

> One of the mysteries of trust is abandoning trust, for abandoning trust allows the "others" to subsist, but trust annihilates the others. In the view of most of the Tribe, the higher is that which annihilates, not that which allows to subsist. But for us, and for our shaykh Abu'l-Suʿūd ibn al-Shibl, Abū ʿAbd Allāh al-Hawwārī of the city of Tunis in the Maghrib, Abū ʿAbd Allāh al-Ghazzāl of Mirya in Andalus, Abū ʿImrān Mūsā ibn ʿImrān al-Mīrtulī of Seville, and for others, the higher is what annihilates appropriately and allows to subsist appropriately in the appropriate state and at the appropriate moment. This was held by ʿAbd al-Qādir al-Jīlī of Baghdad. After all, God annihilates and allows to subsist. He says, *What is at you runs out*, so do not depend upon it; *but what is at God subsists* [16:96], so depend upon God in His subsistence, for He annihilates and allows to subsist. Annihilating was the state of Abū

Madyan at the time of his imamate. I do not know whether or not he moved on after that, for he moved on from his imamate an hour or two before he died. The doubt is mine, because the time is distant. (II 201.16)

In one passage, Ibn al-ᶜArabī cites ᶜAbd al-Qādir's opinion to support his own contention that the prophecy that has come to an end is the specific prophecy of law-giving, whereas the general prophecy, which is the reception of reports from God, continues among the friends of God. The discussion pertains to Ibn al-ᶜArabī's answer to al-Ḥakīm al-Tirmidhī's question, "What is prophecy?"

Abu'l-Badr al-Tamāshikī al-Baghdādī narrated to me from Shaykh Bashīr, one of our masters at Bāb al-Azaj [in Baghdad], that the Imam of the Era, ᶜAbd al-Qādir, said, "Assemblies of the prophets! You have been given the title, but we have been given what you were not given."

As for his words, "You have been given the title," he means that the ascription of the word *prophet* has been interdicted to us, even though the general prophecy pervades the great ones among the Men. And as for his words, "but we have been given what you were not given," this is the meaning of Khaḍir's words, to whose rectitude and priority in knowledge God has given witness. Moses, God's chosen speaking companion brought near to Him, went to the trouble of seeking Khaḍir, even though it is known that the ulama see Moses as more excellent than Khaḍir. Khaḍir said to him, "O Moses, I have a knowledge that God has taught me and that you do not know." This is exactly the meaning of ᶜAbd al-Qādir's words, "We have been given what you were not given."

By "prophets," if he means here "the prophets among the friends," who are the folk of general prophecy, then he has made explicit through this saying that God has given to him what He has not given to them, for God has ranked them as more excellent and less excellent. The like of this is not denied. (II 90.30)

In classifying the Men of Number, Ibn al-ᶜArabī mentions one Man who has a special relationship with the divine name Subjugating (*qāhir*), and he cites ᶜAbd al-Qādir as an example.

Among them is one Man, though it may be a woman, in every time. His verse is *He is the Subjugating above His servants* [6:18], and this Man is overbearing toward everything except God. He is audacious, courageous, bold, and great in claims through a *ḥaqq*. He speaks a *ḥaqq* and he judges by justice. The companion of this station was our shaykh ᶜAbd al-Qādir al-Jīlī in Baghdad. He was forceful and overbearing through a *ḥaqq* toward the creatures. He was great in the task [of being a Man], and reports of him are famous. I did not meet him, but I did meet the companion of our own time [who dwelt] in this station. However, ᶜAbd al-Qādir was more complete in other affairs than this individual whom I met, and now the other has passed away. I have no knowledge of who took charge of this station after him until now. (II 14.18)

Ibn al-ᶜArabī devotes Chapter 30 to "The true knowledge of the first and second strata of the Poles, the Mounted [*rukbān*]." He explains at the beginning that in common usage, those who ride noble camels are called "the Mounted," and he cites a well-known poem from *Dīwān al-ḥamāsa* to prove his point. He says that everyone rides horses, but only the Arabs ride camels, and the Arabs are lords of eloquence, heroism (*ḥamāsa*), and generosity. These are precisely the attributes of the friends of God who are the topic of this chapter. Among them are those who are mounted on noble aspirations and others who are mounted on noble works, which is why they are divided into two strata. The Shaykh then identifies the Mounted with the Solitaries, and he goes on to explain that they stand outside the rule of the Pole. Having explained the attributes that are found in the Solitaries, he tells us that among the Solitaries, certain of them are themselves "Poles," which is to say that they are the highest ranking Solitaries, and he tells us that one day in Mecca he met more than seventy of them. He tells us that Solitaries of this sort have no students. Then he writes,

It is said that Abu'l-Suᶜūd ibn al-Shibl was one of them. I did not meet him or see him, but I smelled that he had a pleasant aroma and a perfumed breath. It has also reached me that ᶜAbd al-Qādir al-Jīlī, who was a man of justice, the Pole of his moment, gave witness that Muḥammad ibn Qāʾid al-Awānī had this station. Such has been transmitted to me, and the responsibility belongs with the transmitter. (I 201.20)

After this, Ibn al-ʿArabī recounts how Ibn Qāʾid saw no one before him in the path, while ʿAbd al-Qādir was concealed in the "Chamber," a passage that was quoted in Chapter 4 (p. 145). Then he turns back to explaining the attributes of these sorts of Solitaries, and at the end of the chapter he explains why he calls them "Poles." He writes,

The companions of this station possess control and free activity in the cosmos. The first grade among them leave the free activity to God in His creation, despite the fact that the Real has given them the ability and appointed them as ruler over it. They do this not by a command, but as an offer. They clothe themselves in the curtain and enter into the pavilions of the absent. They become curtained by the veils of habits and cling to servitude and poverty. They are the chivalrous, the graceful, the Blameworthy, the hidden, the innocent. Abu'l-Suʿūd was one of them. He was one of those who follow God's command in His words, *So take Him as a trustee* [73:9]. It is the Trustee who possesses the free activity, so if He commands, the servant follows the command. This is one of their characteristics. As for ʿAbd al-Qādir, what is manifest from his state is that he was commanded to exercise free activity, which is why it prevailed over him. This is the [proper] conjecture concerning him and his peers.

As for Muḥammad al-Awānī, he was mentioning that God had given him free activity and he received it, so he exercised free activity. But he was not commanded, so he was afflicted. He was deficient in knowledge in the measure that Abu'l-Suʿūd was lifted above him in it. Thus Abu'l-Suʿūd spoke with the tongue of the first stratum of the tribe of the Mounted.

We name them "Poles" because of their fixity and because this station—I mean the station of servanthood—revolves around them. I do not mean by their Polehood that they have a group who are under their command, of whom they would be the chiefs and for whom they would be Poles. They are more majestic and higher than that. They have no chieftainship whatsoever in themselves, because they have realized their servanthood and a divine command through priority.

When something arrives at them and it is imperative for them to obey it because of the realization of servanthood that is theirs, they undertake it in the station of servanthood by observing the command of their Master. As long as they are given choice and the offer is made, or they are seeking to gain the station, then no one makes [free activity] manifest save he who has not realized the station of servanthood for which he was created. (I 201.27)

In his chapter on knowledge, Ibn al-ʿArabī divides knowledge into seven sorts, the fourth of which is knowledge of perfection and imperfection in *wujūd*. He soon turns to explaining the attributes of the most perfect of all created things, the perfect human being, and he points out that this specific perfection makes human beings worthy of God's vicegerency. It is the vicegerency that allows people to exercise free activity and ruling control through Aspiration. He then cites ʿAbd al-Qādir and Abu'l-Suʿūd as contrasting examples. Both had the vicegerency, but the first was commanded to manifest it, so he did so, and the second was given the choice, so he chose not to make it manifest.

Thus the perfection of the human being is through the preparedness for this specific self-disclosure [of the Divine Presence itself]. He becomes manifest through the names of the Real in their contrariety. In what God has clarified for him [through revelation], He has given him the proper applications [of these names]. Thus he becomes manifest through that which He who has taken him as a vicegerent becomes manifest. In the vicegerency, this is called the "*ḥaqq*" and the "justice." God says to David, *O David, We have appointed you a vicegerent in the earth, so judge among people through the* ***ḥaqq****, and follow not caprice* [38:26]. After all, caprice takes its follower away from this degree for which you have been made worthy and which has been made worthy for you and your peers. . . .

When someone is given ruling control in the cosmos, this is the vicegerency. If he wills, he exercises ruling control and makes it manifest, like ʿAbd al-Qādir al-Jīlī, and if he wills, he surrenders and abandons free activity to his Lord in His servants, though inescapably he has the ability in that, like Abu'l-Suʿūd ibn al-Shibl—unless the divine command becomes linked to it, as in the case of David. Then there is no way to reject God's command, for that would be the "caprice" that he was forbidden from following. . . .

When a divine command is linked to someone's ruling control, then it is incumbent upon him to make it manifest, and he will never cease being confirmed. But when a divine command is not linked to it, he has a choice. If he wills to make it manifest, he makes it manifest through a *ḥaqq*, and if he wills, he does not make it manifest, so he curtains through a *ḥaqq*. The abandonment of manifestation is more appropriate.

The friends have been linked with the prophets specifically in the vicegerency, but they are not linked with them in messengerhood and prophecy, for the gate to these two is blocked. (II 307.35)

In one passage where the Shaykh is being critical of those who exercise free activity, he tells us that one sort among the Folk of God act because they are "sheer servants." Then he writes,

To such a one we have nothing to say, for he was commanded. This is our conjecture concerning ʿAbd al-Qādir al-Jīlī, for this was his station—and God knows best—given his exercise of free activity in the cosmos. (I 588.2)

Despite his great respect for ʿAbd al-Qādir, Ibn al-ʿArabī does seem to have considered Abu'l-Suʿūd superior, at least in certain respects. This comes out, for example, in a discussion of the disobedience and shortcomings of the gnostics in Chapter 39, which is called "On the true knowledge of the waystation where the friend dismounts after the Real drives him from His neighborhood." One of the attributes the gnostics may make manifest is "presumptuousness" (*idlāl*). This is taken as a near synonym of the conceit (*zahw*) that is referred to in the saying of ʿUtbat al-Ghulām, "How should I not be conceited, since He is my Patron, and I am His servant?" (see Chodkiewicz, *Illuminations* 288).

Nothing holds the servants back from presumptuousness and from being in this world just as they are in the last world save religious prescription. Thus they are occupied with the commands of their Master until they have finished with them. When no occupation remains, they stand in the station of the presumptuousness that is required by servanthood—but this will come to be only in the last world, for prescription remains with them in every breath in the abode of this world. Every companion of presumptuousness in this abode has fallen short of true knowledge of God in the measure of his presumptuousness, and he will never reach the degree of others who have no presumptuousness. After all, many breaths have escaped him in the state of his presumptuousness, and in them he has been absent from the prescription that is required of him. Occupation with the prescription contradicts presumptuousness. So this world is not the abode of presumptuousness.

Do you not see that when death was made present to ʿAbd al-Qādir al-Jīlī and when the breaths that remained for him in this abode left him with little time, he placed his face on the earth? He confessed that what he was now on was the *ḥaqq* that was appropriate for the servant in this abode. The occasion for this was that at certain moments he was the companion of presumptuousness, because of the [future] occurrences among engendered things concerning which the Real had instructed him.

God preserved his student Abu'l-Suʿūd from this presumptuousness, so he clung to the servanthood that is prescribed for every breath until the time of his death. It has not been narrated that his state changed at death, as did the state of his shaykh ʿAbd al-Qādir.

Someone we consider reliable has narrated to us that Abu'l-Suʿūd said, "Among the paths of the friends, the path of ʿAbd al-Qādir was strange [*gharīb*], and our path, within the path of ʿAbd al-Qādir, was strange." God be pleased with all of them and allow us to benefit from them! (I 233.22)

Ibn al-ʿArabī refers to this "strangeness" of ʿAbd al-Qādir's path in a passage where he compares him with Abū Madyan. The point seems to be that whatever sort of free activity God offered to these two friends, they would take it and make it manifest, and that contradicted the "normal" activity of God's friends:

Our shaykh Abū Madyan in the Maghrib had abandoned his profession and sat with God, depending on what God would open up for him. He was upon a strange path with God in this sitting, for he would not reject anything that was given to him through Him. He was exactly like the imam ʿAbd al-Qādir al-Jīlī. However, ʿAbd al-Qādir was more energetic in the manifest domain, because of what was given by eminence [his public role?]. (I 655.28)

Ibn al-ʿArabī calls Chapter 136 "The true knowledge of the station of truthfulness [*ṣidq*] and its mysteries." He tells us at the beginning that the person who realizes this station is able to act through Aspiration. At the end of the chapter, he compares the truthfulness realized by ʿAbd al-Qādir with that of Abu'l-Suʿūd, and he places the latter in a higher category, since he accords to him the "station" of truthfulness, in contrast to the "state" that he accords to ʿAbd al-Qādir. In the second passage, he makes a parallel point while answering one of al-Tirmidhī's questions. Note that in these passages, the term *state* is used both in its general sense, as referring to any situation (including *station* in the technical sense), and in its technical sense, as a term that is contrasted with *station* (see SPK 264).

According to what has been transmitted to us of his states, the Imam ʿAbd al-Qādir possessed the state of truthfulness, not its station. The companion of the state has unruly utterances [*shaṭḥ*], and indeed he did—God be pleased with him! But the Imam Abu'l-Suʿūd ibn Shibl, the student of ʿAbd al-Qādir, had the station of truthfulness, not the state. In the cosmos he was an unknown man who was not recognized, an ignored one who did not let himself be known—in contrast to ʿAbd al-Qādir. This was a realized incapacity, because he had ability in the station of truthfulness with God. In the same way, ʿAbd al-Qādir was a realizer and was given the ability in the state of truthfulness. God be pleased with both of them! We have not heard in our own time that anyone is the like of ʿAbd al-Qādir in the state of truthfulness, nor the like of Abu'l-Suʿūd in the station of truthfulness. (II 223.3)

At that time, according to what has been narrated to us, the Men were under the subjugation of ʿAbd al-Qādir, and he used to say this about himself, for his state had been delivered over to him. After all, his own witness gave witness to him concerning the truthfulness of his claim. He was the companion of a state that exercised lordly traces for the length of his life, but he was not the companion of a station. He did not pass on to the state of Abu'l-Suʿūd, though he was his student, except at his death, and this was the greatest state. But this state accompanied Abu'l-Suʿūd throughout his life, for he was a sheer servant, whose servanthood was not contaminated by any lordship. (II 80.18)

Presumptuousness before the Real is a discourtesy, and thus it is blamed, but like free activity, it becomes praiseworthy if it is accompanied by a command, or if it derives from realization. Thus, although Ibn al-ʿArabī constantly praises courtesy (*adab*) and defines it in terms that make it strictly analogous if not identical with *taḥqīq* (see SPK 175ff.), he also praises abandoning it, if this is motivated by a *ḥaqq*. He cites ʿAbd al-Qādir as someone who abandoned courtesy through a *ḥaqq* in Chapter 169, "On the true knowledge of the station of abandoning courtesy and its mysteries." Clearly, he is not speaking about ordinary discourtesy, but rather about the discourtesy of those among God's friends who have already realized the station of courtesy.

He who abandons courtesy is courteous in a respect that is not known, for he is with unveiling and its property, not with those who are veiled concerning this. He views God's knowledge eye-to-eye in the flow of the determined measures before they occur, so he hastens to them. Then the tongue of the homestead ascribes to him that he is discourteous with the Real, since he is in opposition [to God's commands]. On the contrary, this is the furthest limit of courtesy with the Real, but most of them are not aware. Among them is he who is placed in the station of presumptuousness, like ʿAbd al-Qādir in Baghdad, the master of his moment. (II 286.9)

When defining deception (*makr*) in the longer version of his *Iṣṭilāḥāt al-ṣūfiyya*, Ibn al-ʿArabī tells us that Abu'l-Suʿūd was the only member of the school of Iraq (perhaps meaning ʿAbd al-Qādir's circle) to escape it:

[Deception] is the continuation of blessings despite [the servant's] opposition [to God's command] (and we have seen that in certain individuals) and [His] making the state subsist despite discourtesy (which has overcome the folk of Iraq; none of them was delivered from it, so far as we know, save Abu'l-Suᶜūd ibn al-Shibl, the master of his moment) and the [servant's] manifestation of signs and charismatic gifts without a command or limit. In our view, these are "breaking of habits," not "charismatic gifts," unless the one who talks of them intends to talk of the blessings. But dread holds back the gnostics from the like of this. (II 131.22)[3]

In Chapter 25, Ibn al-ᶜArabī classifies the Men of God into four types according to the saying that makes the meanings of the Koran pertain to four levels—"There is no verse of the Koran that does not have a manifest sense, a nonmanifest sense, a limit, and an overview." He writes that Ibn Qāʾid alluded to the Men of the Manifest Sense in his words to Abu'l-Suᶜūd: "O Abu'l-Suᶜūd! God has divided the kingdom between me and you. Why do you not exercise free activity in it as I do?"

Abu'l-Suᶜūd replied, "O Ibn Qāʾid! I have given you my share. We have let the Real exercise free activity for us" (I 187.24). Ibn al-ᶜArabī may be referring to the same saying of Abu'l-Suᶜūd when he cites it as, "I was given free activity, and I abandoned it so as to act gracefully" (II 121.5; *Dhakhāʾir* 188). He also cites it in the following passage:

The master of the Tribe, the rational man of his time, he who achieved the equitable balance through his state, Abu'l-Suᶜūd ibn al-Shibl, was equitably balanced when he said, "We have let the Real exercise free activity for us." Thus he did not jostle the Divine Presence. Had he been commanded, he would have halted with the command, and if [a free activity] had been designated for him, he would have halted with that designation. (I 588.8)

In this classification of the Men into four types, Ibn al-ᶜArabī places Abu'l-Suᶜūd among the highest type, the Men of the Overview (*rijāl al-muṭṭalaᶜ*):

As for the Men of the Overview, they are those who have free activity in the divine names, through which they call down from them whatever God wills. No one else possesses this. Through the names they call down everything that is under the free activity of the three sorts of Men—the Men of the Limit, of the Manifest Sense, and of the Nonmanifest Sense. These are the greatest of the Men, and they are the Blameworthy. This is in their power, but nothing of this prevails over them. Among them were Abu'l-Suᶜūd and others. In the manifestation of incapacity and outward habits, they and the common people are the same.

Among these Men, Abu'l-Suᶜūd had a distinction, or rather, he was among the greatest of them. Abu'l-Badr, according to what he narrated to us orally, heard him say, "Among God's Men, some speak of [others'] thoughts, but they are not with the thoughts." In other words, such a person has no knowledge of his companion and has no intention of making the thoughts known. (I 188.6)

Ibn al-ᶜArabī offers some clarification of his point here in his book *al-Tajalliyyāt* ("The Self-Disclosures") in his discussion of "the self-disclosure of conjectures" (*tajallī al-ẓunūn*).

The conjectures of God's friends hit the mark, because these are unveiled to them from behind the veil of the body. They find something in themselves all at once, but they do not know from whence it has come, though they know its station. Hence they know that it belongs to someone else. They speak of it, but it is the state of another. This, in our view, is a "conjecture." In this station are the great ones among us, but in their case it is not a conjecture. God causes to pass on their tongues the state of the person present with them. The person says, "The shaykh has spoken my thoughts!" But the shaykh is not with the thoughts. Were it said to him, "What is in the mind of this person?," he would not know. Abu'l-Suᶜūd al-Baghdādī was asked about this station. He said, "God has a Tribe who speak of thoughts, but they are not with the thoughts." (*Tajalliyyāt* 23; cf. II 574.23)

Continuing his discussion of Abu'l-Suᶜūd in Chapter 25, Ibn al-ᶜArabī writes,

When ᶜUmar al-Bazzāz, Abu'l-Badr, and others described to us the state of this shaykh, we saw him flowing with the states of this high sort of the Men of God. Abu'l-Badr said to me,

"He often recited a certain verse, and we never heard any other from him." It was this:

He placed His foot in the pool of death
and said to it: "Below your hollow will be
the Uprising."[4]

He used to say: "There is nothing but the five *ṣalāt*s and waiting for death." Beneath these words is a great knowledge.

He used to say, "With God, the Man is like a rushing bird—a busy mouth and running feet."

All this belongs to the greatest states of the Men with God, since the great one among the Men is he who deals with each homestead as is its *ḥaqq*. It is not possible for the realizer to deal with the homestead of this world save as this shaykh has mentioned. When other than this dealing becomes manifest in this abode from a Man, it is known inescapably that there is a self, unless he should be commanded to do what has become manifest from him. These are the messengers and the prophets. It may also happen that some of the inheritors be commanded to that, at a certain moment. But this is a hidden deception, since it is a parting from the station of servanthood for which the human being was created. (I 188.10)

Ibn al-ʿArabī repeats most of the sayings of Abu'l-Suʿūd cited in Chapter 25 in Chapter 185, "On the true knowledge of the station of abandoning charismatic gifts." He adds the following while explaining that free activity is the root of such acts:

Abandoning charismatic gifts may occur from the beginning. That is when the friend is not able to do any of this from himself, even though he is one of the great ones among His servants. I mean here [by charismatic gifts] the outward breaking of habits, not knowledge of God. It may happen that God has given the friend the ability to do this in himself, but he abandons it all to God, such that nothing of it becomes manifest from him. We have seen a group standing on this foot. Thus, our master, Abu'l-Suʿūd ibn al-Shibl, the rational man of his moment, was asked by someone from whom he did not conceal some of his state, "Has God given you free activity?"—and that is the root of charismatic gifts. He replied, "Yes, since fifteen years. But we have abandoned it so as to act gracefully, so the Real acts freely for us." He meant that he observed God's command in taking Him as a trustee. Then the questioner asked, "What then is there?" He replied, "The five *ṣalāt*s and waiting for death." (II 370.29)

Ibn al-ʿArabī also cites sayings from Abu'l-Suʿūd concerning "listening" to music (*samāʿ*), the "rational madmen" (*ʿuqalāʾ al-majānīn*, see SPK 266), and a group of the Folk of God known as the "Men of Water." The second of these sayings helps explain why Ibn al-ʿArabī often calls Abu'l-Suʿūd "the rational man [*ʿāqil*] of his time [*zamān*]" or his "moment" (*waqt*).

"Listening" in an unqualified sense cannot be abandoned. What the great ones abandon is only the well-known, qualified listening, that is, singing. It was said to our master Abu'l-Suʿūd ibn al-Shibl al-Baghdādī, "What do you say concerning listening?"

He replied, "It is forbidden for beginners, and those at the end have no need for it."

It was said to him, "Then whom is it for?"

He said, "For the people in the middle, the companions of the hearts." (II 368.26)

It was said to Abu'l-Suʿūd ibn al-Shibl al-Baghdādī, the rational man of his time, "What do you say about the 'rational madmen' among the Folk of God?"

He said, "They are comely, but the rational among [the Folk of God] are more comely."[5]

It was said to him, "How can we distinguish between the Real's madmen and others?"

He replied, "The traces of power prevail over the Real's madmen, but those who are rational witness the Real through witnessing them."

This was reported to me from him by his companion Abu'l-Badr al-Tamāshikī. He was reliable, accurate, and a knower of what he transmitted. He never put a *but* in the place of an *and*.

Then the shaykh said, "When someone witnesses what the [rational madmen] witness and his rational faculty is allowed to subsist, this is more beautiful and greater in ability, for he has been given a station and given strength near to what was given to the messengers." (I 248.15)

Among them are the Men of the Water. They are a tribe who worship God in the depths of the oceans and the rivers. Not everyone knows of them. Abu'l-Badr al-Tamāshikī al-Baghdādī—who was truthful, reliable, knower of what he transmitted, accurate, and one who memorized what he transmitted—reported to me from Shaykh Abu'l-Su^cūd ibn al-Shibl, the imam of his moment in the path, that he said: "I was on the bank of the Tigris in Baghdad, and the thought occurred to me, 'Does God have servants who worship Him in water?' I had not completed the thought when suddenly the river split open over a man. He greeted me and said, 'Yes, Abu'l-Suᶜūd! God has Men who worship Him in the water, and I am one of them. I am a man of Tikrit, but I have left because after so many days, such and such will happen.' He mentioned an affair that would occur there, then he disappeared in the water."

[Abu'l-Badr continued:] "When fifteen days had passed, that affair occurred in the form that the man had mentioned to Abu'l-Suᶜūd. He gave me knowledge of what the affair was." (II 19.3)

Ibn al-ᶜArabī refers to Abu'l-Suᶜūd in one other context which, because of the issues that form its backdrop, deserves more detailed attention. He calls Chapter 284 "On the true knowledge of the waystation of the eminent contest [*mujārāt*] and its mysteries." The chapter corresponds with Sura 100, "The Chargers." As Chodkiewicz has shown, the 114 chapters of this fourth part of the *Futūḥāt* are arranged as a *miᶜrāj*, beginning with the last sura, *al-Nās* or "People" and ending with the first sura, *al-Fātiḥa*, "The Opening." In each chapter, Ibn al-ᶜArabī explains the various sciences that were disclosed to him when he realized the relevant sura in his own being. The reference to Abu'l-Suᶜūd in the present context occurs in Chapter 283 and 284, which correspond to suras 101 and 100.

Sura 100 begins with the verses, *By the snorting chargers, by the strikers of fire, by the dawn-raiders, blazing a trail of dust, cleaving there with a host!* Ibn al-ᶜArabī takes these verses as an allusion to the seekers on the path of God, who are running in a race to become the Preceders (*al-sābiqūn*; see Chapter 1, note 22). He begins the chapter by telling us that the Koran refers to the same sort of thing in verses such as 23:61: *These vie in good works, outracing each other to them.* Towards the end of the chapter, he mentions another sort of knowledge contained in this waystation, and that is knowledge of the secrets of the hearts. He clearly has in mind the last three verses of the sura: *Knows he not that when that which is in the tombs is overthrown, and that which is in the breasts is brought out, surely on that day their Lord shall be aware of them?* (100:9-11). When the Folk of God come to be given full knowledge of this Koranic chapter, they will know what is in people's breasts already in this world. Indeed, the saying already quoted from Abu'l-Suᶜūd—"Among God's Men, some speak of thoughts, but they are not with the thoughts"—pertains to the same sort of discussion.

From this waystation you will know, my son, the affairs sheltered by the hearts, the thoughts that flow within them, and what their souls speak about by way of enumerating what has passed. So much is this so that the realizer of this waystation knows all that the individual's heart contains and that to which his desire attaches from the time of his birth and his movement seeking the breast to the time of his sitting before him. This includes what that individual does not know himself, because he was too small, because of the forgetfulness that has overtaken him, and because of his failure to look closely at everything that has overtaken his heart and everything about which his soul has spoken, because the time is long since past. The companion of this waystation knows this from him with a sound knowledge concerning which he has no doubt and no disquiet, neither from himself, nor from anyone who is before him or present in his thoughts. This is a state that overtakes the servant.

We have heard concerning the shaykh Abu'l-Suᶜūd ibn al-Shibl that he had this waystation. Our companion Abu'l-Badr narrated to us that Shaykh ᶜAbd al-Qādir was mentioned before Abu'l-Suᶜūd, and the person went on and on mentioning him and lauding him. The speaker intended by this to give knowledge to Shaykh Abu'l-Suᶜūd and those present concerning the waystation of ᶜAbd al-Qādir, but he went to extremes. Abu'l-Suᶜūd said to him, "How long will you talk, loving to give us knowledge of the waystation of ᶜAbd al-Qādir?," as if he were rebuking him. "By God, I know how the state of ᶜAbd al-Qādir was with his folk, and how it is now in his grave!" This is known only through this waystation. (II 627.17)

Chapter 283, in which Ibn al-ʿArabī also refers to this episode, is called, "On the true knowledge of the waystation of the Shatterers [*qawāṣim*] and their mysteries." It corresponds to Sura 101, "The Clatterer." Ibn al-ʿArabī's introductory remarks concerning this waystation are especially interesting, because they suggest the nature of the experience that he underwent in ascending on the *miʿrāj* that gave him the knowledge of the sciences concealed in the Koran. Note in particular that the knowledges appeared to him in appropriate images and that he did not know the interpretation of the images until a number of years had passed.[6]

Know that, when I reached this waystation at the moment of my *miʿrāj* on which He took me so that He *might show me* whatever *of His signs* [17:1] that He willed—and along with me was the angel—I knocked on its door. I heard from behind the door a speaker saying, "Who is that knocking on the door of this unknown waystation, which is not known except through God's instruction?"

The angel said, "It is the servant of the Presence, your servant, Muḥammad the son of Light." The door was opened, and I entered the waystation. Then the Real instructed me in everything within it—however, some years after my witnessing it. So this was a formal witnessing, without instruction. Then, after that, instruction concerning it occurred.

When He instructed me that it was an unknown waystation, my back was shattered [in fear?]. When the instruction concerning it occurred, I saw it all as Shatterers, except that God protected me from what I saw. I was afraid, but God stilled my mind through what He disclosed to me.

In this waystation I saw the transmutation of sensory forms within corporeal forms, just as spiritual beings assume shapes in forms. I imagined that those first forms had gone. I realized my gaze at them, but I did not perceive them until I was given strength over them. Then they underwent transmutation, and I perceived the sought object, and I beheld that there were two sorts of transmutation.

The first sort gave a strength through which you display the traces of whatever forms you will in the eye of the viewer—whatever you love to make manifest to him in them. He sees you only according to them even though you, in yourself, accord with your own form. You have not changed, neither in your substance, nor in your form, except that you have no escape from making that form in which you desire to become manifest to the viewer present in your imagination. Thus the eyesight of the viewer perceives it in your imagination just as you imagine it, and this view at that moment veils him from perceiving your customary form. This is one path.

The other path is entailed by this waystation. It is that the form that you have is an accident in your substance. God takes away that accident and clothes you in the forms of those accidents through which you desire to become manifest, such as a serpent, a lion, or another human individual. Your substance remains, and your spirit that governs your substance keeps what it had of reason and all the faculties. Thus the form is the form of an animal, a plant, or an inanimate thing, but the rational faculty is a human rational faculty, so he has the ability to speak rationally and converse. If he wills, he speaks, and if he wills, he does not speak—in any tongue that the Real wills to make him speak. Thus his property is the property of the form itself in what is customary.

From this door is known the rational speech of inanimate things, plants, and animals, while they remain in their forms and you hear them like the rational speech of human beings. In the same way, when the spirit embodies itself in the form of a mortal, it speaks the speech of mortals, because the form's property rules over it. The spiritual being has no strength to speak in other than the speech of the form in which it becomes manifest—in contrast to human beings when they are in other than human form....

Another path in transmutation in form is that the form of the individual subsists as it was, but his soul puts on the form of a spiritual being. Then this spiritual being is found in any form in which the individual wills to become manifest to the viewer. The individual himself becomes absent within the form, while it covers him like the air that surrounds him. Then the eye of the viewer falls upon the form of a lion, a dog, a monkey, or whatever it might be. All of this is by *the determination of the Exalted, the Knowing* [6:96].

Another path is that the individual makes the air surrounding him take the shape of any form that he wills, while he is the nonmanifest side of this form. Hence perception falls on that airy form that has been shaped in the form within which he desired to become manifest. However, if that form should speak, this occurs only in the tongue recognized by the viewer. He hears

> the sound and recognizes it, but he sees the form and denies it. The person who has this state cannot rid himself of his own voice. (II 620.28, 621.22)

Ibn al-ʿArabī devotes most of this chapter to explaining different types of obscuration (*talbīs*) that can occur for the travelers in their imaginal visions. This is one of his longer discussions of the function of the jinn and Satan, and he offers an interesting interpretation of the strange figure Ibn Ṣayyād, a companion of the Prophet who is mentioned in several hadiths as the recipient of false visions. He also discusses the "mark" (*ʿalāma*) and the "clear sign" (*bayyina*) through which God's friends are protected from misinterpreting their visions. In this context he quotes Abu'l-Badr al-Tamāshikī concerning a Shaykh Raghīb al-Raḥbī, who did not see the mark in what he saw. Then he turns to the episode of Abu'l-Suʿūd just mentioned, and considers it in terms of the "clear sign."

> As for Shaykh Abu'l-Suʿūd ibn al-Shibl, the shaykh of the mentioned Abu'l-Badr, what has been described of his states is that he stood *upon a clear sign from his Lord* [11:17]. However, he was the most rational of the folk of his time. Were it not for what the above-mentioned Abu'l-Badr has narrated about him—that he rebuked an individual concerning the mention of ʿAbd al-Qādir with rage, not with stillness and calm, and he let the person know that he knew how ʿAbd al-Qādir's state was among his folk and how it was in the grave—he would have been a sheer servant. However, he lived on after this, so it is possible that he did become a sheer servant.
>
> After all, he did not rebuke this individual because he had done something forbidden by the Shariah—he had only described the states of ʿAbd al-Qādir and magnified his waystation. Had he fallen into something forbidden by the Shariah and then Abu'l-Suʿūd rebuked him and became wrathful toward him, that would not have brought him out of being a sheer servant. So glory be to Him who gave to Abu'l-Suʿūd what He gave! For he was the unique one of his time in his task. Indeed, had the mentioner been his student, rebuking him would have been incumbent upon him, for rebuking him would be part of his training. So, if he was one of his students, that rebuke did not bring him out of his servanthood. If Abu'l-Suʿūd's rebuke derived from a divine command by which he was addressed within himself for achieving the wholesomeness of the moment in the case of whoever it might be, or because of God's jealousy toward a station, then the one who spoke about it [to me] has been discourteous, since Abu'l-Suʿūd's rebuking is part of what realizes his servanthood, not what removes him from it. This is the [proper] conjecture concerning the state of Abu'l-Suʿūd, not what we mentioned first.
>
> I only mentioned the latter, the former, and what is between the two so as to achieve fully my words concerning this station, through what the various aspects require according to their perfection. Inescapably, this shaykh had one of them, and he cannot be judged to have had any other. Thus have we bestown the benefit of the true knowledge of this station and its states upon him who comes to understand this book.
>
> God has not reported to me concerning any of the states of Abu'l-Suʿūd so that we might link him to his waystation. God knows best what that was. However, I am certain that among the shaykhs his scale was given preponderance. May God benefit us with love for him and with love for the Folk of God!
>
> Thus have we cited in this waystation some of what is entailed by the Shatterers, all of which instill fear. *And God speaks the **ḥaqq**, and He guides on the path* [33:4]. (II 624.16)

APPENDIX II: TRANSLATION OF TECHNICAL TERMS

Listed below are the more important technical terms whose English translation differs here from what it was in SPK.

Arabic term	**SPK**	**SDG**
ahl Allāh	Folk of Allah	Folk of God
ākhira	next world, hereafter	last world
arkān	elements	pillars
athar	effect	trace
dahr	Time	Aeon
dalāla	denotation, evidence, proof	signification, proof
dalīl	denoter, proof	signifier, proof
dhātī	inherent, intrinsic	essential
dhilla	lowliness	abasement
fiṭra	primordial nature	innate disposition
ghayb	unseen	absent
halāk	destruction	perishment
himma	Resolve	Aspiration
ḥiss	sense perception	sensation
ḥudūd	bounds	limits
ḥudūth	temporal origination	new arrival
ḥādith	temporally originated	newly arrived
muḥdath	temporally originated	newly arrived
ikhtiṣām	dispute	quarrel
ikhtiṣāṣ	designation, singling out	specification
iṭlāq	nondelimitation	unboundedness
muṭlaq	nondelimited	unbound, absolute, unqualified
ittisāᶜ	vastness	all-embracingness
ᶜizza	inaccessibility	exaltation
ᶜazīz	inaccessible	exalted
jabarūt	invincibility	domination
jabbār	overbearing	all-dominating
jamᶜ	all-comprehensiveness, coincidence, concentration	bringing together
jawāriḥ	organs	bodily parts

Arabic term	**SPK**	**SDG**
jibilla	innate disposition	natural disposition
kibriyā'	magnificence	greatness
mutakabbir	magnificent, arrogant	self-great
ladhdha	enjoyment	pleasure
mādda	substratum	matter
makāna	rank	placement
malakūt	dominion	sovereignty
maraḍ	disease, illness	illness
mawṭin	abode	homestead
munāsaba	affinity	correspondence, correlation
nafs	self, soul, ego	self, soul
nāṭiq	rational	rationally speaking
nisba	relationship	relation
niẓām	order	arrangement
qadar	destiny	measuring out
qahr	severity, overwhelming power	subjugation
qahhār	overwhelming	all-subjugating
qiyām	to subsist	to abide
riḍā	approval	good-pleasure
sabab	secondary cause	occasion
ṣanʿa	art	artisanry
ṣāniʿ	maker	artisan
shahāda	visible	witnessed
shahwa	passion	appetite
sirr	(inmost) consciousness	secret heart
ṣudūr	emergence	procession
taḥqīq	verification	realization
taqwā	godfearingness	godwariness
taqyīd	delimitation	binding
muqayyad	delimited	bound, qualified
tartīb	hierarchy	order
taṣarruf	free disposal	free activity
tawajjuh	attentiveness	face-turning
taʿẓīm	to acknowledge the tremendousness, to venerate	to magnify
thubūt	immutability	fixity
thābit	immutable	fixed
ʿulamā' al-rusūm	exoteric scholars	the ulama of the tracings
ʿurf	common usage	common language
wārid	inrush	arriver
zamn (zamān) fard	individual moment	solitary time

NOTES

Introduction

1. Surprisingly little has been written on cosmology per se in Ibn al-ʿArabī's writings, even though cosmological themes are found throughout his works. The earliest scholar to pay close attention to cosmology was H. S. Nyberg in his still useful study, *Kleinere Schriften des Ibn al-ʿArabī.* However, he focuses mainly on the content of the three short Arabic texts that he edited there, works which, although important, are early and not representative of the full range of Ibn al-ʿArabī's teachings. One of these, *Inshāʾ al-dawāʾir,* has recently been translated into English by Paul B. Fenton and Maurice Gloton as "The Book of the Description of the Encompassing Circles." Titus Burckhardt meditates on the significance of Ibn al-ʿArabī's cosmological symbolism in *Mystical Astrology According to Ibn ʿArabī.* Sachiko Murata has investigated the manner in which Ibn al-ʿArabī and his commentators deal with complementary principles in her *Tao of Islam,* especially Chapter 6.

2. See, for example, Morris, "'Seeing God's Face': Ibn ʿArabi on Right Action and Theophanic Vision, Part I;" idem, "How to Study the *Futūḥāt*: Ibn ʿArabi's Own Advice."

3. *Encyclopedia of Cosmology* 116.

4. On the historical career of the expression *waḥdat al-wujūd,* see Chittick, "Rūmī and Waḥdat al-Wujūd."

5. On the spread of Ibn al-ʿArabī's teachings among all levels of Islamic society, see Michel Chodkiewicz, *An Ocean without Shore,* introduction. On the issue of his "friendship" with God, see idem, *The Seal of the Saints.*

6. On the "profitability" of knowledge, in keeping with the Prophet's saying, "I seek refuge in God from a knowledge that has no profit," see my *Faith and Practice of Islam* 15–16.

7. The order is that already established by the grammarian al-Sībawayh (d. ca. 180/796). See the article "Makhāridj" in the new *Encyclopaedia of Islam* 6:129–30.

8. For an explanation of how this works, see Burckhardt, *Mystical Astrology,* Chapter 5.

9. It is misleading for two major reasons. First, in English the term *essence* is employed to differentiate between the reality of the thing and its phenomenal or accidental appearance. In contrast, the *ʿayn* of a thing is no different from what appears to us, and it is not irrelevant here that one of the standard meanings of the term in Arabic and in Ibn al-ʿArabī's vocabulary is "identical with." The entity, which is fixed in God's knowledge, is not the thing's "essence," but the very thing itself. There is no difference between the entity in God's knowledge and the entity in the world save that with God the entity is fixed and nonexistent in relation to itself and others, but in the world it is existent in relation to itself and others. Thus, the *ʿayn thābita* or "fixed entity" is also called the *ʿayn maʿdūma* or "nonexistent entity." This nonexistent, fixed entity is identical with the *ʿayn mawjūda* or "existent entity" in every respect, except that the existent entity exists in the external world, but the fixed entity does not. The second reason for avoiding "essence" is that we need a word in English to render *dhāt,* which is rarely synonymous with *ʿayn.* "Essence" is well established as the English rendering of *dhāt,* and it is an appropriate translation, because *dhāt* is typically contrasted with *ṣifāt* or "attributes" and *afʿāl* or "acts." Thus a thing's essence is different from its attributes and its acts, but its existent entity is identical with its nonexistent, fixed entity, except when viewed in

terms of *wujūd*. The fixed entity, then, is the quiddity or "whatness" (*māhiyya*) of a thing, a term that is contrasted with its *wujūd*. It is true that *māhiyya* also has often been translated as "essence," but again, we need English terms that help us make the same differentiations that are made in Arabic.

Chapter 1

1. For this passage in context, see Chodkiewicz et al., *Illuminations* 106–7.

2. On the important role that faith plays in Ibn al-ʿArabī's teachings, see Chittick, SPK, Chapter 12 and passim.

3. See Murata, *Tao* 147 ff.

4. Literally, "speaking about passing thoughts" (*al-kalām ʿalā al-khawāṭir*).

5. *Al-akl min al-kawn*. Perhaps the Shaykh has in mind things such as the manna and quails that were given to the people of Moses in the wilderness (Koran 2:57, 7:160, 20:80).

6. Compare the definition and explanation of God's deception in Chapter 231 (II 529.33, partly translated in SPK 267–69).

7. Usually the word *ibl* in this verse is understood to mean "camel," but a minority of scholars have understood it to mean "clouds," and in a passage where the Shaykh comments on the verse (II 402.12), he follows the latter reading.

8. On seeking stations and avoiding states (*aḥwāl*), see SPK 263–70.

9. One may object that ignorance also pertains to the cosmos and therefore should be venerated. For the continuation of this passage, where the Shaykh answers this objection, see SPK 290.

10. See Chittick, "Rumi and *Waḥdat al-wujūd*."

11. On these two sorts of creation, see pp. 47–48.

12. On belief as knotting, see Chittick, *Imaginal Worlds*, Chapters 9 and 10.

13. "Locus" (*maḥall*) is a synonym in this context for heart—the place in which God's self-disclosure is perceived. See Chittick, *Faith and Practice* 199.

14. Here Ibn al-ʿArabī is alluding to the Koranic verse, *If you are wary of God, He will assign you a discrimination* (8:29).

15. The "unobstructed" (*sādhij*) seem to be the same as the "unlettered" (*ummī*) whom Ibn al-ʿArabī sometimes discusses. Compare this passage with his description of the "God-given" knowledge of the friend of God (SPK 235–38). There he cites Ghazālī as a friend who was not able to reach the stage of the unlettered, because his understanding was blocked by the considerative sciences that he had learned.

16. See Chodkiewicz, *Seal* 31–32.

17. For a good survey of philosophical and theological views on the term *ʿilla*, with detailed reference to the philosophical position that Ibn al-ʿArabī rejects, see the article "*ʿIlla*" in the new *Encyclopedia of Islam*.

18. See H. A. Davidson, *Alfarabi, Avicenna, and Averroes* 75 ff.

19. On this term, see SPK 132–34.

20. Ibn al-ʿArabī mentions in several places that both the Ash'arites and the Folk of Ḥusbān or the Ḥusbāniyya, whom he identifies with the Sophists (*sūfisṭāʾiyya*), had perceived the renewal of creation at each instant, though the Ash'arites understood it to occur only in accidents, not in substances. See III 398.2 ff. (translated on p. 249) and III 525.26 ff. (p. 117); Izutsu, *Sufism* 212–13; *Fuṣūṣ* 125 (Austin, *Bezels* 154).

21. For some of the implications of this teaching, see Chittick, "The Divine Roots of Human Love."

22. By "racetrack of precedence" (*ḥilbat al-sabq*) Ibn al-ʿArabī has in mind the imagery connected both with God's mercy that takes "precedence" over His wrath and with the Koranic verse, *Race to forgiveness from your Lord* (57:21). He develops this imagery in a number of passages. For example, in explaining the meaning of the verse, *Do they reckon, those who do ugly deeds, that they will precede Us*? (29:4), he writes: "When people disobey, they expose themselves to vengeance and affliction. They are running a race to vengeance for what has occurred from them. But God races against them in this racetrack in respect of the fact that He is All-Forgiving, Pardoning, Overlooking, Compassionate, and Clement. Through disobedient acts and ugly deeds, the servants race the Real to vengeance, and the Real precedes them. He will have preceded them when they arrive at vengeance through ugly deeds. God passes by them through the All-Forgiving and its sisters among the divine names. When the servants reach the end of the race in this racetrack, they find vengeance, but the All-Forgiving has passed it by and has come between it and the disobedient. They had been judging that they would reach it before this. This is indicated by God's words, *Do they reckon, those who do ugly deeds, that they will precede Us*, that is, that they will precede My forgiveness and My mercy's envelopment through their ugly deeds? *Ill they judge!* [29:4]. On the contrary, precedence belongs to God through mercy toward them. This is the furthest limit of generosity" (III 252.7). See also II 673.30.

23. This is a reference to the practice of marking (*ishʿār*) the sacrificial animal by stabbing it in the right side of the hump so that the blood will announce that it is destined for sacrifice.

24. Reference to the verse, *So take Him as a trustee* (73:9), concerning which much will be said in the next chapter.

25. This is a reference to the hadith of God's self-transmutation at the resurrection, according to which people will keep on denying Him until He appears to them with the "mark" that they recognize. See the index of hadiths, under "Is there between you and Him a mark?"

26. For a more detailed explanation of the mutual waystations, see Chapter 384, translated on pp. 114–20.

27. On "equality" (*sawāʾ*) in this sense, see SPK 318.

28. In this passage Ibn al-ʿArabī has in view the sound hadith, "Loving kindness [*birr*] is beauty of character, while sin is what is woven into your breast."

29. According to al-Sarrāj (*Lumaʿ* 44–45), the saying is by Ibn Sīrīn. There seems to be a textual problem here, and I have corrected it by following the version of the saying given by al-Sarrāj. In place of the clause translated here as "Whenever something disquiets me," the printed text of *Futūḥāt* has a clause that can be translated as "Whenever something becomes woven into myself," though there is also an Arabic phrase, *lahu,* that seems to be extraneous. The corrected text corresponds exactly with the hadith that Ibn al-ʿArabī quotes next.

30. Allusion to the words of Satan that Ibn al-ʿArabī often quotes in this sort of context: *So do not blame me, but blame yourselves* (14:22); also relevant is the *ḥadīth qudsī,* "When someone finds good, let him praise God, and when someone finds other than that, let him blame none but himself."

31. For this saying and Ibn al-ʿArabī's references to it, see SPK 409n6.

32. For the various verses and hadiths which Ibn al-ʿArabī has in mind, see the notes to the parallel passages in SPK 70–76.

33. For some clarification concerning this "mark" perceived by the gnostic, see Chittick, *Imaginal Worlds* 85–87.

34. For a similar commentary on this first line of the *Futūḥāt,* see II 281.3, translated in SPK 103.

35. The personification of an absolute nothingness here is perhaps strange in English but not so in Arabic, where the word for jealousy is *ghayra,* derived from the word *ghayr* (other). Thus in Arabic one immediately understands that the "jealousy" of absolute nonexistence is that it insists upon remaining "other" than *wujūd,* whereas things that are relatively nonexistent possess a mode of identity with *wujūd.*

36. According to a hadith, reciting this chapter is equivalent to reciting one-quarter of the Koran (Tirmidhī, Faḍāʾil al-qurʾān 10).

37. The "Pegs" (*awtād*, pl. of *watad*) are among the several groups of the Men of Number (*rijāl al-ʿadad*) whom the Shaykh describes in rather enigmatic fashion in the *Futūḥāt.* See Chodkiewicz, *Seal,* Chapter 6, "The Four Pillars," that is, the Four Pegs.

38. The "waystation of waystations" is Part 4 of the *Futūḥāt.* Specifically, the Shaykh seems to be referring to Chapter 275, "On the knowledge of the waystation of declaring oneself quit of idols," which corresponds to Surah 109. The separate fascicle (*juzʾ*) to which he refers is probably the unpublished *Kitāb Manzil al-manāzil.* See Chodkiewicz, *Ocean* 65.

39. "Mountedness" renders *tarkīb,* which is normally translated as "composition" or "compoundedness." The term is used in philosophy and the natural sciences to refer, for example, to the fact that corporeal things are compounded of the four elements. The basic sense of the term is to mount something on a horse or a camel, or to put something on top of something else. The Koran uses the term in the one verse that employs the word *form* in the singular: *In whatever form He willed He mounted you* (82:8). Ibn al-ʿArabī's explanation of the term suggests that he is understanding it in its Koranic sense, though of course he also has the philosophical meaning in mind.

40. These are two sorts of tree whose wood ignites quickly when used as tinder. Lane cites a proverb which he translates as follows: "In all trees is fire, but the *markh* and *ʿafār* yield much fire" (see Lane, *Lexicon,* under *ʿafār*).

41. The reference here is to the engendering command and the prescriptive command (see SPK 291–94).

42. On the difference between commentary by "allusion" and ordinary exegesis of the Koran, see SPK 242–50.

43. It should be clear from this passage (and many similar passages) that in Ibn al-ʿArabī's view Jesus' unique status as a prophet has little to do with the fact that he is the word of God. As he explains elsewhere, it is the ascription to God in this verse that is significant, not the fact of his being a word: "God's words are His existent things, and that is why the seas run out before they run out through the writing. Hence Jesus did not gain eminence over the existent things in respect of being a word, but rather in respect of being *[His word] that He cast to Mary* [4:171]. As for you, you were cast by your father" (*ʿAbādila* 57).

44. Here Ibn al-ʿArabī is looking at the etymological sense of the word *taklīf,* "to prescribe [the Shariah]," as in the "prescriptive command." Literally, *taklīf* is to place a burden or a discomfort (*kulfa*) on someone. This last clause can also be

translated as "through us He carries the burden of burdening us."

Chapter 2

1. Ibn al-ᶜArabī cites the hadith in III 295.16, translated in Chittick, *Imaginal Worlds* 107.

2. The term *Dancers* (*al-rāqiṣāt*) presumably refers to certain stars (Lane gives *rāqiṣ* as the name of the star on the tongue of Draco, *Lexicon*, q.v.). A parallel Koranic usage is *rabb al-shiᶜrā*, "the Lord of Sirius" (53:49). The term "concealer" (*kafūr*), employed a dozen times in the Koran, is an intensive form of *kāfir*, an unbeliever or an ingrate. But, as Izutsu explains, etymologically the word *kufr*, from which it is derived, means to conceal or cover up. Hence Ibn al-ᶜArabī reads the recurring Koranic phrase *hum alladhīna kafarū* to mean not "those who disbelieve," but "those who cover and veil." "Thus it is an expression referring to people who, by their 'absence,' conceal the Absolute behind the curtain of their own selves" (Izutsu, *Sufism* 33).

3. See Addas, *Quest* 249.

4. He is referring here to the hadith of God's self-transmutation (*taḥawwul*) at the resurrection, according to which God will keep on disclosing himself to people, but they will keep on denying Him until He discloses Himself in the form that they recognize, which is the form that accords with their own measure of understanding. If the Buddha appears at the resurrection to a Baptist, one can hardly expect the Baptist to recognize him as his God. Ibn al-ᶜArabī discusses this hadith further in a passage that will be cited shortly (see also the Index of Hadiths, under "Thou art our Lord;" also SPK 38, 99–100, 336, 387n9).

5. Reference to a standard understanding of the Koranic verse, *God spoke directly to Moses* (4:164).

6. The Shaykh cites part of the hadith, "We are through Him and for Him."

7. For a translation of the passage just summarized, see SPK 336.

8. For some of Ibn al-ᶜArabī's views on these debates, see SPK 205–11.

9. See SPK, Chapter 7.

10. The term *corporeous* (*jasadī*) is roughly synonymous with "imaginal"; it is contrasted with "corporeal" (*jismānī* or *jismī*), which is the attribute of bodily things in the external, physical world. See Chapter 8.

11. The reference is to the shadow play. Compare this passage with III 68.18 (translated in Chittick, "Two Chapters," p. 102), where Ibn al-ᶜArabī provides a longer description of the shadow play and how it is set up as a lesson for "those with eyes."

12. Reference to the hadith, "The Sarus, the Pyramus, the Euphrates, and the Nile are among the rivers of the Garden."

13. Much of the remainder of this chapter, having to do mainly with continual creation and transmutation, is translated in SPK 100–2.

14. Ibn al-ᶜArabī refers to days of diverse lengths in many passages. The shortest of all days is this "solitary time" (*al-zamn* or *al-zamān al-fard*), known as "the Day of the Task" (*yawm al-shaʾn*). It is identical with the indivisible instant in which the new creation constantly appears (I 292.16 [Y 4:338.12]; II 82.6 [Y 12:359.10], 206.8, 384.31; III 434.3). Collectively, the solitary times are called the "Days of the Breath" (III 287.21, 564.1). The Shaykh sometimes calls the normal, twenty-four-hour day the "small" or the "smallest day," and he explains that all other days are "determined" (*taqdīr*) or measured in terms of this day. "The smallest of the days is that which is counted by the movement of the encompassing sphere, within whose day become manifest night and daytime. Thus the smallest day for the Arabs, that is, this day, belongs to the greatest sphere" (I 121.24). He explains in some detail the rationale for speaking of these diverse days in Chapter 59, "On the true knowledge of the existent and the determined time [*zamān*]": "Night and daytime differentiate the day, so from the rising of the sun until its setting is named 'daytime,' from its setting until its rising is named 'night,' and this differentiated entity is named 'day'. The most manifest of these days is the *wujūd* of the greatest movement, and there is nothing in entified *wujūd* save the *wujūd* of the moving, nothing else, but this is not identical with time. What we gain from all this goes back to the fact that time is an imagined affair, without any reality. Once this is stipulated, the intelligible, determined day is called 'existent time,' and through it become manifest the weeks, the months, the years, and the aeons. These are all named 'days,' and they are determined by this smallest, habitual day, which night and daytime differentiate. Thus the 'determined time' is anything in addition to this smallest day through which all the great days are determined. Hence it is said, 'In a day whose measure is *one thousand years of what you count* [22:47].' God says, [*'The Possessor of the Stairs—the angels and the Spirit ascend to Him*] *in a day whose measure is fifty thousand years* [70:3–4]. The Prophet said concerning the days of al-Dajjāl, 'A day is like a year, a day like a month, and a day like a week, and the rest of his days are like your days'" (I 291.35). Typically, the Shaykh names the various days in keeping with the divine names or cosmic realities with which they are associated, such as the longest of days, which is the fifty-thousand-year "Day of

the Possessor of the Stairs," or the one-thousand-year "Day of the Lord" (II 441.33; III 45.28, 434.3). He says, "Each divine name has a day" (II 441.34), and "These very days are the ruling properties of His names in the cosmos, for each name has days, and these days are the time of the name's ruling property" (III 201.13). Each of the spheres has a specific day, from the twenty-eight-day "day of the moon" to the 36,000-year day that pertains to the fixed stars (II 441.32; III 549.2). See also II 438.9; III 201–202, 238.11, 461.10; and the treatise *Ayyām al-sha*ʾ*n*. For a fine overview of Ibn al-ʿArabī's teachings on time, see Böwering, "Ibn al-ʿArabī's Concept of Time."

15. For a translation of the first part of this passage, see SPK 82–83. For a parallel passage, see Chapter 66, translated in Chittick, *Imaginal Worlds* 130–36.

16. According to Ibn al-ʿArabī's reading of the traditional accounts of paradise, the Dune of White Musk is located in the Garden of Eden, which is the highest of the gardens, and within it people come together for the vision of God (I 319.10 [Y 5:71.1]). There they will stand in four degrees: messengers and prophets; God's friends, who are the inheritors of the prophets in words, deeds, and states; the knowers of God by way of rational demonstration; and the faithful, who follow the authority of the knowers in their *tawḥīd* (I 320.2; Y 5:75–76). For further discussion, see I 756.21 (Y 11:210.3); II 81.13 (Y 12:353.6), 84.28 (Y 12:378.3), 157.27 (Y 13:408.1), 173.4 (Y 13:523.8), 442.10; III 434.26, 442.10, 465.17; IV 15.14, 44.10, 245.24.

17. For a good example, closely related to the present discussion, see II 552.12, translated in SPK 153–54.

18. The reference is to a hadith which describes how a sparrow dipped its beak in the ocean while Moses and Khaḍir were together. Then Khaḍir said to Moses, "My knowledge and your knowledge fall short of God's knowledge just as the pecking of this sparrow falls short of the ocean."

19. The object of love and desire must always be nonexistent in relation to the one who loves and desires. If we have the object, we no longer desire to have it, or we desire its continuation, which is nonexistent. This principle holds true both for God and creatures. In the case of God, it is shown, inter alia, by the hadith of the Hidden Treasure; the objects of His love are nonexistent fixed entities, which "have never smelt, and will never smell, a whiff of *wujūd*." For a detailed explanation of Ibn al-ʿArabī's position, see Chittick, "The Divine Roots of Human Love."

20. The statement, "we give existence to a Lord," is of the sort that easily raised hackles among Ibn al-ʿArabī's critics. Naturally, he does not mean to say that we—who have no *wujūd*—give *wujūd* to Him who does. Rather, his point is that there is no Lord without a vassal, no Creator without a creation, no God (*ilāh*) without a divine thrall (*ma*ʾ*lūh*). See SPK 59–62.

21. On the "commingling" (*imtizāj*) of the attributes of the Real and creation and the appearance of opposing divine attributes in all things, compare I 120.15 (Y 2:229.9), translated in Chodkiewicz et al., *Illuminations* 87–88.

22. Reference to the verse, *God commands you to deliver trusts back to their owners* (4:58).

23. This is one of several passages in the *Futūḥāt* where Ibn al-ʿArabī integrates the categories into his own perspective. J. N. Mattock writes, "It might well be thought that the *Categories* received more attention from the earlier Islamic philosophers than it merited, particularly in view of the difficulty of determining precisely what it is about" ("al-Maḳūlāt," *Encyclopaedia of Islam*, new edition, 6:204). For his part, Ibn al-ʿArabī had no doubt concerning "what it is about," though his interpretations would probably surprise many philosophers. His treatment of the categories is typical of the way in which he takes over well known terminology from other schools of thought and harmonizes it with his own vision of the Koranic universe. For two detailed examples of his use of the categories, see III 11.1, translated on p. 360; and I 121.8, translated into English in Chodkiewicz, *Illuminations* 90. For further references, see II 211.32, 429.18, 435.9, 481.10, 516.8; III 197.32, 279.32; IV 255.19; *Inshā*ʾ 18, 21, 24, 32.

24. On "states" (*aḥwāl*) in the general sense that the Shaykh has in mind here, see SPK 264.

25. On the distinction between knowledge (*ʿilm*) and true knowledge or gnosis (*maʿrifa*) in Ibn al-ʿArabī's writings, see SPK 147–49.

26. The allusion is to the hadith, "[The surah] Hūd and its sisters have whitened my hair." Ibn al-ʿArabī explains that Hūd contains the verse just mentioned that is addressed to Muhammad, *Go thou straight as thou hast been commanded* (11:112), and this made him experience personally the conflict between the engendering command and the prescriptive command. See SPK 291–303, especially p. 300.

27. The person in question here is his companion Aḥmad al-ʿAṣṣād al-Ḥarīrī. See another version of this account in I 276.19 (Y 4:248.4), translated on pp. 321–22.

28. On Ibn al-ʿArīf, see SPK 398n5; Addas, *Quest*. The sentence is found in his *Maḥāsin al-majālis* 76, with a slight textual discrepancy (*yataʿayyan* in place of *yatabayyan*).

29. On Abū Madyan, see Vincent Cornell, *The Way of Abū Madyan*; Addas, *Quest*, passim; SPK 414n19.

30. In the notice where this saying is cited, al-Qushayrī also refers to him as Abu'l-ʿAbbās al-Sayyārī and gives his date of death as 342/953–54 (*Risāla* 168).

31. See SPK 342–43.

32. Presumably by *Maḍnūn* the Shaykh means Ghazālī's short work, *al-Maḍnūn bihi ʿalā ghayr ahlihi,* "That which should be withheld from other than its folk."

33. This seems to be a reference to Koran 2:167: *Oh if only we might return again and disown them.*

34. For some instances of Ibn al-ʿArabī's explanation of triplicity in the syllogism, see Murata, *Tao* 152.

Chapter 3

1. On this important concept, see SPK, Chapter 19, and Chittick, *Imaginal Worlds,* Chapter 9.

2. Lane cites the same verse in witness to this meaning of the word (*Lexicon,* q.v., form 4, p. 1524).

3. The verb *khafiya,* typically said to mean "to be hidden," is one of many Arabic words included among those with opposite meanings (see Lane, *Lexicon,* q.v.).

4. The Shaykh understands the expression "to have the Koran rooted in the memory" (*istiẓhār al-qurʾān*) to mean the reception of the Koran directly from God by His sending it down (*inzāl*) into the heart (II 258.23 [Y 14:589.4]), or "finding the pleasure of the sending down from the absent domain in the heart" (III 414.28). The friend of God receives this as an inheritance from Muhammad, so he is a follower (*tābiʿ*), while the Prophet is followed (*matbūʿ*). Usually the Shaykh refers to having the Koran rooted in the memory in relation to Abū Yazīd. "The messengerhood that has been cut off is the descent of the divine ruling on the heart of mortal man through the intermediary of the Spirit, as we have explained. This is the door that has been closed and the messengerhood and prophecy that have been cut off. However, casting [of knowledge by the spirit into the heart] without law-giving has not been interdicted, nor are divine instructions concerning the soundness or corruption of the stipulated ruling. This has not been cut off. In the same way, the descent of the Koran upon the hearts of the friends has not been cut off, while it has been preserved [in memory] by them. Even so, they have the tasting of the sending down—that is, some of them have it. This is why it has been mentioned that Abū Yazīd did not die until the Koran had been rooted in his memory. In other words, he took it through a sending down" (II 258.19). In describing a group of the friends of God known as the "Koran reciters" (*qurrāʾ*), the Shaykh writes, "They are the Folk of God and His elect, and they are not restricted to any number. The Prophet said, 'The Folk of the Koran are the Folk of God and His elect.' The Folk of the Koran are those who have preserved the Koran through putting it into practice and have preserved its letters in memory. Hence they have had it rooted in the memory through preservation and practice. Abū Yazīd Basṭāmī was one of them. Abū Mūsā al-Dabīlī narrated that Abū Yazīd did not die until he had the Koran rooted in his memory. Those whose character is the Koran are among its folk, and those who are among the Folk of the Koran are among the Folk of God, because the Koran is the speech of God, His speech is His knowledge, and His Knowledge is His Essence. Sahl ibn ʿAbd Allāh al-Tustarī reached this station when he was a boy of six. That is why his beginning in this path was the prostration of the heart" (II 20.15). See also II 447.22; IV 78.18, 105.35; and especially III 94.11; Addas, *Quest* 91–92; Qushayrī, *Risāla* 80. On Sahl and the prostration of his heart, see SPK 407n18. Abū Mūsā was a disciple of Abū Yazīd from Dabīl in Armenia. Many sources record his name as Daybulī, which would suggest that he came from Daybul, a city in India, but this is incorrect. See G. Böwering, "Besṭāmī," *Encyclopaedia Iranica* 4:183.

5. Reference to the hadith, "O God, Thou art the companion in travel and the vicegerent in the family."

6. By the two interpretations of the word *minhāj*[an], typically translated as "way," the Shaykh apparently means the usual interpretation, and what he specifically calls an "allusion" (*ishāra*) that he finds in the Arabic word—not an "exegesis" (*tafsīr*). This allusion is that the word can also be read as the clause *min-hā jāʾ*, "from it he came." Then the verse would be understood to mean, *To each of you We have appointed a shariah, and from it* [that is, from that shariah, a word that literally means path], *he came.* In other words: Each of you prophets came by way of the specific path that We appointed. Thus, Ibn al-ʿArabī writes, "These words are an allusion to the root from which he came. This root is his nourishment. In the same way, the branch of a tree takes nourishment only from the root" (*Fuṣūṣ* 201). Austin (*Bezels* 255) has obscured the meaning of the passage.

7. Elsewhere the Shaykh explains that the servant should take everything given by the Prophet, but he must exercise discrimination in taking what is offered by God. "Your taking from the Messenger is unqualified, but your taking from God is qualified" (IV 186.24). For this sentence in more of its context, see Chittick, *Imaginal Worlds* 146.

8. *Ijtihād* is the exercise of independent judgment in interpreting the rulings of the Shariah; the

person who exercises this judgment is called a *mujtahid*. The Shaykh repeatedly refers to the legitimacy of *ijtihād* and the reward of those who exercise it, and he criticizes the ulama for maintaining that the "gate of *ijtihād*" is closed (III 336.12). Nonetheless, he also praises them for closing it: "Had they opened this gate for themselves, disorder would have entered the religion from those who make claims and have personal desires. . . . So they did an excellent thing!" (II 79.25 [Y 12:341.4]). He sometimes quotes the well-known formula, often cited in the early discussions of *ijtihād*, "Every *mujtahid* is correct" (II 165.33 [Y 13:468.5]). He commonly refers to the hadith, "When the ruler issues a ruling . . . ," according to which the *mujtahid* receives a wage for making the independent judgment, and another wage if his judgment is correct. For an overview of the Shaykh's views on *ijtihād*, see Muqdād Mansiyya, "al-Ijtihād ᶜind Muḥyi'l-Dīn ibn al-ᶜArabī."

9. On the hadith of supererogatory and obligatory works and the manner in which these works bring about the nearness by which God becomes the servant's hearing and eyesight, see SPK 325–31.

10. A "severed exception" (*istithnāʾ munqaṭiᶜ*) is the use of the word *except* in a context where what is excepted is wholly different in kind from the general term (Wright, *Grammar* 2:336A). In the example given by the Shaykh, *except Iblis* is "severed" because Iblis is wholly different in kind from the angels, since he was a jinn. If one does not recognize this (and some commentators do not), then the verse is saying indirectly that Iblis was one of the angels. If we read the verse, *Each thing is perishing except its face*, the exception is severed because the "face" of a thing is not a thing. If we read it Each *thing is perishing except His face*, it is severed because God's face is not a thing. It is in view of considering this latter a severed exception that the Shaykh can negate thingness from God's Essence. Otherwise, if it were a "joined exception" (Wright, *Grammar* 2:335D), the Koran would be saying indirectly that God's face—His Essence—is a thing.

11. Although a book by this title ascribed to Ibn al-ᶜArabî has recently been published, it does not correspond with this work. See G. Elmore's review in *Journal of the Muhyiddin ibn ᶜArabi Society*.

12. Concerning those who possess the station of having "a face with no nape" as an inheritance from Muhammad, see Chapter 4, note 31.

13. Reference to the *ḥadīth qudsī*, "I am with those whose hearts are broken for My sake." Ibn al-ᶜArabī comments on this hadith in a number of places, as in III 481.6, where he writes, "God says, 'I am with those whose hearts are broken,' for when you come to him whose heart is broken, you will find no one sitting with him save God, in state and speech" (III 481.6). See also IV 103.30.

14. One of the properties of jealousy (*ghayra*) is to ascribe divine attributes that appear in the "other" (*ghayr*) to their Owner. See SPK 388n25.

15. See the Shaykh's discussion of this episode in III 18.20, translated in SPK 315–17.

16. The mention of *islām, īmān,* and *iḥsān* alludes to the famous hadith in which the Prophet delineates the three basic dimensions of Islam (for an extended commentary on the hadith, see S. Murata and W.C. Chittick, *The Vision of Islam*). The Shaykh often refers to it and employs it to give structure to his book *Mawāqiᶜ al-nujūm*.

17. Here the Shaykh alludes to the verse, *All that dwells upon the earth is annihilated, and there subsists the face of thy Lord, Possessor of Majesty and Generous Giving* (55:27).

18. Compare this passage: "The Garden is named 'Garden' because it is a curtain and a veil between you and the Real, for it is the locus of the appetites of the souls. When He desires to show you your essence, He veils you from your appetite and He lifts the curtain from your eye. Then you become absent from your Garden while you are in it, and you see your Lord. Hence the veil over you is from you, so you are the cloud over your sun. So know the reality of your self!" (*ᶜAbādila* 101).

19. For more details on imaginal self-disclosure by human beings, see Chapter 311 of the *Futūḥāt*, translated into English in Chodkiewicz et al., *Illuminations* 287–300; also Chapter 6 of Chittick, *Imaginal Worlds*, "Meetings with Imaginal Men."

20. Al-Ḥasan Qaḍīb al-Bān al-Mawṣilī (d. 570/1174) was well-known for his ability to appear in diverse forms, sometimes sequentially, and sometimes at once. Another person "like him" was the master of Awḥad al-Dīn Kirmānī described in Chapter 311 (translated into English in Chodkiewicz et al., *Illuminations* 292–94). Ibn al-ᶜArabī was invested with the *khirqa* of Khaḍir by one of Qaḍīb's disciples in Mosul in 601/1204 (Addas, *Quest* 145, 236). Al-Nabhānī devotes the longest notice in *Jāmiᶜ karāmāt al-awliyāʾ* (2:23–31) to Qaḍīb and his miraculous form-changing, though most of the notice is taken up by a *fatwā* quoted from the famous scholar Jalāl al-Dīn al-Suyūṭī (d. 911/1505) on the possibility of such changes and their legal implications. Al-Suyūṭī quotes the opinions of several jurists, and most of them mention Qaḍīb as an example of the phenomenon. Ibn al-ᶜArabī refers to such form-changing in his answer to Tirmidhī's questions 37 and 38: "Among the loci of manifestation, some know that they are loci of

manifestation, but others do not know that they are loci of manifestation, so they imagine that they are outsiders to the Real. The mark of those who know that they are loci of manifestation is that they have loci of manifestation wherever they will in engendered existence—like Qaḍīb al-Bān, for he had loci of manifestation in whatever he willed of engendered existence, though not wherever he willed in engendered existence. Indeed, among the Men are those who have manifestation in whatever they will of engendered existence, but not wherever they will. But those who have manifestation wherever they will in engendered existence also have manifestation in whatever they will. Thus one form comes to be manifest in diverse places; or many forms in succession clothe one essence in the eye of those who perceive it" (II 65.29). See also I 259.34 (Y 4:153.11); II 333.33, 632.7; III 42.24.

21. The Shaykh held al-Mahdawī in high esteem, and it is to him that he dedicated the *Futūḥāt*. See Addas, *Quest* 113–17.

22. A number of hadiths mention that the Prophet saw Gabriel in a form that "blocked the horizon" (e.g., Muslim, Īmān 290; Bukhārī, Badʾ al-khalq 21; Aḥmad 1:407).

23. The poem is also quoted by Ibn al-ʿArīf, *Maḥāsin al-majālis*, p. 76; French translation, p. 31.

24. In a looser sense, any created thing can be addressed by it; the Koran speaks, for example, of God's revelation to the bees. See SPK 403n18.

25. Once again the poem is quoted by Ibn al-ʿArīf, *Maḥāsin al-majālis*, p. 76; French translation, p. 31.

26. For a reference to the "look at the One Entity" that determines the character of his own writing, see II 548.14, translated in SPK xiv and, in a fuller context, SPK 221.

27. The passage in which Ibn al-ʿArabī discusses this heat is translated in SPK 262.

28. See Chodkiewicz's study of these and related issues in *Seal*.

29. Al-Ḥakīm supports this derivation by an allusion to the word made by Ibn al-ʿArabī in *Dhakhāʾir al-aʿlāq* as well as an explicit explanation made by the Shaykh's commentator al-Nābulusī. See al-Ḥakīm, *Muʿjam* 402, 405. See also Yahia's edition of the *Futūḥāt*, vol. 3, footnotes on pp. 119 and 310.

30. Ibn al-ʿArabī employs the term *fahwāniyya* at the very beginning of his work *Kitāb al-ʿabādila*, "The Book of the Godservants," and its usage there may help illustrate the sense in which he employs it here. The word *ʿabādila* is a broken plural of ʿAbd Allāh, but it is not synonymous with the normal plural, *ʿibād Allāh*, "The servants of God." The latter means simply those who follow the prophets in general or Muhammad in particular, but by *ʿabādila* Ibn al-ʿArabī means those who have attained the station of human perfection, thereby realizing and manifesting the name God (Allah), in the form of which they were created. Thus the title of the work reminds us of the structure of the *Fuṣūṣ al-ḥikam*, the first chapter of which the Shaykh calls "A Ringstone of Divine Wisdom [i.e., the wisdom pertaining to the name God] in the Adamic Word;" he explains there that the perfect human beings, epitomized by Adam, manifest the divine name God. In the remaining twenty-six chapters of the *Fuṣūṣ*, he elucidates the wisdom of twenty-six perfect human beings, most of whom are well known prophets, and each of whom manifests the properties of one of God's names or attributes. In *Kitāb al-ʿabādila* he describes ninety-six Godservants (though the printed text is faulty, and most likely there were originally 114, corresponding to the number of the Koran's chapters [Chodkiewicz, *Ocean* 81]). Each of them has a "proper name" beginning with ʿAbd Allāh and then, in most cases, mentioning the father (a prophet or a friend of God) and the grandfather (a servant of one of God's names). In eleven instances, including seven of the first ten, the order of the second two names is reversed, and in one instance, there are two divine names but no human name (on the diverse divine names as archetypes of the perfect human beings, see SPK 369ff.). Thus, a typical name, ʿAbd Allāh ibn Mūsā ibn ʿAbd al-Qādir, means "Godservant, son of Moses, son of the Servant of the Powerful." By employing this name, Ibn al-ʿArabī wants to designate the wisdom of a perfect human being who manifests the specific qualities of Moses inasmuch as these display the properties and traces of the divine name Powerful. Under each proper name, the Shaykh mentions sayings from the mentioned individual (he mentions sayings from himself in much the same style in many of the "Mysteries" of Chapter 559). For example, the first Godservant is ʿAbdallāh ibn ʿAbdallāh ibn Muḥammad ibn ʿAbdallāh, and this name presumably designates the most perfect of these perfect men. This is the only instance in which four names are mentioned, so the Shaykh probably adds "ibn ʿAbd Allāh" at the end because "Muḥammad ibn ʿAbd Allāh" is the full name of the Prophet, and, in the context of the text's structuring principles, Muhammad's father's name, ʿAbd Allāh, now has an added significance, since it reminds us that Muhammad's wisdom manifests the all-comprehensive name God, given that his wisdom is epitomized in the all-comprehensive revealed book, the Koran, "That which brings everything together" (on *qurʾān* in this sense, see SPK 239–42). Thus we have a double ascription to

the name God and an ascription to Muhammad. This probably means that the perfect man in question manifests the name God in both modes of his perfection (on the two perfections of the perfect human beings, see SPK 366–69). The second saying of the first ʿAbd Allāh will sound familiar to readers of this book: He says: *"Cosmos* derives from *mark,* so each reality of the cosmos is a mark that signifies a divine reality. In its coming into existence, the [cosmic] reality is supported by the [divine] reality, and once it departs, its place of return is to it. So, when God mentions the 'cosmos,' consider to which [divine] reality He has ascribed it. Then you will know which of the worlds He means" (*ʿAbādila* 42).

To come back to the term *fahwāniyya,* Ibn al-ʿArabī tells us in the short introduction to *Kitāb al-ʿabādila* that he heard these sayings from these men on the tongues of the *fahwāniyya,* which is to say that he received them in various mutual waystations from the specific, imaginal configuration of divine realities that are designated by these names. He also alludes to the fact that these wisdoms are aspects of the knowledge that he has been given as the full inheritor of Muhammad. Indeed, the first person he mentions, ʿAbdallāh ibn ʿAbdallāh ibn Muḥammad ibn ʿAbdallāh, surely designates his own station as the Seal of the Muhammadan Friends. As he says in the second chapter, dedicated to the wisdom of ʿAbd Allāh ibn ʿAbd al-Raḥmān ibn Ilyās, "When someone describes you with something, that description abides in him, so he is more worthy of it" (*ʿAbādila* 46); having described these Men, Ibn al-ʿArabī himself is more worthy of their wisdoms than they are themselves. He also alludes to this at the beginning, employing the symbolic language of the text, when he says that the "spokesman" (*tarjumān*) in this book—that is, himself—is an "all-comprehensive son" (*ibn jāmiʿ*) of a "delimited" or "qualified" father (*ab muqayyad*). In other words, the author of the book is a full inheritor of the Prophet, while the Prophet in turn delimits and qualifies God's wisdom in the most perfect manner (cf. the Shaykh's statement, "Your taking from the Messenger is unqualified, but your taking from God is qualified" [IV 186.24], which is to say that you should take whatever the Messenger offers you, because he delimits and qualifies God's reality in a manner that will lead you to your felicity, but if you take whatever God offers you—without the qualification of Muhammad's guidance—you will fall into error and end up in wretchedness).

Ibn al-ʿArabī's words in the introduction to *Kitāb al-ʿabādila* are as follows: "To begin: In this book we have mentioned what the tongues of the Godservants spoke when they realized what the Real gave them to realize in their inmost secrets, and [we have mentioned] what the hearts of the gnostics brought near [to God] expressed from the tongues of the Elocution on the basis of the Word of the Presence before it was delivered over to their consciousness. Thus they spoke clearly about the affair as it is, both in the absent and the witnessed, both in knowledge and in servanthood. The spokesman in this book is an all-comprehensive son taking from a qualified father. Hence the affair is between sonship and fatherhood, inclusive of the state of friendship, prophethood, and messengerhood. Since ʿAbd Allāh is a name that comprehends all the levels of highness, we made him a spokesman, since the spokesman comprehends all the tongues. Then we ascribed him to the station of a servant who has gained one of the levels of the name God, and we ascribed him to a perfect individual, whether prophet or friend" (*ʿAbādila* 39). Concerning this passage and the hidden structural relationship between *Kitāb al-ʿabādila* and the Koran as well as other works of Ibn al-ʿArabī, see Chodkiewicz, *Ocean* 80–82.

31. In this context, by "the earth created from the leftover ferment of Adam's clay," the Shaykh means the whole cosmos considered as God's dream, or Unbounded Imagination (compare his statement here with II 313.12, translated in SPK 118). For more details on this earth, see pp. 357–58. There is an allusion here to the saying, sometimes cited as a hadith, "God fermented Adam's clay in His two hands for forty mornings." Ibn al-ʿArabî comments on this hadith in the process of discussing how the "pillars," that is, the four elements, gave rise to the progeny—minerals, plants, and animals—but not to the human being. "No form became manifest among the elements for the human being, who is the object sought from the *wujūd* of the cosmos. Hence He took sticky earth and mixed it with water, thus making it into a clay with His two hands—as is proper to His majesty, since *Nothing is as His likeness* [42:11]. He left it for a period so that it might ferment through the hot air that permeated the parts of its clay and was passing over it. Hence it fermented, and its scent changed. Then it became *stinking mud,* changed in odor. . . . God says, *We created the human being from a dry clay of stinking mud* [15:26]" (III 296.33).

32. The "specific face" is the face of God unique to each creature. See pp. 135–55.

33. On the role of these "prophets among the friends" (*anbiyāʾ al-awliyāʾ*), see SPK 250–52.

34. On commentary by allusion and Ibn al-ʿArabī's objections to *taʾwīl,* see SPK 246–50, 199–202; Chodkiewicz, *Ocean* 19–20, 35 ff.

35. The word *ṭūr* or "mount" derives from a root that means to approach something and to

hover around it. The Shaykh takes the etymological sense as an allusion to the bodily nature's inclinations, which draw it toward things that it desires.

36. The Shaykh differentiates the "command spirit" (*al-rūḥ al-amrī*) from the divine spirit that is blown into Adam's clay. The first is sent with specific messages, the second is the root of the self or soul. See pp. 276–77.

37. Ibn al-ʿArabī provides another account of this vision of the Antichrist in the following passage: "Nothing more marvelous than the property of mercy can be seen. Do you not see the physician who has mercy toward someone with [the skin disease called] *akila*? He has no power to put mercy into effect save by causing pain. The physician suffers pain in himself in the measure of his mercy toward the companion of this infirmity, because his mercy cannot be put into effect in the person without causing him pain. Were it not for his mercy toward the person, he himself would not suffer pain. Do you not also see that the person seeking the cure does not feel pain, but rather pleasure? So ponder what I have mentioned to you in the divine science! I saw this in a sound unveiling and an explicit locus of witnessing, while the Messenger of God was with me. God had commanded him to slay al-Dajjāl because of his claiming divinity. But he was weeping and apologizing to him for the punishment, saying that none of it was in his own hand. His weeping is like the pain in the soul of someone who is merciful but does not have the power to put his mercy into effect because of something that prevents it" (III 497.29).

38. On the two kinds of mercy, that of necessity or obligation and gratuitous favor or free gift, see SPK 130.

39. Allusion to the verse, *God caused their hearts to swerve* (61:5).

40. The idea that the heart is open to the suggestion (*lamma*) of both the angel and the satan (that is, the specific satan given charge of the person in question) is common in Islamic thought. One of its earliest formulations is in the hadith, "The satan has a suggestion to the child of Adam, and the angel has a suggestion."

Chapter 4

1. The word *ʿafw* or "pardon" is one of many in Arabic that has opposite meanings (*aḍdād*), since it means both to efface, eliminate, and overlook, and to increase, make many, and bestow. The servants "pardon" by overlooking ugly deeds, and they receive a recompense for pardoning when God overlooks their ugly deeds. The Shaykh seems to be saying here that God "pardons" His servants not only by overlooking their sin, but also by bestowing gifts.

2. On occasions, see the discussion of secondary causes in SPK 44–46, 175–77, and passim.

3. The "difficulty" is that the version accepted as sound by the Hadith authorities has the pronoun *his*, and this can be—and usually is by non-Sufis—read as referring back to Adam rather than to God. Hence the hadith would mean, for example, that when God created Adam, He created him in his full, adult form, not as an infant. For an example of Ibn al-ʿArabī's recognition of the validity of this reading, see SPK 399n4.

4. The "infirm person" is everyone other than God. "Everything other than God is an effect, and every effect is ill. So clinging to the Physician is a necessary obligation" (IV 401.9).

5. For another passage in which the Shaykh suggests that envy is the basic reason for rejecting the prophets, see III 83.12, translated in SPK 196.

6. This "someone" may be Ibn al-ʿArabī himself, since he provides a parallel argument elsewhere without ascribing it to anyone: "Among what is comprised by this waystation is the mercy that God has made manifest in the forgetfulness found in the cosmos. If not for it, the situation would be great and hard. It is enough for this to be mentioned. The root of this is the establishment of the veil between the cosmos and God in the homestead of prescribing the Law, for acts of disobedience and opposition are measured out in God's knowledge. Inescapably they must occur from the servant. If they were to occur along with self-disclosure and unveiling, that would be excessive shamelessness before God, since the person would be witnessing Him and seeing Him, while the measuring out would demand the occurrence. Thus He veiled Himself out of mercy toward the creatures, because of the severe calamity. Do you not see what happens to people in affairs that are governed by reason and that flow in accordance with rational propriety? God desires to carry out His decree and measuring out in some affair, but within it He hides the wisdom and knowledge that He is bringing to pass but which rational consideration does not demand. Having carried out the affair, He returns people's rational faculties to them. Thereby they may know that God has had mercy upon them through the disappearance of reason in that, because of the lifting of responsibility. The Prophet said, 'When God desires to put His decree and measuring out into effect, He strips the rational faculties from the possessors of rational faculties until, when He has carried out His decree and measuring out within them, He returns the faculties to them, so that they may take heed.' He also said, 'Error and forgetfulness have been lifted from

my community,' so God will not take them to account for it in this world or the last world" (II 684.35).

7. Allusion to the hadith, "The womb is a branch of the All-Merciful."

8. The reference here is to three sorts of interrelationship between night and daytime mentioned in the Koran, each of which has sexual undertones: *God makes the night enter into the daytime, and He makes the daytime enter into the night* (22:61); *He makes the night cover the daytime* (7:54); and *He wraps night about the daytime, and He wraps daytime about the night* (39:5). For more passages from Ibn al-ʿArabī on the theme of the children of daytime and night, see Murata, *Tao* 144 ff.

9. Reference to the sound *ḥadīth qudsī*, "When someone comes to Me running, I come to him rushing."

10. Allusion to the verse, *The men have a degree above them* (2:228), i.e., above the women. For a detailed discussion of Ibn al-ʿArabī's understanding of this degree, see Murata, *Tao* 179 ff.

11. On freedom, see Chapters 140–41, translated into English in Chodkiewicz et al., *Illuminations* 255–64.

12. For practical purposes "servitude" (*ʿubūda*) and "servanthood" (*ʿubūdiyya*) can be considered synonymous, but sometimes Ibn al-ʿArabī distinguishes between the two. See SPK 310–11.

13. For the introduction to this chapter and the section dealing with the talisman of imagination, see SPK 184–86; on the station of the Blameworthy, see SPK 372 ff.

14. For some of Ibn al-ʿArabī's teachings on the breaking of habits, see SPK, index under *habit*.

15. See SPK 373–74.

16. For more on this type of knowledge, see the translation of the first third of Chapter 289 in SPK 235–38.

17. II 19.18 (Y 11:358–59). For more details and a few references, see SPK 413n23.

18. For more on these, see SPK 406n6.

19. The Garden of Deeds is that of reward for good deeds in this world. The Garden of Specification is alluded to in the just-quoted Koranic verse, *God specifies for His mercy whomsoever He will* (2:105), and the Garden of Inheritance is mentioned in the verse, *That is the Garden that We shall give as an inheritance to those of Our servants who are godwary* (19:63). Ibn al-ʿArabī describes these Gardens briefly as follows: "The Gardens are three Gardens: The Garden of Divine Specification is the Garden entered by children who have not reached the limit of deeds. They reach this limit gradually from the time of birth until they complete six years. On whomever He wills among His servants God bestows whatever He wills of the Gardens of Specification. Among the folk of these Gardens are the mad who have not had the rational faculty, the folk of cognitive *tawḥīd* [cf. SPK 197], the folk of the gaps [between prophets], and those who have not been reached by the call of any messenger. The second Garden is the Garden of Inheritance that is attained by all those I have mentioned as entering the Garden and by the faithful. It is the places that would have been designated for the folk of the Fire had they entered [the Garden]. The third Garden is the Garden of Deeds, within which people dwell in keeping with their deeds. He who is more excellent than others, in the various sorts of ranking in degrees of excellence, has more of this Garden" (I 317.32). "The Gardens are three: the Garden of recompense for deeds; the Garden of Inheritance, which is that which the associator would have rightly claimed had he had faith; and the Garden of Specification, which is other than these two. I do not know if the Garden of Specification includes everyone or if it is for specific servants of God. As for those [mentioned in the hadith] 'who never did any good whatsoever' in terms of the Shariah, they have the Garden of Inheritance, but I do not know whether or not they have a Garden of Specification, as I said. As for the Garden of Shari'ite Deeds in respect of their being shari'ite—not in respect of their being existent—they have no share in that, for there may be among them those who have noble character traits but who have not put them into practice in respect of their being Shari'ite" (II 599.33). See also I 302.30–303.12 (Y 4:398–400).

20. Allusion to the complaint of the angels when God announced that He was placing Adam in the earth: *What, wilt Thou place therein one who will work corruption therein and shed blood?* (2:30).

21. The link is in the word *glory*, since the Shaykh takes *glorification* (*tasbīḥ*) as a synonym for *tanzīh* (see SPK 71). To be a servant is the counterpart of *tanzīh*, because asserting God's greatness and incomparability is to acknowledge human smallness and insignificance. In the same way, vicegerency is the counterpart of *tashbīh*, since asserting God's similarity and nearness is to recognize the human role in representing Him in the cosmos.

22. On Muḥammad ibn Qāʾid, see Appendix I. For more on the incident of the chamber discussed in the passage, see II 80.4 (Y 12:344.3).

23. Usually Ibn al-ʿArabī says that the gnostics affirm the truth of all positions from the perspective of unveiling, but deny some of these positions from the point of view of both the Shariah and reason (as we saw in the chapter on Realization, translated on pp. 96–98). For a clear and explicit statement of this position, see II 605.14, translated in SPK 243 and, more briefly, in *Imaginal Worlds* 10.

24. Ibn al-ʿArabī often tells us that the term *rajul* (pl. *rijāl*), employed for the Folk of God, may refer to women as well as men. See, for example, II 588.6, translated in Murata, *Tao* 268.

25. On the contrast between *tanzīh* and the attributes of Acts, which pertain to *tashbīh*, see SPK 58.

26. On states and stations, see SPK 263–69, 278–83, and passim.

27. These two states, *hujūm* and *bawādih* (plural of *bādiha*), are the topic of Chapter 259 of the *Futūḥāt* and are defined next to each other in the *Iṣṭilāḥāt* 10 (*Futūḥāt* II 131.31 [Y 13:201.4]).

28. See SPK 402n18.

29. Aḥmad al-Sabtī, a son of Hārūn al-Rashīd, had "the reins of affairs in his hands" because he was the Pole of his time. See Chittick, *Imaginal Worlds* 92–94.

30. For the hadith, see the index under "I have a moment. . . . "

31. Eyesight becomes bound by "all the directions" only in a certain type of visionary experience inherited from Muhammad, who said, "I see you from behind my back." In this station, the servant achieves "faceness" (*wajhiyya*, I 491.6 [Y 7:266.9]), which presumably means that he is a face turned toward every direction. Thus the Shaykh tells us that when he reached this station, "With my entire essence I became one eye, so I saw from all my directions" (I 491.7). "I did not see that I possessed a back or a nape, and in that vision I did not differentiate among my directions. On the contrary, I was like a globe. I did not understand any direction for myself save through supposition, not through finding" (II 486.25). For this vision in its historical context, see Addas, *Quest* 149.

32. By knowledge of the "tracings" (*rusūm*, pl. of *rasm*), Ibn al-ʿArabī means all the details of the religious sciences that form the course of study for the ulama. The tracings are the external signs, words, definitions, rules, and other basic components of any discipline. The Shaykh often contrasts the "ulama of the tracings" with the Folk of God; later on in this passage, he divides the ulama into two basic groups, those of the tracings and those of the hearts, who are the gnostics. Most often, he mentions the "ulama of the tracings" with a note of derision, since they are not able to see beyond the superficial meaning of what they have learned, but in this passage he acknowledges their importance and legitimacy. In SPK I translated "ulama of the tracings" as "exoteric scholars," which is more or less adequate, but it raises the unnecessary complication of the relation between "exoterism" and "esoterism." Neither of these terms can find a happy equivalent in Ibn al-ʿArabī's vocabulary, so it is best to avoid the suggestion that they might be adequate to deal with the extraordinarily diverse issues that arise in his elucidations of the nature of religious knowledge. For several instances of his use of the term *rusūm*, see the index of SPK under "exoteric."

33. In contrast to most authorities, Ibn al-ʿArabī is not satisfied with a simple majesty/beauty polarity. On majesty and beauty, see Murata, *Tao* 69–76 and passim. For some of the Shaykh's discussions of the contrast between beauty and the majesty of beauty, see Chodkiewicz et al., *Illuminations* 97–98, 506–7; Ibn al-ʿArabī, "On Majesty and Beauty" 6–8.

34. Reference to the hadith, "You shall see your Lord."

35. The Koranic phrase here is part of God's address to Iblis, after he had refused to prostrate himself to Adam: *What prevented you from prostrating yourself to him whom I created with My own two hands? Are you claiming greatness, or are you among the high ones?* Ibn al-ʿArabī provides some explanation for his identification of these "high ones" with the enraptured spirits in the following passage: "God may mean by *the high ones* the angels who are enraptured in God's majesty, those who do not come under the command to prostration. They are in fact spirits, not angels, for the angels are the messengers among the spirits, such as Gabriel and his peers, since the word *alūka* [from which *malāʾika*, "angels," is derived] means 'message' in the language of the Arabs. Hence the angels are specifically the messengers among these spirits. There remained no angel who did not prostrate itself, because they are the ones to whom God said, *Prostrate yourselves to Adam* [2:34]. But the enraptured spirits did not enter among those who were addressed to prostrate themselves, for God did not mention that He addressed any but angels. That is why He says, *So the angels prostrated themselves, all of them together* [15:30]" (III 294.16).

36. Here by "obligation and its supererogation" the Shaykh means the Real and creation. In the Shariah, obligatory works must be performed and supererogatory works are left to the servant's choice. God's supererogatory works are His creatures, since He is Independent of the worlds. "So we are His supererogatory work, and He is our root" (II 167.4). For some of the Shaykh's teachings on these two basic kinds of Shari'ite activity, see SPK 325–31.

37. Presumably the "contender" is a person who would try to argue that it is not incumbent on people to observe the Shariah. The Shaykh probably has this verse in mind: *We have appointed for every community a way of ritual that they shall observe, so let them not be in contention with you in the matter* (22:67).

38. The Koran says, *None feels secure against God's deception but the people who are losers* (7:99). If one reads this verse as having a universal application, then no station can give security from deception. But clearly the Shaykh does not consider the verse to be without exceptions.

Chapter 5

1. Compare the following passage from *Kitāb al-ʿabādila*, which derives from the all-comprehensive wisdom of ʿAbd Allāh ibn ʿAbd Allāh Muḥammad ibn ʿAbd Allāh (cf. Chapter 3, note 31). "He says: 'When the Real refers to Himself with the singular and He refers to you with the plural, this pertains to His oneness and your manyness in respect of your lack of independence and the fact of your poverty. But when He refers to Himself with the plural, like His words *Surely We* and *We*, this pertains to the realities of the divine names. When He makes you singular, then He is addressing one of your meanings, not all of you, so recognize who of yourself He is addressing, and open your hearing to His address" (*ʿAbādila* 42). Cf. Chodkiewicz's discussion of this passage in *Ocean* 36.

2. There is a reference here to a hadith in which it is mentioned that the Prophet was speaking about whispered prayers and saying, "One of you draws near to your Lord until He places His wing [*kanaf*] over him and says, 'Did you do such and such?' "

3. Reference to the hadith, "Make your rows solid. . . . "

4. Given that Ibn al-ʿArabī mentions "the angels" here and "other created things" earlier in the passage, by the term *umma* he does not mean religious communities, but rather each group of creatures, in keeping with the Koranic verse, *No crawling thing is there on the earth, no bird flying with its wings, but they are communities like you* (6:38).

5. See the Index of Hadiths and Sayings under "I knew God. . . . "

6. For the Shaykh's teachings on the duality that pervades the universe, see SPK, especially the last chapter. Many additional texts, both from Ibn al-ʿArabī and his followers, have been quoted and analyzed by Murata in *Tao*.

7. The two divine watchers (*raqība*) are the two sets of names. The duality becomes manifest on a lower level in the two "writing angels," who record the deeds of the servants. The word "watcher" (*raqīb*) in Koran 50:18 is commonly said to refer to these angels.

8. So says the text; however, in the standard reading, the pronoun is masculine in both cases. Fakhr al-Dīn al-Rāzī cites the remarks of one commentator on this verse that the Prophet used to recite it with the feminine pronoun throughout, but this is a minority opinion. If the text of the *Futūḥāt* is correct here, the Shaykh is following a third reading of the verse. In any case, his basic point—that sometimes the word *nafs* is feminine in the Koran and sometimes masculine—is obvious, and Rāzī remarks upon it in commenting on this verse (*al-Tafsīr al-kabīr* 7:274).

9. The Koranic verse is usually understood to refer to Christians—*They are unbelievers who say, "God is the third of three"* (5:73).

10. Here the Shaykh alludes to the Koranic statement that *The present life is naught but a play and a sport* (6:32, 29:64, 47:36), but he gives the idea a twist that would discomfort many exegetes.

11. The Shaykh's exposition here would clearly appear audacious to many theologians and jurists, especially in this particular sentence, because he chooses language from a well-known hadith that he frequently cites. The reference could hardly be missed by any reader. See the Index of Hadiths under "When someone lays down a beautiful sunnah. . . . "

12. On Ibn Qasī and Ibn al-ʿArabī's view of him, see Addas, *Quest* 53, 55–57; SPK 386n6.

13. Compare Ibn al-ʿArabī's explanation of why the rich are the poorest of all people, SPK 316.

14. On the idea that all poverty and need are for God alone, see SPK 45–46 and passim.

15. See SPK 38, and index, under *reality*.

16. The Cloud is not mentioned in the list itself, but later on in the text it is explained as if it had been mentioned there (II 174.17 [Y 13:534.10]).

17. After mentioning the two opposites, the Shaykh breaks the pattern of his statements and says, "And He chose mercy over wrath."

18. Compare the following two passages: "God has made one of the surahs of the Koran [i.e., Surah 36] its heart, and He has made this surah equivalent to the Koran ten times over [see Tirmidhī, Faḍāʾil al-qurʾān 7]. He has appointed to the verses of the Koran one verse upon which He has bestowed mastership over all the verses of the Koran. Among the surahs of the Koran He has appointed one to be equal to a third of it [i.e., Surah 112], half of it [Surah 99], and a fourth of it [Surah 109; Tirmidhī, Faḍāʾil al-qurʾān 10]. This is because of what is given by the waystation of that surah, yet all is His speech. Hence, in respect of being His speech, there is no ranking in excellence, but in respect of what is spoken about, ranking in excellence takes place because of the diversity of the arrangement" (III 96.3). "Ranking in excellence among the verses is well-known in the manner in which it has come. The excellence goes back to the reciter during recitation in respect of the fact that

what the verse contains is spoken, not in respect of the fact that it is the speech of God, for there is no ranking in excellence in the latter respect. Ranking in excellence occurs only in what is spoken" (IV 79.1).

19. Bahāʾ al-Dīn ibn Shaddād (d. 633/1235) was the chief *qāḍī* of Aleppo, while Ibn al-Ustādh (d. 636/1238) was his successor (Addas, *Quest* 262).

20. Time, of course, is a central problem in cosmology, but it cannot be addressed specifically and directly in the present volume. See Böwering, "Ibn al-ʿArabī's Concept of Time."

21. For more on *ṣalāt* and *muṣallī* in this sort of context, see SPK 343–44.

22. The discussion here and in the next paragraph has to do with fine points of the Shariah related to *ṣalāt*. The issue is *taktīf* (or *takattuf*)—placing one hand on the other and placing both on the stomach during the *ṣalāt*, an act performed by some Muslims and not by others. Thus, for example, when standing during the *ṣalāt* and reciting the *munājāt* or "whispered prayer," Ḥanafīs observe *takattuf*, but Mālikīs do not. Ibn al-ʿArabī's short discussion of this issue in his chapter on *ṣalāt* helps clarify what he is saying here: "The ulama have disagreed about putting one hand on the other during the *ṣalāt*. Some of them have considered it reprehensible during the obligatory [*ṣalāt*], but permissible during the supererogatory. Another group sees that it is one of the sunnahs of the *ṣalāt*. This act has been related from God's Messenger, just as it has been related, in the description of his *ṣalāt*, that he did not do it. It is also affirmed that people commanded the doing of it. Among the Folk of God, the metaphorical interpretation [*iʿtibār*] in this is as follows: The person who does the *ṣalāt* has diverse states before his Lord in his standing, in keeping with the diversity of what he whispers in prayer. If what he whispers requires *taktīf*, then he does it, and if it requires *sudl*, which is letting the two hands fall, he lets them fall. In the same way, if the verse requires asking forgiveness, he asks forgiveness; if it requires supplication, he supplicates; if it requires magnifying the High Side, he magnifies; if it requires happiness, he is happy; and if it requires reverent fear, he is reverently fearful. Thus he accords with his whispered prayer. Hence it does not behoove the person who performs the *ṣalāt* to bind himself in his whispered prayer by a specific attribute. That is why those who have upheld choice in this issue have upheld it. All these guises are permissible and beautiful" (I 439.30). Earlier in the same chapter, the Shaykh mentions *taktīf* in the context of explaining part of the whispered prayer that is recited in the *ṣalāt*, that is, the *tawjīh* or "face-turning," which begins with the words, *I have turned my face to Him who originated the heavens and the earth, with pure faith, and I am not of those who associate* (6:79). Part of this prayer is the words, "Thou art the King—there is no god but Thou." In explaining the sense of these words, the Shaykh writes, "God has called the servant to stand before him, and it is not appropriate that any call him to this attribute save kings. Hence this name [King] is specific to the *tawjīh* apart from any other. This is why *taktīf* was set down as Shariah in the *ṣalāt* in the state of standing, for it is the place of the standing of the servant before the King" (I 419.6).

Chapter 6

1. That God selected or "chose" Friday from among the days of the week was mentioned in the table of God's choices that is cited on p. 189, but the rationale for the relation that Ibn al-ʿArabī sees here between the First and Friday remains unclear to me, especially since he connects Friday explicitly with the name Last in another context: "Friday is the last of the days of creation. On Friday was created he whom God created in the Form, that is, Adam; so through it became manifest the perfection of the completion of creation and its furthest limit. Through it became manifest the most perfect of the creatures, who is the human being, the last of the progeny. Through him God preserved the name Last for the Divine Presence, and through the name Last He preserved him, for among the divine names it is this name that gazes upon him. Since God brought together the creation of the human being in this day, through His configuring in him the bringing together of the two forms—the form of the Real and the form of the cosmos—God named it with the language of the Shariah 'the day of coming together' [*yawm al-jumʿa*]" (I 645.17). See also II 173.15 (Y 13:526.10).

2. Yahia knows of no other reference to this work (*Histoire* 175).

3. Reference to the hadith, "If allegiance is sworn to two caliphs, the other should be killed."

4. Concerning Ibn al-ʿArabī's teachings on these points, see Chittick, *Imaginal Worlds*, Chapter 7.

5. On striking likenesses or similitudes for God, see Chittick, *Imaginal Worlds* 76–77.

6. Authors typically read this hadith to mean, "Even if you do not see Him, He sees you," but Ibn al-ʿArabī offers this as an alternative reading in some passages. Cf. James Morris, "Seeking God's Face," Part I, p. 12. However, contrary to what Morris suggests, Ibn al-ʿArabī does not always read the hadith to mean "If you are not. . . . " For examples of the more usual reading, see II 344.11 and III 309.7.

7. Reading *ghāfilīn* for *ᶜārifīn*. This is demanded by the meaning of the passage and confirmed by the last paragraph of this section, where the Shaykh again refers to "the hearts of the heedless."

8. Ibn al-ᶜArabī calls these four questions "the mothers of the questions": "*Whether* is a question about *wujūd, what* a question about the reality, called the 'quiddity'; *how* a question about the state; and *why* a question about the cause and the occasion" (I 193.31 [Y 3:218.11]). In the continuation of this passage, he discusses the pros and cons of employing these questions to ask about God.

9. On Idris and his being lifted up to a high place, see *Fuṣūṣ* 75–76 (Austin, *Bezels* 83–85); II 445.15; *Dhakhāʾir* 193.

10. There are allusions here both to the hadith of supererogatory works and to the Prophet's supplication, "Make me into a light."

11. Reference to Satan's refusal to prostrate before Adam and his words offered as excuse, *I am better than he* (7:12, 38:76).

12. Riḍwān is the angel who guards over paradise, Mālik the angel in charge of hell.

13. The cursing of these tribes for one month is mentioned in many hadiths, including several quoted by Muslim and Bukhārī (see *Concordance* 8:82, under Riᶜl).

14. For most of this passage, see SPK 362 (III 274.25).

15. The seven attributes are life, knowledge, desire, power, speech, hearing, and sight, though Ibn al-ᶜArabī sometimes replaces the last two with munificence and justice. These are considered the "mothers" or the "leaders" of the other names, because the others can all be seen as falling under their scope and deriving from them (SPK 408n14; cf. III 398.22, translated on p. 249). For some of Ibn al-ᶜArabī's views on how these attributes interrelate, see his *Inshāʾ al-dawāʾir*, translated by Fenton and Gloton. Chodkiewicz has shown that the seven attributes provide the rationale for the overall structure of the *Futūḥāt* (*Ocean* 97–98).

16. On triplicity in Ibn al-ᶜArabī, see Murata, *Tao* 151–53.

17. I read *al-wajh al-khāṣṣ*, following the variant given by Yahia. The text has *al-wajh al-ḥāṣil*, "the actual face" or "the face that is actually present." The latter is not one of Ibn al-ᶜArabī's technical terms, and even if it is the correct reading, the Shaykh means by it the specific face.

18. As pointed out elsewhere (SPK 411n4), Koran interpreters read this verse in various ways. Many of them understand the subject of the verb *He came down* to be Gabriel, not God.

19. It is true that the Shaykh provides a definition for *ill* in his *Iṣṭilāḥāt al-ṣūfiyya*, but, as is the case with many of the terms he defines there, he rarely employs it; or, if he does employ it, he employs it in another sense. In this particular case, he tells us in *Iṣṭilāḥāt* that *ill* is synonymous with the suffix *īl* on the names of various angels (in accordance with the etymological sense of these words, as recognized by some of the Arab lexicographers [see Lane, *Lexicon*, s.v.]). He writes in explanation of the term that *ill* means "Every divine name that is ascribed to an angel or a spiritual, such as Gabriel [Jibraʾīl], Michael [Mīkāʾīl], or ᶜAbdaʾill" (II 130.4; *Iṣṭilāḥāt* 14 [reading *ill* for *āliyya*]; the version in *Iṣṭilāḥāt* itself provides the definition without the examples). The identity of ᶜAbdaʾill (so vocalized by Yahia) is unknown to me.

20. For a longer version of this anecdote and Ibn al-ᶜArabī's explanation, see p. 257.

21. Compare the classification provided in *Inshāʾ al-dawāʾir* 20–21 ("The Book of the Description" 27–28).

22. "Drinking" (*shurb*) is a more permanent sort of perceiving the absent world than "tasting." See SPK 220.

Chapter 7

1. On two modes of witnessing that correspond to the vision of the sun and the moon, see II 632.29, translated in SPK 217–18.

2. Ibn al-ᶜArabī often declares that the vision of God in the form of Muhammad is the most complete and perfect vision of God. This should not be surprising, given the identification he makes between God's total self-disclosure, that is, the Breath of the All-Merciful, and the Muhammadan Reality (see SPK, Chapter 8; and, on Muhammad as God's most perfect self-disclosure, SPK 239–42, 351–52). Compare these passages: "In this station, we long for the vision of the Real through the Muhammadan vision in the Muhammadan form, for it is the most complete and the most truthful vision. This Presence belongs to those who associate nothing with God" (IV 203.8). "So seek not to witness the Real save in the mirror of your Prophet—God bless him and give him peace" (III 252.1). "Know that *some* of the *prophets* have been *ranked in excellence over others* [17:55], so their mirrors are inescapably ranked in excellence. The most excellent, balanced, and correct of mirrors is Muhammad's mirror, so God's self-disclosure within it is more perfect than any other self-disclosure that there may be. So, struggle to gaze at the Self-Disclosing Real in the mirror of Muhammad so that He may be imprinted in your mirror. Then you will see the Real in a Muhammadan form through a Muhammadan vision, and you will not see Him in your form" (IV 433.9). "[Jesus] will be among

those who, on the day of resurrection, see their Lord as the Muhammadan vision in the Muhammadan form" (IV 116.32). In this context Ibn al-ᶜArabī sometimes relates an anecdote about Abū Yazīd (IV 184.28, 203.4, 433.12): Two Sufis were talking, and one asked the other if he had seen Abū Yazīd. He replied, "I have seen God, so I have no need to see Abū Yazīd." The other said to him, "Were you to see Abū Yazīd once, it would be better for you than seeing God a thousand times." When the man finally did see Abū Yazīd, he died on the spot. When Abū Yazīd was told about the man's earlier statement, he said, "He was seeing God in his measure, but when he saw us, the Real disclosed Himself to him in our measure, so he was not able to bear that and he died." Ibn al-ᶜArabī concludes: "Given that such is the affair, we come to know that our vision of God in the Muhammadan form through the Muhammadan vision is the most complete vision that there may be. So we never cease encouraging people to achieve it, both orally and in this book" (IV 184.31). See also III 560.20, translated on p. 302.

3. The essential limits (*al-ḥudūd al-dhātiyya*), or the "essential definitions," are the attributes of things that distinguish them from other things.

4. Bāqillānī was a famous Ash'arite theologian (d. 403/1013).

5. See SPK 408n14.

6. On these two commands, see SPK 291–94; Chittick, *Imaginal Worlds* 142–44.

7. On various distinctions that he draws between knower and gnostic, see SPK 148–49.

8. The poet is Imru'l-Qays (I 602.9 [Y 9:99.3]), and the argument depends on the various ways in which the word *ṣawm* or "fasting" is used in Arabic. Literally, the word means to abstain, to hold back from, to rise beyond.

9. The term *Footstool* (*kursī*) is understood in a number of ways, "God's knowledge" being the most general. More commonly, Ibn al-ᶜArabī gives it a cosmological sense as the complement of the Throne.

10. Gerhard Böwering cites three other versions of this anecdote from a variety of sources (*Mystical Vision* 56–57).

11. For the continuation of this passage, which explains the difference between eyesight and insight, see SPK 223–24.

12. For an English translation of most of Chapter 311, which deals mainly with imagination and of which these two paragraphs are a part, see Chodkiewicz et al., *Illuminations* 287–300.

13. See the detailed study by K. Nakamura, "Imām Ghazālī's Cosmology Reconsidered, With Special Reference to the Concept of *Jabarūt*." It would be difficult to agree with Nakamura's statement, "The *jabarūt* [for Ghazālī] is quite different from the *ᶜālam al-mithāl* that is understood by Ibn ᶜArabī" (p. 44).

14. Ibn al-ᶜArabī considers al-Ḥallāj as the first to use the terms *height* and *breadth* in this sense, as he acknowledges in the continuation of the passage (I 169.6 [Y 3:95.4]).

15. Reference to the *ḥadīth qudsī*, "While His two hands were gripped tight. . . . "

16. Reference to the hadith, "Our Lord descends to the closest heaven every night."

17. The sunset prayer, which has three cycles, is the only mandatory *ṣalāt* with an odd number of cycles. The morning *ṣalāt* has two, both daylight *ṣalāts* have four, and the night prayer has four.

Chapter 8

1. Compare III 67.7, where Ibn al-ᶜArabī says that every form has a governing spirit, but life remains when the spirit leaves at the form's destruction. On the analogy between the spirit and the ruler, see I 294–296 (Y 4:353–65), where it is developed in detail. Ibn al-ᶜArabī's treatise *al-Tadbīrāt al-ilāhiyya fī iṣlāḥ al-mamlakat al-insāniyya* ("The divine governings: On making wholesome the human empire") is based largely on this analogy.

2. After bowing in the *ṣalāt*, the person straightens up and recites the formula, "God hears him who praises Him." Concerning these words, the Prophet said, "God says on the tongue of His servant, 'God hears him who praises Him.'"

3. Ibn al-ᶜArabī says "corporeous" (*jasadī*) rather than "corporeal" (*jismānī*) because he employs the former term in a broad sense to refer to every kind of body—the light bodies of the angels, the fire bodies of the jinn, the dust body of Adam, and the vile-water body of Adam's offspring. "Vile water" is a Koranic expression for sperm, as in the verse, *He originated the creation of the human being from clay, then He made his descendants from an extraction of vile water* (32:7–8).

4. For a passage that makes a clear distinction between these two spirits, see III 125.12, translated in the next chapter (p. 342).

5. The reference is to the well-known hierarchy of spiritual attainment posed in terms of certainty (*yaqīn*)—"the knowledge of certainty," "the eye of certainty," and "the *ḥaqq* of certainty." Often these three stages are compared to knowledge of fire, seeing fire, and being consumed by fire.

6. The thing emplaced "in" the place is confined to the place and determined by it, in which case the place (*makān*) can be called "spatial confines" (*aḥyāz*), and the emplaced thing (*mutamakkin*) "the spatially confined" (*mutaḥayyiz*).

Thus the Shaykh writes, "Place is that *on* [*ʿalā*] which—not *in* [*fī*] which—emplaced things become settled. If they become settled *in* it, that is spatial confines, not place" (II 458.2).

7. See III 154.18, translated in SPK 276.

8. There is reference here to several Koranic passages, such as the following: *If you call them to the guidance, they do not hear; and thou seest them looking at thee, but they do not see* (7:198); *Deaf, dumb, blind—so they do not use intelligence* (2:171); *Deaf, dumb, blind—so they do not return* (2:18).

9. Ibn al-ʿArabī has in mind Koranic verses such as 2:143 and relevant hadiths. For example, the Prophet said, "On the day of resurrection Noah will be called and he will reply, 'At Thy service, my Lord.' He will be asked, 'Did you convey the message?' and he will reply that he did. His people will be asked whether he conveyed the message to them and they will say that no warner came to them. He will be asked who his witnesses are and he will reply that they are Muhammad and his people. They will bear witness that he conveyed the message, *that the Messenger may be a witness against you*." Then he recited, *Thus We appointed you a midmost community that you might be witnesses against the people, and that the Messenger may be a witness against you* (2:143).

10. For the four categories and a brief explanation of the first, see SPK 211.

11. On the correspondence between the one hundred fourteen waystations and the chapters of the Koran, see Chodkiewicz, *Ocean* 64–76.

12. This definition of allusion is also found in Ibn al-ʿArīf, *Maḥāsin al-majālis* 76.

13. The Shaykh refers to the *noble writers* (82:11)—the angels who write down the good and evil deeds of God's servants.

14. As mentioned in the introduction, Ibn al-ʿArabī speaks of four basic modes of order in the cosmos, depending on whether we consider it in terms of time, space, qualitative hierarchy, or the letters articulated in the Breath of the All-Merciful.

15. A reference to the three stages of certainty mentioned above, note 5.

16. Reference to the hadith, "Prophecy and messengerhood. . . . "

17. On rooting the Koran in the memory, see Chapter 3, note 4.

18. The "seal" of the affair is Jesus at the end of time. See Chodkiewicz, *Seal*, Chapter 8.

19. The beginning of this sentence says literally, "he says," not "one says." Ibn al-ʿArabī may be referring to himself in the third person. Earlier in the *Futūḥāt* he has written, "Part of the perfection of *wujūd* is the *wujūd* of imperfection within it, since, were there none, the perfection of *wujūd* would be imperfect through the nonexistence of imperfection within it" (II 307.11). For this passage in context, see SPK 296.

20. That the mountains are "pegs" with which God keeps the earth from quaking is explained in the hadith literature and in commentaries on Koran 78:6–7: *Have We not made the earth as a cradle and the mountains as pegs?* See also the hadith, "He created the mountains. . . ."

21. Compare Ibn al-ʿArabī's words, "Among the pillars, [air] is nearest in relation to the Breath of the All-Merciful" (II 451.13). He calls air the "greatest element, the root of all the elements" (III 437.12). As scriptural support for air's importance, he often refers to a hadith in which the Prophet enumerates a list of things, each stronger than the previous—mountains, iron, fire, water, wind (or air), and the child of Adam. In commenting on this hadith, he says, "There is nothing stronger than air [*hawāʾ*], except the human being, in respect of his ability to curb his caprice [*hawā*] through his rational faculty" (II 451.1). For the hadith, see index under "He created the mountains. . . ."

22. On these two figures, see Appendix I.

23. Abu'l-ʿAbbās Aḥmad ibn Jaʿfar al-Sabtī, who died in Egypt in 601/1205, is a famous Moroccan saint. For biographical details and references to many studies, see H. Bencheneb, "Sabtī," *Encyclopaedia of Islam* (new edition) 8:691–93. For a brief notice concerning his relationship with Ibn al-ʿArabī, see Addas, *Quest* 176–77. For some of Ibn al-ʿArabī's references to him, see Appendix I.

24. The text here has Sulaymān al-Danīlī, but other passages in the *Futūḥāt* refer to him as al-Danbulī. Yahia in his critical edition (Y 10:55.6) gives his first name as Salmān, but also notes Sulaymān as a reading of one of the manuscripts. Apparently nothing is known about him save what Ibn al-ʿArabī mentions. Three of the four passages referring to him tell us that al-Danbulī never had an ugly thought for fifty years. Thus, in discussing the four sorts of (passing) thoughts (*khāṭir*), Ibn al-ʿArabī explains that prophets have the divine, angelic, and soul-derived sorts, but not the satanic sort. Then he writes, "This may also happen for some of God's friends—those who have a full part of prophecy, such as Sulaymān al-Danbulī. I met him, and he was one of those who have this state. He reported to me about himself that for fifty-some years, no ugly thought had occurred to him; but most of the friends have these thoughts" (I 666.22; cf. IV 35.4, 58.6). A fourth passage tells that the Shaykh asked al-Danbulī about his cheerful conversation (*mubāsaṭa*) with God, and he replied as follows: "One day He conversed with me cheerfully in my secret heart. He said to me, 'My kingdom is magnificent,' and I said to Him, 'My kingdom is more magnificent than Your kingdom.'

He said to me, 'How do you say that?' I said to Him, 'The like of You is in my kingdom, but the like of You is not in Your kingdom. So who has the more magnificent kingdom?' He said, 'You have spoken the truth'" (IV 64.11).

Chapter 9

1. See Murata, *Tao* 147–48.

2. On the two Imams, see Chodkiewicz, *Seal* 96–97.

3. That is, when the night is the male and the day is the female. On the sexual imagery of this "covering" of the day by the night and vice versa, see Murata, *Tao* 146–47.

4. Ibn al-ᶜArabī discusses the three meanings of the word in the chapter of Jacob in the *Fuṣūṣ* (see Austin, *Bezels* 113–16).

5. The Shaykh is referring here to the hadith, "You should fast, for it has no likeness." He explains: "Thus the Prophet negated that any act of worship that God set down as Shariah for His servants be like fasting. Those who know that fasting is a negative description—since it is the abandonment of things that break the fast—will know for certain that it has no likeness, since it has no entity that is qualified by the *wujūd* that is rationally understood. That is why God says, 'Fasting is Mine.' In reality, it is neither an act of worship nor a deed. When the name *deed* is ascribed to it, this is done metaphorically [*tajawwuz*], like the ascription, understood by us as a metaphor, of the word *existent* to the Real. After all, since His *wujūd* is identical with His Essence, attributing *wujūd* to Him is not similar to attributing *wujūd* to us, for *Nothing is as His likeness* [42:11]" (I 602.14).

6. Iyās and Bāqil are proverbial references to cleverness and stupidity. The former, Abū Wāthila Iyās ibn Muᶜāwiya ibn Qurra ibn Iyās al-Mazanī (d. 122/740), was a *qāḍī* in Basra. The latter, Bāqil al-Ayyādī, was a bedouin of the Age of Ignorance.

7. See Chodkiewicz, *Ocean* 116–18.

8. In other contexts, *himma* may refer to this same power of concentration as employed by the gnostic to bring about the miraculous breaking of habits. See Izutsu, *Sufism and Taoism*, Chapter 17. Corbin writes, "The force of an *intention* so powerful as to project and realize ("essentiate") a being external to the being who conceives the intention, corresponds perfectly to the character of the mysterious power that Ibn al-ᶜArabī designates as *himma*" (*Creative Imagination*, p. 222). Both Izutsu and Corbin, in their detailed discussions of *himma*, give a distorted picture of what the term involves, focusing as they do on the extraordinary and miraculous side of this power. *Himma* in the sense in which they understand it is rather a bit player in Ibn al-ᶜArabī's overall cosmodrama.

9. For Ibn al-ᶜArabī's views on Rābiᶜa, see Appendix I.

10. These represent one version of the "four journeys" that are often discussed in the later literature. Mullā Ṣadrā's magnum opus, *al-Asfār al-arbaᶜa* ("The Four Journeys"), is structured in terms of these. In his *Isfār ᶜan natāʾij al-asfār*, Ibn al-ᶜArabī says, however, that "There are three journeys, without any fourth that the Real has affirmed—a journey beginning at Him, a journey to Him, and a journey in Him" (3). See the French translation of this work by D. Gril.

11. Reference to the famous hadith, "Three things of this world of yours were made lovable to me: women, perfume—and the delight of my eye is in the *ṣalāt*."

12. On al-Ḥarīrī, see Addas, *Quest*, passim.

13. The Shaykh alludes here to the hadith, "It is newly acquainted with my Lord."

14. The clause in brackets is found in the Cairo edition of the text, but not in Yahia's critical edition.

15. There is a reference here to the hadith, "The child belongs to the bedding," which, in Islamic law, is taken to mean that the child belongs primarily to the father.

16. Al-Ḍurāḥ, which means literally something like "the distant," is the Inhabited House (*al-bayt al-maᶜmūr*) in the seventh heaven (the first heaven below the sphere of the fixed stars).

17. This would have been in the year 599/1202–3 (II 262.3). Little is known about al-Qabbāb, except that he was a Cordovan disciple of Abu'l-Ḥasan ibn Ḥirzihim in Fez (IV 96.5). He is mentioned as an auditor on some manuscripts of the Shaykh's works (Addas, *Quest* 222).

18. See IV 214–15, a section called "The Presence of letting down the curtains, which belongs to the names All-Forgiving, Forgiver, and Forgiving."

Chapter 10

1. For the continuation of this passage, see II 310.17, translated in SPK 126.

2. The Shaykh explains later in this passage (I 285.22 [Y 4:298.14]) that *khabīr* (translated here as "Experienced") takes the form *faᶜīl* and, like other words of this form, can have the sense of *mafᶜūl*, i.e., that which is experienced by us. Usually, he understands the name to signify that God gains knowledge from experience, that is, by putting His creatures through testing and trial. See index, *Experienced*.

3. Ibn al-ᶜArabī seems to be saying that rational thinkers are able to prove on the basis of their own premises that certain things are impossible, but in

their daily lives they recognize that such things are in fact possible, as when they see them in dreams.

4. As noted earlier, the object of desire, like the object of love, remains always nonexistent. See Chittick, "The Divine Roots."

5. See SPK 160–61.

6. Among other things, the Shaykh no doubt has in mind his own experience when, because of the presence of his Beloved, he could not eat for several weeks, but nevertheless grew plump. See II 325.20, translated in Chittick, "Ebno'l-ʿArabi as Lover."

7. For further clarification of the manner in which possibility (*imkān*) accompanies the soul in the spiritual ascent, see the Shaykh's remarks on the talisman of imagination, translated in SPK 184–85.

8. The lines are from Ibn al-ʿArabī's *Tarjumān al-ashwāq* 38–39 (for Nicholson's English version, see Nicholson, *The Tarjumān* 130).

9. For the continuation of the passage, see SPK 351–52.

10. For his two entrances into this abode (in 591/1195 and 593/1196), see Addas, *Quest* 140.

11. Much of the wording derives from a hadith found in several versions in Muslim (Tawba 17–21) and elsewhere.

12. Hadiths to this effect are found in Muslim (Tawba 21) and Aḥmad 3:56.

13. Allusion to the verse, *The word of my Lord will be realized against the unbelievers, that they are the companions of the Fire* (40:6).

14. The Companion in question is ʿAlī ibn Abī Ṭālib, as the Shaykh recognizes elsewhere (III 131.23, 223.23).

15. On the circularity of trusteeship, see pp. 76–77.

16. For a brief review of his teachings on this earth and the fact that he identifies it with "God's all-embracing earth," of which mention was made earlier, see Addas, *Quest* 117–18. See also Henry Corbin's discussion in *Spiritual Body and Celestial Earth* 135–43.

17. For the context of this discussion, see SPK 204–5.

18. For parallels with what he has to say about imagination, compare this passage with SPK, Chapter 7, especially the last section, "The Manifestation of the Impossible."

19. "Tenuities" (*raqāʾiq*) are subtle forms or relations that tie together various levels of existence. See SPK 406n6.

20. About half of this chapter is translated in SPK. See the page references cited in the Index of Sources, SPK 420.

21. Hadiths from which this account is probably derived are found in Muslim (Ruʾyā 14–16), Ibn Māja (Ruʾyā 5), and Aḥmad (3:315).

22. On the categories, see Chapter 2, note 23.

23. This particular category is usually rendered as "position" or "posture," but the Arabic word is *waḍʿ*, which means literally to put or to place. In any sort of technical context, I have been translating the term as "establish," as when God "establishes" the occasions on the basis of wisdom. If the term were to be translated here as "position," the point that Ibn al-ʿArabī makes later on—that all the shariahs are the *waḍʿ* of God through His speech—would be lost.

24. Reference to the hadith, "Our Lord descends. . . . "

25. As noted, this chapter is based on the sciences contained in Surah 82 of the Koran, which has nineteen verses. At the end of the chapter (III 13.22), Ibn al-ʿArabī provides a brief list of these sciences, and these can be enumerated as sixteen. The connection between the verses and the mentioned sciences is far from clear. In the present instance, by mentioning the "eighth degree," he seems to be referring to the eighth verse of the surah, which is mentioned later on in the discussion: *[O Man! What deceived you as to your generous Lord, who created you, then proportioned you, then balanced you—] in whatever form He willed He mounted you?*

26. This is a reference to the rites of the hajj. See I 709.32 (Y 10:356.3).

27. In his account of abstinence (*waraʿ*) in *Kitāb al-Lumaʿ*, Abū Naṣr al-Sarrāj provides accounts of this sort concerning the Sufis Jaʿfar al-Khuldī and Bishr al-Ḥāfī (ed. by Nicholson, p. 45; translated in J. Nurbakhsh, *Sufism IV* 38–39).

28. Allusion to this verse: *As for those unto whom already the most beautiful has gone forth from Us, they shall be kept from* [*Gehenna*] (21:101).

29. "Engendered existence" translates *al-kawn*. It may be that Ibn al-ʿArabī means by this term "all that is," including both God and the cosmos. Then, when we "leave aside" the totality, we observe the two sides. However, although the word *kawn* can apply to the *wujūd* of God in some contexts, *al-kawn* is typically a technical term meaning everything other than God, everything that has come to be as the result of the divine command *kun*. If Ibn al-ʿArabī has this is mind, as I think he does, he means by "creation" and "Real" the two sides of reality as we experience it and as he has been discussing it. Thus "creation" would mean everything that manifests the side of nonexistence and darkness, and "Real" would mean everything that manifests the side of *wujūd* and light. The combination of the two sides gives rise to the cosmos.

30. "Ineffectuality" (*taʿṭīl*) is a well-known heresy, so mentioning its name is sufficient to dismiss it from consideration. It is the idea that God leaves

aside governing His creation even for an instant. See the article "*Tashbīh*" in the *Encyclopedia of Islam*.

Appendix I

1. Not only does the saying accord with the general tenor of the sayings related from her, but also the famous eleventh/seventeenth-century scholar ʿAbd al-Ra'ūf al-Munāwī explicitly cites this passage from the *Futūḥāt* as a criticism of Rābiʿa (*Ṭabaqāt al-awliyāʾ*, quoted in J. Nūrbakhsh, *Zanān-i sūfī* 52). If Ibn al-ʿArabī does not mention her name, this is no doubt out of respect for her.

2. One wonders what Trimingham means here by the word *Sufi*. Although Ibn al-ʿArabī certainly does not define the word in the same way as Trimingham, he might agree with his statement, since he places the Sufis among the middle level Folk of God (see SPK 373–74), while he considered ʿAbd al-Qādir to belong to the highest level.

3. On deception, compare II 529.33, translated in SPK 267.

4. The line is from a *qaṣīda* by Abū Tamām (Yahia's note).

5. This saying is also cited in II 522.32.

6. For more on such imaginal experiences, see especially Chittick, *Imaginal Worlds*, Chapter 6; and Chodkiewicz et al., *Illuminations* 287–300.

BIBLIOGRAPHY

Listed here are cited works and a few editions and studies too recent to be mentioned in the bibliographies of SPK or Addas, *Quest.*

Abū Dāwūd. *al-Sunan.* Ed. A. S. ʿAlī, Cairo: Muṣṭafā al-Bābī al-Ḥalabī, 1952.

Abū Nuʿaym al-Iṣfahānī, al-Ḥāfiẓ, *Kitāb Dalāʾil al-nubuwwa.* Third edition, Hyderabad: The Dāiratu'l-Maʿārifi'l-Osmania, 1977.

Addas, Claude. *Quest for the Red Sulphur: The Life of Ibn ʿArabī.* Cambridge, England: The Islamic Texts Society, 1993.

Aḥmad ibn Ḥanbal. *al-Musnad.* Beirut: Dār Ṣādir, n.d.

Austin. *Bezels.* See Ibn al-ʿArabī, *Fuṣūṣ.*

Böwering, Gerhard. "Besṭāmī." *Encyclopaedia Iranica* 4:183.

———. "Ibn al-ʿArabī's Concept of Time." *God Is Beautiful and He Loves Beauty.* Edited by Alma Giese and J. Christoph Bürgel. New York: Peter Lang, 1994, 71–91.

———. *The Mystical Vision of Existence in Classical Islam: The Qurʾānic Hermeneutics of the Ṣūfī Sahl at-Tustarī (d. 283/896).* New York: de Gruyter, 1980.

Brockelmann, Carl. *Geschichte der Arabischen Litteratur.* Leiden: E. J. Brill, 1937–49.

Bukhārī, al-. *al-Ṣaḥīḥ.* N.p.: Maṭābiʿ al-Shuʿab, 1378/1958–59.

Burckhardt, Titus. *Mystical Astrology According to Ibn ʿArabī.* Gloucestershire: Beshara Publications, 1977.

Chittick, William C. "The Divine Roots of Human Love." *Journal of the Muhyiddin ibn ʿArabi Society* 1995, 17:55–78.

———. "Ebno'l-ʿArabi as Lover." *Sufi* 1991, 9:6–9.

———. *Faith and Practice of Islam: Three Thirteenth Century Sufi Texts.* Albany: State University of New York Press, 1992.

———. "Ibn ʿArabī." *History of Islamic Philosophy.* Edited by Seyyed Hossein Nasr and Oliver Leaman. London: Routledge, 1996, 497–509.

———. "Ibn al-ʿArabī and his School." *Islamic Spirituality: Manifestations.* Edited by S. H. Nasr. New York: Crossroad, 1990, 49–79

———. *Imaginal Worlds: Ibn al-ʿArabī and the Problem of Religious Diversity.* Albany: State University of New York Press, 1994.

———. "Notes on Ibn al-'Arabī's Influence in India." *Muslim World* 1992, 72:218–41.

———. "Rūmī and *Waḥdat al-wujūd.*" *Poetry and Mysticism in Islam: The Heritage of Rūmī.* Edited by A. Banani, R. Hovanisian, and G. Sabagh. Cambridge: Cambridge University Press, 1994, 70–111.

———. "The School of Ibn ʿArabī." *History of Islamic Philosophy.* Edited by Seyyed Hossein Nasr and Oliver Leaman. London: Routledge, 1996, 510–23.

———. *The Sufi Path of Knowledge: Ibn al-ʿArabī's Metaphysics of Imagination.* Albany: State University of New York Press, 1989.

———. "Two Chapters from the *Futūḥāt.*" *Muhyiddin Ibn ʿArabi: A Commemorative Volume.* Edited by S. Hirtenstein and M. Tiernan. Shaftesbury: Element, 1993, 90–123.

Chodkiewicz, Michel. *An Ocean Without Shore: Ibn Arabi, the Book, and the Law.* Albany: State University of New York Press, 1993.

———. *The Seal of the Saints.* Cambridge, England: The Islamic Texts Society, 1993.

Chodkiewicz, Michel, W.C. Chittick, Cyrille Chodkiewicz, Denis Gril, James W. Morris. *Les Illuminations de La Mecque/The Meccan Illuminations: Textes Choisis/Selected Texts.* Paris: Sindbad, 1988.

Concordance. See Wensinck.

Corbin, Henry. *Creative Imagination in the Ṣūfism of Ibn ʿArabī*. Princeton: Princeton University Press, 1969.

———. *Spiritual Body and Celestial Earth: From Mazdean Iran to Shīʿite Iran*. London: Taurus, 1990.

Cornell, Vincent. *The Way of Abū Madyan: Doctrinal and Poetical Works of Abū Madyan Shuʿayb ibn al-Ḥusayn al-Anṣārī*. Cambridge: Islamic Texts Society, 1996.

Dārimī, al-. *al-Sunan*. N.p.: Dār Iḥyāʾ al-Sunnat al-Nabawiyya, n.d.

Davidson, H.A. *Alfarabi, Avicenna, and Averroes: Their Cosmologies, Theories of the Active Intellect, and Theories of the Human Intellect*. New York: Oxford University Press, 1992.

Deladrière, Roger. "The Dīwān of Ibn ʿArabi." *Journal of the Muhyiddin ibn ʿArabi Society* 1994, 15:50–56.

Elmore, G. Review of *Kitâb al-maʿrifah*, attributed to Ibn al-ʿArabî. *Journal of the Muhyiddin ibn ʿArabi Society* 1966, 20:86–88.

Ernst, C. "The Man Without Attributes: Ibn ʿArabi's Interpretation of Abu Yazid al-Bistami." *Journal of the Muhyiddin ibn ʿArabi Society* 1993, 13:1–18.

———. *Words of Ecstasy in Sufism*. Albany: State University of New York Press, 1985.

Ghazālī, Abū Ḥāmid Muḥammad al-. *Iḥyāʾ ʿulūm al-dīn*. Cairo: Maṭbaʿat al-ʿĀmirat al-Sharafiyya, 1326–27/1908–09.

———. *al-Maḍnūn bihi ʿalā ghayr ahlihi*. *al-Quṣūr al-ʿawālī*, Cairo: Maktabat al-Jundī, 1970, 2: 125–69

Ḥakīm, Suʿād al-. *al-Muʿjam al-ṣūfī*. Beirut: Dandara, 1981.

———. *Ibn ʿArabī wa mawādd lugha jadīda*. Beirut: Dandara, 1991.

Hirtenstein, S. and M. Tiernan (eds.). *Muhyiddin Ibn ʿArabi: A Commemorative Volume*. Shaftesbury: Element, 1993.

Ibn al-ʿArabī. *al-ʿAbādila*. Edited by ʿA. A. ʿAṭā. Cairo: Maktabat al-Qāhira, 1969.

———. *Alif, Kitāb al-*. In *Rasāʾil*

———. *Ayyām al-shaʾn*. In *Rasāʾil*.

———. *Dhakhāʾir al-aʿlāq*. Edited by M. ʿAbd al-Raḥmān al-Kurdī, Cairo, 1968.

———. *Dīwān*. Bombay: Mirza Mohamed Shirazi, n.d.

———. *Fuṣūṣ al-ḥikam*. Edited by A. ʿAfīfī. Beirut: Dār al-Kutub al-ʿArabī, 1946; English translation by R.W.J. Austin. *Ibn alʿArabī: The Bezels of Wisdom*. Ramsey, N.J.: Paulist Press, 1981.

———. *al-Futūḥāt al-makkiyya*. Cairo, 1911. Reprinted Beirut, Dār Ṣādir, n.d. Partial critical edition by O. Yahia. Cairo: al-Hayʾat al-Miṣriyyat al-ʿĀmma li'l-Kitāb, 1972–.

———. *al-Isfār ʿan natāʾij al-asfār*. Edition and French translation by Denis Gril. *Le dévoilement des effets du voyage*. Combas: Editions de l'éclat, 1994.

——. *Iṣṭilāḥāt al-ṣūfiyya*. In *Rasāʾil*. Longer version in *Futūḥāt* II 128–34.

———. *al-Jalāl wa'l-jamāl, Kitāb al-*. In *Rasāʾil*. Translation by Rabia Terri Harris. "On Majesty and Beauty." *Journal of the Muhyiddin ibn ʿArabi Society* 1989, 8:5–32.

———. *al-Isrā ila'l-maqām al-asrā*. Edited by Suʿād al-Ḥakīm. Beirut: Dandara, 1988.

———. *Mashāhid al-asrār al-qudsiyya*. Edition and Spanish translation by Suad Hakim and Pablo Beneito. *Las Contemplaciones de los Misterios*. Murcia: Editora Regional de Murcia, 1994.

———. *Mawāqiʿ al-nujūm*. Cairo: Maktaba Muḥammad ʿAlī Ṣabīḥ, 1965.

———. *Mishkāt al-anwār*. Arabic text with French translation by Muhammad Valsan, *La Niche des Lumières*. Paris: Les Editions de l'Oeuvre, 1983.

———. *Naqsh al-fuṣūṣ*. Edited by W.C. Chittick in ʿAbd al-Raḥmān Jāmī. *Naqd al-nuṣūṣ fī sharḥ naqsh al-fuṣūṣ*. Tehran: Imperial Iranian Academy of Philosophy, 1977.

———. "On Majesty and Beauty." See *al-Jalāl wa'l-jamāl*.

———. *Rasāʾil Ibn ʿArabī*. Hyderabad-Deccan: The Dāiratu'l-Maʿārifi'l-Osmania, 1948.

———. *Rāzī, Risālat al-Shaykh ila'l-imām al-*. In *Rasāʾil*.

———. *Risāla Lā yuʿawwal ʿalayhi*. In *Rasāʾil*.

———. *al-Tadbīrāt al-ilāhiyya fī iṣlāḥ al-mamlakat al-insāniyya*. In Nyberg, *Kleinere Schriften*.

———. *al-Tajalliyyāt al-ilāhiyya*. In *Rasāʾil*. Also edited by Osman Yahia. Tehran: Markaz-i Nashr-i Dānishgāhī, 1367/1988.

———. *Tarjumān al-ashwāq*. Edited and translated by R. A. Nicholson. *The Tarjumān al-Ashwāq: A Collection of Mystical Odes by Muḥyi'ddīn ibn al-ʿArabī*. London: Theosophical Publishing House, 1978.

———. *Traité de l'amour*. Translated by Maurice Gloton. Paris, Albin Michel, 1986.

———. *Wasāʾil*. See Ibn Sawdakīn.

Ibn Māja. *al-Sunan*. Edited by M.F. ʿAbd al-Bāqī. Cairo: Dār Iḥyāʾ al-Kutub al-ʿArabiyya, 1952.

Ibn Sawdakīn, *Wasāʾil al-sāʾil*. Edited by M. Profitlich. *Die Terminologies Ibn ʿArabīs im "Kitāb wasāʾil al-sāʾil" des Ibn Saudakīn*. Freiburg im Breisgau: Klaus Schwarz Verlag, 1973.

Izutsu, Toshihiko. *Sufism and Taoism*. Los Angeles: University of California Press, 1983.

Jandī, Mu'ayyid al-Dīn. *Nafḥat al-rūḥ*. Edited by N. Māyil Harawī. Tehran: Mawlā, 1362/1983.

Lane, E. W. *Arabic-English Lexicon*. Cambridge, England: The Islamic Texts Society, 1984.

Mansiyya, Muqdād. "al-Ijtihād ʿind Muḥyi'l-Dīn ibn al-ʿArabī." *Qaḍiyyat al-ijtihād fi'l-fikr al-islāmī*. Tunis: al-Markaz al-Qawmī al-Jāmiʿī li'l-Tawthīq al-ʿIlmī wa'l-Taqannī, 1987, 125–46.

Mattock, J. N. "al-Maḳūlāt," *Encyclopaedia of Islam*, new edition, 6:204.

Maybudī, Rashīd al-Dīn. *Kashf al-asrār wa ʿuddat al-abrār*. Edited by ʿA. A. Ḥikmat. Tehran: Dānishgāh, 1331–39/1952–60.

Morris, James Winston. "How to Study the *Futūḥāt*: Ibn ʿArabi's Own Advice." *Muhyiddin Ibn ʿArabi: A Commemorative Volume*. Edited by S. Hirtenstein and M. Tiernan. Shaftesbury: Element, 1993, 73–89.

———. "Listening for God: Prayer and the Heart in the *Futūḥāt*." *Journal of the Muhyiddin ibn ʿArabi Society* 1991, 13:19–53.

———. "'Seeking God's Face': Ibn ʿArabi on Right Action and Theophanic Vision," Part I, *Journal of the Muhyiddin ibn ʿArabi Society* 1994, 16:1–38. Part II, 1995, 17:1–39.

Murata, Sachiko. *The Tao of Islam: A Sourcebook on Gender Relationships in Islamic Thought*. Albany: State University of New York Press, 1992.

Murata, Sachiko and W. C. Chittick. *The Vision of Islam*. New York: Paragon, 1994.

Muslim. *al-Ṣaḥīḥ*. Cairo: Maṭbaʿa Muḥammad ʿAlī Ṣabīḥ, 1334/1915–16

Muwaṭṭa'. By Mālik ibn Anas, as cited in Wensinck, *Concordance*.

Nabhānī, Yūsuf ibn Ismāʿīl. *Jāmiʿ karāmāt al-awliyāʾ*. Edited by I. ʿI. ʿIwaḍ. Cairo: Muṣṭafā al-Bābī al-Ḥalabī, 1962.

Nakamura, K. "Imām Ghazālī's Cosmology Reconsidered, with Special Reference to the Concept of *Jabarūt*." *Studia Islamica* 1994, 80:29–46.

Nasā'ī, al-. *al-Sunan*. Beirut: Dār Iḥyāʾ al-Turāth al-ʿArabī, 1348/1929–30.

Nicholson. *Tarjumān*. See Ibn al-ʿArabī.

Nurbakhsh, J. *Sufism IV*. London: Khaniqahi-Nimatullahi Publications, 1988.

———. *Zanān-i ṣūfī*. London: Khaniqahi-Nimatullahi Publications, 1363/1984.

Nyberg, H. S. *Kleinere Schriften des Ibn al-ʿArabī*. Leiden: E. J. Brill, 1919.

Rāzī, Fakhr al-Dīn al-. *al-Tafsīr al-kabīr*. Istanbul: Dār al-Ṭibāʿat al-ʿĀmira, 1307–08/1889–91.

Robson, James (translator). *Mishkat al-masabih*. Lahore: Muhammad Ashraf, 1963–65.

Rosenthal, Franz . "Ibn ʿArabī between 'Philosophy' and 'Mysticism,'" *Oriens*, 1988, 31:1–35.

Qushayrī, Abu'l-Qāsim al-. *al-Risālat al-Qushayriyya*. Edited by ʿAbd al-Ḥalīm Maḥmūd and Maḥmūd ibn al-Sharīf. Cairo: Dār al-Kutub al-Ḥadītha, 1966.

Sarrāj, Abū Naṣr al-. *Kitāb al-lumaʿ fi'l-taṣawwuf*. Edited by R. A. Nicholson. London: Luzac, 1914.

Sells, Michael A. *Mystical Languages of Unsaying*. Chicago: University of Chicago Press, 1994.

SPK. See Chittick, *The Sufi Path of Knowledge*.

Suyūṭī, al-. *al-Jāmiʿ al-ṣaghīr*. In al-Munāwī, *Fayḍ al-qadīr: Sharḥ al-jāmiʿ al-ṣaghīr*. Beirut: Dār al-Maʿrifa, 1972.

Tirmidhī, al-. *al-Jāmiʿ al-ṣaḥīḥ, wa huwa sunan al-Tirmidhī*. Edited by A. M. Shākir. Cairo: al-Maktabat al-Islāmiyya, 1938.

Trimingham, J. Spencer. *The Sufi Orders in Islam*. Oxford: Clarendon Press, 1971.

Wensinck, A. J., J. P. Mensing, and J. Brugman. *Concordance et indices de la tradition musulmane*. Leiden: E. J. Brill, 1936–1969.

Wolfson, H. *The Philosophy of the Kalam*. Cambridge: Harvard University Press, 1976.

Wright, W. *A Grammar of the Arabic Language*. Third edition, Cambridge: Cambridge University Press, 1971.

Yahia. O. *Histoire et classification de l'oeuvre d'Ibn ʿArabī*. Damascus: Institut Français de Damas, 1964.

Zamakhsharī, al-. *al-Mustaṣqā fī amthāl al-ʿarab*. Beirut: Dār al-Kutub al-ʿIlmiyya, 1987.

INDEX OF SOURCES

Numbers in italics indicate that the passage represents a complete chapter, section, or subsection.

al-Futūḥāt al-makkiyya

Volume I

Volume IV

INDEX OF KORANIC VERSES

INDEX OF HADITHS AND SAYINGS

Sources are cited to illustrate Ibn al-ᶜArabī's use of the standard hadith collections (those indexed in Wensinck, *Concordance*) and to suggest where he may have found other sayings. Reference is made to SPK to save space and to indicate other examples of Ibn al-ᶜArabī's use and interpretation of the saying in question. *Mishkāt* refers to *Mishkāt al-anwār*, Ibn al-ᶜArabī's own selection of *ḥadīth qudsī*.

Adam forgot, so his offspring forgot; Adam refused, so his offspring refused. 323. Tirmidhī, Tafsīr Sūra 7, 3.

All of God's acts are beautiful. 254

all-comprehensive words. → I was sent with

Alms fall to the hand of the All Merciful. 196. In I 578.28 (Y 8:414.13), Ibn al-ᶜArabī adds the clause, "before they fall to the hand of the requester." Al-Ghazālī provides a slightly different version of the hadith in *Iḥyā*ᵓ 1.5.2 (1:323).

The angels are tormented by everything that torments the children of Adam. 328. Muslim, Masājid 72, 74 (→ *Concordance* 6:268.33). The first part of the hadith (found in many more versions than this specific sentence) says, "Whoever eats of this stinking vegetable [i.e., garlic, onions, leeks] should not come near our mosque."

The angels, the prophets, and the faithful will have interceded. . . . 207, 399n19. Modified section of a long *ḥadīth qudsī* from Muslim (Īmān 302). In *Mishkāt* 16, Ibn al-ᶜArabī quotes a few sentences from the hadith, including the following: "The angels will have interceded, the prophets will have interceded, the faithful will have interceded, and there will remain the Most Merciful of the merciful. He will grasp a gripful of the Fire and remove from it a people who never did any good whatsoever and who had turned into coals. He will cast them into a river at the mouth of the Garden called 'the River of Life.'" For an English translation of most of the hadith, see Robson, *Mishkat al-Masabih*, pp. 1184–86.

As for Gabriel, he swooned at that. → I came to know

As for the folk of the Fire, those who are its folk, they will neither die therein nor live. 188, 274, 289, 295. Muslim, Īmān 306; Ibn Māja, Zuhd 37; Aḥmad 3:5.

The beautiful deeds of the pious are the ugly deeds of those brought near. 217. A well-known Sufi saying (Chittick, *Faith* 250).

before He created His creatures. → He was in a Cloud

Between my grave and my pulpit is one of the plots of the Garden. 62, 363. Aḥmad 3:64. Much more commonly, the text has, "Between my house and my pulpit" (*Concordance* 2:319, under *rawḍa*).

Beware of the face, for God created Adam in His own form. 91. A hadith in Aḥmad (2:244) reads, "When one of you beats someone, avoid the face, for God created Adam in His own form." → God created Adam

blocked the horizon. → 396n22

By Him whose hand holds Muhammad's soul, on the day of resurrection the bad breath. . . . 327. The text is found in all the standard collections (*Concordance* 3:456.38).

The child belongs to the bedding. 406n13. Found in all the standard sources (*Concordance* 5:109.51).

The client of a people is one of them. 336. Bukhārī, Farāᵓiḍ 24 (*Concordance* 7:333.15).

Come near to Me through what I do not possess—abasement and poverty. 185. God's words to Abū Yazīd (SPK 40, 316, 387n11).

A day is like a year, a day like a month, and a day like a week, and the rest of his days are like your days. 392n14. Muslim, Fitan 110, etc. (*Concordance* 7:390.45).

Deeds are judged only by the conclusions. → A man will do the deeds

descends to the closest heaven. → Our Lord descends

Did you indeed see Him? 280. The hadith is not indexed in the *Concordance*. A version relating to ᶜĀᵓisha but not to Ibn ᶜAbbās is cited by Abū Nuᶜaym, *Dalāᵓil* 437.

The distinction lies in abasement and poverty (Abū Yazīd). 15. → SPK 387n11

divided the *ṣalāt*. → I have divided

Do not bestow wisdom on other than its folk, lest you wrong it, and do not hold it back from its folk, lest you wrong them. 159. Al-Ghazālī attributes this saying to Jesus (*Iḥyā*ᵓ 1.1 [1: 56–57]).

Do not curse the aeon, for God is the aeon. 128, 197. Hadiths to this effect are found in Bukhārī (Adab 100, Tawḥīd 35), Muslim (Alfāẓ 2–4), and other sources. → Robson, *Mishkat* 79

Do what you will, for I have forgiven you. 108. This *ḥadīth qudsī* is found in most of the standard collections (*Concordance* 4:531.31). As Ibn al-ʿArabī often points out, it concerns God's forgiveness to those who participated in the Battle of Badr.

Doing what is beautiful is to worship God as if you see Him, for if you do not see Him, He sees you. 56, 92, 115, 351. Bukhārī, Muslim, etc. (SPK 397n13).

Each of the abodes shall have its fill. 293. Bukhārī, Tafsīr Sūra 50, 1. → *Concordance* 6:251.59

Error and forgetfulness have been lifted from my community. 398n6. In Ibn Māja (Ṭalāq 16), a slightly different version of the hadith adds a third category—"that to which they are coerced."

Every child is born in accordance with *fiṭra*; then his parents make him into a Jew, a Christian, or a Zoroastrian. 255. Several versions of the hadith are found in Bukhārī, Muslim, etc. (*Concordance* 5:180.13, 20).

Every *mujtahid* is correct. 96, 154. → 395n8

Everyone who performs the *ṣalāt* is whispering with his Lord. 171, 245, 264. The hadith is found in several slightly different versions in the standard sources (*Concordance* 3:385.48, 3:414.3, 6:364.56, 365.7).

Everything accords with the decree and the measuring out, even incapacity and cleverness. 50. Muslim (Qadar 18) and other sources provide the hadith, but without the words *the decree and.*

Exaltation is My loincloth and magnificence My mantle. When someone contends with Me in either of them, I shatter him. 16. The version given in the standard sources (SPK 410n7) and in Ibn al-ʿArabī's *Mishkāt* (15) has "greatness" (*kibriyāʾ*) in place of "exaltation" (*ʿizza*).

Far away with you, far away with you! 178. In several hadiths (e.g., Muslim, Ṭahāra 39; Bukhārī, Riqāq 53), this is mentioned as the Prophet's imprecation against a group of people who will try to enter his Pool on the day of resurrection. He will send them away because they have changed his teachings.

Fasting is Mine. 406n5. Muslim, Bukhārī, etc. (*Concordance* 3:460.8).

Fāṭima is part of me. What hurts her hurts me, and what makes her happy makes me happy. . . . 152. Hadiths describing these events, with somewhat different wording, are found in Muslim, Faḍāʾil al-Ṣaḥāba 93–96, and Aḥmad 4:326. The other son-in-law was Abu'l-ʿĀṣ ibn al-Rabīʿ, the husband of Zaynab.

A few mouthfuls to firm up his backbone are enough for the child of Adam. 302, 342. Tirmidhī, Zuhd 47; Aḥmad 4:132.

The first that God created was the intellect. 273. Although often cited, especially in Shi'ite sources, it is not considered authentic by the Sunni hadith specialists.

The first to shoot an arrow in the path of God was Saʿd ibn Abī Waqqāṣ. 203. A different version of this saying, quoted in the first person from Saʿd, is found in several hadith collections, including Muslim (Zuhd 12) and Bukhārī (Riqāq 17, Faḍāʾil al-Ṣaḥāba 15, Maghāzī 56).

The first to speak of self-power in Basra was Maʿbad al-Juhanī. 203. This sentence is found in Muslim (Īmān 1) and Abū Dāwūd (Sunna 16). Maʿbad (d. 72/691–92) was an early companion of the Prophet and a banner-carrier on the day of the conquest of Mecca.

the Folk of the Koran. → God has folk

Gabriel sat in one nest, and God's Messenger sat in the other → As for Gabriel

The Garden is encircled with detestable things. 181. Part of a *ḥadīth qudsī* found in Muslim and other sources (*Concordance* 1:479, under *ḥuffat*); *Mishkāt* 5.

The Garden was imaginalized to me in the breadth of this wall. 359. Bukhārī (Adhān 91) gives the following hadith: "The Prophet led us in the *ṣalāt* and then mounted the pulpit and pointed with his hands at the kiblah of the mosque. Then he said, 'I have just seen, since leading you in the *ṣalāt*, the Garden and the Fire imaginalized in the kiblah of this wall. I did not see the good and the evil as today.' He said this three times." Cf. Aḥmad 3:259.

Give him some honey to drink. . . . 330. The hadith is found in Bukhārī (Ṭibb 4, 24), Muslim (Salām 91), and other sources.

Give to each that has a *ḥaqq* its *ḥaqq*. xxiv, 96, 196, 200, 247, 250, 295, 350. Found in most standard sources (SPK 400n12; *Concordance* 1:486).

Glory be to God in the number . . . the ink of His words. 146–47. Nasāʾī, Sahw 94. Cf. Abū Dāwūd, Witr, 24; Ibn Māja, Adab 56.

Glory be to me (Abū Yazīd). 159, 320. SPK 320.

Go out to the creatures . . . magnify Me (God's words to Abū Yazīd). 213

God created Adam in His form. xxi, xxiii, xxxiii, 27, 91, 92, 126, 180, 279, 305, (360). Muslim, Bukhārī, etc. (SPK 399n4).

God created Adam in the form of the All-Merciful. 126

God created the creation in darkness. 49–50. Tirmidhī, Īmān 18; Aḥmad 2:176.

God created the mountains, and He said to them once, "Upon her." Tirmidhī, Tafsīr 96; *Mishkāt* 25 (with a slight discrepancy in the text). For a

complete translation of the hadith and a commentary by Ibn al-ʿArabī's disciple Qūnawī, see Murata, *Tao* 214–15.
God created them for mercy. 220. The saying, "He created them for mercy," is attributed to Ibn ʿAbbās and others in commentaries on the verse, *except those on whom thy Lord has mercy—and for that He created them* (11:119). See, for example, Rāzī, *Tafsīr* 5:146.
God fermented Adam's clay in His two hands for forty mornings. 397n31. Al-Ghazālī cites the saying, with "His hand" in place of "His two hands," in the *Iḥyāʾ* 5:194, without attributing it to anyone specifically.
God has cursed those who alter the boundary marks of the earth. 80. Muslim, Aḍājī 43.
God has curtained that for him—if he would curtain it for himself. 123. Muslim, Tawba 42; Tirmidhī, Tafsīr Sūra 11, 4; Abū Dāwūd, Ḥudūd 31.
God has folk among the people—the Folk of the Koran, who are the Folk of God and His elect. 6, 394n4. Aḥmad (SPK 388n20).
God has ninety-nine names . . . He is odd, and He loves the odd. 175. Bukhārī, Daʿawāt 69; Muslim, Dhikr 4, etc.
God has seventy veils of light and darkness . . . the eyesight of His creatures perceives. 108, 155, 156, 158–59, 162. Found partly in Muslim and other sources (SPK 401n19).
God hears him who praises Him → God says on the tongue
God is and nothing . . . → God was
God is beautiful and He loves beauty. 28, 80. Muslim, Īmān 147; Ibn Māja, Duʿā 10.
God is in the kiblah of the person who performs the *ṣalāt*. 92, 201. Though not indexed in the *Concordance*, it is often quoted by Ibn al-ʿArabī.
God is the aeon → Do not curse
God is the sitting companion → I am the sitting companion
God looks not at your forms, nor at your deeds, but He looks at your hearts. 265. Hadiths to similar effect are found in Muslim, Ibn Māja, and Aḥmad (Chittick, *Faith* 240).
God says on the tongue of His servant, "God hears him who praises Him." 90, 264, 293, 327, 375, 404n2. The hadith, with the words *His Prophet* in place of *His servant*, is found in Muslim (Ṣalāt 62, 63) and Nasāʾī (Taṭbīq 23, 101; Sahw 44); *Mishkāt* 30. The formula "God hears him who praises Him" is recited in every cycle of the *ṣalāt*.
God struck His palm between my shoulders, and I came to know the knowledge of the first and the last folk. 112, 116, 154, 222, 246. Not in the *Concordance* in this exact form (SPK 395n17).
God taught me courtesy, so He made my courtesy beautiful [or: So my courtesy is beautiful]. 103, 154, 155, 221. Suyūṭī, *al-Jāmiʿ al-ṣaghīr* 1:224.
God was [is], and nothing was [is] with Him. 70, 180, 182. Ibn al-ʿArabī invariably gives the hadith in this form, but it is not found in the standard sources. Bukhārī has "God was, and there was nothing other than He" (Badʾ al-khalq 1). As for the clause, "and He is now, and there is nothing," this may be a form of the completion of this saying that has been attributed to Junayd, "and He is now as He was." → SPK 393n13
God was in a Cloud → He was in
God will disclose Himself on the day of resurrection with nothing between them save the mantle of greatness on His face. 105. The closest to this in the standard sources is found in descriptions of paradise that say, "There will be nothing between the people and looking upon their Lord save the mantle of greatness on His face in the Garden of Eden" (Muslim, Īmān 296; *Concordance* 2:250, under *ridāʾ*).
God's mercy → His mercy
The good, all of it, is in Thy hands, but the evil does not go back to Thee. 94, 209, 330, 365. Muslim and Nasāʾī (SPK 408n2).
Good is a habit, and evil is an obstinate persistence. 312–13. Ibn Māja, Muqaddima 17.
Has any of you seen a dream-vision? 345. Abū Dāwūd (SPK 396n10).
Have shame before God as is the *ḥaqq* of shame. 80. Tirmidhī, Qiyāma 24; Aḥmad 1:387.
He created the mountains → God created the mountains
He is a light, how should I see Him? 158, 217. Muslim and Tirmidhī (SPK 403n8).
He loved good omens, and he disliked evil omens. 101. Aḥmad 2:332; cf. Ibn Māja, Ṭibb 43.
He loved to be known. 329 → I was a treasure
He never discloses Himself twice to a single individual in one form, nor to two individuals in one form. 54. This is a form of a saying that Ibn al-ʿArabī often quotes explicitly from Abū Ṭālib al-Makkī (d. 386/996). → SPK 103.
He was, and nothing was with Him → God was
He was in a Cloud. 118, 153, 360. The Prophet's answer to the question, "Where was our Lord before He created the creatures?" Tirmidhī, Ibn Māja, Aḥmad (SPK 397n1).
He was remembering God all the while. 297, 306. Muslim, Ḥayḍ 117; Bukhārī, Ḥayḍ 7, Adhān 19; and other standard sources.

He who has faith will not become perfect until he loves for his brother what he loves for himself. 329. Bukhārī (Īmān 7) gives the text as follows: "None of you will have faith until he loves for his brother what he loves for himself."

He who knows himself best knows his Lord best. 8

He who knows himself knows his Lord. xiv, 7, 8, 21, 23, 37, 42, 65, 79, 120, 133, 157, 173, 179, 229, 235, 252, 269–70, 290, 298, 328, 365, 368. This is rejected by the hadith scholars; SPK 396n22.

He who performs the *ṣalāt*. . . → Everyone who performs

He whose emigration is to God. 302. Part of many hadiths (*Concordance* 7:65.56).

He will lead us only from among us. 144. Muslim (Īmān 246) gives the hadith as follows: "How will you be when the son of Mary descends among you, then leads you from among you?" He then quotes an early explanation: "He will lead you according to the Book of your Lord and the Sunnah of your Prophet."

The heart is between two of the fingers of the All-Merciful. 144. Muslim, Tirmidhī, etc. (SPK 396n18).

The heart of My servant embraces Me 265 → Neither My heaven nor

His character was the Koran. xxxiv. Muslim (SPK 405n13).

His Garden is a Fire, and his Fire is a Garden. 44. Muslim, Fitan 104; Ibn Māja, Fitan 33.

His mercy takes precedence over His wrath. xxii, (225), 287–88. Most versions of this famous hadith give it in the first person as a *ḥadīth qudsī* (Concordance 2:239).

How can he who is sitting with Him be mustered? (Abū Yazīd). 23 → SPK 37

How should I not be conceited. . . ? (ʿUtbat al-Ghulām). 380

Hūd and its sisters have whitened my hair. 393n26. Tirmidhī (SPK 409n12).

I am God (Abū Yazīd). 158, 159, 320. SPK 410n12.

I am his hearing. . . → When I love him

I am pleased with you and I will never be angry with you. 116. This is part of the long hadith beginning "The angels, the prophets."

I am the master of the people → I will be

I am the sitting companion of him who remembers Me. 79, 80, 199. Ibn al-ʿArabī cites the full text of this hadith from *Darajāt al-tāʾibīn* of Ismāʿīl ibn Ibrāhīm al-Harawī (who is, according to Brockelmann [*Geschichte* S1:775], the same as Khwāja ʿAbdallāh Anṣārī, d. 425/1033) as follows: "Moses said, 'My Lord, art Thou far that I should call out to Thee, or art Thou near that I should whisper to Thee?' God replied, 'I am the sitting companion of him who remembers Me, so I am with him.' Moses said, 'Which act is most beloved to Thee, My Lord?' He said, 'You should remember Me much in every state.'" *Mishkāt* 43.

I am with those whose hearts are broken for My sake. 395n13. Maybudī tells us that this *ḥadīth qudsī* is addressed to "one of the prophets," apparently Moses (*Kashf* 1:135, 710; 6:171; 9:283).

I am your Lord. 214 → Thou art our Lord

I came to know his excellence over me in knowledge. 111, 326. Ibn al-ʿArabī (p. 326; II 103.17 [Y 12:511.9]) says that he has taken the hadith from Abū Nuʿaym al-Ḥāfiẓ al-Iṣfahānī, *Dalāʾil al-nubuwwa*, but I did not find it in the printed edition of this work. Elsewhere he explains that the "cushion" (*rafraf*) is "like what we know as a litter [*miḥaffa*]" (III 342.7), and he refers to cushions and Burāqs as two means of ascent to God (I 49.3 [Y 1:220.12]; II 258.33, 278.22; III 110.18). For other examples of his use of the term *rafraf*, see I 41.23 (Y 1:189.7), 226.2 (Y 3:374.6); II 259.29; III 54.24, 104.14, 342.7, 350.23, 505.33, 231.16. *Dhakhāʾir* 11; *ʿUqla* 58, 60.

I came to know the knowledge . . . → God struck

I count not Thy laudations before Thee; Thou art as Thou hast lauded Thyself. 84, 133, 134, 147. Found in most standard sources (SPK 399n19). For the first half, see "I seek refuge."

I encountered the Messenger of God, and he said to me, "O Jābir, why do I see you dejected?" I answered, "O Messenger of God, my father was martyred. He was slain on the day of Uhud and he left a family and debts." He said, "Shall I not give you the good news of how God encountered your father?" I said that he should. He said, "God does not *speak* to anyone except *from behind a veil*, but He brought your father to life, then spoke to him directly. He said, 'O My servant, ask a favor of Me and I will grant it.' He said, 'My Lord, bring me back to life, so that I may be slain a second time.' The Lord said. 'I have already set down that they will not be returned to this world.'" Then he said, "Then God sent down the verse, *Count not those who were slain in God's way as dead, but rather as living with their Lord* [3:169]." Tirmidhī, Tafsīr sūra 3, 18; Ibn Māja, Muqaddima 13, Jihād 16.

I have a knowledge that God has taught to me and that you do not know, and you have a knowledge. . . . 151, 378. Part of a hadith recounting the meeting between Moses and Khaḍir. Bukhārī, ʿIlm 44, Anbiyāʾ 27; Muslim, Faḍāʾil 170.

I have divided the *ṣalāt* into two halves between Me and My servant, so half belongs to Me and half belongs to My servant, and My servant shall have what he requests. 29, 200, 219, 234, 238, 293. Muslim etc. (SPK 410n19; *Mishkāt* 31).

I have a moment when no prophet sent out or angel brought near embraces me (or: when none embraces me other than my Lord). 151, 245. The saying is well attested in Sufi writings, but it is not found in the books of hadith. See, for example, Maybudī, *Kashf* 1:269, 683; 2:328; 6:460; 7:172; 9:238; 10:432.

I have never seen anything without seeing God before it (Abū Bakr). 151, 199. I have never seen anything without seeing God with it (ʿUmar). 199. Although these sayings are often cited by authors after Ibn al-ʿArabī, I have not seen them in earlier writers. In a slightly different form—"I have never seen anything without seeing God in it"—it is ascribed by the fourth/tenth century author al-Kalābādhī to Muḥammad ibn Wāsiʿ (Chittick, *Faith* 205).

I have no morning and no evening. . . (Abu Yazīd). 237. SPK 391n9.

I have not sent thee as an imprecator and a curser. . . . 221. Bukhārī (Adab 38) has this: "The Prophet was not an imprecator, one indecent in speech, or a curser. When he scolded anyone, he would say what would make his forehead cling to the dust [in prostration before God]."

I have prepared for My wholesome servant what no eye has seen, what no ear has heard, and what has never passed into the heart of any mortal. 106, 291. Bukhārī, Muslim, etc. (SPK 413n27; *Mishkāt* 21).

I have seen nothing easier for me than abstinence. Whenever something disquiets me, I leave it aside (Ibn Sīrīn). 26 → 391n29

I knew God only by His bringing together the opposites. 236. Paraphrase of a statement by Abū Saʿīd al-Kharrāz that Ibn al-ʿArabī often cites (→ SPK 391n19).

I loved to be known → I was a Treasure

I mean you, so listen, O neighbor. 103. A proverbial half-line of poetry, attributed to Sahl ibn Mālik al-Fazzāzī. Ibn al-ʿArabī often quotes it, and he dedicates Chapter 359 to its waystation. It refers to a statement that appears to be directed at one person but is actually addressed to someone else. Sahl is said to have recited it to a friend when the friend's sister was close enough to hear him (she was offended, but he did end up marrying her). The full poem reads,

O sister of the best of the desert and the city,
what think you of a youth, a leopard,
who began to long for a perfumed kitten?
I mean you—so listen, O neighbor!
(Zamakhsharī, *Mustaqṣā* 1:450)

I never waver in anything I do the way I waver in taking the soul of a man of faith who dislikes death, while I dislike doing ill to him, but he must encounter Me. 119. Bukhārī (SPK 400n6; *Mishkāt* 91).

I see you from behind my back. 400n31. Muslim, Ṣalāt 110, 111, 125; Bukhārī, Adhān 71.

I seek refuge in God from a knowledge that has no profit. 389n6. Found in most of the standard sources (*Concordance* 6:511.35).

I seek refuge in Thee from Thee. 126. Versions are found in most collections (e.g., Muslim, Ṣalāt 222; Tirmidhī, Daʿawāt 75, 112). The first two clauses of this hadith read "I seek refuge in Thy mercy from Thy wrath, I seek refuge in Thy good pleasure from Thy anger."

I was a prophet when Adam was between water and clay. 154, 296. Tirmidhī and Aḥmad, but with "between spirit and body" (SPK 405n8).

I was a Treasure but was not known, so I loved to be known; I created the creatures and made Myself known to them, so they came to know Me. 21, 22, 70, 211, 329. Not found in the standard collections (SPK 391n14).

I was hungry, but you did not feed Me; I was ill, but you did not visit Me. . . . 126, 348. Muslim etc. (SPK 392n33).

I was ill → I was hungry

I was sent to complete the noble character traits. 375. Versions are found in Bukhārī, Aḥmad, and *Muwaṭṭaʾ* (SPK 409n18).

I was sent with the all-comprehensive words. (116), 154, (222, 249), 296. Bukhārī and Nasāʾī (SPK 395n17).

I will be the master of the people on the day of resurrection, without boasting. 195, 222, 289. Tirmidhī, Aḥmad, etc. (SPK 405n6).

If allegiance is sworn to two caliphs, the other should be killed. 402. Muslim, Amāra 91.

If any of you is afflicted with these filthy things, let him conceal it. 217. A hadith with slightly different wording is found in *al-Muwaṭṭaʾ*, Ḥudūd 12 (*Concordance* 5:330.31).

If not for the excess in your speaking and the tumult in your hearts, you would see what I see and hear what I hear. 363. A similar hadith is related from Abū Umāma al-Bāhilī by Aḥmad, 5:266.

If you are not, you will see Him, for He sees you. 212. This is an alternative reading for the sentence defining *iḥsān* in the hadith of Gabriel. → Doing what is beautiful
If you let down a rope, it will fall upon God. 182, 224, 236, 330. This is part of a hadith that is cited by Tirmidhī (Tafsīr Sūra 57) as a commentary on the verse, *He is the First and the Last and the Manifest and the Nonmanifest* (57:3). The Prophet refers to seven heavens and seven earths and then, at the end of the hadith, says, "If you let down a man with a rope to the lowest earth, he will fall upon God." A slightly different version is offered by Aḥmad 2:379.
in a Cloud → He was in a Cloud
In His hand is the scale; He lets down the just measure and lifts it up. 360. This seems to be a conflation of sentences from two different hadiths. As given by Ibn al-ʿArabī in *Mishkāt* 9 (following Bukhārī, Tafsīr sūra 11:2, Tawḥīd 19), the relevant sentence from the first reads, "What is in His hand is not diminished; *His Throne is upon the water* [11:7]; in His hand is the scale; He lets down and lifts up." A version of the second hadith reads: "God does not sleep, and it is not proper for Him to sleep. He lets down the just measure and lifts it up. The deeds of the night are lifted up to Him before the deeds of the [following] day, and the deeds of the day before the deeds of the night. His veil is light" (Muslim, Īmān 293). → *Concordance* 2:53, under *yakhfiḍ*.
The incapacity to attain perception is itself perception (Abū Bakr). 55, 64, 84, 191. This may be a form of the saying that al-Sarrāj and al-Qushayrī give as "Glory be to Him who assigned the creatures no path to His knowledge save the incapacity to know Him." They tell us that Junayd called this "the most eminent words in *tawḥīd*" (*Lumaʿ* 36, 124; *Risāla* 585).
Is it not a soul? 287. Muslim, Janāʾiz 81; Bukhārī, Janāʾiz 50.
Is not everything other than God unreal? → The truest words
Is there any caller? → Our Lord descends
Is there between you and Him a mark? 54. Part of the long hadith of God's self-transmutation (→ Thou art our Lord). The text in Muslim has *sign* (*āya*) in place of *mark* (*ʿalāma*), and, when quoting the text in detail, Ibn al-ʿArabī cites it so (III 45.7), but he also says explicitly that Muslim's text employs *mark* (I 266.18 [Y 4, 192.5]).
It is newly acquainted with my Lord. 406n13. Muslim, Abū Dāwūd (SPK 405n28).
joining the womb relatives → The womb is the knowledge of the first and the last → God struck
Leave aside yourself and come! 180. God's words to Abū Yazīd. → SPK 319.
Leave what disquiets you for that which does not disquiet you. 26. Bukhārī, Buyūʿ 3; Tirmidhī, Qiyāma 60; Aḥmad 3:153.
Let him blame none but himself → When someone finds good
Like a chain across pebbles. 16, 110, 112. The phrase is from this hadith: "When God decrees the command in heaven, the angels flap their wings in meekness at His words, which are like a chain across pebbles. *When terror is lifted from their hearts, they will say, 'What said your Lord?' They will say, 'The **ḥaqq**, and He is the High, the Great'* [34:23]." Bukhārī, Tafsīr sūra 15,1; 34,1; Tawḥīd 32.
Look at the *ṣalāt* of My servant. . . . 97. Abū Dāwūd, Ṣalāt 145; Ibn Māja, Ṣalāt, 202.
Love God for blessings that come to you in the morning. 311. The rest of the hadith reads, "Love me for the love of God, and love the folk of my house for the love of me." Tirmidhī, Manāqib 32.
love to be known → I was a Treasure
Loving kindness is beauty of character, but sin is what is woven into your breast while you dislike that people should become aware of it. Muslim (Birr 14, 15) and other sources
Make me into a light. 37, 74, 162, 403n10. Part of a prophetic supplication found in Muslim and other sources (SPK 404n20).
Make your rows solid, bring them together, and make your necks parallel. 401n3. Nasāʾī, Abū Dāwūd, Aḥmad (SPK 408n15).
A man will do the deeds of the Folk of the Garden . . . so he will enter the Fire. . . . Deeds are judged only by the conclusions. 25. The first part of this hadith is found in Muslim (Qadar 1), Bukhārī (Qadar 1, Tawḥīd 28), and other standard sources, while the second ("Deeds . . . ") is from Bukhārī (Qadar 5). That the two are part of the same hadith is suggested by the version in Tirmidhī (Qadar 4).
Many a well-dressed woman is naked. 84. Bukhārī gives the text as "Many a well-dressed woman in this world is naked in the last world" (ʿIlm 40, Tahajjud 5, Libās 31, Adab 121, Fitan 6; also Tirmidhī, Fitan 30). Aḥmad gives the text, "Your women are well-dressed and naked" (2:223; cf. 6:297).
May the knowledge benefit you. 245. Ibn al-ʿArabī seems to have in mind a version of this hadith: The Prophet asked Abu'l-Mundhir which verse of the Koran he considered most

magnificent. Abu'l-Mundhir replied with the standard formula, "God and His Messenger know best." The Prophet insisted that he answer by repeating the question, and he recited the Footstool Verse (2:255). Then, Abu'l-Mundhir said, "He tapped my breast and said, 'So that the knowledge may benefit you, Abu'l-Mundhir'" (Muslim, Musāfirīn 258; Abū Dāwūd, Witr 17; Aḥmad 5:142).

Me and her? 375. Muslim, Ashriba 139; Aḥmad 3:123.

Morning becomes clear for the possessor of the two eyes. 121, 122. This is a proverb (Lane, *Lexicon* 286; Zamakhsharī, *Mustaqṣā* 2:190).

My heart narrated to me from my Lord, so I take the text of the Book from Him, O denier (Abū Yazīd). 106

My knowledge and your knowledge fall short of God's knowledge. . . . 393. Part of the hadith cited under "I have a knowledge."

the names of the folk of the Garden . . . → two books

Neither My heaven nor My earth embraces Me, but the heart of My servant with faith does embrace Me. 7, 265, 349. Considered a *ḥadīth qudsī* by many Sufi authors, it is not found in the standard sources (Chittick, *Faith* 198; SPK 396n20).

No one is slain wrongfully without Adam's son being liable . . . . 203. Muslim, Qasāma 27; Bukhārī, Janā᾿iz 32, Iᶜtiṣām 15, Anbiyā᾿ 1 (*Concordance* under *sann*).

None knows God but God. 8, 28, (42). A theological maxim (→ SPK 62).

Nothing makes it impure. 335. The hadith, "Water is pure, and nothing makes it impure," is found in Abū Dāwūd, Ṭahāra 34; Tirmidhī, Ṭahāra 49; Nasā᾿ī, Miyāh 1; Aḥmad 3:31, 86. See also *Concordance* 4:34.14, 6:361.22.

Nothing proceeds from the One but one. 17, 18, (19), 75, 137, 148, 169, 229. A philosophical maxim apparently first used by Avicenna (Davidson, *Alfarabi* 75ff.).

O God, guide my people, for they do not know. 221. The version in the standard sources has "forgive my people" (*Concordance* 4:318.47).

O God, I ask Thee by every name . . . in the knowledge of Thy absent. 206. Aḥmad (SPK 399n18).

O God, place in my hearing a light . . . 37 → make me into

O God, Thou art the companion in travel and the vicegerent in the family. 95. Muslim, Ḥajj 425; Tirmidhī, Daᶜawāt 41.

O God, wash us with snow . . . cold water . . . hail. 112. For several hadiths from the standard sources employing these terms, see *Concordance* 4:501.30

O Muhammad, God says to you . . . → I have not sent

O servant of God, and O son of God's handmaid. 322. Not indexed in the *Concordance*; but see *Muwaṭṭa*᾿ 16.

On the day of resurrection Noah will be called. . . . 405n9. Bukhārī, Tafsīr Sūra 2, 13.

One of you draws near to your Lord until He places His wing over him and says, "Did you do such and such?". . . 401n2. Muslim, Tawba 52; Bukhārī, Adab 60, Tawḥīd 36; Ibn Māja, Muqaddima 13.

Our Lord, and Lord of our fathers and our mothers. 312. Not indexed in the *Concordance*.

Our Lord descends to the closest heaven every night in the last third of the night and He says. . . that I may forgive him. 114, (171), 236, 330, 404n16. Muslim etc. (SPK 388n5).

Over them will occur the resurrection → a pleasant wind

The Physician has made me ill (Abū Bakr). 126

a pleasant wind that will take them beneath the armpits. . . over them will occur the resurrection. 154. The quotations are from a hadith (Muslim, Fitan 110; Ibn Māja, Fitan 33; Aḥmad 4:182). In the several instances in which the *Concordance* cites the term "honeydrop" (*ᶜusayla*) that the Shaykh mentions in the context of this hadith, it is from other hadiths and refers to sexual intercourse.

Prophecy and messengerhood have been cut off, so there will be no prophet after me, and no messenger. Tirmidhī, Aḥmad (SPK 406n8).

a prophet when Adam. . . → I was a prophet

The Real becomes clear when the designation dissolves (Ibn al-ᶜArīf). 86 → 393n28

The retainer of the people is their master. 257

the Riᶜl, the Dhakwān, and the ᶜUṣayya. . . . 221 → 403n13

The Sarus, the Pyramus, the Euphrates, and the Nile are among the rivers of the Garden. 392n12. Muslim, Janna 16; Aḥmad 2: 289, 440.

The satan has a suggestion to the child of Adam, and the angel has a suggestion. 398n40. The hadith continues: "As for the suggestion of the satan, that is promising evil and denying the Real, and as for the suggestion of the angel, that is promising good and acknowledging the Real. If someone finds the latter, he should know that it is from God, so he should praise God; if someone finds the former, he should seek refuge in God from the accursed satan." Then, the narrator tells us, the Prophet recited the verse, *The satan promises you poverty, and bids you unto indecency, and God promises you His pardon and His bounty* (2:268). (Tirmidhī, Tafsīr sūra 2, 35)

Satan withdraws from him, weeping. . . . 201. Muslim, Īmān 133; Aḥmad 2:443.
Seek a pronouncement from your heart. . . . 26. Dārimī, Buyūᶜ 2; a slightly different version is found in Aḥmad 4:228.
Self-disclosure never repeats itself. 31, 261. A Sufi axiom (→ SPK 103).
Sometimes it comes to me in the likeness of a bell's clanging. . . . 112. Muslim, Faḍāʾil 87; Bukhārī, Badʾ al-Waḥy 2, Badʾ al-Khalq 2 (see also *Concordance* 1:338, under *jaras*).
Sometimes the angel becomes imaginalized to me as a man. 366. Bukhārī, Badʾ al-Waḥy 2; *Muwaṭṭaʾ*, Mass al-Qurʾān 7.
The stomach is the house of malady, practicing abstinence is the head of every cure; and the root of every malady is indigestion. 302. Suyūṭī, *Jāmiᶜ* 1:532
The Sufi is the son of the moment. 178. A common Sufi saying; for another instance, see IV 357.28.
Take them back to their castles! 227. This sentence seems to belong to a long hadith that Ibn al-ᶜArabī quotes, with its *isnād*, from his teacher Yūnus ibn Yaḥyā al-Qaṣṣār (I 309.20–311.19, 320.21–321.12; Y 4:436.6–447.7, 5:78.12–82.10). The hadith describes, among other things, fifty waystations on the Day of Resurrection, each of which lasts one thousand years. In his index of hadiths, Yahia maintains that this specific sentence (cited on I 321.19; Y 5:84.1) is part of the hadith, even though Ibn al-ᶜArabī has brought his quotation to an end. The preceding sentences, also not part of the main body of the hadith, describe how God discloses Himself to the servants after addressing them concerning their everlasting stay in the Garden. Elsewhere in the *Futūḥāt*, Ibn al-ᶜArabī explains that this sentence is God's words after the felicitous have been given a vision of Him at the Dune of White Musk. "When God desires their return to the witnessing of their bliss through that vision in their Gardens, He says to the angels and guards of the Dune, 'Take them back to their castles,' so they return in the form of what they had seen, and they find their waystations and their families colored with that form, so they take pleasure through it. After all, at the moment of their witnessing, they had been in the state of annihilation from themselves. No pleasure occurred for them at the time of their vision. . . . So when they see that form in their waystations and their families, the pleasure becomes continuous for them, and they become blissful through that witnessing. Hence they are blissful in this homestead through the very thing that had annihilated them in the Dune" (III 442.31). For an explanation of "castles" (*quṣūr*) as an allusion to their "incapacity" (*quṣūr*), see II 657.22.
There is no actor save God. 254. Al-Ghazālī employs the expression in the *Iḥyāʾ* (4.5.3).
There is no emigration after the conquest. 302. Muslim, Amāra 86; Bukhārī, Ṣayd 10; etc. (*Concordance* 7:67.19).
There is no escape from the subsistence of the tracings of servanthood . . . (Abū Madyan). 86
There is no god but God. 60, 78, 79, 167, 186, 189. Koran and hadith.
There is no power and no strength save through God. 319, 321. Found in numerous hadiths.
There is no target behind God. 134, 214, 225, 226. Not indexed in the *Concordance*. Lane cites it in his *Lexicon* (under *marmā*) from *Tāj al-ᶜarūs*.
There is no verse of the Koran that does not have a manifest sense, a nonmanifest sense, a limit, and an overview. 219. Not found in the standard sources (SPK 412n5).
There is not one of you to whom God will not speak directly, there being no spokesman between Him and him. 245. Ibn Māja (Muqaddima 13) gives the hadith, but without the word *directly* (*kifāḥ*).
There is nothing but the five *ṣalāts* and waiting for death (Abu'l-Suᶜūd). 383
There is nothing in possibility more wondrous than this cosmos (al-Ghazālī). 360 → SPK 409n6
There is nothing in *wujūd* but God. 12, 15, 94, 195
These are for the Garden, and it is no concern of Mine. Those are for the Fire, and it is no concern of Mine. 174. The closest to this in the standard sources is Aḥmad 6:441.
They are neither He nor other than He. 36, 229. This is the well-known "Kullabite" formula of the Ash'arite theologians (→ Wolfson, *Philosophy*, pp. 206ff.). For translations of two other instances in which Ibn al-ᶜArabī cites it, see Chodkiewicz, *Illuminations*, p. 114–15, 320–21.
They will neither die therein nor live → As for the folk of the Fire
Things become distinct through their opposites. 30, 31. This proverbial half-line of poetry can be traced back to the poet al-Mutanabbī (Furūzānfar, note to Rūmī, *Fīhi mā fīhi*, p. 291)
Thou art as Thou hast lauded Thyself → I count not
Thou art our Lord. (54, 214), 215. Part of the hadith of God's self-transmutation in forms (Muslim, Īmān 302; SPK 387n9). In *Mishkāt*

(26), Ibn al-ᶜArabī cites a short version of this hadith as follows: "This community remains, along with its hypocrites, so God comes to them in other than the form that they had been recognizing. He says, 'I am your Lord.' They say, 'We seek refuge in God from you. This is our place until our Lord comes to us. When our Lord comes to us, we will recognize Him.' So God comes to them in the form that they recognize. He says, 'I am your Lord,' and they say, 'Thou art our Lord,' so they follow Him."

Three things of this world of yours were made lovable to me: women, perfume—and the delight of my eye is in the *ṣalāt*. 318, 406n11. Versions are found in Nasāʾī and Aḥmad (Murata, *Tao* 345n43; and on Ibn al-ᶜArabī's frequent references to it, pp. 183ff.).

to complete the noble character traits → I was sent

The truest verse spoken by the Arabs . . . 30, 199. Bukhārī, Muslim, etc. (SPK 397n7).

The Trumpet is a horn of light. (357) Not indexed in the Concordance (SPK 397n12).

Two books [in the Prophet's hand, within which were] the names of the folk of the Garden and the names of their fathers, families, and tribes. . . . 178. Tirmidhī, Qadar 8; Aḥmad 2:167.

the vicegerent in the family → O God, Thou art

was remembering God all the while → He was remembering

The water takes on the color of the cup (Junayd). 324, 337. SPK passim.

We are through Him and for Him. 43, 55, 392n6. Ibn al-ᶜArabī calls this a sound hadith (I 406.19 [Y 6:167.6]), but the words of the text (*naḥnu bihi wa lahu*) are too commonplace to be indexed in the *Concordance*. He often alludes to it or cites it, but I did not start noticing it until years into the *Futūḥāt*. → I 406.19 (Y 6:167.12); II 70.1 (Y 12:271.2); III 312.30, 416.12, 441.1, 538.16; IV 6.7, 63.33, 64.30, 65.12, 87.22, 107.27, 102.6, 160.34, 350.8; *Fuṣūṣ* 113.2.

Welcome to those concerning whom my Lord scolded me! 101, 102. The hadith is cited by Koran commentators in explaining the meaning of the first lines of Sura 80. Rāzī, *Tafsīr* 8:470; Maybudī, *Kashf* 10:381.

Were He to lift them, the glories . . . → God has seventy

Were the covering unveiled, I would not increase in certainty (ᶜAlī ibn Abī Ṭālib). 355

when Adam was between water and clay → I was a prophet

When God desires to put His decree and measuring out into effect. . . . 398n6. Not indexed in the *Concordance*. Suyūṭī (*Jāmiᶜ* 2:201), gives it in these forms: "When God loves to put His command into effect, He strips every possessor of a kernel [*lubb*] of his kernel" (cited from al-Khaṭīb al-Baghdādī, *Taʾrīkh Baghdād*). "When God desires to put a command into effect, He dismisses the rational faculties of the Men until He puts His command into effect. When He has put it into effect, He returns their rational faculties to them, and they become remorseful" (cited from Sulamī, *Sunan al-ṣūfiyya*).

When God loves a servant . . . → When I love him

When I love him, I am his hearing through which he hears, his eyesight through which he sees, his hand through which he holds, and his foot through which he walks. 8, (29, 58, 59, 68, 74, 75, 83, 97), 107, 160, 170, (180, 211, 219, 220), 222, (234), 235, 290–91, 293. Bukhārī, Riqāq 38; *Mishkāt* 91. For the full text of the hadith and several of Ibn al-ᶜArabī's commentaries on it, see SPK 325–31.

When someone comes near to Me by a span, I come near to him by a cubit. 318. Part of a *ḥadīth qudsī* found in Bukhārī, Muslim, etc. (SPK 396n29; *Mishkāt* 27).

When someone comes to Me running, I come to him rushing. 399n9. Part of the hadith, "When someone comes near to Me. . . ."

When someone dies, his resurrection has come. 351, 364. Quoted by al-Ghazālī and others, but not found in the standard sources (Chittick, *Faith* 229).

When someone finds good, let him praise God, and when someone finds other than that, let him blame none but himself. 63, 391n30. Muslim, Birr 55; *Mishkāt* 1.

When someone lays down a beautiful sunnah in Islam that is then practiced, he will have written for him the like of the wage of those who practice it, and nothing will be reduced from their wages; and when someone lays down an ugly sunnah in Islam that is then practiced, he will have written against him the like of the burden of those who practice it, and nothing of their burdens will be reduced. 401n11. Muslim, ᶜIlm 15.

When someone performs the night *ṣalāt* in a gathering, it is as if he has stood half the night. 264. Muslim, Masājid 260; Bukhārī, Adhān 34, etc. (*Concordance* 1:371)

When someone's saying Amen coincides with the angels' saying Amen, he will be forgiven. 63. Muslim, Ṣalāt 72; Bukhārī, Adhān 111, 112, etc. (*Concordance* 1:72).

When the night approaches from there. . . . 253. This hadith seems to be derived from Muslim, Ṣiyām 51–53.

When the ruler issues a ruling, then exercises *ijtihād*, then is correct, he has two wages. . . . 395n8. Bukhārī, Iʿtiṣām 21; Muslim, Aqḍiya 15, etc. (*Concordance* 1:390).

When they are seen, God is remembered. 102, 223. The full text of the hadith is, "The best of you are those who, when they are seen, God is remembered." Ibn Māja, Zuhd 4.

Where are those who go about creating, like My creation? 321. Bukhārī (Libās 90, Tawḥīd 56) and Muslim (Libās 101) give this hadith: "Who is more wrongdoing than those who go about creating, like My creation? Let them create a dustmote, or let them create a grain, or let them create a hair!"

While His two hands were gripped tight, God said to Adam, "Choose whichever you like." Adam replied, "I choose the right hand of the Lord, though both hands of my Lord are right and blessed." Then God outspread it, and within it were Adam and His offspring. 404n15. Tirmidhī, Tafsīr sūra 113, 3; *Mishkāt* 24.

who never did any good whatsoever → the angels have interceded

Whoever supposes that Muhammad saw his Lord has committed a great calumny toward God, for God says, *Eyesights perceive Him not* [6:103]. 246. Muslim, Īmān 287; Tirmidhī, Tafsīr Sūra 6, 5.

Within it is what no eye . . . → I have prepared

The witnessing of the Real is an annihilation within which there is no pleasure (Abu'l-ʿAbbās al-Sayyārī). 86 → 394n30

The womb is a branch of the All-Merciful. 170, 399n7. Bukhārī, Adab 13; Tirmidhī, Birr 16. For the full text of this and three similar hadiths, all of which speak of "joining" the womb relatives, see Murata, *Tao* 215–16.

Worship God as if you see Him → Doing what is beautiful

Would that I had not been created . . . (ʿUmar). 34. Al-Sarrāj gives the saying in this form: "Would that my mother had not given birth to me, would that I were this piece of straw, would that I were nothing" (*Lumaʿ* 125).

Write what has been and what will be until the day of resurrection. 153. Part of a well-known hadith, not found in the standard Sunni sources, that begins, "The first thing God created was the Pen." See Murata, *Tao* 153ff.

You have a knowledge . . . → I have a knowledge

You shall see your Lord. 217, 400n34. Muslim, Bukhārī, etc. (SPK 403n10).

You should fast, for it has no likeness. 406n5. Nasāʾī, Ṣiyām 43; Aḥmad 5: 255, 258.

You take your knowledge dead from the dead, but we take our knowledge from the Living who does not die (Abū Yazīd). xiv, 124

You were correct in some and mistaken in some. 348, 358. Muslim, Ruʾyā 17; Bukhārī, Taʿbīr 47 (→ *Concordance* 2:41).

You will be questioned about the bliss of this day. 365. Hadiths to this effect are found in Tirmidhī, Zuhd 39, and Muslim, Ashriba 140.

You will have a wage for what you spend on them. 312. Muslim, Zakāt 47; also Bukhārī, Nafaqāt 14; Aḥmad 6:292–93, 310, 314.

Your Lord is one, just as your father is one. 73. Not indexed in the *Concordance*.

Your self has a *ḥaqq* upon you . . . → Give to each

INDEX OF PROPER NAMES

INDEX OF ARABIC WORDS

INDEX OF TERMS

divine, 25, 299; infinity of, 67, 68, 223; follows object, 17, 23, 25, 26–27, 43, 51, 186–87; same as Essence, 27, 46, 188, 256, 394n4; & creature's *wujūd*, 48, 73–74, 139, (199), 220, 232; Knower (*ʿālim*), 41, 138, 183, 194, 220, 243, 244, 247, 262, 297, 338, 360, 361; Knowing (*ʿalīm*), xvii, xviii, xxxi, 125, 183, 184, 250, 308, 310, 336, 362

knowledge (human), 4, 104, 120, 150–55, 276–79, 294–99, 316, 325–26, 346, 348–49, 351; complete, 196, 281, (320), 373; disengaged, 368; divine, 296, 312; God-given, 142; real, 120, 150; realized, 117, 291; sound, 37, 211, 334, 348, 373, 384; in form of knower, 23, 48, 57, 377; benefit of, 114, 246; impossibility of (→ Essence); levels (sorts) of, xiii–xv, 15, 43, 56, 81, 84, 186, 230, 341; & vision, 211, 356 (→ certainty, eminence, faith, increase, practice, self, self-evident, witnessing); true knowledge (*maʿrifa*), passim (→ gnosis); knowers (*ʿulamāʾ*), 9, 41, 159, 163, 218, 223, 252, 261, 297, 302, 317, 318, 319, 374; of God, 11, 50, 84, 136, 163, 185, 195, 208, 227, 234, 245, 256, 279, 286, 375, 393n16 → ulama

knowledge-giving (*iʿlām*), 112, 152–53, 244, 246, 277; divine, 293, 299, 342, 347 → teaching

known (thing) (object of knowledge) (*maʿlūm*), 12, 93, 131, 135, 177, 179, 223, 230, 248, 250, 291, 295, 338, 341; (God's), xix, 22, 26, 45, 46, 71, 244, 336

lamp (*sirāj, miṣbāḥ*), 16, 38, 85, 160, 161, 228, 343, 350, 351, 358; & wick, 273, 279, 321–22, (369)

language (*lugha, lisān*), xxxii–xxxv, 18, 42, 115, 193, 197, 302, 316, 318, 400n35, 402n1; common language (*ʿurf*), 228, 278, 295, 299, 356 (→ consent)

Last (*ākhir*), lastness (*ākhiriyya*), xxix, 173, 204 (→ First); last world (*ākhira*) → world

laudation (*thanāʾ*), 133–34, 146–47; 97, 149, 185, 193, 199, 200, 219, 253, 278, 301, 327, 341

law (*nāmūs*), 190, 249; Lawgiver (*shāriʿ*), 6, 8, 38, 61, 90, 146, 154, 159, 188, 229, 263, 274, 299, 317, 327, 335, 353, 363, 368, 372; law-giving (*tashrīʿ*), 113, 154, 279, 378, 394n4 (→ prescription, shariah); lawful (*ḥalāl*) & unlawful (*ḥarām*), 152, (335, 347), 351

length (*ṭūl*), 229; (*qāb*) → bow

letter (*ḥarf*), 5, 64, 193, 196, 239, 240, 260, 264, 294, 295, 296, 316, 348, 349, 362; & breath, 42, 70, 71, 116, 196–97, 292

level (*martaba, rutba*), xxxii, 12, 46, 48, 88, 103, 135, 143, 155, 170, 190, 191, 194–96, 198–99, 200, 203, 216, 250, 279, 294, 299, 310, 326, 329, 344, 345, 353, 356, 365, 369 (→ Essence); intelligible, 168, 195; (& sensory), (10, 304); of cosmos, 10, 42, 43, 86, 185, 207, 214, 230, 261, 264, 289, 295, (337, 339); of names, 204, 207; of *wujūd*, 239–40; mixing of, 195; priority in, 17, 20, 27, 50, 198–99, 204–5; *tawḥīd* of, 46, 175, 225; & nonexistence, 168, 238

life (*ḥayāt*), 45, 92, 149, 204, 226, 258, 272, 273–74, 276, 280, 281, 284, 285, 290, 292, 304, 315, 331; & death, 62, 64, 95, 227, 235, 273, 289, 297, 308, 356–57, 364, 369, 372, 374, 403n15; living (alive) (*ḥayy*), (God as), xvii, xviii, xxxi, 125, 155, 201, 203, (249), 290, 282, 308; (things as), 45, 274, 284, 285, 321, 341 (→ animal); Life-Giver (*muḥyī*), xxxi, 41, (308)

lifting (up) (uplifting) (*rifʿa, irtifāʿ*), 54, 216, 238, 253, 255, 338, 360; & putting down, 29, (76), 238; Uplifter (Uplifted) (*rafīʿ*), 238; in/of Degrees, xxxii, 42, 43, 54, 220, 256 → intermediary, occasion, veil

light (*nūr*), 226–27, 272, 275, 279, 299, 308, 352, 357, 365; (& darkness), 37–38, 49–50, 132–33, 155–61, 228–29, 309–11; 4, 12, 76, 93, 95, 111, 135, 202, 215, 234, 252, 255, (273), 283–84, 321, 326, 334, 350, 351, 369; all-inclusive, 248; assigned, 159, 161, 309; divine, 4, 38, 283; earthly & heavenly, 38; embodied, 332; engendered, 38; essential, 161; glassy, 284; natural, 306; sensory & suprasensory, 161, 284; sheer, 252; solar, 4 (→ sun); stellar, 4; temporal, 310; unadulterated, 309; visual, 37; of Essence, 176–77, of reason, 39, 169, 228, 261, 350; of self-disclosure, 67, (102), 163, (192, 213); of things, 38; of *wujūd*, 49, 67, 85–86, 133, 135, 194, 222; degrees of, 160–61; folk of, 65; God as, xxxi, 16, 160, 163, 217, 220, 222, 226, 228, 255, 283; son of, 385; sorts of, 159–60, 169, 310; transformation into, 74, 163, 220, 352; world of, 258; & mystery, 65; & nature, 259, 309; & shadow, 50, 272, 326, 361 → faith

luminous (*nūrī*), 4, 156, 158, 161, 240, 280; body, 280, 281–83, (292), 304, 306, 332, 358; form, 279, 326, 357; spirit, 43, 196, 277, 280, 318; luminosity (*nūriyya*), 283–84

lightning (*barq*), 90, 156, 160, 219, 228, 301, 302

likeness (*mathal, mithl, mithliyya*), 26, 104, 127, 129, 130, 131, 218, 231, 236, 244, 273, 304, 340, 406n5; affirmation of, 76, 77, 92, 254; humans as, 23, 77, 305, 366; negation of, 29, 38, 43, 44, 95, 107, 133, 179, 210, 305, 316; renewal of, 63, 66, (72), 104, 119, 172, 181, 241, 330, 360; striking (*ḍarb*) of, 15, 16, 38, 42, 77, 90, 94, 131, 177, 189, 210, 213, 250, 253, 293, 352; & opposites, 32, 119, 241, 365; & separation, 64, 77, 81, 172; mutual likeness (*mumāthala*), 104, 107

limit (*ḥadd*), 10, 19, 22, 43, 55–56, 60, 69, 74, 79–81, 84, 89, 93, 106, 108, 115, 129, 147, 176, 204, 208, 211, 212, 213, 218, 219, 221, 223, 235, 247, 293, 299, 303, 305, 314, 334, 336, 345, 382,

Folk of God, 302, 381, 385; tracing (*rasm*), 86, 155, 180, 218, 220, 282; knowledge of, 400n32; 124, 154, 155; ulama of, 155, 215, 345, 372, 375
tradition (*sam*ʿ), 114, 218, 230, 325 → hearing
traits → character
tranquillity (*sakīna*), 151
transferal (*intiqāl*), 209; 11, 23, 33, 34, 46, 49, 51, 57, 59, 61, 62, 64, 66, 68, 126, 133, 205, 207, 217, 221, 253, 262, 265, 276, 284, 294, 295, 300, 338, 339, 343, 347, 352, 353, 355, 356, 357, 358, 362, 364, 365
transformation (*inqilāb*), 259, 356 → fluctuation
transgression (*taʿaddī*), 23, 111, 114, 204, 225, 275, 343; of levels, 250, 295; of Shariah, 88, (100, 217) → limit
translucent (*shaffāf*), 110, 282, 283
transmission (*naql*), 65, 101, 176, 257, 328, 346, 379, 381, 384; (of hadiths), 70, 106, 126, 363
transmutation (self-) (*taḥawwul, istiḥāla*), xxvi, 30, 36, 43, 333, 385; (of cosmos), 60–63, 80, 208, 300; (of God), 53, 177, 207, 215, 217, 235, 243, 264, 276, 296, 325, 335, 336
traveler (*musāfir*), 68, 299, 295, 338 → journey
Treasure (*kanz*), Hidden, 5, 21, 70, 393n19
trial (*balāʾ, ibtilāʾ*), 25, 106, 133, 197, 292, 297, 350; (*muḥākama*), 354
Tribe (*ṭāʾifa, qawm*), 85, 102, 126, 148, 173, 178, 257, 270, 278, 372, 377, 382, 384
triplicity (*tathlīth*), (90), 229,
true (*ḥaqīqī*), 12, 28, 36, 85, 152, 185, 187, 260, 263, 293, 300, 334, 335, 350, 358 → knowledge (true)
trust (*amāna*), 75, 141; (in God, *tawakkul*), 76, 134, 210, 377; Trustee (*wakīl*), 24, 76–78, 355, 356, 379, 383; trusteeship (*wikāla*), 76–78, 356
truthful (*ṣādiq*), truthfulness (*ṣidq*), 381; 29, 32, 43, 83, 84, 85, 86, 87, 95, 96, 150, 190, 199, 209, 299, 303, 330, 336, 341, 347–48, 350, 358, 403n2; of report, 4, 43, 54, 65, 68, (71), 107, 144, 169, (200), 209, 261, 262, 285–86, 336, 365; seat of, 22, 303 → faith
turbidity (*kudūra*), 283, 317, 347–48

ugliness (*qubḥ*), 11, 28, 62, 69, 203, 277, 320, 346, 348,405n24; (*sūʾ*), 122–23, 216–19, 275, 287, 310, 313, 359, 367, 373, 390n22
ulama (*ʿulamāʾ*), 154–55, 169, 196, 235, 249, 261, 271, 278, 287, 306, 346, 348, 378, 402n22; of the hearts, 155 → knowers, tracing
unbelief, disbelief (*kufr*), 55, 139; unbeliever (*kāfir*), 88, 145, 152, 158, 257, 305, 354, 364, 375, 392n2
unboundedness (*iṭlāq*), unbounded (*muṭlaq*), 72, 182; mercy, 178, (244), 295; imagination, 60, 130, 332, 336, 337; binding by, 23, 134, 179, 307; & binding, xxii, 30; 13, 17, 54, 147, 153, 171, 178, 262, 351, 358 → *wujūd*; absolute, unqualified,
understanding (*fahm*), 315–17; 43, 73, 90, 103, 118, 142, 155, 197, 209, 247, 265, 278, 293, 296, 301, 305, 327, 367, 372; folk of, 6, 23, 171, 197, 291
undifferentiation (*ijmāl*), 104, 318 → differentiation
unification (*ittiḥād*), 118, 163, 214, 216
unity (*aḥadiyya*), 167–73, 202; 19, 87, 100, 137, 170, 179, 187, 197, 198, 202; of cosmos, 75, 173; of distinction, 198; of each thing, 44, 137, 169, 176, 198, 202; of Entity (Essence), 80, 94, 168, 169, 171, 176; of manyness, 65, (75), 78, 89, 167–70, 173, 177, 196, 198; of one, 65, 168, (202); of totality, 171–72, 176, 177; declaring unity (*tawḥīd*), 60, 78, 80, 89, 127, 169, 181, 220, 258, 307 (→ *tawḥīd*); unitary (*aḥadī*), 54, 169; units (*āḥād*), 176, 196
universal (*kullī*), 237; Body, 324; Nature, 337; Spirit, 272, 310, 324 → soul
unlawful → lawful
unlettered (*ummī*), 142, 390n15
unqualified (*muṭlaq*), 324; love, 324, 346; & qualified, 231, 367, 383, 394n7
unreal (*bāṭil*), xviii, 30, 71, 79, 98, 199, 209, 249, 344
unruly utterances (*shaṭaḥāt*), 301, 302–3, 381
unveiling (*kashf, mukāshafa*), xiv, xxii, 222, 355–56; 9, 29, 34, 51–52, 57, 59, 68, 69, 80, 84–85, 86, 99, 104, 108, 109, 111, 118, 119, 122, 123, 126, 127, 128, 130, 144, 145, 157, 160, 169, 170, 195, 208, 223, 225, 226, 230, 252, 256, 261, 276, 281, 289, 295, 297, 310, 320, 325, 341, 342, 350, 351, 364, 365, 367, 369, 372, 381, 382, 398n37, 398n6; highest (etc.), 51, 152, 262; & reason (reflection), 4, (5), 6, 13–14, 29, 54–55, 74, 81, 89, 121, 124, 169, 183, 261, 298, 356; folk of, xxiii, 53, 57, 63, 103, 108, 121, 148, 249, 275, 284, 285, 287, 292, 295, 296, 341, 355, 363; & of finding, 4, 11, 99, 292, 301; unveiler (*mukāshif*), 51, 283, 295, 318, 321
Uplifter, uplifting → lifting up
uprightness (*istiqāma*), 7, 293 → straight
Uprising (*baʿth*), xxix, 62, 64, 68, 85, (188, 250, 256), 289, 324, 333, 351, 357, 358, (359, 362), 364, 383; raised-up (*munbaʿith*), (xxix), 153, (298, 375)
upstirring (*nashr*), 41, (212); (day of), 62, 150, 250
usage, common (*iṣṭilāḥ*), 217, 316
usurpation (*ghaṣb*), 75

variation (*tanawwuʿ*), 15, 26, 41, 47, 194, 289, 324; of self-disclosures, 65, 94, 264, 349
variegation (*talwīn*) → stability
vassal (*marbūb*), 126 → Lord
veil (*ḥijāb*), 104–20; 6, 16, 39, 43, 59, 68, 123–30, 134, 138, 151, 155–63, 188, 198, 207, 211, 214, 215, 217–18, 252, 264, 299, 318, 350, 363, 365,

works → deed, obligatory, practice
world (ʿ*ālam*), 3, 241–65; 25, 33, 50, 58, 98, 109, 141, 159, 197, 220, 239, 241, 297, 331, 344, 358, 367, 397n30; elemental, 131, 154, 240, (330); heavenly, 105; human, 138, 203, 281, (342); intellective, xxix; most perfect, 259; two, 145, 174, 241, 242, 258–65, 282; three, 78, 258–65, 304; of accidents, 241; of *barzakh*, 260, 264, 270, 271, 277; of breaths, 149; of disengagement, 292; of composition, 64, 310; of domination, 260; of dust, 258; of engendered existence, 302; of felicity, 174; of fire, 258; of forms, 347; of jinn, 281, 306; of kingdom, 260; of light, (240), 264; of manifestation, 264; of meaning, 260, 265; of purity, 287; of reason, 264, 265; of relations, 13; of shape, 224; of soul, 287; of Sovereignty, 260, 317; of wholesomeness, 254; of words, 170, (349); of wretchedness, 174, 287 → absent, body, command, high (& low), imagination, macrocosm, nature, spirit, sensation
this world (*dunyā*), 54, 101, 130, 150, 198, 225, 334, 343, 344, 355, 372, 373, 383; & last world (*ākhira*), xxix, 204–5; (19), 22, 49, 59, 61, 61–62, 64, 66, 68, 69, 70, 78, 80, 81–82, 94, 104, 131–32, 137, 147, 215, 221, 226–27, 230, 242, (245), 246, (256), 257, 264–65, 271, 276, 278, 284, 287, 291, 292, 293, 296, 299, 317, 320, 321, 330, 336, 341, 346–47, 350, 352, (353), 354, (356, 358, 362, 363, 364), 366, 367, 370, 372, 374, 380, 399n6; last world, 58, 178, 210, 222, 290, 308, 319, 335, 351
worship (ʿ*ibāda*), 55–56, 75, 87–88, 105, 125, 138, 147, 172, 189, 200, 261, 262, 312, 315, 336, 349–51, 375–75, 384, 406n5; essential & commanded, 68, 69, (251), 284, 351, 374; none of One, 168, (375)
wrath (*ghaḍab*) → mercy
wretchedness (*shiqā*ʾ), 147, 330, 363 → felicity
writing (*kitāba*), 5–6, 26, 71, 116, 153, 178, 192–93, 239, 240, 295, 296, 316, 362, 391n43; writer (writing angel) (*kātib*), 123, 402n7, 405n13
wrongdoing (*ẓulm*), 18, 26, 75, 133, 159, 204, 331, 344, 354, 361

yearning (*shawq, ishtiyāq*), 39, 170, 234, 293

zeal (*ḥamiyya*), 119, 314, 315, 344
zodiac, xxx